RESEARCH GUIDE TO BIOGRAPHY AND CRITICISM

WORLD DRAMA

Edited By
Walton Beacham

Research Publishing

Library of Congress
Cataloging in Publication Data

Research guide to biography and criticism: world drama/edited by Walton
Beacham—Washington, D.C.: Research Publishing, 1986.
1 v.; 24 cm.

Bibliography
Includes index.
Includes cumulative index.

Description and evaluation of the most important biographical, autobiographical, and critical sources for 146 dramatists worldwide.

1. Drama—Bio-bibliography. 2. Drama—History and criticism—
Bibliography. 3. Dramatists—Biography—Bibliography.
I. Beacham, Walton, 1943-

Z5781.R47   1986   016.8092   86-6441
(PN1721)

Library of Congress Catalog Card Number: 86-6441

ISBN: 0-933833-06-7

Printed in the United States of America
First Printing, May 1986

PREFACE

With so many biographical and critical works available in most libraries, it is often difficult for students to know which sources relate to their specific needs, or for general readers to know which biographies interest them the most.

The *Research Guide to Biography and Criticism* has been designed to assist students in narrowing and researching topics for term papers and essay exams, and to provide librarians with a tool which will help them lead students to valuable, accessible resources. This guide is especially useful for libraries which have limited holdings, or which are building collections. With clear content descriptions and exact bibliographical information for every book reviewed, it is much easier to determine which works are most appropriate, and to locate them in other libraries.

Because one of the goals is to provide a useful tool for students and librarians, the Research Guide has limited its scope to those authors who are most often studied. The contents in no way reflect any editorial opinion as to the writer's historical importance, or to the quality of his work. The contents were compiled with the assistance and advice of university professors and librarians.

A second criterion for including an author is the amount and availability of biographies, autobiographies, and critical materials about him in English. Some excellent foreign dramatists, many of whom are treated extensively in their own languages, have had little work translated or written about them in English. Similarly, most contemporary writers have no full biographical treatments of their lives.

The first two volumes of the Research Guide contain 335 British, American, and Canadian poets and fiction writers. The drama volume contains 146 world dramatists. It is clear that interest in world drama is increasing and more materials are being made available in English. We hope this interest continues, especially for African, Asian, Latin American, and Indian dramatists.

Contributors to the drama volume have included works which deal with performance, drama theory, drama history and explanation of themes. Many of the biographical entries are interesting for their views of the theatre as well as their subjects. Most of the entries are available in English editions and can be found in American libraries, but essential, untranslated sources are also included so that readers will have a clear overview of the important works.

Research Publishing is continually interested in producing books which are devoted to improving the research capabilities of students and assisting librarians in finding concise, accurate information. We welcome any suggestions for revising this title or ideas for other types of books. Write to: Research Publishing, 2113 "S" Street, NW, Washington, DC 20008.

Walton Beacham

CONTRIBUTORS

Sister Consuelo M. Aherne, S.S.J.

Margaret Ann Baker

Fiora A. Bassanese

James P. Bednarz

Kirk H. Beetz

F.G. Blaha

Robert G. Blake

Harold Branam

Jeannie R. Brink

Mitzi M. Brunsdale

Hallman B. Bryant

Jean-Pierre Cap

Gisela Casines

John R. Clark

Robin A. Clouser

David W. Cole

William Condon

Fred D. Crawford

Peter Davison

Frank Day

Elliott A. Denniston

Phyllis T. Dircks

Richard J. Dircks

Robert DiYanni

William R. Drennan

John J. Dunn

Ann W. Engar

Clara Estow

Robert C. Evans

Christoph Eykman

James Flynn

Anne-Marie C. Foley

John Miles Foley

Howard L. Ford

Robert J. Forman

John Freedman

Robert A. Gates

John K. Gillespie

C. Herbert Gilliland

Joe Glaser

Kenneth B. Grant

Clara Györgyey

Jay L. Halio

Katherine Hanley, CSJ

Todd C. Hanlin

Maryhelen C. Harmon

Stephen Hart

Leo Hecht

William J. Heim

David K. Herzberger

John T. Hiers

Elizabeth A. Holtze

Mary Anne Hutchinson

Ed Jewinski

Gloria Johnson

Sister Irma Kashuba, S.S.J.

Richard Keenan

Raymond LePage

Naomi Lindstrom

James Maloney

Charles E. May

Richard A. Mazzara

Linda E. McDaniel

Amy B. Millstone

Gerald W. Morton

Anna Lydia Motto

John Mulryan

Richard J. Panofsky

Genaro J. Pérez

Janet Pérez

Philippe D. Radley

Elizabeth Molnár Rajec

Edward C. Reilly

Margit Resch

Bonnie Arden Robb

Samuel J. Rogal

Carl E. Rollyson, Jr.

Sven Rossel

Murray J. Sachs

David Sadkin

Harold Schefski

Joachim J. Scholz

Margaret K. Schramm

Wanda Seay

Steven Serafin

Lynne P. Shackelford

John C. Shields

Jack Shreve

R. Baird Shuman

Thomas J. Slater

Marjorie Smelstor

Charlotte Spivack

Michael L. Storey

F.C. St. Aubyn

Thomas J. Taylor

Constantin Toloudis

Nancy Walker

Joan M. West

Faye Pauli Whitaker

Robert F. Willson

Kathryn A. Wixon

Eugene P. Wright

Bruce W. Young

Leon Zolbrod

CONTENTS

AESCHYLUS
525-456 B.C.

Author's Chronology

Born *525 B.C.* in Eleusis near Athens, to father Euphorion and unknown mother; *510-508* age of tyrants ends with establishment of democracy in Athens; *499-496* Aeschylus' first dramatic competition; *490* fights against the Persians in the Battle of Marathon; *484* wins his first dramatic victory 15 years after his initial competition; *472* wins tragic victory for *Persians*; *468* loses tragic contest to Sophocles; *467* wins with *Seven Against Thebes*; *463?* wins with *Suppliants*, while Sophocles is second; *458* wins with the *Oresteia*; *456* death and burial at Gela in Sicily.

Author's Bibliography

Scholars place Aeschylus' total number of plays at between 73 and 90, of which there are 83 known titles. Only seven complete plays survive, all of them formal tragedies: the *Oresteia* trilogy (*Agamemnon*, *Libation Bearers*, *Eumenides*), *The Persians*, *The Seven Against Thebes*, *The Suppliants*, and *Prometheus Bound*. Papyri and citations from other authors indicate that Aeschylus was also well known for his satyr-plays, the comic, colloquial, realistic codas to dramatic tetrologies. Editions of the Greek texts include Herbert W. Smyth, *Aeschylus: Plays and Fragments with an English Translation*, Loeb Classical Library (New York: G.P. Putnam, 1922), 2 vols. (2nd vol. rev. 1957 by Hugh Lloyd-Jones); and Denys Page, *Aeschyli Tragoediae*, 2nd rev. ed. (Oxford: Oxford University Press, 1972). All seven of the tragedies are magnificently translated into English in David Grene and Richmond Lattimore, *The Complete Greek Tragedies*, I-II (Chicago: University of Chicago Press, 1953-1956), with the *Oresteia* also readily available in a workable translation by Lloyd-Jones (Englewood Cliffs: Prentice-Hall, 1970).

Overview of Biographical Sources

Since Aeschylus is generally considered to have begun the ancient Greek—and therefore the European—dramatic tradition, and since ancient commentators showed great ingenuity in inventing fanciful biographical details to supplement the facts of literary figures' lives, there is little reliable biographical information on Aeschylus. Hypothetical relationships between Aeschylus' works and the political, social, and religious aspects of the time and place in which he lived are the subject of such studies as Anthony J. Podlecki's *The Political Background of Aeschylean Tragedy*, George Thomson's *Aeschylus and Athens: A Study in the Social Origins of Drama* (New York: Grosset and Dunlap, 1968), Brian Vickers' *Toward Greek Tragedy: Drama, Myth, Society* (London: Longman, 1973), and Peter Walcot's

Greek Drama in its Theatrical and Social Context. Gerald F. Else's *The Origin and Early Form of Greek Tragedy* gathers up the evidence on pre-Aeschylean, pre-dramatic forms and attempts a rationalization of the disparate facts. For the most thorough collection of evidence on Aeschylus' life, see F. Schoell, ed., *De Aeschyli vita et poesi testimonia veterum* in F. Ritschl, ed., *Aeschylus: Septem adversus Thebas* (Leipzig: B.G. Teubner, 1875), pp. 3-52. A dependably conservative summary may be found in Thomas G. Rosenmeyer, "The Life and Times of Aeschylus," in his *The Art of Aeschylus*, pp. 369-376.

Evaluation of Selected Biographies

Podlecki, Anthony J. *The Political Background of Aeschylean Tragedy*. Ann Arbor: University of Michigan Press, 1966. This book stresses the sociopolitical climate in which Aeschylus lived and created, with special emphasis on the threat of the Persian empire, the democratic liberation of Athens when Aeschylus was fifteen years old, and the changing self-concept of Athens as a political entity.

Walcot, Peter, *Greek Drama in its Theatrical and Social Context*. Cardiff: University of Wales Press, 1976. Walcot seeks to reinvigorate the Greek drama with some of its original force by investigating the staging and the other aspects of production, the audience, the primacy of the spoken word in Athenian life, the art of the fifth-century actor, and the social context of plays and playwrights.

Overview of Critical Sources

From the ancients onward, scholarship on Aeschylus has been both voluminous in quantity and uneven in quality. Until the mid-twentieth century most of this work consisted of textual criticism of the seven complete surviving plays, but in recent years classicists have increasingly felt the need for interpretive scholarship of all kinds. The most thorough summary of scholarship available is A. Wartell, *Bibliographie historique et critique d'Eschyle* (Paris: Les Belles Lettres, 1978); both before and after that date, see also the standard classical bibliography, *L'Année philologique*, for annotated citations on the year's work. Journals in which criticism on Aeschylus regularly appears include *Harvard Studies in Classical Philology*, *Transactions of the American Philological Association*, *Classical Quarterly*, and the *American Journal of Philology*. What follows, then, is merely a highly selective sampling of recent interpretive studies, intended to provide a sense of the variety of approaches taken to Aeschylus' drama.

Evaluation of Selected Criticism

Lebeck, Anne, *The Oresteia: A Study in Language and Structure*. Cambridge: Harvard University Press, 1971. This is a sensitive study of patterns of imagery in the trilogy and of the role of such patterns as bearers of thematic meaning. Lebeck stresses the importance of interpreting each image both in its immediate context and as an expression of the tragic vision of the *Oresteia* trilogy as a whole.

McCall, Marsh H., Jr. ed. *Aeschylus: A Collection of Critical Essays.* Englewood Cliffs, NJ: Prentice-Hall, 1972. McCall brings together reprints of ten classic essays and chapters of books on various aspects of Aeschylean art. Among them are studies of the tragic vision, all of the major plays, and the translation process.

Rosenmeyer, Thomas G. *The Art of Aeschylus.* Berkeley: University of California Press, 1982. This is the single most reliable and insightful study of Aeschylus' dramatic accomplishment. It covers clearly and precisely the areas of text and transmission, production, style, the chorus, characterization, and various thematic aspects of the tragedies. A sizable selected bibliography on all dimensions of Aeschylean studies is appended.

Segal, Erich, ed. *Greek Tragedy: Modern Essays in Criticism.* New York: Harper and Row, 1983. Includes ten essays and book chapters on Aeschylus, ranging from the problem of decision and responsibility to Agamemnon's guilt. Also contains material on Sophocles and Euripides.

Spatz, Lois, *Aeschylus.* Boston: Twayne, 1982. This handy volume includes a brief introduction to Aeschylus' life and times and to Attic drama, followed by chapters on all seven tragedies. A dependable source for consensus judgments, with a very large annotated bibliography.

Taplin, Oliver, *The Stagecraft of Aeschylus: The Dramatic Use of Exits and Entrances in Greek Tragedy.* Oxford: Clarendon Press, 1977. A monumental work of scholarship that seeks to discover the "grammar" of the dramatic technique employed by the Greek tragedians, to provide commentary on the plays of Aeschylus from that perspective, and to relate the discoveries about production and stagecraft to the meaning of the plays. An extremely useful, learned, and interesting compendium.

Other Sources

Beck, Robert H. *Aeschylus: Playwright Educator.* The Hague: Martinus Nijhoff, 1975. Beck probes the moral philosophy of Aeschylus, with chapters on honor and time, moral lessons in the drama, and crime, punishment, and judgment.

Else, Gerald F. *The Origin and Early Form of Greek Tragedy.* Cambridge: Harvard University Press, 1965. This brief study offers a sensible explanation of the puzzle of the origins of the drama in the Dionysiac rite and the now-perished work of Thespis. The final chapter surveys Aeschylus' creation of the tragic drama, with special emphasis on his dramatic innovations.

Havelock, Eric A. *The Literate Revolution in Greece and its Cultural Consequences.* Princeton: Princeton University Press, 1982. One chapter in this book,

"The Oral Composition of Greek Drama" (pp. 261-312), examines the continuity between Homeric oral epic and the Attic drama, concentrating on the mimetic nature of the drama and its function as a reflection of contemporary views and attitudes.

Hogan, James C. *A Commentary on the Complete Greek Tragedies: Aeschylus*. Chicago: University of Chicago Press, 1984. A line-by-line companion to the tragedies, intended primarily for those reading Aeschylus in translation but also of use for classics students.

Kuhns, Richard, *The House, the City, and the Judge: The Growth of Moral Awareness in the Oresteia*. Indianapolis: Bobbs-Merrill, 1962. Attempts to provide insight into the philosophical background of Aeschylus' trilogy. Kuhns is a philosopher by training, and his book offers a fresh and challenging perspective on some of the central problems of the *Oresteia*.

Lesky, Albin, *A History of Greek Literature*. trans. James Willis and Cornelis de Heer. London: Methuen, 1966. The finest general history of ancient Greek literature, with extensive sections of Attic drama and Aeschylus (esp. pp. 241-70).

Lloyd-Jones, Hugh, *The Justice of Zeus*. Berkeley: University of California Press, 1971. In his chapter on "Presocratic Thinkers: Aeschylus," Lloyd-Jones assembles that dramatist's cosmology from the evidence of the extant plays and demonstrates a continuity in the concept of *dike* or "justice" from Homer onward.

Murray, Gilbert, *Aeschylus: The Creator of Tragedy*. Oxford: Clarendon Press, 1940. An older but venerable account of the plays and fragments in their reconstructed Athenian context, with emphasis on Aeschylus as the originator of Greek tragedy and therefore as the father of all European tragedy.

Otis, Brooks, *Cosmos and Tragedy: An Essay on the Meaning of Aeschylus*. ed. E. Christian Kopff. Chapel Hill: University of North Carolina Press, 1981. A text-based work of literary criticism that provides a clear perspective on the *Oresteia*.

Sagan, Eli, *The Lust to Annihilate: A Psychoanalytic Study of Violence in Ancient Greek Culture*. New York: Psychohistory Press, 1979. Includes substantial sections on Aeschylus and on tragedy in general that offer a psychoanalytic view on some of the most significant action and themes in ancient Greek drama.

Sideras, Alexander, *Aeschylus Homericus: Untersuchungen zu den Homerismen der aischyleischen Sprache*. Göttingen: Vandenhoeck and Ruprecht, 1971. A useful study of "Homerisms," that is, Homeric vocabulary, syntax, and style, in the works of Aeschylus.

Simon, Bennett, *Mind and Madness in Ancient Greece: The Classical Roots of Modern Psychiatry*. Ithaca: Cornell University Press, 1978. Within its general interest in reconstructing ancient Greek theories of the mind in healthy and diseased states from the evidence provided by the literary witnesses, this book looks at the model of mind projected by the tragedies and Aeschylean tragedy in particular.

Winnington-Ingram, R.P. *Studies in Aeschylus*. Cambridge: Cambridge University Press, 1983. A detailed examination of all of the tragedies, centering on the destinies of individual, family and city, and the human race. Five chapters are devoted to the *Oresteia*.

John Miles Foley
University of Missouri

LEONID ANDREYEV
1871-1919

Author's Chronology

Born Leonid Nikolaevich Andreyev August 21, 1871 in Orel, Russia; *1891* enters the Law School of St. Petersburg University; *1892* attempts suicide over love affair and leaves university; *1893* enters Moscow University; *1895* first short stories are published; *1897* is awarded law degree and becomes court reporter for two Moscow newspapers; *1899* meets Maxim Gorky who introduces him to literary figures including Tolstoy and Chekhov; *1901* collection of stories which is published attains record-breaking sales; *1902* marries, becomes affluent; *1904* publishes *The Red Laugh* of which 60,000 copies are sold; *1905* imprisoned for several weeks for illegal political activity, leaves Russia and publishes his first play, *To the Stars*; *1907* returns to St. Petersburg where his most successful play, *The Life of Man*, is staged by V. Meyerhold; *1908* publishes most successful novella, *The Story of the Seven Who Were Hanged*; *1909 Anathema* is staged at the Moscow Art Theatre; 1911 completes major novel, *Sashka Zhegulev*; *1911-1913* publishes "Letters on the Theatre" and continues writing plays; critics turn against him; *1916* becomes Literary Editor of the reactionary journal *Russkaia volia*; *1918* moves to Finland to escape Civil War and becomes anti-Communist propagandist; September 12, 1919 dies of a heart attack.

Author's Bibliography

Collections of his short fiction in English translation include: *The Seven That Were Hanged and Other Stories* (New York: Random House, 1958); *The Little Angel and Other Stories* (Freeport, NY: Books for Libraries Press, 1971); *The Crushed Flower and Other Stories* (New York: Alfred A. Knopf, 1916); *Sashka Jigouleff* (New York: R.M. McBride & Co., 1915) (novel).

Critical material written by the author and translated into English includes: *The Shield: Essays and Lectures* (Westport, CT: Greenwood Press, 1975); "Andreyev on Motion Pictures" (*New York Times*, October 19, 1919, VII, 5:1); "Andreyev on the Modern Theatre" (*New York Times*, October 5, 1919, IV, 3:1).

A sampling of his most important translated plays includes: *Plays by Leonid Andreyeff*, which comprises the plays *The Black Maskers*, *The Life of Man* and *The Sabine Women* (New York: Charles Scribner's Sons, 1915); *Anathema—A Tragedy in Seven Scenes* (New York: Macmillan, 1923); *Katerina—A Drama in Four Acts* (New York: Brentano's, 1923); *Savva* and *The Life of Man* (New York: Mitchell Kennerly, 1914); *King Hunger* (Sewanee, CT: University Press, University of the South, 1973); *He Who Gets Slapped* (Westport, CT: Greenwood Press, 1975).

Overview of Biographical Sources

Andreyev was one of pre-revolutionary Russia's most important playwrights. It is therefore understandable that most of the biographical material written about him during his lifetime was in Russian, as were major editions of his collected works. Since he was an avowed enemy of communism, he remained a "non-person" to whom no reference was made in writing during the Lenin and Stalin regimes. It wasn't until the 1960s that the first mention of the writer's name appeared in Soviet literary biographical materials and that a selection of his works was published. In the West, although Andreyev's plays continued to generate interest in the English-speaking countries over the years, relatively little biographical information was collected or published.

Sources of biographical data to be recommended among translated materials are Maxim Gorky's *Reminiscences of Tolstoy, Chekhov and Andreyev* (New York: Viking Press, 1959); and *Letters of Gorky and Andreev* (New York: Columbia University Press, 1958). Biographical works of article length which are particularly helpful include: T. Seltzer, "The Life and Works of L. Andreyev," *The Drama*, February 1914, pp. 5-33; "Leonid Andreev" in D.S. Mirsky, *Contemporary Russian Literature* (London: George Routledge & Sons, 1926); and significant, lengthy multiple references in Marc Slonim, *Russian Theatre from the Empire to the Soviets* (New York: Collier Books, 1962) and in Harold B. Segel, *Twentieth Century Russian Drama* (New York: Columbia University Press, 1979).

Evaluation of Selected Biographies

Newcombe, Josephine M. *Leonid Andreyev*. New York: Frederick Ungar, 1973. It contains a good, albeit short, biographical survey, a good biographical chronology table, and an excellent chronological listing of the writer's works.

Autobiographical Sources

Andreyev did not keep a diary or memoirs. The only first-hand biographical data are his letters (see previous entry on collected correspondence with Gorky). He also did not write any fictionalized documentaries which narrate his own experiences. Of course, some critics have subsequently claimed that a number of his works were based on his personal life. For example, his first published story, "He, She and Vodka," allegedly portrayed his experiences as a child and youth with an alcoholic father, and his own three attempts at suicide. His "Seven Who Were Hanged" is supposedly based on revelations by fellow prisoners whom he encountered during his short stay in jail. His two last plays, *Satan's Diary* and particularly the posthumously published tragedy *Samson in Chains*, purportedly portray the trials and tribulations of the last years of the playwright's own existence. Nevertheless these arbitrary judgments are virtually impossible to substantiate. The two plays in question are highly symbolic and allegorical and make no discernibly realistic statement. His short stories may be interpreted by the beholder without fear of contradiction by any other extant materials, but are therefore also unsubstantiated.

Overview of Critical Sources

Andreyev was always considered a controversial and uneven writer. His early fiction was viewed by critics as clearly realistic and critical of the Czarist system, particularly "Petka at the Dacha" and the "Seven Who Were Hanged." The social critics therefore found Andreyev to be a valuable ally towards social reform. When he started writing plays, the same critics hailed his major products such as *He Who Gets Slapped*, *The Life of Man* and *Anathema* for its resistance to old forms and its innovative spirit in line with the many imported and self-generated "isms" in art which were bombarding Russia at the turn of the century. This love affair was relatively short-lived since these critics soon attacked Andreyev for his extreme fascination with allegory, incomprehensible symbols, lack of social commitment and preoccupation with form rather than with the all-important content necessary for good art. Fellow writers accused him of sensationalism and opportunism apparent in his vividly gory short stories. The best-known comment of the period was by Leo Tolstoy whom Andreyev adored and attempted to emulate. After reading a particularly frightening story which was dedicated to him, Tolstoy stated "Andreyev says 'Boo!' but I'm not scared." The final years of his life saw many more detractors than supporters in Russia and abroad although his better plays continued to be performed regularly.

In general, most of the criticism treated his general work rather than, more specifically, his dramatic output. There are no major critical works in English on his involvement with the theatre although there are several good studies in German and French on his skill as a narrator and playwright, for example Angela Martini's recent work *Erzaehltechniken Leonid Nikolaevic Andreevs* (Munich: 1978).

Similar to the lack of biographical studies, very few critical works other than short notes have been published in the USSR during the past two decades. Andreyev is still too dangerous a writer for Soviet critics to discuss objectively. Even today, Soviets prefer to discard him as a relatively untalented reactionary whose products rape the very essence of Socialist Realism and who is unworthy of serious critical analysis. The most important item they have published to date is a 25-page collection of materials on Andreyev in Russian in a major bibliographical guide on early twentieth century literature, which was distributed in 1963. Since much of worthy Soviet literary criticism is eventually translated into English, the sparcity in the case of Andreyev has greatly diminished the number of such works. Russian emigre publishers have printed some critical materials on Andreyev, however they have not been translated.

Evaluation of Selected Criticism

Kaun, Alexander, *Leonid Andreyev: A Critical Study*. Freeport, NY: Books for Libraries Press, 1973. This is an identical reprint of the 1924 edition, but is still the best critical source in English. It contains an excellent chronological coverage of Andreyev's works starting with his early feuilletons and short stories, and then progresses to a psychological analysis of his main period of productivity— particularly his work as a playwright. It has an excellent bibliography which includes listings of translations of his writings and of a number of critical articles written in English. There are separate bibliographic entries on materials in Russian, German, French, Dutch, Swedish and Spanish sources, and a thorough index.

Jackson, R.L. *Dostoevsky's Underground Man in Russian Literature*. The Hague: Mouton, 1958. A lengthy section of this book (Chapter 8) is allocated to a discussion of the influence of Dostoevsky on Andreyev. Although the segment is well done and makes its point, literary influences are always controversial and difficult to prove, even if it is definitely true that Dostoyevsky was the darling of the Russian avant garde of the first twenty years of the twentieth century and that Andreyev also fell under his spell.

Persky, S. *Contemporary Russian Novelists*. Boston, 1913. This is the only work in English which has a lengthy (50-page) discussion of Andreyev's novels and novellas. Although somewhat outdated, it is quite good and is recommended for a superficial study of his prose.

Woodward, James B. *Leonid Andreev: A Study*. Oxford: Clarendon Press, 1969. This is also an excellent work in that it contains a thorough discussion of philosophical influences and the literary climate of the first two decades of twentieth century Russia. Although it has an inadequate bibliography and no notes of reference, it appears to be much more directed towards the researcher into specifically Slavic materials than the general academic audience.

Other Sources

Although it is in the original Russian, any reference guide would be remiss in not mentioning the definitive edition of Andreyev's collected works: *Polnoe sobranie sochenenii Andreeva*. 17 vols. (St. Petersburg and Moscow: 1913-1917.)

All histories of Russian literature in all languages include sections on Andreyev. An excellent example is Adolf Stender-Petersen's seminal *Geschichte der russischen Literatur* (Munich: Beck, 1957), in which he discusses Andreyev's function as a dramatic neo-realist and symbolist.

Marc Slonim's *From Chekhov to the Revolution* (New York: Oxford University Press, 1962), contains an excellent segment on, and many additional references to, Andreyev's works. It is highly recommended.

A most recent article by Angela Martini entitled "The Syncretism of Dramatic Structure and the Failure of L.N. Andreev's Dramas" in *Theater and Literature in Russia 1900-1930* edited by Lars Kleberg and Nils Ake Nilsson (Stockholm: Almqist & Wiskell, 1984), is also definitely worth reading although the author wastes a great deal of space arguing that no space should be wasted on Andreyev's plays.

All histories of Russian drama and theatre necessarily also concern themselves with a playwright whose popularity rivaled that of Chekhov and Gorky. Examples are Oliver M. Sayler's *The Russian Theatre* (New York; Brentano's, 1922); and, by the same author, *Inside the Moscow Art Theatre* (Westport CT: Greenwood Press, 1970).

Any article on Russian stage design must certainly also discuss a number of Andreyev's most widely performed plays, particularly *He Who Gets Slapped* and *Life of Man*.

A small digression may be a literary travelogue by Olga Andreyev Carlisle entitled *Voices in the Snow* (New York: Random House, 1962). In this book Andreyev's granddaughter looks at Soviet literature through the eyes of her grandfather.

There were also a number of operas based on Andreyev's works which were moderately successful, among them: *Days of Our Life* by Glukhovetsky; *The Abyss* by Rebikov; and *The Black Maskers* by Ilyin. The libretti and program notes are of definite interest.

A similar statement may be made concerning a number of Andreyev's plays were turned into motion pictures, among them: *Anathema*; *He Who Gets Slapped*; and *Katherina Ivanovna*.

Selected Dictionaries and Encyclopedias

Dictionary of Russian Literature, Littlefield, Adams, 1959.

Handbook of Russian Literature, Yale University Press, 1985.

Encyclopedia of Russia and the Soviet Union, McGraw-Hill, 1961.

Leo Hecht
George Mason University

JOHN ARDEN
1930

Author's Chronology

Born October 26, 1930, Barnsley, Yorkshire, England, son of a glassworks manager; attends elementary school in Barnsley, then Terrington Hall, a preparatory school; *1944-1949* attends Sedbergh School, Yorkshire; *1949-1950* serves in British Army Intelligence Corps, attains rank of lance-corporal; *1953* takes B.A., architecture, King's College, Cambridge University; *1955* first production of an Arden play, *All Fall Down* in Edinburgh; *1955* takes diploma in architecture, Edinburgh College of Art; *1955-1957* works in architect's office in London; *1956* wins BBC Northern Region prize for radio play *The Life of Man*; *1957* Royal Court Theatre produces *The Waters of Babylon*; *1957* marries Margaretta D'Arcy, an Irish actress; quits architecture, becomes full-time writer; *1959* wins *Encyclopaedia Britannica* prize for *Serjeant Musgrave's Dance*; *1959-1960* wins *Evening Standard* (London) Most Promising Playwright Award; *1963* moves to Kirbymoorside, Yorkshire; *1966* becomes chairman of *Peace News*; lives in London and County Galway, Ireland; *1967* holds visiting lectureship in politics and drama at New York University, stages (with D'Arcy) a "Vietnam War Carnival"; *1969* resigns as chairman of *Peace News*; *1969-1970* travels in India to study nonviolence, suffers from hepatitis, jailed with family in Assam; *1971* settles in Corrandulla, County Galway, Ireland; *1972* Arden and D'Arcy picket Royal Shakespeare Company production of *The Island of the Mighty*; *1973* Arden and D'Arcy hold visiting lectureship at the University of California, Davis; *1975* serves as writer-in-residence, University of New England, Armidale, Australia; *1982* publishes first novel.

Author's Bibliography

Arden's bibliography is particularly entangled because of his publication of radio or television plays in the same volumes as stage plays and because of his collaborations with Margaretta D'Arcy. Radio plays, television plays, and collaborations are indicated here in parentheses, with the major contributor listed first for collaborations.

Serjeant Musgrave's Dance, 1960; *The Business of Good Government* (Arden/D'Arcy), 1963; *Three Plays*, 1964, including *The Waters of Babylon*, *Live Like Pigs*, and *The Happy Haven* (Arden/D'Arcy); *The Workhouse Donkey*, 1964; *Armstrong's Last Goodnight*, 1965; *Left Handed Liberty*, 1965; *Ars Longa, Vita Brevis* (Arden/D'Arcy), 1965; *Ironhand* (adaptation of Goethe's *Goetz von Berlichingen*), 1965; *Soldier, Soldier and Other Plays*, 1967, including *When Is a Door Not a Door?*, *Soldier, Soldier* (television), *Wet Fish* (television), and *Friday's Hiding* (Arden/D'Arcy); *The Royal Pardon* (Arden/D'Arcy), 1967; *The Hero Rises Up*

(Arden/D'Arcy), 1969; *Two Autobiographical Plays*, 1971, including *The True History of Squire Jonathan and His Unfortunate Treasure* and *The Bagman* (radio); *The Ballygombeen Bequest* (Arden/D'Arcy), 1972; *The Island of the Mighty* (Arden/D'Arcy), 1973; *Plays One*, 1977, including *Serjeant Musgrave's Dance*, *The Workhouse Donkey*, and *Armstrong's Last Goodnight*; *To Present the Pretence* (essays), 1977; *The Non-Stop Connolly Show* (5 vols., D'Arcy/Arden), 1978; *Pearl* (radio), 1979; *The Little Gray Home in the West* (D'Arcy/Arden), 1980; *Vandaleur's Folly* (D'Arcy/Arden), 1981; *Silence Among the Weapons*, 1982 (novel, published in the United States as *Vox Pop: Last Days of the Roman Republic*, (1983).

Overview of Biographical Sources

So far, no biography of Arden has been published. Biographical information is scanty, restricted to brief summaries in reference works and in the pamphlets and full-length studies on Arden. Yet Arden's life offers much interesting material for biographers: his controversial critical reception, his continuing argument with the British theatrical establishment about the nature of theater, his political development and involvement, his travels, his marriage to and collaboration with Margaretta D'Arcy (they have four sons). A sampling of this material can be gleaned from Arden's prefaces and essays, from newspaper accounts of Arden and D'Arcy's 1972 disagreement with the Royal Shakespeare Company, and from D'Arcy's *Tell Them Everything* (London: Pluto, 1981), about her three-month term in Northern Ireland's Armagh Prison. In March, 1965, BBC Television filmed a documentary on the author at home in Kirbymoorside.

Autobiographical Sources

Arden's *Two Autobiographical Plays* (London: Methuen, 1971) are not as revealing as they sound. Allegorical, they provide little solid fact, but *The Bagman* does give a harrowing picture of Arden's state of mind during his mid-career crisis, around 1969-70, when he agonized over playwriting and politics.

More informative are Arden's numerous prefaces and essays. In his prefaces, Arden covers such topics as the genesis of particular plays, their theatrical production, their reception by critics, and his intentions (especially where these were misunderstood). His most important essays—treating the influences on him, his travels to the United States and India, his political development, his and D'Arcy's production of the "Vietnam War Carnival" and *The Non-Stop Connolly Show*, and their dispute with the Royal Shakespeare Company—are collected in *To Present the Pretence* (London: Eyre Methuen, 1977).

Overview of Critical Sources

Arden's work has attracted considerable critical attention, despite a hostile reception of it by many early reviewers and Arden's eventual alienation from the established theater. Critics soon rushed to explain and defend Arden's work, citing its Brechtian and English antecedents. The result is that much Arden criticism focuses on his earlier plays, with *Serjeant Musgrave's Dance* the universal favorite. The main problem is that this criticism is now outdated or at least does not account for Arden's later career, since Arden has continued to write. Arden's career so far divides into two stages: an earlier period (to around the late 1960s) of probing plays which dramatize issues without giving answers and a later period of propagandistic plays (most written with D'Arcy).

Some of Arden's critics also have another problem—inability to distance themselves enough to make careful critical judgments. In particular, a number of Arden's British critics tend to be swayed by political biases and/or to be drawn into the in-fighting. The British critics often have better on-the-spot, detailed information (though sometimes they takes such information for granted), while the American and Continental critics are better at the larger view.

Evaluation of Selected Criticism

Gilman, Richard, "Arden's Unsteady Ground," *Tulane Drama Review*, XI, No. 2 (1966): 54-62. Reprinted in *Modern British Dramatists: A Collection of Critical Essays*, ed. John Russell Brown. Englewood Cliffs, NJ: Prentice-Hall, 1968, pp. 104-116. Covering Arden's work to 1965, this perceptive article on Arden's thematic unity is essential reading. Gilman, an American critic, exercises a fine critical judgment and makes sense of the early plays which baffled his British colleagues. Gilman considers Arden a highly political but not a polemical writer in the early plays: Arden's theme is the nature of political action—its necessity but also its limitations, ambiguities, and consequences—particularly the tragic conflict between abstract political principle and the disorderly energies of human life.

Gray, Frances, *John Arden*. London: Macmillan, 1982. This book, published in paperback in the United States by Grove Press, gives a good general introduction to Arden's "Resources," "Manner," and "Matter" and is especially good on Arden's continuing "debate about theatre" with his audience and the British theatrical establishment. Taking sides in the debate, Gray is more of an advocate than critic of Arden's work. She comments on individual plays mainly to illustrate general points; the only systematic analysis is of four plays selected to demonstrate Arden's range: *Serjeant Musgrave's Dance*, *Ars Longa, Vita Brevis*, *The Island of the Mighty*, and *Pearl*. Biographical information is disappointingly sketchy, and the writing is occasionally sloppy.

Hunt, Albert, *Arden: A Study of His Plays*. London: Eyre Methuen, 1974. Hunt is an effective commentator on Arden's theatrical style, in terms of which he analyzes Arden's plays to 1972, with a postscript on *The Island of the Mighty* production. But Hunt must be read with caution: his own style is rather theatrical, tending towards exaggeration and sweeping generalities: he considers Arden "one of the greatest dramatists in the English language for several centuries." Still, Hunt's brashness (as in the chapter title "Portrait of the Artist as a Reprehensible Coward") makes for entertaining reading.

Page, Malcolm, *John Arden*. Boston: Twayne, 1984. Factual, informative, Page's book is the latest and most useful full-length study of Arden to date. Chapter 1 is a biography, brief but nevertheless the fullest one so far. Subsequent chapters cover all of Arden's twenty-eight plays, even those for radio and television, giving extensive plot summaries, information on performances, and critical reactions. Page is a bit short on critical analysis himself, weakest on thematic analysis. The concluding chapter generalizes about "recurring character types and how they reveal some major themes." There is an excellent bibliography, with brief annotations for secondary sources.

Schvey, Henry I. "From Paradox to Propaganda: The Plays of John Arden," in *Essays on Contemporary British Drama*. ed. Hedwig Bock and Albert Wertheim. Munich: Hueber, 1981, pp. 47-70. Another essential reading, this article by a Leiden University scholar provides the best overall view of Arden's development to date. The title indicates Schvey's thesis on Arden's two-stage development, which picks up where Gilman's article left off. Like other commentators, Schvey examines *The Bagman*, Arden's India trip, and *The Island of the Mighty* as key evidence in Arden's conversion to Marxist commitment, but he also carefully documents his thesis by tracing Arden's work before and after. He concludes that "Arden's excursions into agitprop theatre have compromised his art" and hopes that Arden will soon move on to a third phase.

Other Sources

Branam, Harold, "John Arden," in *Critical Survey of Drama: English Language Series*, 6 vols., ed. Frank N. Magill. Englewood Cliffs, NJ: Salem Press, 1985, I, 41-49. An overview of Arden's career, with a compact analysis of selected plays.

Brown, John Russell, *Theatre Language: A Study of Arden, Osborne, Pinter and Wesker*. New York: Taplinger, 1972. Closely analyzing the theatricality of speeches, characters, and staging in Arden's plays to 1969, Brown finds that Arden uses "artificial theatre" not to simplify issues but to suggest their complexity, not to satisfy conventional expectations but to challenge audiences.

Hunt, Albert, "Arden's Stagecraft," in *Encore*, XII, No. 5 (1965): 9-12. Reprinted in *Modern British Dramatists: A Collection of Critical Essays*, ed. John Russell Brown. Englewood Cliffs, NJ: Prentice-Hall, 1968, pp. 98-103. Sees Arden's work not as "naturalistic" drama played for "illusion and identification" but as direct theater in the tradition of the music hall and Brecht.

Itzin, Catherine, *Stages in the Revolution: Political Theatre in Britain Since 1968*. London: Eyre Methuen, 1980. This excellent study packed with absorbing details contains a chapter tracing Arden's conversion (c. 1968) "from committed pacifism to revolutionary socialism" and its consequences, including more collaboration with D'Arcy and dissociation from the established theater.

Kennedy, Andrew K. *Six Dramatists in Search of a Language*. London: Cambridge University Press, 1975. Examines Arden's attempt to tap a "primitive," "pre-literary" language in ballads, dialect, and colorful prose.

Leeming, Glenda, *John Arden*. Writers and Their Work Series, No. 238. Harlow, Essex: Longman Group for the British Council, 1974. A pamphlet giving a good survey of Arden's first phase, covering work to 1973 and including brief biographical comments.

Taylor, John Russell, *Anger and After: A Guide to the New British Drama*. London: Methuen, 1962. Published in the United States as *The Angry Theater*. New York: Hill & Wang, 1962. Revised and expanded edition, 1969. Contains an early sympathetic defense of Arden against the initially baffled and hostile critical reaction.

Trussler, Simon, *John Arden*. Columbia Essays on Modern Writers, No. 65. New York: Columbia University Press, 1973. Another good introductory pamphlet on Arden's first phase, this one surveying plays to 1971 and including a biographical summary.

Harold Branam

ARISTOPHANES
c. 446-c. 388 B.C.

Author's Chronology

Born c. 446 B.C. at Athens, son of Philippos of Kudathenaion, a naturalized Athenian born in either Rhodes or Egypt; *432* Peloponnesian War begins; *430* plague at Athens; *429* Pericles dies; *427* receives first public recognition with production of *Daitales* (*The Two Sons*), a play no longer extant; play wins second prize; *Babylonians* (not extant) also produced; *425 Acharnians* produced, wins first prize at Lenaea festival; *424 Knights* appears, a parodic attack on Cleon; *Holkades* (not extant) follows, attacks Cleon's followers; *Clouds* given at the Dionysia, polemic on Socrates; *422 Wasps* attacks jury system and "Philocleon;" *421 Peace* appears, emphasizes need for Panhellenism; Peace of Nicias signed ending war; *415 Baptae* (not extant) against Alcibiades; in May, mutilation of the Hermae in which Alcibiades is implicated; July, Sicilian Expedition and flight of Alcibiades; *414 Birds* produced, on founding of "Cloudcuckooland;" *Lysistrata*, strike of women to enforce peace; *410 Thesmophoriazusae* on Euripides' slanders on women; *408* first production of *Plutus*; *406* Euripides and Sophocles die; *405 Frogs* appears, contest between Aeschylus and Euripides for poet's laurel crown; *399* Socrates condemned, executed; c. *392 Ecclesiazusae*, rule by women, parody of Plato's *Republic*; *388* second production of *Plutus*; transition to Middle Comedy, stage attacks on living persons becomes unlawful; traditional date of death.

Author's Bibliography

Numerous editions of Aristophanes' plays are available. They range from scholarly Greek texts with apparatus to idiomatic English translations. The best Greek text with apparatus, although old, is readily available and regularly reissued: 1906-7, F. W. Hall, W. M. Gilbert, 2 vol. (Oxford: Clarendon Press); a verse translation, now somewhat dated but still cited, the Greek text on facing pages but no apparatus by Benjamin Bickley Rogers, 3 vol., Loeb Classical Library (Cambridge: Harvard University Press, 1924); Dudley Fitts' modern translation of *Lysistrata*, *Frogs*, *Birds*, and *Thesmophoriazusae* is very serviceable for modern readers (New York: Harcourt, Brace 1962); D. Barrett provides a good translation of *Wasps*, *Thesmophoriazusae*, and *Frogs* (Harmondsworth: Penguin, 1964); A. H. Sommerstein is engaged in an ongoing series of translations of the eleven extant plays, full edition with Greek text and English commentary (London: Aris and Phillips 1981). Good idiomatic translations of the individual plays appear in the University of Michigan series. Two good annotated bibliographies, listing all major editions and important scholarship, are those of K. J. Dover, "Aristophanes 1938-55" in *Lustrum* 2 (1957-58): 52-112 (arranged by subject and listing 227 items) and C. T. Murphy, "A Survey of Recent Work on Aristophanes and Old Comedy" in *Classical World* 49 (1956): 201-11 (continued in *Classical World* 65 (1972) 261-73 for the years 1957-67); taken together, they effectively survey Aristophanes scholarship to 1967. T. Gelzer, "Hinweise auf einige neuere Bücher zu Aristophanes" in *Museum Helveticum* 21 (1964) cites and comments on several important books, primarily German, which appeared in 1962-63.

Overview of Biographical Sources

There is no purely biographical study of Aristophanes. His life is necessarily treated in the context of the party politics of his day and the important personalities and events which form the stuff of his plays; Socrates, Pericles, Nicias, Cleon, Alcibiades, the tragedians Aeschylus, Sophocles, and Euripides, the Peloponnesian War, the plague at Athens. T. A. Sinclair, *A History of Classical Greek Literature from Homer to Aristotle* (London: Macmillan, 1934; rpt. New York: Collier Paperback, 1962) gives a short biographical sketch with analyses of the eleven extant plays. He emphasizes the historical events which occasioned their writing and provides a good introduction for the general reader. The biography in *Harper's Dictionary of Classical Literature and Antiquities,* H. T. Peck, ed. (New York: Cooper Square, 1963) is likewise excellent. Also easily accessible is the article in the *Oxford Classical Dictionary*, though this has less detail than the Harper's entry. Aristophanes is important in the historical development of Greek drama; indeed, the scathing parodies in his plays hastened the demise of Old Comedy (portrayal of actual persons and events). Marguerite Bieber's *History of the Greek and Roman Theatre* (Princeton: Princeton University Press, 1961) deals with architecture primarily but also treats theatre history. It is profusely illustrated and scholarly, though written straightforwardly and has an appeal for any reader with an interest in classical drama.

Autobiographical Sources

While an ancient *Vita* is attached to several of the manuscripts, this is essentially a compilation of scattered autobiographical references in the plays and is of later composition. The plays themselves were drawn from important events in Aristophanes' life, and Gilbert Murray presents a good discussion of these autobiographical references in the first chapter of his text, *Aristophanes: A Study*. (Oxford: Clarendon Press, 1933; New York: Russell & Russell, 1964).

Evaluation of Selected Biographies

The following studies consider details of Aristophanes' life in relation to important events of Greek civilization, politics, or theatre history. All are more specialized than the works cited above.

Behr, C. A. "Old Comedy and the Free State," in *Harvard Studies in Classical Philology* 65 (1961): 345-348. This is an easily available summary of a dissertation which considers the sources of Old Comedy and how it was repressed in the name of Athenian democracy.

Dornseiff, F. "Aristophanes," in *Altertum* 2 (1956): 170-181. Examines the poet's relationship to the Peloponnesian War and outlines the plays with emphasis on their historical backgrounds.

Dover, K. J. "Aristophanes' Speech in Plato's *Symposium*," in *Journal of Hellenic Studies* 86 (1966): 41-50. This is an unusual and interesting article which examines what Plato's portrait of Aristophanes implies about how the Socratics viewed a man supposedly their antagonist.

Lever, Katharine, *The Art of Greek Comedy*. London: Methuen, 1956. Lever believes that the events of Aristophanes' life allowed him to serve as teacher, prophet, priest, and doctor of his society as well as playwright. These ideas follow a worthwhile introduction to Greek comedy.

Murphy, C. T. "Aristophanes, Athens, and Attica," in *Classical Journal* 59 (1964): 306-323. This article is of special interest to a student visiting Greece or one interested in the places Aristophanes refers to in the plays. Murphy distinguishes between historical locations and those merely invented.

Strauss, Leo, *Socrates and Aristophanes*. New York: Basic Books, 1966. This unusual book deals with what the lives and ideas of each man reveal about the relationship between them. Strauss believes that Aristophanes was not anti-Socratic as might appear to have been the case from the portrait of Socrates in *Clouds*. While Strauss's interpretations of Socratic thought could be questioned, the book sets forth interesting ideas and presents a clever synthesis.

Overview of Critical Sources
Nearly a thousand critical works have appeared since 1945. For the general reader the best critical works are those which combine elements of interpretation and biography. Traditionally the approach in these is to see Aristophanes as a playwright whose career begins with cynical and savage parodies and ends with plays whose meanings are more elusive and subtle. Many of the works cited above for their biographical content can therefore stand as well as studies of Aristophanes' art.

Evaluation of Selected Criticism
Arnott, P. D. *Greek Scenic Conventions in the Fifth Century B.C.* Oxford: Clarendon Press, 1962. Uses evidence from the comedies to support arguments for

a permanent stage altar, a raised stage, and use of the *ekkyklema* (for presenting interior scenes) in the Attic theatre of the fifth century. Arnott, while approaching his subject archaeologically, uses portions of the plays to support his thesis.

Dover, K. J. *Aristophanic Comedy.* Berkeley and Los Angeles: University of California Press, 1972. Designed for the reader with no Greek, this important work provides three brief background essays, then concentrates on analyses of the eleven extant plays. It concludes with final comments on Middle and New Comedy and the problems encountered in translating and studying Aristophanes.

McLeish, K. *The Theatre of Aristophanes.* London: Thames & Hudson, 1980. McLeish is concerned with the historical circumstances which produce New Comedy and believes that the scathingly effective parodies of Aristophanes' plays hastened its onset.

Murray, Gilbert, *Aristophanes: A Study.* Oxford: Clarendon Press, 1933; New York: Russell & Russell, 1964. This reissued study is often cited and readily obtainable. It discusses the plays in relation to historical events and personalities and contains a good chapter on Aristophanes' relationship to Menander.

Whitman, Cedric, *Aristophanes and the Comic Hero.* Cambridge: Harvard, 1964. Whitman believes that the diverse protagonists of the plays may be compared on the basis of their "supreme selfmanship," a reliance on unscrupulous tactics and wit to work their ends. This study has become an often cited study on Aristophanes' characters.

Other Sources

Dale, A. M. "An Interpretation of Aristophanes' *Vespae* 136-210 and Its Consequences for the Stage of Aristophanes," in *Journal of Hellenic Studies* 77 (1957): 205-11. Presents arguments for single house and door as setting for the fifth century stage. The argument is unusual, is based on a brief passage from the *Wasps*, and runs counter to prevailing views such as those of Arnott, Bieber, Lever, and others.

Littlefield, D. J., ed. *The Frogs: Twentieth Century Interpretations.* Englewood Cliffs: Prentice-Hall, 1968. This is a collection of previously printed essays on the play. They are suitable for general readers and provide a good introduction.

Marquardt, M. "Zur Verwendbarkeit des Komödientyps in der sozialistischen Buhnenkunst," in *Altertum* 12 (1966): 242-252. A socialist critic argues that Aristophanes aimed primarily at social reform in his plays, that his real goal was to awaken the Athenian "social conscience."

Okal, M. "Aristophanes et l'armée athenienne," in *Eirene* 1 (1960): 101-124. Okal argues that anti-democratic tendencies of Aristophanes repeatedly emerge in his comedies. The article is open to challenge and could be read against the Strauss and Marquardt works cited above.

Petruzzellis, N. "Aristophanes et la sofistica," in *Dionsio* 20 (1957): 38-62. This article is in two parts, a review of the theories of comedy with an approach to Aristophanes and Aristophanes' treatment of Socrates and the Socratics. The article also examines Aristophanes' relationship to the Sophists. The interpretations of Socratic thought are open to question, but Aristophanes considered in relation to the Sophistic movement makes this an interesting treatment.

Webster, T. B. L. *Greek Theatre Production*. London: Methuen, 1956. Contains brief, clear general treatments of staging conventions, the theatre building, stage, use of masks, nature of costumes, and the like.

Robert J. Forman
St. John's University, New York

ARISTOTLE
384-322 B.C.

Author's Chronology

Born 384 B.C. in Stagira (in northern Greece); may have spent part of boyhood in Macedonia; *367* enters Plato's Academy at Athens and remains for 20 years; c. *348-347* after Plato's death, leaves Athens and joins philosophic circle at court of Hermeias in Assos (Asia Minor); marries Pythias (niece or adopted daughter of Hermeias); c. *344-343* moves to island of Lesbos; c. *343-342* goes to Macedonia and becomes tutor to Alexander, son of King Philip II; c. *340* moves to Stagira; *335* returns to Athens; founds school known as the Lyceum, which becomes location of extensive research and teaching; about this time his wife dies; he takes as a companion Herpyllis, who bears him a son; *323* charged with capital offense of impiety after outbreak of anti-Macedonian feeling following Alexander's death; leaves Athens for Chalcis; *322* dies of stomach ailment.

Author's Bibliography (selected)

Aristotle's most important works include his *Logic* (or *Organon*), *Physics*, *Metaphysics*, *On the Soul*, *Nicomachean Ethics*, *Politics*, *Rhetoric*, and *Poetics*. Exact dates for the composition of his works are not known, but scholars believe many were written during his second stay in Athens (after 335 B.C.). The *Poetics* may date either from that period or earlier, perhaps as early as 360. All of Aristotle's surviving writings may be found in *The Complete Works of Aristotle*, edited by Jonathan Barnes, 2 vols. (Princeton: Princeton University Press, 1984). A good selection is found in *The Basic Works of Aristotle*, edited by Richard McKeon (New York: Random House, 1941). For the *Poetics*, Aristotle's one major work on poetry and drama, several good translations are available: *Poetics*, translated by Gerald F. Else (Ann Arbor: University of Michigan Press, 1967); T.S. Dorsch's translation in *Classical Literary Criticism* (Baltimore: Penguin Books, 1965); and the translations by Butcher, Cooper, and Golden listed below. The *Poetics* is also available in many anthologies of literary criticism, such as Hazard Adams' *Critical Theory Since Plato* (New York: Harcourt Brace Jovanovich, 1971); Walter Jackson Bate's *Criticism: The Major Texts* (New York: Harcourt Brace Jovanovich, 1970); Allan H. Gilbert's *Literary Criticism: Plato to Dryden* (Detroit: Wayne State University Press, 1962); and D.A. Russell and M. Winterbottom's *Ancient Literary Criticism* (Oxford: Clarendon Press, 1972).

Overview of Biographical Sources

The authoritative work on Aristotle's life is Ingemar Düring's *Aristotle in the Ancient Biographical Tradition* (Göteborg, 1957). Düring includes and evaluates all the ancient sources on Aristotle's life and personality and concludes with a short section summarizing what these sources mean. Except for this last section, Düring's book, while essential for scholars, is too technical for the general student. Also rather technical is Werner Jaeger's influential (but widely challenged) *Aristotle: Fundamentals of his Development* (2nd ed.; Oxford: Clarendon Press, 1948), which revolutionized the study of Aristotle by setting his works in the context of his life and asserting that his ideas changed over time. More accessible to most students are the brief sections on Aristotle's life found in most general studies of Aristotle, such as G.E.R. Lloyd's *Aristotle: The Growth and Structure of his Thought* (Cambridge: Cambridge University Press, 1968); John Herman Randall's *Aristotle* (New York: Columbia University Press, 1960); and Sir David Ross's *Aristotle* (5th ed.; London: Methuen, 1966).

Overview of Critical Sources

Most of the general studies of Aristotle just cited include sections on the *Poetics* and other works of interest to students of literature. Ross, for instance, has a chapter on the *Rhetoric* and the *Poetics,* and Randall sets the *Poetics* very usefully in the context of Aristotle's general temper of thought. Other good general discussions of Aristotle's literary views may be found in William K. Wimsatt and Cleanth Brooks' *Literary Criticism: A Short History* (New York: Alfred A. Knopf, 1967), in which chapters on Aristotle relate his ideas to issues of persistent concern in literary theory (such as poetic structure and language and tragedy and comedy as genres); D.A. Russell's *Criticism in Antiquity* (London: Duckworth, 1981), in which chapters on "Mimesis," "Rhetoric," "Classification of Literature," and other topics treat Aristotle along with other ancient critics; G.M.A. Grube's *The Greek and Roman Critics* (London: Methuen, 1965), in which a long chapter on Aristotle discusses the *Poetics,* the *Rhetoric,* and the section of the *Politics* on the social role of music and poetry; and W.J. Bate's long introduction to the *Poetics* in his *Criticism: The Major Texts.*

Since its rediscovery during the Renaissance, the *Poetics* has exercised enormous influence on literary, and specifically on dramatic, theory. The work's influence in Europe from antiquity through the Renaissance and beyond is briefly traced in Lane Copper's *The Poetics of Aristotle: Its Meaning and Influence* (Ithaca: Cornell University Press, 1923); and a thorough discussion of the work's influence in England from the Middle Ages to the early twentieth century is provided in Marvin Theodore Herrick's *The Poetics of Aristotle in England* (New Haven: Yale University Press, 1930). As these books demonstrate, each age has interpreted the *Poetics* after its own fashion, neoclassic critics deriving the influential idea of the three unities (time, place, and action) from hints in Aristotle; later critics taking a less rigid view; and critics of each age taking various views on such Aristotelian concepts as imitation, catharsis, reversal (*peripeteia*), the tragic error (*hamartia*), and the tragic character. The general trend of recent criticism on the *Poetics* has been to move away from notions derived from Aristotle but not clearly present in the text—such as some versions of the "tragic flaw" and of catharsis—and to look more closely at what Aristotle actually wrote.

One of the subjects of greatest dispute has been *hamartia,* the error that Aristotle makes responsible for the tragic character's downfall. The standard view through the nineteenth century was that this error was a moral flaw; many recent critics have suggested that it is instead an error of judgment. Important studies of the question include Philip Whaley Harsh, "*Hamartia* Again," *Transactions of the American Philological Association* 76 (1945): 47-58, who favors the idea of moral culpability; E.R. Dodds, "On Misunderstanding the *Oedipus Rex,*" in *The Ancient Concept of Progress* (Oxford: Clarendon Press, 1973), who takes the opposite view; T.C.W. Stinton, "*Hamartia* in Aristotle and Greek Tragedy," *Classical Quarterly* 25 (1975): 221-254, who argues that *hamartia* may have a range of meanings encompassing both views; and J.M. Bremer, *Hamartia* (Amsterdam: Adolf M. Hakkert, 1969), who surveys the various opinions held on the subject. Another major area of discussion has been catharsis, which has been variously interpreted as a medical or psychological purging, as a religious purification, even as a purifying, not of the audience, but (through artistic imitation) of an otherwise crude and painful story. For this last view, see H.D.F. Kitto, "Catharsis," in *The Classical Tradition,* edited by Luitpold Wallach (Ithaca: Cornell University Press, 1966).

Evaluation of Selected Criticism

Butcher, S.H. *Aristotle's Theory of Poetry and Fine Art.* 4th ed. London: St. Martin's Press, 1911; rpt. New York: Dover, 1951. For almost a century, Butcher's book has been highly influential—for instance, in its description of the tragic hero and in its suggestion that, in catharsis, the emotions are not only relieved, but also purified of their painful and purely personal or self-regarding elements and thus universalized. But on these and other questions, the book has been criticized by many scholars as straying from Aristotle's original meaning. Though it begins with the Greek text and Butcher's translation (on facing pages), the bulk of the book consists of essays on art and nature, imitation, the function of art and tragedy, the unities, the tragic hero, plot and character, poetic universality, and other topics related to the *Poetics.* These essays are illuminating, but often go beyond Aristotle to consider in very general terms the issues he raises.

Cooper, Lane, *Aristotle on the Art of Poetry.* rev. ed. Ithaca: Cornell University, 1947. This translation, accompanied by what amounts to a running commentary, will be helpful both to the beginning student and to anyone looking for insight into difficult passages. Besides frequently expanding the original text in order to make it more readily intelligible, Cooper adds explanatory comments in brackets and introduces illustrations from English literature and other sources to supplement those of Aristotle. The effect, on the whole, is illuminating and stimulating, though sometimes at the cost of pushing the reader toward one of many possible interpretations, occasionally with emphasis on views no longer favored by scholars. On the other hand, Cooper often points out difficulties and possible interpretations the reader might otherwise miss.

Else, Gerald F. *Aristotle's Poetics: The Argument.* Cambridge: Harvard University Press, 1957. Starting from the assumption that the *Poetics* forms "a single coherent piece of argument," Else sets out to analyze that argument point by point. The book presents the Greek text (except for a few of the more technical sections) in segments, each segment followed by an English translation and a detailed, line-by-line analysis. Else examines textual details, considers previous opinions on passages, and offers his own sometimes controversial reinterpretations of such questions as imitation, Aristotle's views on the origins of poetry and comedy, the kinds of tragedy, the "unity of time," and catharsis. He views catharsis, not as the play's effect on the audience's emotions, but as the effect of the play's structure on the tragic act, purifying what would otherwise be morally offensive. Else's book is long and is intended for advanced study, but beginning students may find it useful as a reference tool for understanding particular passages.

Golden, Leon, and O.B. Hardison, *Aristotle's Poetics: A Translation and Commentary for Students of Literature.* Englewood Cliffs, NJ: Prentice-Hall, 1968. Hardison's commentary, which follows Golden's translation, analyzes and discusses the *Poetics* chapter by chapter. This commentary, though serious and detailed, is designed for students coming to the *Poetics* for the first time. In addition to serving as a basic introduction, the book helpfully brings together the views of many important critics of the *Poetics,* while at the same time offering a coherent interpretation of its own. *Hamartia,* for instance, is viewed as a miscalculation rather than a sin (but without denying a possible moral dimension), and catharsis is defined as an "intellectual clarification of the incidents." For this view of catharsis, see also two articles by Leon Golden: "Catharsis," *Transactions of the American Philological Association* 93 (1962): 51-60, and "*Mimesis* and *Katharsis,*" *Classical Philology* 64 (1969): 145-153.

House, Humphry, *Aristotle's Poetics.* London: R. Hart-Davis, 1956. A brief but stimulating introduction to the *Poetics* (originally a series of Oxford lectures), written with clarity and a refreshingly engaging style. After a quick survey of Aristotle's life and thought, House discusses the main ideas of the *Poetics* in chapters on plot, character, catharsis, and pleasure and imitation. He argues persuasively for his view of *hamartia* as an error based on ignorance and of catharsis as an exercising, directing, and balancing of the emotions.

Other Sources
Else, Gerald F. *The Origin and Early Form of Greek Tragedy.* Cambridge: Har-

vard University Press, 1967. A short but solid book offering an alternative both to Aristotle's and to many modern theories of the origin of tragedy.

Jones, John, *On Aristotle and Greek Tragedy.* London: Chatto & Windus, 1962. Though concerned mainly with Aeschylus, Sophocles, and Euripides, Jones begins with a section on the *Poetics,* emphasizing Aristotle's definition of tragedy as an imitation of an action and asserting that the idea of the tragic hero comes, not from the *Poetics,* but from the preconceptions of modern readers.

Kitto, H.D.F. *Greek Tragedy.* 2nd ed. London: Methuen, 1950. A discussion of the major Greek tragedians, with frequent reference to Aristotle's ideas. For Kitto's later, sometimes modified views, see *Form and Meaning in Drama* (London: Methuen, 1956) and *Poeisis: Structure and Thought* (Berkeley: University of California Press, 1966).

Lucas, D.W. *Aristotle: Poetics.* Oxford: Clarendon Press, 1968. This highly respected work of scholarship may be too advanced for some students. The main body of the book (after an introduction to Aristotle's works and the place of the *Poetics* among them) consists of the Greek text of the *Poetics,* followed by a detailed commentary that closely examines words and phrases from the text. Probably of greatest use to beginning students are the appendices, which offer concise and informative discussions of *mimesis, katharsis,* simple and complex tragedy, and *hamartia.*

Lucas, F.L. *Tragedy: Serious Drama in Relation to Aristotle's Poetics.* rev. ed. London: The Hogarth Press, 1957. Examines Aristotle's ideas as they relate to later ideas on tragedy and to examples of tragedy from ancient times to the present.

Olson, Elder, ed. *Aristotle's "Poetics" and English Literature.* Chicago: University of Chicago Press, 1965. A collection of essays in the Aristotelian tradition, ranging from the eighteenth to the twentieth century and including some work from the modern critical movement known as the "Chicago" or "neo-Aristotelian" school.

Selected Dictionaries and Encyclopedias

Ancient Writers: Greece and Rome, Charles Scribners' Sons, 1982. Includes a long article on Aristotle's life, works, and ideas, with a substantial section on the *Rhetoric* and *Poetics.*

Encyclopaedia Britannica: Macropaedia, 1974. Has an extensive article on Aristotle and Aristotelianism, including a detailed account of Aristotle's life and a short section on the *Poetics.*

Oxford Companion to English Literature. 5th ed. Oxford University Press, 1985. Has a brief article on Aristotle noting his influence on English literature.

Bruce W. Young
Brigham Young University

ROBERTO ARLT
1900-1942

Author's Chronology

Born Roberto Godofredo Christophersen Arlt, April 2, 1900, Buenos Aires; grows up in unsettled household of Karl Arlt, lately of Germany, and Ekatherine Iobstraibitzer, from Trieste; *1916* leaves home; *1918* begins writing for popular periodicals; *1922* marries Carmen Antinucci; daughter Mirta, Arlt's literary executrix and posthumous editor, born *1923*; Arlt's fame in journalism grows; *1928* launches the 'Etchings," a famous column in the newspaper *El Mundo* (The World) which rivets the city's readers (English selection appears 1982); *1929* Arlt attracts fame and controversy with his novels, especially *Los siete locos* (*The Seven Madmen*, 1984); *1932* despite enjoying a ready-made audience in journalism and prose fiction, Arlt turns to experimental theater, to which he devotes his main effort subsequently while continuing to work for newspapers and magazines; *1940* wife dies; *1941* marries Elizabeth Shine; *1942* dies of heart attack.

Author's Bibliography

During his lifetime, Arlt was Buenos Aires' star journalist and a much-discussed fiction writer. The drama to which he gave his last ten years had a much smaller public. Arlt's playscripts, never widely circulated in lasting editions, were by the 1960s nearing the status of collector's or archival items. Interest in Arlt and his theater rose abruptly in the 1960s. The demand for accessible playscripts was answered by Schapire Editores, which brought out a two-volume *Teatro completo* (Complete Theater) edited and annotated by Mirta Arlt. It gives established versions of major staged plays. Subsequently *Un hombre sensible* (*A Sensitive Man*) and *La juerga de las polichinelas* (*Punch and Judy Go Wild*) were discovered in the archives of the newspaper *La Nación*. These mid-1930s dramatic sketches appear, together with the reprinted 1968 editions, in volume 2 of Arlt, *Obra completa* (*Complete Works*), published by Carlos Lohlé in 1981. Mirta Arlt details her father's theatrical staging and publishing history, including items in neither of the above collections, in her notes to the 1982 edition of *Trescientos millones* (*Three Hundred Million*; probably Arlt's "classic" play) and *La juerga de las polichinelas*. It should be noted that Arlt wrote many brief sketches in dialogue; the customary editorial practice has been to include these with short prose works. Arlt's works in English are: "Esther Primavera" (short story) in *Doors and Mirrors: Fiction and Poetry from Spanish America 1920-1970* (1972, Grossman; rpt. 1973, Viking); "One Sunday Afternoon" (short story) in *Eye of the Heart, Short Stories from Latin America*, (1973, Bobbs-Merrill; rpt. 1974, Avon); "Small-Time Property Owners" (short sketch with dialogue) in *Contemporary Latin American Short Stories*, (1974, Fawcett); *"Selections from Aguafuertes porteñas"* (Arlt's famous column); and "From *Los siete locos*" (excerpt from novel *The Seven Madmen*) in *Review of the Center for Inter-American Relations*, No. 31 (1982); *The Seven Madmen* (trans. Naomi Lindstrom, Boston: David R. Godine, 1984.)

Overview of Biographical Sources

Because Arlt's strong personality and erratic behavior helped make him a legend of Buenos Aires literary life, and because of the autobiographical strain in his work, there is abundant reference to Arlt's life and person in the writing about him and his work. Examples of this frequently biographical commentary include Nilda Etchenique, *Roberto Arlt* (Buenos Aires: La Mandrágora, 1962); Diana Guerrero, *Roberto Arlt, el habitante solitario* (Buenos Aires: Granica Editor, 1972); Raúl Larra, *Roberto Arlt el torturado* (Buenos Aires: Futuro, 1950); Oscar Masotta, *Sexo y traición en Roberto Arlt* (Buenos Aires: Jorge Alvarez, 1965). These works tend toward speculation about the influence of Arlt's personal idiosyncracies upon his work.

Less such speculation appears in the more straightforwardly biographical section of Eduardo González Lanuza, *Roberto Arlt* (Buenos Aires: Centro Editor de América Latina, 1971); this work also features the legendary anecdotes of Arlt in Buenos Aires. Mirta Arlt's prefaces, especially that accompanying the above-mentioned *Three Hundred Million*, are informative ones.

Evaluation of Selected Biographies (in English)

Dowling, Lee, "Chronology" in *Review of the Center of Inter-American Relations*, No. 31 (1982), pp. 26-28. This year-by year account contains minor errors, but is very usable and the best informative chronicle available in English.

Foster, David William, "Arlt, the Maverick," in *Review of the Center for Inter-American Relations*, No. 31 (1982), pp. 29-30. This interpretive piece examines Arlt's rebellion against literary conventions and standards.

Onetti, Juan Carlos, "Preface to *Los siete locos*," in *Review of the Center for Inter-American Relations*, No. 31 (1982), pp. 34-35. Excerpted from Onetti's preface to the Italian translation of *The Seven Madmen*, this essay gives a celebrated fellow writer's vivid recollections of Arlt's personality and presence on the Buenos Aires scene.

Autobiographical Sources

Arlt's most autobiographical writings are the columns he wrote for *El Mundo* beginning in 1928. The late-1920s and early-1930s "Buenos Aires Etchings" show Arlt as an eccentric strolling observer of his native city. Later etchings include travelogues of Arlt's swings through Spain, North Africa and elsewhere; the Arlt of these travel writings is a more worldly individual than the easily-astonished narrator of the early columns. Losada publishing house of Buenos Aires has a long record of keeping the etchings in circulation, collected in volumes. With the Arlt revival, other publishers launched editions of the etchings. A critical edition with considerable commentary about Arlt's self-portrait as a reader of literature is Daniel C. Scroggins, *Las aguafuertes porteñas de Roberto Arlt* (Buenos Aires: Ediciones Culturales Argentinas, 1981).

Overview of Critical Sources (in English)

The Arlt boom of the 1960s brought this innovative figure, whose readership had dwindled to a virtual cult, to high critical and public visibility. There are currently numerous studies covering all genres. A work devoted entirely to Arlt's theater Raúl H. Castagnino, *El teatro de Roberto Arlt* (La Plata: Universidad Nacional de la Plata, 1964; rpt. Editorial Nova, 1970). In English, Arlt begins to receive attention in the 1970s; for example, he is one of four authors studied at length in David William Foster, *Currents in the Contemporary Argentine Novel* (Columbia: University of Missouri, 1975); English-language commentary on Arlt appears in such journals as *Latin American Literary Review*, *Kentucky Romance Quarterly*, *Romance Notes* and *Chasqui*.

Evaluation of Selected Criticism (in English)

Foster, David William, "Roberto Arlt's *La isla desierta*: A Structural Analysis," in *Latin American Theatre Review*, 11, 1 (1977), pp. 25-34. Foster examines how theatrical dialogue reveals the disaffection and isolation of the characters in *La isla desierta* (*The Desert Island*). The speech of these characters, who are bored office workers fantasizing about a faraway retreat, is characterized by ritualistic repetition of phrases and other signs of non-communicative, fetishistic use of language. Foster's analysis is useful because it suggests how analysis of the structure of dialogue can help explain the famous and oft-noted alienation and isolation of Arlt's characters.

Lindstrom, Naomi, "The World's Illogic in two Plays by Argentine Expressionists," in *Latin American Literary Review*, 4, 8 (1976), pp. 83-88; also in *Literary Expressionism in Argentina*, Tempe, AZ: Center for Latin American Studies, 1977. This commentary on Arlt's posthumously produced and published play *El desierto entra a la ciudad* (*Desert Comes to the City*) examined together with a drama by Armando Discépolo, shows the principles of dramatic expression involved in both works to be strongly akin to the tenets of expressionism. The frequently-made assertion that Arlt's plays were avant-garde is confirmed by linking his dramatic program to that of a major current in the avant-garde. In particular, the expressionist imperative to show the world as a madhouse, devoid of rational order, is fulfilled in Arlt's dramaturgy.

Troiano, James J. "The Grotesque Tradition and the Interplay of Fantasy and Reality in the Plays of Roberto Arlt," in *Latin American Literary Review*, 4, 8 (1976), pp. 7-14. Troiano seeks to specify the elements in Arlt's drama that have been vaguely characterized as bizarre or fantastic. Two factors stand out: Arlt's plays draw upon, and form part of, the long-standing tradition of the grotesque, and they comingle realistic depiction of situations with projections of the characters' hallucinations, longings and fantasies.

Naomi Lindstrom
University of Texas at Austin

JAMES BARRIE
1860-1937

Author's Chronology

Born May 9, 1860, in Kirriemuir, Forfarshire, Scotland, to David and Margaret Ogilvy Barrie; *1867* older brother David is accidently killed—a crucial event in James' life; *1873-1878* attends Dumfries Academy; *1878-1882* enters Edinburgh University and earns M.A. degree; *1833-1885* begins journalistic career, doing free lance work for Fleet Street papers; *1887* publishes first book, *Better Dead*; *1891* production of first play, *Richard Savage*; *1894* marries Mary Ansell, an actress; *1904 Peter Pan* opens for fifty-year run; *1904* receives honorary LL.D from Edinburgh University and divorces wife for adultery; *1913* created a baronet by George V; *1926* accepts honorary doctorates from Oxford and Cambridge; *1930* becomes Chancellor of Edinburgh University; June 19, *1937*, dies and is buried in Kirriemuir.

Author's Bibliography

Barrie was a productive journalist and prolific writer of fiction, miscellaneous prose works, and plays. The majority of his fiction and prose writing is found in the following editions of his works: the Kirriemuir Editions, 10 vols. (London Hodder and Stonghton, 1913); the Thistle Edition, 12 vols. (New York: Charles Scribner's Sons, 1896); and the Peter Pan Edition, vols. 1-11 (New York: Charles Scribner's Sons, 1929). The plays that Barrie wished to preserve are in the so-called "Definitive Edition" entitled *The Plays of J. M. Barrie*, ed. A. E. Wilson (London: Hodder and Stongthton, 1947).

Overview of Biographical Sources

Although Barrie was a public figure for much of his life and wrote with candor about himself, revealing many thinly veiled autobiographical details in his novels and plays, there is still much that is puzzling about the man's character. His early biographers who were fervent admirers or Scottish literary partisans did little to help our understanding of the essential Barrie. Books like Patrick Braybrooke's *J. M. Barrie: A Study in Fairies and Mortals* (London: Drane, 1924) and Sir John Hammerton's *Barrie: The Story of a Genius* (London: Samson Low, 1929) are typical of the sentimental, superficial lives that were produced by Barrie's contemporaries. The earliest full-length study of any merit is Denis Mackail's *The Story of J. M. B.* (1941), which was the standard biography until superseded by Janet Dunbar's *J. M. Barrie: The Man Behind the Image* (1970). Drawing on archival sources such as unpublished letters, diaries, and notes, Dunbar frames her portrait of Barrie on his relationships with four women—his mother, his wife, his secretary, and a friend, Sylvia Davis. Though generally sympathetic, she does not conceal Barrie's problems, which are explained psychologically but without excessive analytical jargon. While not a biography in the strict sense Andrew Birkin's *J. M. Barrie and the Lost Boys* (1979) provides an easy and interesting entry into a phase of Barrie's life. Using photographs and extracts of letters and passages from Barrie's literary works, Birkin reconstructs the middle-aged Barrie's relationship with the five Davies brothers that began in 1901 and resulted in *Peter Pan*, which depicts the boys as characters.

Evaluation of Selected Biographies

Birkin, Andrew, *J. M. Barrie and the Lost Boys*. New York: Potter, 1979. This book is a "spin-off" from a popular BBC series about Barrie's strange involvement with the Davies boys whom he "adopted" or appropriated following the break-up of his childless marriage. Birkin presents a poignant picture of a man who loved children but could not have his own, who also knew the delights and tragedy of never growing up. This is a highly readable account that is interesting without really adding anything new, except the numerous revealing photographs that illustrate the text.

Dunbar, Janet, *J. M. Barrie; the Man Behind the Image*. Boston: Houghton Mifflin, 1970. Dunbar provides much new biographical information but little interpretation of the literary works in what is currently the most comprehensive study of Barrie's life. The literary executors of Barrie's estate made several key documents available to Dunbar such as the diaries of Barrie's private secretary, Lady Asquith, who worked for him for nineteen years and the unpublished diary of Peter Davies (the protype for Peter Pan). Her understanding of Barrie's personality, based on this evidence, is that he was a neurotic case of arrested development, driven by a need to possess and be possessed by people he admired. The only drawback of this fine biography is that from a scholarly standpoint the documentation is not specific enough.

Mackail, Denis, *The Story of J. M. B.* London: Peter Davis, 1941. Commissioned by the Barrie's literary executors, this biography was the first authorized life and was long the standard work about Barrie. Mackail gives a lengthy and full account, but does not write in a readable style nor provide sufficient documentation. Some commentary is given to the works, but the most space is devoted to a review of the surface details of Barrie's life, many of them irrelevant, contributing to the 736-page bulk of the book. There are redundant accounts of weekends in the country with the aristocracy and Barrie's bouts with bronchitis but no explanation of important matters, such as his fixation on his mother or his sexual impotence.

Autobiographical Sources

Barrie's most direct autobiographical writing is found in his memoir of his mother, *Margaret Ogilvy* (1896). Though some of the facts of Barrie's strange childhood are reflected in nearly all that he wrote, here he relates the story in full. Recalling conversations verbatim that he had with his mother, he builds this book around their dialogues, much of it in Scottish dialect. His version of the events surrounding his brother David's accidental death are especially important for understanding Barrie's subsequent physical and psychological development; ironically, the biography of his mother reveals more about him than it does about her. Barrie was a prolific letter writer, but his correspondence has never been collected in a complete edition. Viola Meynell compiled and edited *Letters of J. M. Barrie* (New York: Charles Scribner's Sons, 1947); however, most of these letters ranging in date from 1884 to 1937 are polite correspondence and tell more of Barrie's social calendar than his character.

Overview of Critical Sources

Like the early biographical studies most of the criticism of Barrie was appreciative rather than analytical and many of the critics were too kind to Barrie for his own good. Even today there has been remarkably little serious study of Barrie's literary themes, forms, and techniques. Since so much of Barrie's writing was autobiographical in nature, it has attracted the attention of Freudian critics who have analyzed his works in order to interpret some to the complexities of his character. Psychoanalytical critics have been especially concerned with Barrie's mother worship, his affinity with young boys, and his sexual impotence. Some have shown great ingenuity in tracing his art to his neurotic condition.

Evaluation of Selected Criticism

Blake, George, *Barrie and the Kailyard School*. London: Baker, 1951. Blake makes no attempt at a full-length study of Barrie, but offers perceptive commentary on Barrie's role in the sub-genre of Scottish local color fiction, known as the "Cabbage Patch" or Kailyard School.

Geduld, Harry, *Sir James Barrie*. New York: Twayne, 1971. Geduld advances the thesis that the recurrent fantasies in Barrie's literary work have their origins in "prototypic" psychological experiences. The psychoanalytical approach yields some biographical insights, but causes Geduld to neglect Barrie's artistic techniques and makes the discussion of the literary works reductive. Otherwise, this is a useful guide with elaborate plot synopses, and goes far toward explaining how Barrie was the creator and captive of his sentimental fantasies.

Green, R. L. *Fifty Years of Peter Pan*. London: Peter Davis, 1954. Green gives a survey of the productions of Barrie's most enduring play which ran from 1904 to 1954 and is subject to frequent revivals, the most recent by Sandy Duncan on Broadway. This book contains chapters on the literary sources and biographical genesis of the play.

Other Sources

Adelman, Irving and Rita Dworkin, comp. *Modern Drama: A Checklist of Critical Literature on 20th Century Plays*. Metuchen, NJ: Scarecrow Press, 1967. Gives a selective listing of important general studies and articles on Barrie.

Hunter, Lynette, "J. M. Barrie's Islands of Fantasy," *Modern Drama* 23 (1980), pp. 65-74. Opines that Barrie uses islands as a literary motif to reveal his dual perspective on fantasy worlds, which are presented as both dangerous and attractive.

Karpe, Marietta, "The Origins of Peter Pan," *Psychoanalytic Review* 43 (1956), pp. 104-110. Speculates that Barrie was a classic case of neurotic arrested development which he rationalized through the hero of this play who refuses to grow up.

Lurie, Allison, "The Boy Who Couldn't Grow Up," *New York Review of Books* (6 February 1975), pp. 11-15. Analyzes *Margaret Ogilvy*, the "Tommy" novels and two plays, *Peter Pan* and *Mary Rose*, to show that Barrie's writings are allegories of his emotional life and personal relationships.

Hallman B. Bryant
Clemson University

BEAUMARCHAIS
Pierre-Augustin Caron
1732-1799

Author's Chronology

Pierre-Augustin Caron born in Paris, January 24, 1732; works in his father's shop as a watchmaker; *1754* wins suit from the Academy of Sciences against the watchmaker Lepaute who claims Caron's invention as his own; *1755* appointed watchmaker at the Court of Louis XV; *1756* marries the widow Madeleine-Catherine Franquet, who dies ten months later, and from whose estate he adopts the name Beaumarchais; rapid success at the Court and friendship with the financier Pâris-Duverney; *1764* travels to Spain to avenge his sister's honor; *1768* marries the widow Lévêque, who dies two years later; a son born of this marriage also dies soon after; *1767* his first drama *Eugénie* presented at the Comédie Francaise; *1773-1774* Goezman Affair, involving Beaumarchais's five *Mémoires*; Beaumarchais exonerated from the accusation of debt after Pâris-Duverney's death, but is labeled as a "blâmé"; to clear his name, works as a secret agent for Louis XV and Louis XVI, one of his most famous adventures involving the Chevalier d'Eon, disguised as a woman; *1775 Le Barbier de Sévile* played at the Comédie Francaise; Beaumarchais becomes involved in the War for American Independence, transacting business under the name of Rodrigue Hortalez at Cie; *1777* founds the *Société des Auteurs dramatiques* to seek proper payment for authors (finally granted by the National Assembly in 1791); *1779* undertakes to publish the complete works of Voltaire, a project finished in 1790 at a great financial loss and after much conflict with civil and religious authorities; *1781* involved in the Kornman case, which severely damages his reputation; *1786* marries Marie-Thérèse de Willermaulez, his mistress since 1776 and the mother of his daughter Eugénie; *1789* builds an impressive mansion near the Bastille, to be a cause of provocation during the Revolution; *1792-1794* incurs many accusations, imprisonments, and adventures on the charge of hiding guns, narrowly escapes with his life; *1794-1796* lives at Hamburg; *1796* returns to Paris, to the theater, and to public life; dies suddenly from an attack of apoplexy in Paris, May 17, 1799.

Author's Bibliography

Best known for his two plays, *Le Barbier de Séville* (*The Barber of Seville*, 1775), and *Le Mariage de Figaro* (*The Marriage of Figaro*), written in 1778, but not played until 1784, his fame rests on his own work as well as on the operas by Rossini and Mozart. His other dramatic works are inferior to these two masterpieces. They consist of *Eugénie*, 1767, which soon failed on the stage, and which was preceded by an essay on serious drama, entitled *Essai sur le genre dramatique sérieux*; *Les Deux Amis* or *le Négociant de Lyon* (The two friends, or the Lyon

34

businessman), 1770, likewise a failure; and *La Mère coupable*, a sentimental sequence to the two other Figaro plays, written in 1791 and first presented in 1792 without success, but which had moderate success after the Revolution and in the early nineteenth century. Beaumarchais is also the author of an opera, *Tarare*, written in 1784, and for which Salieri wrote the music, first presented in 1787. From the period 1760-1775 he wrote five *parades*, direct descendants of medieval farces, a genre which was popular in the eighteenth century, and was played in salons. Beaumarchais's *parades*, of which the most popular were *Les Bottes de Sept Lieues* (The seven-league boots), *Léandre*, and *Jean-Bête à la foire* (Jean-Bête at the fair), were probably played when he was in the good graces of M. Lenormand d'Etioles, the husband of Mme de Pompadour. Of equal merit with his best plays are his *Mémoires contre Goezman*, 1774, polemics often compared to Pascal's *Provinciales*. Frequently involved in law suits and similar adventures, Beaumarchais wrote numerous *mémoires*, against La Blache and Kornman, for example. One of his last and more interesting is *Mémoires des dix époques*, written to justify himself in the accusation of hiding 60,000 guns during the Revolution.

Although there are many editions of Beaumarchais's plays, the only editions of his *Oeuvres complètes* date from the nineteenth century. The first, published by his friend Gudin de la Brenellerie by Collin in 1809, was long the standard edition. The edition by Louis Moland, Paris: Garnier, 1874, is also important but incomplete. Of the many editions of the plays, the most accessible is the Pléiade, *Théâtre complet de Beaumarchais*, edited by Maurice Allem and Paul Courant. In English there are numerous editions of *The Barber of Seville* and *The Marriage of Figaro*. The most accessible are the Penguin edition, 1964, and the Appleton-Century-Crofts edition, 1966.

Overview of Biographical Sources

Since the life of Beaumarchais contains more adventures than any of his exciting plays, it is not surprising that many critics attach great importance to it. Guidin de la Brenellerie, Beaumarchais's secretary and friend, wrote a very favorable biography, not always critical, entitled *Histoire de Beaumarchais*, later published by Plon in 1888. The nineteenth-century works by Louis de Loménie *Beaumarchais et son temps* (Paris: Lévy, 1856; trans. Henry S. Edwards, *Beaumarchais and His Times*. New York: Harper, 1857), and Eugène Lintilhac *Beaumarchais et ses oeuvres* (Paris: Hachette, 1887), are still fundamental to an understanding of Beaumarchais, since both had access to family archives and documents in the possession of Beaumarchais's heirs or of the Comédie Francaise. Because of Beaumarchais's numerous political and personal adventures, one can find many works dealing with single aspects of his life. Important examples are Pierre Richard's *La vie privée de Beaumarchais* (Paris: Hachette, 1951), which emphasizes the individual rather than the man of his time; M. Leah Johnson's *Beaumarchais and his Opponents* (Richmond, VA: Dietz, 1936), an analysis of materials related to Goezman, Kornman, and other cases; and Elizabeth Kite's *Beaumarchais and the War of American Independence* (Boston: Badger, 1918). One of the best biographies in English is Cynthia Cox's *The Real Figaro*. Critical works of Beaumarchais's theater, such as those of Pomeau and Van Tieghem, also contain good biographical selections.

Evaluation of Selected Biographies

Cox, Cynthia, *The Real Figaro: The Extraordinary Career of Caron de Beaumarchais*. New York: Coward McCann, 1963. This book is an objective biography and a good use of primary sources, which enable the author to make well-founded conclusions in such complex issues as the Chevalier d'Eon, Beaumarchais and the French and American Revolutions, and the Goezman and Kornman cases. The work is written in a readable style, which does not detract from its factual nature. It contains a bibliography of interesting primary and secondary sources related to Beaumarchais and his times.

Kite, Elizabeth S. *Beaumarchais and the War of American Independence*. Boston: Badger, Gorham Press, 1918; 2 volumes. This admiring biography loses somewhat in its critical nature because of the author's romantic style. She has the honor of being one of the first to point out Beaumarchais's contributions to the American Revolution, and his persuasion of the King to bring aid to the Americans. She notes the later disappointment of the French and of Beaumarchais's heirs that America showed so little gratitude and even recognition of his work on their behalf. Only Chapters XVI-XXII address the American Revolution, and hence shed new light on Beaumarchais; the other materials repeat earlier biographies.

Overview of Autobiographical Sources

Beaumarchais' many *Mémoires* are not really autobiography, but rather polemics, often in the form of letters, addressing the various legal, political, and personal issues in which he was so often involved. The best of them are the *Mémoires contre Goezman*, 1773-1774; the least valuable and the most rapidly written, the *Mémoires contre Kornman*, 1781. The *Mémoires des dix époques*, 1792, give many curious insights into the French Revolution. On the whole, Beaumarchais's *Mémoires* are of more value as documentations of his personality, rather than factual material on his life.

Beaumarchais wrote a number of letters, but given the tumultuous nature of his life, the task of assembling them is still in progress. The best collection, *Correspondance*, in three volumes, was edited by Brian N. Morton (Paris: Nizet, 1969). Gilbert Chimard (Paris: Margraff, 1929), has also collected valuable letters in his *Lettres inédites de Beaumarchais*, which shed important biographical information. The Pléiade edition of Beaumarchais's *Théâtre* contains letters relative to his plays, and also gives Beaumarchais's essays and prefaces to his dramas.

Overview of Critical Sources

Critical works on Beaumarchais address principally his plays, and among them mainly *Le Barbier de Séville* and *Le Mariage de Figaro*, with the greatest number dealing with the latter. René Jasinski discovered sources to *Le Barbier de Séville*, which he published in *Revue d'histoire et de la philosophie*, Lille, 15 avril 1936 ("Sur la tirade de la calomnie dans "Le Barbier de Séville"). Further information on the topic is available in Emile Jules Arnould's *La Genèse du Barbier de Séville* (Paris: Minard, 1965). Among the monographs on *Le Mariage de Figaro* is Félix Gaiffe's *Le Mariage de Figaro* (Paris: Nizet, 1956), which deals with the composition, performance and criticism of Beaumarchais's masterpiece. Jasinski has also written numerous articles and prepared courses on this play. The less popular *La Mère coupable* is the subject of Jacques Vier's article on Beaumarchais in *Histoire de la littérature française du dix-huitième siècle* (Paris: Armand Colin, 1970).

There are a number of general works on Beaumarchais. One of the most practical in English is *Beaumarchais* in the Twayne series, by Joseph Sungolowsky. Edna Frederick's *The Plot and its Construction in the Eighteenth Century Criticism of French Comedy* (Benjamin Franklin, 1973) relates Beaumarchais's theory and practice with Diderot's ideas on the *drame*. French editions by René Pomeau, Philippe Van Tieghem, and Jacques Scherer are very well documented and show up-to-date research. Also to be noted is Auguste Bailly's *Beaumarchais, la vie et l'oeuvre* (Paris: Fayard, 1945). The notes and introduction and chronology to the Pléiade edition, by Maurice Allem and Paul-Courant are also helpful.

Evaluation of Selected Criticism

Pomeau, René, *Beaumarchais, l'homme et l'oeuvre*. Paris: Hatier-Boivin, 1956. Untranslated. This short work by an outstanding French critic is an extraordinary compendium of knowledge about Beaumarchais. The biographical section is quite complete, including many controversial facets of Beaumarchais's turbulent career. The discussion of the works devotes an ample section to *Mémoires* and the *parades*, not always addressed in general studies. The conclusion addresses Beaumarchais's fate in the nineteenth and early twentieth centuries. There is a good bibliography well commented.

Scherer, Jacques, *La Dramaturgie de Beaumarchais*. Paris: Nizet, 1954. Untranslated. Scherer draws on information from all of Beaumarchais's plays, including his *parades*, to examine their structure and essential characteristics. He examines the roots of Beaumarchais's plays in other dramatic works, especially, Molière, Racine, Voltaire, and Diderot. He analyzes the structure of the plays, finding the best of them like Beaumarchais's watches, simple and functional. Beaumarchais's success, according to Scherer, is due to his ability to adapt to public tastes, which in the eighteenth century sought pleasure and virtue, comedy, and political references suitable to the bourgeoisie. Scherer insists especially on the unity of Beaumarchais's theater, noting the relationship of the *parades* to the full-length dramas and comedies, with special attention to the disputed dates of the *parades*.

Sungolowsky, Joseph, *Beaumarchais*. New York: Twayne, 1974. This book presents a general introduction to the life and works of the author, and provides a good overview for the reader who wishes a superficial knowledge of Beaumarchais. The biography is highly simplified, an understandable necessity for such a complex life. All the principal works are addressed, with emphasis on the *Barber of Seville* and *The Marriage of Figaro*. There is a good bibliography included.

Van Tieghem, Philippe, *Beaumarchais par lui-même*. Paris: Seuil, 1960. Untranslated. As is usual in this series, the author presents a brief introduction to Beaumarchais, then allows him to speak for himself through quotations from his various works. Van Tieghem shows Beaumarchais as a man of his times, the sentimental and philosophical eighteenth century. This book is not a complete critique of Beaumarchais, and requires a more direct study to complement it.

Sister Irma M. Kashuba, S.S.J.
Chestnut Hill College

FRANCIS BEAUMONT
c.1584-1616

Author's Chronology

Born c. 1584 in Leistershire, England; father a distinguished lawyer and Justice of Common Pleas; brother to poet John Beaumont; began education at Oxford but left for Inner Temple to study law in 1600; *c.1606* begins writing plays; contributed commendatory verses, along with John Fletcher, to an edition of Ben Jonson's *Volpone* (1607), a play and author whose work he admired; *1608* begins collaboration with Fletcher, possibly with *Philaster*; *1613* marries heiress Ursala Isley and retires from the theater world, but not before composing a spectacular masque for performance at the marriage of Princess Elizabeth and the Elector Palatine; *1616* dies (the same year as Shakespeare) and is buried in Westminster Abbey.

Author's Bibliography

Although scholars have not finally determined which of the many plays attributed to Beaumont and Fletcher were written by Beaumont alone, they generally agree that the playwright began his career without the aid of a collaborator. He apparently also tried his hand at Ovidian poetry with a long narrative titled *Salmacis and Hermaphroditus*, published in 1602. This piece is in the same vein as Marlowe-Chapman's *Hero and Leander* and Shakespeare's *Venus and Adonis*. After the fruitful collaboration with Fletcher, Beaumont composed the *Masque of Gray's Inn and the Inner Temple* (Elizabethan law schools) to celebrate a royal wedding. The entertainment depicts, with the help of Inigo Jones's stage machinery, the "marrying of the Thames to the Rhine." The two complete standard editions of the plays and masque are A. Glover and A.R. Waller, eds., *The Works of Francis Beaumont and John Fletcher*. 10 vols. Cambridge University Press, 1905-12 and Fredson Bowers. ed., *The Dramatic Works in the Beaumont and Fletcher Canon*. 3 (of 10) vols. Cambridge University Press, 1966-1976.

(Plays of sole authorship; dates of composition): *The Woman Hater*, c.1606; *The Knight of the Burning Pestle*, 1607.

(Plays for which a case of sole authorship has been argued): *The Noble Gentleman*, 1607?; *The Coxcomb*, 1608-10; *The Scornful Lady*, c.1610.

(Plays written in collaboration with Fletcher): *Philaster*, 1608-9; *The Maid's Tragedy*, c.1610-11; *A King and No King*, 16ll; *Four Plays in One*, c.1612; *Cupid's Revenge*,1612.

Overview and Evaluation of Biographical Sources

Only one full-scale biography of Francis Beaumont has been written: Charles Mills Gayley's *Beaumont, the Dramatist* (New York: Russell and Russell, 1914).

Though dated, Gayley's account of Beaumont's family and friends paints the picture of a talented gentleman dramatist grown from distinguished British stock. His father's career as Justice of the Court of Common Pleas no doubt prompted Beaumont to enter the Inner Temple in 1600, after an unsuccessful period as a student at Oxford. In evaluating the playwright's collaboration, Gayley makes a strong case for the claim that Beaumont's sure-handed plotting and stately tragic verse provided the anchor necessary for a balanced collaboration with the "effusive, exuberant" Fletcher. Gayley embraces the traditional belief that Beaumont composed the serious scenes, Fletcher the comic and romantic repartee, in their tragicomedies. Of central importance to Beaumont's evolution as well was his friendship with Ben Jonson, whose neoclassical critical attitudes he fervently embraced. As one of many "sons of Ben," he reveals biting contempt for the taste of popular audiences in *The Knight of the Burning Pestle*. With his marriage in 1613 to Ursala Isley, daughter of one of the landed gentry, Beaumont retired to a life of ease that, according to Gayley, suited his genteel manner. Lawrence B. Wallis, *Fletcher, Beaumont and Company: Entertainers to the Jacobean Gentry* (1947; rpt. New York: Octagon Books, 1968) features a lengthy biographical chapter on Beaumont and Fletcher, focusing on their King's Men careers, which began when they decided to room together in 1608. Wallis argues that both men fell under Jonson's influence, which led them to write primarily for audiences of sophisticated tastes.

Overview of Critical Sources

Few major critics discuss the work of Beaumont except that he wrote in collaboration with Fletcher. Yet *The Knight of the Burning Pestle*, his inspired satire of apprentice plays, has received deserved praise in recent years. In addition to his gift for parody, Beaumont's talents as a tragic dramatist can be glimpsed in his shares of *The Maid's Tragedy* and *A King and No King*. The critical consensus seems to be that he was successful in joining the sound of language to the sense of character in whatever he wrote. He was certainly influenced in this regard by the declamatory style of the Roman playwright Seneca. In recent years, however, the work of both playwrights has attracted comparatively little critical attention; their plays are rarely acted in Britain or America. Their themes and characters seem very much of an age. Once concerned with attribution of shares, critics now appear to be less interested in analysis of individual works or comparison of these works with those written by Shakespeare or Webster. The relative brevity of Beaumont's dramatic career (c.1608-1613) probably helps to account for the paucity of commentary on his plays. *The Knight of the Burning Pestle* remains the one exception to this rule.

Evaluation of Selected Criticism

Appleton, William W. *Beaumont and Fletcher: A Critical Study*. London: George Allen and Unwin, 1956. Appleton briefly discusses the early careers of the dramatists, describes their collaborative method, and attempts to assess their influence on Restoration drama. The plot summaries are short and accurate; the character analyses provide a sound understanding of tragicomic types. In the chapter titled "Apprentice Dramatists," Appleton documents Beaumont's career before he met Fletcher, suggesting that his promising but largely unsuccessful early efforts may have prompted the collaboration. Appleton's checklist of plays is dependable.

Danby, John F. *Poets on Fortune's Hill: Studies in Sidney, Shakespeare, Beaumont and Fletcher*. London: Faber and Faber, 1952; rpt. 1964 as *Elizabethan and Jacobean Poets*. Labeling Beaumont and Fletcher "Jacobean absolutists," Danby argues that their plays were stage adaptations of sonnet-like conceits. The resulting dramatic worlds are sophisticated, at the same time reflecting the court of James I and the coming civil war. Danby concludes that the playwrights are "the first of the moderns," exposing decadence and corruption in a manner similar to that of recent dramatists.

Ellis-Fermor, Una, *Jacobean Drama: An Interpretation*. London: Methuen, 1936. This general study includes a perceptive chapter on Beaumont and Fletcher in which the author enumerates the chief themes of their plays and poetry. Most of the topics debated by their characters—friendship, the nature of kingship, honor—were topical and, in Ellis-Fermor's words, delivered in language suitable to "a good leading article in a paper." She concludes that the body of the dramatists' work represents a self-contained world full of "reverberant rhetoric" and "melting cadences of word and music."

Gayley, Charles Mills, *Beaumont, the Dramatist*. New York: Russell and Russell, 1914. This book surveys Beaumont's early life and career, his experiences as a law student at the Inner Temple, and his contributions to the collaboration with Fletcher. Gayley assigns considerable weight to Jonson's influence on Beaumont's aesthetic perspective, concluding that the two men shared many opinions about style and audience taste. The section on the collaboration is not as useful as the evaluations in Appleton and Ellis-Fermor.

Wallis, Lawrence B. *Fletcher, Beaumont and Company: Entertainers to the Jacobean Gentry*. 1947; rpt. New York: Octagon Books, 1968. Attempting to cut away the underbrush of morally inspired criticism, Wallis shows how Beaumont and Fletcher appealed directly to the gentrified tastes of their day. He cites "emotional form" as the controlling element in the tragicomedies, deemphasizing separate analyses of characters, action, and poetry. What the playwrights give us is something close to the 19th century well-made play. Wallis's bibliography is the fullest of any of the critical works cited here.

Other Sources
Bowers, Fredson, ed. *The Dramatic Works in the Beaumont and Fletcher Canon.* 3 (of 10) vols. Cambridge: Cambridge University Press, 1966-1976.

Fletcher, Ian, *Beaumont and Fletcher*. London: Longmans, Green, 1967. A short but useful overview of the playwrights' dramatic output.

Mizener, Arthur, "The High Design of *A King and No King*," in *Modern Philology*, 38 (1940-41): 133-154. Mizener examines the elevated style and formally depicted characters in one of Beaumont and Fletcher's successful tragicomedies.

Waith, Eugene M. *The Pattern of Tragicomedy in Beaumont and Fletcher*. New Haven: Yale University Press, 1952. Waith attempts to define tragicomedy with reference to Jacobean literary forms and a rhetorical tradition leading back to ancient Rome.

Willson, Jr., Robert F. *Their Form Confounded*. The Hague: Mouton, 1975. Contains a chapter that discusses Beaumont's satiric technique in *The Knight of the Burning Pestle*.

Robert F. Willson, Jr.
University of Missouri
Kansas City

JACINTO BENAVENTE
1866-1954

Author's Chronology

Born August 12, 1866, Madrid, Spain, the son of a pediatrician, Mariano Benavente; attends primary and secondary school; constructs toy theaters and writes little plays which he acts out with friends; *1882-1885* attends University of Madrid where he unenthusiastically studies law until his father's death; *1885* dedicates himself to reading and writing; *1892* publishes first work for theater, *Teatro fantástico*; *1894* première of his first play, *El nido ajeno*; *1896* first theatrical success, *Gente conocida*; *1899* edits the journal *Vida literaria*; *1901-1909* produces many plays including several considered his masterpieces; *1909* founds "Teatro de los niños"; *1908-1912* dedicates himself primarily to journalism, publishing weekly articles in *El Imparcial*; *1912* elected to the Spanish Royal Academy, but he was never an active member and so was named an honorary member in 1946; *1922* receives the Nobel Prize for literature for his some one hundred plays to date; travels through Latin America and the United States; *1920-1924* upset by critics, writes no more for the theater; *1924* receives several honors in Madrid and begins to write plays again; *1929* travels in Russia; is named president of the *Montepío* (Pension Fund for Widows and Orphans) of the Union of Authors; *1936-1939* spends the Civil War years in Valencia without writing for the theater; *1944* is offered many tributes and his most famous plays are performed to celebrate fifty years of playwrighting; *1945* sets out for Argentina at the head of a theatrical company; *1948* is awarded the "Mariano de Cavia Prize" for the best Spanish newspaper article of 1947; dies July 14, 1954, in Madrid, having produced three plays that year at the age of 88.

Author's Bibliography

There are 172 plays written and staged by Jacinto Benavente. Readers of Spanish will find them in the author's *Obras completas* (Complete Works) (Madrid: Aguilar, 1941-1958). The following chronological list contains some of his most celebrated plays that have been translated: *The Governor's Wife* (1901, 1921); *The Witches' Sabbath* (1903-1923); *Autumnal Roses* (1905, 1921); *The Evildoers of Good* (1905-1917); *Princess Bébé* (1906, 1921); *The Bonds of Interest* (1907, 1917); *The Lady of the House* (1908, 1921); *His Widow's Husband* (1908, 1917); *The Passion Flower* (1913, 1921). A total of sixteen plays by Benavente can be found in translation in John Garrett Underhill, *Plays by Jacinto Benavente*, Series One-Series Four (New York: Charles Scribners' Sons, 1917-1925). Of the non-dramatic writings of Benavente, the *Complete Works* contain the original Spanish of many of his articles, lectures, letters, works of literary criticism and short stories.

Overview of Biographical Sources

Most of what little has been written of the life of Benavente is in Spanish. Among the best are Ángel Lázaro, *Vida y obra de Benavente* (Life and Works of Benavente) (Madrid: A. Aguado, 1964), with a prologue by Benavente himself, and Federico Carlos Sáinz de Robles, *Jacinto Benavente* (Madrid: E. Madrileños, 1954), a brief but interesting study. In English one may profitably consult Julio Brouta, "Spain's Greatest Dramatist," *Drama* (November, 1915), pp. 555-567, and Marcelino C. Peñuelas, *Jacinto Benavente*, tr. Kay Engler (New York: Twayne, 1968), esp. pp. 13-22. Between the two Spanish studies mentioned above, the one to be preferred is perhaps Sáinz de Robles' because of its focus on the man and its greater objectivity. In English Peñuelas' work is more complete in that all quotations from the Spanish are translated.

Autobiographical Sources

Jacinto Benavente's *Recuerdos y olvidos: Memorias* (Things Remembered and Forgotten: Memoirs) (Madrid: Aguilar, 1962) has not been translated. He has written a great deal about himself, his ideas, attitudes, and temperament, but very little about his private life, as have few other Spanish writers. Only concerning his childhood does he relate the very personal details that demonstrate his prodigious memory. The rest consists of memories, anecdotes, and facts about people he knew and impressions of the Madrid of his time.

His plan, as he himself explained was to divide his *Memoirs* into three parts: the first, from 1866 to 1886; the second, from 1886 until the end of the nineteenth century; and the last, "as far as I go into the twentieth century." He began to write them during the Civil War, in 1937, under circumstances which were hardly conducive to reminiscence and serene reflection. The first part comprises 428 pages; the second, only twenty-three. They end abruptly, perhaps because of circumstances resulting from the Civil War. Unfortunately, he never wrote, as was his intention, the very important part concerning his literary career and his relationships with the public, actors and critics. In any event, the *Memoirs* are interesting in that they make known some important facets of his personality.

Overview of Critical Sources

As probably the outstanding Spanish dramatist of the late nineteenth and over half of the twentieth centuries, Jacinto Benavente has had much written about him. Eager to have his work known and most influential, he was much discussed in all Hispanic countries in his long lifetime and since his death. As a recipient of the Nobel Prize he was the object of much attention also in the world at large. There are several significant studies of his work in English.

Evaluation of Selected Criticism

Peñuelas, Marcelino C. *Jacinto Benavente*, tr. Kay Engler. New York: Twayne, 1968. Peñuelas has tried to place Benavente, the man and the writer, in the age in which he lived; to study his relationship with the Spanish and European theater of his time; and to analyze the similarities and differences between Benavente and the other writers of his and later generations. He has attempted to discover what Benavente's work meant at the beginning of the century and what it means today in the Spanish and European theater. Through detailed analysis of his most representative plays, and through considerations of a more general nature, Peñuelas has pointed out the positive and negative qualities of his theater; to study the nature of his themes and techniques; to make a classification of his plays and to outline the philosophical, moral and ideological position which, implicitly or explicitly, the author takes in his plays.

Sheehan, Robert Louis, *Benavente and the Spanish Panorama, 1894-1954*. Chapel Hill: Estudios de Hispanófila, 1976. The purpose of this study is to attempt to fill a need for a complete analysis of Benavente's works in terms of their esthetic, political, and social ideas, and in relation to the important historical events of his time. Sheehan fills that need both through detailed analysis of the essays of representative Benavente criticism over a period of more than six decades, and through analysis of the dramatist's works during the same period. By contrasting the ideals present in the drama with what Benavente himself said, Sheehan shows that in his esthetics he was revolutionary in form, tending toward modernism, but at the same time could be identified with the preoccupation of the Generation of '98. It is seen also that in his social outlook he was humane, progressive and reform-minded. In politics, Benavente was a nationalist and an ardent patriot. He believed that a constitutional monarchy with an enlightened king was the most effective way to bring about social reforms, since in his opinion, there is no fundamental incompatibility between a monarchy and socialism. However, he mistrusted both formal socialism and republicanism, looking instead for a revolution "desde arriba" (from above), in which the middle and upper classes seek to lead the way in aiding the poor and the disinherited. Finally, Sheehan observes that despite the apparent veering from left to right and back again often criticized in his plays and essays, these characteristics are consistently in evidence through every period of literary activity in Benavente's long and productive career as a dramatist and commentator on the Spanish panorama.

Starkie, Walter, *Jacinto Benavente*. London: Oxford University Press, 1924. The question of Benavente's position on World War I greatly influenced the opinions of Walter Starkie. Whereas Ángel Lázaro in his aforementioned book defends Benavente in his insistence that he was indeed neutral during the war, but denies that the dramatist had demonstrated much idealism in the Generation of '98 period, the opposite is true of Starkie. The latter's British sensibilities seem to have been wounded by what he considered Benavente's hostility to Britain. On the other hand, he does identify Benavente with the Generation of '98, although he believes that he was too conservative to be passionately involved with the political reforms espoused by the group. Nevertheless, as a generationist Benavente was responsible for the restoration of humor to the Spanish stage, and for bringing to Spain the revolution in the drama which was taking place throughout western Europe during the period from 1887 to 1893. In Starkie's opinion it was Benavente who destroyed the aside and the soliloquy, introducing in their stead the quick, jerky dialogue of ordinary speech. Furthermore, it was Benavente who prepared the way for Chiarrelli and Pirandello. *Bonds of Interest* may be taken as a progenitor of the brilliant grotesque theater that sprang up in Italy during the great War, through the instrumentality of Chiarrelli and Pirandello. Starkie, therefore, seems generous in his evaluation of Benavente in strictly theater terms, but reluctant to praise his social attitudes because of what he believes had happened during the war.

Underhill, John Garrett, *Plays by Jacinto Benavente*, Series One-Series Four. New York: Charles Scribners' Sons, 1917-1925. In the introductions to each of his four volumes of translations of sixteen outstanding Benavente plays, John Garrett Underhill continually emphasizes the dramatist's contributions in form and content to the development of the modern drama. Like Azorin, Underhill places Benavente in a leadership role in the Generation of '98, stating that while he was in no sense a promoter of the movement, Benavente had been the most stimulating and compelling figure in this latter-day renaissance. According to Underhill, Benavente is the last of the moderns, going beyond Ibsen whose theater ideas were already coming into disfavor. Unlike his predecessors, Benavente does not depend upon stage effects, scenery or descriptions of characters to create dramatic tension, but does so through the use of language alone. The Spaniard was also among the first dramatists in Europe to exploit the newly discovered world of the subconscious, and the first in his own country to see the stage as a medium of social protest. Rejecting the idea put forth by others that Benavente was anti-social or indifferent to the plight of the poor in Spain, Underhill says that on the contrary, the author calls our attention to the unbelievable poverty, the absolute, hopeless destitution which there prevails; poverty of means, poverty of surroundings, poverty of mind, poverty of will. Underhill also points out the unreliability of much of the early Benavente criticism and its disproportionate influence in moulding subsequent critical opinion both in Spain and abroad. In his judgment many of the critical articles were occasional in nature and composed in haste at the time of the première performances of the plays in order to meet newspaper deadlines. These were later published unrevised in book form, and achieved unwarranted authority especially in foreign countries.

Other Sources
Alarcón, Mariano, "Benavente as an Interpreter of Woman," in *Poet Lore*, XXIX (1918): 201-205. Previously published in *Coram Populo*, Madrid, 1916. On the meaning of woman in Benavente's theater.

"Benavente and Chekhov," in *The London Times Literary Supplement*, September 18, 1924, p. 324. An anonymous article which includes comments on four of Benavente's plays. It establishes an interesting parallel between the theater of Benavente and Chekhov.

Dos Passos, John, *"Benavente's Madrid,"* in *The Bookman*, no. 53, (1921): 226-230; rpt. in *Rosinante to the Road Again*. New York: G. H. Doran, 1922, pp. 182-95. A look at Madrid through the eyes of a traveler passionately involved with Europe between the wars.

Jameson, Storm, *Modern Drama in Europe*. London: Collins, 1920, pp. 239-45. An excellent commentary on Benavente's theater.

Richard A. Mazzara
Oakland University

UGO BETTI
1892-1953

Author's Chronology

Born February 4, 1892, Camerino, Italy, to Tullio Betti, a physician, and his wife; *1901* the family moves to Parma where Tullio becomes director of the municipal hospital; *1910* completes the lyceum, enters the University of Parma to study law and publishes a translation from Catullus; *1914* receives a doctorate in jurisprudence with a thesis on law and revolution; *1915* volunteers to serve after Italy enters World War I, becoming an artillery officer at the front; *1917* taken prisoner of war after the Italian defeat at Caporetto; *1919-1921* repatriated, continues his legal studies and enters the judiciary; *1922* publishes his first book of poetry, *Il re pensieroso* (*The Thoughtful King*); *1920s* holds a series of judicial appointments in small towns and in Parma and continues to write poetry, short stories, and drama, notably *La padrona* (*The Mistress*, 1926 premier); *1930* marries Andreina Frosini and moves to Rome after being appointed magistrate of the Appellate Court; *1932 Un albergo sul porto* (*An Inn on the Harbor*) is awarded first prize in a national drama competition and *Landslide* (produced 1936, tr. 1964) is composed; *1934-1940* writes a series of comedies and farces including *Summertime* (1937, tr. 1956) which Betti calls "a diversion"; *1941-1953* in a burst of creative activity, writes thirteen plays, among them his generally recognized masterpiece, *Corruption in the Palace of Justice* (composed 1944-45, tr. 1962) and the internationally acclaimed *Goat Island* (1946, tr. 1961) and *The Queen and the Rebels* (1949, tr. 1961); *1949 Corruption in the Palace of Justice* is awarded first prize by the Istituto del Dramma Italiano as that season's best play; June 9, 1953, Betti dies of cancer after receiving the last rites of the Catholic Church.

Author's Bibliography

All of Ugo Betti's theatrical production, totalling 26 plays, is collected in *Teatro completo* (Bologna: Cappelli, 1971). Other volumes in Italian contain his poetry, short stories, and minor works, including a movie script and a libretto. A number of Betti's plays have been produced in Great Britain and the United States with great success; some of these have been published, others have not. Both *Irene innocente* (pub. 1950) and *Acque turbate* (pub. 1955) were produced in English—respectively titled *Time of Vengeance* and *Troubled Waters*—but have not been printed. There are a number of edited English collections of Betti's plays, generally accompanied by introductory essays. Two translations of *Delitto all'Isola delle capre* are available: one by Henry Reed and another by Gino Rizzo and David Gullette. The former, *Crime on Goat Island*, appears independently in a volume published by Chandler (San Francisco, 1961) and is reprinted in *Masterpieces of the Modern Italian Theatre*, ed. Robert Corrigan (New York: Collier, 1967); it displays a definite British flavor in the language. More colloquial, *Goat Island* is included in *Ugo Betti: Three Plays*, ed. Gino Rizzo (New York: Hill and Wang, 1966), a collection which also has *The Inquiry* (1941) and *The Gambler* (1951). Another Bettian anthology, *Three Plays on Justice*, ed. G.H. McWilliam (San Francisco: Chandler, 1964) includes: the masterly *Landslide*, *Struggle Till Dawn* and the playwright's final work, *The Fugitive*. British translator Henry Reed prepared his renditions of the political plays, *The Queen and the Rebels* and *The Burnt Flower-Bed*, as well as the farcical *Summertime*, for the Third Programme of the BBC. Altered for stage production and further revised for publication, this trio composes *Three Plays by Ugo Betti* (New York: Grove Press, 1958). This translation of *The Queen and the Rebels* was also published in *Three European Plays*, ed. E. Martin Browne (London: Penguin, 1965) and in *Makers of the Modern Theater*, ed. B. Ulanov (New York: 1961). Betti's best known drama, *Corruption in the Palace of Justice*, in another Reed translation, was published in Robert Corrigan's *The New Theatre of Europe*, Vol. I (New York: Dell, 1962) and in *Classics of Modern Theater*, ed. Alvin Kernan (New York: Harcourt, Brace, and World, 1965). In addition to these English-language translations of the plays, the *Tulane Drama Review* has also published some of Betti's non-fictional material. In the December, 1960, issue both the "Preface to *The Mistress*" (a short discussion of man's dark side) and the important essay, "Religion and the Theatre", appear. The latter is also included in Corrigan's *Masterpieces of the Modern Italian Theatre* and *The New Theatre of Europe*, previously cited. The spring 1964 number of the journal contains "Essays, Correspondence, Notes" by Ugo Betti, short pieces the dramatist had prepared for various periodicals, private letters, and jottings about his plots and characters; these are important sources for the study of Betti's drama.

Overview of Biographical Sources

No biography of Betti has yet appeared, although most works dealing with his theater also give some space to his life and times. The best source for biographical data and information about the creation, production, and publication of his works is Antonio Di Pietro's *L'opera di Ugo Betti*, 2 vols. (Bari: Centro Librario, 1968). A somewhat detailed, if brief, description of the playwright's life and its relation to his opus is offered in G.H. McWilliam's "Introduction" to *Three Plays on Justice* and in Gino Rizzo's "Introduction" to *Ugo Betti: Three Plays*. Critics always stress the importance of Betti's career in the judiciary to the recurrent motif of investigations and trials in his plays and often analyze his adherence, or lack thereof, to the Fascist regime. Referring to his professional experiences, Betti himself noted that his work owed "Nothing in particular, everything in general" to his legal background.

Autobiographical Sources

Some insight into Betti, the inner man, can be found in the writer's poetry, notably in the autobiographical compositions of *Ultime liriche (1938-1953)*. While these lyrics offer glimpses of the poet's meditations on childhood, youth, and family, they are not documents but subjective and nostalgic outpourings. Betti's poetry has not been rendered in English. The essays, letters, and notes published by the *Tulane Drama Review*, VIII, 3 (Spring 1964) provide some information about Betti's personal views on his writing and his position in Italian theater. Thoughts on the nature of art, his reactions to theatrical successes and failures, a discussion of his personal interests, as well as comments on his dramatic career, his Catholicism, and his artistic intentions, are all covered, if only in a fleeting manner. Betti's religious concerns, as they relate to his plays and to drama in general, are eloquently discussed in his essay, "Religion and the Theatre."

Overview of Critical Sources

It is generally, if not universally, conceded that Ugo Betti is Italy's greatest dramatist after Pirandello. Critics have noted his debt to, or similarity with, a variety of literary and philosophical trends effecting European drama: Symbolism, Naturalism, Expressionism, and Existentialism. Most agree that Betti's theater is predominantly moral in tone, stressing the themes of justice, passion, sexuality, transgression and punishment, isolation, spiritual chaos, and desire for redemption. The problem of evil, the discovery of salvation in love, and the need for judgment dominate these plays, leading many scholars to view Betti, sometimes negatively, as a "Catholic" writer; often this Christian interpretation is exaggerated and extraneous to the texts under analysis. While Betti's plays may be "religious", they are not dogmatic. The somber colors, obsessed characters, and dark messages of Betti's drama did not endear him to Italian audiences until he achieved international renown in the 1950s with the French and English premieres of his dramas. Betti became a celebrity abroad before achieving national stature, as had happened to Pirandello thirty years before. The majority of serious criticism dedicated to the playwright, as well as the translations of his works, date from the 1950s and 1960s. Unfortunately, the greater part of Bettian studies available in English are located in literary and theatrical periodicals rather than in books.

Evaluation of Selected Criticism

Licastro, Emanuele, *Ugo Betti. An Introduction*. Jefferson, NC: McFarland, 1985. This is the only book-length study devoted to Betti available in English. While clearly being introductory, it is very thorough and embraces not only Betti's theater but the minor prose and lyric works as well. Licastro has organized the text chronologically in "Part I. The Theater," following a short presentation of the dramatist's biography. The chapters are divided somewhat thematically, pinpointing the phases in Betti's theatrical career. Each play is introduced and succinctly analyzed in short sections, with careful attention paid to the presentation of standard characters, motifs, and scenes as they first appear in the playwright's *opus*. The critic also discusses the diverse forms employed by Betti: fable, naturalist drama, trial plays, farce, comedy of manners, and tragedy. Some mention is made of the playwright's original stagecraft and personal symbolism as well. Licastro's stress is on the epistemological concerns the Italian dramatist demonstrates in his plots and characterizations. The book functions well as a initiation to Betti studies.

McWilliam, G.H. "Introduction," to *Crime on Goat Island*, by Ugo Betti. trans. Henry Reed. San Francisco: Chandler, 1961. The most extensive and developed of McWilliam's various prefaces to Betti's works, the critic discusses Betti's life, philosophical and literary influences, interests, and basic themes. McWilliam focuses on the Bettian thesis that it is impossible to achieve true justice in a social context, leading to a need for compassion, love, and redemption. *Crime on Goat Island* is interpreted as a tragedy of errors in the classical manner, played out in a primitive world where sexual instinct has power to destroy man's moral awareness.

Rizzo, Gino, "Regression-Progression in Ugo Betti's Drama," in *Tulane Drama Review*, vol. 8., no. 1 (Fall 1963): 101-129. Rizzo attempts to elucidate the inherent paradox and incongruities in Betti's plays by analyzing the dramatist's dynamic utilization of a "regression-progression" pattern. The characters are interpreted as moving inwards (backwards) in order to discover the primal motivations for their human suffering and, thereby, to move toward awareness only to be hampered by the constant forward motion of life itself. Rizzo analyzes the child-motif, or Jungian child archetype, in Betti as an example of the pre-concious in act, from the earliest play, *La padrona*, to the teleology of *Landslide* and the religious symbolism of *Corruption in the Palace of Justice*, concluding in *The Burnt Flower-Bed*. This is an excellent study of the subtle patterns in Betti's works which allow the incongruous and sub-conscious to emerge.

Other Sources

Corrigan, Robert W. "Five Dramas of Selfhood," in *The New Theatre of Europe*. New York: Dell, 1962, pp. 9-31. Betti is one of five dramatists represented who sought to "find a metaphor for universal modern man," which could be communicated to the audience. Corrigan stresses the problem of evil and its solution in the redemptive power of love (as the perfect system of justice) and in the creative force of imagination.

Gatt-Rutter, John, "Ugo Betti: The Whore as Queen," in *Writers and Politics in Modern Italy*. New York: Holmes & Meier, 1974, pp. 17-21. A political reading of the plays, the critic doubts Betti's ability at social analysis, offering some controversial interpretations in a socio-historical vein.

MacClintock, Lander, *The Age of Pirandello*. New York: Kraus Reprint, 1968. A reprint of a 1951 edition. In the chapter titled "Post-Pirandello," the author presents Betti as a continuator of the Italian verist tradition (a somewhat controversial position) and reiterates the presence of the problem of good and evil in the plays. Criticizing Betti's theater as being unsuitable for the stage because of its abstract qualities, MacClintock appears to dislike both the plots and the characters because of their sordidness and Freudian overtones.

McWilliam, G.H. "Interpreting Betti," in *Tulane Drama Review*, Vol. 5, no. 2 (December 1960): 15-23. Offers, then interprets, some of Betti's remarks on his anti-realism, ideal audience, and characterizations, as well as in the role of actors and producers as seen from the dramatist's viewpoint. It is an essay on the playwright's role in the realization of his works, illuminating Betti's attitudes and prejudices.

Markey, Constance, "The Theatre of Ugo Betti: New Critical Approaches and New Questions," in *Theatre Annual*, vol. 39 (1984): 35-44. Markey offers a panoramic view of Betti criticism while emphasizing the treatment of religion in the plays. It is an informative essay.

Salmon, Eric, "Ugo Betti's *Troubled Waters*," in *Modern Drama*, XI, no. 1 (May 1968): 97-108. This is a theatrical insider's view of the difficulties involved in interpreting Betti on the stage, given the naturalistic conventions and mode of dialogue and the abundance of ideas in the text. Having directed *Troubled Waters* in New York, Salmon emphasizes the need to explore the depths and subtleties of the script to make its modernity emerge.

Scott, J.A. "The Message of Ugo Betti," in *Italica*, XXXVII (March 1960): 44-57. An analysis of *The Inquiry*, *The Queen and the Rebels*, and *The Burnt Flower-Bed* which seeks to explore the deeper meanings these plays offer the public, expressed somewhat subjectively.

Usmiani, Renate, "Twentieth-century Man, the Guilt-Ridden Animal," in *Mosaic*, Vol. 3, no. 4 (Summer 1970): 163-178. Using Kafka as a starting point, the author explores the use of the trial motif in Betti and Dürrenmatt, noting that modern man's guilt is rendered as a metaphysical malaise and that, paradoxically, sin is not sin in a dogmatic sense but a means to self-awareness through culpability.

Watts, Harold H. "Ugo Betti: The Theater of 'Shame'," *Modern Drama*, Vol. XII, no. 1 (May 1969), 64-79. A study of the Bettian use of the inter-related motifs of crimes, investigations, judgment, and shame. Watts stresses the religious implications of the plays, highlighted by the presence of God in indirect and direct ways, as He operates through the protagonists' sense of guilt and expiation.

Fiora A. Bassanese
University of Massachusetts
Boston

DION BOUCICAULT
1820?-1890

Author's Chronology

December 27, 1820 is perhaps the most plausible of five dates advanced for Boucicault's birth in Dublin; his mother was Anne Maria Darley Boursiquot; his father may have been her husband, Samuel Smith Boursiquot, a wine merchant, or her lover, Dr. Dionysius Lardner, a writer, lecturer, university professor and civil engineer; *1838-1840* serves an apprenticeship in provincial theatres; *1841* comedy of manners, *London Assurance*, met with great success; *1841-1845* remains in London, working as an actor and dramatist and living prodigally; *1845* marries a French widow who dies under unclear circumstances sometime during the next three years. *1848* declares bankruptcy; *1852* writes *The Corsican Brothers* for Charles Kean and soon after elopes with Kean's ward, actress Agnes Robertson; *1853* travels with Robertson to America and subsequently manages her career, acts himself, and writes prolifically: adaptations of novels and French dramas; spectacular melodramas, e.g. *The Poor of New York* (1857); and plays of more artistic merit, i.e. *The Octoroon* (1859) and *The Colleen Bawn* (1860); he and Robertson and their growing family (they would eventually have six children) return to England where they enjoy great prosperity; *1872* in London Boucicault writes and produces the extravanganza *Babil and Bijou*, one of the most spectacular stage pieces of the century; the play is a popular success but a financial failure because of extraordinary costs of production; Boucicault and Robertson return to New York, where Boucicault, always a philanderer, sets up housekeeping with a mistress; *1874* employs David Belasco as a secretary on tour, and writes *The Shaughraun*, perhaps his greatest artistic achievement and his last great financial success; *1876* promotes the fireproofing of stage scenery; *late 1870s* and *1880s* continues to write, with less and less popular success, and to act and direct plays; *1880-1883* contests divorce proceedings initiated by Robertson; *1885* before obtaining a divorce, marries Louise Thorndyke, a twenty-one year old actress in his touring company; September 18, 1890, still writing and working as a teacher of acting, dies of pneumonia and cardiac problems, in New York City.

Author's Bibliography

Boucicault sometimes overstated and sometimes minimized or denied his contributions to dramatic works. These contributions in fact varied widely from work to work. Estimates of the number of works which might be considered his vary from about a hundred to over four hundred; the best estimate is about one hundred fifty. Many of these were published in acting editions in the nineteenth century. Modern collections containing some of Boucicault's more important plays include *British*

Plays of the Nineteenth Century, ed. J.O. Bailey, New York: Odyssey Press, 1966 (containing *London Assurance, After Dark*); *The Dolmen Boucicault*, ed. David Krause, Dublin: Dolmen Press, 1964 (containing *The Colleen Bawn, Arah-na-Pogue, The Shaughraun*); *Plays by Dion Boucicault*, ed. Peter Thompson, London: Cambridge University Press, 1984 (containing *Used Up, Old Heads and Young Hearts, Jessie Brown, The Octoroon, The Shaughraun*); and *Representative American Plays from 1767 to the Present Day*, ed. Arthur Hobson Quinn, New York: Appleton, Century, Crofts, 1953 (containing *Rip Van Winkle, The Octoroon*).

Overview of Biographical Sources

Perhaps the earliest biography is Charles Lamb Kenney's *Career of Dion Boucicault* (New York: The Graphic Co., n.d.). Subsequent biographies include Townsend Walsh, *The Career of Dion Boucicault* (New York: The Dunlop Society, 1915); Robert Hogan, *Dion Boucicault* (1969); and Richard Fawkes, *Dion Boucicault* (1979). Mention should also be made of Sven Eric Molin and Robin Goodfellow, eds., *Dion Boucicault, The Shaughraun: A Documentary Life, Letters and Selected Works* (Newark, DE: Proscenium Press, 1979).

Evaluation of Selected Biographies

Fawkes, Richard, *Dion Boucicault*. London: Quartet Books, 1979. Detailed, readable and authoritative (based in part on previously unused sources), this is now the standard biography of Boucicault.

Folland, Harold F. "Lee Moreton: The Debut of a Theatre Man," in *Theatre Notebook*, 23 (Summer 1969): 122-129. A detailed account of the very early apprenticeship of Boucicault on the stage, from June 1838 until the production of *London Assurance*.

Hogan, Robert, *Dion Boucicault*. New York: Twayne, 1969. Readable and sensible, this book is fairly comprehensive but not exhaustive. It contains a fuller critical discussion of the major plays and a better bibliography than Fawkes' book.

Walsh, Townsend, *The Career of Dion Boucicault*. New York: The Dunlop Society, 1915. Walsh is often unreliable in details, but quite successfully suggestive of the ethos of Boucicault's theatrical milieu.

Autobiographical Sources

Boucicault wrote "Debut of a Dramatist," in *North American Review*, 148 (April 1889): 454-463, and "Early Days of a Dramatist," also in *North American Review*, 148 (May 1889): 584-593. According to Louise Thorndyke he was also responsible for the account of his life published by his friend Charles Kenney. Intensely interested in self-promotion, Boucicault is not always a reliable source about the facts of his life. Nonetheless, his testimony is essential for anyone wishing to understand him and his career.

Overview of Critical Sources

Boucicault has not been extensively studied. However, the increased attention given to nineteenth century drama by scholars in recent years has extended to Boucicault and his work. Scholars have considered him both as a literary figure—the author of comedy, melodrama and plays of social significance—and as a theatrical figure—a technical innovator, a leader in the development of unified dramatic productions, a teacher of acting, and an important figure in the evolution of authorial rights in the theatre.

Evaluation of Selected Criticism

Lynaugh, John Broderick, *The Forgotten Contributions and Comedies of Dion Boucicault.* Unpublished doctoral dissertation, University of Wisconsin, 1974. Lynaugh treats Boucicault as a theatrical innovator and argues that he was "more a comic playwright who wrote melodramas than a melodramatist who wrote comedies."

Nicoll, Allardyce, *A History of English Drama, 1660-1900*: Vol.V, *Late Nineteenth Century Drama, 1850-1900*. Cambridge: Cambridge University Press, 1959. Nicoll's respectful treatment of Boucicault as a melodramatist is a useful introduction to Boucicault's work, and the fourth and fifth volumes of the *History* taken together help to place his work in the context of nineteenth century drama. Nicoll's list of Boucicault's plays is less complete than Fawkes' list.

Other Sources

Booth, Michael R. *Victorian Spectacular Theatre, 1850-1910*. Boston: Routledge & Kegan Paul, 1981. This work, by a leading authority on the Victorian theatre, treats of Boucicault only incidentally, but makes a fascinating introduction to the technical aspects of nineteenth century theatre for students whose appreciation of drama is largely limited to literary aspects. Such an introduction is essential to any understanding of Boucicault's work.

Degan, John A. "How to End *The Octoroon*," in *Educational Theatre Journal*, 27 (May 1975): 170-178. A description and analysis of both the original tragic ending of *The Octoroon* written for the play's American production and the subsequent happy ending forced on Boucicault by public demand during the play's London run. The article discusses Boucicault's reasons for the original ending (artistic, not polemical) and the theatrical pragmatism which the revision reveals.

Faulkner, Seldon, "The *Octoroon* War," *Educational Theatre Journal*, 15 (March 1963): 33-38. An account of Boucicault's 1859-60 lawsuit, which helped to establish the legal force of dramatic copyright.

_____, "The Great Train Scene Robbery," in *Quarterly Journal of Speech*, 50 (February 1964): 24-28. An account of Augustin Daly's 1868 lawsuit against the American producers of Boucicault's *After Dark*. The court determined that the sensation scene of *After Dark* had been plagiarized from Daly's *Under the Gaslight*.

Kaplan, Sidney, "*The Octoroon*: Early History of the Drama of Miscegnation," in *Journal of Negro Education*, 20 (Fall 1951): 547-557. Kaplan describes the social and political controversy surrounding the original American production of *The Octoroon* and criticizes Boucicault's pecuniary motivations throughout.

McMahon, Sean, "The Wearing of the Green: the Irish Plays of Dion Boucicault," in *Eire-Ireland*, 2 (Summer 1967): 98-111. A general treatment of Boucicault's career and a synopsis and evaluation of his three major Irish plays—*The Colleen Bawn*, *Arrah-na-Pogue*, and *The Shaughraun*—which usefully supplements David Krause's excellent introduction to the Dolmen Press edition of these plays.

David W. Cole
University of Wisconsin Centers

BERTOLT BRECHT
1898-1956

Author's Chronology

Born February 10, 1898, Augsburg, Germany, the son of a clerk at a papermill; *1917* enrolls at the University of Munich as a student of medicine; *1918* serves as a medical orderly in an Augsburg army hospital and writes his first play, *Baal*; *1919* has his first child, an illegitimate son; *1922* receives the Kleist Prize, awarded to the most promising young dramatist of the year, for his second play, *Drums in the Night*; accepts position as dramaturg in Munich and marries the opera singer Marianne Zoff, who bears him a daughter shortly afterwards; *1924* moves to Berlin, becomes dramaturg under Max Reinhardt and has an illegitimate son with his future wife, the actress Helene Weigel; *1926* becomes interested in the writings of Karl Marx; *1927* is granted a divorce from Marianne Zoff; *1928* *The Threepenny Opera* opens in Berlin to great acclaim; *1929* marries Helene Weigel, who gives birth to his second daughter in 1930; *1933* escapes from the Nazis and settles in Denmark; *1935* is officially deprived of his German citizenship by the Hitler regime; *1939* leaves Denmark for Sweden; *1940* leaves Sweden for Finland, where he awaits a visa to the United States; *1941* settles near Hollywood; *1945-1947* collaborates closely with the actor Charles Laughton in the production of *Galileo*; *1947* is subpoenaed to appear before the House Committee for Un-American Activities and leaves the United States for Europe immediately afterwards; *1948* settles in Switzerland; *1949* applies for Austrian citizenship but goes to East Berlin as the artistic advisor of the *Berliner Ensemble*, a company of actors under the official direction of his wife; *1951* is awarded the East German National Prize; *1954* becomes vice president of the East German Academy of Arts and wins the Stalin Peace Prize; August 14, 1956 dies of a heart attack.

Author's Bibliography (selected)

Baal, 1922, tr. 1970 (play); *Drums in the Night*, 1923, tr. 1970 (play); *In the Jungle of the Cities*, performed 1923, published in revised form 1927, tr. 1970 (play); *Man equals Man*, 1927, tr. 1979 (play); *A Manual of Piety*, 1927, tr. 1966 (poems); *The Threepenny Opera*, 1929, tr. 1979 (ballad opera, with music by Kurt Weill); *Rise and Fall of the City of Mahagonny*, 1930, tr. 1979 (epic opera with music by Kurt Weill); *The Measures Taken*, 1931, tr. 1959 (didactic play); *St. Joan of the Stockyards*, 1932, tr. 1962 (play); *The Threepenny Novel*, 1934, tr. 1956 (novel); *Fear and Misery of the Third Reich*, performed 1938, published in revised form 1948, tr. 1970 (dramatic scenes); *Mother Courage and Her Children*, performed 1941, published 1949, tr. 1962 (chronicle play); *The Life of Galileo*, performed 1943, published 1955, tr. 1960; *The Good Woman of Setzuan*, performed 1943, published 1953, tr. 1961 (parable play); *Herr Puntila and his Man Matti*, performed 1948, published 1956, tr. 1962 (folk play); *The Caucasian Chalk Circle)*, 1949, tr. 1960 (parable play).

Overview of Biographical Sources

There was little of the recluse about Brecht. All his life he thrived on the company and collaboration of friends and associates even during his creative moments. Writers like Lion Feuchtwanger and Sergei Tretyakov, the stage designer and lifelong friend Caspar Neher, critics like Walter Benjamin and Herbert Ihering, the singer Lotte Lenya, the composers Hanns Eisler and Paul Dessau, and several of his devoted women friends have written about their acquaintance and association with the dramatist. Thirty-eight of these sketches are now available in *Brecht As They Saw Him*, ed. by Hubert Witt, tr. by John Peet (London: Lawrence and Wishart, 1975). What this collection reveals more than anything else is, however, that those who knew Brecht best seemed least interested in speaking about him as a private individual while those who did, frequently fell victim to his well-developed sense of self-dramatization. The Brecht Archive, established in Brecht's apartment in East Berlin after his death, seemed to offer prospects of a sheer limitless supply of information but remained almost inaccessible to scholars as East Germany's regime nervously monitored Brecht's rising fame in the West. As a result, the first studies of Brecht's life and work provided no more than a literary biography, such as Frederic Ewen's *Bertolt Brecht: His Life, His Art, and His Times* (1967); or they simply relegated the biography to an introductory chapter, as did Martin Esslin in his pioneering *Brecht: The Man and His Work* (Garden City, NY: Doubleday, 1960). Biographical knowledge about Brecht has increased dramatically over the last several years with the publication of no less than three impressively researched studies which complement each other in important ways: Klaus Völker's *Brecht: A Biography* (1978), James K. Lyon's *Bertolt Brecht in America* (1980), and Ronald Hayman's *Brecht: A Biography* (1983). Still, too much of Brecht's complex and contradictory personality remains unexplored to support any of the rival claims to a definitive portrayal.

Evaluation of Selected Biographies

Cook, Bruce, *Brecht in Exile*. New York: Holt, Rinehart and Winston, 1982. After advancing his own version of a conspiracy theory, according to which Brecht's international fame is the creation of a clique of critics, theater people, and campus academicians, Cook proceeds in eleven disjointed chapters to expose Brecht as an unpleasant fellow, a fact which has long been a commonplace even among the dramatist's ardent admirers. In spite of the book's title, its author writes extensively about Brecht's life in Germany, yet summarizes on a few pages the long years of exile in Denmark, Sweden, and Finland. Though Cook's gossipy approach and racy style might hold the reader's attention for a while, even the most embarrassing information about Brecht can be studied more reliably in other biographies.

Ewen, Frederic, *Bertolt Brecht: His Life, His Art, and His Times.* New York: Citadel Press, 1967. The first full treatment of Brecht's life and times in English, this study remains a most fascinating and readable literary biography. Written for a non-German public, Ewen's presentation profits from its author's wide and solid literary background. Brecht's role in the exciting and tumultuous culture of the Weimar Republic is depicted in lively detail. Strictly personal affairs in Brecht's life, however, are touched on only marginally. Brecht's travails during his exile are less vividly captured as the interpretation of his major plays dominates Ewen's discussion. The dramatist's last years in East Germany are treated with commendable objectivity.

Hayman, Ronald, *Brecht: A Biography.* New York: Oxford University Press, 1983. More persistently than previous biographies, Hayman's work is in pursuit of the private individual Brecht. The young man is brought to life as never before, and many of Brecht's own attempts to reconstruct this phase of his career are corrected. Brecht's legendary sexual exploits are recorded in detail, yet without undue censoriousness. Only when Hayman seems satisfied to explain Brecht's political convictions from a psychological perspective does his approach become incomplete. In spite of this important reservation, Hayman's study is the most thorough biography of Brecht to date.

Lyon, James K. *Bertolt Brecht in America.* Princeton: Princeton University Press, 1980. Though the importance of Brecht's stay in America between 1941 and 1947 has been recognized, it took the evidence of Lyon's fascinating book to shed broad light on what had remained a rather obscure period in the artist's life. Refraining from psychological speculations on his part, the author relies on the careful exploration of a great number of Brecht's personal relations as he draws the picture of an obdurate man who would rather offend than compromise. Unflinching in his account, Lyon clearly sympathizes with his subject's principled stubbornness.

Völker, Klaus, *Brecht: A Biography.* Translated from the German by John Nowell. New York: Seabury Press, 1978. Painstakingly researched and providing numerous new details, Völker's efforts fall short of creating a thoroughly convincing picture of Brecht's peculiar individuality. Chapters analyzing several of the plays are helpful but tend to lengthen the work unduly. Völker's record of the six years Brecht spent in America is surprisingly cursory. Most convincing is the attempt to view Brecht's political convictions within the shifting contexts of his turbulent times. The strength and limitation of this biography lie in the fact that Brecht, who considered any psychological investigation a typically bourgeois preoccupation, might not have been dissatisfied with Völker's emphasis.

Autobiographical Sources

Brecht never made any effort to disguise his contempt for those who felt the need to bare their souls. In part this highhanded disregard belonged to his favorite pose

of tough resilience; in part extreme discretion became a necessary virtue in someone of Brecht's sexual liberality. Above all, it served him as a strategy of self-
defense in an unstable and hostile world. As a result, only two autobiographical
writings are available and only one has so far been translated into English. *Bertolt
Brecht: Diaries 1920-1922*, ed. by Herta Ramthun, tr. by John Willett (New York:
St. Martin's Press, 1979) was begun when Brecht was still a literary unknown and
ends several months before his *Drums in the Night* established him as one of
Germany's most promising talents. Still a medical student in Munich but already
intent on pursuing a career in literature, the young man openly writes here about
his ebullient egoism, his obsession with sex, his unconventional creativity. In the
work journal Brecht kept from 1938 to 1955, he had long done with such un-
guarded introspection. His *Arbeitsjournal*, 3 vols., ed. by Werner Hecht
(Frankfurt/Main: Suhrkamp, 1973) is clearly composed with an eye to publication
and records Brecht's reflections on his work, on books he read and people he met.
During the years of World War II, the documentation of the momentous course of
events gains prominence. Though not designed as a diary, this journal gives an
excellent idea of Brecht's artistic and political passion and intelligence.

Overview of Critical Sources
   Thirty years after his death, Brecht is widely respected as one of the most
important and influential dramatists of this century. Yet in 1956, his fame was by
no means a foregone conclusion. In the East, where his political allegiance ought
to have made him a major culture hero, critics labored uneasily under the attempt
to accommodate his work to the prevailing party line while in the West his art was
perceived as having been spoiled by the unfortunate bend of his political creed. To
a wider public in the English-speaking world, Brecht's work was introduced three
years after his death in two pioneering studies, John Willett's *The Theatre of Bertolt
Brecht* (London: Methuen, 1959) and Martin Esslin's *Brecht: A Choice of Evils*
(London: Eyre & Spottiswoode, 1959), rpt. for the American market under the
considerably more innocuous title *Brecht: The Man and His Work* (1960). If, on
the whole, Esslin's study proved more influential, this was because its author
advanced an argument which saved Brecht's art for the Western critic by relegating
Brecht's political commitments to the realm of the irrelevant. Under Esslin's flag of
a divide and conquer, Brecht scholarship devoted itself for the next fifteen years to
the task of interpreting Brecht's plays as expressions of a radical but enlightened
humanism. Fine studies in this tradition are John Fuegi's *The Essential Brecht*
(1972) and Claude Hill's *Bertolt Brecht* (1975). Critics who insisted on the playwright's avowed Marxism and deduced from it a secondary literary talent, as did
the German Gerhard Szczesny in *The Case against Bertolt Brecht* (New York:
Ungar, 1969) and the Austrian Willy Haas in *Bert Brecht* (New York: Frederick
Ungar, 1970), soon found themselves fighting a losing battle. The last ten years
have, nevertheless, seen a return to the question of the relationship between politics

and art in Brecht's work. Attempts at viewing both aspects in constructive complementarity are Keith A. Dickson's *Towards Utopia: A Study of Brecht* (1978) and, in an even more radical vein, several scholars in *Bertolt Brecht: Political Theory and Literary Practice*, ed. by Betty Nance Weber and Hubert Heinen (Athens, GA: University of Georgia Press, 1980).

Evaluation of Selected Criticism

Dickson, Keith A. *Towards Utopia: A Study of Brecht*. Oxford: Clarendon Press, 1978. It is the author's contention that Brecht's work cannot be understood without careful consideration of the playwright's optimistic views on the perfectability of man and society. Dickson discusses, therefore, Brecht's developing concepts of nature, man, society, and history; shows how Brecht exposes the stultifying powers of religion, law and literature; and concludes with an analysis of the artistic modes which Brecht thought most capable of arousing an activist response in audience or reader. The book's thematic approach is constantly detailed by interpretations of a wide range of Brecht's works and checked against a full array of scholarly opinions. Only the longer of many quotations are translated in endnotes. Dickson's is an illuminating and challenging work for the more advanced student of Brecht.

Esslin, Martin, *Brecht: The Man and His Work*. Garden City, NY: Doubleday, 1960. Possibly the most influential study on Brecht in English, Esslin's work has not so much become outdated as it has become incomplete. Its central thesis of a divided personality in Brecht, which allowed him to be a humanist in his art and a communist in his politics, has been greatly qualified by subsequent research and can no longer be taken at face value. Esslin's arrangement of his material into what in fact are several loosely connected essays makes for some repetition. No longer commendable as an introduction, this intriguing portrait still is immensely stimulating.

Fuegi, John, *The Essential Brecht*. Los Angeles: Hennessey & Ingalls, 1972. Fuegi starts from the once highly unorthodox position that Brecht's theatrical theories did not determine, but were determined by Brecht's development as a playwright. Dividing the dramatist's career into four major stages, Fuegi analyzes eight plays from the different periods as he integrates in his evaluation their literary sources and merit, the theatrical theory that informed them as well as their definitive staging by Brecht. More than eighty photos, most of Brecht's *Berliner Ensemble*, add an important dimension. This convincing and well-written book is a must for any serious student of Brecht.

Gray, Ronald, *Brecht the Dramatist*. Cambridge: Cambridge University Press, 1976. As the title suggests, Gray does not discuss the playwright's poems or prose writings. An excellent chapter on the tradition of political theater in Germany and its relation to Marxism precedes a chronological examination of the plays. His survey demands, of course, that Gray cover some well-trodden ground, but he does so with vitality and imagination. An epilogue traces Brecht's influence on the political theater in England and America. Gray's compact assessment of the dramatist has become a standard introduction.

Hill, Claude, *Bertolt Brecht*. Boston: Twayne, 1975. This admiring, yet not uncritical study traces Brecht's work for and in the theater against the background of the dramatist's biographical, literary, and political developments. Hill's conviction that Brecht's theatrical theory has too often been stressed at the expense of his plays leads to a balanced approach. Though other scholarly opinions are referred to, the author's own interpretations remain clear and concise. His chapter on Brecht's poetry might have seemed adequate at a time when the vast majority of the poems was not yet available in English, but cannot be considered so now. Despite this flaw, Hill's book continues to represent an excellent starting point for the nonspecialist.

Parmalee, Patty Lee, *Brecht's America*. Columbus, OH: Published for Miami University by Ohio State University Press, 1981. Parmalee shows how Brecht's early fascination with America was shaped by his reading of works by Upton Sinclair, Frank Norris, Sherwood Anderson and a number of lesser known writers. She continues by proving that Brecht's interest in America led him to study economics and ultimately Marx, an effort which transformed his cynical rebelliousness into a commitment to revolutionary social change. Parmalee's research stops with the year 1931 and does not deal with the playwright's experiences as an exile in America. For American students of Brecht, this informative and enjoyable book should be obligatory.

Schoeps, Karl H. *Bertolt Brecht*. New York: Frederick Ungar, 1977. A brief introduction to Brecht's life and theory of the theater is followed by a chronological survey of thirty-nine of his plays, supplying for each plot summaries, biographical and literary contexts, production histories and critical reviews. Schoeps' own evaluations of the plays are too perfunctory to allow this book to serve as an adequate introduction. Its reliable information, its photos of many different performances, and its extensive bibliography and index make it, nevertheless, a much-welcome reference guide not just for the beginner.

Other Sources

Bartram, Graham and Waine, Anthony. eds. *Brecht in Perspective*. London: Longman, 1982. Thirteen essays on Brecht's own literary tradition and his influence on those of Germany and England.

Bentley, Eric, *The Brecht Commentaries 1943-1980*. New York: Grove Press, 1981. A collection of articles by America's first Brecht scholar.

Demetz, Peter. ed. *Brecht*. Englewood Cliffs, NJ: Prentice-Hall, 1962. An early collection of fifteen essays on all aspects of Brecht's work.

Hiley, Jim, *Theatre at Work: The Story of the National Theatre's Production of Brecht's 'Galileo'*. London: Routledge & Kegan Paul, 1981. An instructive account of what went into the staging of one of Brecht's plays.

Mews, Siegfried and Knust, Herbert, eds. *Essays on Brecht: Theater and Politics*. Chapel Hill: University of North Carolina Press, 1974. Thirteen essays by international Brecht scholars.

Speirs, Ronald, *Brecht's Early Plays*. Atlantic Highlands, NJ: Humanities Press, 1982. Close analyses of Brecht's pre-Marxist plays.

Weber, Betty Nance and Heinen, Hubert, eds. *Bertolt Brecht: Political Theory and Literary Practice*. Athens, GA: University of Georgia Press, 1980. Fifteen essays exploring the impact of Brecht's politics on his art and its reception.

Selected Dictionaries and Encyclopedias

Encyclopaedia Britannica, 1984. Succinct biography and assessment, extensive bibliography of Brecht's works.

Encyclopedia of World Drama, McGraw-Hill, 1984. Brief introduction, plot summaries of all plays, publication and production dates, bibliographies of secondary literature in German and English.

Joachim J. Scholz
Washington College

EUGÈNE BRIEUX
1858-1932

Author's Chronology

Born January 19, 1858, Paris, France, to working class parents; orphaned age 14; leaves school to work as a bank clerk but continues education on his own; *1879* first staged production (*Bernard Palissy*), a one-act play written in collaboration with Gaston Salandri; leaves Paris and works as journalist, eventually becomes editor of the *Nouvelliste de Rouen*; writes three plays while in Rouen; *1890* André Antoine stages *Ménages d'artistes* at the Théâtre Libre; *1892* Antoine stages *Blanchette*, Brieux successfully launched as playwright, returns to Paris; *1893-1899* serves as music and drama critic of *La Vie Contemporaine*; as soon as well-established, leaves Paris and settles in provincial countryside; *1909* elected to French Academy; *1910-1913* travels extensively in the Orient and North Africa; during World War I serves as President of Committee for Rehabilitation of Blind Soldiers; *1929* awarded the Legion of Honor; December 6, *1932* dies in Nice.

Author's Bibliography

Of Brieux's twenty-seven published plays, only nine have appeared in English translation. *Blanchette* (1892) and *The Escape* (1896) were published together with a preface by H.L Mencken, trans. Frederick Eisemann, 1913; *Three Plays by Brieux* with preface by Bernard Shaw, 1911, includes two versions of *Maternity* (1903), trans. Mrs. Bernard Shaw and John Pollock; *The Three Daughters of Monsieur Dupont* (1897), trans. St. John Hankin, and *Damaged Goods* (1901, censured in France after one performance; 1902 Belgium), trans. John Pollock; a second volume of *Three Plays by Brieux* with preface by Brieux appeared in 1916: *Woman on Her Own* (1913), trans. Mrs. Bernard Shaw, *False Gods* (1909), trans. J.F. Fagan, and *The Red Robe* (original version 1900, new version 1909), trans. A. Bernard Miall; *Artists' Families* (1890), trans. by Barrett H. Clark, intro. by J.R. Crawford, 1918.

Overview of Biographical Sources

No biographies of Brieux exist in English, and few have appeared in French. The reason for this is twofold: on the one hand, Brieux was an intensely private individual and considered that his personal life was of no concern to the public; on the other, the somewhat didactic nature of his plays caused critics to be interested in his ideas rather than in his life.

Overview of Critical Sources

Brieux criticism is extensive, but, for the most part, is confined to his lifetime. Moreover, book-length studies of Brieux are virtually non-existant. Most criticism in English shows the influence of Bernard Shaw's essay which generated international interest in the playwright. For this reason, the book chapters and articles discussed in the criticism section all reflect the same basic views, with only nuanced differences of interpretation. Noted American intellectuals who wrote on Brieux include H.L. Mencken and William Dean Howells; Upton Sinclair wrote the screenplay of a film based on a Brieux play.

Evaluation of Selected Criticism

Bacourt, Pierre De and J.W. Cunliffe, *French Literature During the Last Half-Century*. New York: Macmillan 1923, pp. 204-240. The chapter on Brieux is an excellent introduction to his work. After reviewing the plays in chronological order, focusing on theme and discussing the literary merits of each, the authors briefly discuss Brieux's reputation in the United States, England and France because he has been so differently perceived in the three countries.

Scheifley, William, *Brieux and Contemporary French Society*. New York: G.P. Putnam's, 1917. In this excellent sociological study, Scheifley focuses on the social themes treated by Brieux. Each chapter is devoted to a different problem and is divided in two parts. In the first section, the author discusses the problem within the context of French society, often providing extensive legal and historical background on the subject. In the second part, he discusses literary treatments of the theme by Brieux and contemporaneous writers. One strength in Scheifley's approach is that he deliberately includes novels due to his interest in ideas rather than literary form. The greatest difficulty in using this book is that it calls for great familiarity with authors who are, for the most part, unknown today.

Shaw, Bernard, "Preface" in Eugène Brieux, *Three Plays*. English versions by Mrs. Bernard Shaw, St. John Hankin and John Pollock. New York: Brentano's, 1911. Shaw's seminal essay represents the core of Brieux criticism in English. Starting from the premise that Brieux is "incomparably the greatest writer France has produced since Molière," he discusses the evolution of the scientific spirit in the nineteenth century and the effect of this new philosophy on literature, the French tradition of the well-made play, censorship in France and England, and concludes that Brieux must be read and performed not only because he rejects conventionality in the theatre, but also because he alone dares present uncomfortable realities on the stage.

Smith, Hugh Allison, *Main Currents of Modern French Drama*. New York: Holt, 1925. The thesis of Smith's chapter on Brieux is that Brieux is the French dramatist whose works could best be studied for the purpose of understanding the French theatre of that period as well as the recent trend in dramatic taste in England and the United States. He focuses particularly well on the problems inherent in explaining Brieux's popularity, and he often raises possible explanations merely in order to dispel them.

Van Erde, John, "Brieux's Realism," in *College Language Association Journal*, II (Dec. 1958): 111-127. This is the only major article on Brieux written long after the dramatist's death. Van Erde focuses on Brieux's detailed use of environment rather than dialogue to present dramatic situations and is the only critic to discuss comic elements as an integral element of Brieux's realism.

Other Sources

Clark, Barrett H. *Contemporary French Dramatists*. Cincinnati: Steward and Kidd, 1916. In his chapter on Brieux, Clark predicts that Brieux will be considered among the foremost dramatists of his generation, though not for the plays that Shaw selects as the most important.

Courtney, W.L. *Old Saws and Modern Instances*. New York: E.P. Dutton, 1918, pp. 218-235. Courtney labels Brieux as a moralist and sees him as interesting because his didactic aims as a dramatist do not always coincide with influences which led him to pursue certain topics.

Howells, William Dean, "Plays of Eugène Brieux," in *North American Review*, CCI (March 1915): 402-411. Howells is clearly of the Shaw school in seeing Brieux as an important dramatist but he attributes Brieux's greatness to his delineation of character and not merely to his preoccupation with social problems.

Pratz, Claire de, "M. Brieux and his Works," in *Contemporary Review*, LXXXI (March 1902): 343-357. The author of this early article focuses on two plays— *Blanchette* and *The Three Daughters of Monsieur Dupont*—in order to show what traits characterize Brieux's theatre. At the same time, she considers these two plays "epoch-making" because they embody many feminist ideas. She concludes in a similar vein to Howells, claiming that Brieux is more interested in the study of character than in the presentation of dramatic action.

Santa Vicca, Edmund F. *Four French Dramatists: A Bibliography of Criticism of the Works of Eugène Brieux, François de Curel, Emile Fabre and Paul Hervieu*. Metuchen, NJ: Scarecrow Press, 1974. The author provides short biographical introductions to the authors and a complete bibliographic listing of plays by the author including date and place of first staging, books and articles dealing with the author, criticism devoted to each play, articles dealing with Brieux's election to the French Academy, and obituaries. A good reference work.

Scott, Temple, "Brieux," in *Forum*, XLVII (April 1912), 403-418. The author's intent is to explain why Brieux's work has elicited extreme and contradictory opinions. After dismissing Shaw's assessment on grounds that Shaw merely sees in Brieux a reflection of his own theories, Scott clearly explains Brieux's dramatic principles based on the playwright's own statements. He then discusses the issue of propriety in the theatre and concludes that if Brieux is to be criticized, it should be on the grounds of his over-insistence on the value of science and philosophy at the expense of genuine artistic expression.

Mencken, H.L. "Preface" in Brieux, *Blanchette and the Escape*. Boston: Luce, 1913. The brief summary of Brieux's dramatic production until 1913 offers nothing new. The only point of interest, aside from the fact that Mencken wrote the preface, is the discussion of the literary influence of Ibsen and Zola on Brieux.

Amy B. Millstone
University of South Carolina

GEORG BÜCHNER
1813-1837

Author's Chronology

Born October 17, 1813, at Goddelau, near Darmstadt, Germany, into the professional class; his father, Ernst, is appointed court physician to Grand Duke Ludwig I in Darmstadt shortly thereafter; at the local gymnasium (high school) Büchner produces a notable address defending suicide; *1831* enters the University of Strasbourg, France, to study medicine, becomes involved in politics; *1833* secretly engaged, to Whilhelmine (Mina) Jaeglé, whom he never marries. *1834* moves to the University of Giessen in Hessen and becomes a member of radical circles, including the Society of the Rights of Man, which advocated abolition of property rights and violent rebellion; writes his *Hessian Peasant Courier*, a call to arms; an informer betrayed members of Büchner's group, some of whom were tortured; returns to Darmstadt under surveillance. *1835* writes *Danton's Death* in five weeks; March *1835*, escapes to Strasbourg without a passport, an exile; resumes studies, producing philosophical essays, neurological lectures, translations of two Victor Hugo plays, a dissertation on the nervous system of the barbel (a European carp), *Lenz*, and *Leonce and Leona*; fall *1836* receives doctorate and moves to Zürich as teacher of comparative anatomy; works on *Woyzeck* until he contracts typhus in early 1837; dies February 19, 1837, at the age of 23.

Author's Bibliography (selected)

Hessian Peasant Courier, 1834 (revolutionary pamphlet); *Danton's Death*, 1835 (play); *Lenz*, 1836 (unfinished novel); *Leonce and Leona*, 1836 (play); *Woyzeck*, 1837 (play). Only *Danton's Death* and the *Hessian Peasant Courier* were published during Büchner's lifetime. Posthumous publication of the other works was overseen by Büchner's brother Ludwig, who tried to tone down their revolutionary sentiments. As a result, only recent editions are trustworthy. The standard German-language edition is *Sämtliche Werke und Briefe (Historisch-kritische Ausgabe mit Kommentar)*, ed. Werner R. Lehmann (1967; Munich: Hanser, 1979), but this four-volume work is not widely available. Translations of individual Büchner plays abound, including a recent collected edition in English, *George Büchner: The Complete Collected Works*, trans. H.J. Schmitt (New York: Avon, 1977), which includes Büchner works previously unavailable in English. For the plays alone, *The Plays of Georg Büchner*, trans. Victor Price (London: Oxford University Press, 1971), is highly thought of.

Overview of Biographical Sources

Büchner is still not a household name in the English-speaking world, but a good deal of material on his brief life is to be found in the biographical chapters of general books on his works. Although Büchner's life was short, there is little dispute about its important details. However, even the brief accounts that are available in English differ in emphasis. Reliable accounts are contained in Herbert Lindenberger's *Georg Büchner* (1964); Ronald Hauser's *George Büchner* (1974); William C. Reeve's *George Büchner* (1979); and, most recently, Julian Hilton's *Georg Büchner* (1982).

For those familiar with German, *Georg Büchner Sämtliche Werke und Briefe*, ed. Werner R. Lehmann, includes the prose and letters. An adventurous choice might be *Ein Dichter*, ed. Anton Büchner (Darmstadt: Darmstädter Schriften, 1964) which is an unfinished novel by Luise Büchner, the playwright's sister, based on Büchner's life. Finally, new documents having to do with Büchner's life were brought to light by Heinz Ludwig Arnold and Thomas Michael Mayer (eds.) in *Text und Kritik Georg Büchner* (Munich: Edition Text und Kritik, 1979). A general account of the Büchner family is Anton Büchner's *Die Familie Georg Büchners* (Darmstadt: Edward Roetner Verlag, 1963).

Much of what these sources say about Büchner's experience will require some understanding of the politics of his time and place. Good accounts are Jaques Droz' *Europe Between Revolutions 1815-1848* (London: Fontana, 1967), and David Thompson's *Europe Since Napoleon* (Harmondsworth: Pelican, 1966).

Evaluation of Selected Biographies

Hauser, Ronald, *Georg Büchner*. Twayne World Authors Series #300. New York: Twayne, 1974. Hauser gives the fullest account of Büchner's difficulties with the police.

Hilton, Julian, *Georg Büchner*. New York: Grove Press, 1982. Hilton's treatment of Büchner's career takes into account the latest scholarship, and Hilton is a good source for Büchner's relationship to such earlier writers as Lessing, Lenz, Schiller, Tieck, and Grabbe.

Lindenberger, Herbert, *Georg Büchner*. Carbondale: Southern Illinois University Press, 1964. Lindenberger is especially interested in Büchner's schooling and academic career. His thoughtful and readable comments on Büchner's work go on to establish a convincing picture of the author's ideas and psychological states during his short working career.

Reeve, William C. *Georg Büchner*. New York: Fredrich Ungar, 1979. Reeve is interested in Büchner's political beliefs and gives an analysis of the *Hessian Peasant Courier*, along with an outline of Büchner's activities as a would-be revolutionary.

Autobiographical Sources

Büchner's life is reflected only indirectly in his imaginative works; however his *Hessian Courier* and other prose works are available in *Georg Büchner: The Com-*

plete Collected Works, trans. H.J. Schmitt. Selected letters are reproduced in "Some Büchner Letters in Translation," trans. Karl W. Maurer, *German Life and Letters*, 1 (1954/55): 50-55, and "From Georg Büchner's Letters," trans. Maurice Edwards, *Tulane Drama Review*, 6 (1961/62): 132-35.

Overview of Critical Sources

Critics of Büchner's works generally take one of two approaches: either they view him as a man of letters and discuss the internal qualities of his works and their place in tradition (especially theatrical tradition); or they concentrate on his political and philosophical beliefs. In both areas Büchner is increasingly regarded as a seminal figure, anticipating the surrealism, psychological truth, and social relevance of modern drama and modern literature as a whole. Büchner's alienated characters and his concern for social justice are especially important for later dramatists. But Büchner is much more than just a forerunner of modern writers. His plays in particular are still memorably effective theatrical works, making him an outstanding literary figure in his own right.

Evaluation of Selected Criticism

Benn, Maurice, *The Drama of Revolt: A Critical Study of Georg Büchner*. Cambridge: Cambridge University Press, 1976. Benn gives the fullest account of Büchner's philosophical preoccupations under the headings "Political Revolt," "Metaphysical Revolt," and "Aesthetic Revolt." He analyzes the plays as literature rather than as pieces for staging and finds in Büchner a profound anticipation of modern concerns and literary themes.

Hauser, Ronald, *Georg Büchner*. Twayne World Authors Series, #300. New York: Twayne, 1974. Hauser emphasizes the bleakness of Büchner's vision and explains in detail his handling of such themes as nihilism, powerlessness, madness, and death.

Hilton, Julian, *Georg Büchner*. New York: Grove Press, 1982. Hilton gives the best accessible account of Büchner's place in the German theatrical tradition up to his time. This book is also rich in discussions of staging problems and conventions affecting Büchner plays and their production history.

Lindenberger, Herbert, *Georg Büchner*. Carbondale: Southern Illinois Press, 1964. Like Benn, Lindenberger is especially interested in the imagery and themes of Büchner's works. He gives detailed accounts of each work, tracing the parallels between them to justify his thesis, that Büchner was building toward a new way of writing drama with the imagination and freedom of poetry. Lindenberger offers a convincing presentation of Büchner's own growth as a personality and excellent last chapter on Büchner's place in literary history.

Richards, David G. *Georg Büchner and the Birth of the Modern Drama*. Albany: State University of New York Press, 1977. Richards analyzes Büchner's contributions to the modern stage, especially such modern movements as Naturalism, Expressionism, Documentary Theater, and Theater of the Absurd.

Other Sources

Büchner, Georg, "Woyzeck." A BBC production hosted by Jose Ferrer, available in videotape from Films Inc., Film and Tape Division, 733 Green Bay Road, Wilmette, IL 60091. Mr. Ferrer in the character of Georg Büchner himself comments on the play and the production.

Hamburger, Michael, "Georg Büchner," *Evergreen Review* #1 (1957): 68-98. A general appreciation by one of Büchner's translators.

Knight, Arthur H. J. *Georg Büchner*. Oxford: Oxford University Press, 1951. A rather dry account of Büchner's life. Extensive quotations in German.

Schmidt, Henry J. *Satire, Caricature, and Perspectivism in the Works of Georg Büchner*. The Hague: Mouton, 1970. Discussion of non-representational techniques in Büchner's writing and Büchner's expressive distortions of reality.

Selected Dictionaries and Encyclopedias

McGraw-Hill Encyclopedia of World Drama. 2nd ed. McGraw-Hill, 1984. Synopses of Büchner's works, including photographs of the plays in production.

The Reader's Encyclopedia of World Drama. Thomas Crowell, 1969. Short biography and appreciation of Büchner's plays. `

Joe Glaser
Western Kentucky University

ANTONIO BUERO VALLEJO
1916

Author's Chronology

Born September 29, 1916, in Guadalajara, Spain; *1934-1936* attends San Fernando School of Fine Arts to study painting, but with the outbreak of the Spanish Civil War (1936-1939) he enlists in the Republican army as a medic; *1939* he is sentenced to death by the Nationalist victors, but serves six years in prison and is released in 1945; *1949* performance of his first play, *Historia de una escalera*, winner of the important Lope de Vega Prize; *1954* Censor's office prohibits the premiere of *Aventura en lo gris; 1957 Hoy es fiesta* wins National Theater Prize; Buero is denied exit visa to France by the Spanish government; *1958 Las cartas boca abajo* receives National Theater Prize; *1959* marries the actress Victoria Rodríguez; *1960* signs public letter condemning censorship in Spain; *1966* visits the United States and lectures on Spanish drama; *1968 The Double Case History of Doctor Valmy* performed in English in Chester, England after being banned in Spain; *1971* elected to Spanish Royal Academy; *1984 The Dream of Reason* performed by the Center Stage of Baltimore, the first professional production in the United States of an important postwar Spanish play.

Author's Bibliography

Buero's plays are easily accessible in the original Spanish. They have been published individually and in various collections, though the complete works have yet to be published in a single volume. His most important plays include the following: 1949 *Historia de una escalera;* 1950 *En la ardiente oscuridad;* 1952 *La tejedora de sueños;* 1956 *Hoy es fiesta;* 1957 *Las cartas boca abajo;* 1960 *Las Meninas: Fantasía velazqueña en dos partes;* 1967 *El tragaluz;* 1968 *The Double Case History of Doctor Valmy;* 1970, 1984 *The Sleep of Reason;* 1974, 1983 *The Foundation.* Since contemporary Spanish theater has only recently begun to win recognition in the United States, few of Buero's plays have been translated into English. Many of his works, however, have been performed in translation in Germany, Italy, France, Portugal, Holland, Norway, Hungary, Yugoslavia, and Japan. In the United States, Marion P. Holt has done the two most important translations, *The Foundation* and *The Sleep of Reason.*

Overview of Biographical Sources

With the exception of Federico Garcia Lorca, few twentieth century Spanish playwrights have been the subject of in-depth biographical studies. Buero Vallejo has been among the most scrutinized of Spanish writers, but his complete biography remains to be written. The best sources for information about his life are the chapters in Martha Halsey's *Antonio Buero Vallejo* (Boston: Twayne, 1973) and Carmen González-Cobos Dávila's *Antonio Buero Vallejo: El hombre y su obra*. The former offers an overview of Buero and his times and a chronology of important dates; the latter includes a more detailed examination of crucial events in Buero's life and how they relate to his theater.

Autobiographical Sources

Buero has given numerous interviews since the early 1950s in newspapers and magazines, and these are the best source of his perspective on life and art. The interviews have not been collected in a single volume nor have they been translated into English.

Overview of Critical Sources

Buero's theater has inspired more critical commentary than any other postwar Spanish playwright, and his work has been examined at close range by scholars in Italy, France, Germany, Spain, and the United States. Since Buero has continued to write and evolve as a dramatist, it is precipitate to reach definitive conclusions about the meaning of his work and its impact on the contemporary Spanish theater. To date, much of the critical work has focused on the form and technique of Buero's plays and on his conception of tragedy. As more of his plays have become known in the United States, his work has begun to attract attention in relation to modern American and European playwrights.

Evaluation of Selected Criticism

Domenech, Ricardo, *El teatro de Buero Vallejo*. Madrid: Editorial Gredos, 1973. Domenech is not only an astute literary scholar of Buero Vallejo's theater, but he has also had the opportunity to see most of his works performed. The book is useful for its interpretive insights and for its data on the premieres, actors, and directors of Buero's plays. It also contains a complete bibliography of critical studies through 1971.

Dowd, Catherine Elizabeth, *Realismo trascendente en cuatro tragedias sociales de Antonio Buero Vallejo*. Chapel Hill: Estudios de Hispanófila, 1974. The linking of Buero's theory and practice of writing tragedy is a legitimate one, though Dowd ties both to a somewhat diffuse and problematic definition of realism. She studies four of Buero's tragedies and envisions them as an instrument for positive social change in an abulic society.

González-Cobos Dávila, Carmen, *Antonio Buero Vallejo: El hombre y su obra*. Salamanca: Ediciones Universidad de Salamanca, 1979. González-Cobos Dávila divides her study into several sections on characters and character types, and studies their relationship to society, politics, war, and other recurring themes in Buero's theater. The book is useful, but has been superseded by the more recent work of Luis Iglesias Feijoo.

Halsey, Martha, *Antonio Buero Vallejo*. Boston: Twayne, 1973. The first study in English that offers an overview of Buero's life and times, as well as an analysis of his plays through 1970. Halsey's critical posture is eclectic and covers the major ideas and forms of Buero's theater. Halsey is the preeminent Buero scholar in the United States, and her book serves as a valuable introduction to Buero and his work.

Iglesias Feijoo, Luis, *La trayectoria dramática de Antonio Buero Vallejo*. Santiago de Compostela: Universidad de Santiago de Compostela, 1982. This is the most in-depth and complete study to date of Buero's theater. Iglesias Feijoo frames his work in Buero's dramatic theory and offers an intrinsic analysis of each of Buero's plays through 1979. Emphasis is on changing thematic and technical elements of Buero's theater as he evolves as a playwright.

Nicholas, Robert L. *The Tragic Stages of Antonio Buero Vallejo*. Chapel Hill: Estudios de Hispanófila, 1972. Nicholas views the early theater of Buero as essentially tragic and asserts that the diverse ways in which tragedy is played out in Buero's theater parallels the changing norms of the author's aesthetics. This is a perceptive and well-written study that emphasizes the link between the artistic and the ethical in Buero's theater.

Other Sources

Borel, Jean-Paul, "Buero Vallejo o lo imposible concreto e historico." in *El teatro de lo imposible*. trans. G. Torrente Ballester. Madrid: Ediciones Guadarrama, 1966. Philosophical analysis of Buero's plays from an existential point of view.

Halsey, Martha T. "Buero Vallejo and the Significance of Hope," *Hispania*, 51 (1968): 57-66. Studies hope as a key element of Buero's tragedies, both for understanding existential dilemmas and the transcendent order of the universe.

Herzberger, David K. "The Painterly Vision of Buero Vallejo's *El sueño de la razón*," *Symposium*, 34 (1985): 93-103. Studies the importance of art and imagination as a source of hope and creation.

Kronik, John, "Buero Vallejo's *El tragaluz* and Man's Existence in History," *Hispanic Review*, 41 (1973): 371-396. Perceptive analysis of Buero's view of war, history, and existential meaning.

O'Connor, Patricia, "Censorship in the Contemporary Spanish Theater and Antonio Buero Vallejo," *Hispania*, 52 (1969): 282-288. Discusses the problem of censorship in postwar theater and its impact on Buero.

Roeple, Joelyn, *Antonio Buero Vallejo: The First Fifteen Years*. New York: Eliseo Torres, 1972. General study of Buero's early theater.

David K. Herzberger
University of Connecticut

PEDRO CALDERÓN DE LA BARCA
1600-1681

Author's Chronology

Born January 17, 1600, in Madrid, Spain, third of five children, to a civil servant; *1608* or *1609-1614* studies with Jesuits at Alcalá; *1614-1620* studies canon law at Salamanca, which gave him a solid education in Catholic theology; *1620* returns to Madrid; *1623* writes first known play *Amor, honor y poder*; *1624* probably travels to Flanders and northern Italy, both colonies of Spain; *1625* enters service of the Duke of Frías; *1635* Philip IV appoints him official court dramatist; *1637* is made Knight of Santiago and enters service with Duke of Infantader; *1642* Philip IV awards him monthly pension; *1644-1645* is in Toledo; *1645-1649* is in service to the Duke of Alba, may have fathered an illegitimate child during these years; *1651* is ordained priest and becomes chaplain of the New Sovereign in Toledo, but continues writing both secular and religious plays; since *1656* lives more or less continuously at court; *1663* is named King's Chaplain; dies March 25, 1681.

Author's Bibliography

Calderón was a prolific writer, but many of his plays have been lost. During his lifetime seven *Partes de las comedias* were published, the last three composed of rather corrupt texts and of plays not by Calderón. The dates for the first four volumes are 1636, 1637, 1664, 1672 and are now available in facsimiles edited by Don W. Cruikshank and J. E. Varey (London: Gregg International, 1973). The two most easily available collections are J.E. Hartzenbusch's edition for the Bibliotecas de Autores Españoles (vols. 7, 9, 12, 14) and the superior edition by Angel Valbuena Briones, the three-volume *Obras completas*: Vol. I—Dramas, Vol. II—Comedias, Vol. III—Autos sacramentales. An edition of Calderón's plays with full textual apparatus is sorely needed.

Overview of Biographical Sources

Like Shakespeare and unlike modern writers, Calderón did not collect his letters, nor did he have a Boswell-type admirer to write his biography. As a matter of fact, there is not a standard full-size biography of Calderón; all there exists are a few details, which, when brought together, do not offer a coherent view of the playwright, his work, and his beliefs. Cristóbal Pérez Pastor's *Documentos para la biografía de Don Pedro Calderón de la Barca* (Madrid: Estableermiento Tipográfico de Fortanet, 1905) collects official documents relating to Calderón and his immediate family. Emilio Cotarelo y Mori coherently discusses the little information available in *Ensayos sobre la vida y las obras de Calderón* (Madrid: Tipografía de la *Revista de Archivos, Bibliotecas y Museos*, 1924). Harry Lund's hard to find *Calderón de la Barca: A Biography* (Edinburgh, Texas: privately printed, 1952) ought to be avoided because of its lack of historical accuracy.

Evaluation of Selected Biographies

Cotarelo y Mori, Emilio, *Ensayo sobre la vida y obras de D. Pedro Calderón de la Barca.* Madrid: Tipografía de la *Revista de Archivos, Bibliotecas y Museos*, 1924. Although Cotarelo y Mori promised a second part where he would discuss Calderón's work, he never completed it. This first volume focuses on Calderón's biography. A bit outdated, this is the most comprehensive and best biography of Calderón.

Lund, Harry, *Pedro Calderón de la Barca: A Biography.* Edinburgh, TX: privately printed, 1952. The style of this amateurish biography is purile. Not a scholarly work, this biography ought not to be consulted by serious students of Calderón.

Pérez Pastor, Cristóbal, *Documentos para la biografía de D. Pedro Calderón de la Barca.* Madrid: Establecimiento Tipografico de Fortanet, 1905. This collection contains mostly official documents relating to Calderón and his immediate family. Most interesting of these is the list made after Calderón's death of his belongings.

Autobiographical Sources

Autobiographical information on Calderón de la Barca is scant. In Emilio Cotarelo y Mori's *Ensayo sobre la vida y obras de D. Pedro Calderón de la Barca* (Madrid: Tipografía de la *Revista de Archivos, Bibliotecas y Museos*, 1924), there is a famous letter where he answers critics of the theater who chastize him for writing plays even after he took the religious vows. The only other autobiographical information is that which can be surmized from his plays, a practice the student of Calderón should avoid.

Overview of Critical Sources

Calderón is now beginning to receive the critical attention he deserves. Because of the large number of plays that he wrote, scholars concentrate their attention of a relatively small number. Book-length studies of his plays have so far focused their attention on the honor plays and the *autos sacramentales*. But of all of his plays, *La vida es sueño (Life is a Dream)* has been the subject of many articles and usually forms part of any book-length analysis of the Calderonian canon.

Evaluation of Selected Criticism

Bryans, John V. *Calderón de la Barca: Imagery, Rhetoric and Drama.* London: Tamesis, 1977. Although at times rather technical, the first part of this study analyzes the stylistics of a speech or a scene in twelve of Calderón's plays. Later, Bryans suggests how these rhetorical devices work within the larger context of the play. One of the strengths of the book is the variety of plays that Bryans has chosen to focus on.

Cascardi, Anthony J. *The Limits of Illusion: A Critical Study of Calderón*. Cambridge: Cambridge University Press, 1984. Cascardi discusses Calderón's use of illusion, certainly a pervasive and important aspect of Calderón's works. By analyzing nine plays, representing the different types of plays that Calderón wrote, Cascardi suggests how Calderón uses the Christian theology he knew so well to answer the skepticism of his age.

Honig, Edwin, *Calderón and the Seizures of Honor*. Cambridge: Harvard University Press, 1972. Studying five of Calderón's honor plays, Honig suggests that in each play Calderón deals differently with that very problematic question of honor. Implicitly arguing against the readings of the plays offered by E. M. Wilson and A. A. Parker, Honig declares that these plays do not necessarily teach a particular lesson about the effect of this code of conduct but rather it is used to develop the characters' self awareness.

Parker, Alexander A. *The Allegorical Drama of Calderón: An Introduction to the Autos Sacramentales*. Oxford: Dolphin, 1943. This is a seminal study of Calderón's short religious plays. After first giving an excellent introduction to the *autos*, Parker analyzes three of the best and the most easily accessible *autos*. Although the *autos* are the most didactic of Calderón's dramas, they have definite artistic merits, which Parker amply demonstrates.

Sloman, Albert E. *The Dramatic Craftsmanship of Calderón: His Use of Earlier Plays*. Oxford: Dolphin, 1958. This is one of the earliest full length and still one of the finest studies of Calderón's art and genius. Like Shakespeare, Calderón did not invent many of his plots, but rather frequently chose to rewrite what was available. His versions, however, are very much his own and not just mere editing of his sources. Sloman focuses on plays and their sources to point out Calderón's artistry.

ter Horst, Robert, *Calderón: The Secular Plays*. Lexington: University of Kentucky Press, 1982. After evaluating some eighty plays, ter Horst concludes that Calderón's secular canon can be best understood if seen in terms of myth, honor, and history. For each of the divisions, he focuses on one play while freely bringing in others to supplement his argument.

Other Sources
Honig, Edwin, tr. *Four Plays*. New York: Hill and Wang, 1961. A fine translation of four of Calderón's most important plays: *A secreto agravio, secreta venganza, La devoción de la cruz, El alcalde de Zalamea*, and *La dama duende*.

McGaha, Michael D. ed. *Approaches to the Theater of Calderón*. Lanham, MD: University Press of America, 1982. McGaha collects essays presented at a West Coast symposium commemorating the tercentenary of the death of Calderón. Although the quality of the essays varies, a large number of the most important and influential Calderonian scholars are included.

Muir, Kenneth, tr. *Four Comedies by Pedro Calderón de la Barca*. Lexington: University of Kentucky Press, 1980. Muir has provided very readable translations of *Peor está que estaba, El secreto a voces, No siempre lo peor es cierto*, and *Dicha y desdicha del nombre*.

Parker, Jack H. and Arthur M. Fox, comp. *Calderón de la Barca Studies, 1951-1969*. Toronto: University of Toronto Press, 1971. An annotated bibliography of primary and secondary sources published between 1951 and 1969. Although the compilers at times provide their own commentary in the notations, they frequently excerpt from book reviews.

Wardropper, Bruce W. *Critical Essays on the Theatre of Calderón*. New York: New York University Press, 1965. Wardropper reprints eleven of the finest articles on Calderón by noted scholars such as A. A. Parker, E. M. Wilson, and Evertt W. Hesse. Probably one of the best collections of reprinted articles available anywhere.

Gisela Casines
Florida International University

ALBERT CAMUS
1913-1960

Author's Chronology

Born November 7, 1913, Mondovi, Algeria, to Lucien Camus, a French winery worker, and Catherine Sintès of Minorcan descent; *1914* father dies in Battle of the Marne; Camus and his older brother Lucien are raised in poverty in the working-class district of Belcourt in Algiers by his almost totally deaf mother and domineering grandmother; *1918-1923* attends grade school in Belcourt; *1923-1930* attends the Algiers high school on a scholarship; plays soccer; *1930* suffers his first attacks of tuberculosis; *1931* enrolls in the University of Algiers and meets Jean Grenier, the philosophy professor who becomes his friend and mentor; his studies over the next five years are frequently interrupted by poor health; he supports himself with various odd jobs; *1933* involves himself in the antifascist movement; *1934* joins the Communist party, but quickly becomes disenchanted; marries Simone Hié, only to be divorced two years later; *1935* founds the *Théâtre du travail* (Work Theatre), soon to become the *Théâtre de l'Equipe* (Team Theatre), in Algiers and serves as actor-director-playwright; collaborates on a group theatrical endeavor *The Revolt in Asturia*, which is banned from production in Algiers because of its revolutionary theme; *1936* receives the *diplôme d'études supérieures* (Masters degree) in philosophy, but for reasons of poor health is unable to take the examinations for the *agrégation*, or university teaching degree; *1937* works as a reporter for the *Alger Républicain* newspaper, and publishes his first work in Algiers, *The Wrong Side and the Right Side*, a collection of essays; *1940* marries Francine Faure; resides briefly in Lyon, France, until 1941; *1942* publishes his first novel *The Stranger*; leaves Algeria again to join the French Resistance; *1942-1947* edits the Movement's newspaper *Combat* (clandestine until the liberation in 1944); *1943* joins the Gallimard publishing firm in Paris as an editor, a position he holds until his death; *1944* meets Jean-Paul Sartre; his first play is produced in Paris, *The Misunderstanding*; *1945* birth of his twins Jean and Catherine; *1946-1947* lectures in the United States; *1947* publishes *The Plague*, an instant success; *1949* his health fails even more following a lecture tour of South America; *1951* publishes *The Rebel*, a long philosophical essay which sparks a bitter polemic with the literary and political left; a rift with Sartre ensues in 1952; embittered, Camus retires briefly from most literary and political activity; *1955* returns to journalism for the *Express*; *1957* receives the Nobel Prize for Literature; *1959* is appointed by Minister for Cultural Affairs André Malraux to direct a new, state-supported, experimental theatre in Paris, and begins work on a new novel *The First Man* (unfinished); January 4, 1960 dies in an automobile accident.

Author's Bibliography (selected; see also Autobiographical Sources)

Caligula, 1938, performed 1945 (play); *The Stranger*, 1942, trans. 1946 (novel); *The Myth of Sisyphus*, 1943, trans. 1955 (essay); *The Misunderstanding*, also translated as *Cross Purpose*, 1944 (play); *The Plague*, 1947, trans. 1948 (novel); *State of Siege*, 1948 (play); *The Just Assassins*, 1949 (play); *The Rebel*, 1951; trans. 1954 (essay); *The Fall*, 1956, trans. 1957 (novel); *Exile and the Kingdom*, 1957, trans. 1958 (short story collection). All of the English translations of Camus's major works are published in New York by Alfred A. Knopf. His four original plays are published in one edition, *Caligula and Three Other Plays* (1958), with a preface by Camus. Of his six adaptations for the theatre produced between 1953 and 1959, only his play of Dostoevsky's *The Possessed*, 1959, exists in English translation (1960).

Overview of Biographical Sources

Camus's sudden death at the age of 46 in 1960 interrupted a literary career that many critics believe was just coming to fruition following a rather sterile period between 1952 and 1956 in the wake of the polemic surrounding the publication of *The Rebel* in 1951. Camus did not gain worldwide attention until the early 1940s, with the publication of *The Stranger* and *The Myth of Sisyphus*. Thus, the first overall studies of the man and his work did not begin to appear until the mid-1950s. Camus was widely heralded as the moral conscience of his time, depicting on a philosophical scale man struggling to survive in an absurd cosmos and on a political scale the individual making a stand against all forms of modern tyranny. Therefore, early studies of him tended to be conventionally encomiastic literary biographies which interpreted the man as a function of the evolving thought expressed in his works. Albert Maquet's 1955 study *Albert Camus: The Invincible Summer* (New York: George Braziller, 1958) typifies this approach to the author. The book idealizes Camus as a purist in the midst of the contemporary political society. "The work of Albert Camus is of the kind that requires us to be worthy of it," Maquet states in an author's note. In this same vein of the semi-biographical, semi-critical study, but a more sincere effort at an objective appraisal of his art, is Germaine Brée's *Camus*, originally published in 1959, and then revised in 1964 after his death. This blurred line between biography and criticism characterizes almost all of the book-length studies of Camus in the fifties and sixties and is due in part to a lack of information concerning the important events of his life and an ignorance of the genesis of his works while he lived. Therefore, as Roger Quilliot, editor of Camus's complete works, points out, "It was a risky business in the early stage at least, to set apart the dramatist from the man of action and the journalist from the poet and novelist." Camus worked simultaneously as a polemicist, novelist and playwright, and this led some critics to facile conclusions regarding the relationship of the man's life to his works. Several other treatments of Camus deal with him as a spokesman for human rights, a polemicist interested in the social and political problems of his time. Emmett Parker's *Albert Camus, the Artist in the Arena* (Madison: University of Wisconsin Press, 1965) provides a discussion of Camus's political thought and the beliefs that inspired it. Relating Camus's politics to his fiction, Susan Tarrow's *Exile from the Kingdom: A Political Rereading of Albert Camus* (University, AL: University of Alabama Press, 1985) constitutes an interesting update of Parker's study. In the wake of these eulogistic tributes to the man and his work Camus's popularity diminished in the seventies, particularly in France, when attention shifted away from Existentialist and philosophically-oriented literature to the technically aesthetic innovations of the "new" novel and theatre. Camus has retained his appeal to the American public, however, and his work has been undergoing a new and more critically distant evaluation in the eighties. Proof of this Camusian revival are two recent biographies in English: an immense work by Herbert R. Lottman, *Albert Camus* (1979), and Patrick Mc-Carthy's *Camus* (1982). Both are far more truly biographical in scope than any previous treatments of Camus. For the reader of French, the Pléiade edition of Camus's complete works in two volumes, edited and extensively annotated by Roger Quilliot, contains an enormous amount of biographical material, as well as almost all of Camus's writings, speeches and interviews.

Evaluation of Selected Biographies

Brée, Germaine, *Camus*. New Brunswick, NJ: Rutgers University Press, 1959, rev. ed. 1964. This is, primarily, a study of Camus's works, generically organized, but the first chapters center on Camus's life. Brée often presents a sympathetic Camus, a man struggling with himself and his times, reflective of the laudatory studies of the late fifties and sixties. Her book reveals a personal understanding of Camus—whom she knew—and reflects her access to unpublished material; her style is clear and readable. The detailed and well-organized bibliography is divided into French and English-language books on Camus.

Lottman, Herbert R. *Albert Camus: A Biography*. Garden City, NY: Doubleday, 1979. This is a relatively effective attempt at a definitive biography—more than seven hundred pages of detail documenting with painstaking fidelity all the events of Camus's life. Lottman concentrates on externals, often giving the literary scholar far more concrete detail than necessary—eleven pages, for example, on the exact circumstances of Camus's fatal auto accident. The book is excellent on the specifics of Camus's personal relationships and the historical context, particularly that of the Second World War and the Resistance, out of which his literature arose. Well-indexed, it provides a fine resource on almost any aspect of Camus's life.

McCarthy, Patrick, *Camus*. New York: Random House, 1982. A fitting complement to the Lottman work, McCarthy is direct and graceful where Lottman is sometimes turgid and heavy, penetrating where Lottman is often superficial. The book is essentially a psychological study, illuminating the emotional complexity of Camus and exploring in depth the intricate relationship between the public, often mythic, image of the writer and the contradictory and neurotic but fascinating real man.

Quillot, Roger, *The Sea and Prisons: A Commentary on the Life and Thought of Albert Camus*. trans. Emmett Parker. University, AL: University of Alabama Press, 1970. Quilliot considerably revised and updated his original 1956 study for this English translation of the work. It follows the usual approach of most of the works on Camus, dealing with the man in relation to his works. Thus, like Brée's, it is not a true biography. However, since Quilliot was a personal friend of Camus's from 1948 on, and also the director of the Pléiade edition of Camus's complete works, he had access to a wealth of information on Camus's life. The work is a positive but candid appraisal of Camus and his works. It makes interesting reading, because Quilliot quotes extensively from Camus and analyzes his works chronologically as an outgrowth of Camus's personal experience or "mindset" at each stage of his career. Quilliot devotes two chapters to Camus's drama and also provides a very detailed, annotated biographical chronology of the author's life.

Autobiographical Sources

Camus's *Notebooks*, published in two volumes, 1935-1942 and 1942-1951, are his most clearly autobiographical work (Alfred A. Knopf, 1963 and 1965). The notebooks constitute a spontaneous, random collection of philosophical thought, social commentary, poetic fancy, ideas for works in progress or projected works, and simple reminders. Moreover, because Camus was an essayist and journalist as well as a novelist and playwright, many of his essays and articles contain autobiographical material. In addition to his two well-known, long philosophical essays *The Myth of Sisyphus*, published in English in *The Myth of Sisyphus and Other Essays* (Alfred A. Knopf, 1955), and *The Rebel* (Alfred A. Knopf, 1954), there are several other collections of Camus's essays in English translation. *The First Camus and Youthful Writings* (Alfred A. Knopf, 1976) collects essays Camus wrote between 1932 and 1934 on art, philosophy and his impoverished youth in Algiers. *Resistance, Rebellion and Death* (Alfred A. Knopf, 1961) represents a selection of essays chosen for English translation by Camus himself from the three volumes of his *Actuelles* (1950, 1953, 1958), which constitute his essays and articles on political issues of his day. *Lyrical and Critical Essays* (Alfred A. Knopf, 1969) contain the translations of his published essay collections *The Wrong Side and the Right Side* (also translated as *Betwixt and Between*), 1937, *Nuptials*, 1939, and *Summer*, 1954, essays which are commentaries on Camus's own immediate experience and highlight his Mediterranean sensualist side. This book also contains his essays on literary and aesthetic topics, particularly Camus's writings on other authors such as Sartre, Gide, Faulkner and Melville. Of particular relevance here to Camus's theatre are the essay "On the Future of Tragedy" and the "Foreword" to his stage adaptation of Faulkner's *Requiem for a Nun*.

Overview of Critical Sources (drama only)

Despite Camus's lifelong passion for and involvement with the theatre as actor, director and playwright, the overwhelming critical consensus is that his plays are largely failures, certainly insofar as staged theatre. His conception of drama is too purist; his plays too intellectual, and thus they are better read than produced. Camus is far better known and acclaimed for his essays and fiction. Consequently, while scholarly criticism of Camus abounds, most critical commentaries on his theatre consist of chapters in general studies of Camus's art. The earlier of these analyses tend to highlight the content of his plays: characters, plot, themes. Only more recently have scholars attempted to analyze the reason for Camus's failure as a dramatist in studies of his theatre. Critics almost uniformly relate Camus's four original plays, all produced between 1944 and 1949, although written between 1938 and 1949, to his two major philosophical essays. They see in *Caligula* and *The Misunderstanding* the dramatic expression of the absurd, as elaborated in *The Myth of Sisyphus*, while *State of Siege* and *The Just Assassins* represent specific illustrations of Camus's concept of revolt as enunciated in *The Rebel*. For the reader of French, Raymond Gay-Crosier's *Les Envers d'un échec: étude sur le théâtre d'Albert Camus* (Paris: Lettres Modernes—Minard, 1967) is still by far the most complete treatment of Camus's theatre in all its aspects, and the bibliography is an excellent source for reviews (some in English) of the plays when they were first produced. Also in French is Ilona Coombs' book *Camus, homme de théâtre* (Paris: Nizet, 1968). Roger Quilliot's notes and commentary to the critical edition of Camus's theatre in Volume I of the Pléiade edition, Albert Camus, *Théâtre, récits, nouvelles* (Paris: Gallimard, 1962) represent a most important critical source as well.

Evaluation of Selected Criticism

Brée, Germaine, *Camus*. New Brunswick, NJ: Rutgers University Press, rev. ed. 1964. Brée devotes three consecutive chapters to Camus's plays, first treating his concept of drama and its sources, then giving the genesis of each of his four original plays and summarizing the action, before analyzing them as stage productions. Finally she moves to a detailed analysis of the themes of each. She stresses the importance of the dramatic adaptations in the development of Camus's concept of theatre and provides an extensive discussion of Camus's adaptation of Faulkner's *Requiem for a Nun*. Unlike most critics, Brée foregoes the usual coupling of *Caligula* and *The Misunderstanding* as theatre of the absurd, and *State of Siege* and *The Just Assassins* as theatre of revolt. She sees *State of Siege*, instead, as a social amplification of the more metaphysical *Caligula*, while *The Just Assassins* becomes for her a second *Misunderstanding* presented in terms of a concrete political action. Brée believes *The Just Assassins* most clearly highlights the issues of deepest concern to Camus. She claims that in Camus's hands the stage becomes the "*décor* of a mental universe."

Cruickshank, John, *Albert Camus and the Literature of Revolt*. London: Oxford University Press, 1959. Like Brée's work, this is again a literary biography divided into three parts. In the first and most biographical section, Cruickshank posits revolt as Camus's attitude to life, then applies this notion of revolt to Camus's political beliefs, and finally, to his literature. In a chapter devoted to Camus's theatre, Cruickshank emphasizes the traditional philosophical dichotomy of the four plays and supports the prevailing thesis that *Caligula* and *The Just Assassins* are Camus's best. He analyzes the unmitigated failure of *State of Siege*, believing this to be the main critical interest of the play. He provides a solid analysis of Camus's philosophical attitude toward the function of the drama. In Cruickshank's estimation Camus's failures are due more to inadequate control of his dramatic gifts than to a lack of ability as a playwright.

Freeman, E. *The Theatre of Albert Camus: A Critical Study*. London: Methuen, 1971. Instead of condemning Camus's theatre outright, Freeman attempts to assess objectively Camus's place in what he terms the "renaissance" of French theatre which began in the 1930s. The book is therefore an excellent introduction to the French theatre of the first half of the century as well as the most complete analysis in English of Camus's drama. After an introduction devoted to Camus's preoccupation with the theatre and his aims, Freeman divides Camus's drama into three phases. The first, 1935-39, represents Camus's dramatic apprenticeship in Algeria and includes a lengthy treatment of *The Revolt in Asturia*. The second phase, 1944-49, deals with Camus's four original plays in separate chapters, and the third, 1950-60, treats the stage adaptations. In a final synthetic chapter Freeman evaluates whether or not Camus was successful in creating the modern tragedy and judges the merit of Camus's work as theatre. Freeman comes to the same conclusions as most critics of Camus's drama, but his study is far more analytically detailed. He views Camus's theatre as one of static situation, lacking in effective dramatic exploitation, and he stresses the notion of the absurd as fundamental to it. Freeman avoids the mistake that so many Camusian scholars have made and attempts above all "to appraise Camus's theatre as theatre rather than as philosophical literature in dramatic form." The book also contains an excellent bibliography of articles in French and English relating specifically to Camus as a dramatist and of general works on modern theatre with sections devoted to Camus.

Lazere, Donald, *The Unique Creation of Albert Camus*. New Haven: Yale University Press, 1973. In a chapter entitled "The Drama: An Unmastered Form," Lazere analyzes Camus's failure as a dramatist, subscribing to the widely held belief that the plays make better reading than staged pieces. This work is a good analysis of the failings of Camus's plays in production and of their reception by drama critics. Lazere finds *Caligula* to be Camus's most successful effort. Lazere's study is particularly geared to Camus's reputation in America.

Rhein, Phillip H. *Albert Camus*. New York: Twayne, 1969. Intended as a complete composite critical/analytical introduction to the works of the author, in this volume of Twayne's World Authors Series Rhein devotes two chapters to Camus's theatre, dividing the four major plays into the conventional pairings of *Caligula* and *The Misunderstanding* as theatre of the absurd, and *State of Siege* and *The Just*

Assassins as theatre of revolt in the context of Camus's two philosophical essays. Rhein prefaces his analysis of the action and themes of the individual plays with a brief introduction to Camus and the theatre, Camus's theory of tragedy, and a brief discussion of the contemporary intellectual and political scene, and concludes by relating each of the plays to Camus's other works. He believes *The Just Assassins* is the best of the plays and the one that comes closest to Camus's notion of modern tragedy.

Other Sources (drama only)

Block, Haskell M. "Albert Camus: Toward a Definition of Tragedy," in *University of Toronto Quarterly*, vol. 19 (1950): 354-60.

Couch, J.P. "Camus' dramatic adaptations and translations," in *French Review*, no. 33 (1959-60): 27-36.

Fowlie, Wallace, *Dionysus in Paris: A Guide to Contemporary French Theater*. New York: Meridian, 1960. Contains a chapter on Camus in the section devoted to the "theater of ideas." Sees Camus's plays as "the spectacle of his thought as it tried to comprehend that other spectacle of contemporary society lost in its political machinations."

Guicharnaud, Jacques, *Modern French Theatre from Giraudoux to Genet*. New Haven: Yale University Press, 1967. Contains a chapter on the existentialist theatre of Sartre and Camus, emphasizing the symbolic nature of the conflict in Camus's drama.

Nagy, Moses M. "The Theatre of Camus: A Stage for Destiny," in *Claudel Studies*, vol. 9 (1982): 17-25.

Popkin, Henry, "Camus as Dramatist," rpt. in *Camus: A Collection of Critical Essays*. ed. Germaine Brée. Englewood Cliffs, NJ: Prentice-Hall, 1962.

Reck, R.D. "The Theatre of Albert Camus," in *Modern Drama*, vol. 1, no. 4 (May 1961).

Roeming, Robert F. *Camus: A Bibliography*. Madison: University of Wisconsin Press, 1975. A useful reference tool.

Sonnenfeld, Albert, "Albert Camus as Dramatist: The Sources of His Failure," in *Tulane Drama Review*, no. 5 (Summer 1961): 106-123.

Thody, Philip, *Albert Camus, 1913-1960*. New York: Macmillan, 1962. An early critical study of Camus's works, emphasizing their philosophical content.

Kathryn A. Wixon
Lafayette College

KAREL CAPEK
1890-1938

Author's Chronology

Born January 9, 1890, Male Svatonovice, Bohemia (now Czechoslovakia) to Antonin Capek and Bozena Capekova; *1907* moves to Prague; *1915* receives doctorate in philosophy at Charles University; *1916* co-produces first book, *The Luminous Depths*, with his brother Josef; *1920* first full-length play, *The Outlaw*, is produced; falls in love with one of the play's understudies, Olga Scheinpflugova, whom he does not marry until 1935 because of his continually bad health; *1921* *R.U.R.* (*Rostum's Universal Robots*) establishes Capek as an internationally known writer; *1921-1923* directs the Prague Municipal Theatre; *1933-1934* writes *Hordubal*, *Meteor*, and *An Ordinary Life*, a trilogy, cited by some as a masterpiece; *1938* becomes increasingly anxious over Nazi aggression in Europe; December 25, 1938 dies of a lung inflammation.

Author's Bibliography

R.U.R., 1921 (*Rostum's Universal Robots*) (drama); *The Makropoulos Secret*, 1922 (drama); *The Insect Play*, 1922 (with Josef Capek); *Adam the Creator* (with Josef Capek), 1927 (drama); *Hordubal*, 1933 (novel); *Meteor*, 1934 (novel); *An Ordinary Life*, 1934 (novel); *War With the Newts*, 1936 (novel).

Overview of Biographical Sources

Czechoslovakia's troubled political history has seriously hindered the amount of scholarship about Karel Capek. When Nazi troops entered Prague on March 15, 1939, Capek's widow, Olga Scheinpfulgova, hurriedly burned all of his personal correspondence. However, she later included several personal reminiscences in her biographical novel *Cesky Roman* (Czech Novel) (Prague: F. Borovy, 1947). Unfortunately, this book is not available in English. Since the war, Czechoslovakia's restricted intellectual life has certainly limited the number of full-length studies of Capek's life. Therefore, the best biography remains the first chapter of William E. Harkins' *Karel Capek* (1962).

Evaluation of Selected Biographies

Harkins, William E. *Karel Capek*. New York: Columbia University Press, 1962. Harkins' first chapter provides a valuable twenty-two page biography of Capek, the most comprehensive available. Harkins describes Capek's childhood as happy, but plagued by ill-health. He mainly focuses on Capek's method of writing, including his close relationship and frequent collaborations with his brother Josef, and the highlights of his literary career. But Harkins also discusses Capek's long relationship and eventual married life with Olga Scheinpflugova, his love of travel (Capek wrote several travel books), and his political struggles during the 1930s. Throughout, Harkins's attitude is one of respect and sympathy for a man who struggled greatly to express his ideas and enlighten mankind.

Autobiographical Sources

Two major sources exist. The first is an autobiographical preface by Karel and Josef Capek to *The Garden of Krakonos*, a collection of sketches and aphorisms co-authored between 1908-1912 and published in 1918. This volume, however, is also unavailable in English. The other source is Karel Capek's novel *An Ordinary Life*, originally published as the second volume of a trilogy in 1934 and later republished in English as part of a collective edition entitled *Three Novels* (New York: A. A. Wyn, 1948). *An Ordinary Life* contains recognizable portraits of Capek's father and mother.

Overview of Critical Sources

Karel Capek was deeply concerned with the major social, political, and philosophical issues of his times: technology, Communism, Fascism, and man's struggle to retain his humanity in the face of these. His works reveal his concerns, both to their benefit and hindrance. At the time of their original productions, plays such as *R.U.R.* and *The Insect Play* addressed these issues in powerfully creative fashion. Early criticism like Ashley Dukes' (*The Youngest Drama: Studies of Fifty Dramatists.* London: Ernest Benn Limited, 1923) and H.T. Parker's ("Introduction" to Capek's *The Makropoulos Secret.* Boston: John W. Luce and Co., 1925), cited these qualities as very positive. These critics also provide a valuable service in revealing more about Capek's dramatic techniques than later commentators.

As early as 1936, however, critics such as Rene Wellek (in an essay reprinted in *Essays on Czech Literature*, 1963) began to see Capek's dramas as dated and philosophically faulty. Although Capek is still known as the father of Czech drama, most critics now agree that his novels, though also seriously flawed, are far superior to his plays. William E. Harkins' *Karel Capek* (1962) does Capek a great service while still pointing out the flaws in his writing. Alexander Matuska's *Karel Capek: Man Against Destruction: An Essay* (1964) is a thorough explanation of the immensity of Capek's thought. It is a work capable of sparking great new interest in Capek, although it has not done so yet.

Overview of Selected Criticism

Harkins, William E. *Karel Capek.* New York: Columbia University Press, 1962. Harkins concerns himself primarily with Capek's philosophical ideas, and secondarily with artistic structure, devices, and innovations in form. Taking a chronological approach, Harkins devotes much space to the development of Capek's ideas in his minor works from 1908-1920. Harkins often refers to Capek's essays to outline the ideas expressed in his plays, novels, and other works. Harkins also describes Capek's blending of symbolism and realism and his influences from other artistic mediums. In conclusion, Harkins finds some of Capek's most popular works flawed by the writer's reliance on relativism while Capek's works containing some sense of the Absolute are the most powerful.

Matuska, Alexander, *Karel Capek: Man Against Destruction: An Essay*. London: George Allen and Unwin, 1964. Where other writers mention Capek's influences and comment on the ambiguities in his philosophy, Matuska explores every aspect of Capek's work in depth. Capek had a desire to know "everything," and so his influences include more than they exclude. But Capek sought a creative dynamism for his own life and country and not a mere chronicling of the past. Matuska takes the typical labels of Capek as "individualist," "terrestrial," and "optimist," and fully explains all the divergencies that other critics see as inconsistent thinking. He then goes on to give a thorough analysis of Capek as an artist apart from his philosophy. Matuska's is a brilliant study that illuminates an artist, a nation, and an era.

Wellek, Rene. *Essays on Czech Literature*. The Hague: Mouton Publishers, 1963. Wellek goes further than most other critics in providing concise insights to the full range of Capek's work. Wellek notes the philosophical weaknesses and dated nature of Capek's plays, but he also comments on their theatrical qualities. Most valuably, he reviews Capek's travel books and fairy tales as well, which reveal the bright side of the writer's personality.

Other Sources

Bradbrook, B.R. "Karel Capek's Contribution to Czech National Literature," in *Czechoslovakia Past and Present Vol. 2: Essays on the Arts and Sciences*. ed. Miloslav Rechcigl, Jr. The Hague: Mouton, 1968. 1002-1011. This brief essay confirms Capek as an artist who enriched Czech literature by infusing it with new ideas gained from international writers such as Shaw, Wells, and Chesterton. Bradbrook provides insightful comments about Capek's work in each literary genre.

Chandler, Frank W. *Modern Continental Playwrights*. New York: Harper and Brothers, 1931. Chandler describes the plots of *R.U.R., The Makropoulos Secret, The Insect Play,* and *Adam the Creator* and gives a brief interpretation of each.

Moskowitz, Sam. *Explorers of the Infinite: Shapers of Science Fiction*. Cleveland: The World Publishing Co., 1963. Moskowitz describes the influence of Capek on world literature of the 1920s and 1930s. With *R.U.R.*, Capek created the first truly successful science fiction stage production and also popularized the term "robot." Moskowitz discusses Capek's influences and the origins for his major science fiction works.

Nemecek, Zdeneck. "Karel Capek," in *World Literature*. Freeport, NY: Books for Libraries Press, 1956, pp. 53-65. A brief, biographically based account of Capek's work, highlighting his devotion to democracy, belief in pragmatism, and main themes.

Suvin, Darko. *Metamorphosis of Science Fiction: On the Poetics and History of a Literary Genre*. New Haven: Yale University Press, 1979. Suvin places Capek within the entire history of science fiction, drawing his influences to as far back as Swift and Voltaire. Suvin traces Capek's philosophical development, finding his plays to be the most inconsistent and dated works and his later novels, particularly *War With the Newts*, to be the most brilliant statements. In these works, Capek moved from an almost blind support of working- and middle-class values to a complex anti-fascism and anti-militarism in which the social and political outcomes were left uncertain.

Thomas J. Slater
Northwest Missouri State University

EMILIO CARBALLIDO
1925

Author's Chronology

Born May 22, 1925, in Córdoba, a provincial city in the Mexican state of Veracruz to Francisco Carballido and Blanca Rosa Fentanes; *1926-1939* lives with his mother in Mexico City; *1946* writes his first play *Los dos mundos de Alberta*; *1948* publishes *The Intermediate Zone* and sees his first two dramas performed, *El triángulo sutil* and *La triple porfía*; *1950* receives a Rockefeller fellowship to study in New York; after the unsuccessful production of *la sinfonía doméstica* (1953) Carballido experiences a prolonged period of disillusionment; as Assistant Director of the School of Theater at Xalapa (1954) writes *The Golden Thread, Felicidad, La danza que sueña la tortuga* and several short stories; *1955* receives three national literary awards: El Nacional, INBA (Instituto Nacional de las Bellas Artes), and UNAM; as public relations advisor for the National Ballet spends most of 1957 travelling through Europe and Asia; *1957* receives the Juan Ruiz de Alarcón Award for *Felicidad*; during the 1960s many of his works are translated and anthologized in Germany, Italy, Russia, and the United States; *1962* wins the Casa de las Américas Prize for *A Short Day's Anger*; travels three times to Cuba where he serves on the Casa de las Américas jury; *1965* visiting professor at Rutgers; *1966 I Also Speak of the Rose* wins both the Heraldo and Juan Ruiz de Alarcón Awards; *1967 Te juro Juana* wins the Heraldo Prize; *1968* travels to Spain; *1970* visiting professor at the University of Pittsburgh; *1971* participates in the *International Theater Festival* in Calí; *1975* named the Director of Cultural Programs at the University of Veracruz; *1977* receives the Sociedad de críticos y cronistas Award for *A Short Day's Anger*; the decade of the 1980s brings increased national and international recognition, and at age 61, Carballido is universally recognized to be Mexico's most prominent living dramatist.

Author's Bibliography (selected drama)

For the most complete bibliographical information concerning Carballido refer to Margaret S. Peden's "Emilio Carballido, Curriculum Operum," in *Texto crítico*, 2, no. 3 (January-April, 1976): 94-112. The following is a selective bibliography of Carballido's most important plays that have been translated into English. *The Clockmaker from Córdoba*, 1960, tr. 1971; *Conversation Among the Ruins*, produced but not published; *The Day They Let the Lions Loose*, 1957, tr. 1971; *The Golden Thread*, 1956, tr. 1971; *The Intermediate Zone*, 1948, tr. 1971; *I Too Speak of the Rose*, 1966, tr. 1969; *Medusa*, manuscript in the Pan American Society of New England; *The Mirror*, 1971; *A Short Day's Anger*, produced but not published; *Theseus*, 1962, 1971; *The Time and the Place*, 1957, 1971; *The Sun*, unpublished translation by Margaret S. Peden; *The Golden Thread and Other*

Plays, Austin: University of Texas Press, 1971. Peden translates six of Carballido's plays: *The Mirror, The Time and the Place, The Golden Thread, The Intermediate Zone, The Clockmaker from Cordoba*, and *Theseus*.

Overview of Biographical Sources

The first, and to date the only, full-length study in English on Carballido's life and works is Margaret S. Peden's *Emilio Carballido*, 1980. Two published interviews, one with Marco Antonio Acosta in the November 12, 1972 edition of *El Nacional* (Mexico City) and the other with Joseph F. Vélez in the Fall, 1973 issue of *Latin American Theater Review* allow those who read Spanish to hear first hand some of Carballido's ideas concerning drama.

Evaluation of Selected Biographies

Peden, Margaret S. *Emilio Carballido*. Boston: Twayne, 1980. This is the most complete and accurate source of biographical material on Emilio Carballido. As the principal translator of Carballido's works Peden brings to her study a knowledge of both the man and his works that only years of professional association can produce. Peden's focus is both biographical and critical, and as such, remains the best source for acquiring a general overview of Carballido's life and literary development. The study is of manageable size (192 pp.) and Peden's style is clear and direct.

Overview of Critical Sources

Along with Rodolfo Usigli and Xavier Villaurrutia, Carballido is one of Mexico's leading dramatists of the twentieth century and unquestionably her most distinguished living dramatist. Since many of his plays have been translated or produced in other languages (English, French, German, Italian, Norwegian, Polish, Russian), scholars throughout the world have had the opportunity to analyze and to interpret critically Carballido's theater. What follows therefore, is only a representative sampling of the more important critical studies which have been published in English on his drama.

Evaluation of Selected Criticism

Holzapel, Tamara, "A Mexican Medusa," in *Modern Drama*, 12 (1969): 213-237. Holzapel's article compares *Medusa* to Sartre's *Les mouches*. Her study focuses on the political and philosophical elements present in both works.

Oliver, William I. ed., tr. and intro. *Voices of Change in the Spanish American Theater*. Austin: University of Texas Press, 1971. Included in this anthology of six contemporary Latin American plays is Carballido's *The Day They Let the Lions Loose*.

Peden, Margaret S. "Theory and Practice in Artaud and Carballido," in *Modern Drama*, 11 (1968): 132-142. Focusing on *The Golden Thread* and the trilogy *The Time and the Place* Peden compares Carballido's dramas to that of Artaud's theater of the senses.

_____, *Emilio Carballido*. Boston: Twayne Publishers, 1980. To date, the best source of acquiring a general overview of Carballido's life and literary development.

Peterson, Karen, "Existential Irony in Three Carballido Plays," in *Latin American Theater Review*, 10, no. 2 (Spring, 1977): 29-35. Peterson demonstrates how *Medusa*, Theseus, and *Las estatuas de marfil* reflect the existential irony characteristic of Sartre's drama.

Skinner, Eugene R. "The Theater of Emilio Carballido: Spinning a Web," in *Dramatists in Revolt: The New Latin American Theater*, ed. Leon F. Lyday and George W. Woodyard. Austin: University of Texas Press, 1976. An intelligent study of *The Intermediate Zone*, *Rosalba*, *The Golden Thread*, and *La rosa* that sees in these four plays a progressive allegory about man.

Woodyard, George, ed. and intro. *The Modern Stage in Latin America: Six Plays*. New York: E.P. Dutton, 1971. Woodyard presents five English translations of various contemporary Latin American plays; among them appears Carballido's *I Too Speak of the Rose*.

Other Sources

Dauster, Frank, *Ensayos sobre teatro hispanoamericano*. Mexico City: SepSetentas, Secretaria de Educación Pública, 1975. In this general study (in Spanish) on the Spanish American theater Dauster dedicates a chapter on Carballido's contribution to contemporary drama. In particular, he focuses on Carballido's technical innovations and his deep sense of humanity.

Vázquez Amaral, Mary, *El teatro de Emilio Carballido (1950-1965)*. Mexico City: B. Costa-Amic, 1974. Ph.D. dissertation, Rutgers University, 1970. This is a detailed analysis of Carballido's drama from 1950 to 1965. According to Peden this is the most important work to date devoted to Carballido.

Richard Keenan
University of Idaho

SUSANNA CENTLIVRE
1669-1723

Author's Chronology

Probably born 1669, the daughter of William and Anne Freeman (once thought the daughter of Edward Freeman of Holbeach, Lincolnshire); baptized in Whaplode, Lincolnshire on November 20, 1669; *1681-1687* probably orphaned, may have married a nephew of Sir Stephen Fox and been widowed; believed to have married a Mr. Carroll and been widowed a second time; *1700* settles in London; *Familiar and Courtly Letters* published; *The Perjured Husband* produced at Drury Lane; *1701 Familiar and Courtly Letters*, Volume II, and *Letters of Wit, Politics, and Morality* published; *1702 The Beau's Duel*, and *The Stolen Heiress* acted at Lincoln's Inn Fields; *1703 Love's Contrivance* produced at Drury Lane; *1705 The Gamester* acted at Lincoln's Inn Fields, and *The Basset Table* at Drury Lane; *1706* meets Joseph Centlivre at Bath, where *Love at a Venture* is presented; *The Platonic Lady* produced at the Queen's Theatre; *1707* marries Joseph Centlivre; *1709 The Busie Body* acted at Drury Lane, and *The Man's Bewitched* at the Queen's Theatre; *1710 A Bickerstaff's Burying*, and a sequel to *The Busie Body*, *Marplot*, presented at Drury Lane; *1712 The Perplexed Lovers* offered at Drury Lane; *1713 The Masquerade*, a poem, published; *1714 The Wonder* produced at Drury Lane; celebrates the accession of George I in two poems; *1715* the Lord Chamberlain refuses to license two farces, *The Gotham Election* and *A Wife Well Managed*; *The Cruel Gift* produced at Drury Lane; *1717* publishes *Epistle to the King of Sweden*; *1718 A Bold Stroke for a Wife* presented at Lincoln's Inn Fields; *1720* publishes *A Woman's Case*; contributes political abstracts to the *Weekly Journal*; *1722 The Artifice* produced at Drury Lane; *1723* dies and is buried in St. Paul's, Covent Garden; *1724 A Wife Well Managed* produced at the Haymarket; Joseph Centlivre dies.

Author's Bibliography

The Perjur'd Husband, 1700 (tragedy); *The Beau's Duel*, 1702 (comedy); *The Stolen Heiress*, 1703 (comedy); *Love's Contrivance*, 1703 (comedy); *The Gamester*, 1705 (comedy); *The Basset-Table*, 1706 (comedy); *Love at a Venture*, 1706 (comedy); *The Platonic Lady*, 1707 (comedy); *The Busie Body*, 1709 (comedy); *The Man's Bewitched*, 1709 (comedy); *A Bickerstaff's Burying*, 1710 (farce); *MarPlot*, 1711 (comedy); *The Perplexed Lovers*, 1712 (comedy); *The Masquerade*, 1713 (poetry); *The Wonder*, 1714 (comedy); *A Poem Most Humbly Presented to his Sacred Majesty*, 1715 (poetry); *The Gotham Election*, 1715 (farce); *A Wife Well Manag'd*, 1715 (farce); *The Cruel Gift*, 1717 (tragedy); *An Epistle to the King of Sweden from a Lady of Great Britain*, 1717 (poetry); *A Bold Stroke for a Wife*, 1718 (comedy); *A Woman's Case*, 1720 (poetry); *The Artifice*, 1723 (comedy).

Overview of Biographical Sources

Few biographical studies of Susanna Centlivre exist and only two full-length books on the dramatist have been published in the twentieth century, those of John Wilson Bowyer(1952) and F.P. Lock (1979). Both books contain both biographical information and extensive critical material. The major modern biographical study of Centlivre is that of Bowyer, but his work has left many problems unanswered. The chief difficulty in the study of her life is the absence of documentary material that can definitively indicate the names of her parents, her place of birth, and the true facts concerning her two possible early marriages. Records concerning these matters are scant and much speculation has taken place regarding them. In addition, stories of wild living in her younger years are found in early biographical accounts without substantial hard evidence being presented regarding their accuracy. The problems the student faces in determining the facts of her early life are well summarized in F.P. Lock's study of Mrs. Centlivre in the Twayne English Author's series. Because after 1700 records of the theatre, advertisements concerning performances and the publication of books in the newspapers, and the existence of contemporary diaries are increasingly more numerous than in the preceding forty years, Centlivre's life after coming to London at the turn of the eighteenth century is well documented, and the details of her theatrical career are mainly available. The student must rely largely on early accounts of her life for most of the useful information about her, but modern scholarship has provided apparatus for the evaluation of such material, and all data from early sources should be evaluated in the light of subsequent scholarly opinion. While the account of her life in *The Dictionary of National Biography* is a convenient starting point for the biographical study of Centlivre, it has been greatly modified by the work of Bowyer and Lock, and should be considered relatively unreliable in details about the dramatist's early life. It should be read with the awareness that matters regarding her life before coming to London are open to various interpretations.

Evaluation of Selected Biographies

Baker, David Erskine, Isaac Reed and Stephen Jones, *Biographia Dramatica*. London, 1812; rpt. AMS 1966. This eighteenth-century source of information on the theatre of the period contains (pp. 97-100) an early account of Mrs. Centlivre's life. As an account that is close to the period in which she lived, it is valuable for that reason, but has the limitation of relying on material that was at least partly rumor at the time. It should therefore be read in the light of the improved evaluation techniques of subsequent scholarship.

Bowyer, John Wilson, *The Celebrated Mrs. Centlivre*. Durham, NC: Duke University Press, 1952. The first major modern study of Susanna Centlivre. Bowyer attempts to bring together all biographical material available and to evaluate it in the light of twentieth-century biographical approaches. Bowyer makes use of those details about her early life that can be gleaned from eighteenth-century accounts and from records that still exist, makes use of her letters as biographical sources, and also frequently quotes from her non-dramatic work, including her poetry. Much information regarding the writing, production, and publication of her plays is presented, and although accurate in most respects, such information has been substantially added to and up-dated by the subsequently published *The London Stage*, Part II, ed. Emmett L. Avery, Carbondale, IL: Southern Illinois University Press, 1960. Bowyer's work should, therefore, be checked against this now-available source of theatrical information.

Jacob, Giles, *The Poetical Register*. London, 1719. The *Register* includes a brief account of Susanna Centlivre, written while she was still alive, and is of interest for that reason. The author maintains that most of the biographies included in the volume were composed by the individuals themselves. It is uncertain whether or not Centlivre was the author of hers, but it bears special attention because of that possibility. Students should be aware that the reservations due any autobiographical statement because of the possibility of an author's attempting to justify his life should be observed in this case.

Lock, F.P. *Susanna Centlivre*. Boston: Twayne, 1979. Although this is primarily a critical study, the introductory chapter contains a good summary of the facts and speculations regarding Mrs. Centlivre's life and sets much of the scholarly controversy concerning it in perspective. Lock includes in the discussion of Centlivre's early life a considerable portion of Jacob's account, one that is sometimes difficult to obtain.

Mackenzie, John H. "Susan Centlivre," in *Notes and Queries*, 198 (September 1953): 386-390. Contains information concerning the biography of Mrs. Centlivre, particularly the place and date of her birth, thus contributing significantly to the knowledge of one of the most ambiguous aspects of her life.

Sutherland, James R. "The Progress of Error: Mrs. Centlivre and the Biographers," in *Review of English Studies*, XVII (1942): 167-182. Attempts to evaluate the evidence concerning questions of Centlivre's life that have often led to relatively unsupported speculation. It deals, in a conservative way, with the problems concerning Mrs. Centlivre's biography and is useful in presenting, at times, a different analysis from that of Bowyer. It should be read as a supplement to Bowyer's study.

Overview of Critical Sources

Significant critical comment is to be found in the two modern full-length studies of Centlivre, by Bowyer and by Lock. Considerable incidental critical comment is contained in most studies dealing with comedy during the early part of the eighteenth century, with consideration often given to individual plays. For example, a consideration of *The Gamester* may be found in Ernest Bernbaum's *The Drama of Sensibility* (Boston: Ginn and Co., 1915) and in Arthur Sherbo's *English Sentimental Drama* (East Lansing: Michigan State University Press, 1957); Robert Hume provides a discussion of *The Busie Body* in *The Development of English Drama in the Late Seventeenth Century* (Oxford: The Clarendon Press, 1976); and Joseph Wood Krutch deals with Centlivre's posthumously published comedy, *The Artifice*, in *Comedy and Conscience after the Restoration* (New York: Columbia University Press, 1924). The studies of Bowyer and Lock contain the most comprehensive consideration of Centlivre's plays set within the context of her life that is available.

Evaluation of Selected Criticism

Bateson, F.W. "Mrs. Centlivre," in *English Comic Drama*. Oxford: The Clarendon Press, 1929, 61-77. Within the context of a general study of the comic drama, Bateson devotes a substantial portion to the work of Centlivre. He reviews significant biographical problems and presents a careful and detailed study of the most important plays, focussing on *The Gamester*, *The Bassett Table*, *The Busie Body*, and *The Wanderer*. Bateson, although he recognizes that Centlivre's plays often do not read well, notes that they were excellent acting vehicles and concludes that in dealing with disguise and mistaken identity in comedy, conventions much in use on the Restoration and early eighteenth-century stage, Mrs. Centlivre is a "master-mechanic of dramatic construction."

Boas, Frederick S. *Eighteenth-Century Drama, 1700-1780*. Oxford: The Clarendon Press, 1953. This general study is a comprehensive treatment of the drama of the period, which devotes a substantial part of Chapter Four to a discussion of Centlivre's plays (pp. 110-116). In assessing the overall significance of her work during the period, Boas focusses his criticism on what he considers to be the dramatist's most significant comedies., *Marplot*, *The Wonder*, and *A Bold Stroke for a Wife*.

Lock, F.P. *Susanna Centlivre*. Boston: Twayne, 1979. Contains significant critical commentary on most of Mrs. Centlivre's plays. Although the English Author's Series does not offer an opportunity for extensive original approaches, Lock is successful in providing an overview of Centlivre's work while providing useful discussions of many individual plays. The work contains a bibliography of both Centlivre's work and of secondary material essential for its study.

Loftis, John, *Comedy and Society from Congreve to Fielding*. Stanford, Stanford University Press, 1959. In Chapter 3, pp. 43-76, Loftis considers changes in the attitude toward society manifested in Centlivre's plays, noting in particular her moving from stereotypes regarding merchants and tradesmen in her early plays to portraits in her later plays that conform more realistically to changing social conditions. The study provides a framework for understanding the manner in which Centlivre related to the society of her day.

anna Centlivre*

Other Sources

Norton, J.E. "Some Uncollected Authors, XIV: Susanna Centlivre," in *Book Collector*, VI (1957): 173-178; 380-285. Gives detailed bibliographical information regarding first editions of the plays, with transcriptions of the title pages. Norton provides records of publication advertisements in the newspapers. Additional information on this subject is provided in subsequent issues of *Book Collector* by Alan D. McKillop (VII : 79-80); D.G. Neill (VII : 189-190); and Jacqueline Faure (X ; 68-69).

Richard J. Dircks
St. John's University
New York

MIGUEL de CERVANTES SAAVEDRA
1547-1616

Author's Chronology

Born September 29 (?), 1547, Alcelá de Henares, Spain, to Rodrigo de Cervantes and Leonor de Cortinas, the fourth of seven children; baptized October 9; *1569* poems of Cervantes published in commemoration of the death of the Queen, Isabel de Valois; Cervantes in Rome in the service of Cardinal Giulio Acquaviva; *1571* fights heroically under Don Juan of Austria against the Turks at Lepanto; wounded twice and loses the use of his left hand; *1575* on return trip to Spain is captured by Turks and taken to Algiers as a slave; *1575-1580* held captive in Algiers, organizes four unsuccessful escapes with fellow Christians; *1580* ransomed by a Trinitarian friar; *1581-1587* attempts career as playwright in Madrid; love affair with Ana Franca de Rojas produces daughter, Isabel de Saavedra; *1584* publishes *La Galatea*, marries Catalina de Salazar y Palacios, resides in La Mancha; *1587* becomes minor commissary for the Spanish Armada; *1597* jailed in Seville for alleged malfeasance; *1602* investigated and perhaps jailed again; *1605 Don Quixote*, Part I, published in Madrid, two editions in the same year; Cervantes moves to Valladolid; *1612* the *Novelas ejemplares* (*Exemplary Novels*) published; *1614 Viaje al Parnaso* (*Journey to Parnassus*) published; the false *Quixote* appears; *1615 Don Quixote*, Part II, published; also *Ocho comedias y ocho entremeses* (Eight Comedies and Eight Interludes) that had never been performed; dies April 23, *1616*, in Madrid; 1617 *Los trabajos de Persiles y Sigismunda* (The Trials of Persiles and Sigismunda) published posthumously.

Author's Bibliography

Cervantes' *Obras complⁿtas* (Complete Works), ed. Angel Valbuena Prat, 2 vols. (Madrid,1975), is a compact yet complete edition of all of his work in Spanish. Following are some translations of Cervantes' key works: *The Ingenius Gentleman Don Quixote de la Mancha*, tr. Samuel Putnam, 2 vols. (New York, 1949); *The Adventures of Don Quixote*, tr. J.M. Cohen (Baltimore, 1963) (more modern language); *Three Exemplary Novels*, tr. Samuel Putnam (New York, 1950); *Exemplary Stories*, tr. C.A. Jones (Hamondsworth, 1972); *Journey to Parnassus*, tr. James G. Gibson (London, 1883); *The Wanderings of Persiles and Sigismunda*, tr. Louisa Dorothea Stanley (London, 1854). Unfortunately, as Cervantes is not internationally recognized for his fine comedies and excellent interludes, only the latter have been translated into English: *Interludes*, tr. Edwin Honig (New York, 1959). See also Remigio Ugo Pane's *English Translations from the Spanish* (Rutgers, 1944) for earlier translations of Cervantes' works.

Overview of Biographical Sources

As shown in his chronology, Cervantes led much of his life in the public eye; there are numerous documents by which the broad outline of his biography are known. Cristóbal Pérez Pastor, Francisco Rodríguez Marín, and Luis Astrana Marín have through their indefatigable research added greatly to the first scholarly basic biography produced in 1819 by Martín Fernández de Navarrete. A great deal may be learned from these scholars if one reads Spanish, particularly from Marín's *Vida ejemplar y heroica de Miguel de Cervantes Saavedra* (The Exemplary and Heroic Life of Miguel de Cervantes Saavedra), 7 vols. (Madrid, 1948-1958), despite its frequent verbosity and excessive personal bias.

James Fitzmaurice-Kelly's *Miguel de Cervantes Saavedra. A Memoir* (Oxford, 1913) is brief but scrupulously thorough for the time it was written. Richard L. Predmore's *Cervantes* (New York, 1973), a well illustrated work, is admirably balanced. Manuel Durán's *Cervantes* (New York, 1974) is a good, compact study of his subject, in the format characteristic of the Twayne World Authors Series. (See more below.) Albert F. Calvert's *The Life of Cervantes* (London, 1976) has some curious but potentially useful illustrations and bibliographies. Melveena McKendrick's *Cervantes* (Boston, 1980) is written with great thoroughness and insight.

Evaluation of Selected Biographies

McKendrick, Melveena, *Cervantes*. Boston: Little, Brown, 1980. Melveena McKendrick has used every scrap of evidence to create a remarkable portrait of the man Cervantes, who emerges as both complex and deeply human. She uses his works to give added depth and understanding to his character—for he was born a compulsive writer and wrote far, far more than *Don Quixote*. Nor does she miss any of the moments of irony that tend to thread all writers' lives, and realizes, too, how accidental works of genius can be. The abilities of a writer find, almost by chance, the vehicle for their genius. This is particularly true of *Don Quixote*, for what began as a short parody of the romances of chivalry became the first great modern novel, largely because a hack writer wrote a spurious Part Two, which goaded Cervantes into finishing his epic novel. That whirligig of Fate which tossed Cervantes around through so much of his life at the same time gave him penetrative insight into the hopes, the despairs, the wonderful endurance of men and women.

Predmore, Richard L. *Cervantes*. New York: Dodd, Mead, 1973. As one does not have for Cervantes the kind of personal papers and letters so often available for prominent writers, Predmore has sought to compensate for this deficiency by judicious use of his published writings. Aware that there are pitfalls in using a man's fiction to illuminate his life, he has nonetheless considered it both possible and desirable to do so. He has quoted liberally form Cervantes' works, because it seemed fitting that his own voice should be heard in the telling of his story; he has, however, tried to guard against the easy assumption that whatever his characters say, feel and do necessarily reflects their creator's personal experience. Finally, he has included some critical comment on Cervantes' outstanding works, because he cannot imagine trying to re-create the life of a writer without paying some attention to what he wrote.

Autobiographical Sources

Cervantes reveals himself openly in the prologues to some of his works which may be found in Spanish in his *Complete Works*, ed. Angel Valbuena Prat (Madrid: Aguilar, 1975).

Overview of Critical Sources

Because Cervantes enjoyed some considerable success in his lifetime and enormous success thereafter, there are many critical works treating every aspect of *Don Quixote*. In addition to the books referred to above that combine biography with criticism, in English one may profitably consult Angel Flores and M.J. Bernadette, eds. *Cervantes Across the Centuries* (New York, 1947), containing first-rate essays by Leo Spitzer, Américo Castro, and many other important scholars, and Lowry Nelson, ed. *Cervantes. A Collection of Critical Essays* (Englewood Cliffs, 1969), an excellent anthology of essays by Blanco Aguinaga, W.H. Auden, Harry Levin, Thomas Mann, E.C. Riley, Leo Spitzer, and others. However, the criticism devoted to Cervantes' drama is quite limited even though he was considered a good dramatist in his time, overshadowed only by Lope de Vega. The works cited below contain chapters on Cervantes' drama, or deal with *Don Quixote*'s dramatic elements.

Evaluation of Selected Criticism

Durán, Manuel, *Cervantes*. New York: Twayne, 1974. Duran's work is an effort to bring the vast bibliography on Cervantes up to date. Moreover, he is convinced that a succinct analysis of all the aspects of the author's life and works may show their interrelationship and shed much needed light on Cervantes' masterpieces. One chapter is devoted to the dramatic works.

Flores, Angel, and Bernadette, M.J. eds. *Cervantes Across the Centuries*. New York: The Dryden Press, 1947. As the literature of the sixteenth century came to be better understood, scholars and scholarly critics began to make separate studies of the various problems posed by *Don Quixote*. Sensitive objective criticism assumed the leadership, and thanks to the work of many students and lovers of Cervantes, scholars are now in a position to discern some of the meanings of Spain's first genius. Samples of this rich harvest are offered in English for the first time in the pages of this book. The serious reader, the student, the teacher, and the critic will find in the essays of Menéndez-Pidal, Joaquín Casalduero, and Helmut Hatzfeld analyses of the first order centering around the possible original idea which developed into the work we know as *Don Quixote*. For the first time these readers will experience the pleasure of surprise in discovering the architectural design and style of a literary monument. Readers familiar with the drama will be able to draw parallels between the dramatic structure of the novel and the plays.

Nelson, Lowry, Jr. *Cervantes. A Collection of Critical Essays.* Englewood Cliffs, NJ: Prentice-Hall, 1969. Of great aesthetic interest are the vast number of imitations, adaptations and translations of Cervantes' fictional discoveries since 1605, but of considerable cultural moment, too, is the history of the shaping and reshaping of the image of Don Quixote, for example, across the centuries. Such a chronicle would begin with a rather crude conception of a comical man (laughing-stock), who becomes for Romantics such as Bryon, Ludwig Tieck, and Jean Paul a mournful sufferer and scapegoat, an inwardly heroic Knight of the Sad Countenance. Later in the nineteenth century, Cervantes' novel received the ministrations of textual critics and philologists. These, while keeping bright the letter, went far toward encumbering and embalming the text with misplaced notes and irrelevant references, thus compounding the tendency to see the novel either as a children's story or simply as a scholar's example of seventeenth-century Spanish prose. A more recent aberration of "criticism" has been the use of *Don Quixote* as a textual ground for expansive speculation on large philosophical and existential issues not necessarily unrelated to Cervantes' text though certainly uncontrolled by it. Only in the twentieth century has a body of true literary criticism begun slowly to accumulate. If criticism of *Don Quixote* in the past seems rather thin, scattered, and unimpressive, modern readers will find some excellent and profound criticism.

Other Sources

Ford, J.D.M. and Ruth Lansing, *Miguel de Cervantes Saavedra: A Tentative Bibliogrpahy of His Works and of the Biographical and Critical Material Concerning Him.* Cambridge: Harvard University Press, 1931.

Grismer, Raymond L. *Cervantes; A Bibliography.* New York: H.W. Wilson, 1946. Volume II: Minneapolis: Burgass-Beckwith, 1963.

Madariaga, Salvador, *Don Quixote: An Introductory Essay in Psychology*; Oxford: The Clarendon Press, 1935. An intelligent, perceptive essay on the Don Quixote-Sancho relationship.

McGaha, Michael D. ed. *Cervantes and the Renaissance.* Easton, PA: Juan de la Cuesta-Hispanic Monographs, 1980. The fourteen papers in Spanish and English contained in this volume were first presented at the Pomona College Symposium on

Cervantes and the Renaissance in 1978 to provide an opportunity for some of the world's leading Cervantes scholars to reassess his work within the context of Renaissance thought and art.

Ortega y Gasset, José, *Meditiations on Quixote*, tr. Evelyn Rugg and Diego Marín. New York: W.W. Norton, 1963. The original Spanish text of the celebrated thinker and writer, *Meditacioines del Quijote*, was first published in 1914.

Riley, E.C. *Cervantes' Theory of the Novel*. Oxford: The Clarendon Press, 1962. A perceptive analysis of Cervantes' ideas on literature and the way they affected his writings.

Unamuno, Miguel de, *The Life of Don Quixote and Sancho According to Miguel de Cervantes Saavedra*, tr. Homer P. Earle. New York: Alfred A. Knopf, 1927. The original Spanish text by the famous thinker and writer, *Vida de don Quijote y Sancho según Miguel de Cervantes Saavedra*, dates from 1905.

Richard A. Mazzara
Oakland University

ANTON CHEKHOV
1860-1904

Author's Chronology

Born January 16 or 17, 1860 (Russian Calendar) in Taganrog, third of Pavel and Evgeniya Chekhov's six children; *1876* remains in Taganrog to complete high school after rest of dispossessed family join bankrupt father in Moscow; *1879* enters Moscow University medical school; *1880* first stories published in humorous magazines; *1884* earns medical degree and publishes first collection of short stories; *1887 Ivanov* produced; story collection *In the Twilight* published; *1888* receives Pushkin Prize; *1889* brother dies of tuberculosis; *The Wood Demon* fails on stage; *1890* makes trip through Siberia to Sakhalin Island; *1891* travels in Europe; *1892* purchases country estate at Melikhova, where he practices medicine; *1894* sojourns in Yalta for his health; *1895* meets Tolstoy; *1896* "fiasco" of *Seagull* opening; *1897* acute hemorrhaging leads to hospitalization for tuberculosis; *1898* after father's death, decides to build villa at Yalta; *1899* meets Stanislavsky and actress Olga Knipper at Moscow Art Theater; *1901* Moscow premier of *Three Sisters*; *1901* marries Olga Knipper; *1904* honored at *Cherry Orchard* premiere; travels to Germany for his failing health; dies in Badenweiler on July 2.

Author's Bibliography (selected)

"The Kiss," 1887 (story); "The Steppe," 1888 (story); *The Bear*, 1888 (play); "The Duel," 1891 (long story); "Ward No. 6," 1892 (story); *The Seagull*, 1896 (play); "Peasants," 1897 (story); *Uncle Vanya*, 1897 (play); "A Lady with a Dog," 1899 (story); *Three Sisters*, 1901 (play); *The Cherry Orchard*, 1903-1904 (play).

English translations: *Tales* and *Plays*, 1916-1923, trans. Constance Garnett; *Lady with Lapdog and Other Stories*, 1964, trans. David Magarshack; *The Oxford Chekhov*, 1964-1980, trans. Ronald Hingley.

Overview of Biographical Sources

Numerous biographies in various languages indicate the fascination Chekhov holds for readers, but despite a wealth of source materials, several obstacles prevent a definitive portrait of the author. First, Chekhov's habitual discretion and reserve about personal matters left many questions unanswered. Memoirs and recollections abound, but they often give contradictory views. A representative sampling of them appears in *Anton Tchekhov: Literary and Theatrical Reminiscences*, trans. and ed. S.S. Koteliansky (London: Routledge & Kegan Paul, 1927; rpt. Benjamin Blom, 1965). In the most controversial account by an acquaintance, *Chekhov in My Life*, trans. David Magarshack (New York: Harcourt, Brace, 1950), Lydia Avilov claims a secret love affair with the author. In addition to these hindrances, each Russian regime censors passages or suppresses letters to and from Chekhov, according to official ideology or prudery.

Furthermore, while political considerations have often colored Russian pictures of a national monument, reminiscences and biographies in general have perpetuated the "Chekhov legend" of the sad and suffering soul. For instance, Princess Nina Andronikova Toumanova's version in *Anton Chekhov: The Voice of Twilight Russia* (New York: Columbia University Press, 1937) follows the movement of a "gentle soul" from "disillusionment" to serene pessimism as he recorded his gloomy times. An interpretive breakthrough occurred in English scholarship in 1950 with the publication of Ronald Hingley's *Anton Chekhov: A Biographical and Critical Study* (rev. ed. New York: Barnes & Noble, 1966), which countered the myths with a fuller view of the man and the work. After 1962, Ernest Simmons' *Anton Chekhov*, drawn in main part from the greatly expanded Soviet editions of 1944-1951, became the basic biographical reference for scholarship in English. As unpublished materials gradually come to light, biographers continue to rearrange and fit together intriguing puzzle pieces and to present a less saintly, but more realistically complex and human figure, as in Ronald Hingley's *A New Life of Anton Chekhov* (1976). The thirty-volume *Works and Letters* issued in Moscow (1974-1982) may correct and discover details to further clarify the portrait of Chekhov.

Evaluation of Selected Biographies

Hingley, Ronald, *A New Life of Anton Chekhov*. New York: Alfred A. Knopf, 1976. This clear, well-organized and documented account of the life by the authority who first challenged the one-sided Chekhov legend in 1950 and who translated *The Oxford Chekhov* presents a credible account of a great writer and humanitarian, who could also complain, get bored, or have premarital love affairs. Photographs, remarks on Russian editions in the Preface, an index of Chekhov's works, and Appendices on "Chekhov in English" and phases of his career add to the value of this book.

Melchinger, Siegfried, *Anton Chekhov*. trans. Edith Tarcov. World Dramatists Series. New York: Frederick Ungar, 1972. Though he presents uneven summaries and interpretive remarks in later chapters, Melchinger provides an incisive introductory "Biographical Essay," which places Chekhov in his Russian milieu, relates his artistic development, and examines the relation of his medical practice to his literary career.

Simmons, Ernest J. *Chekhov: A Biography*. Boston: Little, Brown, 1962. Simmons' lengthy biography remains the most thoroughly detailed account of the development of the writer and his art. While his recreation of scenes and dialogue makes for readable narrative, his research provides particulars documenting the many sides and moods of Chekhov. Simmons offers logical assessments of available information when varying sources prove confusing or contradictory. His "Bibliographical Survey" includes useful information.

Autobiographical Sources

Because of the diversity of opinions about his life and works, Chekhov's letters prove the best touchstone for evaluating interpretations. Despite problems of censorship and translation, the letters available afford a fair sampling of the author's remarkable correspondence. The best collections in English, selected from over four thousand letters published in expanded Soviet editions (1944-51, 1963-64), provide insights into Chekhov's medical, literary, and theatrical concerns. Flavored with humor, banter, bawdy and figurative language, they elaborate his artistic and critical theories or entertain with poetic travelogues, intriguing character sketches, and observations of the contemporary scene.

Simon Karlinsky's excellent introductions and helpful annotations establish contexts for Chekhov's correspondence in *Anton Chekhov's Life and Thought: Selected Letters and Commentary*, trans. Henry Heim in colloboration with Simon Karlinsky (Berkeley: University of California Press, 1975). Each of the selected letters appears in its fullest known form, including less familiar observations by the doctor/author on medicine and biology. *Letters of Anton Chekhov*, trans. Avrahm Yarmolinsky, Bernard Guilbert Guerney, and Lynn Solotaroff (New York: Viking Press, 1973), offers a selection "intended for the common reader" and includes important, frequently quoted letters with obscure passages excised, confusing phrases altered, and footnotes kept to a minimum. Each edition contains over four hundred letters and an index.

Also available in shortened form is the epistolary record of the author's love and marriage in *The Letters of Anton Pavlovitch Tchehov to Olga Leonardovna Knipper*, trans. and ed. Constance Garnett (New York, 1925; rpt. Benjamin Blom, 1966). This collection suggests the joys and problems of the relationship, as Chekhov writes of his daily and literary activities, his travels and illness.

Overview of Critical Sources

Because the resolutely objective artist left his audience to answer the questions posed in his works, critics have often furnished a bewildering array of contradictory, even mutually exclusive interpretations. For example, Chekhov wrote either optimistic or pessimistic, idealistic or cynical, gloomy or satirical stories and plays. More balanced treatments examine Chekhov's blending of tragedy and comedy, stress the relation and importance of the fiction in understanding the dramatic work, and demonstrate responsible readings of the texts. In the 1950s, important contributions by David Magarshack in *Chekhov the Dramatist* (1952) and by Ronald Hingley in his previously mentioned biography (1950) led to better focused argument and more comprehensive interpretations, with subsequent studies benefitting from their research and opinions. Hingley's explanatory notes and appendices in *The Oxford Chekhov* (1964-1980) also serve as valuable aids to coherent interpretations. Continued and growing interest in Chekhov has also made more translations of significant Russian and European scholarship available.

Evaluation of Selected Criticism

Bristow, Euguene K. trans. and ed. *Anton Chekhov's Plays*. Norton Critical Editions. New York: W.W. Norton, 1977. This casebook makes convenient annotated translations of the four major plays together with informative essays illustrating a gamut of approaches to interpreting and staging the plays, ranging from prominent criticism to a definition of *poshlust* by Vladimir Nabokov.

Hahn, Beverly, *Chekhov: A Study of the Major Stories and Plays*. Cambridge: Cambridge University Press, 1977. Basing sensible interpretations on the concept of Chekhov's "humanism," Hahn's approach assimilates negative and positive characteristics of major works and suggests more universal application of his themes than either/or views permit. The book also contains useful chapters on Chekhov's female characters and on his association with Tolstoy.

Kirk, Irina, *Anton Chekhov*. Boston: Twayne, 1981. Kirk furnishes a condensed, balanced review of Chekhov's life in the Chronology and opening chapter, then discusses the stories and plays chronologically, placing them in biographical context. Clear style, basic review, and cogent commentary make this a profitable introduction to the man and the work.

Magarshack, David, *Chekhov the Dramatist*. 1952; New York: Hill & Wang, 1960. Magarshack's seminal study distinguishing between the plays of direct and indirect action contains useful, readable discussions with clarifying remarks on characters and structural "architecture" and devices. Advanced students may wish to consult his complementary volume, *The Real Chekhov: An Introduction to Chekhov's Last Plays* (London: George Allen & Unwin, 1972).

Pitcher, Harvey, *The Chekhov Play: A New Interpretation*. New York: Barnes & Noble, 1973. Pitcher advances a fresh view of dramatic action and dialogue by focusing on the "emotional network" of the characters. Coherent discussions of the plays include worthwhile analysis of the functions of imagery and structure and of "outsiders" and "philosophizing" characters.

Valency, Maurice, *The Breaking String: The Plays of Anton Chekhov*. 1966; New York: Schocken Books, 1983. After scholarly background on European and Russian stage traditions and developments preceding Chekhov, Valency presents thought-provoking analyses of seven plays, noting biographical circumstances, drawing parallels between stories and plays, and theorizing on the philosophical implications of Chekhov's understated complexities.

Other Sources

Bruford, W.H. *Chekhov and His Russia.* 1947; rpt. Hamden, CT: Archon Books, 1971. Helpful for clarifying and pointing out significance of descriptions of nineteenth-century life in Russia, such as beds on the stove or bearded men, which might puzzle or escape the Western reader.

Gillès, Daniel, *Chekhov: Observer Without Illusion.* trans. Charles Lam Markmann. New York: Funk & Wagnalls, 1968. A lively translation of the Belgian critic's biography portraying a cool, detached author whose "only real passion" was his art. Engrossing discussions of Chekhov's interaction with women.

Gottlieb, Vera, *Chekhov and the Vaudeville: A Study of Chekhov's One-Act Plays.* Cambridge: Cambridge University Press, 1982. Discursive, academic discussion of earlier Russian comedy and of Chekhov's one-act plays with comments on how they developed from his idea of "sad comicality."

Jackson, Robert Louis, ed. *Chekhov: A Collection of Critical Essays.* Englewood Cliffs, NJ: Prentice-Hall, 1967. Reviews trends in Russian criticism before introducing a broad spectrum of distinguished essays by Russian and Western commentators.

Llewellyn Smith, Virginia, *Anton Chekhov and the Lady with the Dog.* London: Oxford University Press, 1973. Impressive research makes available previously inaccessible information of Chekhov's love life. Informed scholarly speculation and argument often falter though, as when she argues Chekhov's "misogyny" by quoting his characters. Interesting chapter on Chekhov's "heroines."

Magarshack, David, *Chekhov: A Life.* New York: Grove Press, 1952. Explores effects of unhappy childhood and long illness on Chekhov's life and work. Accepts authenticity of Lydia Avilov's account of an unhappy love affair. Includes Bibliographical Index of Chekhov's complete works with publication dates and English translations.

Styan, J.L. *Chekhov in Performance: A Commentary on the Major Plays.* Extended, often revealing explication of the plays by putting them on the stage.

Welleck, Rene and Nonna D. Wellek, eds. *Chekhov: New Perspectives.* Englewood Cliffs, NJ: Prentice-Hall, 1984. Includes introductory discussion of Chekhov's reception in England and the United States and seven essays, worthwhile if not "new."

Winner, Thomas, *Chekhov and His Prose.* New York: Holt, Rinehart & Winston, 1966. Structural and stylistic analysis of stories in academic style to show how Chekhov's art evolved.

Selected Dictionaries and Encyclopedias

Handbook of Russian Literature. New Haven: Yale University Press, 1985. Brief review of Chekhov's life and literary career.

Linda McDaniel
University of South Carolina

CHIKAMATSU MONZAEMON
1653-1725

Author's Chronology

Born to a family of hereditary warriors; surname, Sugimori; birthplace uncertain; presumed year of birth calculated by counting back from time of death; ca. *1664-1670* father abandons feudal service and moves or returns with family to Kyoto, where Chikamatsu benefits from familiarity with both high and popular culture; *1671* verse appears in haiku collection; serves as page for Prince Ichijō, ninth son of Emperor Goyōsei; *1672* prince dies; leaves service; spends time at Kinshōji ("Chikamatsu-*dera*") temple; *1673* possibly writing plays; certainly doing so by 1675-76; *1675-1684* writing plays for *jōruri,* or "puppet play," chanter, Uji Kaganojō (1635-1711), who opens new puppet theatre; *1683* writes *Yotsugi Soga* (The Soga Heir), which the chanter, Takemoto Gidayū (1651-1714) in 1684 presents in Osaka; *1684-86* involvement with Kabuki; perhaps writes Kabuki play, *Yūgiri shichinenki* (The Seventh Anniversary of Yūgiri's Death), for actor, Sakata Tōjurō (1645-1709); perhaps writes Kabuki play, *Fujitsubo no onroyō* (Fujitsubo's Malicious Ghost); *1685* writes puppet play, *Shusse Kagekiyo* (Kagekiyo Victorious) for Takemoto, and close association lasts till the latter's death; ca. *1688* composes puppet play, *Semimaru* (personal name); *1688-1703* devotes talent to Kabuki; *1702 Keisei Mibu dainenbutsu* (Courtesans and the Great Recitation of the Name of Buddha at the Mibu Temple), reportedly his best Kabuki play; *1703* vendetta of the famous forty-seven loyal retainers; within three years writes two plays on the topic, setting them in an earlier age to avoid censorship and give impetus to eventual production of *Chūshingura* (Storehouse of Loyal Hearts); with composition of *Sonezaki shinjū* (The Love Suicides at Sonezaki) attention shifts to puppet plays; ca. *1705-1706* lives primarily in Osaka and writes for Takemoto; *1715 Kokusenya kasen* (The Battles of Coxinga), his most ambitious historical play and greatest commercial success, is produced for Takemoto's successor; *1725* January 6, by the Western calendar, dies, his reputed last words being, "I was born in a hereditary warrior house but left the military calling, and on intimate terms I served three puppet masters and the Ninth Prince. I die without regrets . . .," or alternatively, ". . ., I held no rank. . . ."

Author's Bibliography

During the eighteenth and early nineteenth century in Japan chant books for puppet plays occasionally appeared in wood-block printed editions. More often manuscript texts in a characteristic calligraphic style with a modicum of musical notation were used ceremoniously, with subsequent playwrights and chanters making revisions with different titles for revivals on stage. Only toward the end of the nineteenth century did a tradition of scholarly, moveable-type editions develop. As part of a series of moveable-type texts, the *Teikoku bunko* (Imperial Library), in the 1890s some of Chikamatsu's pieces were published, allowing new readers to savor Chikamatsu's rich language. Between 1925 and 1928 Fujii Otoo edited the *Chikamatsu zenshū* (Chikamatsu's Complete Works; 12 volumes; Osaka: Osaka Asahi Shimbunsha). Other texts appeared in series and collections, and by the late 1920s and early 1930s scattered notes were included for readers, who found the plays hard to comprehend, owing to the transformation of Japanese society under the impact of Western civilization.

By the early 1920s Miyamori Asatarō was translating puppet plays into English, which Tsubouchi Shōyō (1859-1934), the first translator of the complete works of Shakespeare into Japanese, acknowledged as contributing to a movement wherein "Western drama . . . [may] make a new departure in form and technique." Miyamori's *Masterpieces of Chikamatsu: The Japanese Shakespeare* (1926) made it possible for English-speaking readers to get some idea of Chikamatsu's genius.

After the end of World War II carefully edited texts in Japan based on the best and oldest available manuscripts or early wood-block printed editions appeared in series such as *Nihon koten bungaku taikei* (1955-61, Compendium of Japanese Classical Literature). The *Chikamatsu jōruri-shū, jō* (1958, Collection of Chikamatsu's Puppet Plays, Vol. I), edited by Shigetomo Ki, contains fourteen plays out of twenty-four domestic pieces together with an admirable scholarly apparatus. Volume Two (1959), edited by Shūzui Kenji and Ōkubo Tadakuni, includes six historical plays out of about seventy or more and an annotated passage of Chikamatsu's conversations on the art of the puppet theatre (first published, 1738). Shortly after Shigetomo, Shūzui, and Ōkubo's texts appeared Keene published *Major Plays of Chikamatsu* (1961) with eleven dramas translated under UNESCO sponsorship.

The first of two translations of *Kokusenya kasen* (1715) by Keene appeared (1951), and Shively's re-translation of a famous domestic play, *Shinjū ten no Amijima* (1720, The Love Suicide at Amijima) was published. More recently, Susan Matisoff, in 1978, published a translation of *Semimaru* (ca. 1688).

Overview of Biographical Sources

Although the idea of biography in East Asia is as old as the *Shih chi* (Records of the Grand Historian) in the first century B.C., in China, attention to the lives of individuals, especially of the ordinary classes, never developed as an independent genre. Even after the Western concept of individualism entered Japan in the twentieth century, biography as a branch of humanistic scholarship remained a low priority. The case of Chikamatsu is no exception. Paucity of records combined with a relative lack of interest in the study of an individual's life for its own sake has militated against production of biographical sources. As with Zeami, no full-length biographical study exists in English, and in Japanese virtually the same situation prevails. Miyamori's observation in *Masterpieces of Chikamatsu* (1926) that "much of the life . . . remains . . . shrouded in mystery," and, "No certainty exists as to where he was born and where his bones lie; nor is anything known of his parents, wife and children," remains almost as true six decades later. Keene's discussion in *World Within Walls* (1976) evaluates the conflicting claims as to the place of birth and the site of his last remains. In Japan established scholars as well as budding researchers seem to take it for granted that little new information about Chikamatsu's life will likely come to light. Research focuses mainly on the plays, the theatrical forms (both Kabuki and the puppet plays), and the social setting.

Evaluation of Selected Biographies

Kawatake, Shigetoshi, *Chikamatsu Monzaemon*. Tokyo: Yoshikawa Kōbunkan, 1958. Untranslated. A comprehensive monograph, Kawatake's approach is eclectic but with emphasis on Chikamatsu's literary achievements rather than his character or personality. The style is clear, concise, and relatively colloquial with little stuffiness. There is no sign of the work's being superseded, and it could well form the base of a valuable monograph in English. Kawatake covers the early life, apprenticeship to the performing arts, relations with the three chanters with whom Chikamatsu had lifelong association, involvement with the Kabuki theatre, analysis of a representative stock situation—namely usurpation of family control by a tyrant or illegitimate heir—and the crowning achievements of the last twenty years as a playwright for the Osaka puppet theatre. Kawatake evaluates Chikamatsu's dramaturgy and personality in terms of a persona, or role, to the extent that the underlying identity of Sugimori Nobumori is completely eclipsed.

Kawatake Toshio, *Chikamatsu Monzaemon*. Tokyo: Japanese National Commission for UNESCO, 1974. A brief pamphlet in English on Chikamatsu's life, works, and artistic principles, the text was prepared for the 250th anniversary of the playwright's death. It is uncertain whether it was written in English or translated from Japanese. Although not widely available, Kawatake Toshio's work supplements the Chikamatsu chapter in Keene, *World Within Walls* and the material in Matisoff, *The Legend of Semimaru* (1978).

Autobiographical Sources

As implied above, there is little autobiographical material except a few scattered letters. Even the authenticity of the inscription on a portrait with Chikamatsu's last words is suspect. Otherwise, the nearest thing to an autobiographical source is a passage of conversation published in 1738 by a Confucian scholar, Hozumi Ikan (1695-?), which Donald Keene has translated as "Chikamatsu on the Art of the Puppet Stage," in his *Anthology of Japanese Literature from the Earliest Era to the Mid-Nineteenth Century* (1955). In Keene's translation the most famous passage reads, "Art is something which lies in the slender margin between the real and the unreal." As another version puts it, "Art occupies the narrow margin between truth and falsehood." The role of the playwright has subsumed the identity of the individual.

Overview of Critical Sources

Along with Bashō (1644-1694) and Saikaku (1642-1693), Chikamatsu is feted as one of three exemplars of Japanese literary and artistic life in the first half of the Tokugawa period (1600-1868). This evaluation has endured for a century since Japanese scholars began to study their own tradition within a framework of Western scholarship. By modern standards Chikamatsu's domestic tragedies are celebrated as the crowning achievement of his genius. The historical pieces have been relatively denigrated or ignored. Chikamatsu's principal theme as embodied in the three-act domestic plays rather than the five-act historical dramas, involves the plight of ill-fated lovers, trapped between the call of public duty and the desire of private passion. As in Racine, for example, the conservative ideals of duty and honor conflict with the instincts of love. The ideal is sustained, and the audience approves, even though saddened at the tragic cost to the individual. As in nineteenth-century European tragedy, the plays may be read as studies of how the combined pressure of a reactive society without and a disorganized soul within frustrate and smother basic human emotions and instincts. Tragedy lies in how nothing save suicide promises to reintegrate the soul.

Scholarship on Chikamatsu also stresses how the plays offer vivid insight and description of a unique age and that they represent the first mature tragedies written about the common man. The plays have been called "living newspapers," because so many of them were inspired by actual occurrences. Each year in Japan brings a fresh harvest of books, articles, and editions of the plays. Chikamatsu is rightfully paired with Zeami as one of two outstanding playwrights and theoreticians. Whereas in the realm of surviving dramatic texts Chikamatsu was the more prolific, in terms of his theoretical writings Zeami remains beyond compare.

Evaluation of Selected Criticism

Keene, Donald, *The Battles of Coxinga: Chikamatsu's Puppet Play, Its Background and Importance*. London: Taylor's Foreign Press, 1951. "Cambridge Oriental series," No. 4. Historical and critical exegesis are superbly balanced in the first extensive treatment in English of one of Chikamatsu's plays. Along with a fluent translation, Keene supplies an account of the Japanese puppet theatre and the historical background of the play as well as abundant information on the Japanese and Chinese institutions and people mentioned in the text. He touches on details about piracy, intrigue, conquest, international relations, and above all, human passion, ambition, and suffering, which lie at the heart of the play. Besides a detailed study of Chikamatsu's career and an imaginative literary analysis of the text, Keene supplies over 200 notes of a historical and philological nature as well as a detailed bibliography of Japanese secondary sources and a glossary of Japanese terms. The text is retranslated in *Major Plays of Chikamatsu* (1961).

_____. *World Within Walls: Japanese Literature of the Pre-Modern Era, 1600-1867.* New York: Holt, Rinehart and Winston, 1976. Here Keene provides brief summaries and analyses of several plays. He describes the typical pattern of a domestic tragedy or love suicide, pointing out that Chikamatsu's typical hero is a sincere young man of weak character. The heroine is a generous and passionate woman. Duty and affection bind three main characters in a triangle with ties of love and responsibility too strong to break. The Japanese qualities of *giri*, or "obligation," and *ninjō*, or "human feeling," are shown to underlie the dramatic structure, which accounts for both the strength and limitations of Chikamatsu's drama. Keene also discusses the nature of tragedy in Chikamatsu's plays, as well as the role of social class. Finally, he touches on the historical plays, Chikamatsu's views on the art of the puppet theatre, and his use of language and style.

_____. "Characteristic Responses to Confucianism in Tokugawa Literature." Peter Nosco, ed., *Confucianism and Tokugawa Culture*. Princeton: Princeton University Press, 1984. A discourse on the role of Confucian values in Chikamatsu's plays focuses on three specific titles. Merchants are seen to be admirable not for their business acumen but for their ability to act like samurai. Human feelings always triumph, even in death, as Chikamatsu imparts to his heroes and heroines something of the grandeur of tragedy. Purity of soul is found to compensate for all manner of deceit and abrogation of social or personal responsibility. In historical plays, as *Kokusenya Kasen* suggests, the call of duty is emphasized in an exaggerated and absolutistic way in order to emphasize nobility and generosity.

Matisoff, Susan, *The Legend of Semimaru: Blind Musician of Japan.* New York: Columbia University Press, 1978. Besides a careful, annotated translation of Chikamatsu's historical play, *Semimaru*, Matisoff presents a wealth of information and criticism. For instance, she discusses the Buddhist temple, Kinshōji (Chikamatsu-dera)—the playwright's namesake for his pseudonym—and its association with reciters, many of whom were blind, like the hero of the play. She treats the sketchy details of Chikamatsu's life, date of the play, and circumstances of authorship and setting. Emphasizing the five-act structure and the overall theme of *Semimaru*, Matisoff touches on specific stage effects, connections with earlier legendary sources and dramatic productions, including a Noh play of the same name attributed to Zeami. Following an act-by-act analysis of the play, the author concludes with the argument that devotion to duty on the one hand and private emotional concerns on the other hand furnish the underlying conflict, with the private element in the foreground, as in the later domestic dramas. Passion and jealousy are seen as the principal unifying impulses. Matisoff complements and extends Keene's work on Chikamatsu, in effect demonstrating that further study and translation of the surviving dramas can enhance the appreciation and understanding of the playwright's achievement.

Shively, Donald Howard, *The Love Suicide at Amijima: A Study of a Japanese Domestic Tragedy by Chikamatsu Monzaemon.* Cambridge: Harvard University Press, 1953. A literal approach to translation lies at the heart of this monograph and text. It includes an extended introduction on the Japanese puppet theatre, Chikamatsu's career, the historical and domestic plays, the institution of the pleasure quarter, social mores and ethical teachings, and the faddishness of love suicide. Shively's analysis of character treats elements of stereotyping as well as the degree of individualistic delineation. He also touches on the overall structure and setting as well as the underlying religious beliefs. A thorough description of Chikamatsu's style emphasizes the playwright's indebtedness to the conventions of Noh and the technical devices of traditional Japanese poetry. Attention to the textual history reminds readers of the extensive revision that took place for subsequent performances and for presentation of puppet plays on the Kabuki stage, owing to the constant demand for new treatment of familiar themes. In the end, Shively's translation is labored and lacking in elegance, marked sometimes by excessive use of colloquial diction, sometimes by stiff and unidiomatic expressions, and on every page by stultifying literalism and brackets. Students learning to read Chikamatsu's difficult and obsolescent style are the main beneficiaries of Shively's version of the play. The annotations are a marvel of patience and erudition, drawing on the wealth of Japanese secondary sources available at the time of writing.

Other Sources

Besides those listed here and above, numerous Japanese secondary sources exist, of which readers of that language may avail themselves. Space does not allow their mention here.

Adachi, Barbara, *The Voices and Hands of Bunraku.* Tokyo: Kodansha International, Ltd., 1979. More a book of illustrations than text, this title sets Chikamatsu in a theatrical tradition that attracts theatre-goers and scholarly investigators alike. Like Ando (1970) and Keene (1965), a book for basic information and understanding.

Ando, Tsuruo, *Bunraku: The Puppet Theatre, with an Introduction by Charles J. Dunn.* New York and Tokyo: Walker/Weatherhill in Collaboration with Tankosha, Kyoto, 1970. First published in Japanese, the book addresses a general audience and serves as a brief introduction. Although containing many fine illustrations of historical material on the puppet theatre, it is inferior to Keene, *Bunraku* (see below).

Dunn, C.J. *The Early Japanese Puppet Drama.* London: Luzac and Co., Ltd., 1966. A scholarly introduction to the historical background and development of the puppet theatre in Japan, the treatment stops with the emergence of Chikamatsu as Uji Kaganojō and Takemoto Gidayu's playwright.

Jones, Stanleigh, *Sugawara and the Secrets of Calligraphy.* New York: Columbia University Press, 1985. Translation of a historical play by Chikamatsu's eighteenth-century successors.

Keene, Donald, *Bunraku: The Art of the Japanese Puppet Theatre . . . , Photographs by Kaneko Hiroshi, with an Introduction by Tanizaki Junichiro.* Tokyo: Kodansha International, Ltd., 1965. With 360 superlative plates, including eleven in color, Keene describes the history of the form, giving detailed explanations of texts, music, puppets, and gestures with reference to Chikamatsu scattered throughout. Still the best general introduction.

_____, trans. *Major Plays of Chikamatsu.* New York and London: Columbia University Press, 1961. An authoritative literary translation of eleven plays, this book is the standard text in English.

_____, trans. *Four Major Plays of Chikamatsu.* New York: Columbia University Press, 1961. A selection of titles from the above, useful for students.

Kirkwood, Kenneth P. *Renaissance in Japan: A Cultural Survey of the Seventeenth Century.* Tokyo: Meiji Press, 1938; new ed., with a foreword by Arnold J. Toynbee. Tokyo: Charles E. Tuttle, 1970. Three chapters deal with Chikamatsu and his career in a perceptive and fluent account by a Canadian diplomat posted in Japan, 1929-1939. In spite of various superficialities, worth consulting for some details not available elsewhere and for analogies with sixteenth and seventeenth century European theatre.

Miyamori, Asatarō, *Masterpieces of Chikamatsu: The Japanese Shakespeare,* translated by Asatarō Miyamori . . ., revised by Robert Nichols . . ., with 74 Illustrations. London and New York: Kegan Paul, Trench, Trubner and Co; E.P. Dutton, 1926. Two domestic plays and three historical pieces are translated with a lengthy introduction. The translations remain readable and are reasonably close to the Japanese originals. Disparaged by some scholars, Miyamori's versions nonetheless deserve respect and attention. Several plays are otherwise unavailable in English.

Scott, A.C. *The Puppet Theatre of Japan.* Tokyo: Charles E. Tuttle, 1963. For the study of Chikamatsu the chief value of this book lies in a synopsis and description of a 1712 play, *Yūgiri Izaemon kuruwa bunshō* (Vicissitudes of Yugiri and Izaemon).

Shively, Donald H. "Chikamatsu's Satire on the Dog Shogun," in *Harvard Journal of Asiatic Studies,* Vol. 23 (1955): 159-180. A study of historical aspects of the 1714 puppet play, *Sagami nyūdō sembiki inu* (The Sagami Lay Monk and the Thousand Dogs), the article analyzes the use of contemporary historical detail and earlier sources to create a historical play that treats political satire on Shogun Tsunayoshi (1646-1709), whose misguided efforts to protect dogs and living creatures led to widespread human suffering and resentment toward the government.

Leon Zolbrod
University of British Columbia

COLLEY CIBBER
1671-1757

Author's Chronology

Born November 6, 1671 to Caius Gabriel and his second wife, Jane Colley Cibber; *1682* sent to the free school at Grantham, Lincolnshire; *1688* serves in the army under the Earl of Devonshire at Chatsworth; *1690* first recorded acting at Drury Lane as unpaid probationer; *1693* marries Katherine Shore, who bore him ten children; *1695* on the reopening of the Theatre Royal, Cibber recites a Prologue of his own composition; *1696* successfully acts role of Sir Novelty Fashion in his first play, *Love's Last Shift*; *1697* success in another fop role, Lord Foppington in *The Relapse*; *1700* becomes adviser to Christopher Rich in the management of Drury Lane Theatre; *1704* signs a five-year contract for acting and managing at Drury Lane; *1706* plays Sir Fopling Flutter in *The Man of Mode*, among other successful roles; acts at the Haymarket Theatre, subsequently sued by Rich for breach of contract; *1708* Drury Lane and Haymarket companies unite, with management of Drury Lane delegated to Wilks, Cibber and Estcourt; Drury Lane temporarily closed from October 26 to December 14 "by reason of Prince George's illness and death"; *1709* actors, opposing Christopher Rich, enter into covert agreement with Owen Swiney, planning to move to the Haymarket; Drury Lane closed; Cibber continues to act successfully in a variety of roles; *1712* Drury Lane reopens with Wilks, Cibber and Doggett as managers; *1714* new license issued to Steele, Wilks, Doggett, Cibber and Booth; *1715* patent assigned to Wilks, Cibber, Booth; first performances of *Venus and Adonis*, *Myrtillo*, and *Bulls and Bears*; *1717* his comedy, *The Non-Juror*, very successful; *1719 Ximena*, first acted 1712, published; preface angered the Lord Chamberlain, who suspended Cibber from acting at Drury Lane; suspension later revoked; *1721* first performance of comedy, *The Refusal*; publishes collected plays, *Plays Written by Mr. Cibber*; *1724* first performance of *Caesar in Aegypt*; *1728* first performance of *The Provok'd Husband*; Cibber mentioned in Pope's first *Dunciad*; *1729* first performances of *Love in a Riddle* and *Damon and Phillida*; *1730* Cibber named Poet Laureate; *1732* sells share in Drury Lane to John Highmore; *1733* officially retires as actor; *1734-1735* six performances in favorite roles; first performance of *Polypheme*; *1735* Cibber attacked in Pope's *Epistle to Dr. Arbuthnot*; *1740* publishes *An Apology for the Life of Mr. Colley Cibber*; *1742* Cibber attacked by Fielding in *Joseph Andrews*; Cibber publishes *A Letter from Mr. Cibber to Mr. Pope*; *1743* Pope publishes *The Dunciad* with Cibber as hero; *1744* Pope-Cibber controversy halted by death of Pope; *1745* first appearance of *Papal Tyranny in the Reign of King John*; Cibber's last appearance on stage; *1747* enjoys social prominence; *1750* seriously ill but recovers; *1757* dies.

Author's Bibliography (selected)

Love's Last Shift, 1696 (play); *Xerxes*, 1699 (play); *The Tragical History of King Richard III*, 1700 (play); *Love Makes a Man, or the Fop's Fortune*, 1701 (play); *She Wou'd and She Wou'd Not, or the Kind Impostor*, 1702 (play); *The Careless Husband*, 1704 (play); *Venus and Adonis. A Masque*, 1715; *Myrtillo. A Pastoral Interlude*, 1715; *The Non-Juror*, 1718 (play); *Ximena, or the Heroick Daughter*, 1719 (play); *The Refusal, or the Ladies Philosophy*, 1721 (play); *Plays Written by Mr. Cibber*, 1721; *The Provok'd Husband, or a Journey to London*, "Written by the Late Sir John Vanbrugh and Mr. Cibber," 1728 (play); *Love in a Riddle. A Pastoral*, 1729 (play); *Damon and Phillida. A Ballad Opera*, 1729 (play); *An Ode to His Majesty, for the New Year 1730/31*, 1730 (poem); *An Ode for His Majesty's Birthday, October 30, 1731*, 1731 (poem); *Polypheme. An Opera*, 1734; *The Blind Boy*, c.1735 (poem).

Overview of Biographical Sources

The most useful and basic general studies of Cibber's life appear in two brief biographical sketches, one in the *Dictionary of National Biography* and the other in *A Biographical Dictionary of Actors, Actresses, Musicians, Dancers, Managers and Other Stage Personnel in London, 1660-1800* (1973-   ). Both provide authoritative, straightforward accounts of Cibber's lengthy and complicated professional life, the first focusing on his literary output and the second emphasizing the interrelatedness of his activities. Aspects of Cibber's troubled tenure as manager of Drury Lane during the period 1706-1715 are studied and documented in *Vice Chamberlain Coke's Theatrical Papers, 1706-1715*, edited by Judith Milhous and Robert D. Hume (Carbondale: Southern Illinois University Press, 1982). The most authoritative full-length study of Cibber's life is Richard Barker's *Mr. Cibber of Drury Lane* (New York: Columbia University Press, 1939).

Evaluation of Selected Biographies

Highfill, Philip H., Jr., Kalman A. Burnim, and Edward A. Langhans, eds. "Colley Cibber," in *A Biographical Dictionary of Actors, Actresses, Musicians, Dancers, Managers, and Other Stage Personnel in London, 1660-1800*. This recent work is a stimulating study of the interrelatedness of Cibber's roles as actor, manager and playwright. The approach is chronologiccal, allowing the reader to grasp some of the simultaneity of Cibber's activities. The plays, often with their performance histories, are noted and the chief roles are briefly described. The complexities of Cibber's position as manager of Drury Lane are noted and useful background information on the day-to-day activities of the triumvirate management of Cibber, Wilks and Doggett is given. Details of the Cibber-Dennis feud and the Cibber-Pope controversy are duly cited.

Knight, Joseph, "Colley Cibber," in *Dictionary of National Biography*. Knight's essay is a carefully researched, clearly written account of Cibber's long and varied life. Knight traces Cibber's acting career from his first appearance through his many successes until his retirement in 1733 and after, when he was called upon to perform favorite roles on stage. He identifies and dates plays written by Cibber, as well, and details the complicated history of Cibber's tenure as theatrical manager. His remarks on *The Non-Juror* are especially pertinent. Knight is dispassionate in detailing the later attacks on Cibber by Pope and Fielding, allowing that "Cibber's treatment of Pope in the pamphlet warfare which he waged is creditable, if only on the score of discretion." He is enthusiastic about Cibber's dramatic writing: "In his comedies Cibber all but stands comparison with the best of the successors of Congreve." Admitting that Cibber's plays lack wit, he maintains that they are marked by a "smartness of dialogue and animal spirits" that are "an acceptable substitute." However, he makes no literary defense of Cibber's work as laureate, believing his odes to be "among the most contemptible things in literature." Knight attempts to view his subject comprehensively and his conclusions are positive: "He was a sparkling and successful dramatist, a comedian of high mark, a singularly capable and judicious manager, . . . and an unequalled critic of theatrical perform-ances."

Autobiographical Sources

An Apology for the Life of Mr. Colley Cibber, Comedian, and Late Patentee of the Theatre-Royal. With an Historical View of the Stage during His Own Time. Written by Himself. (London: 1740). The *Apology* is a lively, candid, though bi-ased, account of theatrical life in the early eighteenth century. Besides providing abundant information on himself and his activities, Cibber has given the reader a collection of character sketches and anecdotes of contemporary actors and ac-tresses. His critical reviews of plays in performance are informative and his general observations on actors and acting are acute. The *Apology* has long been acknowl-edged as one of the most important theatrical books ever written.

Overview of Critical Sources

Although Cibber's overall theatrical contributions have been widely acknowl-edged, there is only one full-length recent critical study of his plays, Leonard R.N. Ashley's *Colley Cibber*. Recent Cibber criticism has developed in two directions: 1) those studies that consider one play as a single entity; and 2) those studies that attempt to establish Cibber's importance as a dramatist by linking him with major playwrights of the period. The first group includes Paul Parnell's essay, "Equivoca-tion in Cibber's 'Love's Last Shift' " (*Studies in Philology*, VII, 519-534), and Albert E. Kalson's "The Chronicles in Cibber's *Richard III* (*Theatre Survey*, 16, 42-55). The second direction may be seen in Shirley Strum Kenny's "Humane Comedy" (*Modern Philology*, 75) in Alan Roper's "Language and Action in *The Way of the World, Love's Last Shift,* and *The Relapse*" (*English Literary History*,

40: 44-69), and Robert D. Hume's *The Development of English Drama in the Late Seventeenth Century* (Oxford: Clarendon Press, 1976).

Evaluation of Selected Criticism

Ashley, Leonard R.N. *Colley Cibber*. New York: Twayne, 1965. A critical and analytical study of the entire Cibber canon, Ashley's book examines each work, placing it within its literary and theatrical context. The works are related to biographical elements and the whole is scrupulously documented.

Hume, Robert D. *The Development of English Drama in the Late Seventeenth Century*. Hume evaluates Cibber's work candidly, noting both its weaknesses and its contributions to a period of lively dramatic activity. Links Cibber with Vanbrugh, Steele, and Centlivre.

Kenny, Shirley Strum, "Humane Comedy," in *Modern Philology*, 75 pp. 29-43. Kenny links plays by Cibber with works of Farquhar, Steele, Vanbrugh and Congreve, ascribing the term "humane comedy" to all of them. She notes characteristics of style, dialogue, plot and characterization that were common to these plays, which were among the most popular stage pieces of the entire eighteenth century.

Other Sources

Boas, Frederick S. *An Introduction to Eighteenth-Century Drama 1700-1780*. London: Oxford University Press, 1953. Detailed discussions of *The Careless Husband*, *The Non-Juror*, and *The Provok'd Husband*.

Broadus, Edmund Kemper, *The Laureateship: A Study of the Office of Poet Laureate in England*. Oxford: The Clarendon Press, 1921. Scholarly discussion of Cibber as Poet Laureate, including some of the poems written by him in that capacity.

Hopkins, Kenneth, *The Poets Laureate*. Carbondale: Southern Illinois University Press, 1954. Discussion of Cibber as Poet Laureate, including some of the poems written by him in that capacity. Written for the general reader.

Potter, Lois, "Colley Cibber: the Fop as Hero," in *Augustan Worlds*, ed. J.C. Hilson, M.M.B. Jones and J.R. Watson. New York: Harper and Row, 1978. Study of Cibber's use of the fop persona as an element in his personal life.

Phylllis T. Dircks
Long Island University

PAUL CLAUDEL
1868-1955

Author's Chronology

Born August 6, 1868, Villeneuve-sur Fère (Aisne), France, to Louis-Prosper Claudel, a fiscal functionary, and Louise Cerveaux, daughter of a physician and niece of the priest of Villeneuve; this comfortable middle-class family which included also two daughters, Camille born in 1864 and Louise born in 1866, moves three times before settling in Paris in 1882 so as to enable Camille to study sculpture; Paul Claudel studies at Louis-le-Grand, undergoes a serious philosophical crisis; *1883* loses his faith; *1884* passes first part of baccalauréat (after having failed the previous year) and passes the second half in philosophy in 1885; *1886-1890* studies at the Ecole des Sciences Politiques; *1886* writes his first work, *L'Endormie;* reads very extensively including Rimbaud's *Illuminations; 1886* finds his faith again and formally converts in 1890; *1888* writes *Une Mort prématurée; 1890* takes first place on the entrance examination to the diplomatic service; *1893-1895* takes up his first consular posts in New York and Boston, translates *Agamemnon* and writes *L'Echange; 1895-1899* first assignment in China; *1900* returns to France, finishes *La Jeune Fille Violaine* (2nd vers.) and after retreats at Solesmes and Ligugé returns to China; en route he meets a young married woman, "Ysé" travelling with her husband and two children whom she leaves to follow Claudel; *1905* breaks with "Ysé" and returns to France where he marries Reine Sainte-Marie Perrin with whom he has five children; *1906* returns to China for a third time; *1909* is sent to Prague; *1912* is sent to Frankfurt and Hamburg; *1913* writes the farce *Protée;* the same year his father dies and his sister Camille, Auguste Rodin's student and mistress, is confined; *1914* completes *Coronal* begun in 1887 and *Crusts; 1915* serves in Paris and Rome; *1913-1915* translates *The Choephori* and *The Eumenides; 1917-1918* mission in Rio de Janeiro; *1919-1921* mission in Copenhagen; *1921-1927* in Tokyo for his first ambassadorship; 1924 completes *The Satin Slipper* begun in 1919; *1925-1926* visits to Europe; *1927-1933* ambassador to Washington; during this period he publishes *The Book of Christopher Columbus* (1927); *1929* death of his mother; *1933-1935* ambassador to Brussels; *1935-1955* retirement with residences in Paris and Brangues; writes numerous works of exegesis, poems and new "versions of plays"; dies February 23, 1955.

Author's Bibliography (selected)

Most of Claudel's vast *oeuvre* was published during his lifetime, including the several versions of a number of his major plays. The two major editions of Claudel's works were published by Gallimard: one is in the "Pléiade" series and includes two volumes of dramatic works, one of poetry, one of prose and two volumes of diaries; the other is the *Oeuvres complètes* in 29 volumes (1950-1985).

Although Claudel's major works have been translated into English, his complete works are not being published systematically in English.

Tête d'or, 1890 (1st version), 1901 (2nd version), tr. 1916 (2nd version), (play); *The City,* 1903 (1st version), 1910 (2nd version), tr. 1920 (both versions), (play); *The East I Know,* 1900, tr. 1914 (poetry); *Poetic Art,* 1907, tr. 1948 (poetry); *Break at Noon,* 1906 (1st version), 1918 (1st "version for stage"), 1949 ("new version for stage"), tr. 1960 (play); *Five Great Odes,* 1910, tr. 1967 (poetry); *The Hostage,* 1911, tr. 1917, 1945 (play); *The Tidings Brought to Mary,* 1912 (1st version), 1948 ("definitive verison"), tr. 1916, 1960 (play; both versions first written and published as poetry entitled *La Jeune Fille Violanine* [1892-1893] and *La Cantate à trois voix* [1898-1900]); *Protée,* 1914 (play); *Coronal,* 1915, tr. 1943 (poetry); *Crusts,* 1918, tr. 1945 (play); *The Humiliation of the Father,* 1920, tr. 1945 (play); *The Satin Slipper,* 1928-1929 (1st version), 1944 (1st "version for stage"), tr. 1931, 1945 (play); *Feuilles de saints,* 1925 (poetry); *The Book of Christopher Columbus,* 1929, tr. 1930 (libretto); *Conversations dans le Loir-et-Cher,* 1929 (dialog); *Au milieu des vitraux de Apocalypse,* 1966 (dialog); *Positions et propositions I,* 1928, tr. 1933 (essays); *Positions et propositions II,* 1934 (essays); *Joan at the Stake,* 1934 (libretto); *A Poet before the Cross,* 1938, tr. 1958 (poem) *Figures et Paraboles,* 1936 (essays); *L'Histoire de Tobie et de Sara,* 1942 (play); *Contacts et circonstances,* 1947 (essays); *Paul Claudel interroge l'Apocalypse,* 1942 (essays); *Lord, Teach us how to Pray,* 1942, tr. 1948 (poetry); *Three Poems of the War,* 1915, tr. 1919 (poetry); *The Eye Listens,* 1946, tr. 1950 (essays); *Introduction à l'Apocalypse: Le Livre de Job,* 1946 (essay); *La Rose et le rosaire,* 1947 (essay); *Accompagnements,* 1949 (essays); *Emmaüs,* 1949 (essays); *Le Cantique des cantiques,* 1948 (essay); *Discours et remerciements,* 1947 (essay); *L'Evangile d'Isaïe,* 1951 (essay); *Trois figures saintes pour le temps actuel,* 1951 (essay); *Mémoires improvisés,* 1954, 1969 (memoirs); *The Essence of the Bible,* 1955, tr. 1957 (essays); *Journal,* 2 v. 1968-1969 (diary); a number of miscellaneous works can only be found in the *Oeuvres complètes* in 29 v.

Overview of Biographical Sources

Claudel died at the age of 87 in 1955, having had a distinguished career as diplomat and having been one of the greatest writers of the century. Before leaving France for his first diplomatic post, in addition to his unfinished first play, he had written the first version of three of his major plays. He had attended also Mallarmé's literary gatherings (his "mardis") where he not only learned from the Symbolist master, but met some of his most distinguished future confrères: André Gide and Paul Valéry. Although these beginnings brought him close to literary greatness, Claudel attracted little attention in France prior to World War I. This was due both to the novelty of his style and to his profession which required that he be away from France and Paris literary circles most of the time from 1893 and his retirement in 1935. The other major obstacles Claudel had to overcome were ideological: his strong reaction against rationalism and his fervent Catholicism which at first conservative Catholics found insufficiently orthodox and even more numerous anti-Catholics found and continue to find unpalatable. In spite of all obstacles, by the thirties the early acclaim of Jacques Rivière and Georges Duhamel between 1907 and 1912, and Jacques Madaule's excellent study (*Le Génie de Paul Claudel*, 1933) as well as numerous other studies and performances of his dramas had vastly enlarged Claudel's audience. Since the Second World War he has been acclaimed and revered as a classic in France and increasingly regarded as an author of world stature. Since the publication of Georges Duhamel's *Paul Claudel* in 1919, numerous general studies have been dedicated to Claudel's life and works. Jacques Madaule's *Le Génie de Paul Claudel* (1933) and *Le Drame de Paul Claudel* (1936, revised editions in 1947, 1952, 1964) remain the best overall studies of Claudel's works with essential information and explanation on numerous aspects of the poet's life. Wallace Fowlie's *Claudel* (1957) is the first introductory study to Claudel in English. Paul-André Lesort's *Paul Claudel par lui-même* (1963) is the best short biographical introduction. Henri Guillemin's *Le Gonverti Paul Claudel* must be mentioned because it elucidates definitively the circumstances of the most important event in Claudel's life: his conversion. Louis Chaigne's *Paul Claudel: The Man and Mystic* (1961) is the best biography to date in English, although Harold A. Waters' *Paul Claudel* (1970) contains more penetrating criticism and factual information. There is no definitive biography of Claudel as yet.

Evaluation of Selected Biographies

Chaigne, Louis, *Paul Claudel: The Man and the Mystic*. tr. Pierre de Fontnouvelle. Mâme, 1961; New York: Appleton Century Crofts, 1961. This chronological biography was written by someone who knew Claudel well and admired him greatly. Chaigne stresses the positive development of Claudel and avoids discussion of the poet's religious wavering and the adulterous episode in his life. It is a very readable and useful introduction in English.

Fowlie, Wallace, *Claudel*. London: Bowes and Bowes, 1957. This is the first general introduction to Claudel in English. It treats selective aspects of Claudel's thought and work. Still useful for its explanation of Catholicism in Claudel's works.

Lesort, Paul-André, *Paul Claudel par lui-même*. Paris: Le Seuil, 1963. Untranslated. This very concise presentation is perhaps the most complete and practical as well as the fairest general introduction to Claudel's life and works.

Waters, Harold A. *Paul Claudel*. New York: Twayne, 1970. As a leading Claudel scholar, Waters has thorough command of Claudel's life and times. He shows also depth and originality in his interpretations of the works which he studies in three genre chapters. Although certain parts are exceedingly short, this is the most useful and practical general introduction to Claudel in English.

Autobiographical Sources

With the exception of *Break at Noon,* few of Claudel's plays were directly inspired by his life. The same can be said of his lyric poetry. On the other hand, such prose works as *Contacts et circonstances* (1947), *Positions et propositions I* (1928) trans. as *Ways and Crossways* (1933) and *Positions et propositions II* (1934), found in the Bibliothèque de la Pléiade editions of Claudel's *Oeuvres en prose* (Paris: Gallimard, 1965), are full of information on his activities and thought. Naturally, his *Mémoires improvisés* (Paris: Gallimard, 1954 and the more complete and accurate edition of 1969) and his *Journal* (2 v., Paris: Gallimard, 1968-1969) contain essential biographical information. The extensive introduction to the *Journal* by François Varillon is especially rich in biographical information and candid in its approach. Lastly, since he was abroad most of the time between 1893 and 1935, he kept a very extensive correspondence. Numerous correspondences of a strictly personal or religious nature have not been published, with one major exception: A. du Sarment. *Lettres inédites de mon parrain Paul Claudel (1925-1955)* (Paris: J. Gabalda, 1959). On the other hand, most of his literary correspondences have been published in excellently annotated editions. They are:

Correspondance Paul Claudel—Jean-Louis Barrault (1939-1954). Paris: Gallimard, 1974.

Correspondance avec Copeau, Bourdet, Dullin, Jouvet. Cahier Paul Claudel VI. Paris: Gallimard. 1966.

Correspondance Paul Claudel—André Gide (1899-1926). Paris: Gallimard, 1949.

The Correspondences, 1899-1926, between Paul Claudel and André Gide. ed. Robert Mallet. Pref. and tr. by John Russel. New York: Pantheon, 1952.

Correspondance Paul Claudel—Francis Jammes—Gabriel Frizeau (1897-1938). Paris: Gallimard, 1952.

Correspondance avec Lugné-Poe (1910-1928), in *Cahier Paul Claudel V.* Paris: Gallimard, 1964.

Correspondance Paul Claudel—Darius Milhaud (1912-1953) in *Cahier Paul Claudel III.* Paris: Gallimard, 1961.

Correspondance Jacques Rivière—Paul Claudel (1907-1914). Paris: Plon, 1926. tr. as *Letters to a Doubter* by Henry Longan Stuart. New York: A. & C. Boni, 1927. New and complete edition: *Correspondance Paul Claudel—Jacques Rivière (1907-1924).* Paris: Gallimard, 1984, in *Cahiers Paul Claudel XII.*

Correspondance André Suarès—Paul Claudel (1904-1938). Paris: Gallimard, 1951.

Thus at this time, most of the autobiographical material has been published and constitutes an unusually large and rich corpus.

Overview of Critical Sources

Claudel scholarship is voluminous; all his works, especially his drama and poetry have been studied seriously and with increasing intensity during the past four decades. It also reflects use of most of the major approaches of twentieth century literary criticism. The publication of the *Oeuvres complètes* (Paris: Gallimard, 1950-1985, 29 v.) have made readily available to scholars of Claudel's works. This explains in part the considerable growth of Claudel criticism. The other factor is that alongside Gide, Proust and Valéry, Claudel has clearly emerged as a major figure in French and world literature. The following is merely a sampling of Claudel criticism.

Evaluation of Selected Criticism

Alter, André, *Paul Claudel*. Paris: Seghers, 1968. This introductory study is useful for its comments on Claudel's concept of drama, synopsis of his plays, stylistic qualities, quotations from Claudel and numerous critics, chronologies and a bibliography.

Chiari, John, *The Poetic Drama of Paul Claudel*. London: Harvill, 1954. Studies symbolism in Claudel's plays, their structure and the significance of characters. Admires Claudel as a poet of great vision rather than as a dramatist.

Eméry, Léon, *Claudel*. Lyon: Cahiers libres, 1967. Hails Claudel as a supreme artist and as "the Hugo of the twentieth century." This very dense and suggestive study was influential especially in France.

Farabet, René, *Le Jeu de l'acteur dans le théâtre de Claudel*. Paris: Lettres Modernes, 1960. Untranslated. Study of the problems encountered by actors in performing Claudel's plays. The appendix is most valuable, for it contains all essential information about the production of Claudel's plays from 1912 to 1959.

Freilich, Joan, *Paul Claudel's "Le Soulier de Satin": A Stylistic, Structuralist and Psychoanalytic Interpretation*. Toronto: University of Toronto Press, 1973. Study of the effectiveness of imagery based on analysis of stylistic elements. The structure is studied from a psychocritical perspective.

Lioure, Michel, *L'Esthétique dramatique de Paul Claudel*. Paris: Armand Colin, 1971. Untranslated. The most extensive study of Claudel's dramatic esthetics and genius. It contains systematic studies of Claudel's beginnings as a dramatist including early influences and experiments, the various phases of his development, and an analysis of the elements of Claudelian drama.

Madaule, Jacques, *Le Drame de Paul Claudel*. Paris: Desclée De Brouwer. 1936, 1947, 1952, 1964. Untranslated. Generally recognized as the clearest and the best overall study of Claudel's drama. It contains detailed analysis of all plays in chronological order.

Matheson, William H. *Claudel and Aeschylus*. A Study of Claudel's Translation of the Orestia. Ann Arbor: University of Michigan Press, 1965. Matheson assesses the accuracy of Claudel's comprehension and translation of Aeschylus. He believes that Aeschylus' influence on Claudel was very important and he finds evidence of it in *Tête d'or* and in the trilogy.

Other Sources

Barrault, Jean-Louis, "Paul Claudel." in *Nouvelles réflexions sur le théâtre.* Paris: Flammarion, 1959. Untranslated. An extremely perceptive director discusses the problems and collaboration while staging Claudel's plays.

Berchan, Richard, *The Inner Stage. An Essay on the Conflict of Vocations in the Early Works of Paul Claudel.* East Lansing: Michigan State University Press, 1966. Study of the conflict in Claudel between his religious and poetic vocations as reflected in the works *Partage de Midi* and *Cinq grandes odes.*

Brunel, Pierre, *Claudel et Shakespeare..* Paris: A Colin, 1971. Untranslated. Excellent influence study which shows Claudel continued to admire Shakespeare throughout his career as a dramatist.

Claudel et l'Amérique. Ottawa: Editions de l'Univ. d'Ottawa, 1964. Untranslated. This volume contains essays on Claudel's experiences in Boston, New York, Washington and Rio de Janeiro, as well as his friendship with Agnes Meyer, and commentaries on Claudel's works written in or about America.

Critiques de notre temps et Claudel. Paris: Garnier, 1970. Untranslated. Excellent selection of articles on Claudel's life and works.

Hatzfeld, Helmut, "Critical Revision of Claudel as a Catholic Poet," in *Cross Currents* 5 (1955): 109-114. In the context of the Catholic revival, Claudel's poetic vision is compared to Dante's and his missionary zeal to Calderon's.

MacCombie, John, *The Prince and the Genie.* A Study of Rimbaud's Influence on Claudel. Amherst: University of Massachusetts Press, 1972.

Madaule, Jacques, *Claudel et le langage.* Paris: Desclée De Brouwer, 1968. Untranslated. Important study of Claudel's theory and use of language, especially in *L'Echange.*

Madaule, Jacques, *Paul Claudel, dramaturge.* Paris: L'Arche, 1956. Untranslated. A very good introduction to Claudel's theater which contains summaries and commentaries for all major plays in alphabetical order.

Mercier-Campiche, Marianne, *Le Théâtre de Claudel, ou la puissance du grief et de la passion.* Paris: Pauvert, 1968. Untranslated. In-depth study taking into account all major interpretations of Claudel's plays.

Moreau, Pierre, "Etat présent des études claudéliennes en France" in *Information littéraire* 22 (1970): 22-32. Untranslated. Useful critical bibliographic data on critical editions, biographical studies, as well as an analyses of themes and language in Claudel's poetry and theater.

Nagy, Moses, "La Condition surnaturelle de l'homme et la souffrance terrestre dans le théâtre de Claudel," in Revue de l'Université *Laval* 15 (1960): 131-151. Untranslated. An especially good study of suffering in Partage de midi.

Petit, Jacques, *Pour une explication du "Soulier de satin.* Paris: Lettres modernes, 1965. Untranslated. An invaluable study of Claudel's most important and complex play.

Waters, Harold A. "Situation de Claudel aux Etats-Unix," in Bulletin de la *Société Paul Claudel* 50 (1973): 34-38. Untranslated. The little interest in Claudel in the United States prior to 1968 is on the rise as indicated by the increase in the number of doctoral dissertations on Claudel.

Watson, Harold, *Claudel's Immortal Heros. A Choice of Death.* New Brunswick, NJ: Rutgers University Press, 1971. Important study of death in a number of Claudel's plays. Excellent treatment of *Partage de midi.*

Jean-Pierre Cap
Lafayette College

JEAN COCTEAU
1889-1963

Author's Chronology

Born Clément Eugène Jean Maurice July 5, 1889, Maisons-Laffitte; *1889* his father shoots himself to death; his mother with her three children moves to Paris; Jean enters the Lycée Condorcet; *1906* a reading of Cocteau's poems is organized at the Théâtre Fémina by Edouard de Max; *1912* begins associating with Serge Diaghilev and Igor Stravinsky; *1916* frequents Montparnasse with Modigliani, Apollinaire and his friends, meets Picasso; *1917 Parade,* his first work for the stage, is produced at the Chatelet, with sets and costumes by Picasso and music by Satie; *1918* meets Raymond Radiguet, precocious adolescent poet and novelist introduced to him by Max Jacob; *1921 The Wedding on the Eiffel Tower* is produced at the Théâtre des Champs-Elysées; *1922* publishes *Plain-Chant,* and *Thomas the Impostor; Antigone* is produced at the Théâtre de l'Atelier, with sets by Picasso and music by Honegger; *1924* becomes addicted to opium; *1925* is briefly tempted by Catholicism; *1926 Orpheus* is produced at the Théâtre des Arts; completes filming *The Blood of a Poet,* his first film; *The Human Voice* is produced at the Comédie Française; *1931* taken seriously ill in Toulon; *1934 The Infernal Machine* is produced at the Théâtre des Champs-Elysées, with Louis Jouvet and Jean-Pierre Aumont; *1938 Intimate Relations* is produced first at the Théâtre des Embassadeurs, then judged scandalous by the Municipal Council and forced to move to the Bouffe-Parisiens where it becomes an instant success; *The Holy Terrors* is produced at the Théâtre Michel; *1941* violent demonstrations at the re-opening of *The Holy Terrors; The Typewriter* is produced at the Théâtre Hébertot, subsequently banned by the German authorities; *1945* writes the script for *La Belle et la Bête,* subsequently filmed under his direction; *1946 The Eagle With Two Heads* is produced at the Théâtre Hébertot; *1947* decides to settle in Milly-la-Forêt, in a house bought jointly with Jean Marais; *1948* travels in the United States; *1955* is elected member of the Académie Française; *1956* receives an honorary Doctor's degree at Oxford University; decorates the Saint-Pierre chapel, in Villefranche; *1963* dies October 10 of an attack of pulmonary edema, at Milly-la-Forêt.

Author's Bibliography (selected)

The Wedding on the Eiffel Tower, 1923, tr. 1964 (drama); *Thomas the Impostor,* 1923, tr. 1925 (novel); *The Miscreant,* 1923, tr. 1958 (novel); *Orpheus,* 1927, tr. 1963 (drama); *Antigone,* 1927, tr. 1962 (drama); *Oedipe Roi,* 1928 (drama); *The Children of the Game,* 1929, tr. 1955 (novel); *The Human Voice,* 1930, tr. 1951 (drama); *The Infernal Machine,* 1934, tr. 1963 (drama); *The Knights of the Round Table,* 1937, tr. 1963 (drama); *Intimate Relations,* 1938, tr. 1962 (drama); *The*

Holy Terrors, 1940, tr. 1962 (drama); *The Typewriter,* 1941, tr. 1947 (drama); *Renaud et Armide,* 1943 (drama); *The Eagle With Two Heads,* 1946, tr. 1962 (drama); *Bacchus,* 1952, tr. 1963 (drama).

English translations of Cocteau's works have been done by a variety of the author's devotees in England and the US. Among the translators particularly favored by Cocteau are Wallace Fowlie and Mary C. Hoeck. The latter was an ardent admirer and intimate friend of the poet.

Overview of Biographical Sources

With very few exceptions, biographers have generally been kind to Cocteau, so far. It is not without significance, however, that there is a lot of factual information yet to be brought into the open which may in time induce bolder approaches to assessing what Cocteau, the man, really amounts to. Some Cocteau biographies are products of complacent, self-indulging gossip-collectors. But professional, scholarly biographies are also available. The latter are often penetrating, offering stimulating insights into the spirit and idiosyncrasy of a man whose entire life was an unrelenting struggle promoting an ever changing, preposterous myth about himself, manufactured with countless masks and disguises, in a maze of shadows, forever fleeing from the predictable, the expected, the conventional. A man of theater par excellence, Cocteau will no doubt continue to tempt the chroniclers of an era that produced the essence of modernism, in a pre-war Paris that worshiped the unabashed esthetes of "scandal and parade," the Picassos, the Stravinskys, the artists and impressarios of ballets and circuses, catering to a new breed of insatiable thrill seekers. And as the myth Cocteau so intensely belabored to assert himself continues to be reinvented, the definitive biography of Cocteau is probably something impossible to contemplate.

Evaluation of Selected Biographies

Brown, Frederick, *An Impersonation of Angels. A Biography of Jean Cocteau.* New York: The Viking Press, 1968. This is a well written account of Cocteau's life and works based mainly on published documents, but also on conversations with Cocteau's acquaintances and some unpublished correspondence. As a biography, it is less thorough than some that were written after it (such as Kihm's, or Steegmuller's). It is also less detached, less reticent about the thrust of its author's conclusions and evaluations. The sense Brown conveys most clearly is that he simply does not admire most of his subject's attributes. In fact, his candor borders on utter cruelty as he speaks of a Cocteau "fertile in stillbirths," "lacking the confidence or the energy to make a statement of its own touting," "mourning its own sterility." Nonetheless, he shows himself more than capable of going beyond the temptation of mere malicious gossip and assesses Cocteau as an artist -intensely aware, versatile, witty, troubled, tragically flawed both as a man and as a poet, yet undeniably gifted and successful enough to have made himself a part of every significant artistic and literary event of his time.

Crosland, Margaret, *Jean Cocteau*. New York: Alfred A. Knopf, 1956. This is a rather summary account of Jean Cocteau's life and accomplishments, marred with some unfortunate inaccuracies, errors and misrepresentations. Of only moderate value as a biography, Crosland's book seems to offer testimony only to the Cocteau of a legend created either by Cocteau himself or by the gossip his extravagant life generated everywhere he made his presence felt. Despite the claim in the introduction that the author attempted to relate Cocteau's work to his life and experience, the attempt is only partially successful, weakened by uncritical presentations of major works, by lists of works simply mentioned in passing, and by a lack of any discernible effort to either trace an evolution or introduce new information. The book has nevertheless the merit of a succinct, readable presentation of Cocteau, based on conversations with him and many of his friends.

Sprigge, Elizabeth and Jean-Jacques Kihm, *Jean Cocteau: The Man and The Mirror*. London: Victor Gollancz, 1968. This is a richly documented biography written by two very knowledgeable Cocteau experts who knew Cocteau personally and managed to earn his trust. It seems that the authors' intent was to write an "objective" biography in order to separate the real human being Cocteau was from the myriad mirror-images that perpetrate Cocteau's legend. The book chronicles most of the important events of Cocteau's life, with noticeable concern for accuracy and detail but with an emphasis on the positive. It comes through as a gentle, polite, sympathetic treatment of a Cocteau that the authors have come to like. It is particularly rich in details on the circumstances surrounding the production of some of Cocteau's films and about his work as a visual artist.

Steegmuller, Francis, *Cocteau. A Biography*. Boston: Little, Brown, 1970. A very well documented scholarly study of Cocteau's life and art, this has been heralded by critics as an exceptional achievement and is the best biography of Cocteau so far. Written by a distinguished biographer/critic, the book earned added recognition by receiving the National Book Award. It is based on interviews, unpublished letters, Cocteau's published and unpublished texts, and critical writings on Cocteau. Steegmuller establishes Cocteau as an extremely complex man but not necessarily a mystery. He does not ignore Cocteau's flaws: his obsessive self-centeredness, his mean back-biting, his waspishness, his childish hero-worship, his shaky sense of style, the frivolousness of his Jack-of-all-trades approach to creativeness. But the biographer is favorably predisposed and invariably given to defending Cocteau. Without the slightest equivocation, he dismisses the suggestion that Cocteau is but a third rate writer, and treats him as no less than a real creative genius. The amount of detailed information collected for this task is unprecedented. It covers the entire background of Cocteau's most diverse activities, it probes into the psychology of his unwavering loyalties and savage quarrels, it offers detailed accounts of his friendships and love affairs, including a delightful diversion reserved in an appendix, a meeting with Barbette, the American trapeze artist and female impersonator admired by Cocteau in the 1920s, whom Steegmuller tracked down—with some ingenious detective work—in Austin, Texas.

Autobiographical Sources

The autobiographical material Jean Cocteau has made available to his biographers is abundant and irresistible. However artificial, manipulated, deliberately packaged for an effect, the already published portion of it does help throw light on some important aspects of his personality. Cocteau has often indicated that it would be impossible for him to write his memoirs. Nevertheless, he has written several texts which, when put together, come rather close to being just that. In *Opium* (1930), he left a diary of a disintoxication, a book that is crucial for understanding Cocteau's state of mind in the 1920s. In *Portraits-Souvenirs*, published in 1935, several articles published in the literary section of *Le Figaro* offer a lot of material useful for the biographer. In *The Difficulty of Being* (1947, 1966), an explicitly autobiographical narrative, Cocteau calmly speaks of his life, his youth, his work, his style, his legend, and of some of the people who played an important role in his life: Radiguet, Diaghilev, Nijinsky, Apollinaire, among others. In *Journal d'un inconnu* (1953) there is a succession of essays where the poet explains what he considers poetry, a work of art, relations between art and morality, and explanations of his quarrel with François Mauriac during the controversy stirred by the latter's violent attack on *Bacchus,* Cocteau's last play.

A good deal of Cocteau's personal papers are still unavailable to the public eye. A large part of his correspondence with his mother (it is known that he wrote over 1000 letters to her), and with many of his numerous friends and acquaintances, also remains unpublished.

Overview of Critical Sources

The critical studies that have been written on Cocteau so far bring out the multifaceted character of his professional achievements. Poet, draftsman, novelist, playwright, cineast, mystifier, prophet, dilettante, Cocteau had drawn fairly early in his career a great deal of attention, both from the critics of the press and from a variety of academics representing practically all of the fields encompassed in the vast domain of his creative "genius." In evaluating his work, critics have focused on his theater often with marked emphasis but not exactly unanimously. Between those who consider his cinema as his best work and those who favor his theater on the stage, opinions are somewhat divided. Lack of unanimity is also noticeable among those who probed into Cocteau's attempt to transform old, well-known myths. Though generally thought of as a "man of dialogue," Cocteau's manner of reworking the components of established myths has been viewed as ambivalent, lacking dialectic force and direction by some or as evidence of startling originality by others.

Evaluation of Selected Criticism

Brosse, Jacques, *Cocteau.* Paris: Gallimard, 1970. Brosse offers a comprehensive, detailed account of Cocteau's life and works, particularly useful for its summaries of key works and extensive documentation. Based on certain Freudian assumptions, focused sharply on Cocteau's treatment of the Oedipus myth, Brosse's thesis is constructed with interpretations of Cocteau's psychological complexion, in a manner that places the author in a most favorable light and undermines Cocteau's reputation as a liar or lacking seriousness. What the critic genuinely admires in Cocteau is the immensely gifted writer who has the courage to face up to his inner truth lucidly, relentlessly.

Crowson, Lydia, *The Esthetic of Jean Cocteau.* Hanover, NH: The University Press of New England, 1978. Written in a clear, very readable language, this essay attempts a lucid discussion of Cocteau's art based almost exclusively on his theater. Although the author claims to avail herself on the lessons of structuralists, her critical analysis of Cocteau's works is not in any strict or technical sense inspired by concepts derived from linguistic models. Rather, through a series of juxtapositions, the critic offers some very valid assessments of familiar Coctelian motifs, particularly in connection with his notions of truth and untruth, reality and illusion, the fragmentary nature of reality, and the effect and function of myth in artistic creation.

Dubourg, Pierre, *Dramaturgie de Jean Cocteau.* Paris: Grasset, 1954. Untranslated. This is the first comprehensive, detailed study of Cocteau's theater written by a fervent admirer. The author's stated intent is to dispel some misunderstandings about Cocteau, of the type that hastily and uncritically cast him as an insignificant clown. What he sees as Cocteau's major themes are the mystery of the unknown that surrounds us, the forces that guide us in spite of ourselves, the enigma or illusion of Free Will. His main argument is that the central theme of Cocteau's works is the drama of the poet's destiny. The critic concludes his study with a penetrating analysis of the film version of *Orpheus* which he treats as a summary of Cocteau's total artistic production. Indeed, Dubourg's book is successful in subverting the myth of Cocteau the joker, or Cocteau the juggler. It helps explain how Cocteau is solemn, dead serious.

Fowlie, Wallace, *The History of a Poet's Age.* Bloomington: Indiana University Press, 1966. This is one of the important books on Cocteau's life and works written by someone who knew the author personally and who also published several translations of Cocteau's texts with the latter's collaborations. With his characteristic, direct approach, Fowlie offers a generalized, sketchy overview of Cocteau's works which he views as manifestations of "poetry" in the sense Cocteau used that term. In Cocteau's creative achievements on record, the critic sees but one process, governed by the same laws in different media, by the poet as a novelist, the poet as a dramatist, the poet as a verse maker, the poet as a film-maker, etc. The book is also rich with biographical data, including a brief account of Picasso's role in Cocteau's art and an "epilogue" consisting of an account of a meeting with the author in Paris, three years before the latter's death. Fowlie's criticism is of a special kind: he comments on and describes only those aspects of Cocteau's work that he decided he can be positive and sympathetic about. In that respect, he typifies the "professorial" kind of critic, the kind who adjusts to the requirements for a teacher's mission in an American university classroom.

Oxenhandler, Neil, *Scandal and Parade: The Theater of Jean Cocteau.* New Brunswick, NJ: Rutgers University Press, 1957. This is by far the best study of Cocteau's theater to date. With a keen sense of relevance, the author discusses Cocteau's plays at length, occasionally giving some consideration to his films, assessing with a thoroughly professional objectivity Cocteau's indebtedness to Baudelaire, Apollinaire, Surrealism, and Expressionism. On another plane, his general assessment of Cocteau by reference to concepts of Existentialist psychoanalysis and the Sartrian concepts of liberty and commitment is also quite impressive. Oxenhandler aptly demonstrates that Cocteau's notion of liberty is different from Sartre's in that it is limited to the "liberty not to choose." Thus Cocteau's drama is situated in its historical context and judged with criteria reflecting a moralist's point of view, in what the critic convincingly establishes as the most relevant context for his subject, given the general cultural climate in Cocteau's lifetime. Thus, Cocteau's notion of the play as a poem, his orphism in the choice of images and metaphors, the suppressed theme of homosexuality and persecution, the ambiguity of his moral vision and in general his using art as an expiatory ritual against the despair of alienation, attest, according to Oxenhandler, to a special vision of the tragic, a vision that Cocteau derives from what he sees as "the tragedy of impotent will." By its conclusions, Oxenhandler's book is generally an unequivocal panegyric, finding cause for praise even in Cocteau's most obvious failures and contradictions.

Other Sources

Chiari, Joseph, *The Contemporary French Theater.* London: Rockliff, 1958. A study of twentieth century French playwrights including a chapter on Cocteau, strongly disapproving of the latter's tampering with old masterpieces and myths.

Evans, Arthur B. *Jean Cocteau and His Films of Orphic Identity.* Philadelphia: The Art Alliance Press, 1977. An informative, though rather brief and limited treatment of Cocteau's cinematic art.

Fraigneau, André, *Cocteau par lui-même*. Paris: Seuil, 1957. A competent biographical essay, enriched with attractive photographic illustrations.

Grossvogel, David, *Twentieth Century French Drama*. New York: Columbia University Press, 1961. A competent study on French theater, with a chapter on Cocteau.

Guicharnaud, Jacques, *Modern French Theater*. New Haven: Yale University Press, 1961. An enlightening overview of twentieth century French theater with a chapter on Cocteau.

Kihm, Jean-Jacques, *Cocteau*. Paris: Gallimard, 1960. A very thorough, comprehensive study written with the collaboration of Cocteau, by a friend and lucid admirer.

Knapp, Bettina L. *Jean Cocteau*. New York: Twayne, 1970. An incisive study of Cocteau and his works, written by a scholarly and very knowledgeable critic.

Magnan, Jean-Marie, *Cocteau*. Paris: Desclée de Brouwer, 1968. An interesting book attempting to define Cocteau's religious attitude through an analysis of key texts.

Mourgue, Gérard, *Cocteau*. Paris: Editions Universitaires, 1965. A very general, somewhat uncritical essay on Cocteau's works.

Peters, Arthur King, *Jean Cocteau and the French Scene*. New York: Abbeville, 1984. A collection of well written, short essays by known Cocteau enthusiasts and cognoscenti.

Surer, Paul, *Cinquante ans de théâtre*. Paris: Société d'Edition d'Enseignement Supérieur, 1969. Untranslated. A general study on important twentieth century playwrights including a chapter on Cocteau.

Selected Dictionaries and Encyclopedias
Hartnoll, Phillis, ed., *The Oxford Companion to the Theater*. 3rd ed. London: Oxford University Press, 1967. A very short entry on Cocteau as playwright.

Lemaître, Henri, *Dictionnaire Bordas de littérature française et francophone*. Paris: Bordas, 1985. A succinct but very thorough exposé on Cocteau's life and career followed by an annotated, comprehensive listing and summaries of selected works.

Quéant, Gilles, *Encyclopédie du Théâtre Contemporain*. Paris: Olivier Perrin, 1959. A brief survey of Cocteau's theater.

Constantin Toloudis
The University of Rhode Island

WILLIAM CONGREVE
1670-1729

Author's Chronology

Born January 24, 1670, at Bardsey, Yorkshire, England; *1681* in Ireland, enters Kilkenny College; *1686* enters Trinity College in Dublin; becomes interested in drama; *1691* studies law at the Middle Temple; becomes acquainted with John Dryden; *1692* publishes *Incognita* and other minor works; *1693* stages *The Old Batchelor* and *The Double Dealer*; meets Anne Bracegirdle; *1693-1694* publishes several minor poems; *1695* produces *Love for Love*; receives sinecure as a commissioner for licenses for hackney coaches; *1696* receives M.A. from Trinity; *1697* stages *The Mourning Bride*; replies to Jeremy Collier with *Amendments of Mr. Collier's False and Imperfect Citations; 1700* stages *The Way of the World; 1701* meets the Duchess of Marlborough; *1702* appointed as one of the heads of the new theater in Haymarket; *1705* becomes Commissioner for Wines; retires from active work in theater; *1710* almost blind, receives visit from Jonathan Swift; *1714* appointed Secretary to Jamaica and Searcher of Customs; *1723* Duchess of Marlborough gives birth to a daughter, probably Congreve's; *1726* receives visit from Voltaire; *1729* dies January 19.

Author's Bibliography (selected)

Incognita, 1692 (novel); *The Old Batchelor*, 1693 (comedy); *The Double Dealer*, 1693 (comedy); *Love for Love*, 1695 (comedy); "The Mourning Muse of Alexis," 1695 (pastoral poem); *The Mourning Bride*, 1697 (tragedy); *Amendments of Mr. Collier's False and Imperfect Citations* (essay); *The Way of the World*, 1700 (comedy); *The Judgment of Paris*, 1701 (masque); "A Hymn to Harmony in Honour of St. Cecilia's Day," 1701 (poem); *Semele*, 1707 (opera libretto).

Overview of Biographical Sources

The earliest biography of Congreve appeared in Giles Jacob's *The Political Register* (London: E. Curll, 1719); Jacob received much of his information directly from Congreve. Shortly after Congreve's death, Charles Wilson (a pseudonym) published *Memoirs of the Life, Writings, and Amours of William Congreve* (London: E. Curll, 1730); in spite of its closeness to the time of Congreve's life, the work is of very little value, being based in large part on hearsay. The first significant lengthy biography was the *Life of William Congreve*: Great Writers Series (New York: Thomas Whittaker, 1888), by Sir Edmund Gosse; the study had some inaccuracies and a large number of gaps. A revised and enlarged edition appeared in 1924; some new facts were added, but this volume also suffered from incompleteness. (Gosse's work was reissued in 1972 by the Kennikat Press of Port Washington, New York, but, amazingly, the very inadequate 1888 edition was used.) The critical biography by a Roumanian scholar, Dragos Protopesco, *Un classique moderne: William Congreve; sa vie, son ouevre* (Paris: editions La Vie Universitaire, 1924) contains some useful information but devotes too much attention to conjectures about sources; the work is not readily available in smaller libraries. The biography of D. Crane Taylor, *William Congreve* (1983) mildly criticizes Gosse's weaknesses, but it also contains factual inaccuracies and is of limited value. The standard biography is John C. Hodges, *William Congreve, The Man: A Biography From New Sources*: MLA General Series, No. 11 (1941); this study by one of the most notable of Congreve scholars is highly authoritative.

Evaluation of Selected Biographies

Hodges, John C. *William Congreve, The Man: A Biography From New Sources*. MLA General Series, No. 11. New York: Modern Language Association of America, 1941. Hodges corrected many previous blunders and introduced several new facts. In particular, he discovered the legal maneuvering surrounding Congreve's will, several points of which had been openly doubted by Taylor. The Hodges study is readable; it is organized well, has good documentation and an extensive index.

Taylor, D. Crane. *William Congreve*. London: Humphrey Milford, 1931. Taylor devoted two years to his book, beginning in 1921. Although not published immediately, it probably was largely finished by 1923, before Gosse's revised edition of 1924. Taylor added a preface expressing slight criticism of Gosse. Taylor corrected some old errors about Congreve and uncovered some new facts, but his work has been termed "extremely unreliable in both its facts and judgments."

Autobiographical Sources

Congreve wrote no autobiography, but in 1719 he welcomed the visit of Giles Jacob and supplied him with many facts for a proposed biographical sketch in *The Poetical Register*. Congreve's letters provide useful information about him; they appear in John C. Hodges' edition, *William Congreve: Letters and Documents* (New York: Harcourt, Brace and World, 1964).

Overview of Critical Sources

Until recent years full-length studies of Congreve were lacking because scholarship tended to discuss the Restoration dramatists as a group. The first major study in this century of Congreve and the other Restoration playwrights was John Palmer's *The Comedy of Manners* (London: G. Bell and Sons, 1913), which was the first work to attempt a careful definition of the term "comedy of manners" as it applied to Restoration drama. Since comedies of manners deal with the values and customs of a particular class and period, Palmer's work encouraged further studies of Restoration comedies in relation to the milieu in which they were produced.

Kathleen Lynch, in *The Social Mode of Restoration Comedy* (New York: Macmillan Company, 1926), studied the tradition of preciosity, defined as a very narrow and rigid code of love, and argued for its influence on Congreve. Dale Underwood's *Etherege and the Seventeenth Century Comedy of Manners*: Yale Studies in English, No. 135 (New Haven: Yale University Press, 1957) presents extremely valuable insights into the libertinism which influenced the thought of Restoration comic writers. Other writers have dealt with both the *préciosité* and the libertinism (or Neo-Epicureanism) of the age.

Palmer had been criticized by some for not adequately answering the charges of immorality which had frequently been made against Restoration comedy. Bonamy Dobrée, *Restoration Comedy 1660-1720* (Oxford: Oxford University Press, 1924) argued that the Restoration comic writers were satirizing the loose behavior of the age; he maintained that several of the comedies illustrate the enlightened values of an "honest man" and that they attempt to illustrate the foolish excesses of the age. The question of the morality of the Restoration playwrights remained an issue. Sister Rose Anthony in *The Jeremy Collier Stage Controversy 1698-1726* (Milwaukee: Marquette University Press, 1937) took the side of Collier in his famous attack of the Restoration theater; although the Anthony volume has its faults—factual inaccuracies and relatively weak criticism—it is still the most detailed analysis of the whole controversy in which Congreve was deeply involved. Attacks of Restoration drama on either moral or aesthetic grounds continued. The most significant of these attacks came in an essay by L. C. Knights "Restoration Comedy: The Reality and the Myth," *Explorations* (London: Chatto and Windus, 1946), and Knights' lines of argument were supported by D. R. M. Wilkinson, *The Comedy of Habit* (Leiden: Universitaire Pers, 1964) and John Wain, in "Restoration Comedy and Its Modern Critics," *Essays in Criticism*, VI (1965): 367-85. Opposition to Knights and his line of argument was expressed by Marvin Mudrick, in "Restoration Comedy and Later," *English Stage Comedy*, ed. W.K. Winsatt (New York: Columbia University Press, 1955), and by F. W. Bateson, in "Second Thoughts: L. C. Knights and Restoration Comedy," *Essays in Criticism*, VII (1957): 56-67, which asserts the basic seriousness of the intentions of the Restoration playwrights and uses Congreve's attitudes as expressed in *Love for Love* for a major part of his argument. In the past few decades several individual studies have appeared. Among those of a general nature are Bonamy Dobrée's *William Congreve*: Writers and Their Work, No. 164 (London: British Council, 1963), Kenneth Muir's "The Comedies of William Congreve," *Restoration Theatre*, ed. John Brown and Bernard Harris, Stratford-upon-Avon Studies, No. 6 (London: Shakespeare Institute, 1955), and Harold Love's *Congreve*: Plays and Playwrights Series (Totowa, New Jersey: Rowman and Littlefield, 1975). Studies with a narrower focus belong to Paul and Miriam Mueschke, *A New View of Congreve's Way of the World*: University of Michigan Contributions in Modern Philology, No. 23 (1958) and W. H. Van Voris, *The Cultivated Stance: The Designs of Congreve's Plays* (1965), both of which analyze aspects of the aesthetics of Congreve's work.

Evaluation of Selected Criticism

Mueschke, Paul and Miriam, *A New View of Congreve's Way of the World*. University of Michigan Contributions in Modern Philology, No. 23. Ann Arbor: University of Michigan Press, 1958. This brief study calls Congreve's final play the masterpiece of all Restoration comedies. It insists that the excellence of the play lies in carefully balanced structure, the ingenuity with which adultery is exposed through the integration of character, plot, and dialogue, and in the brilliance of its wit.

Novak, Maximillian E. *William Congreve*. New York: Twayne, 1971. Novak presents a good overview of Congreve's career. An opening chapter on the facts of and myths about Congreve's life precedes a chapter on his critical theory; then one separate chapter is given to each of Congreve's six major works (including *Incognita*). The work is readable and includes significant notes, a useful bibliography, and a good index. It also has some careless mistakes.

Van Voris, W. H. *The Cultivated Stance: The Designs of Congreve's Plays*. Dublin: The Dolmen Press, 1965. The work analyzes the structure of Congreve's plays, including his masque and opera, focusing mainly on the handling of time. The author attempts to clarify Congreve's basic personal and social values and his assumptions about art and nature. The "cultivated stance" was the role Congreve adopted: that of what Dobrée called "the honest man." The analyses of the plays are interesting, and the work is very readable; but it does not have sufficient documentation, and it lacks both a bibliography and an index.

Other Sources

Fujimura, Thomas H. *The Restoration Comedy of Wit*. Princeton: Princeton University Press, 1952. Fujimura's often-complimented work analyzes the significance of wit in Restoration comedy, arguing that the term "comedy of manners" does not fit the drama as well as "comedy of wit" would do; he finds that many of Congreve's characters, and indeed the characters of most Restoration comedy, are either Witlesses, Witwouds, or Truewits, this last group representing the heroes of the age.

Holland, Norman, *The First Modern Comedies*. Cambridge: Harvard University Press, 1959. Holland presents an excellent study of the difference between appearance and reality in Restoration plays.

Leech, Clifford, "Congreve and the Century's End." *Philological Quarterly*, XLI (1962): 275-293. The essay analyzes Congreve's difficulty as a writer of the 1690s, a time of significant change as the drama moved from the older comic traditions toward the new practices which would dominate the early 1700s.

Morris, Brian, ed. *William Congreve*. Totowa, NJ: Rowman and Littlefield, 1972. The volume contains nine papers delivered by Congreve scholars honoring the tercentenary of Congreve's birth.

Perry, Henry Ten Eyck, *The Comic Spirit of Restoration Drama*. New Haven: Yale University Press, 1925. Perry's early work emphasizes the plays as dramas rather than as social or moral commentaries.

Selected Dictionaries and Encyclopedias

British Writers, Vol. 2 (*Thomas Middleton to George Farquahar*), Charles Scribner's Sons, 1979. Rather substantial biographical and critical overview of Congreve by Bonamy Dobrée, with substantial bibliography.

Critical Survey of Poetry: English Language Series, Vol. 2. Salem Press, 1982. Concise biography with analysis of Congreve's literary career.

Howard L. Ford
North Texas State University

PIERRE CORNEILLE
1606-1684

Author's Chronology

Born June 6, 1606, of middle-class parents at Rouen, in Normandy; *1615* enters that city's Jesuit school, one of the best in France at the time; *1622* begins his study of law and passes the bar examination two years later; soon abandons his career in law for that of dramatist; *1629* writes his first play, *Mélite*, followed by six successful plays culminating with *Le Cid* (1637), his masterpiece; remains silent for three years after harsh criticism of *Le Cid* by the French Academy; *1640* renews writing for the theater with *Horace*, followed by *Cinna* (1641) and *Polyeucte* (1642), each considered to be among his greatest plays; *1643* weds Marie de Lamperiére; *1643-1650* produces seven new plays among which is the well- known *Rodogune* (1647); *1647* elected to the French Academy; *1650-1652* writes three more plays including *Nicomède* (1651), and publishes the first twenty chapters of the *Imitation of Jesus Christ* (1651); *1656* completes the *Imitation* and helps his younger brother, Thomas, launch his own career as a playwright; *1660* publishes three "Discours" on dramatic art; *1661-1667* composes seven more plays of unequal merit; *1671* produces two new plays, one of which (*Psyché*) is a collaborative effort with Quinault and Molière; *1672 Pulchérie* performed; *1674* writes his last tragedy, *Suréna*, and retires as a playwright; *1674* loses his government pension, which he regains in 1682; September 30,1684, dies in Paris.

Author's Bibliography

There were seven editions of Corneille's plays during his period of life, the most important being the editions of 1644 and 1660 since they incorporate many textual changes and variants as well as commentaries by the author. Corneille wrote 32 plays (excluding the play that he wrote jointly with Quinault and Molière.) Of these, the most important are: 1636 *L'Illusion comique*; 1636 *Le Cid*; 1640 *Horace*; 1641 *Cinna*; 1642 *Polyeucte*; 1645 *Rodogune*; 1650 *Nicomède*. Although dated, the standard definitive French edition of Corneille's works is Marty-Laveaux's, in the series Les Grands Ecrivains de la France, 12 volumes (1862-1868).

Corneille holds the distinction of being the first French playwright to be translated into English during his lifetime. Performances of his plays in translation were common during the first decades of the Restoration in England. There is no edition of his complete dramatic works in English. The best modern edition of his principal plays in English is that of Lacy Lockert, *The Chief Plays of Corneille* (Princeton University Press, 1957; rpt. 1971). It includes six of the seven above-mentioned major plays (*L'Illusion comique* excepted.) Paul Landis has translated two of these plays (*Le Cid* and *Cinna*) for the Modern Library edition of *Plays of Corneille and Racine* (New York: Random House, 1931). The best English translation of his masterpiece, *Le Cid*, is by John C. Lapp for the AHM Crofts Classics Series (AHM Publishing, 1955).

Overview of Biographical Sources

Curiously enough, little is known about the life of this great playwright. He was a very private individual who shunned even socializing with the *literati* of the period. He lived the ordinary, drab life of a good bourgeois family man. Indeed, there is no relationship between his own uneventful life and the existence of those superheroes and heroines that he created for the stage. Because his life seems to have had minimal effect upon the plays, scholars, critics and students have concentrated instead on his literary output. The few books which attempt to shed light on his existence are mostly in French. One of the earliest studies, Auguste Dorchain's *Pierre Corneille* (Paris: Garnier, 1918) is still the best complete study of Corneille's life. Robert Brasillach's *Pierre Corneille* (Paris: Fayard, 1961) is a penetrating study which combines biography and criticism. One of the best studies in English of Corneille's life and works is Henry Carrington Lancaster's "The Period of Corneille", II, vol. I in his monumental *A History of French Dramatic Literature in the XVIIth century*, 9 vols. (Baltimore: Johns Hopkins University Press, 1929-1942). Claude Abraham's *Pierre Corneille* (New York: Twayne, 1972) has a good chapter on the author's life which should satisfy the general reader.

Evaluation of Selected Biographies

Couton, Georges, *Corneille*. Paris: Hatier, 1958; rev. ed. 1969. This is a first-rate study in French on Corneille, an indispensable guide for biographical and historical facts. The work shows this scholar's own contribution to the literary historian's critical method.

Yarrow, P.J. *Corneille*. New York: St. Martin's Press, 1963. A good introduction to Corneille done in English. The author gives the reader a concise picture of the dramatist's career and of his milieu. However, some critics feel that this work is highly opinionated and judgmental which, in turn, could lead the non-expert astray.

Autobiographical Sources

Critics have usually turned to Corneille's "prefaces" and the "examens" of his own plays for any clues concerning major biographical or historical points. The correspondence in which he engaged was slight by seventeenth-century standards and provides very little information on his theatrical output.

Overview of Critical Sources

As one would expect, the scholarship on a major writer during France's so-called "Classical Age" of literature is prodigious. Cioranescu alone lists over 1200 entries and his listings are only up to 1960! The last twenty years have seen a richness of Anglo-American research and publication on Corneille's works. The following is a sampling of some of the better studies done in English, with preference given to the more general ones.

Evaluation of Selected Criticism

Fogel, Herbert, *The Criticism of Cornelian Tragedy: A Study of Critical Writing from the Seventeenth to the Twentieth Century*. New York: Exposition Press, 1967. Students should find this book helpful since it surveys the major French critical attitudes towards Corneille down through the centuries as well as the various schools of criticism. Although incomplete in its treatment, the work is a useful reasearch tool.

Harwood, Sharon, *Rhetoric in the Tragedies of Corneille*. New Orleans: Tulane University Press, 1977. This is another examination of Corneille's style of writing. The author shows that Corneille was not interested in imitating the Aristotelian concepts of terror and pity in tragedy, but appealed rather to his audience's liking of certain rhetorical devices as practiced by Cicero and Quintilian. The critic probes into some of the major rhetorical devices found in Corneille.

Mallinson, G.J. *The Comedies of Corneille: Experiments in the Comic*. Manchester: Manchester University Press, 1984. One of the more recent and best studies on Corneille's comedies, this is a very thorough reappraisal of the eight comedies that he wrote, showing the special comic features of each. A lot of emphasis is placed on rhetoric, such as Corneille's techniques of ambiguity along with his use of parody.

Muratore, Mary Jo, *The Evolution of the Cornelian Heroine*. Madrid: Porrua Turanzas, 1982. The companion study to Nelson's work on the Cornelian hero, this book traces the evolution from Corneille's early "idealist" heroines to the later more "reactive" heroines. The author examines the ethical and psychological complexity of characters in their relations with others and themselves.

Nelson, Robert J. *Corneille, His Heroes and Their Worlds*. Philadelphia: University of Pennsylvania Press, 1963. The general reader should begin by reading this excellent book. It is an interesting and stimulating study of Corneille's dramatic universe, in particular his tragic heroes. The book focuses as much on the youthful works as it does on the more mature plays.

Other Sources

Cabeen, David C. and Jules Brody, *A Critical Bibliography of French Literature, Volume III: The Seventeenth Century*. Syracuse: Syracuse University Press, 1961.

Also supplemental Volume IIIA: 1983. An annotated compilation of selected Cornelian scholarship. Very useful to the general reader and specialists of the period.

Cioranescu, Alexandre, *Bibliographie de la littérature francaise du dix-septième siècle*. 3 vols. Paris: CNRS, 1965-66. This major bibliography contains the most comprehensive listings of Cornelian scholarship. Coverage of primary and secondary sources to 1960.

Vedvik, Jerry D., *et al. Descriptive Bibliography of French Seventeenth-Century Studies*. Fort Collins, CO: Colorado State University, 1953 to date. This on-going annual bibliography is a good supplement to the Cabeen for information on Corneille. Although not "critical", it contains elaborate commentaries on the works listed.

Raymond LePage
George Mason University

GABRIELE D'ANNUNZIO
1863-1938

Author's Chronology

Born March 12, 1863, in Pescara, Italy, to Francesco Paolo Rapagnetta D'Annunzio and Luisa de Benedictis; *1874* having received the best possible elementary education available in his provincial backwater, is sent to boarding school in Prato where he shines for intelligence and audacity; *1879* father has his first collection of lyric poetry published, *Primo Vere*; *1881* completes secondary studies and enrolls at the University of Rome, leaving the first in a long series of loves behind; *1882* D'Annunzio quickly abandons his studies for an intense journalistic and artistic life, publishing in major Roman periodicals and entering the sophisticated world of high society; *1883* in the midst of a whirlwind existence of articles, poems, love affairs, social engagements, and duels, meets and seduces the young duchess, Maria Hardouin, whom he marries after a romantic elopement; *1884-1891* resides alternately in Rome and in his native region, the Abruzzi; separates from wife after the birth of three sons; enters into a devastatingly passionate love story with Barbara Leoni who inspires some of his best poetry and figures prominently in the novel cycle, the Romances of the Rose, which includes *The Child of Pleasure* (1889, 1898), *The Intruder* (1892), and the *Triumph of Death* (1894, 1896); dabbles in writing lyrical dramatic pieces; *1891-1893* moves to Naples to write for a newspaper and meets the princess Maria Gravina Anguissola who abandons her family and eventually bears D'Annunzio two children; *1893-1896* retreats to the Abruzzi to work, often living with the painter Francesco Paolo Michetti and devoting himself to writing and travels in Greece and Venice where he befriends the celebrated actress, Eleonora Duse; *1897* elected deputy to the Italian Parliament from the Abruzzi, marking the start of D'Annunzio's political involvement and produces his first real play, *Sogno d'un mattino di primavera*, initiating his long artistic collaboration with Duse as his leading lady; *1898* settles permanently at the opulent villa, La Capponcina, outside Florence with Duse as his neighbor, friend and mistress, has his first major play, *The Dead City* (1902), produced in France with Sarah Bernhardt starring; *1899-1904* Duse continues to work for D'Annunzio the playwright, presenting his tragedies to an often resistant public, among them *La Gioconda* (1899) and the successful *Francesca da Rimini* (1901, 1902), but the two separate after a series of personal betrayals by the writer who had published a fictionalized account of their affair in the novel *The Flame of Life* (1900) and later offered the lead role in his best drama, *The Daughter of Jorio* (1904, 1907) to a younger actress; *1910* forced to abandon Italy because of his extraordinary debts, D'Annunzio leaves for France where he resides until 1915, continuing his notorious existence and composing in French, notably *Le martyre de Saint Sébastien* (1911)with music by Debussy; *1915* returns to Italy on the eve of war to carry on a nationalistic campaign for intervention; volunteers for military service, becoming a hero and achieving the rank of colonel after receiving five silver and one gold medal but also losing an eye; *1919* invades and occupies the city of Fiume with a group of followers as a protest against the "mutilated victory", becoming virtual dictator of that area until January 28, 1921; *1921-1938* goes into permanent retirement at a villa on Lake Garda renamed the Vittoriale degli Italiani which he transforms into a living museum of his life and interests; his isolation is interrupted by rare visits, the grant of a patent of nobility as Prince of Montevevoso (1924) and the accession to the presidency of the Fascist Italian Royal Academy (1937); March 1, 1938, D'Annunzio dies suddenly of a cerebral hemorrhage at his lake retreat.

Author's Bibliography

A prolific and self-revealing writer, D'Annunzio's works fill many volumes and include numerous poetry collections, several lengthy novels, novellas, short stories, essays, diaries, remembrances, orations, political writings, a biography, newspaper articles, fifteen plays, and a few lyric pieces in dialogue form. The complete works were published during the author's lifetime as *Opera omnia* in 48 volumes with an Index in vol. 49 (Milano: Mondadori, 1926-1937). The third section of this vast work includes all of D'Annunzio's theatrical production: "III. Tragedie, misteri e sogni" (vols. XX-XXXIV). The Mondadori publishing house also issued a more accessible, commercial edition in ten books, under the aegis of the Fondazione "Il Vittoriale degli Italiani," which specializes in D'Annunzian memorabilia: *Tutte le opere*, ed. Egidio Bianchetti, 10 vols. (Milano: Mondadori, 1939-50). *Tragedie, sogni e misteri* comprise two volumes of this edition. D'Annunzio's plays were all individually published between 1897 and 1920 in the original language of composition. The most popular of these dramas were quickly translated into English as well, due in part to the playwright's notoriety and in part to Duse's stirring renditions of her D'Annunzian roles. The famous theater specialist, Arthur Symons, translated both *Francesca da Rimini* and *La Gioconda* while another admirer of D'Annunzio, Charlotte Porter, was responsible for *La figlia di Jorio*. Besides the early editions of these translations, a number of reprints have quite recently appeared, signalling a renewed international interest in the Italian playwright. *Francesca de Rimini*, in an English verse version, was first published in New York by Frederick A. Stokes in 1902; it is also included in *Continental Plays*, ed. by T.H. Dickinson, vol. 1 (Boston, 1935). *La Gioconda* can be found in *Chief Contemporary dramatists, second series, vol. 2* (Boston: Houghton Mifflin, 1921), another anthology prepared by T.H. Dickinson, and in *Types of Domestic Tragedy*, ed. R.M. Smith (New York, 1928). Both *Francesca de Rimini* and *La Gioconda*, in Symons' translations, were reprinted by the Foundation for Classical Reprints (Albuquerque) in 1983. D'Annunzio's dramatic masterpiece, *The Daughter of Jorio*, was translated soon after it premiered in 1904 by Charlotte Porter, Pietro Isola, and Alice Henry (Boston: Little Brown, 1907). This rendering was reprinted by Greenwood Press (Westport, CT.) in 1968 and can also be found in

Representative Continental Drama, ed. Montrose J. Moses (Boston: Little Brown, 1926). Finally, *The Dead City* was given English dress by G. Mantellini (Chicago: Laird and Lee, 1902), later published in *The Eleonora Duse Series of Plays*, ed. O.M. Say (New York, 1923). The probable reason for so few translations of D'Annunzio's plays into English (most were quickly rendered into French and other languages) lies with the dramatist's language, themes, and politics. D'Annunzio's vocabulary is both elaborate and recondite, punctuated with lyrical rhythms and poetic phrasing. The sensationalism, violence, and erotic nature of his subject matter linked to the rhetorical flourish of his idiom made D'Annunzio's works somewhat unappealing to the Anglo-American audiences, even at the time of the great Duse's performances. In addition, D'Annunzio's association with Fascism made him ideologically distasteful during and following the Second World War. Besides the plays listed, much of D'Annunzio's better poetry and his novels have been translated into English.

Overview of Biographical Sources

    Gabriele D'Annunzio's life was a series of extraordinary exploits: literary, political, amorous, and military. His name constantly appeared in newspapers and magazines: on the front page, in the society column, in the literary section, in political and cultural editorials. He was a legend in his own time, feted and courted, detested and adored. Both his life and his books caused scandal and invited polemics. By 1900 he was the most famous (and infamous) living writer in Europe. Therefore, it is not surprising that he became a biographical subject quite early in his long career. With the advent of Fascism, D'Annunzio was an official symbol of the new order which he had helped create in both word (the numerous political writings) and deed (the daring warrior and the dictator of Fiume); consequently, he became the hero of a number of admiring biographies written in Italian. At the same time, his relationship with another living legend, Eleonora Duse, also made him one of the principals in her biographies. In point of fact, much of the best information about D'Annunzio and the theater is to be found in books dedicated to his celebrated mistress. The man, perhaps more than the writer, exerted much fascination on the Anglo-American world. The titles of two of these biographies speak for the contents: Federico Nardelli and Arthur Livingston's *Gabriel the Archangel* (New York: Harcourt, Brace, 1931) and Anthony Rhodes' *The Poet as Superman: A Life of Gabriele D'Annunzio* (London: Weidenfeld & Nicolson, 1959). The emphasis on anecdote and adventure also appears in those works centering on Duse or the Duse-D'Annunzio affair. However, in these books, there are two Gabrieles: a positive figure and a romantic villain. Jeanne Bordeux opts for the former in her *Eleonora Duse: The Story of her Life* (New York: George H. Doran, 1925); this biographer's D'Annunzio is The Lover and his Beloved is an extraordinary woman—together they are "two great souls" joined in their artistic and intellectual bond. Unfortunately, Bordeux invents conversations and is not exceptionally insightful, informative, or accurate. Others are also caught up in the mythic love story to the detriment of historical judgment, often choosing sides. In *Age Cannot Wither: The Story of Duse and D'Annunzio* (Philadelphia and New York: Lippincott, 1947), Bertita Harding paints D'Annunzio as Egotist, stressing Duse's mission and self-immolation to his art because of her great love. A happier mean is to be found in Emil Alphons Rheinhardt's *Life of Eleonora Duse* (London: Martin Secker, 1930) and Frances Winwar's *Wingless Victory* (Westport, CT: Greenwood Press, 1974 [reprint of 1956 edition]), which are much more factual and less biased. Winwar's volume stresses the life of D'Annunzio and offers numerous interviews, letters, and documents but also utilizes the novels and poetry as biographical sources. More recent, Giovanni Pontiero's "Introduction" to *Duse on Tour. Guido Noccioli's Diaries, 1906-07* (Amherst: University of Massachusetts Press, 1982) emphasizes the artistic collaboration of the lovers and briefly critiques the works in which Duse appeared in order to clarify the spirituality of the actress in her approach to these dramas. Finally, there is Jeffrey Meyers' study of writers and politics: *A Fever at the Core: The Idealist in Politics* (London and New York: Barnes and Noble, 1976). D'Annunzio is analyzed and compared to the other subjects of the book: Blunt, Graham, T.E. Laurence, Casement, and Malraux.

Evaluation of Selected Biographies

Antongini, Tom, *D'Annunzio*. Freeport, NY: Books for Libraries Press, 1971 (reprint of a 1938 edition). Antongini was D'Annunzio's personal secretary for more than thirty years. This book of memories offers anecdotes, reminiscences, and documents in order to examine the man and "lift the veil which covers this mysterious personality" (p. vi). The text blends gossip and psychological interpretation by an actual witness to many of the events in the dramatist's life. Not chronological, it offers a series of themes such as "D'Annunzio and money" or "D'Annunzio and the theatre" which, taken as a whole, give much insight into the "private" man rather than the exalted public figure more visible during the Fascist regime. Although Antongini purports objectivity, there is a grudging admiration for "the Poet" (as D'Annunzio is often called) as well as a sincere belief in the writer's genius. It is an amusing journey into the secret life and foibles of an international celebrity told by someone of wit and intelligence.

Jullian, Philippe, *d'Annunzio*. London: Pall Mall, 1972. Translated from the French, this is doubtlessly the best available biography in English. The element of scandal is ever-present for Jullian enjoys underlining the erotic nature of D'Annunzio's existence, depicting him in his metamorphosis from young Faun to modern Tiberius at Capri (the Vittoriale). The dramatist is presented as a petty bourgeois who "succeeded in living his wildest dreams" as a new Don Juan, the perfect aesthete, daring aviator, and modern dictator. The biographer seeks to balance the legend and the reality of the man yet gives significance to D'Annunzio's cult of

beauty, lyricism, and modernity. In the discussion of the works, French comparisons are stressed as is the connection between D'Annunzian decadence and romanticism.

    Weaver, William, *Duse. A Biography*. New York: Harcourt, Brace, Jovanovich,
1984. "Part Two 1894-1904" follows the gradual development of the Duse-
D'Annunzio affair and collaboration, using many of Duse's letters and other significant documentation. Their artistic pact is outlined and detailed: he would write
great plays to reform Italian theater and she would be their interpretive soul.
Weaver notes that Duse and D'Annunzio were joined as much in their love of art as
in their mutual attraction.

Autobiographical Sources

    Many of D'Annunzio's writings are autobiographical, particularly those com-
posed during the final years of his life, among them: the *Notturno* (1921), *Le
faville del maglio* (1924-1928), the *Libro segreto* (1935), and *Solus ad solam*
(1939). Unfortunately, these meditations, diaries, and thoughts have not been translated into English—nor have the thousands of letters of his vast epistolary. Editions
of his letters to Eleonora Duse, Barbara Leoni, and Benito Mussolini have appeared in Italian during the last few decades. However, in D'Annunzio the distinction between life and art is often blurred and his novels and poetry are transfigured
fictions of his experiences offering some indication of his erotic tendencies, liai-
sons, and psychological make-up. Naturally, the reader must take care not to con-
fuse the writer with the protagonist: the two are not totally interchangeable. The
other sources of autobiographical writings in English are the books cited above,
since the biographers of D'Annunzio and Duse were obliged to translate the documents quoted in their texts.

Overview of Critical Sources

    D'Annunzio's popularity with literary critics has undergone a series of reversals
and transformations. At the turn of the century, there was a marked tendency to
condemn the writer on moral grounds, while the great Italian scholar Benedetto
Croce set the intellectual tone by accusing D'Annunzio of "psychic dilettantism"
and artificiality. Less severe critics noted early on the bond joining art and life and
the beauty of the author's language. One thing was immediately clear, even by
1910: Italian letters had been permanently influenced and marked by Gabriele
D'Annunzio. The writer's popularity naturally grew under the Fascist regime,
which he seemed to personify artistically, and declined with Mussolini's fall. The
Italian tendency to read D'Annunzio biographically, morally, and politically was
repeated abroad. In the English-speaking world, D'Annunzio was analyzed and
interpreted according to the critic's ethical and ideological biases: extolled or deni-

grated. As the attitudes towards the Fascist state deteriorated, so did D'Annunzio's fortunes abroad. Very little has been written on D'Annunzio in English since the 1930s. What was written is often superficial and prejudiced. There has been a Renaissance in D'Annunzio studies in Italy post-1960 due in large measure to the changing trends in literary criticism. In a seminal work, Carlo Salinari placed D'Annunzio firmly in the historical reality of fin-de-siècle Italy, beginning a trend in the socio-cultural interpretation of the writer's *opus*. At the same time, structuralists and semioticians have been analyzing D'Annunzio's unique language while marxist critics have been judging the writer's historical position and ideological references. There are literally dozens of books and thousands of articles published on Gabriele D'Annunzio in Italian and French. Indeed, a number of extensive bibliographies have been prepared and some will be cited later in this essay. It should be noted, however, that D'Annunzio's theater remains the least studied of his works. Most criticism is directed to either his poetry or his fiction.

Evaluation of Selected Criticism

Gullace, Giovanni, *Gabriele D'Annunzio in France. A Study in Cultural Relations*. Syracuse: Syracuse University Press, 1966. Although this work is clearly French-oriented, it is one of the few available books in English dedicated to D'Annunzio's works rather than to his life. Part II deals exclusively with the subject as dramatist, emphasizing his intense lyricism, rejection of realism, symbolism, and cult of beauty. Gullace notes the lack of character development and dramatic action as serious theatrical flaws but admires the evocative qualities and emotional depth of the language. The critic points to the Nietzschean influences on the playwright, the depiction of a superman-hero and destructively beautiful female protagonists, as well as D'Annunzio's desire to re-create Greek tragedy in modern garb. The plays are all described and analyzed (with a tendency to making comparisons with French writers) for their dramatic worth and inherent qualities and flaws. The approach is fair and unclouded by individual biases.

Hastings, R. "D'Annunzio's Theatrical Experiment," in *The Modern Language Review*, Vol. 66 (1971): 85-93. This is a significant article devoted to the dramatist's desire to create an "orgiastic experience" with a cathartic, religious (not Christian) function similar to that offered by ancient Greek tragedy as described by Nietzsche. Hastings describes D'Annunzio's means to this end: naked elemental passions, succubus figures, shock tactics such as spectacle, sound effects, ritual elements, provocation, scandal, fostering of atavistic fears about sexuality and incest, sado-masochism, and excitement. The critic also notes that the playwright has failed because of his lack of dramatic sense.

MacClintock, Lander, "Gabriele D'Annunzio," in *The Contemporary Drama of Italy*. Boston: Little, Brown, 1920. pp. 94-134. This is a portrait of D'Annunzio as an (un)Italian dramatist. A standard depiction of the playwright's qualities and defects with a psychological tinge, the chapter shows D'Annunzio as the embodiment of his nation's dying past, with a genius for poetry and description but a lack of drama. MacClintock notes the eloquence, splendor, and pageantry of the plays while criticizing their erotic excesses. The critic demonstrates how the plays integrate Nietzschean ideas, particularly that of the superman, while suffering from "a state of ecstatic immobility". Knowledgeable about matters theatrical, MacClintock offers reasonable explanations for the failure of many of D'Annunzio's works on the stage, concluding that most should be read not seen.

Praz, Mario, *The Romantic Agony*. 2nd ed. New York: Oxford University Press, 1951. A seminal book, Praz's study of European Decadentism clearly situates D'Annunzio within this cultural movement: indeed he is its "most monumental figure." The dramatist appears mostly in the chapters "La Belle Dame Sans Merci" and "Byzantium," the former being an analysis of the *femme fatale* and how this figure is portrayed in D'Annunzian novels, poetry and plays. Praz is one of the first to note the Italian writer's debt to French and Anglo sources, notably Flaubert and Swinburne, and to tie his sado-erotic motifs (blood lust, incest, transgression, barbarity) to his Abruzzese origins.

Other Sources

Carlson, Marvin, *The Italian Stage from Goldoni to D'Annunzio*. Jefferson, NC: McFarland, 1981. This book concludes with a short study of how D'Annunzio breaks with realism in theater and presents the Duse-D'Annunzio affair.

Dukes, Ashley, "Italy. Gabriele D'Annunzio," in *Modern Dramatists*. Chicago: Charles H. Seigel, 1911. Dukes emphasizes the dramatist as a "word-painter" who has ties with Symbolist theater and has revolted against the bourgeois theater then in vogue.

Forcella, Roberto, *D'Annunzio*. 4 vols. New York: Burt Franklin, 1973. A reprint of 1926-1927 bibliography of D'Annunzian studies. Extensive data.

Fucilla, Joseph C. and J.M. Carrière. *D'Annunzio Abroad*. 2 vols. New York: Institute for French Studies, 1935-1937. This work contains more than 2500 entries in a bibliography covering non-Italian sources.

Getto, Giovanni, *Tre studi sul teatro*. Caltanisetta: Sciascia, 1976. One of Getto's three theatrical studies is dedicated to *The Dead City*, using modern critical techniques.

Herrmann, Oscar, *Living Dramatists: Pinero Ibsen and D'Annunzio*. New York: Gordon Press, 1977. A reprint of a 1905 edition. Interesting because it offers insight into the reactions to D'Annunzio's theater at the time it was produced. It does not cover the later plays.

MacClintock, Lander, "The Decline of the Realist Tradition," in *The Age of Pirandello*. New York: Indiana University Press, 1968. A reprint of a 1951 edition. D'Annunzio as a superb craftsman of language and lover of beauty who appeals to the senses in opposition to the realism of earlier Italian drama.

Porter, Charlotte, "Introduction," to *The Daughter of Jorio. A Pastoral Tragedy*, by Gabriele D'Annunzio. New York: Greenwood Press, 1968. A reprint of a 1907 edition. Porter emphasizes the primitive and tragic beauty of this play based on folklore noting its picturesqueness and spirit of mystery.

Salinari, Carlo, *Miti e coscienza del decadentismo italiano*. Milano: 1960, pp. 29-107. An important work, done with considerable historical accuracy, which places the D'Annunzian myths in an exact historical context.

Sharp, William, *Studies and Appreciations*. Freeport, NY: Books for Libraries, 1967. A reprint of a 1912 edition. The critic dedicates some thirty pages to the earlier plays of D'Annunzio, especially *The Dead City* and *La Gloria*.

Symons, Arthur, "Introduction," to *Francesca da Rimini*, by Gabriele D'Annunzio. New York: Frederick A. Stokes, 1902. Discusses the difficulty of translating the dramatist into English and analyzes the play as a love tragedy but also a "study of an age of blood," the Italian Middle Ages.

Fiora A. Bassanese
University of Massachusetts
Boston

THOMAS D'URFEY
c. 1653-1723

Author's Chronology

Born Devonshire about 1653 (documentary evidence unavailable) to Severinus and Frances D'Urfey; *1676* after period as scrivener's apprentice, receives acclaim of Charles II on the performance of his first comedy, *Madam Fickle*, and becomes attached to the court; *1676-1682* entertains nobility with his songs at Whitehall, Winchester, Newmarket, Windsor, and establishes friendship with composers Henry Purcell, Thomas Farmer, and Dr. John Blow; *1681-1683* writes four political satires on Shaftesbury and the Whigs; *1683-1685* attains fame and wealth through the publication of song collections, with music, both in single sheets and in volumes; *1689* spends summer as singing teacher at Josias Priest's boarding school for girls at Chelsea and there writes epilogue for the Tate-Purcell opera, *Dido and Aeneas*; *1690-1691* establishes newspaper, *Momus Ridens: or, Comical Remarks on the Publick Reports*, facetious poems on recent news events; publishes four political satires, three of them anonymously, in service of the Whigs; *1694* enjoys greatest dramatic success in the first two parts of *The Comical History of Don Quixote*, for which Purcell had written the music; *1695* writes "Gloriana, A Funeral Pindarique Ode," in memory of Queen Mary; *1698* attacked by Jeremy Collier in *A Short View of the Immorality and Profaneness of the English Stage* because of Collier's objections to *Don Quixote*; responds to Collier in a song "New Reformation begins through the Nation!" which he placed in the "Preface" to *The Campaigners*. Indictment brought against him by justices of Middlesex for having written *Don Quixote*; *1704* publishes *Tales Tragical and Comical*, the first group of the thirteen narrative tales in prose and verse, which also include *Stories Moral and Comical* (1706) and *New Operas* (1721); *1713* benefit performance of his comedy *A Fond Husband: or The Plotting Sisters* at Drury Lane, arranged for him by Joseph Addison and Richard Steele; *1714* benefit performance of his comedy *Court Gallantry: or, Marriage A-la-Mode* at Drury Lane; *1719* publishes *Songs Compleat, Pleasant and Divertive*, reissued later that year as *Wit and Mirth: or, Pills to Purge Melancholy*; *1723* dies in poverty on February 26; buried at St. James Church, Piccadilly, at the expense of the Earl of Dorset.

Author's Bibliography (selected)

Madam Fickle, 1677 (comedy); *A New Collection of Songs and Poems*, 1683 (songs); *Momus Ridens*, 1690 (newspaper); *The Comical History of Don Quixote*, 1694 (comedy); *A New Opera, call'd Cinthia and Endimion*, 1697 (dramatic opera); *The Famous History of the Rise and Fall of Massaniello: or A Fisherman a Prince*, 1700 (tragedy); *Tales Tragical and Comical*, 1704 (narrative tales); *Wonders in the Sun: or, The Kingdom of the Birds*, 1706 (dramatic opera); *Wit and Mirth: Or Pills to Purge Melancholy*, 1719 (songs).

Overview of Biographical Sources

Although Thomas D'Urfey was one of the most prolific playwrights of his time, as well as one of the most accomplished lyricists, and although he traveled in the company of the social luminaries of his day, no biographer has written a full-length study of his life. Three reliable brief accounts of his life are available, however: J.B. Ebsworth's sketch of his life in *The Dictionary of National Biography*: Cyrus Lawrence Day's "Life," which serves as a partial introduction to his edition, *The Songs of D'Urfey*, (1933) and an entry in *A Biographical Dictionary of Actors, Actresses, Musicians, Dancers, Managers, and Other Stage Personnel in London, 1660-1800*, edited by Philip H. Highfill, Jr., Kalman A. Burnim, and Edward A. Langhans (1975).

Biographical entries on D'Urfey in recent literary dictionaries give useful, though brief, accounts of the playwright. *Everyman's Dictionary of Literary Biography, English and American*, compiled after John W. Cousin by D.C. Browning (London: J.M. Dent, 1958) contains a short, though balanced, sketch of D'Urfey. *British Authors Before 1800: A Biographical Dictionary*, edited by Stanley J. Kunitz and Howard Haycraft (New York: H.W. Wilson, 1952) contains a brief, insightful biography.

Evaluation of Selected Biographies

Day, Cyrus Lawrence, "Life" in *The Songs of Thomas D'Urfey* (Cambridge: Harvard University Press, 1933). Day's biography, the fullest biographical account of the playwright to date is painstakingly researched. Day provides a thorough social and historical context for D'Urfey's life and works. Day's treatment of D'Urfey's transferring of political loyalties to William, as soon as the poet was assured of the permanence of the monarch's reign, is candid.

Ebsworth, J.B. "Thomas D'Urfey," in *A Dictionary of National Biography* is a straghtforward summary of the most important events of D'Urfey's life. The particular value of Ebsworth's life is that it covers all facets of D'Urfey's life and career as playwright, poet, songster, and political satirist, without bias and without reticence. Ebsworth's comments on the plays are critically acute and give the reader a sense of the relative merit of D'Urfey's accomplishments. He notes, for instance, that D'Urfey's early comedies "were full of bustle and intrigue, lively dialogue, and sparkling songs," and that "his comedies were not more licentious than Dryden's or Ravenscroft's." Ebsworth was one of the first critics to note the importance of *Wonders in the Sun: or, the Kingdom of the Birds* as a comic opera and to cite D'Urfey's innovations in costuming actors to look like parrots, crows, and other birds, to create a farcical effect. Through a careful citation of his plays, he charts the decline of D'Urfey's popularity as a dramatist in the early eighteenth century and the attempts of loyal friends, such as Addison and Steele, to hold benefit nights for him. D'Urfey's songs, however, maintained their popularity throughout his lifetime. Ebsworth notes the salutary effect on D'Urfey's career of his relationship to four successive monarchs and to various influential aristocrats and men of letters.

Highfill, Philip H., Kalman A. Burnim, and Edward A. Langhans, eds. *A Biographical Dictionary of Actors, Actresses, Musicians, Dancers, Managers, and Other Stage Personnel in London, 1660-1800* (Carbondale: Southern Illinois University Press, 1975-). The life of D'Urfey would not normally be included in the *Biographical Dictionary*, which focuses on performers and other stage personnel, rather than playwrights, of the period in London. However, on May 8, 1676, one Thomas D'Urfey was sworn a comedian in the King's Company under the manager Thomas Killigrew. Since "comedian" simply indicated that one was a member of the theatrical company, D'Urfey may have served the company in any capacity, as singer, actor, or house playwright. The biographical account thus included is complete and lively, supplying detail on D'Urfey's political attachments and personal life not given by Ebsworth. The editors chart the increasing difficulties faced by D'Urfey upon the death of Charles II, despite the fact that the talented dramatist had written plays "by the dozens" (at least thirty-two works) and song lyrics "by the hundreds." Details of his tenure as singing master to the girls at Josias Priest's school in Chelsea and of his changing political loyalties under James and William provide a fuller picture of the man, as do the many illustrations of his pretensions to the life of fashion and literary renown. The editors' final picture of D'Urfey is that of an aging playwright, author of plays no longer popular, reciting flattering "orations" or prologues to royalty, in an attempt to curry favor.

Overview of Critical Sources

Although Thomas D'Urfey cannot be overlooked in any critical view of late seventeenth century drama, he has commanded only one book-length survey of his work, Robert Forsythe's *A Study of the Plays of Thomas D'Urfey* (Western Reserve University bulletins, NS 19 (May 1916). This is a useful, if unenthusiastic, account of D'Urfey's thirty-two plays; Forsythe views the dramatist as "distinctly a third-rate writer." General critical opinion of D'Urfey, which ranged from condemnatory to tepid throughout most of the nineteenth century, has become increasingly positive in this century as critics as diverse as Allardyce Nicoll, *A History of Restoration Drama 1660-1700* (1969), John Harold Wilson, *The Influence of Beaumont and Fletcher on Restoration Drama* (1928; rpt. New York: Benjamin Blom, 1968), Eric Rothstein, *Restoration Tragedy*, (Madison: University of Wisconsin Press, 1967), and Robert D. Hume, *The Development of English Drama in the Late Seventeenth Century*, (1976) have noted the excellences in D'Urfey's work.

Evaluation of Selected Criticism

Hume, Robert D. *The Development of English Drama in the Late Seventeenth Century*. Oxford: Clarendon Press, 1976. In his discussion of seventeenth-century comedy, Hume identifies D'Urfey as a playwright who favors plot and humor rather than wit in his comedies. He writes a spirited defense of *Don Quixote*, which had been denigrated by earlier critics, such as Nicoll. Hume characterizes the play as "a roistering low comedy" with "vitality, bite and humor"; he is appreciative of Purcell's "lovely" songs and finds the piece effective in that "it teems with life." He also has high praise for *The Fond Husband*, which he considers "brilliantly plotted" and very influential, "a key play in determining the directions taken in comedy at the end of the seventies" toward sex-comedy. Hume comments on most of D'Urfey's important works, placing them within the context of the dramatic activity of other playwrights of his time. Because of D'Urfey's lack of ideological commitment, Hume sees him as a barometer of late seventeenth-century taste.

Nicoll, Allardyce, *A History of Restoration Drama 1660-1700.* Cambridge: Cambridge University Press, 1923. Nicoll was the first important critic to examine D'Urfey's works in detail. He distinguishes different periods of artistic development: the early or Jonsonian period, in which D'Urfey wrote humors comedies; the second period, in which he produced comedies of manners; and the final period, in which he moved towards sentimental drama. He notes that D'Urfey was "endowed with considerable ability."

Sprague, Arthur Colby, *Beaumont and Fletcher on the Restoration Stage.* Cambridge: Harvard University Press, 1926. Sprague gives extensive attention to the three plays which D'Urfey adapted from Beaumont and Fletcher, *Trick for Trick, A Commonwealth of Women*, and *A Fool's Preferment*. Sprague comments on D'Urfey's emphasis on clarity of exposition in his adaptations, on his attempt to impose unity of action on his play, and on his overall concern with dramatic form. This allies him, he believes, with "the better writers of his time." He also notes D'Urfey's tendency to embroider a situation with licentiousness and to move an improbable dramatic situation towards farce.

Other Sources

Brown, Laura, *English Dramatic Form, 1660-1760: An Essay in Generic History.* New Haven: Yale University Press, 1981. Brown ascribes considerable importance to D'Urfey in anticipating the moralization that took place in comedy in the early eighteenth century. She likens his work to Southerne's and Cibber's in that all display the impetus to write moral comedy "before the means has evolved to make that comedy coherent."

Gewirtz, Arthur, *Restoration Adaptations of Early 17th Century Comedies*, Washington, DC: University Press of America, 1982. Gewirtz is the first critic to pay special attention to D'Urfey's use of music and its contribution to his farce.

Holland, Peter, *The Ornament of Action.* Cambridge: Cambridge University Press, 1979. Holland stresses D'Urfey's dramatic craftsmanship in manipulating audience expectations; he notes that D'Urfey achieves satirical effect by crossing those expectations.

The London Stage 1660-1800, 11 vols. Carbondale: Southern Illinois University Press, 1960-1968. Part 1, ed. William Van Lennep, with a Critical Introduction by Emmet L. Avery and Arthur H. Scouten (1965). Part 2, ed. Emmet L. Avery (1960). A calendar of plays, entertainments and afterpieces, listing casts, box-office receipts and contemporary comment which has been compiled from the playbills, newspapers and theatrical diaries of the period of D'Urfey's greatest popularity. Indispensable in evaluating the impact of his plays on the social and dramatic community.

Phyllis T. Dircks
Long Island University

THOMAS DEKKER
1572?-1632

Author's Chronology

Born 1572? in London of unknown parentage; *1589-1593?* may either have been a seaman or an apprentice to a tradesman; *1592?* marries; *1593?* probably begins writing plays for the Lord Admiral's Men; *1594* his child is baptized in St. Giles, Cripplegate; *1598* Henslowe mentions him for the first time and he is cited in Francis Meres' *Palladis Tamia* as one of the best English writers of tragedy; February *1598* is imprisoned for debt; *1599* is arrested on January 30 for money owed to the Lord Chamberlain's Men, which Henslowe pays; *1600-1601* writes for the Children of Paul's and becomes a participant in the Poets' War against Jonson, in the service of the Chamberlain's Men, although he still writes for the Admiral's Men as well; *1603-1604* issues two pamphlets on the plague; *1604* when theatres re-open writes for Admiral's Men, the Children of Paul's, and probably the Prince's Men, while collaborating with Middleton and with Webster; *1606-1609?* argues with Prince's Men, Children of Paul's breaks up, and he returns to writing pamphlets; *1610-1612* becomes playwright for the Queen's Men; moves to Clerkenwell; *1613-1619* in King's bench prison for debt; *1616* his wife, Mary, dies; *1620-1624* composes for Players of the Revels, for the Palsgrave's Men, collaborating with Massinger, Day, Ford, and Webster; *1625* when plague closes theatres he writes pamphlets; *1626-1629* probably again in debt, he publishes tracts, writes Lord Mayor's pageants, and works on plays; *1630* plague again forces him to earn a living pamphleteering; *1632* dies and is buried on August 25, having resided in St. James' parish, Clerkenwell.

Author's Bibliography (selected)

The Play of Sir Thomas More, 1595-1596 (with Munday, Chettle, Heywood, and Shakespeare); *The Shoemakers' Holiday*, 1599 (play); *Patient Grissill*, 1599 (play, with Chettle and Haughton); *The Whole History of Fortunatus*, 1599 (play); *Satiromastix*, 1601 (play, with Marston); *The Wonderful Year*, 1603 (pamphlet); *The Honest Whore*, 1604 (play, with Middleton); *Roaring Girl*, 1605 (play, with Middleton); *The Bellman of London*, 1608 (pamphlet); *The Gull's Hornbook*, 1608 (pamphlet).

Overview of Biographical Sources

The best biography of Dekker is available only in French. Marie Jones-Davis' *Un Peintre de la vie Londonienne: Thomas Dekker*, 2 volumes (Paris, 1958) is an exhaustive and encyclopedic study of his life and work, both dramatic and non-dramatic, in relation to Elizabethan society and culture. Outside of this book, Gerald Bentley's essay in *The Jacobean and Caroline Stage* (1956) incorporates the most important updated findings, including Mary Hunt's observations in *Thomas Dekker* (1911), F.P. Wilson's "Three Notes on Thomas Dekker," *Modern Language Review*, XV (1920): 82-85, and Mark Eccles "Thomas Dekker: Burial Place," *Notes and Queries*, CLXXXVII (1939): 157. A good recent account of Dekker's career can also be found in E.D. Penry's introduction to a selection of his pamphlets: *Thomas Dekker* (London: Edward Arnold Publishers, 1967).

Evaluation of Selected Biographies

Bentley, Gerald, *The Jacobean and Caroline Stage*. Volume 3, pp. 241-145. Oxford: Clarendon Press, 1956. In his section on "Plays and Playwrights," Bentley sums up the life, provides historical record of the plays, performances and publications, and lists doubtful works. Bentley is a careful and thorough scholar.

Hunt, Mary, *Thomas Dekker*. New York: Columbia University Press, 1911. Attempting a unified account of the man and writer, Hunt's chapters focus on Dekker's early life, earliest plays, dealings with Henslowe, quarrel with Jonson, influence of Middleton, prose, plays from 1610-1619, imprisonment, and final years. Hunt's cogent and clear explication analyzes Dekker's blend of idealism and realism in both his personality and literary efforts.

Price, George, *Thomas Dekker*. New York: Twayne, 1969. This is a well-written biography with paraphrases of the major plays aimed at the general reader. The book fuses the life and works, and is divided into four chapters dealing with: 1) independently written dramas 2) dramatic collaborations, 3) non-dramatic works, and 4) explication of his religious and social thought.

Small, R.A. *The Stage-Quarrel Between Ben Jonson and the So-Called Poetasters*. Breslau: H. & M. Marcus, 1899. This excellent short volume covers Dekker's contribution to Marston's attack on Jonson in *Satiromastix*. It is still authoritative and judicious, for those interested in dramatic rivalry at the turn of the seventeenth century.

Autobiographical Sources

Dekker reveals very little about himself in the prefatory material he attaches to his published works. He does state that he was born in London in *The Seven Deadly Sinnes* (1600) and in *A Rod for Runneaways* (1625). In the dedication to *Match Me In London* (1631), he writes, "I have beene a priest in Apollo's temple many yeares, my voice is decaying with my age." If a passage in the preface to his *English Villainies* (1637) is correct, in which he speaks of "my three score years," he would be born in 1577. The most provovative act of self-reference appears in

Satiromastix, in which Dekker portrays himself as Demetrius Fannius, who with Crispinus (John Marston) punishes Horace (Ben Jonson) for his abusive satire and forces him to repent. In 1620 he published *Dekker his Dreame* in which he describes how, lifted by poetic enthusiasm, he saw a vision of heaven and hell. This kind of writing is highly conventional, however. The title page bears a woodcut, nonetheless, of the author lying in bed.

Overview of Critical Sources

Although Dekker was a prolific writer and composed in a wide variety of forms, most criticism deals with him as a "professional," who often combines elements of realism and pathos, able at times to rise to moments of great lyrical beauty, but often uneven in his effect. Both of these charges, of being a hack and of being far too scattered in his dramatic structure, have been answered by recent criticism. However, of his many works two are usually selected for highest praise: *The Shoemakers' Holiday* and the *Gull's Hornbook*. With the exception of *Satiromastix*, because of its place in the Poets' War between Marston and Jonson, and *Sir Thomas More*, because Shakespeare apparently wrote about fifty lines of it still preserved in his handwriting, the rest of Dekker's plays have been largely neglected, except by specialists. Dekker is particularly important for scholars who investigate the rise of "Citizen Comedy" and those interested in the way the middle class became increasingly an object of dramatic representation in the theatre. The *Hornbook* is an essential document in theatre history, revealing much about the social setting of the bankside playhouses; it is included in most surveys of the Elizabethan stage.

Evaluation of Selected Criticism

Bush, Douglas, *English Literature in the Earlier Seventeenth Century, 1600-1660*. Oxford: Clarendon Press, 1945. The second chapter of this volume presents an excellent assessment of Dekker's non-dramatic work.

Chandler, Frank, *The Literature of Roguery*. 2 volumes. New York: Burt Franklin, 1958. Chandler studies Dekker's debt to the literature of theft, gulling, and cozening, from which the dramatist's analysis of Elizabethan street life derives.

Conover, James, *Thomas Dekker: An Analysis of Dramatic Structure*. The Hague, Mouton, 1969. Conover's thesis is that although Dekker has often been faulted for a lack of ability to provide adequate form for his plays, this is not the case. This book subjects six plays to close structural analysis to force a re-evaluation, allowing a sense of tight structure to develop along with Dekker's already acknowledged talents for characterization, lyricism, and comic effect. Conover concentrates on works completely written by Dekker: *The Shoemakers' Holi-*

day, Old Fortunatus, The Second Part of the Honest Whore, The Whore of Babylon, If This Be Not a Good Play, The Devil is In It, and *Match Me In London.*

Knights, L.C. *Drama and Society in the Age of Jonson.* London: Chatto & Windus, 1937. Asserting that Dekker's approach is neither medieval nor modern, Knights gives a valid assessment of the playwright's "citizen morality," but censures him for incompetence.

McKerrow, R.B. *The Gull's Hornbook.* London: De la More Press, 1904. The introduction to this edition and notes provide a superb treatment of this delightful work, which is one of Dekker's most memorable pieces. McKerrow brings an important document in stage history to life.

Shirley, Peggy, *Serious and Tragic Elements in the Comedy of Thomas Dekker.* Salzburg: University Press, 1975. The analysis here focuses on serious elements in *The Shoemaker's Holiday,* tragic elements in *Old Fortunatus,* and tragic and comic fusion in *If This Be Not a Good Play.* The author maintains that comdey can often present simultaneously a vision of the tragic nature of experience.

Tolliver, Harold, "The Shoemaker's Holiday: Theme and Image," in *Boston University Studies in English,* V (1961): 208-218. Tolliver illustrates the often overlooked complexity of Dekker's skill as a dramatic craftsman.

Other Sources

Adler, Doris Ray, *Thomas Dekker: A Reference Guide.* Boston: G.K. Hall, 1983. This annotated bibliography covers studies of and references to Thomas Dekker from 1800 through 1980. The survey demonstrates the revival of interest in Dekker's writing that was initiated by Charles Lamb's comments in *Specimens of English Dramatic Poets Who Lived About the Time of Shakespeare,* published in 1808. A reference book of this kind is indispensible for an understanding of the critical tradition that stands behind the interpretation of Dekker's enormous production of works and his collaborations with major contemporary writers.

Bowers, Fredson, *The Dramatic Works of Thomas Dekker.* 4 volumes. Cambridge: Cambridge University Press, 1953-1961. The standard volume of plays with an introduction concerning their transmission and printing.

Chambers, E.K. *The Elizabethan Stage.* Vol. 3. Oxford: Clarendon Press, 1923. After furnishing a short biography and listing collections of Dekker's works, Chambers lists plays that exist with early publication and performance dates.

Hoy, Cyrus, *Introduction, Notes, and Commentaries to Texts in the Dramatic Works of Thomas Dekker,* Edited By Fredson Bowers. 4 volumes. Cambridge: Cambridge University Press, 1980. Splendid introductions and painstaking analysis—line by line—of cruxes in the plays.

Routh, Harold, "London and the Development of Popular Literature," in *Cambridge History of English Literature*. Volume IV. New York: G.P. Putnam's Sons, 1910. Routh places Dekker's work in the generation of professional writers, including Greene, Lyly, and Nashe, who turned to their own times for the settings and plots of the popular literature they created.

James P. Bednarz
Long Island University

DENIS DIDEROT
1713-1784

Author's Chronology

Born October 5, 1713, Langres, Champagne, France, to Didier Diderot and Angélique Vigneron; *1723-1728* attends Jesuit college in Langres; *1728* leaves for Paris, attends either Collège Louis-le-Grand (Jesuit) or Collège d'Harcourt (Jansenist); *1732* awarded master of arts degree; *1743* Didier Diderot uses *lettre de cachet* in vain attempt to prevent his son from marrying Anne-Toinette Champion; *1747* Diderot and d'Alembert commissioned as co-directors of *Encyclopédie; 1748* writes *Les Bijoux Indiscrets; 1749* imprisoned for three months at Vincennes because of his *Pensées philosophiques; 1755* begins correspondence with Sophie Volland; *1757* publishes his first play, *Le Fils Naturel,* along with a theoretical work on the theater, *Entretiens sur le Fils Naturel;* friendship with Rousseau ends in bitterness; *1758* D'Alembert quits position of co-editor of *Encyclopédie;* Diderot publishes second play, *Le Père de Famille,* and *Discours sur la poésie dramatique; 1759* father dies; *1760* Diderot and other *Encyclopédie* collaborators ridiculed in Palissot's play, *Les Philosophes,* at Comédie Française; writes novel *La Religieuse* (pub. 1796); *1761 Le Père de Famille* presented at Comédie Française with only moderate success but great controversy; writes *Le Neveu de Rameau* (first published 1821, re-translated from German); *1765* sells his library to Catherine the Great, who leaves him use of it for his lifetime, and grants him a pension; *1769* writes *Le Paradoxe sur le Comédien* (pub. 1831) and *Le Rêve de d'Alembert* (pub. 1830); *1771-1778* writes *Jacques le Fataliste* and *Supplément au Voyage de Bougainville* (pub. 1796); *1773-1774* travels to Russia at Catherine's invitation; *1778* writes play *Est-il bon? Est-il méchant?;* July 21, *1784* dies without having published many of his later works, and therefore known to contemporaries principally as director of the *Encyclopédie* and a playwright/theoretician.

Author's Bibliography

At the beginning of his career, Diderot published his works anonymously for the most part, although his authorship became known and caused him trouble. His first work, the *Pensées philosophiques,* was condemned by the Parlement of Paris and publicly burned as contrary to religion and morals. This work, along with *Les Bijoux Indiscrets* and *Lettre sur les Aveugles,* landed him in prison in 1749. The *Encyclopédie* was printed 1751-1766, each volume as it was prepared, by the publisher Le Breton, Briasson, the elder David, and Durand, this publication also requiring much courage and persistence on the part of Diderot as editor, since anti-Encyclopedist attacks brought about suppression of the first two volumes in 1752 and temporary revocation of the license to print in 1759. Diderot published his first

163

two plays, accompanied by works of dramatic theory; his *Salons* were published in Grimm's *Correspondance littéraire,* which delivered them to a select, but very small audience. Battle weary, Diderot chose not to publish most of his later writings, entrusting to posterity the works which it has indeed judged to be his greatest masterpieces. In 1798, Diderot's disciple Naigeon published the first edition (15 vol., incomplete) of his works. *Oeuvres,* 1821-1834, 26 vol., ed. J.L.J. Brière; *Oeuvres complètes,* 1875-1877, 20 vol., ed. J. Assézat and M. Tourneux (incomplete); *Oeuvres complètes,* 1969-1973, 15 vol., ed. Roger Lewinter; *Oeuvres complètes,* 1975-Herman edition. Specialized editions include: *Oeuvres philosophiques,* 1956, ed. Paul Vernière; *Oeuvres esthétiques,* 1959, ed. Paul Vernière; *Oeuvres romanesques,* 1962, ed. Henri Bénac.

A limited number of Diderot's works are available in English translation, including *The Nun,* translated by L. Tancock (Harmondsworth, 1974), *Jacques the Fatalist and his Master,* translated by J. Robert Loy (New York, 1959), and *The Encyclopedia: Selections,* translated by S.J. Gendzier (New York, 1967). *Diderot's Early Philosophical Works,* translated by M. Jourdain (Chicago, 1916), includes his *Philosophic Thoughts, Letter on the Blind,* and *Letter on the Deaf and Dumb.* Another collection, *Rameau's Nephew and Other Works,* translated by J. Barzun and R.H. Bowen (New York, 1956), includes *D'Alembert's Dream, Supplement to Bougainville's Voyage,* the important article "Encyclopedia" from the *Encyclopedia,* and other shorter works. Of Diderot's theatrical writings, there is only *The Paradox of Acting,* translated by W.H. Pollock (London, 1883; rpt. New York, 1957.)

Overview of Biographical Sources

There has been plenty of documentary evidence on Diderot's life for biographers, except for the period of his early formative years in Paris, about which little has been discovered. The earliest account was that written by his daughter, Mme de Vandeul, the year he died. Although inaccurate on some points, her "Mémoires pour servir à l'histoire de la vie et des ouvrages de Diderot" (published in vol. 1 of Assézat-Tourneux) have been a valuable source of information for subsequent biographers. Jacques-André Naigeon, Diderot's disciple and friend during the last twenty years of his life, published his *Mémoires historiques et philosophiques sur la vie et les ouvrages de D. Diderot* (Paris: Brière, 1821; reprint ed., Geneva: Slatkine Reprints, 1970), useful because of the author's close association with his subject but, again, not always reliable. André Billy's *Diderot* (Paris: Editions de France, 1932; revised and expanded 1943 as *Vie de Diderot*), the first significant twentieth-century biography of Diderot, was based on firsthand documents, but novelized. Franco Venturi's *La Jeunesse de Diderot* (1939) interpreted Diderot's early career from a Marxist point of view. Lester Crocker's *The Embattled Philosopher: A Biography of Denis Diderot* (East Lansing: Michigan State College Press, 1954) provided a much-needed, comprehensive biographical study at a time when scholarly interest in the *philosophe* was beginning to grow rapidly. The most complete book on Diderot's life is Arthur M. Wilson's *Diderot* (1972), an invaluable, indeed classic, work of scholarship which supersedes all previous biographies. In a smaller format, Otis Fellows's *Diderot* (1977) presents a judicious overview of Diderot's life and works and examines Diderot's and posterity's views of his career. Jacques Chouillet's *Diderot,* which also appeared in 1977, is a masterful study of the man through his works.

Evaluation of Selected Biographies

Chouillet, Jacques, *Diderot.* Paris: Société d'Edition d'Enseignement Supérieur, 1977. Untranslated. Written by an eminent Diderot scholar, this biography is centered on Diderot's works, with careful analyses which provide new insight into Diderot's thought processes and into the social and political implications of his texts. In French, the book contains a bibliography of major reference works with a listing of books and articles published since 1972.

Fellows, Otis, *Diderot.* Boston: Twayne, 1977. This book provides an excellent introduction to Diderot and his age for the general reader. Fellows draws on his extensive scholarship to present the life of the Encyclopedist, tracing the crucial points in Diderot's development and situating these events in the larger historical context. He gives an excellent summary of the ideas and arguments of Diderot's major works and a sampling of critical opinion. The book also contains a very helpful annotated bibliography.

Wilson, Arthur M. *Diderot.* New York: Oxford University Press, 1972. The first part of this book was published in 1957 under the title *Diderot: The Testing Years, 1713-1759,* and is republished in this volume with Part II, *The Appeal to Posterity.* The work incorporates data from all available sources to present a detailed account of Diderot's life and a balanced view of the complexities of his personality and thought. Historical background is accurately provided, the *milieux* in which Diderot moved are brought alive. Diderot's works are examined, sometimes at length, with particular attention given to the importance of the *Encyclopédie* and Diderot's role as editor. The book is richly annotated and there is a full bibliography. Indispensable for scholarly research, the work is also immensely readable.

Autobiographical Sources

Diderot habitually made his presence felt in his writings, where autobiographical references occur directly in the form of occasional anecdotes or examples drawn from his own experience and, more ambiguously, in his appearance as character in a number of his works. The major autobiographical source, however, is Diderot's correspondence, which was, typically for the age, extensive, and which reveals the activities and thoughts, frustrations and victories, friendships and antagonisms of a long career, and sheds light on the genesis and elaboration of many of Diderot's writings. A complete and critical edition of the *Correspondance* was edited by Georges Roth and Jean Varloot (Paris: Editions de Minuit, 1955-70, 16 vol.). The letters to Sophie Volland are of particular interest and have been published separately in *Les Lettres de Diderot à Sophie Volland,* ed. Yves Florenne (Paris: Club français du livre, 1965). A translation of a number of these is found in *Diderot's Letters to Sophie Volland: A Selection,* by Peter France (London: Oxford University Press, 1972).

Overview of Critical Sources

Although esteemed in Germany, (in the late eighteenth and early nineteenth centuries even Goethe, Schiller, and Gessner saw fit to translate various of Diderot's manuscripts before they were even published in France), Diderot's talent in France was long questioned and his work depreciated as undisciplined by many scholars. While such views persisted well into the twentieth century, Diderot has over the last few decades come to be considered one of the Englightenment's most brilliant and most modern writers. As appreciation of his wide-ranging genius has grown, so has the corpus of Diderot scholarship and the multitude of critical approaches. Diderot's drama, somewhat overshadowed by his posthumous masterpieces, has nevertheless been the object of numerous articles in the past two decades, in addition to treatment within particular chapters of broader studies on Diderot. Although the *drames* themselves have generally been judged disappointing, the importance and wide influence of Diderot's works of dramatic theory have been universally recognized.

Evaluation of Selected Criticism

Chouillet, Jacques, *La Formation des Idées Esthétiques de Diderot, 1745-1763.* Paris: Colin, 1973. In a chapter devoted to Diderot's plays and theories of 1757 and 1758, Chouillet attempts to identify essential, dialectic elements of Diderot's theater. Emphasizing the importance of the theory of the ideal model in *De la poésie dramatique* as an attempt to resolve the antithesis between natural and artistic truth, Chouillet's analysis is very helpful to an understanding of Diderot's theater and the relationship of his dramatic theories to the esthetic theories of the age.

Dieckmann, Herbert, "Currents and Crosscurrents in *Le Fils Naturel,*" in *Linguistic and Literary Studies in Honor of Helmut A. Hatzfeld.* Washington, DC: Catholic University of America Press, 1964, pp. 107-116. Examining the circumstances surrounding Diderot's composition of *Le Fils Naturel* and the *Entretiens,* Dieckmann suggests that, consciously or unconsciously on Diderot's part, his relationship with Rousseau was an important factor. The article, by a major Diderot scholar, is especially useful for the perspective it offers on the nature of Diderot's preoccupation with the theater.

Lacoue-Labarthe, Phillipe, "Diderot, le paradoxe et la mimésis," in *Poétique* 43 (1980): 266-281. Unlike those who have sought to reconcile the paradoxes of Diderot's esthetics, Lacoue-Labarthe posits in this study of *Paradoxe sur le comédien* that the logic of the paradox, with its equation of opposites, is also the logic of mimesis, and is therefore its necessary, though unsettling, formulation.

Lewinter, Roger, "Diderot et son théâtre: pour une psychocritique formelle," in *Temps modernes* 24 (1968): 698-721. Lewinter studies *Le Fils Naturel* and *Le Père de Famille* using a psychoanalytical approach, asserting that the subconscious motivations underlying the creative process produced a complex, multiple distribution of Oedipal roles among the characters, and exploring different levels of meaning in the plays.

Niklaus, Robert, "La Portée des théories dramatiques de Diderot et de ses réalisations théâtrales," in *Romanic Review* 53-54 (1962-63): 6-19. In a study which provides a good overview of Diderot's theories and proposed reforms for the theater, Niklaus sees in Diderot's conception of and ambition for the *drame* the factors responsible for his morally simplistic plays. He finds in the theoretical *Entretiens*, however, a measure of the morally complex, provocative dialogue which was to become Diderot's distinctive mode of expression and which, argues Niklaus, made his novels and tales his best "theater."

Undank, Jack, "The Open and Shut Case of *Est-il Bon? Est-il Méchant?*" in *Diderot Studies* 20 (1981): 267-285. Undank, editor of *Est-il Bon? Est-il Méchant?* in the Hermann edition of the *Oeuvres complètes*, here views the play, with its protagonist as both manipulator and servant of his friends, as revealing Diderot's view of his own relationship with his audience. Undank offers excellent insights into Diderot's perception of the literary and moral dilemma of the writer, caught between convention and invention, writing and living.

Whitmore, Richard Prescott, "Two Essays on *Le Père de Famille*," in *Studies on Voltaire and the Eighteenth Century* 116 (1973): 137-209. Refuting the common assumption that the language of *Le Père de Famille* is identical to that of *Le Fils Naturel*, Whitmore differentiates the two plays, arguing that the dialogue of Diderot's second play was less sermonizing and more supportive of effective characterization and plot development.

Other Sources

Archer, William, *Masks or Faces? A study in the psychology of acting.* London: Longmans, Green, 1888; rpt. New York: Hill and Wang, 1957. An investigation of Diderot's *Paradoxe sur le Comédien,* based on actors' testimony of their own experience.

Braun, Theodore E.D. "La Conscience de la présence des spectateurs dans la comédie larmoyante et dans le drame," in *Studies on Voltaire and the Eighteenth Century* 192 (1981): 1527-1534. A study contrasting the *drame* to the *comédie* and *comédie larmoyante* of the period.

Creech, James, "Diderot's 'Ideal Model'," in *Diderot: Digression and Dispersion*. Lexington, KY: French Forum, 1984, pp. 85-97. In a collection rejecting the attempt to integrate the diversity of Diderot's thought, this article examines the theory of the ideal model as a source of mimetic plurality.

Cru, R. Loyalty, *Diderot as a Disciple of English Thought*. New York: AMS Press, 1966. English influence in all areas of Diderot's work, with a chapter devoted to its manifestations in Diderot's theater and dramatic theories.

Fellows, Otis E., (vol. 1 and 2) Norman L. Torrey, (vol. 3) Gita May, and (vol. 8-) Diana Guiragossian Carr, ed. *Diderot Studies*. Syracuse, NY: Syracuse University Press, 1949-52; Geneva: Droz, 1961- . An important collection of studies on all aspects of Diderot's work. Twenty-one volumes since 1949.

Jourdain, Eleanor F. *Dramatic Theory and Practice in France, 1690-1808*. New York: Benjamin Blom, 1921; rpt. New York: Benjamin Blom, 1968. A history of *comédie, tragédie,* and *drame* in the eighteenth century, with emphasis on the latter's increasing importance and influence on the other genres.

Lewinter, Roger, "L'Exaltation de la vertu dans le théâtre de Diderot," in *Diderot Studies* 8 (1966): 119-169. Study of the evolution of the notion of virtue in Diderot's theater, from dogmatism to pragmatism, with an appendix corrolating this evolution to that of Diderot's relationship with his father.

Spear, Frederick A., ed. *Bibliographie de Diderot*. Geneva: Librairie Droz, 1980. Comprehensive listing of critical works to 1975, some later; updated in *Diderot Studies* 22 (1983): 139-153.

Undank, Jack, *Diderot: Inside, Outside & In-Between*. Madison, WI: Coda Press, 1979. Three chapters deal with the psychology of imitation in *Le Fils Naturel* and the *Entretiens*.

Bonnie Robb
University of Delaware

ALEXANDRE DUMAS (*FILS*)
1824-1895

Author's Chronology

Born July 27, 1824, in Paris, the illegitimate son (or "infant naturel") of the hedonistic Alexandre Dumas the Elder (or *père*) who would become the prolific and popular Romantic novelist and dramatist, and Marie Catherine Labay, a Belgian seamstress; left to be reared by his mother; *1831* paternity acknowledged by Dumas père, who attempts to make some financial arrangement for his son's support and education, and gains custody of the child; sent to a boarding school where he experienced cruelty and neglect for the first time in his life; *1841* abandons his formal education and begins living with his father, observing his prodigality; restless, lives for a time in Marseille, returns to Paris and meets Alphonsine Plessis (known as Marie Duplessis), an elegant and beautiful young woman, once a provincial shopgirl, but now the toast of society, also a gambler and suffering from tuberculosis, and she becomes his mistress, but they soon break the relationship; returns to live with his father; *1846* travels to Spain and Orient with his father and friends; *1847* Marie Duplessis dies; writes the novel *The Lady of the Camellias* (known in English as *Camille*) based on their love affair; *1849* adapts *Camille* for the stage; *1850* begins affair with the married Russian countess Lydia Nesselrode and tries to follow her to Russia; *1852 Camille* appears on the Paris stage after being delayed by censorship and with its success he provides for his mother; *1853* begins series of fifteen "thesis" or problem plays dramatizing social problems and their solutions (examples: *Diane de Lys*, 1853, *The Demi-Mode*, 1855, *The Illegitimate Son*, 1858, *The Prodigal Father*, 1859); *1864* marries Nadejda Naryschkine who had borne him an illegitimate daughter in 1860; *1866* published *The Clémenceau Affair*, an autobiographical novel recounting his unhappy early life; *1867* a second daughter born; *1868* his mother dies; *1870* his father dies; *1874* elected to French Academy; *1895* Madame Dumas dies; *1895* marries Henriette Regnier and dies five months later, November 17, 1895.

Author's Bibliography (selected)

The complete works are available in several editions, both in French and English. The first collection to appear in French was *Théâtre complet* in five volumes in 1868 and later in seven volumes in 1880. After the dramatist's death a new edition was published in 1896. Another collection is dated 1923.

Translations have not been as successful as the originals, as it is the consensus that "no English adaption had done justice" to them. An early and distorted version of *The Lady of the Camellias* appeared as *Camille* in 1853, with an improved translation published in 1856. *Camille* is available in English in these versions: in *Nineteenth-Century French Plays*, J.L. Borgenhoff, ed., New York: Century, 1831, and in *Chief Plays of the Nineteenth Century*, E.M. Grant, ed., New York: Harper, 1934. *The Demi-Monde* was translated in 1858 and appears in *The Chief European Dramatists*, B. Matthews, ed., Boston: Houghton Mifflin, 1916; and again by B.H. Clark in 1921 with the title *The Outer Edge of Society* and in the *World Drama* vol 2, New York: Appleton, 1933, later reprinted in 1956. Another play of Dumas *fils* available in an English translation is *Madam Aubray's Ideas* included in *Nineteenth-Century French Plays*.

Overview of Biographical Sources

Because of the enormous world popularity of the sentimental *Camille*, combined with Dumas *pere's* flamboyant life and wide reputation, there have been numerous accounts of his life, beginning almost during his own lifetime in biographies about his father. Although Dumas *fils* lived his life so as to make it difficult for his biographers, such reticence challenged his biographers to discover both the inconsistencies in his life as well as his remarkable accomplishments, and to present them in chronologies of varying merit.

Evaluation of Selected Biographies

Endore, Guy, *King of Paris: Lives of Alexandre Dumas pere and fils*. New York: Simon and Shuster, 1956. Endore treats the famous scenario of the elder Dumas challenged both artistically and personally by his son by emphasizing their significance in the development of the novel and drama of nineteenth-century France. The father was a man of tremendous energy and extravagance, filled with a passion for life's pleasures. Gathering an immense popularity, he was indeed, in his time, an uncrowned "king of Paris." The son, however, was more of a craftsman, and of a temperament that prompted him to be a moral critic. Victor Hugo's evaluation of father and son is instructive: "It was the father who was the genius . . . he had more genius than talent. The son was "just the reverse . . . the embodiment of talent . . . but is nothing more than talent."

Gribble, F.H. *Dumas Father and Son*. London, 1930. There is no material here that cannot be found elsewhere. Although readable, it lacks the narrative quality of other biographies.

Maurois, André, *The Titans: A Three-Generation Biography of the Dumas*. tr. Gerard Hopkins. New York: Harper and Brothers, 1957. Maurois' focus is Dumas *père*, a writer he claims was "the delight" of his boyhood; however he argues that the son too is worthy of study, and he feels that too little is known of his life. To rectify this ommission, he claims to utilize a great deal of hitherto unpublished material in his portrayal of the son. Maurois strives to find similarities within the family, particularly their joint suffering from prejudice, in spite of appearances of dissimilitude. For one interested in a well-written, illustrated presentation of this remarkable family and the place of Dumas *fils* in it, this is a very readable biography.

Saunders, Edith, *The Prodigal Father*. London: Longmans, Green, 1951. Somewhat overly sentimental, this study focuses on "the history of Dumas *fils* and his play *The Lady of the Camellias*." Complete with illustrations and prolific anecdotes, Saunder's books links Dumas *fils* with other famous men and women of his time—writers, musicians, actors, and celebrities—so that an overall view of nineteenth-century French cultural life in the Second Empire is presented. Her emphasis on the melodramatic, the histrionic, however, is excessive. Saunders relies too heavily on personal relationships, contriving conversations to portray the dramatic confrontations. For the serious scholar it reads too much like a romantic novel.

Autobiographical Sources

In addition to his novels and plays, Dumas *fils* wrote a series of moralizing yet instructive prefatory essays based on both his own experience and observation, often appearing long after the plays were published but to which they were appended. Sometimes of more interest to the sociologist than the literary critic, they dealt with two major subjects: contemporary social problems and the moral crises they generated, along with self-analyses of his theories of dramaturgy. They are extremely useful both for their illumination and expansion of the author's convictions as well as of nineteenth-century French drama in general. To the student of this period they have inestimable value. In these prefaces Dumas *fils*, as a crusading theatrical innovator, analyzed popular and critical reaction to each of his plays, and then defended, in this light, his purpose for dealing with his controversial subject. In addition to being literary documents, thus they are ultimately autobiographical, for they reveal the creative, sensitive consciousness that produced the creative work. There was no playwright of the nineteenth century who set up such a dialogue with his public concerning his art with more freedom, and these prefaces form a unique phase of his work. Other autobiographical insight can be gained from examining both the plots of certain plays (*Camille*, for example) to decide how much of Dumas *fils* himself is in the role of the lover, as well as of his affair with Marie Duplessis, the consumptive heroine. Also much of his subject matter is obviously based on his personal situation and the environment in which he lived: *The Illegitimate Son*, *The Demi-Mode*, and *A Prodigal Father* are examples. Dumas *fils* wished to live inconspicuously, not surprising for two reasons: the notoriety of his flamboyant father, and the truth that the events of his private life did not square with his unbending public position on morality.

Overview of Critical Sources

Opinion of Dumas *fils* has irrevocably been linked with that of his more famous father. As the son of one of the most romantic nineteenth-century writers, he represents a remarkable transition from the elder's rousing novels and plays of action and amour in his emphasis on realism in his social dramas. Nevertheless, a number of major studies combine the biographies of father and son, one, *The Titans* by Maurois, expanding to examine the lives of three generations of Dumas, beginning with Thomas-Alexandre, the grandfather, an army general. Because of this dynastic situation and the close yet difficult relationship between the son and father, it is almost impossible to focus exclusively on one figure biographically. Another problem from the English-speaking student is the lack of secondary material. Bibliographies in French are extensive, but few of the works have been translated. A recent bibliographer complained that "English contributions are in the main a poor lot and unreliable."

Evaluation of Selected Criticism

Schwarz, H. Stanley, *Alexandre Dumas fils, Dramatist*. New York: New York University Press, 1927. Having its origin as the author's dissertation, it claims to be the first "volume of any considerable dimensions" devoted to an examination and analysis of the dramatic works of the writer. Schwarz admits that interest in the dramatist "waned lamentably" since his death, but that despite critical opinion of his play, "his influence upon the drama of his day, and upon subsequent French drama, was inestimable," and that Dumas *fils* should be recognized both for that reason and "as a leading exponent of the realistic drama, as an earnest moralist, and as an important student of social questions." A systematic study of the work of Dumas *fils* that focuses on both his originality in his creative achievements as well as his moral positions, the work is summed up by Schwarz thusly: "we have attempted to be impartial, indicating frankly the deficiencies of Dumas *fils* as well as his virtues; and if we have erred in either direction, we have defeated our own purpose of presenting a true picture of the work of the dramatist." This critic does present a balanced study, and it is a commendable piece of work.

Other Sources

Bell, A. Craig, *Alexandre Dumas: A Biography and Study*. London: Cassell, 1950. In this biography of the father, the author despairs about the tangle made of the life by the truth being mixed with legend and calumny, "libels and half-truths." He feels a need for "a just, critical and serious biography," thus defending his attempt. The events of the son's life are recorded as they coincide with he father's, and at the end, when the father is dying, Bell offers his opinion that "the son was the father and the father the son," as the old man stood in awe of his moral didactic son.

Chandler, Frank W. *Modern Continental Playwrights*. New York: Harper and Brothers, 1931, pp. 142-143. Chandler places Dumas *fils* within the context of

"The Theatric and the Naturalistic in France,: especially how he adapts the principles of the "well-made plays" of Eugène Scribe.

Gorman, Herbert, *The Incredible Marquis Alexandre Dumas*. New York: Farrar and Rinehart, 1929. The flamboyant style of Alexandre Dumas seems to engender the same rhetoric in his biographers, and Gorman's book is no exception. The famous quotation of the son about his father is emphasized: "My father is a great baby of mine—born when I was quite a little child." Succinctly this biographer evaluates the relationship: the son "was worried about his father because he loved him and enraged at him because he disapproved of his lack of morals." This book is valuable for such insights.

Hemmings, F.W.J. *Alexandre Dumas: The King of Romance*. New York: Charles Scribners' Sons, 1979. The elder Dumas is the subject of this rather novelistic narrative, but both biographical and literary information about the son and his work runs throughout. The father's resentment of the son's literary reputation forced him to use the designation *père*, and this suggestion of age particularly galled him. The dissolute life father and son led when living and travelling together precedes the years when "the younger man would eventually evolve into the pompous moralist he became under the Second Empire," and suggests exactly what Dumas *fils* would inveigh again later in his fashionable plays. Hemmings gives a good account of this difficult relationship.

James, Henry, *Notes on Novelists*. New York: Charles Scribners' Sons, 1914, pp. 362-384. Written in 1895 just after the death of Dumas *fils*, this memoir includes James' opinion that his work appealed to him, and brings back memories of his own youth when he first experienced the excessive sentiments of *Camille*. James ranks the play "an astonishing production," and voices his regret that the playwright "really never figured among us all again." This essay is highly personal, but does shed some light on opinion of Dumas *fils* by a celebrated critic.

Matthews, Brander, *French Dramatists of the Nineteenth Century*. New York: Benjamin Blom, pp. 136-171. A good review of Dumas *fils* and his work, this chapter sees him as "a fresh force" in French drama, one breaking from tradition.

Maurois, André, *Alexandre Dumas: A Great Life in Brief*. New York: Alfred A. Knopf, 1955. In this rather dramatized version of the life of the father, episodes are related that involve the son. Particularly interesting are scenes relating to the son's desire to follow his father in writing for the stage, but in a radically different way. Especially affecting is the description of the elder's last days, tenderly cared for by the son in a final reconciliation.

Smith, Hugh Allison, *Main Currents of Modern French Drama*. New York: Henry Holt and Co., 1925, pp. 122-150. In this chapter "Dumas *fils* and Realistic Social Drama," Smith argues that *Camille* launched realism on the stage, an important epoch in French dramatic history, and this form persisted far into the twentieth century and influenced plays written in other countries. Negatively, he faults the playwright for relying too much on logic and turning the drama toward propaganda.

Stanton, Stephen, ed. *Camille and Other Plays*. New York: Hill and Wang, 1957. In this anthology is one of the better English versions of Dumas' *fils* first and most famous play, by Edith Reynolds and Nigel Playfair. In addition to a comprehensive bibliography, there is also a good critical introduction as well as the history of the play's productions.

Selected Dictionaries and Encyclopedias

European Authors 1000-1900, H.W. Wilson, 1967. A brief but inclusive review of the life and works of Dumas *fils*.

McGraw Hill Encyclopedia of World Drama, vol. 2, McGraw Hill, 1972. A very thorough review of all aspects of Dumas *fils*: his life, works, and importance. The emphasis here is also on performance, and a list of first stagings of the various plays is included. There are also illustrations.

The Oxford Companion to French Literature, Clarenden Press, 1959. A dependable brief biography and itemization of the major plays and novels, with emphasis on his technique and significance as the bridge figure between Romanticism and Realism in French drama.

Maryhelen C. Harmon
University of South Florida

WILLIAM DUNLAP
1766-1839

Author's Chronology

Born February 19, 1766, Perth Amboy, New Jersey, to Samuel and Margaret Sargeant Dunlap; *1778* becomes blind in one eye; *1783* meets George Washington and paints his portrait; *1784-1787* goes to England to study art but spends more time at the theatre; *1789* marries Elizabeth Woolsey and has his first play performed; *1791* frees the family's slaves when his father dies; *1793* becomes friends with Charles Brockden Brown, novelist; *1798* becomes manager-director of a theatre company; *1805* becomes bankrupt and turns to painting for a livelihood; *1806* returns to the theatre; *1810* works with George Frederick Cooke, actor; *1816* becomes a full-time painter again; *1823* begins friendship with James Fenimore Cooper, novelist; September 28, 1839, dies and is buried in Perth Amboy.

Author's Bibliography

William Dunlap wrote, adapted, and translated over fifty plays. Not all his plays are extant, and some works have been incorrectly attributed to him. His plays include *The Father*, 1789; *Andre*, 1798; *The Fatal Deception or Leicester*, 1807; *The Italian Father*, 1810; *The Glory of Columbia—Her Yeomanry!*, 1817; *A Trip to Niagara*, 1830. No complete collection of Dunlap's extant works exists, but the Readex Microprint edition of Early American Imprints published by the American Antiquarian Society includes many of his plays. Dunlap himself prepared one volume of *The Dramatic Works of William Dunlap* in 1806 and two more volumes in 1816; the collection was never finished. His non-dramatic publications include, *Memoirs of the Life of George Frederick Cooke*, 1813; *The Life of Charles Brockden Brown*, 1815; *History of the American Theatre*, 2 vols. 1832; *History of the Rise and Progress of the Arts of Design in the United States*, 2 vols. 1834; *Diary of William Dunlap*, 1930, 3 vols., ed. Dorothy C. Barck.

Overview of Biographical Sources

Two important biographies exist on William Dunlap, *William Dunlap: A Study of His Life and Works and of His Place in Contemporary Culture* by Oral Sumner Coad (1917) and *William Dunlap* by Robert H. Canary (1970). Since the authors emphasize different aspects of the playwright's life and reach different conclusions about him, the Dunlap student should read both. Accounts of Dunlap's friendship with literary figures can be found in such biographies as *Charles Brockden Brown: American Gothic Novelist* by Harry R. Warfel (Gainesville: University of Florida Press, 1949) and *The World of Washington Irving* by Van Wyck Brooks (New York: E.P. Dutton, 1944).

175

Evaluation of Selected Biographies
    Canary, Robert H. *William Dunlap*. New York: Twayne, 1970. In his account of
Dunlap's early life, Canary finds it significant that the playwright wrote highly of
Thomas Bartow, the man who introduced him to literature and art, but wrote little
about his father. Canary qualifies Dunlap's influence on the theatre by stating that
his contributions were largely inevitable or unimportant. Nonetheless, Canary does
not deny that Dunlap is the Father of American Theatre. He acknowledges that
Dunlap was the best historian of the American theatre during his time and that
Andre is better than the first American novels. Dunlap's best works, in Canary's
opinion, are *History of the American Theatre* and *History of the Rise and Progress
of the Arts of Design in the United States*.

    Coad, Oral Sumner, *William Dunlap: A Study of His Life and Works and of His
Place in Contemporary Culture*. New York: The Dunlap Society, 1917. Coad,
unlike Canary, does not emphasize Thomas Bartow's influence on Dunlap and
assumes that his relationship with his father was good. He admits that Dunlap, as a
playwright, was a borrower rather than an original author. He also admits that
Dunlap's inexperience and unassertiveness were partly to blame for his bankruptcy.
Nonetheless, Coad states that Dunlap richly deserves to be called the Father of
American Theatre because he developed the art of scenery, encouraged the production of plays written by Americans, and brought a cosmopolitan influence to the
United States stage by translating German and French plays. He further asserts that
Dunalp made important contributions in sentimental drama, the patriotic play,
ballad-opera, tragi-comedy, and Gothic drama. Coad's well-documented book includes an act-by-act synopsis of many of the plays and provides important information about the history of the American theatre and biography before Dunlap made
his own contributions in these areas.

Autobiographical Sources
    Dunlap apparently wrote about thirty volumes for his diary, but only eleven were
found for publication in *Diary of William Dunlap*. These volumes begin in 1786
with a recount of a walking trip from London to Oxford. The volumes from 1797 to
1798 describe Dunlap's work as manager as the Old American Company of Come-
dians and his ensuing money troubles. It also reveals such personal details as his
devotion to his children and his love of gardening. The 1806 diary contains letters
he wrote to his wife while he was an itinerant painter and entries he made when he
briefly returned to the theatre. The remaining volumes include entries on George
Frederick Cooke, the subject of one of his biographies; his life as a painter; and his
work on his histories of art and the theatre.
    Besides being an important source for Dunlap's contribution to the theatre, *His-
tory of the American Theatre* has two chapters about Dunlap's life before he wrote
plays and after bankruptcy forced him from the theatre. In the first volume of

History of the Rise and Progress of the Arts of Design in the United States, Dunlap includes three chapters on himself. They detail his childhood, trip to England, and life as a painter after he left the theatre.

Overview of Critical Sources
The biographies by Coad and Canary provide important criticism on Dunlap's works. Criticism can also be found in histories and anthologies of early American drama. Critics agree that *Andre* is one of Dunlap's finest plays and that *History of the American Theatre* is one of his most important contributions.

Evaluation of Selected Criticism
Moses, Montrose J. *The American Dramatist*. New York: Benjamin Blom, 1939. Moses repeats the salient points of Coad's biography. Like Coad, he concludes that, while Dunlap was an unoriginal playwright, he fully deserves to be called the Father of the American Drama. Two of Dunlap's best works, according to Moses, are *Andre* and *History of the American Theatre*.

Quinn, Arthur Hobson, *A History of the American Drama from the Beginning to the Civil War*. New York: Appleton-Century-Crofts, 1943. Quinn skillfully blends biography and criticism to give an excellent account of Dunlap's life and career. He provides cogent analyses of many of his plays including *The Father*, *The Fatal Deception or Leicester*, *Andre*, and *The Italian Father*. Quinn praises Dunlap for being a prolific, versatile writer who wrote dignified blank verse.

Vaughn, Jack A. *Early American Dramatists from the Beginnings to 1900*. New York: Frederick Ungar, 1981. Vaughn's chapter on Dunlap concentrates on two plays, *Andre*, and *A Trip to Niagara*. He admires the former for its successful blank verse, effective characterization and well-structured plot. Vaughn praises the latter for the characterization of Amelia and its restrained sentimentality. In his admiration for Dunlap, Vaughn ignores or minimizes the playwright's limitations.

Other Sources
Blanck, Jacob, *Bibliography of American Literature*, Vol. II. New Haven: Yale University Press, 1957. Accurate list of Dunlap's works.

Moody, Richard, ed. *Dramas from the American Theatre 1762-1909*. Cleveland: World Publishing, 1966. Introduction to *The Glory of Columbia: Her Yeomanry!* provides a short biography of Dunlap's life, compares *The Glory of Columbia* to *Andre*, and evaluates Dunlap's contribution to American theatre. The introduction to *A Trip to Niagara* discusses the spectacle of dioramic scenery.

Quinn, Arthur Hobson, ed. *Representative American Plays from 1767 to the Present Day*. New York: Appleton-Century-Crofts, 1953. Introduction to *Andre* provides a biography of Dunlap and a brief discussion of his plays.

Margaret Ann Baker
Iowa State University

FRIEDRICH DÜRRENMATT
1921

Author's Chronology

Born January 5, 1921, in Konolfingen, Switzerland, to Reinhold Dürrenmatt, a Protestant minister, and Hulda Dürrenmatt-Zimmermann; grandfather Ulrich Dürrenmatt active in politics; attends secondary school in Grosshochstetten, then the *Gymnasium* in Bern; *1941* graduates from the Humboldtianum and begins studies at Zurich, then in Bern, in literature and philosophy; *1943* produces paintings and first writings, including the unpublished *Komodie; 1945* publishes "The Old Man" in Bern newspaper *Der Bund,* and begins first play, *It Is Written; 1947* marries Lotti Geissler; *1948 The Blind Man* performed in Basel; moves to Ligerz on Lake Biel; *1948-1952* establishes reputation as short story writer, novelist, and playwright, settles in Neuchâtel (present residence) with wife and three children; *1962 The Physicists* performed in Zurich, Berlin, Hamburg and Hanover; international reputation grows with Gore Vidal's adaptation of *Romulus the Great* in New York; *1969* travels to America; *Play Strindberg* performed in Basel; *1972* publishes critical writings since *Theater-Schriften* (1966); *1976 Writings on Theatre and Drama* in English published in London.

Author's Bibliography

Only a portion of Dürrenmatt's writings in theatre, radio plays, short stories, mysteries, essays, and other work are translated into English, but his most important plays are available in several anthologies and collections. Individual editions, notably *Four Plays,* translated by Gerhard Nellhous ("Problems of the Theatre" and *Romulus the Great*), Michael Bullock (*The Marriage of Mr. Mississippi*), William McLewee (*An Angel Comes to Babylon*), and James Kirkup (*The Physicists*), published in 1964 (London: Jonathon Cape), and a series of single works by Dürrenmatt published by Grove Press, have introduced him to English speaking readers. Volkmar Sander edited *Romulus* (the Nellhaus translation), *The Visit* (tr. Patrick Bowles), and some prose essays including "Problems of the Theatre" (New York: Continuum Press, 1982) as #89 in the German Library Series. Current work is published simultaneously by Jonathan Cape in London and Grove Press in New York.

Biographical Sources

While no purely personal biography of Dürrenmatt has been written to date, introductions to his collected works give some personal information. In the process of discussing Dürrenmatt's earlier prose works, Murray B. Peppard, in *Friedrich Dürrenmatt's* (New York: Twayne, 1969) and Armin Arnold, in *Friedrich Dürren-*

matt (New York: Frederick Ungar, 1972) both point to Dürrenmatt's religious upbringing and his experiences as a small-town child in Switzerland. The Biographical accounts in chronological form give some public career details, in these sources and in *Dürrenmatt; A Study of His Plays,* by Urs Jenny (London: Eyre Methuen, 1978). No autobiography is among Dürrenmatt's work to date, in German or English.

Overview of Critical Sources

The intensely intellectual bias of Dürrenmatt's work, especially for the stage, lends itself to critical analyses on many fronts, but the single major thrust of all the scholarship surrounding his success moves toward Dürrenmatt's particularly cynical view of man's relation to God. The "Deus absconditus" element of the existential view has no better spokesman than Dürrenmatt, so that critics concentrate on his dramatic and theatrical recapitulation of the hopelessness of the human endeavor to improve humanity itself. A "writer in extremis," Dürrenmatt presents God and man as totally irreconcilable, echoing post-war absurdist ideas as well as (critics suspect) Dürrenmatt's own observations about the ineffectuality of religious zeal. Whether specifically dealing with the dramatic works or ranging to the stories and mysteries, critics always note Dürrenmatt's irrepressible sense of humor in the face of meaninglessness existence.

Evaluation of Selected Criticism

Arnold, Armin, *Friedrich Dürrenmatt.* New York: Frederick Ungar, 1972. This graceful, uncluttered essay examines the early drama, major plays, radio plays, and critical writings from the perspective of Dürrenmatt's notions of reality as partially obscured by the character's automatic belief in a benevolent (or at least attentive) deity. The absurdity of human endeavors, according to Arnold, makes for both the distressing and the comic thematic slants in his work. Arnold divides the playwright's work into major periods, from *Romulus* to *The Visit,* demonstrating a turn away from the comic to the socially tragic.

Jenny, Urs, *Dürrenmatt: A Study of His Plays.* London: Eyre Metheun, 1978. Putting the stress on Dürrenmatt's work as it reflects the times after World War II, Jenny treats the playwright's fundamental pessimism as it is reflected in his inclination for comedy. Moving through the major dramatic work chapter by chapter, devoting each section to a single play, Jenny's critical analysis is the most thorough available in English, since he concentrates on only the dramatic work and leaves the prose to others. Particularly valuable is Jenny's discussion of the treatment of "chance" as an anti-structural element in both playwriting and social theory; using *The Physicists* as the model of Dürrenmatt's interest in chance as a formative aspect (usually the opposite of human planning) in his plays, Jenny builds an argument Dürrenmatt's work goes from anger to desperation, and points out that *Portrait of a Planet,* written in 1970, was the first play in twenty years that Dürrenmatt did not call a comedy. Two special features of this critical work are its thorough chronology of all dramatic work at the beginning of the book, and the vital discussion of the changes Dürrenmatt added during the actual production of his plays; this last section has no parallel in English criticism and as such places Jenny's work among the indispensable sources for Dürrenmatt in English.

Peppard, Murray B. *Friedrich Dürrenmatt.* New York: Twayne, 1969. This critical study avoids personal comparisons between Dürrenmatt's life and work, noting Dürrenmatt's request that, even in his interviews, his personal life be kept apart from his public life. Peppard extends the discussion of the more popular plays to an examination of the prose pieces and critical writings of Dürrenmatt as well; starting with the years of apprenticeship, Peppard shows how Dürrenmatt's intellectual view of God's indifference colored his work in all genres. He traces the influence of Bertolt Brecht, Max Frisch, and even Thornton Wilder on Dürrenmatt's work, especially in *It Is Written* and *The Physicists.* Depicting Dürrenmatt as a stern moralist, the study concludes that Dürrenmatt's theoretical work constitutes a general statement regarding his thinking about the world as much as about the creative writing process, and that, as a moralist, he holds to his belief that critics should look not to his "explanations" but to the works themselves for answers to what they are about. Peppard quotes Dürrenmatt in *Problems Of the Theatre:* "Misunderstandings creep in because people desperately search the henyard of my dramas for the egg of explanation which I steadfastly refuse to lay."

Tiusanen, Timo, *Dürrenmatt: A Study in Plays, Prose, Theory.* Princeton: Princeton University Press, 1977. One of the longest and most recent of complete studies of Dürrenmatt as thinker as well as creative writer, Tiusanen's work also can claim the most scholarly approach to the subject, listing no less than three hundred entries in its bibliography. This ambitious study identifies several important features of Dürrenmatt's work, such as the "demonic grotesque," "parodic grotesque," and "absolute grotesque." This differentiation clarifies a great deal of the playwright's complex world view, and explains the relationship between the serious and the comic in his work, coupled with the concept of "scenic units" which Tiusanen discusses as well. His treatment of the dramaturgical skills that Dürrenmatt employs to get his philosophical point across demonstrates Tiusanen's familiarity with theatrical rules and structures as well as his critical skills in literary analysis. Dürrenmatt was his own *dramaturg,* according to Tiusanen, separating the creative process from the critical process by going back into his work with a cold and unforgiving eye, sacrificing the pet phrase or scene in the interests of structure, clarity, and impact. Unlike Jenny's neutral discussion of Dürrenmatt's stage work, Tiusanen incorporates the production changes that Dürrenmatt insisted on with his total intellectual signature; the final chapter, "Dürrenmatt and the

Stage," brings together all the central themes winding through this complex but very readable major critical work.

Other Sources

Askew, Melvin W. "Dürrenmatt's *The Visit of the Old Lay,*" in *Tulane Drama Review* (June 1961): 89-105. A study of the rituals and myths, especially the castration myth, imbedded in the play.

Benedikt, Michael, and George E. Wellwart, eds. *Postwar German Theatre.* London: Macmillan, 1968. A strong introductory essay that puts Dürrenmatt's work in perspective with his contemporaries, especially Brecht and Frisch, together with *Incident at Twilight,* which Dürrenmatt wrote in 1959.

Brustein, Robert, *The Theatre of Revolt.* London: Metheun, 1965. Reviews of Dürrenmatt's New York productions, tying his work into the movement toward alternative theatre on the legitimate stage. A fiery and personal book by one of theatre's best critics and practitioners.

Diller, Edward, "Dürrenmatt's Use of the Stage as Dramatic Element," in *Symposium* (Fall 1966): 201-202. A continuation of the critical interest in Dürrenmatt's close contact with the actual productions, as opposed to the literary publications, of his work. Diller has published several other articles on Dürrenmatt in *Modern Language Quarterly* and elsewhere.

Esslin, Martin, *The Theatre of the Absurd.* London: Eyre & Spottiswood, 1962. The absurdist movement discussed thoroughly; although Esslin concentrates on non-German absurdists, he also treats Dürrenmatt's contributions.

Heilman, Robert Bechtold, *The Iceman, the Arsonist, and the Troubled Agent,* Seattle: University of Washington Press, 1973. A readable discussion of Europen themes as reflected in Dürrenmatt, Frisch, and many other playwrights. Puts Dürrenmatt's work among the most important creative outbursts of post-war literature.

Klarmann, Adolf D. "Friedrich Dürrenmatt and the Tragic Sense of Comedy," in *Tulane Drama Review* (May 1960). A good analysis of the hero and non-hero in the plays, especially *An Angel Comes to Babylon;* Klarmann notes that the non-hero must survive in order to prevent "the grim pursuit of duty."

Sharp, Sister Corona, "Dürrenmatt and the Spirit of Play," in *University of Toronto Quarterly* (Oct. 1969): 73-74. Puts Dürrenmatt's plays into larger perspective of "the spirit of play," and notes Dürrenmatt's characters' predilection to games.

Wellwarth, George, "Friedrich Dürrenmatt and Max Frisch," in *Tulane Drama Review* (March 1962): 24-32. A comparison of the two Swiss playwrights whose work has been more exhaustively compared in only German criticism.

Whitton, Kenneth S. *The Theatre of Friedrich Dürrenmatt.* New York: Humanities Press, 1980. Examines Dürrenmatt in light of his later works and his growing critical reputation.

Thomas J. Taylor
Purdue University

JUAN DEL ENCINA
1468-1529?

Author's Chronology

Born Juan de Fermoselle to a poor shoemaker, probably in Salamanca, Spain on July 12, 1468; *1484* is made chorister at the Cathedral of Salamanca under the name Juan del Encina (*encina* means "holm oak" and suggests the bucolic literary connotations that were in vogue at the time); *1492* enters the household of Don Fadrique, second Duke of Alba as court musician; *1496* applies for the post of precentor at the Cathedral of Salamanca and loses it to his rival Lucas Fernández, whereupon he goes to Rome and becomes a singer in the chapel of Spanish Pope Alexander VI; *1502* appointed by papal bull to the prebendary of the Cathedral of Salamanca; *1508* is appointed by Pope Julius II to the archdeaconry of Málaga; January 6, *1513* his *Egloga de Plácida y Victoriano* is performed at Rome before the Spanish ambassador; *1519* appointed prior of León and makes a pilgrimage to the Holy Land, is ordained and celebrates his first mass in Jerusalem; *1523* takes up residence in Leon; 1529 or 1530 (before January 10) dies, probably in Leon.

Author's Bibliography (selected)

Cancionero, 1496 (a compendium that includes the essay *Art of Castilian Poetry*; his paraphrase of Virgil's ten eclogues; his original pastoral verses called *villancicos*; and eight plays); *Egloga de amores I* (*The Courtier Turned Shepherd*, trans. by R. Lima in *Early Spanish Plays*, ed. R. O'Brien, vol. 1, 1964); *Egloga de amores II* (*The Shepherds Turned Courtier*, trans. by R. Lima in *Early Spanish Plays*, ed. R. O'Brien, vol. 1, 1964); *Egloga de las grandes lluvias*, 1507 (*Eclogue*, trans. by Willis Knapp Jones in *Spanish One Act Plays in English*, 1934); *Egloga de los tres pastores*, 1509? (*The Eclogue of the Three Shepherds*, trans. by R. Lima in *Early Spanish Plays*, ed. R. O'Brien, vol. 1, 1964); *Auto del repelón*, 1509? (The Hair-Pulling Skit; untranslated); *Egloga de Plácida y Victoriano*, 1514 (*The Eclogue of Placida and Victoriano*, trans. by H.A. Herter in *Early Spanish Plays*, ed. R. O'Brien, vol. 1, 1964); *Trivagia o Sacra Via de Hierusalem* (Sacred Voyage to Jerusalem; untranslated autobiographical essay in verse), 1520.

Overview of Biographical Sources

The details of Encina's early life and origins are contained in R. Espinosa Maeso's "Nuevos datos biográficos de Juan del Encina" in *Boletin de la Real Academia Española* 8 (1921): 640-56, and the years of his residence in Malaga are covered by R. Mitjana y Gordón in *Sobre Juan del Encina músico y poeta. Nuevos datos para la biografía* (Malaga, 1895). The psychology of his later years can be filled in from his own *Trivagia* (most recent edition is *Viage y peregrinacion a*

Jerusalem (Madrid: Pantaleón, 1786), where the playwright gives up seeking a patron for devotion to Christ and the Virgin and declares, not without bitterness, that for centuries past unresponsive patrons have allowed poets to languish in poverty. Chapter 2 of John Lihani's *Lucas Fernández* (New York: Twayne, 1973) portrays Encina as seen by this contemporary playwright during the years of their rivalry.

Evaluation of Selected Biographies

Andrews, Richard J. *Juan del Encina. Prometheus in Search of Prestige.* Berkeley: University of California Press, 1959. As is implied by the subtitle, the composite impression of Encina's personality is not a favorable one. Andrews provides an especially insightful chapter of commentary on the playwright's autobiographical *Trivagia* but, although there is a substantial section of footnotes, there is no bibiography.

Sullivan, Henry W. *Juan del Encina*. Boston: Twayne, 1976. Although not blind to Encina's flaws as a social climber and sycophant, Sullivan chooses to stress the multifaceted personality of this Renaissance man as cleric, pilgrim, composer, impresario, linguist, playwright, editor, translator, critic and preceptist within the context of his times, and what emerges is a far more sympathetic portrayal of the man than is achieved by Andrews. There is a nearly exhaustive bibliography.

Overview of Critical Sources

It has been said that Encina's work in drama unfairly overshadows his contributions to music and poetry, but these fields as well as drama have been amply explored in English; his musical work, for example, is analyzed by R.M. Stevenson in *Spanish Music in the Age of Columbus* (The Hague; Nijhoff, 1960) and the Virgilian aspect of his poetry by James A. Anderson in *Encina and Virgil* (University, MS: Romance Monographs, 1974). Besides analyses of the plays themselves, such as are available in chapters 4, 5 and 6 of Sullivan and chapters 8 and 9 of Andrews, speculation on the sources of Encina's various plays is a fertile area of critical study; Crawford (see below) demonstrates the interdependence of Encina's *Egloga de los tres pastores* and a contemporary eclogue of Antonio Tebaldeo and Donald McGrady points out a similarity between *Egloga de Plácida y Victoriano* and Giovan Francesco Straparola's *Le piacevoli notti* (in "An Unperceived Popular Story in Encina's 'Plácida y Vitoriano' " in *Bulletin of the Comediantes*, vol. 32, no. 2, Fall 1980, 139-141).

A special critical problem is the study of Encina's *sayagués* "dialect" that the playwright uses in the mouths of his rustic characters for humorous effect and indeed may well have brought into vogue among his dramatic colleagues by his own elaboration. The term, which became a sloppy all-inclusive designation for non-

Castilian speech used in 16th and 17th century drama, derives from its mistaken identification with the village of Sayago in the southwestern region of Zamora near the Portuguese border. Lihani deals extensively with the characteristics of *sayagués* (e.g., rhotacism, *hue* for *fue*) in *Lucas Fernández*, pp. 74-76, and more generally in his article, "Some Notes on Sayagués" in *Hispania*, 41 (1958), 165-169. Encina's *sayagués* is also studied by Charlotte Stern in "Sayago and Sayagués in Spanish history and literature" in *Hispanic Review*, 29 (1961), 217-37, and by Paul Teyssier in *La langue de Gil Vicente* (Paris: Klincksieck, 1959). So important is the role of this *sayagués* dialect that its linguistic inconsistencies in *Auto del repelón*, regarded as Encina's one true farce and as the ancestor of the *entremés*, were the basis of an unsuccessful attempt to discredit its authorship by Encina (see Sullivan, p. 94).

Evaluation of Selected Criticism

J.P. Wickersham Crawford, *Spanish Drama before Lope de Vega*. Philadelphia: University of Pennsylvania Press, 1937. Chapter 2 is devoted to Encina and analyzes the plays individually. Noting that Encina's canon comprises every differenct form of dramatic entertainment known in 15th century Spain, Crawford willingly concedes to him the title of founder of Spanish drama. There is an unannotated bibliography.

Selected Dictionaries and Encyclopedias

European Authors, 1000-1900: A Biographical Dictionary of European Literature, H.W. Wilson, 1969. Standard short-entry synopsis of Encina's life and contribution to Spanish literature.

McGraw-Hill Encyclopedia of World Drama, McGraw-Hill, 1984. Furnishes an extensive bibliography and dates for *both* the writing and publication of fourteen of Encina's plays.

Jack Shreve
Allegany Community College

SIR GEORGE ETHEREGE
1634?-1691?

Author's Chronology

Birthplace and date unknown; *1654* apprenticed to attorney at Beaconsfield; *1659* went to Clement's Inn to read law; *1664* success of *The Comical Revenge* or *Love in a Tub* brings membership in inner circle of court wits; *1668 She Wou'd If She Cou'd* produced; *1668-1671* serves as secretary to Sir Daniel Harvey, English Ambassador to Turkey; *1676* writes last play *The Man of Mode* and serves Mary of Modena, wife of future James II; *1679?* marries rich widow and knighted; *1685* begins diplomatic post of English Resident to the Diet of the Holy Roman Empire at Ratisbon; *1691?* dies in Paris(?).

Author's Bibliography

The first collected edition of the plays was printed in 1704 in London and sold by J. Tonson and T. Bennet. This version was reprinted in 1715, in 1723, and again in 1735. The first modern (1888) edition of the plays was based on the 1704 text and edited by A. W. Verity. The standard edition for many years was *Dramatic Works*, edited by H. F. B. Brett-Smith in two volumes (1927). More recently, Michael Cordner has edited *The Plays of Sir George Etherege* for Cambridge University Press (1982). Separate modern editions of the plays include *She Wou'd If She Cou'd* (ed. Charlene M. Taylor, Regents Restoration Drama Series, 1972) and *The Man of Mode* (ed. John Barnard, Norton, 1979).

Overview of Biographical Sources

As the number of question marks in the Author's Chronology section indicates, there are many gaps in the knowledge of Etherege's life, even such basic information as his date and place of birth, his marriage date, and his date and place of death. There is no full scale biography of his life. The first attempt at a biography of Etherege's life was not made until 1750 when William Oldys prepared an entry on Etherege for *Biographia Britannica*. Edmund Gosse used Etherege's diplomatic correspondence written at Ratisbon for his sympathetic biography of Etherege in *Cornhill Magazine* (1881), and Bonamy Dobree's short biography of Etherege in *Essays in Biography, 1680-1726* (1925) similarly concentrates on the diplomatic years. The best account of Etherege's life is a short sketch written by Frederick Bracher for his introduction to *Letters of Sir George Etherege* (1974).

Autobiographical Sources

The chief source for information about Etherge's life is his letters. Two of his official letter books are at Harvard University; other letters can be found in the

Middleton Papers at the British Museum. *The Letterbook*, edited by Sybil Rosen-feld (Oxford: Oxford University Press, 1928; rpt. New York: Benjamin Blom, 1971), contains Etherege's letters from Ratisbon written from 1685 to 1688. Six years later, in 1934, Rosenfeld published 134 letters not included in *The Letterbook* in "Sir George Etherge in Ratisbon," *Review of English Studies* 10:177-189. In 1952, Rosenfeld published "The Second Letterbook of Sir George Etherege" in *Review of English Studies* 3:19-27, which contains over ninety more letters and a list of 29 letters from February 20 to September 28, 1689. Frederick Bracher's *Letters of Sir George Etherge* (Berkeley: University of California Press, 1974) reprints the most important letters from these three collections plus others, though eighty still remain in manuscript. Bracher provides translations from Latin and Italian in the notes and the manuscript source for each letter. The chief strength of Bracher's work is the biographical sketch of Etherege he provides.

Overview of Critical Sources
Despite Etherege's small output of only three plays, an increasing number of articles and especially dissertations have been written about his work. Early com-mentary concentrated on the "immorality" of his works; modern critics have been more interested in Etherege's rake heroes, strong-minded heroines, "type" charac-ters, his treatment of marriage, and his sources.

Evaluation of Selected Criticism
Mann, David D. *Sir George Etherege: A Reference Guide*. Boston: G. K. Hall, 1981. This thorough bibliography is arranged chronologically from 1664 to 1980, covers writings both by and about Etherege, and contains short summaries of the contents and value of each entry. The introduction provides helpful notes on Etherege's biography, the texts, general critical trends in the study of Etherege, and topics for criticism in the individual plays.

Underwood, Dale, *Etherege and the Seventeenth-Century Comedy of Manners*. New Haven: Yale University Press, 1957. The best of the critical studies, this book defines the forces in seventeenth-century thought and society which influenced Etherege (the heroic tradition, Christian humanism, Hobbes), reinterprets the plays as literary and comic art, and shows how the plays modify some of the principal traditions of Elizabethan and Jacobean drama.

Other Sources
Brown, Laura S. "The Divided Plot: Tragicomic Form in the Restoration," in *English Literary History*, 47 (1980): 67-79. Comparison of *Love in a Tub* with Dryden's *Marriage A-la-Mode*.

Corman, Brian, "Interpreting and Misinterpreting *The Man of Mode*," in *Papers in Language and Literature*, 13 (1977): 35-53. Dorimant as comic hero forced to undergo comic punishments.

Fujimura, Thomas H. *The Restoration Comedy of Wit*. Princeton: Princeton University Press, 1952. Chapter 5 establishes Etherege as a "true wit" and examines the "wit" of the characters in Etherege's plays.

Holland, Norman, *The First Modern Comedies: The Significance of Etherege, Wycherley, and Congreve*. Cambridge: Harvard University Press, 1959. Study of Etherege's comedy and place among Restoration writers.

Hume, Robert D. "The Myth of the Rake in 'Restoration' Comedy," in *Studies in Literary Imagination*, 10 (1977): 25-55. Dorimant in *Man of Mode* as exception to rakes as comic exaggerations and satiric butts.

Hughes, Derek, "Play and Passion in *The Man of Mode*," in *Comparative Drama*, 15 (Fall 1981): 231-257. Discussion of game and religious imagery.

Mann, David D. ed. *A Concordance to the Plays and Poems of Sir George Etherege*. Westport, CT: Greenwood Press, 1985. A study of Etherege's language use, including place names, French usages, allusion, and frequency of individual word use.

Ann W. Engar
University of Utah

EURIPIDES
485(?) B.C.-406(?) B.C.

Author's Chronology

Born in 484(?) B.C., the son of Mnesarchus or Mnesarchides and of Clito; father came from the deme (township) of Phyla in Attica; his parents, according to the comic poets, are shopkeepers, but less biased sources describe the family as land-owners in Salamis where Euripides grew up; he may have been a disciple of Anaxagoras whose doctrines appear in some of his writings; seems to have known other intellectual leaders of Athens and to have been influenced by them; Packard-Cambridge mentions Prodicus of Ceos and Archelaus, who, like Euripides, was a pupil of Anaxagoras; Socrates himself admired Euripides; fathers three sons; post-humous production of some later tragedies is attributed to one of them; holds minor offices: a priesthood at Phyla, membership in an embassy to Syracuse, and he fulfills the usual military obligations; toward the end of his life Euripides leaves Athens, and at the invitation of Archelaus, King of Macedonia (413-399 B.C.) as part of the latter's policy of hellenization, settles in Pella (or Magnesia (?) in Thessaly) where he writes *The Bacchae*; after his death a cenotaph is erected in his honor at Athens.

Author's Bibliography (all dates are B.C.)

Ancient sources ascribe ninety-two plays to Euripides. Of these, seventeen trage-dies are extant:

Alcestis, produced 438; *Medea*, 431; *Heraclidae*, c. 430; *Hippolytus*, 428; *Andromache*, c. 425; *Hecuba*, c. 424; *The Suppliants*, c. 424; *Ion*, c. 418-17; *Electra*, 417 or 413; *Hercules furens*, c. 417; *The Trojan Women*, 415; *Iphigenia in Tauris*, c. 413; *Helen*, 412; *Phoenissae*, between 412-408; *Orestes*, 408; *Bacchae* and *Iphigenia in Aulide* (the last two produced posthumously), c. 405; *Rhesus* is ascribed to him and *Cyclops* is a satyr play. Among his lost or fragmentary works are fifty-eight titles, seven of which are identified as satyr plays.

Overview of Biographical Sources

The source materials on Euripides' life describe his preference for a life devoted to reflection and writing. The comic poets exaggerated his reclusiveness (e.g., describing him as living in a cave at Salamis), and ridiculed his tragedies and his person. Aristophanes hints that Euripides' marriage failed. He describes Euripides in *The Frogs* as the owner of a large library.

As an author Euripides was not popular with Athenian audiences. He criticised the conduct of the gods and thus opened himself to the suspicion of atheism. His plays won twenty prizes; only five times did he win first prize, once posthumously.

Nonetheless, there is evidence that his poetry was loved and memorized by many during his lifetime. For example, there is an account of Athenian prisoners freed after the siege at Syracuse when their captors heard them recite passages from Euripides. His indubitable apotheosis occurred after his death: he was by far the most popular of the Greek tragedians in the Hellenistic period. His appeal rests upon his profound psychological insights; his empathy with human suffering, his censure of the moral and spiritual inadequacy of Greek religion made him a herald of the new thought, of the new emphasis on the individual. As creator of the "happy ending" he foreshadowed the New Comedy developed by Menander. Some authors believe that Euripides left Athens at Archelaus' invitation to escape the jibes of the comic poets.

In the absence of source material on Euripides' life, biographers are content to repeat the few certain—or even uncertain—facts "What biographical material we possess is unreliable; most of it obviously stems from comic travesties." (*Cambridge History of Classical Literature*, I, 768); *cf.* M. Lefkowitz, *The Lives of the Greek Poets* (Baltimore: Johns Hopkins Press, 1981, pp. 88-105).

Autobiographical Sources
Although Euripides left no autobiographical data, strictly speaking, he nonetheless reveals through his drama his convictions in regard to every aspect of life and thought that concerned him: religion and myth, women and war, politics and power.

Overview of Critical Sources
The bibliography on Euripides is understandably extensive. Each of the tragedies has been carefully edited. Translations of each play into English are available in prose and in verse forms. Studies of Euripides describe his style, his use of meter, his dramatic form. An even larger corpus of writings studies individual plays. There is finally a concordance of Euripides which gives an alphabetical list of the important words used by him with references to the passages in which they occur (*cf.* the bibliography on Euripides in *Cambridge History of Classical Literature*, I, 769-772).

Evaluation of Selected Criticism
Bates, William N. *Euripides, a Student of Human Nature*. Philadelphia: University of Pennsylvania Press, 1930; rpt. 1969. Bates analyzes the special characteristics of Euripides' drama, especially the child motif.

Conacher, D.J. *Euripidean Drama*: Myth, Theme and Structure. Toronto: University of Toronto Press, 1967. Conacher describes in seven sections the mythological tragedy, using *Hippolytus*, *The Bacchae* and the *Heracles* considering in each case a critique of other views; political tragedy under which he considers *The Suppliants* and the *Heraclidae*; war and its aftermath are considered in relation to *The Trojan Women*, *Hecuba* and *Andromache*. Realistic tragedy, *tragédie manquée*, romantic tragedy and satyr plays are developed with the same meticulous illustration and analysis.

Lucas, F.L. *Euripides and His Influence*. New York: Cooper Square Publishers, 1963. Lucas describes the dramatist in his own setting and his impact on literature and thought in antiquity, the Middle Ages, the Renaissance and up until the present which he sees as a new Greek renaissance.

Mechlinger, Siegfried, *Euripides*. New York: Frederick Ungar, 1973. Mechlinger gives a chronology of Euripides' life and the events in Athenian political and intellectual life which affected him. Mechlinger describes the Athenian theater and gives an analysis of each of the tragedies.

Segal, Erich, ed. *Euripides*: A Collection of Critical Essays. Englewood Cliffs, NJ: Prentice Hall, 1968. In his introduction Segal throws a new light on Euripides' unpopularity, completely reversing the picture: he cites as Euripides' greatest admirer Aristophanes, usually considered his greatest enemy. Among the authors of critical essays which make up Segal's work is Jean-Paul Sartre's essay, "Why the Trojan Women?" It serves as an introduction to the play of the same name and shows the reader the problems of a translator in adapting language, style and culture itself to the content of the play. There is a one-page chronology of important events in Euripides' life and times and an identification of the contributors to this volume of essays.

Webster, T.B.L. *Greek Theatre Production*. London: Methuen, 1956. This work discusses the specific aspects of producing tragedy and comedy on the Greek stage.

Other Sources

Cambridge History of Classical Literature, Vol. I: Greek Literature, ed. P.E. Easterling and B.M.W. Knox. Cambridge: Cambridge University Press, 1985.

Murray, Gilbert, *Euripides and His Age*. 2nd ed. New York: Oxford University Press, 1965. A classical treatment by the poet-translator of *The Trojan Women*, *The Bacchae*, *Rhesus*, and *The Frogs* of Aristophanes.

Oates, Whitney J. and Eugene O'Neill, Jr., eds. *The Complete Greek Drama*, 2 vols. New York: Random House, 1938. Besides a lengthy general introduction to Greek drama (I, xiii-xlix) by Eugene O'Neil, Jr., there are introductions to each play by the editors. The editors have endeavored to choose the best available translation for each individual play, and to bring together in a single work the complete corpus of extant Greek drama available in the past only in individual translation.

Packard-Cambridge, Arthur Wallace, "Euripides", in *Oxford Classical Dictionary* Oxford: Clarendon Press, 1949, pp. 347-350. An encyclopedic survey by an eminent scholar of Euripides.

Taplin, Oliver, *Greek Tragedy in Action*. Berkeley, California. University of California Press, 1978. Taplin's work could serve as a handbook for contemporary productions of Greek plays, so detailed and specific is his study of staging, costumes, masks and other phases of production.

Consuelo Maria Aherne, S.S.J.

EVERYMAN-AUTHOR
late 1400's

Author's Chronology

The English morality play *Everyman* is now generally held to be a translation of a Dutch play written in the late fifteenth century entitled *Elckerlijc*. The earliest known edition of the Dutch play appeared in Antwerp in approximately 1495. The first English translation was printed between 1510 and 1525. Both the author of the Dutch play and the translator of the English are anonymous. *Everyman*, and its Dutch original, developed from sermon literature of the late Middle Ages. The homiletic topic of the play is the Christian's proper preparation for death and judgment, as defined by late medieval Catholic theology. Given this topic and treatment and taking into account the internal evidence of the "power of priesthood" passage, it seems likely that the original author was a member of the Catholic clergy. The story of Everyman's abandonment by his friends is derived from a collection of tales of oriental origin entitled *Baarlaam and Josaphat*. This collection was often used by medieval preachers as a source book for moral *exempla*. The author of *Elckerlijc* and the translator of *Everyman* succeed in shaping the didactic tale and the theology into a powerful dramatic work. The stark dignity of action and character and the plain, clear diction of *Everyman* have made it the most well-known example of the English morality play.

Author's Bibliography

Everyman, late fifteenth century; first printed c. 1510-1525. The standard edition is edited by A. C. Cawley. Manchester: Manchester University Press, 1961.

Overview of Critical Sources

Most scholarship written in the latter nineteenth century and the first half of the twentieth century has concentrated on attempting to establish the priority of composition of *Everyman* or the Dutch play *Elckerlijc*. A.C. Cawley conveniently summarizes this debate in his introduction to the standard edition of *Everyman*. The general consensus now is that the Dutch play came first. Interpretive analyses of the play may be said to begin with Lawerence V. Ryan's essay "Doctrine and Dramatic Structure in *Everyman*" which appeared in 1957, an intelligent discussion of the relation between the doctrine and the drama of the work. Later commentators such as Conley, Kolve, Jambeck, and Van Dyke have brought facets of the medieval theological and/or literary background of the play to bear in their analyses, which point to a rich complexity of ideas and dramatic movement in this apparently simple and otherwise austere play. Critical opinion continues to be divided over the interpretation of the character Knowledge. Does it represent intellectual and/or theological Knowledge, the product of reason, or does it represent acknowledgement of sinfulness as a necessary prerequisite to completing the sacrament of penance? Helpful summaries of this debate may be found in the essays by Thomas, Kolve, and Jambeck.

Evaluation of Selected Criticism

Brooks, Cleanth and Robert B. Heilman, *Understanding Drama*. New York: Holt, 1948, pp. 100-111. Describing *Everyman* as a "dramatized parable," Brooks and Heilman provide a thorough "new critical" analysis of key dramatic elements of the play.

Cawley, A.C., ed. *Everyman*. Manchester (England): Manchester University Press, 1961. Cawley's introduction to this standard edition is a comprehensive, yet concise, treatment of the play's relation to its medieval background and of its meaning and style.

Conley, John, "The Doctrine of Friendship in *Everyman*," *Speculum*, 44 (1969): 374-382. Drawing on classical, Biblical, and medieval sources, Conley explains how the doctrine of friendship in the play reflects medieval commonplace attitudes on the subject. The commonplaces are adapted to reflect two central thrusts of the play: 1) the necessity, for salvation, of good works, and 2) divine judgment after death.

Cormican, L. A. "Morality Tradition and the Interludes," *The Pelican Guide to English Literature: The Age of Chaucer*, ed. Boris Ford. Baltimore: Penguin Books, 1954, pp. 186-194. Cormican provides a general, and somewhat superficial, introduction to the play, citing its medieval qualities and distinguishing it at several points from Elizabethan drama.

Jamback, Thomas J. "*Everyman* and the Implications of Bernardine Humanism in the Character 'Knowledge,' " in *Medievalia et Humanistica*, no. 8, ed. Paul Maurice Clogan. Cambridge: Cambridge University Press, 1977, pp. 103-123. Jambeck draws on the sermons of St. Bernard of Clairvaux to show how the playwright reflects Bernard's penitential piety, especially in its emphasis on the "potentialities of human nature . . . as the operative principle in the redemptive process." Everyman's psychological experience of attempting to understand his plight prepares him for the appearance of Knowledge, who represents, in the Bernardine system, knowledge both of self and of God. This view of active human nature, shaping to an extent its own destiny, anticipates later dramatic protagonists and a "humanism that is implicitly modern."

Kaula, David, "Time and Timelessness in *Everyman* and *Dr. Faustus*," *College English*, 22 (1960): 9-14. This is a brief, but suggestive article which explains the contrasting treatments of time and evil in the two plays as reflecting basic shifts in ideas on these topics between the Middle Ages and the post-Reformation. In the medieval play, *Everyman*, time is seen as a medium of moral growth and fulfillment, while in the post-Reformation *Faustus* time is presented as a destructive force, reflecting the problematic view of time in the later period.

Kolve, V. A. "*Everyman* and the Parable of the Talents," in *Medieval Drama*. ed. Sandro Sticca. Albany: SUNY Press, 1972, pp. 69-98. In an impressive essay, Kolve draws upon patristric commentary on Jesus's parable of the talents (Matthew 25: 14-30) to explain key features of the play's plot, characterization, language, and doctrine. Kolve claims that the parable is the "source behind the sources." The play is not, Kolve argues, about the art of dying but is about how to ready and render spiritual accounts; that is, it is a "play about holy living."

Potter, Robert A. *The English Morality Play: Origins, History, and Influence of Dramatic Tradition*. London: Routledge & Kegan Paul, 1975. Potter provides some helpful commentary on the play in relation to other moralities. For the student of *Everyman*, most interesting is Potter's account of the play's famous productions and its reception and influence in the twentieth century.

Ryan, Lawerence V. "Doctrine and Dramatic Structure in *Everyman*," in *Speculum*, 32 (1957): 722-735; rpt. *Middle English Survey: Critical Essays*, ed. Edward Vasta. Notre Dame: University of Notre Dame Press, 1965, pp. 283-307. In a thorough and elegant essay, Ryan provides a detailed analysis of the theology of the play, showing how the theology "gives the play its characters, structure, significance, and even its dramatic impressiveness."

Van Dyke, Carolynn, "The Intangible and Its Image: Allegorical Discourse and the Cast of *Everyman*," in *Acts of Interpretation: The Text in its Contexts. 700-1600*. eds. Mary J. Carruthers and Elizabeth D. Kirk. Norman, OK: Pilgrim Books, 1982, pp. 311-324. This is an illuminating article about the nature of the allegorical program of the play, based on a close reading of the text. Van Dyke distinguishes between allegorical characters such as Death, Fellowship, and Cousin who "teach" Everyman to "understand particularities through the categories whose names they bear" and the later-appearing characters such as Good Deeds, Knowledge, and Confession who "reveal the force and meaning of universals in the phenomenal world."

Van Laan, Thomas F. "*Everyman*: A Structural Analysis," in *PMLA*, 78 (1963): 465-475. Van Laan discovers a two-part structure in the play: the falling action of the first half of the play, as Everyman's fortunes decline, and the rising action that culminates in his salvation. The descent-ascent pattern is related to Maude Bodkin's theory of archetypes and to the "Christic action" of descent into the world, death, resurrection, and ascent as a pattern for all Christians.

Other Sources

Cawley, A. C. and others, *The Revels History of Drama in English, Volume I: Medieval Drama*. London: Metheun, 1983. A brief treatment of *Everyman* appears in the chapter on morality plays.

Davenport, W. A. *Fifteenth-century English Drama*. Cambridge and Totowa, NJ: D. S. Brewer and Rowman & Littlefield, 1982. Davenport includes a brief discussion of *Everyman* in his survey.

Houle, Peter J. *The English Morality and Related Drama: A Bibliographical Survey*. Hamden, CT: Archon Books, 1972. Houle provides a list of editions of *Everyman*, a plot summary, and a list of critical studies.

Thomas, Helen S. "The Meaning of the Character Knowledge in *Everyman*," in *Mississippi Quarterly*, 14 (1961): 3-13.

_____, "Some Analogues of *Everyman*," in *Mississippi Quarterly*, 16 (1963): 97-103.

Tigg, E. R. *The Dutch Elckerlijc is Prior to the English Everyman*. London, 1981. The definitive pamphlet on the topic.

James Flynn
Western Kentucky University

GEORGE FARQUHAR
1677?-1707

Author's Chronology

Born in Londonderry, Ireland in 1677 or 1678, the son of an Anglican minister; between *1684-1686* he may have entered the Free Grammar School in Londonderry, leaving between 1688 and 1690; *1689* family property may have been destroyed by Catholic supporters of James II; *1689 or 1690(?)* father dies; *1694* enters Trinity College in Dublin as a sizar—an indigent student who performed menial chores for the college; *1696* leaves college without a degree when his sponsor, the Bishop of Dromore, dies; also *1696* joins Smock Alley Theatre in Dublin as an actor; *1697* wounds a fellow actor on stage through carelessness with a sword and therefore quits acting; travels to London; *1698* Jeremy Collier's attack on Restoration drama, *A Short View of the Immorality and Profaneness of the English Stage*, published, influencing Farquhar; first play, *Love and a Bottle*, produced at Drury Lane in London; *1700* visits Holland; *1703* marries Margaret Pemell, a widow with two children; *1704* commissioned a lieutenant in the army; *1706* leaves army; dies in May 1707 in London, leaving behind his wife, her original two children, and two daughters of his own.

Author's Bibliography (selected)

Love and a Bottle, 1698 (comedy); *Adventures of Covent-Garden*, 1698 (novella); *The Constant Couple, or a Trip to the Jubilee*, 1699 (comedy); *Sir Harry Wildair*, 1701 (comedy); *The Inconstant, or The Way to Win Him*, 1702 (comedy); *The Twin-Rivals*, 1702 (comedy); *Love and Business*, 1702 (verse and letters); *The Stage-Coach*, 1703 (farce); *The Recruiting Officer*, 1706 (comedy); *The Beaux' Stratagem*, 1707 (comedy); "Barcelona," 1710 (poem); *The Complete Works of George Farquhar*, edited by Charles Stonehill, 1930; rpt. 1967.

Overview of Biographical Sources

Very little is known of Farquhar's childhood and youth; most of the known details of his life focus on his career as a playwright. His friend who performed in his plays, Robert Wilkes, provided W.R.Chetwood with some memoirs for the 1728 edition of his works. This memoir, along with Farquhar's published letters (see Autobiographical Sources) and the claims of Mrs. Farquhar, form the basis of most subsequent biographical accounts. In 1775, Thomas Wilkes published "The Life of George Farquhar" as part of an edition of Farquhar's works. Wilkes drew his information from a few elderly survivors of Farquhar's time and from the traditions that had grown up around the playwright.

Not until 1904 was another significant account published: that of D. Schmid in *George Farquhar: Sein Leben und seine Original-Dramen* (Vienna: Braumüller, 1904). This work, written in German, provides a coherent rendering of Farquhar's life, as well as unremarkable criticism of Farquhar's works. The only full-length biography was published in 1949 (see Connely, below). Since then, scholars have made slow progress in uncovering the missing details of Farquhar's life; much work still needs to be done.

Evaluation of Selected Biographies

Connely, Willard, *Young George Farquhar: The Restoration Drama at Twilight*. London: Cassell, 1949. The "young" in the title refers to Farquhar's early death at the age of twenty-nine or thirty, not to an emphasis on his early years. Connely provides an engagingly written narrative of Farquhar's life that has not fully satisfied literary scholars because he includes conjectures and speculations to fill in the gaps between records of the dramatist's activities. Many of the names, dates, and places in this biography have been revised since its publication. In addition, Connely's claims for Farquhar's influence seem exaggerated. Nevertheless, both highschool and college students will find Connely's prose clear and accessible; Connely presents the basics of Farquhar's life in an appealing manner. Serious scholars will wish to check Connely's assertions against subsequent studies before accepting them as fact.

Autobiographical Sources

The writing of letters was a significant literary form in Farquhar's era. He contributed letters for publication in two miscellanies, *Familiar and Courtly Letters Written by Mr. Voiture* in 1700 and *Letters of Wit Politicks and Morality* in 1701. It is from these letters that biographers learn about Farquhar's trip to Holland and other events, as well as of his views about the society of his day and the human condition in general. In addition to contributing to the two miscellanies, Farquhar wrote *Love and Business*, published in 1702. *Love and Business* contains verse and letters, including a letter entitled "A Discourse upon Comedy," which explains Farquhar's views on the art of comedy. "A Discourse upon Comedy" has become an important resource for students of Restoration and eighteenth-century drama; *Love and Business* is a fundamental reference for those researching the biography of Farquhar.

Overview of Critical Sources

Farquhar's plays have been consistently popular with audiences from his day to the present, yet critics have been slow to warm to them. When compared to the number of articles written about Farquhar's contemporaries William Congreve and William Wycherley, the number of critical studies of Farquhar is very small. Commentators of the eighteenth century generally agreed with Alexander Pope's assessment of Farquhar: "What pert low Dialogue has Farqu'ar writ!" Critics believed that Farquhar's plays suffered from excessive vulgarity. In the nineteenth century, critics not only accepted the judgment of their predecessors but added to it their disapproval of the sexual themes found not only in Farquhar's plays, but those of his contemporaries, as well. Some critics saw Farquhar's plays as transitional works grounded in the crudities of Restoration comedies while pointing the way to the more sensitive comedies of eighteenth-century playwrights, such as Richard Brinsley Sheridan.

Modern critics are divided in their assessments of the merits of Farquhar's plays, although most agree that his writings deserve much more attention than they have as yet received. Some critics treat Farquhar as strictly a Restoration dramatist whose efforts are best analyzed in terms of the conventions of Restoration comedy. Other critics see Farquhar as a playwright who showed much promise before dying; they see Farquhar's plays as immature products of a talented writer. Still other critics argue that Farquhar attempted to respond to the angry complaints of such critics as Jeremy Collier, who in 1698 attacked Restoration comedy as immoral; they argue that Farquhar's last two plays, *The Recruiting Officer* of 1706 and *The Beaux' Stratagem* of 1707, are the works of a mature literary artist whose sensitive characterizations and sophisticated themes presage the comedies of later playwrights, thus making Farquhar a truly transitional figure between the Restoration and the eighteenth century, as well as an innovator. This latter view is the one subscribed to by most modern critics, in large part because of the influence of Eric Rothstein's *George Farquhar* (see below).

Four good editions of Farquhar's last two plays have made them accessible to students: two editions of *The Recruiting Officer*, one edited by Michael Shugrue (Lincoln, NB: University of Nebraska Press, 1965, for the Regents Restoration Drama Series) and the other edited by A. Norman Jeffares (Edinburgh: Oliver and Boyd, 1973, for the Fountainwell Drama Texts); two editions of *The Beaux' Stratagem*, one edited by Michael Cordner (New York: W.W. Norton, 1976, for the New Mermaids series) and the other edited by Charles N. Fifer (Lincoln, NB: University of Nebraska Press, 1977, for the Regents Restoration Drama Series). All four texts have informative introductions by their editors; Jeffares' comments are notably excellent and would provide students with a sound understanding of the themes and dramatic conventions of *The Recruiting Officer*; Cordner's introduction is superb and is ideal reading for anyone new to the works of Farquhar because Cordner summarizes Farquhar's life and then presents a clear and full critical introduction to *The Beaux' Stratagem*. The commentaries of Shugrue and Fifer lean toward the bibliographical but do provide insight into the conventions of the plays.

Evaluation of Selected Criticism

James, Eugene Nelson, *The Development of George Farquhar as a Comic Dramatist*. The Hague: Mouton, 1972. Some readers are likely to be put off by the tone of this book; it reads like a dissertation. In addition, the redundant assertions of the need for a book-length critical study of Farquhar are wearisome. The introduction presents an excellent history of critical views of Farquhar, although his statement, "As far as I know, there have been no full length critical studies by English or American scholars on George Farquhar," makes one wonder what else Nelson missed besides Rothstein's book. The rest of the book is given over to thorough analyses of the various plays, with an emphasis on structural analysis. This book is clearly intended for a scholarly audience; much of it would likely bewilder high-school students and would possibly mystify college students. However, this book is must reading for graduate students and scholars, and teachers would find it a good resource for preparing to teach Farquhar's plays.

Raymond A. Anselment, ed. *Farquhar: The Recruiting Officer and The Beaux' Stratagem: A Casebook*. London: Macmillan, 1977. This book is a gathering of previously published commentaries on Farquhar's two best-known plays. It is divided into three parts: "Part One: Critical Comments, 1706-1924," "Part Two: Modern Studies," and "Part Three: Comment on Production." The first part presents those commentaries that have been most often referred to by critics and scholars, including influential remarks by William Hazlitt in 1819 and Leigh Hunt in 1840, as well as those of Alexander Pope in 1737. "Part Two" begins with an essay first published in 1963 and ends with one first published in 1973; two of the commentaries are chapters from Eric Rothstein's *George Farquhar*. The criticism in the second part varies enough in point of view to give readers an idea of the disagreements critics have had about the merits of Farquhar's plays. "Part Three" provides two essays that would help anyone who wishes to stage the plays. Overall, this book shows just how thin the criticism of Farquhar's writings has been and indicates that there is a need for many more critical studies of Farquhar's achievement. As a basic reference, this book is invaluable to college students for researching term papers and handy for those libraries that do not have all the old magazines and journals, as well as out-of-print books, from which Anselments selections have come. In addition, Anselment provides a good summary of critical views in his introduction.

Rothstein, Eric, *George Farquhar*. New York: Twayne, 1967. This is the most important study of Farquhar. Although part of Twayne's English Authors Series, which is directed at student readers, *George Farquhar* has had an influence far beyond that of its intended audience. Rothstein provides a thoughtful summary of the playwright's life and follows with critical analyses of not only the comedies but of the verse and prose, as well. The book is written in clear prose without sacrificing details of the contradictions and confusions found in the study of Farquhar. Rothstein's book remains the standard critical reference for its subject not only because it covers works not discussed in similar detail elsewhere but because Rothstein's judgments have proven to be sound and helpful for scholars as well as high-school and college students. This is the first book to which readers unfamiliar with Farquhar should refer.

Other Sources

Farmer, A.J. *George Farquhar*. London: Longmans, Green, 1966. Some of its assertions have been superseded by more recent scholarship, but it presents sound summaries of the playwright's life, verse and prose, and plays, as well as a good bibliography.

Tynan, Kenneth, ed. *The Recruiting Officer: The National Theatre Production*. London: Hart-Davis, 1965. This book discusses and presents the script for the successful National Theatre production of the play. It includes photographs. Drama teachers would find this book to be helpful for staging the play.

Kirk H. Beetz
National University, Sacramento

JOHN FLETCHER
1579-1625

Author's Chronology

Born December 1579 at Rye, Sussex, England; father a clergyman who became Bishop of London in 1594; two cousins, Giles and Phineas, gained fame by writing long Spenserian poems; attended Cambridge but did not graduate; *1608-1609* began playwriting career with *The Faithful Shepherdess*, preface to which defined new form of play—tragicomedy—that he claimed to be introducing into England; Ben Jonson, his mentor, affixed dedicatory verses to published play; *1608* begins collaboration with Francis Beaumont that produced many plays—*Philaster, A King and No King*—in the new style; *1613* when Beaumont retires, Fletcher collaborates with other playwrights but also composed plays such as *Bonduca* and *The Wild Goose Chase* on his own; generally regarded as Shakespeare's successor with the King's Men; dies, probably from effects of plague, in August 1625.

Author's Bibliography

(Plays of sole authorship; dates of first performance): *The Faithful Shepherdess*, 1608; *The Woman's Prize, or The Tamer Tamed*, 1611; *The Humorous Lieutenant*, 1619; *The Island Princess*, 1621; *The Wild Goose Chase*, 1621; *Rule a Wife and Have a Wife*, 1624.

(Plays in collaboration with Francis Beaumont): *Philaster, or Love Lies a Bleeding*, 1608; *Cupid's Revenge*, 1608; *The Maid's Tragedy*, 1610; *A King and No King*, 1611; *The Scornful Lady*, 1613.

(Plays in collaboration with Philip Massinger): *The Double Marriage*, 1620; *The Custom of the Country*, 1620-21; *The Elder Brother*, 1625.

(Plays in collaboration with William Shakespeare): *Henry VIII*, 1613; *The Two Noble Kinsmen*, 1613.

Fletcher also appears to have collaborated with Nathaniel Field, Thomas Middleton, and James Shirley, among others. See Ian Fletcher, *Beaumont and Fletcher* (London: Longmans, Green and Co., 1967) for a listing of ascriptions.

Overview and Evaluation of Biographical Sources

Very litle factual evidence about Fletcher's life survives. The only critical biography is Orie Latham Hatcher's *John Fletcher: A Study in Dramatic Method* (Chicago: University of Chicago Press, 1905), and the author focuses mainly on the plays. She attempts to discount the essentially literary and moral approaches to Fletcher's work, electing instead to praise their stageworthiness. She also recommends Fletcher's verse for its musical qualities and its variety; whether the dramatic situation called for gravity or lightness, Fletcher artfully depicted the required mood. Hatcher's assessment of the playwright's stagecraft and verse is upheld and expanded by Lawrence B. Wallis' *Fletcher, Beaumont and Company: Entertainers to the Jacobean Gentry* (1947; rpt. New York: Octagon Books, 1968). In the chapter "The Time, the Place, the Men," Wallis traces the early lives and careers of Fletcher and Beaumont, who roomed together while both men wrote plays for the King's Men. Wallis makes a case for their falling under the influence of Ben Jonson; their work reflects much of his contempt for popular taste. Although Fletcher's father was a clergyman, he apparently shared Beaumont's aristocratic attitudes about life and art.

Overview of Critical Sources

Most Fletcher criticism concerns his collaboration with Francis Beaumont in the composition of tragicomedies that won them fame as entertainers of the Jacobean court. As a comic playwright, Fletcher mirrored the sophisticated lifestyle of Stuart courtiers, composing plays depicting gender conflict and lovers' pursuits. Fletcher's lyricism and genteel wit distinguished plays that were acknowledged forerunners of Restoration comedies of manners. But to speak of one John Fletcher would be incorrect; there are at least three phases of his career. He was the Beaumont collaborator responsible for designing the love plots of their tragicomedies; the Shakespeare collaborator charged with bringing his special comic gifts to the brand of romance represented by *The Two Noble Kinsmen* and *Henry VIII*; and the leading composer of sophisticated comedy for the King's Men. Throughout his career, however, he was a dependable entertainer, skillfully employing the talents of his company and the devices of the Blackfriars stage.

Evaluation of Selected Criticism

Appleton, William W. *Beaumont and Fletcher: A Critical Study*. London: George Allen and Unwin, 1956. Appleton discusses the early careers of the dramatists, describes their collaborative method, and attempts to assess their influence on Restoration drama. The plot summaries are short and accurate; the character analyses provide a solid understanding of tragicomic types. In the chapter titled "Fletcher's Unaided Work," Appleton identifies the elements of theme and style—especially tests of chastity—that are readily identifiable in the plays written with Beaumont.

Danby, John F. *Poets on Fortune's Hill: Studies in Sidney, Shakespeare, Beaumont and Fletcher*. London: Faber and Faber, 1952; rpt. 1964 as *Elizabethan and Jacobean Poets*. Labeling Beaumont and Fletcher "Jacobean absolutist," Danby argues that their plays were adaptations to the stage of sonnet-like conceits. The resulting dramatic worlds are sophisticated, at the same time reflecting the court of James I and the coming civil war. Danby concludes that the playwrights are "the first of the moderns," exposing decadence and corruption in a manner similar to that of recent dramatists.

Ellis-Fermor, Una, *Jacobean Drama: An Interpretation*. London: Methuen, 1936. This general study includes a perceptive chapter on Beaumont and Fletcher in which Ellis-Fermor explores the chief themes of their plays and poetry. Most of the topics debated by the characters—friendship, the nature of kingship, honor—are popular and, in the critic's words, delivered in language suitable to "a good leading article in a paper." She concludes that the body of the dramatists' work represents a self-contained world full of "reverberant rhetoric" and "melting cadences of word and music."

Leech, Clifford, *The John Fletcher Plays*. Cambridge, MA: Harvard University Press, 1962. Leech carefully studies Fletcher's "dramatic mode" in the three genres of comedy, tragicomedy, and tragedy. He cites *The Humorous Lieutenant*, a comedy, as Fletcher's most appealing play, in part because of the contrast between the innocent Celia and the worldly court of Antigonus. Leech also analyzes the collaboration of Fletcher and Shakespeare with skill, piecing out the distinguishing features of each writer's style. An appendix consisting of a chronological list of Beaumont and Fletcher plays is particularly useful.

Wallis, Lawrence B. *Fletcher, Beaumont and Company: Entertainers to the Jacobean Gentry*. 1947; rpt. New York: Octagon Books, 1968. Attempting to cut away the underbrush of morally inspired criticism, Wallis endeavors to show how Beaumont and Fletcher appealed directly to the gentrified tastes of their day. He cites "emotional form" as the controlling element in the tragicomedies, deemphasizing separate analyses of characterization, action, and poetry. What the playwrights give us is something close to the 19th century well-made play. Wallis's bibliography is the fullest of any critical works cited here.

Other Sources

Bowers, Fredson, ed. *The Dramatic Works in the Beaumont and Fletcher Canon*. 3 (of 10) vols. Cambridge: Cambridge University Press, 1966-1976.

Mizener, Arthur, "The High Design of *A King and No King*," in *Modern Philology*, XXXVIII (1940-1941): 133-154. An analysis of the elevated style and characters in one of Beaumont and Fletcher's successful tragicomedies.

Waith, Eugene M. *The Pattern of Tragicomedy in Beaumont and Fletcher*. New Haven: Yale University Press, 1952. Waith's outline of the history and rhetorical style of tragicomedy is astute and illuminating.

Robert F. Willson, Jr.
University of Missouri
Kansas City

DENIS FONVIZIN
1745-1792

Author's Chronology

Born April 3, 1745 in Moscow, Russia, to Ivan Adreeevich and Ekaterina Vasilievna Fonvizin (or Fon-Vizin, as it was sometimes written until the early 1900s); *1755-1762*? attends Moscow University, pursuing traditional classical education; *1763* takes position of translator in the Foreign Office in St. Petersburg; *1764* his translation/adaptation of Jean Baptiste Gresset's play *Sidnei* (Russian title: *Korion*) is staged; *1766-1769*? writes his first original play, *The Brigadier* (date of first staging unknown); *1769-1781* serves in employ of Nikita Panin at court of Catherine II; *1773* meets Denis Diderot in St. Petersburg; *1774* marries Ekaterina Ivanovna Khlopova; August *1777*-November *1778* travels in Germany and France where he meets Benjamin Franklin and Voltaire, attends seminars and lectures on philosophy and experimental physics, and delivers lectures on Russian language and culture; January-February *1782* finishes *The Minor* (staged in September); July *1784* leaves for Italy and Germany where he suffers light stroke (February 1785); August *1785* suffers paralyzing stroke; *1786* father dies while Denis is in Austria for health reasons; *1787* returns to Russia; *1788* unsuccessfully attempts to publish his collected works; December 1, *1792* dies in St. Petersburg, Russia.

Author's Bibliography

Fonvizin produced a rather large opus of which his dramatic works form only a small portion. His literary legacy included, among other things, travel letters, translations from drama, fiction and social commentary from the German and French, some poetry, and satirical and philosophical essays. His first dramatic work to be published in English was *The Choice of a Tutor*, included in *Five Russian Plays with One from Ukrainian*, ed., Carl E. B. Roberts, 1916; *The Minor* was first translated by George R. Noyes and George Z. Patrick as *The Young Hopeful* in 1933, and re-issued in 1961 in the collection *Masterpieces of the Russian Drama*; a second translation of *The Minor* was published by F. D. Reeve in 1961 in *An Anthology of Russian Plays: Vol. 1*; a third version of *The Minor* appeared along with translations of *The Brigadier* and two dramatic fragments of lesser importance in *Dramatic Works of Fonvizin* ed., by Marvin Kantor, 1974; the first appearance of *The Brigadier* in English was a 1967 translation by Harold B. Segel included in *The Literature of Eighteenth-Century Russia: Vol. 2*.

Overview of Biographical Sources

The time Fonvizin spent at the Foreign Office and in the employ of Nikita Panin, adviser to Catherine II, made much of his adult life a highly political one. Consequently, there is a close interrelation between his biography and his writings. Deeply impressed by the ideas of The Enlightenment, he considered literature in all of its facets to be a means to fulfilling certain social obligations. As a result, the vast majority of his translations, plays, essays and letters were written at least in part for the purpose of educating and edifying his readers and audiences. For this reason, many of his writings provide an excellent insight at least into the type of life he would have liked to have lived. Further, since Fonvizin was a serious and frequent letter writer, there is a good, if naturally biased, source of factual information. Unfortunately, there are few objective third-party accounts of Fonvizin's life. Most modern accounts of his life are derived from his correspondence, from official government documents, and from satirical journals which flourished in Russia in the 1770s, to which Fonvizin contributed and in which he occasionally polemicized with Catherine II herself. Biographical accounts of Fonvizin's life naturally exploit this close connection between Fonvizin's life and work, combining biographical information with critical treatments of his literary activity.

Evaluation of Selected Biographies

Kantor, Marvin, "Life" in *Dramatic Works of D. I. Fonvizin*. Bern: Peter Lang, 1974. The first attempt at an overview of Fonvizin's life and work in English, this biographical introduction is quite complete despite its brevity, and contains several observations not to be found in other sources.

Moser, Charles A. *Denis Fonvizin*. Boston: Twayne, 1979. Chapter 1, "Biography", is the most extensive concentrated treatment of Fonvizin's life in English. Moser's account of Fonvizin's life mixes many an interesting anecdote with a good deal of hard factual information. It is especially good for achieving an understanding of the general social and personal surroundings in which Fonvizin lived and worked. The following 7 chapters present biographical information as it relates to his literary activity.

Autobiographical Sources

Fonvizin's published correspondence from his trips abroad not only forms an important autobiographical source, but is now considered to be one of the best examples of epistolary prose in eighteenth century Russia. A small selection from his first journey is included in *Anthology of Russian Literature*, ed. Leo Wiener, 1902 (pp. 355-58), while a far more substantial selection from his second and third journeys may be found in *The Literature of Eighteenth-Century Russia*, ed. Harold B. Segel, 1967 (pp. 301-351). Perhaps anticipating the spiritual crises which would affect many of the great Russian writers of the nineteenth century, Fonvizin underwent a conversion of sorts late in his life which he set out to describe in *An Open Hearted Confession*, although he never finished the work. Excerpts from this document may be found in the Leo Wiener *Anthology of Russian Literature* (pp. 351-355).

Overview of Critical Sources

Scholarly interest in Fonvizin is primarily restricted to the twentieth century, although one striking exception is the full-length critical biography (in Russian), *Fon-Vizin*, published in St. Petersburg by Prince Petr Viazemskii in 1848. This is an opinionated, occasionally unfriendly and severely dated work, though fascinating for the historical perspective it provides. Kiril Pigarev's excellent *Tvorchestvo Fonvizina* (*Fonvizin's Creative Work*), 1954, is the modern standard Russian treatment of Fonvizin's life and work. The occasional concessions to forced ideological readings do not in any way diminish Pigarev's stimulating and insightful commentary. The most detailed and comprehensive book of all is in French: *Denis Fonvizine* by Alexis Strycek, 1976, although English-language criticism of Fonvizin has grown substantially in the last two decades.

Evaluation of Selected Criticism

Alexandrov, Vladimir E. "Dialogue and Rousseau in Fonvizin's *The Minor*," *Slavic and East European Journal*, XXIX, 2, (1985), pp. 127-143. To date, *The Minor* has primarily been seen as a work of satire aimed specifically at contemporary late eighteenth century Russian life. This article suggests that the scope of the play may be somewhat larger, and may in fact be a reaction to, and dialogue with, certain specific European writers, particularly Rousseau.

Kantor, Marvin, "Fonvizin and Holberg: A Comparison of *The Brigadier* and *Jean de France*," *Canadian Slavic Studies*, VII, 4, (1973): 475-484. Examined here is the connection between Ludwig Holberg's play about Gallomania in Denmark and Fonvizin's first full-length original play, which, among other things, treats a similar topic in a Russian setting.

Kantor, Marvin, "Writings" in *Dramatic Works of D. I. Fonvizin*. Bern: Peter Lang, 1974. This essay provides quite detailed historical and critical readings of Fonvizin's two major plays, and puts them into a proper context with his other writings and with his less important dramatic works. In his effort to remain objective, Kantor occasionally is severe in his judgments.

Moser, Charles A. *Denis Fonvizin*. Boston: Twayne, 1979. This useful study of all of Fonvizin's works is the primary English-language source of information about the playwright. The readings of the two important plays are conservative, but solid. The generous selection of Notes and References and the Selected Bibliography at the end of the book are a gold mine of information for those seeking to do more extensive research. The book begins with a short Chronology of Fonvizin's life.

Patterson, David, "Fonvizin's *Nedorosl* As a Russian Representative of the *Genre sérieux*," *Comparative Literature Studies*, XIV, 3, (1977), pp. 196-204. Patterson examines the elements of Diderot's theory of morally and socially engaged comedy in Fonvizin's best-known play, *The Minor*.

Other Sources

Brown, William Edward, "Denis Fonvizin and the Comedy," in *A History of 18th Century Russian Literature*. Ann Arbor: Ardis, 1980, pp. 219-245. This chapter presents an overview of Fonvizin's biography, including some information not mentioned in other biographical sources, and opinionated evaluations of his literary works. Browns' sometimes harshly judgmental approach causes some errors and occasionally permits an original observation.

Karlinsky, Simon, "Denis Fonvizin" in *Russian Drama from Its Beginnings to the Age of Pushkin*. Berkeley: University of California, 1985, pp. 151-171. Karlinsky focuses primarily on Fonvizin's best-known play, *The Minor*, after an introductory treatment of the playwright's first two dramatic efforts, *Korion* and *The Brigadier*. His critical and historical evaluations of the play are always insightful.

Welsh, David J. *Russian Comedy: 1765-1823*. The Hague: Mouton, 1966. This survey of the beginnings of Russian comedy is an excellent starting point for study of Fonvizin. Although Fonvizin is not the book's focal point, he figures prominently in it and the reader is provided a good social and artistic context in which to place Fonvizin in relation to his contemporaries.

John Freedman
Harvard University

JOHN FORD
1586-1640(?)

Author's Chronology

Born in April, 1586 (exact birthdate not known but baptized April 17) into a branch of an old Devonshire family living at Ashburton; *1602* admitted to the Middle Temple; temporarily expelled for debt but readmitted; few details known about his life at the Middle Temple but published poems in 1606; *1610* as second son inherits a small legacy at the death of his father; long residence at the Temple but degree as barrister is never taken; publishes several long poems but no plays written before 1621; *1621-1625* collaborates with Thomas Dekker in his first play-wrighting efforts; *1628-1639* as an independent dramatist writes eight more plays; nothing is known of his life while a playwright; exact date and place of his death are unknown; dies sometime after his last recorded play in 1639; probably dies c. 1640; in *1656* a couplet in *The Time Poets* refers to him; "Deep in a dump John Ford was got/ With folded arms and melancholy hat."

Author's Bibliography

Only two of the plays written in collaboration with Dekker survive, *The Witch of Edmonton*, 1621 and *The Sun's Darling*, 1624. The plays written solely by Ford are, in chronological order, *The Lover's Melancholy, 1628; The Broken Heart*, ca. 1629-1633; *'Tis Pity She's a Whore*, ca. 1629-33; *Love's Sacrifice*, ca. 1630-32; *Perkin Warbeck*, 1625-34; *The Fancies Chaste and Noble*, 1635-36; *The Lady's Trial*, 1638-39; *The Queen*, n.d.

Overview of Biographical Sources

Basic biographical information appears in the section on John Ford in Gerald Eades Bentley, *The Jacobean and Caroline Stage*, Vol. 3 (1956). M. Joan Sargeaunt's *John Ford* (1935) contains a discussion of virtually all of the little information available. R. G. Howarth, "John Ford," *N&Q* 4 (1957), pp. 241 argues that Ford was still living in 1640 because of two contemporary works which allude to him.

Evaluation of Selected Biographies

Sargeaunt, M. Joan, *John Ford*. Oxford: Basil Blackwell, 1935. Sargeaunt's introductory chapter on Ford's early life contains the little available biographical information. She speculates cautiously on the basis of this evidence that Ford did not become a barrister but that he may well have practised some sort of legal career because of his long time at the Middle Temple. The paucity of details about his later years is partly because "John Ford" is a very common name at that time particularly in the area of Devonshire where he probably lived. There are also no autobiographical sources available.

Overview of Critical Sources

John Ford has been the subject of serious critical attention since the early nineteenth century when Charles Lamb and William Hazlitt wrote commentaries on his major plays. Unfortunately the standard edition, *The Works of John Ford*, ed. William Gifford and Alexander Dyce, also dates from the 19th century (1869, reissued 1965) and is not adequate. Most of the modern criticism, therefore, tends to focus on the three major plays which have appeared in single work editions (*The Broken Heart*, *'Tis Pity She's a Whore*, and *Perkin Warbeck*). Several books have appeared about Ford, however, with a range of critical approaches. Starting with Sargeaunt's work in 1935, these studies offer useful and varied insights into the achievements of this Caroline playwright, the last major dramatist before the closing of the theaters in 1642.

Evaluation of Selected Criticism

Anderson, Donald K. *John Ford*. Bloomington: Indiana University Press, 1972. An effective introduction to all of Ford's works, plays and poetry, this book attempts to unify the artistic achievement through emphasis on love and specifically on "the threatened marriage." Separate chapters on *The Lover's Melancholy* and *Love's Sacrifice* offer original views of these usually neglected plays, citing the theme of art vs. nature in the earlier play and finding the sin of lust central to the latter.

Davril, Robert, *Le Drame de John Ford*. Paris: Librairie Marcel Didier, 1954. The longest and most thorough of all the books about Ford, this study in French is most valuable. Separate chapters treat Ford's sources, themes, characterization, language, and theatrical techniques. Davril also denies the charge of decadence which many critics have leveled against Ford.

Ewing, S. Blaine, *Burtonian Melancholy in the Plays of John Ford*. Princeton: Princeton University Press, 1940. This monograph is a close study of the indebtedness of Ford's plays to Robert Burton's *The Anatomy of Melancholy* (1628 edition). The first section provides a detailed summary of Burton; the second examines in detail Ford's use of Burton's material; the third analyzes the significance of Ford's use of melancholy. This work effectively presents Ford as an expert in the theories of abnormal psychology of his time, thereby illuminating his characterization and placing his sensationalism in an intellectual context. It is sound in its historical scholarship.

Leech, Clifford, *John Ford and the Drama of His Time*. London: Chatto and Windus, 1957. This brief study of Ford focuses on his relationship to the dominant dramatic types of the Jacobean and Caroline periods in which he was writing. Leech views *'Tis Pity She's a Whore* as the epitome of the Jacobean tragic spirit. He stresses the aristocratic code of behavior which suited the private theater audience for whom Ford wrote, noting that the playwright exalts but does not censure human beings who suffer. Ford is a writer who dignifies human passion.

Oliver, Harold J. *The Problem of John Ford*. Melbourne University Press, 1955. A critical assessment of Ford's dramatic and non-dramatic works, this work approaches the playwright both in terms of his dramatic context and his continual experimentation. Ford is seen as one forced to write within a defined tradition which was at odds with his own special skills and interests in psychological drama. A gifted amateur rather than a professional playwright, Ford was a near-genius in subtle character analysis as well as a gifted poet.

Sargeaunt, M. Joan, *John Ford*. Oxford: Basil Blackwell, 1935. This pioneering study of Ford is still one of the best. Mainly a critical study, it also contains the little biographical information available. The first five chapters consider Ford's writings in chronological order; the remaining three are devoted to the setting of the plays, the use and development of their dramatic verse, and the playwright's literary reputation. In addition two appendices provide a summary of evidence concerning Ford's authorship of the anonymous *The Queen* and a bibliography of Ford's works, including variant editions. The critical substance of this book is balanced and reliable.

Sensabaugh, George F. *The Tragic Muse of John Ford*. Stanford University: Stanford University Press, 1944. Viewing Ford in the context of early seventeenth century thought, this work argues that his plays are vehicles of both scientific determinism and unbridled individualism. The author therefore finds that Ford's tragic muse speaks directly to the modern consciousness, which has been influenced by these same theories. The ethical impasse of his dramatic world is prophetic of modern problems.

Stavig, Mark, *John Ford and the Traditional Moral Order*. Madison: University of Wisconsin Press, 1968. An historically based critical study, this work takes issue with critics who find Ford a rebel and extremist. Stavig places Ford solidly within the Renaissance traditions of Christian humanism. He finds Ford's principal themes introduced in his non-dramatic writings, concerned with the themes of love, honor, resolution, and ambition. The philosophical assumptions found there carry over into the plays, with a continuing emphasis on the importance of moral and ethical choice. Throughout his career Ford values honesty, rationality, simplicity, and naturalness.

Other Sources
Farr, Dorothy M. *John Ford and the Caroline Theater*. New York: Harper and Row, Barnes and Row Import Division, 1979. The focus of this study is Ford's

relationship with the Caroline theater. The playwright's uniqueness is interpreted as the result of his position between two theatrical worlds, the Jacobean and the Caroline. Since Ford wrote five of his plays specifically for the Phoenix theater, it is important to take the features of that theater into account. References in his plays to such matters as stage lighting make it clear that they should be read in terms of their theatrical environment.

Kaufman, R. J. "Ford's Tragic Perspective," *Texas Studies in Literature and Language* I (1960): 522-537. An analysis of Ford's characters as self-defining and non-political, not so much rebellious as indifferent to society's standards.

Neill, Michael, " 'Anticke Pageantrie': The Mannerist Art of Perkin Warbeck," *Renaissance Drama* N. S. 7 (1976): 117-150. A study of the play as an example of Mannerist art, self-referential and conceptually paradoxical.

Orbison, Tucker, *The Tragic Vision of John Ford.* Salzburg: Salzburg Studies in English Literature, 1974. A study suggesting that Ford moved away from the tensions and problems inherent in a tragic vision, thus handling major themes ambivalently.

Rosen, Carol, "The Language of Cruelty in Ford's *'Tis Pity*," *Comparative Drama* 8 (1974): 356-68. An article influenced by French critic Antonin Artaud, who argued that Ford's play exemplifies what he considers the resemblance between the theater and the plague, i.e., that both exteriorize the evils latent in society and human nature. This essay stresses the use of language in that context.

Charlotte Spivack
University of Massachusetts

MAX FRISCH
1911

Author's Chronology
Born in Zurich, Switzerland, the youngest of three children, to a self-made architect; writes his first play, *Strahl,* while in high school; *1931* enrolls at the University of Zurich to study literature; *1933* father's death forces him to give up his studies; supports himself as a free-lance journalist and by writing travel reports from the Balkan states and Turkey (to this day, he uses the press to voice his political views); *1934* publishes his first novel, *Jürg Reinhart;* supported by a friend, begins studying architecture; *1937* shortly after the publication of *Antwort aus der Stille. Erzählung aus den Bergen* (Answer from Silence: a Story from the Mountains) Frisch burns all his manuscripts and ceases to write; *1939* during his service in the Swiss army, resumes his literary career with an account of his experiences as a recruiter, *Blätter aus dem Brotsack: Tagebuch eines Kanoniers* (Pages from a Knapsack: Diary of an Artilleryman), the first of a series of diaries; *1940* concludes his studies and opens an architectural office which he operates until 1954 when his success as a writer makes him financially independent (although he continues to be involved in architectural issues, particularly urban renewal); travels all over the world, including the USSR, South America, Mexico, Japan, China, residing for long periods in Rome, Berlin, and New York; *1958* receives the prestigious Georg Büchner Prize; the Grand Prize of the Swiss Schiller Foundation (1974), and the Peace Prize of the German Book Trade (1976).

Author's Bibliography (in English)
Narrative Prose: *Sketchbook 1946-1949,* 1950, tr. 1977; *I'm not Stiller,* 1954, tr. 1958; *Homo faber,* 1957, tr. 1959; *A Wilderness of Mirrors,* 1964, tr. 1965; *Sketchbook 1966-1971,* 1972, tr. 1974; *Montauk,* 1975, tr. 1976; *Man in the Holocene: A Story,* 1979, tr. 1980.

Plays: *Now They Sing Again,* 1946, tr. 1972; *The Chinese Wall,* 1947, tr. 1961; *When the War Was Over,* 1949, tr. 1967; *Count Oederland,* 1951, tr. 1962; *Don Juan, or The Love of Geometry,* 1953, tr. 1967; *The Firebugs,* 1958, tr. 1963 (also called *The Fire Raisers,* 1962); *The Great Rage of Phillip Holtz,* 1958, tr. 1967; *Andorra,* 1961, tr. 1962; *Biography: A Game,* 1967, tr. 1969.

Overview of Biographical Sources
No genuine biography about Frisch is available, either in German or in English. J. H. Petersen, *Max Frisch* (in German), a study of Frisch's work from various perspectives, provides a detailed chronology and an excellent introduction to Frisch's life and career. As far as English texts are concerned, both C. Petersen

Max Frisch, translated from a German 1966 edition, and Ulrich Weisstein, *Max Frisch* (New York: Twayne, 1967), not only deal primarily with Frisch's work and thought, but are out-of-date and sometimes factually incorrect. However, they provide an introduction into the early years of Frisch's life and career that is, overall, still valid.

Autobiographical Sources

Frisch cultivated the art of keeping a diary and, thus, not only allowed his readers generous insight into his life and work, but also helped this literary genre attain unexpected popularity. He also made frequent use of the diary form in his fiction which points to the autobiographical character of his entire work. *Blätter aus dem Brotsack* (Pages from the Knapsack, 1939), *Tagebuch mit Marion* (Diary with Marion, 1947), but particularly his sketchbooks from the 1940s and 1960s (which are available in English) reveal a great deal about his experiences, his ideas, and his work.

Sketchbook 1946-1949, an expanded version of *Tagebuch mit Marion,* contains not only descriptions of and reflections on the post-war years in Europe, but allows insight into his philosophy and aesthetics. The most seminal of his writings, it can be considered a "writer's workshop" that reveals the themes, motifs, and plots for many of his later works such as *The Firebugs* and *Andorra.*

Sketchbook 1966-1971 differs from the previous diaries in that Frisch contemplates and assesses his activities and writings. He also deals extensively with the themes of aging and death which become the focal point of his work in the 1970s.

The most revealing autobiographical account is the novel *Montauk,* first published in 1975 and translated into English in 1976, in which, according to Frisch, the author himself is the focal point and the content. The novel is unique in literary history for its utter lack of fiction. It is an honest, often shockingly frank portrayal of the man and writer Frisch. It contains a wealth of information about Frisch's experiences, such as his relationship with his two wives, his affair with the poet Ingeborg Bachmann, the background of the Jewish bride in *Homo faber,* and many more.

Overview of Critical Sources

Frisch's most popular and critically acclaimed work is the novel *Stiller* (1954), shortly followed by the other two major novels, *Home Faber* (1957) and *A Wilderness of Mirrors* (1964) in which he elaborates on one of his dominant themes, the individual's search for identity in the face of the multiplicity of roles assigned to us by society. Variations of this theme are also found in his plays *When the War Was Over* (1949), *Don Juan* (1953), *Andorra* (1961), and *Biography* (1967). Frisch's most successful play is *The Firebugs* (1958), a modern morality play and a fortuitous blend of the theater of the absurd with Brecht's didactic theater. His more recent concern is with aging and death. In *Triptychon* (1978), death is presented as the agent of an "eternity of that which happened," a view of a paradoxically imminent transcendence. Frisch, a realist and moralist, rejects all ideologies, questions established order and tradition, and explores critically modern life, its contradictions, its lack of security. Influenced by Wilder and Brecht, whom he met in 1947, his plays employ alienating and dialectic elements and show a predilection for farce and the grotesque.

The scholarly studies of Max Frisch's work to date are so numerous that the recent *MLA International Bibliography* shows more entries under his name than for Böll and Grass, two famous German post-war writers, together. Most criticism is written in German. Of the German book-length editions, Th. Beckerman, *Über Max Frisch* and W. Schmitz, *Über Max Frisch II* contain useful studies of Frisch's major works from diverse viewpoints. J. H. Petersen, *Max Frisch,* attempts to describe the evolution of Frisch's opus, investigating individual works within the context of his creative development. While there are few published book-length studies in English, there are quite a few excellent dissertations and articles available that investigate and assess Frisch's work from a variety of perspective (see bibliography in *Perspectives on Frisch,* eds. G. F. Probst and J. F. Bodine. The following describes the books and selected dissertations that are published in English and may be of interest to the student of Frisch's dramatic works.

Evaluation of Selected Criticism

Butler, Michael, *The Novels of Max Frisch.* London: Oswald Wolff, 1976. The aim of the book is to reconcile the needs of the specialist and the general reader. Butler presents a clear and concise interpretation of Frisch's novels, *Jürg Reinhart, Die Schwierigen* (The Difficult Ones), *I'm not Stiller, Homo Faber, A Wilderness of Mirrors,* and *Montauk.* In each case, Butler describes the genesis of the novel from its inception, develops its set of distinctive issues, and places it within the general thematic and linguistic complex of Frisch's work. His conclusions are supported by ample quotation both in German and in English translation. The bibliography constitutes a comprehensive record of secondary literature in German and English on Frisch's novellistic work. Butler's treatment of the thematic content of Frisch's narrative work is of value to the student of his plays.

Holley, John F. *The Problem of the Intellectual's Ethical Dilemma as Presented in Four Plays by Max Frisch.* Diss., Tulane University, 1965. This study examines the problematic features common to the intellectual characters in the four plays *Now They Sing Again, The Chinese Wall, Count Oederland,* and *Don Juan.* The dilemma rests in the inability of the intellectual to resolve the conflict between the dictates of his intellect, the rational side, and the demands of his ethical and irrational side. The intellectual's reason frequently contradicts his conscience or some basic instinct and, consequently, the character finds himself divided against himself. The appendix of the dissertation contains a personal interview with Frisch in which he answers questions pertinent to the theme of the study.

McCormick, Dennis R. *Max Frisch's Dramaturgical Development.* Diss., University of Texas at Austin, 1972. Most criticism of Frisch's plays focuses on thematic questions of private concern or of social significance. McCormick examines the dramatic works, in chronological order, in regard to their dialectical relationship between form and content. The author follows Frisch's dramaturgical development from its point of naiveté in theatrical matters where form is totally determined by the requirements of the theme (e.g., *Santa Cruz*) to the point of sophistication where the theme is largely subject to the dictates of dramaturgical theory (e.g., *Biography*).

Probst, Gerhard F. and Jay F. Bodine, *Perspectives on Max Frisch.* Lexington: University Press of Kentucky, 1982. In thirteen essays, eminent Frisch scholars treat a variety of issues such as Frisch as diarist and narrator, his use of the notion of fairy tale in *Die Schwierigen* and *Montauk,* "I'm not Stiller as a Parody of *The Magic Mountain*" (Thomas Mann's famous novel). The volume includes an essay which traces the development of Max Frisch the playwright as well as studies of the protagonist in *Don Juan* and the marriage theme in the *Phillip Holtz* and *Count Oederland.* Some essays were originally written in German. Unfortunately, an inadequate translation has rendered them difficult to understand. A valuable contribution of this book is its comprehensive bibliography of the author's works, presented by genre, and of secondary literature which is divided by books, dissertations, and articles, the later being subdivided according to the genre and the work that they investigate. It also includes a list of Frisch's works that are available in English translation.

Ruppert, Peter, *Existential Themes in the Plays of Max Frisch.* Diss., University of Iowa, 1972. The study proceeds from the premise that Frisch's plays revolve around the questions central to Existentialist philosophy: "What is the quality of our freedom? Is authenticity possible?" Investigating all of Frisch's plays published before 1972, the author arrives at the conclusion that Frisch does not provide ready answers and solutions to the problems of modern man, but that he does reiterate his belief in man's ability to cope, at least, with the responsibility of freedom and the demand for authenticity.

Weisstein, Ulrich, *Max Frisch.* New York: Twayne, 1967. This volume presents a critical-analytical study of Frisch's work, providing a brief chronology, a short introduction to Frisch's life and career, and a critical appraisal of the early prose, the novels *I'm not Stiller, Home Faber, A Wilderness of Mirrors,* and of the plays written up to and including *Andorra.* The author devotes one chapter to each of the novels, providing a short summary and a text analysis that suffices as an introduction to the themes and structure of the works. The plays are discussed thematically under appropriate headings in two different chapters. Other studies need to be consulted to gain access to the complexity of the plays. Weisstein follows Frisch's literary career from his journalistic beginnings in 1932 to 1967 and comes to the conclusion that his strength is in the narrative genre with *I'm not Stiller* being the masterpiece, while his plays, except for *Andorra* and *The Firebugs*, are less successful or even downright artistic failures, such as *The Chinese Wall*.

Zakrison, Gordon W. *The Crisis of Identity in the Works of Max Frisch*. Diss., University of Nebraska, 1975. In his analysis of both the dramatic and the narrative works of Frisch, the author found evidence that Frisch is primarily concerned with the individual's struggle for identity. Born free, a person is soon exposed to the limitations and demands of society at large and the institution of marriage and the state in particular, and he is not only forced to adopt a role that is contradictory to his natural identity, but he also loses his individual freedom. The only solution to the identity crisis is love or escape from the forces that seek to transform the individual.

Margit Resch
University of South Carolina

ATHOL FUGARD
1932

Author's Chronology

Born June 11, 1932, in Middleburg, Cape Province, South Africa, to South African Dutch mother and English immigrant father; named Harold Athol Lannigan Fugard; *1935* moves to Port Elizabeth; *1945-1950* attends Port Elizabeth Technical College; *1950-1953* studies philosophy and social anthropology at University of Cape Town; *1953* hitch-hikes from Capetown to Cairo with a friend; arrested and sent back to imprisonment in the Sudan; *1954* returns home by way of a tramp steamer trip around the world; *1956* marries Sheila Meiring; produces first play, *Klaas and Devil*; *1958* moves to Johannesburg; writes and directs first full-length play, *No-Good Friday*; hired as stage manager for National Theater Organization; *1959* spends year in London; *1960* daughter Lisa is born; *1965* founds and directs Serpent Players; *1967-1971* denied passport; *1971* receives Obie Award; *1972* cofounds the Space experimental theater with Brian Astbury; *1974* moves to The Ashram on Sardinia Bay; *1980* spends semester on fellowship at Yale.

Author's Bibliography (selected)

The Blood Knot, 1963 (play); *Boesman and Lena*, 1969 (play); *Hello and Goodbye*, 1971 (play); *Statements: Two Workshop Productions Devised by Athol Fugard, John Kani, and Winston Ntshona: "Sizwe Bansi Is Dead" and "The Island"; and a New Play: "Statements after an Arrest under the Immorality Act,"* 1974 (plays); *"Dimetos" and Two Early Plays*, including *Nongogo* and *No-Good Friday*, 1977; *Tsotsi*, 1980 (novel); *A Lesson from Aloes*, 1981 (play); *"Master Harold" . . . and the Boys*, 1983 (play); *Notebooks: 1960-1977*, 1984 (autobiography).

Overview of Biographical Sources

The first book devoted to Fugard was *Athol Fugard*, ed. Stephen Gray (1982), which contains interviews of interest to students of Fugard's life. Dennis Walder's *Athol Fugard* (1984) is a short study in the Macmillan Modern Dramatists series, with a chapter devoted to "Career and Personal Influences." Russell Vandenbroucke's *Truths the Hands Can Touch: The Theatre of Athol Fugard* (1985) is a full and important account of Fugard's life and work.

Evaluation of Selected Biographies

Vandenbroucke, Russell, *Truths the Hands Can Touch: The Theatre of Athol Fugard*. New York: Theatre Communications Group, 1985. Vandenbroucke gives a richly detailed account of Fugard's career, including a production chronology listing opening dates of world and American premieres through 1983. This indispensable study provides a lengthy bibliography.

Walder, Dennis, *Athol Fugard*. London: Macmillan, 1984. While not a biography, Walder's well-written brief study covers Fugard's life succinctly, noting the influence on him of his reading of Camus. Walder includes excellent plates and a useful bibliography.

Autobiographical Sources

Fugard gives an absorbing account of his reflections and preoccupations in *Notebooks: 1960-1977* (New York: Alfred A. Knopf, 1984). Among the topics are his reading of Camus, his work with such plays as *Waiting for Godot* and *The Caucasian Chalk Circle*, and his on-going meditations on the philosophy of the theater. Fugard's "Introduction" to *"Boesman and Lena" and Other Plays* (London and New York: Oxford, 1978) complements the *Notebooks* with some autobiographical remarks.

Overview of Critical Sources

The works by Walder and Vandenbroucke offer much useful analysis while being more descriptive and appreciative than critical. Stephen Gray's collection of essays and interviews in *Athol Fugard* (Johannesburg: McGraw-Hill, 1982) brings together much helpful work. Vandenbroucke's bibliography in *Truths the Hand Can Touch* includes reviews, articles, and interviews—many of them in South African publications.

Evaluation of Selected Criticism

Berner, Robert L. "Athol Fugard and the Theatre of Improvisation," in *Books Abroad* (Winter 1976): 81-84. Berner stresses the influence on Fugard of the Polish theorist Jerzy Grotowski, whose improvisational techniques Berner thinks have helped Fugard shape his accounts of social struggle into artistic wholes.

Green, Robert, "South Africa's Plague: One View of *The Blood Knot*," in *Modern Drama* (February 1970): 331-345. Green finds that *The Blood Knot* has "universal resonances" that go beyond its allegorizing of South African politics. He identifies Fugard as a major modern dramatist whose most prominent theme is human loneliness.

Kauffmann, Stanley, *Persons of the Drama*. New York: Harper & Row, 1976, pp. 208-211. Kauffmann praises *Boesman and Lena* but expresses disappointment at *Sizwe Banzi Is Dead* and *The Island*. Kauffmann also thinks that Fugard spends too much time working with actors and thereby wasting his best talent, which is writing. *Boesman and Lena* is superior to *Sizwe Banzi Is Dead* and *The Island* because it rises above the subject of South African blacks and their troubles and becomes "a small epic of contemporary man."

Weales, Gerald, "The Embodied Images of Athol Fugard," in *The Hollins Critic* (February 1978): 1-12. Weales ranks Fugard with Wole Soyinka as the two African playwrights who have earned a place among modern world dramatists. Weales surveys the plays in terms of Fugard's own remark that "The starting-point to our work was always at least an image, sometimes an already structured complex of images about which I, as a writer, was obsessional" (from the introduction to *Statements*).

Other Sources

McLaren, Dorrian, *Athol Fugard and His Work*. Dissertation. University of Leeds 1974. A useful, early academic study.

Marks, Jonathan, "Interview with Athol Fugard," *Yale/Theater* (Winter 1973): 64-72. One of the more readily available of the numerous interviews.

Selected Dictionaries and Encyclopedias

Contemporary Dramatists, St. Martin's Press, 1977. Bibliography with an appreciative discussion of the plays, with especial high praise for *The Blood Knot*.

Frank Day
Clemson University

BENITO PÉREZ GALDÓS
1843-1920

Author's Chronology

Born May 10, 1843 to Sebastián Pérez, a retired Army officer, and Dolores Galdós, in Las Palmas (Canary Islands); *1860- 1862* while finishing his secondary education, begins to contribute articles to periodicals in Las Palmas; *1862* enrolls as a student at the University of Madrid; *1865* begins journalistic work for *La Nación*. *1867* first trip to Paris; writes *La sombra*; *1868* the "Glorious Revolution," in which Queen Isabel II was deposed in a bloodless coup, inspires some of Galdós's later works, and marks the beginning of his lifelong involvement in liberal movements and causes; *1871* becomes general editor of *El Debate*, a liberal newspaper; *1872* Galdós leaves *El Debate* to become editor of a more culturally-oriented periodical, *La Revista de España*; *1873* gives up most journalistic involvement to begin writing the first series of *Episodios Nacionales* (novelized modern Spanish history, finishing four volumes in 1873; *1876* writes *Doña Perfecta*, the first of his contemporary thesis novels; *1880* reads Zola and begins a period of attenuated Naturalism with *La desheredada* in 1881, lasting until 1885; *1883* first trip to England; *1886* elected to Congress as a Liberal; *1887* mother dies; publication of the first two volumes of his masterpiece, *Fortunata y Jacinta*; *1887-1888* travels to England, northern Europe and Italy; *1889* elected to the Royal Spanish Academy; *1892* his first play, *Realidad* (Reality) premieres followed in 1894 by his first major success in the theater, *La de San Quintín* (The Duchess of San Quintín); *1895* affected by a spiritual revival sweeping Europe, and perhaps under the influence of Tolstoy, Galdós writes two spiritually oriented novels, *Nazarín* and *Halma*, followed by one of his most significant novels, *Misericordia* (Compassion) in 1897; *1893* suffering financial stress, Galdós attempts to set up his own publishing firm, and writes a potboiler *Episodios Nacionales*; *1901* *Electra*, produced and is a theatrical triumph, but more for political than literary reasons; *1905* suffers a stroke, and in 1906, Lorenza Cobián, the mother of his illegitimate daughter María, commits suicide; *1906-1912* Galdós undergoes unsuccessful eye operations; *1907* returns to politics when he was elected a Republican (anti-Monarchical) Representative for Madrid; *1907-1912* writes six volumes of his unfinished Fifth Series of *Episodios Nacionales*; a campaign to award Galdós the Nobel Prize fails because of his liberal politics which were anathema to the monarchy in Spain; *1914* elected a Republican representative for Gran Canaria; *1915* writes his last novel, *La razón de la sinrazón*; *1918* his last play, *Santa Juana de Castilla*, is produced; *1919* a statue in his honor is unveiled in Madrid's Retiro Park; *1920* dies on January 4, and despite efforts by the government to silence the event, his funeral was attended by multitudes of the common people whose cause he had served.

Author's Bibliography

The most commonly-used "official" edition of Galdós's works is the 1941 Aguilar version in six volumes, frequently reprinted (the 1958 printing is preferred). It has an introduction, with biography, and catalogues of characters by Federico Carlos Sainz de Robles. Unfortunately, the lack of uniform pagination between the various printings limits the usefulness of the character indexes which appear at the end of volumes III and VI. Most of Galdós's seventy-seven novels are also available separately and in various combinations. The twenty-two works of theater are less easy to find outside the collected works, and no complete edition of Galdós's theatrical works is available. American editions and translations of specific works of theater include *The Duchess of San Quintín*, in *Masterpieces of Modern Spanish Drama*, ed. Barrett H. Clark (New York: Duffield, 1917); *La loca de la casa*, a comedy in four acts edited with introduction, notes and vocabulary by J. Warshaw (New York: Holt, 1924); *Electra*, edited with notes and vocabulary by Otis Gridley Bunnell (New York: American Book Company, 1902); *Mariucha*, a comedy in five acts, edited with introduction, notes and vocabulary by S. Griswold Morley (Boston and New York: D.C. Heath, 1921); *El abuelo*, a drama in five acts, edited with introduction, notes and vocabulary by H. Chonon Berkowitz (New York and London: Century, 1929).

Overview of Biographical Sources

The best and most complete source in English is H. Chonon Berkowitz, *Benito Pérez Galdós: Spanish Liberal Crusader* (Madison: University of Wisconsin Press, 1948), a lengthy and occasionally ponderous compilation of most of the then-known biographical data. Berkowitz has two special interests, Galdós's liberalism, and his "dark side," the thesis that the author's novels reflect little-known but real inadmissible, hidden passions or real-life affairs. A major source in Spanish is Joaquín Casalduero, *Vida y obra de Galdós* (2nd ed.; Madrid: Gredos, 1931). See also "Galdós íntimo," *La lectura*, vol. 1 (1920), 64-88, for the insights of Gregorio de Marañón, a distinguished writer and essayist in his own right and Galdós's personal physician in his old age. Walter T. Pattison also provides data on Galdós's biography, in his *Benito Pérez Galdós* (Boston: G.K. Hall/Twayne, 1975) and *Benito Pérez Galdós and the Creative Process* (Minneapolis: University of Minnesota Press, 1954). In addition, a good deal of relevant material can be found in the correspondence of Galdós with friends and a number of important intellectuals of his day, listed below in the discussion of autobiographical sources.

Several additional sources focus on specific aspects of the life of Galdós, a number of these on his strong-willed and dominant mother, who is considered a decisive force in the lives of her ten children, only two of whom ever married. See Donald F. Brown, "More Light on the Mother of Galdós," *Hispania* 39 (1956): 403-408, as well as the Casaldúero and Marañón items listed above. Alfonso Armas Ayala, "Galdós y sus cartas," *Papeles de Son Armadans*, XL (Jan-Mar 1966):

9-36, contains a biographical study and letters from the novelist to his friend Cámara, focusing primarily upon the relatively little-known early years spent in Madrid. Antonio Regalado García, *Benito Pérez Galdós y la novela histórica española: 1868-1912* (Madrid: Insula, 1966) also contains considerable biographical information. Certainly, the best sources are those already listed, i.e., Casalduero, Berkowitz and Pattison in English, followed by a host of other sources, predominantly in Spanish, or dealing with minor, specific aspects of the writer's life.

Evaluation of Selected Biographies

Alarcón Capilla, A. *Galdós y su obra*. Madrid: Matheu, 1922. Untranslated. Provides an early overview of the life and works together with a defense of the novelist's art.

Altamira y Crevi, Rafael, "Galdós," in *Arte y realidad*. Barcelona: 1920, pp. 51-77. Untranslated. Discusses at some length why he decided to enter the theater. The same writer, in *De historia y arte* (Madrid: Suárez, 1893), pp. 275-314 provides some of the earliest contemporary studies of *Realidad* and *La loca de la casa*, stressing Galdós's innovations in theater, the relationships between his novelistic and dramatic characters, and influences of Tolstoy.

Antón del Olmet, Luis and Arturo García Carraffa, *Los grandes españoles: Galdós*. Madrid: Alrededor del mundo, 1912. Untranslated. Includes a biography, interviews with Galdós, elucidating his opinions on literature and political questions, his education, travels, and methods of writing.

Arroyo, César, E., *Galdós*. Madrid: Sociedad General Española de Librería, 1930. Untranslated. Provides an extensive biography.

Berkowitz, H. Chonon, *La biblioteca de Benita Pérez Galdós*. Untranslated. Las Palmas: Museo Canario, 1951. Offers a catalogue of the books in Galdós's personal library, preceded by an introductory study which includes biographical details, and emphasizes his erudition and reading habits.

Casalduero, Joaquín, *Vida y obra de Galdós*. Madrid: Gredos, 1951. Untranslated. The fundamental biographical study in Spanish; also provides a methodology of classifying the novels and studies of each.

Cimorra, Clemente, *Galdós*. Buenos Aires: Nova, 1947. Untranslated. Offers a biography which emphasizes the writer's youth, arrival in Madrid, relation to the Nineteenth-Century philosophy of Krausism, and a general review of the works.

Donoso, Armando, "Al margen de Pérez Galdós," in *Dostoievski, Renan, Galdós*. Madrid: Calleja, 1925, pp. 191-157. Untranslated. Includes a biographical sketch emphasizing the revolutionary-radical phase of Galdós's early literary career, the influence of Romanticism and *costumbrismo*, but also devotes attention to the activities of the novelist in the theater.

Gullón, Ricardo, *Galdós, novelista moderno*. Madrid: Taurus, 1960. Untranslated. Contains a fundamental study of Galdós, together with a biography emphasizing literary relations, psychology, and their relationship to style.

Gutiérrez, Gamero y de Laiglesia, Emilio, *Galdós y su obra*. Madrid: Blas, 1934. Untranslated. Contains a thorough study of the author's life and works, including the theater.

Mesa, Rafael, *Don Benito Pérez Galdós. Su familia, sus mocedades, su senectud*. Madrid: Pueyo, 1920. Untranslated. Offers a biographical focus with emphasis on the beginnings and end of the writer's life, his birth, family, friends, and doctors, as well as his friendship with Tolosa and Marañón.

Pattison, Walter T. *Benito Pérez Galdós and the Creative Process*. Minneapolis: University of Minnesota Press, 1954. Stresses the sources used by Galdós, the influence of Krausism and religious problems.

Pérez Vidal, José, *Galdós, crítico musical*. Madrid-Las Palmas: Patronato de la Casa de Colón, 1936. Untranslated. Provides an overview of the writer's life and works, but stresses his musical preparation and interests as seen in his literary works and articles as well as a study of documentary evidence from the libraries of Galdós. The same critic's *Galdós en Canarias, 1843-62* (Las Palmas, 1952) is primarily a biography stressing the youth of Galdós, his first literary endeavors, schools, teachers, the atmosphere of his upbringing, and comments on the manuscripts of his first writings.

Walton, L.B., *Pérez Galdós and the Spanish Novel of the 19th Century*. New York: E.P. Dutton, 1927. Contains an extensive survey of the author's life and works, emphasizing national problems, religious, racial and sexual problems.

Autobiographical Sources

A major autobiographical source is the correspondence of Galdós, much of which has been published, none of which has been translated: see Armas Ayala, Alfonso, "Galdós y sus cartas," *Papeles de Son Armadans*, 40 (Jan-Mar 1966): 9-36; Nuez, Sebastián de la and Schraibman, José, *Cartas del archivo de Galdós* (Madrid: Taurus, 1967), and by the same scholars, "Unamuno y Galdós en sus cartas," *Insula*, 19, nos. 216-217 (1964): 29; Ortega, Soledad, *Cartas a Galdós* (Madrid: Revista de Occidente, 1965); Schmidt, Ruth, *Cartas entre dos amigos del teatro: Manuel Tolosa Latour y Benito Pérez Galdós* (Las Palmas: Ediciones del Cabildo de Gran Canaria, 1969); Shoemaker, William H., "Una amistad literaria: la correspondencia epistolar entre Galdós y Narciso Oller," *Boletín de la Real Academia de Buenas Letras de Barcelona*, 30 (1963-64): 247-306; and Varela Hervías, Eulogio, *Cartas de Pérez Galdós a Mesonero Romanos* (Madrid: Artes Gráficas Municipales, 1943). Additional autobiographical data may be found in the posthumous works of Galdós, published as *Obras inéditas* in a multi-volume series which may still be appearing. Particularly useful for personal, autobiographical data are the two volumes entitled *Política española*, which throw light on Galdós's own involvement in national politics, as well as his attitudes and ideology; *Cronicón*, in two volumes, containing much information of the personal journal sort, and his reflections on travel, *Viajes y fantasías*, as well as his *Memorias* (Memoirs).

Mention should also be made of the existence of the Casa-Museo de Galdós (Galdosian Library and Museum) in Las Palmas, which contains not only memorabilia, private papers, photographs, and a most extensive compilation of works from the author's several libraries, but also the most complete assortment of secondary sources, and invaluable early manuscripts of juvenilia and unfinished or unpublished works.

Overview of Critical Sources

The criticism on Galdós is vast, and much of it is only very marginally relevant for those interested specifically in the writer's theatrical output. Several bibliographies of Galdosian criticism exist, and some at least are readily available to the American reader: Theodore A. Sackett, *Pérez Galdós: An Annotated Bibliography* (Albuquerque: University of New Mexico Press, 1968) is a very useful critical tool for those whose interest is general, or primarily in the novels of Galdós. Sackett's selective focus has excluded studies of other aspects, and thus the only studies of plays included are those which also investigate a relationship to the novels, or to aspects of general interest (e.g., Galdós's theater vis-a-vis the Generation of 1898). Sackett emphasizes that critics have displayed a predominance of interest in Galdosian biography at the expense of other aspects. This work of Sackett was updated five years later by Jon V. Blake in his "Bibliography of Galdosian Research in the Last Five Years," a master's thesis at the University of North Carolina, 1973. Hans Hinterhauser, *Los 'Episodios nacionales' de Benito Pérez Galdós* (Madrid: Gredos, 1963, translated by José Escobar), contains a survey of the current state of Galdosian criticism at the time of writing, together with extensive bibliography. Antonio Regalado García, *Benito Pérez Galdós y la novela histórica española, 1868-1912* (Madrid: Insula, 1966), with a prologue by Manuel Durán, contains extensive bibliography and an epilogue on the history of Galdosian literary criticism. Finally, one of the most useful sources in English is Hensley C. Woodbridge, "Benito Pérez Galdós: A Selected Annotated Bibliography," *Hispania* 53 (1970): 899-971.

Basic and indispensable sources in English continue to be the two works of Walter T. Pattison, *Benito Pérez Galdós and the Creative Process* (Minneapolis: University of Minnesota Press, 1934) and his book for the Twayne World Authors Sries, *Benito Pérez Galdós* (New York: Twayne, 1975), as well as the monumental study of Berkowitz, *Benito Pérez Galdós: Spanish Liberal Crusader* (Madison: University of Wisconsin Press, 1948). In addtion, of special interest for Galdós's own ideas on literature, see W.H. Shoemaker, *Los prólogos de Galdós* (Mexico: University of Illinois Press/Ediciones de Andrea, 1962).

Evaluation of Selected Criticism

Finkenthal, Stanley, *El teatro de Galdós*. Madrid: Editorial Fundamentos, 1980. Untranslated. Finkenthal follows an extrinsic critical method, utilizing the sociological methodology of George Lukács to analyze selected dramas. Both, regrettably, give little attention to aesthetics, textual elucidation, but Finkenthal has as a positive point the exploration of ways in which Galdós attempted to revolutionize the theatre of his time through the introduction of more psychologically and ideologically complex characters. The work of Finkenthal and the two volumes of Menéndez Onrubia will provide an excellent point of departure for the intrinsic aesthetic analysis of Galdós's theater which still remains to be done.

Menéndez Onrubia, Carmen, *El dramaturgo y los actores: Epistolario de Benito Pérez Galdós, María Guerrero y Fernando Díaz de Mendoza*. Madrid: Consejo Superior de Investigaciones Científicas, 1984. Untranslated. In more than 350 pages, the relationship between Galdós as dramatist and two of the leading theatrical personalities of Spain in the early twentieth century is elucidated, together with many insights into his ideas on the productions of his works, and related matters. The same author and publisher are responsible for the other volume, a revised doctoral dissertation published as a monograph which is entitled *Introducción al teatro de Benito Pérez Galdós*. Menéndez Onrubia's extensive research with the manuscripts in the Casa-Museo Pérez Galdós in Las Palmas provides new information on his creative process, with tables of documentation on the invention, composition, adaptation and staging of his plays. The critic points out various ways in which the *Episodios Nacionales* lead to certain plays. Several individual plays are studied, and an extensive Appendix includes unpublished correspondence between the dramatist and friends, actors and other writers, in each case related to a given play. A drawback is the emphasis on extra-literary matters (biography, Spanish society and politics, psychology), but this is the most recent work devoted to Galdós's theater, and only the second book-length study of his drama in any language.

Janet Pérez
Texas Tech University

FEDERICO GARCÍA LORCA
1898-1936

Author's Chronology

Born on June 5, 1898, in Fuente Vaqueros, a town in Granada in southern Spain, oldest of four children; father Federico García Rodríguez, a landowner of considerable means, mother Vicenta Lorca Romero, a former teacher; *1909* family moves to Granada, and García Lorca begins high school at Colegio del Sagrado Corazón; *1914* enrolls in University of Granada in both the Schools of Arts and Sciences and Law; *1918* publication of first book, *Impresiones y paisajes; 1919* moves to the Residencia de Estudiates in Madrid, center of intellectual activity in the city; *1920* in Madrid première of his first play, *El maleficio de la mariposa; 1921* publishes his first book of poetry, *Libro de poemas; 1927* with other poets travels to Seville and participates in festivities celebrating the tricentenary of the death of the Spanish poet Góngora; *1928* founds the literary magazine *Gallo* in Granada and breaks long standing friendship with painter Salvador Dalí; *1929* arrives in New York and enrolls in classes at Columbia University, lectures, and writes what will eventually become *Poeta en Nueva York; 1930* gives four lectures in Havana, Cuba, returns to Spain to find political strife; *1932* under governmental auspices establishes the theater repertory group, La Barraca, to perform drama classics in the provinces and later in the year travels to Buenos Aires to give a series of lectures and to supervise production of several of his plays; *1934* early in the year goes to Montevideo and then returns to Spain; *1936* soon after his leaving Madrid for Granada, the Civil War begins; on August 19 is shot by Nationalists near Viznar and is buried in a mass grave.

Author's Bibliography (selected)

During his lifetime, García Lorca published several books of poetry, prose, and plays: *Impresiones y paisajes,* 1918 (prose); *Libro de poemas,* 1921 (poetry); *Canciones,* 1927 (poetry); *Primer romancero gitano,* 1928 (poetry); *Poema del cante jondo,* 1931 (poetry); *Bodas de sangre,* 1936 (play); *Primeras canciones,* 1936 (poetry). After his death many of his plays were published. The first collection of his works, *Obras completas de Federico García Lorca,* was edited by Guillermo de la Torre (8 vols. [Buenos Aires: Editorial Losada, 1938-1942]). The more definitive collection is Arturo de Hoyo's edition, *Obras completas de Federico García Lorca* (Madrid: Aguilar, 1954). Helpful because of its extensive textual apparatus is Miguel García-Posada's collection of García Lorca's poetry: *Poesía* (2 vols. [Madrid: Akal, 1980]).

Overview of Biographical Sources

Since García Lorca's death, not as many of his contemporaries have written biographies or reminiscences as would be expected, for reasons not quite clear, but perhaps having to do with his homosexuality. The first scholar to discuss this issue was Jean-Louis Schonberg, *Federico García Lorca: El hombre, la obra* (tr. Jean Cassou [Mexico City: Compañía General de Ediciones, 1959]). The most extensive and scholarly work has been done by Ian Gibson, who first investigated the circumstances of García Lorca's death in *The Death of Lorca* (Chicago: J. Philip O'Hara, 1973) and who has just published the first volume of his definitive biography of the poet, *Federico García Lorca* (Barcelona: Grijalbo, 1985).

Evaluation of Selected Biographies

Adams, Mildred, *García Lorca: Playwright and Poet.* New York: Braziller, 1977. Adams, who met García Lorca during his stay in New York, is perhaps not as critical or objective as scholars have come to expect because this is not really a critical biography; consequently, those who wish to consult this work ought to do so with great care. The section on the poet's visit to New York, as would be expected, is the most interesting. Although it contains a bibliography, its lack of an index is a definite weakness.

Gibson, Ian, *The Death of Lorca.* Chicago: J. Philip O'Hara, 1973. Gibson presents an engrossing account of the political situation in Granada and the events that led to García Lorca's death. Also of interest is the account of how the country reacted to García Lorca's death and how the Nationalists tried to cover up what turned out to be a major mistake since after his murder García Lorca became a martyr in the Republican cause.

————, *Federico García Lorca.* Barcelona: Grijalbo, 1985. Gibson has finally published the first volume of this much awaited biography, by far the best and most scholarly. Detailed, but quite readable, it includes many photographs of the poet and a very extensive bibliography that will be of great help to any student of García Lorca. Volume I ends with Gracía Lorca's visit to New York. In Spanish.

Schonberg, Jean-Louis, *Federico García Lorca: El hombre, la obra.* tr. Jean Cassou. Mexico City: Compañía General de Ediciones, 1959. Schonberg was the first to bring out into the open the question of García Lorca's sexual preference and its significance, if any, to the study of his work. In the two parts of this study (Part I is biographical; Part II is analytical), this issue dominates.

Umbral, Francisco, *Lorca, poéta maldito.* Madrid: Biblioteca Nueva, 1968. Umbral sees García Lorca as a Romantic figure, at odds with his society. Not strictly either a biography or a critical analysis, this book makes for engaging but not scholarly reading because Umbral offers practically no documentation.

Vázquez Ocaña, Fernando, *García Lorca: Vida, cántico y muerte.* Mexico City: Biografías Gandesa, 1957. Although providing some very important biographical information, Vázquez Ocaña embellished whatever details are available to provide a smooth narrative. It must be used with care.

Autobiographical Sources

During his short life, García Lorca did not publish any works that might later on assist biographers in their task, although one might certainly argue that his poetry and drama closely reflect events and interests in his life. For example, born out of his experiences and feelings of alienation while in New York, *Poeta en Nueva York* in symbols and abstraction represents the spiritual journey he underwent. Antonio Gallego Morell's collection of García Lorca's *Cartas, postales, poemas y dibujos* (Madrid: Editorial Moneda y Crédito, 1968) offers some letters and drawings and can be considered a companion piece to the two complete works edition. García Lorca's letters have yet to be completely collected. Christopher Maurer has collected some of them in his two-volume *Epistolario* (Madrid: Alianza Editorial, 1983). David Gershator has collected and translated some of García Lorca's letters in *Federico García Lorca: Selected Letters* (New York: New Directions, 1983).

Overview of Critical Sources

Because García Lorca is equally famous for his poetry and drama, there does not exist the usual partiality for one genre over the other. Receiving most attention are *Poema del cante jondo* and *Bodas de sangre,* but not to the exclusion of other works. So far, most of the studies have approached the Lorguian canon from a structural or mythological perspective.

Evaluation of Selected Criticism

Allen, Rupert C. *The Symbolic World of Federico García Lorca.* Albuquerque: University of New Mexico Press, 1972 and *Psyche and Symbol in the Theater of Federico García Lorca.* Austin: University of Texas Press, 1974. In these two studies Allen examines how García Lorca's fascination with Spanish folklore and myth was worked into his poems and plays. Rather Jungian in his approach, Allen convincingly demonstrates the symbolism in García Lorca's works.

Edwards, Gwynne, *Lorca: The Theatre beneath the Sand.* London: Marion Boyars, 1980. Edwards postulates that, for all its variety, García Lorca's theater has a unity of vision. By devoting a chapter to each of the plays, he offers a close reading that interprets the works as well as giving a close reading. This analysis of the themes and dramatic techniques is quite valuable.

Higginbotham, Virginia, *The Comic Spirit of Federico García Lorca.* Austin: University of Texas Press, 1976. In this study of the changing use of humor by García Lorca, Higginbotham argues that the writer's humor developed into a grotesque humor which he used to suggest the despair and lack of meaning in the modern world. By discussing both plays and poems, Higginbotham is able to chronicle García Lorca's changing attitudes toward the use and meaning of humor.

Londré, Felicia Hardison, *Federico García Lorca.* New York: Frederick Ungar, 1984. This work forms part of a series which seeks to introduce foreign writers to an English-speaking audience. However, the sophistication of this study is far superior to others of the genre and particularly those written in the 1940s and 1950s. After the obligatory chapter on the author's life, Londré studies not only the plays and the poetry, but also discusses García Lorca's interest in the visual arts and his use of folk motifs.

Loughran, David K. *Federico García Lorca: The Poetry of Limits.* London: Tamesis, 1978. The "limits" of this study are the images that are most frequently found in García Lorca's poetry. Of particular importance are the images associated with Andalusia, one of the most picturesque regions in Spain. Loughran ends the study with a thorough analysis of García Lorca's four major books of poetry.

Stanton, Edward F. *The Tragic Myth: Lorca and Cante jondo.* Studies in Romance Languages, 20. Lexington: University Press of Kentucky, 1978. *Cante jondo,* García Lorca's major poetic achievement, is given an exhaustive study. Although focusing on the mythic aspects, Stanton examines García Lorca's use of music and studies the Andalusian and gypsy motifs so important to the poem. This excellent study will be quite useful even to those very familiar with Spanish culture.

Other Sources

Colecchia, Francesca, ed. *García Lorca: A Selectively Annotated Bibliography of Criticism.* New York: Garland, 1979. This annotated bibliography collects secondary sources up to and including 1975. Although a different compiler was in charge of each section, the bibliography manages to have coherence. The section on Lorca's music and art is particularly useful. The annotations are descriptive rather than critical.

Durán, Manuel, ed. *Lorca: A Collection of Critical Essays.* Englewood Cliffs, NJ: Prentice Hall, 1962. Now a bit outdated, this collection remains a useful grouping of essays. Included is an infrequently reprinted essay by William Carlos Williams; other authors represented are Dámaso Alonso, Edwin Honig, and Ángel del Río.

García Lorca, Francisco and Donald M. Allen, eds. *The Selected Poems of Federico García Lorca.* New York: New Directions, 1961. The editors have culled the best known poems from each of García Lorca's books of poetry. The poems have been translated by several hands. This bilingual collection's weakness is the inadequate representation from García Lorca's excellent collection, *Poema del cante jondo.*

Graham-Luján, James and Richard L. O'Connell, trans. *Three Tragedies of Federico García Lorca.* New York: New Directions, 1947 and *Five Plays: Comedies and Tragicomedies.* Norfolk, CT: New Directions, 1963. These two collections present the most important plays by García Lorca. In addition, Graham-Luján and O'Connell provide translations for the songs and include the music of the plays.

Laurenti, Joseph L. and Joseph Siracasa, eds. *Federico García Lorca y su mundo: Ensayo de una bibliografía general.* Scarecrow Author Bibliographies, 15. Metuchen, NJ: Scarecrow Press, 1974. This bibliography focuses on the biography of García Lorca and on the writings associated with events in his life. It begins with a detailed chronology of García Lorca's life, year by year. The only annotations provided are citations for reviews.

Zdenek, Joseph W., ed. *The World of Nature in the Works of Federico García Lorca.* Winthrop Studies on Major Modern Writers, 2, 1980. This collection of thirteen essays selected from papers presented at the second Winthrop Symposium on Major Modern Writers is a valuable grouping on a significant topic. Generally, the quality of the essays is high, and included are major scholars such as Gustavo Correa, Robert ter Horst, and María Teresa Babin.

Gisela Casines
Florida International University

JOHN GAY
1685-1732

Author's Chronology

Born June 30, 1685, at Barnstaple, Devon, England; *1694* after parents die, given over to uncle Thomas Gay; *1702* apprenticed to silk mercer in London; *1707* becomes secretary to Aaron Hill; *1708* publishes *Wine*, a comic imitation of Milton; *1711* begins friendship with Pope; *1712* becomes secretary and domestic steward to Duchess of Monmouth; *1713* helps form Scriblerus Club and writes greater part of *The Shepherd's Week; 1714* appointed secretary to Lord Clarendon, Ambassador to Court of Hanover; *1715 The What D' Ye Call It* performed with notable success; *1717* writes *Three Hours After Marriage* with Pope and Arbuthnot; *1719 Acis and Galatea* with music by Handel performed privately at Cannons, estate of Duke of Chandos; *1720* loses profit from *Poems on Several Occasions* in South Sea Bubble stock crisis; *1723* appointed Commissioner of Lotteries; *1724* writes *The Captives*, an orthodox Augustan tragedy; *1728 The Beggar's Opera* runs continuously for 60 performances, but its sequel *Polly* refused license for performance; 1732 dies December 4 in London and buried in Westminster Abbey.

Author's Bibliography

The most recent edition of Gay's works, *Poetry and Prose* (ed. V. A. Dearing and C. E. Beckwith, Oxford: Clarendon Press, 1975) does not contain his plays. Several of the plays and fragments of others can be found in *The Poetical Works of John Gay*, ed. G. C. Faber (London: Oxford University Press, 1926). Other plays can be found in *The Plays of John Gay*, 2 vols., Abbey Classics (London: Chapman and Dodd, 1923). *Three Hours After Marriage* can be read in two separate editions, one edited by Richard Morton and William Peterson (Painesville, OH: Lake Erie College Studies, 1961) and the other by John Harrington Smith for the Augustan Reprint Society, nos. 91 and 92 (Los Angeles; Clark Library, 1961). Editions of *The Beggar's Opera* which include its music can be found in the Regents Restoration Drama series, ed. Edgar V. Roberts, music ed. Edward Smith (1969) and *British Dramatists from Dryden to Sheridan*, 2nd ed. rev. by George W. Stone, Jr. (1969). Recordings of *The Beggar's Opera*, in which the music usually reflects later theatrical tradition rather than the performance practice of Gay's own time, include Frederic Austin's arrangement conducted by Richard Austin (London A-4245) or orchestrated by Sir Malcolm Sargent (Seraphim S113-6023). One recording with all the airs, which are arranged by Max Goberman, is Everest 6127/2 and 3127/2. The most recent recorded version was put out by Decca, with Angela Lansbury as Mrs. Peachum, Joan Sutherland as Lucy, and Kiri Te Kanawa as Polly. *The Beggar's Opera* film version with Sir Laurence Olivier as Macheath was released in 1953.

Overview of Biographical Sources

The first biography of John Gay, issued in 1733, was written by Edmund Curll without any assistance from Gay's friends. The fact that Gay had attacked Curll in "Epistle to the Right Honorable Paul Methuen, Esquire" makes the biography even more untrustworthy. An "Account of the Life and Writings of the Author" prefixed the 1760 volume of "Plays Written by Mr. Gay," but more helpful is the biographical sketch which introduces "Gay's Chair" (1820) and was written by Rev. Joseph Baller, Gay's nephew. The best modern biography is William Irving's *John Gay: Favorite of the Wits*.

Evaluation of Selected Biographies

Irving, William Henry, *John Gay: Favorite of the Wits*. Durham, NC: Duke University Press, 1940. This is the standard life. It includes careful research notes, uses letters, and carries out an in-depth factual study. Irving carefully notes contemporary reactions to Gay's works. At times, though, Gay's actual life is overwhelmed by background material, and Irving's critical judgments are sometimes weak.

Melville, Lewis, pseud. for Lewis S. Benjamin. *Life and Letters of John Gay*. London: Daniel O'Connor, 1921; rpt. Folcroft, PA: Folcroft Press, 1969. A short biography of Gay, this book is valuable chiefly for an appendix which chronologically lists letters to and by Gay. The last three chapters of the biography, covering the years 1729-1731, are all correspondence, mostly letters by Gay but a few from Pope, Swift, and the Countess of Suffolk.

Autobiographical Sources

John Gay kept no diary and wrote no autobiography. His letters were never preserved carefully as were those of other eighteenth-century writers. For over two hundred years the letters were widely scattered; some appeared in collections of correspondence of Swift and of Pope, others appeared in appendices to Gay's *Works*, and still others were published in scholarly journals when discovered. In 1966, *The Letters of John Gay*, ed. C. F. Burgess (Oxford: Clarendon Press) containing 81 of Gay's letters appeared, but it is clear that a considerable number are still missing. The major disadvantage of Burgess's work is that it contains no letters *to* Gay, though those of Pope and Swift are readily available.

Overview of Critical Sources

Most recent scholarly work on Gay has been in producing reliable and complete editions of his works. Though only a few articles and even fewer books have been entirely devoted to Gay's work, a number of works on eighteenth-century literature and theater contain important comments on Gay's plays.

Evaluation of Selected Criticism

Empson, William, *Some Versions of the Pastoral*. London: Chatto and Windus, 1935; 2nd imp. 1950. Chapter 6, "*The Beggar's Opera*: Mock-Pastoral as the Cult of Independence," has often been cited and praised by succeeding critics. Empson examines the complex tone of the play, discusses Gay's use of double irony, and claims that the essential process behind the opera is an exploration of conflicting views and a resolution of heroic and pastoral into a "cult of independence."

Noble, Yvonne, ed. *Twentieth Century Interpretations of The Beggar's Opera*. Englewood Cliffs, NJ: Prentice-Hall, 1975. This collection consists of ten essays or chapter excerpts on *The Beggar's Opera*. Only a few of the excerpts are fully developed arguments, partly because one-third of the book is devoted to Chapter 6 of Empson's *Some Versions of the Pastoral*. Excerpts include comments on *The Beggar's Opera* as Christian satire, its Hobbesian world vision, its characterization, and its burlesque of Italian opera.

Spacks, Patricia M. *John Gay*. New York: Twayne, 1965. The best critical study of Gay's work, Spacks' book describes Gay's struggle to find an appropriate poetic stance, to progress from hiding behind masks to manipulating them. Spacks' comments on *The Beggar's Opera* are particularly helpful: she describes the complexity of disguises and levels of imagery in the play.

Warner, Oliver, *John Gay. Writers and Their Work*, no. 171. London: Longmans, Green, 1964. This pamphlet, published for The British Council and the National Book League, contains a very brief biography and introduction to Gay's works through the use of many quotations. It is mostly an appreciation rather than a careful scholarly study.

Other Sources

Bateson, F. W. *English Comic Drama, 1700-1750*. Oxford: Clarendon Press, 1929; rpt. New York: Russell & Russell, 1963. Reviews of Gay's plays and his treatment in the eighteenth century.

Berger, Arthur V. "*The Beggar's Opera*, the Burlesque, and Italian Opera," in *Music and Letters* 17 (1936): 93-105. Discussion of influence of Italian opera on Gay's burlesque.

Boas, Frederick S. *An Introduction to Eighteenth-Century Drama*. Oxford: Clarendon Press, 1953. General review of Gay's dramatic works.

Bronson, Bertrand Harris, "*The Beggar's Opera*," in *Studies in the Comic, University of California Publications in English*, 8 (1941): 197-231. Examination of the satire and characterization in *The Beggar's Opera* and discussion of Gay's sources in popular song and Italian opera.

Fiske, Roger, *English Theatre Music in the Eighteenth Century*. London: Oxford University Press, 1973. Discussion of Gay's mockery of Italian opera and explanation of how music was handled during performance in eighteenth century.

Salmon, Richard J. "Two Operas for Beggars: A Political Reading." *Theoria* 57 (Oct. 1981): 63-81. Comparison of Gay's play to those of Brecht and Bertolt.

Ann W. Engar
University of Utah

JEAN GENET
1910-1986

Author's Chronology

Born December 19, 1910, in Paris, son of a prostitute, Gabrielle Genet, who abandoned him; raised in welfare institutions; indentured to a peasant family in the Morvan region southeast of Paris; *1926* sent to the infamous Mettray reformatory for theft where he remained until 1929; *1932-1940* wanders as a vagrant through much of Europe; *1942* publishes his first poem *The Man Sentenced to Death* and his first novel *Our Lady of the Flowers*, the latter of which launched his career as an important writer; *1946* his first work for the theater is a ballet *'Adame Miroir*, the same year as his novel *Miracle of the Rose*; *1947* the novels *Funeral Rites* and *Querelle of Brest* follow; his plays *The Maids* and *Deathwatch* date from 1947 and 1949; *1948* is threatened with life imprisonment but pardoned by President Vincent Auriol at the entreaty of Jean-Paul Sartre, Jean Cocteau, and others; *1949* his autobiography *The Thief's Journal* published; *1952* Sartre's canonization of Genet, *Saint Genet, Actor and Martyr*, altered Genet's concept of himself and his art; his last three plays, *The Balcony* (1956), *The Blacks* (1958), and *The Screens* (1961), reveal Genet's dramatic talent at its best; aside from a few interesting essays Genet has produced nothing of importance since 1961; enormously popular at one time, Genet's theater must now stand the test of time; dies April 14, 1986.

Author's Bibliography

All of Genet's plays have been published by Grove Press in New York in Bernard Frechtman's admirable translations: the 1962 revised version of *The Balcony* with photographs by Martha Swope (1966), *The Blacks* (1960), *The Maids* and *Deathwatch*, Introduction by Jean-Paul Sartre, and *The Screens* (1962). *The Balcony* in Frechtman's translation was also recorded in 1967 by The Theatre Recording Society of New York (Caedmon TRS-316-S [A-F]). Genet's *Letters to Roger Blin: Reflections on the Theater*, tr. Richard Seaver with photographs by Jacques Sassier (Grove Press, 1969), reveal a great deal about Genet's ideas on all aspects of play production and the theater. The "Letters" in the same translation were republished by Faber & Faber in London (1972) under the title *Reflections on the Theatre and Other Writings* which include the essays "The Strange word *Urb . . .*" on the theater and "What remains of a Rembrandt" on art and eroticism. Other volumes published by Grove Press in Frechtman's translations include: *Funeral Rites* (1969), *Miracle of the Rose* (1960), *Our Lady of the Flowers*, Introduction by Jean-Paul Sartre (1963), and *The Thief's Journal*, Foreword by Jean-Paul Sartre (1964). A pirated, unreliable translation of *Our Lady of the Flowers* was published by André Levy (Philadelphia, 1955) as *The Gutter in the Sky* with "Preparatory Notes On an Unknown Sexuality" by Jean Cocteau, with no indication of the translator, and interesting only for Cocteau's two-page introduction. Genet's last novel exists in two translations: *Querelle of Brest*, tr. Gregory Streatham (London: Anthony Blond, 1966), and the much preferable *Querelle*, tr. Anselm Hollo (Grove Press, 1974). Genet's collected poems appeared in a bi-lingual edition called *Treasures of the Night*, tr. Steven Finch (San Francisco: Gay Sunshine Press, 1981). While the poems are hardly great works, they help complete the literary portrait of Genet.

Autobiographical Sources

The Thief's Journal purports to recount Genet's life from his birth, probably in 1910, to the publication of the *Journal* in 1949 but is not always reliable. He revealed a few details of his life to Sartre and others in interviews here and there but no one has explained satisfactorily, least of all Genet, how he acquired or perfected the literary talent evidenced by his novels and plays. Genet's life has ceased to be of much interest since the publication of the *Letters to Roger Blin* in 1966. Mohamed Choukri in *Jean Genet in Tangier*, Introduction by William Burroughs, tr. Paul Bowles (New York: Ecco Press, 1974), recounts twenty-eight brief encounters with Genet between November 1968 and November 1970 which reveal something about his apparently aimless wandering. The ideas Genet expresses about French writers are too brief and too casual to be of much import. Aside from the essays mentioned earlier and "The Atelier of Alberto Giacometti" of 1963, Genet's imagination seems to have failed him long ago. The definitive biography remains to be written.

Evaluation of Selected Criticism

Brooks, Peter and Joseph Halpern, eds. *Genet, A Collection of Critical Essays*. Englewood Cliffs, NJ: Prentice-Hall, 1979. Includes seven essays on Genet's theater. Among them are: (1) Bernard Bort, "Genet: The Struggle With Theater," tr. Ruth Goldfarb, pp. 114-128, proposes that Genet's negation of the theater is a catharsis that is the reverse of classical catharsis; (2) Raymond Federman, "Jean Genet: The Theater of Hate," tr. Frank Abetti, pp. 129-45, believes that Genet attempts to give back to the theater a more meaningful orientation by destroying the distorted image it has offered heretofore and re-establishing the true relationship between men which is hate, not love; (3) Odette Aslan, "Genet, His Actors and Directors," tr. Elaine Ancekewicz, pp. 146-55, provides an interesting, concise account of Genet's relations with the actors in and the producers of his plays; (4) Michèle Piemme, "Scenic Space and Dramatic Illusion in *The Balcony*," tr. Kathryn Kinczewski, pp. 156-71, proposes that Genet's theater denounces its own means of production as well as the product it engenders to arrive at a victory of appearance; (5) Jean Gitenet, "Profane and Sacred Reality in Jean Genet's Theater," tr. Janie Vanpée, pp. 172-77, says that the primary truth of Genet's theater is that everything is profane and sacred. His plays leap into the void between the two to find that death is the guarantee of the sacred and the negation of the profane.

Cetta, Lewis T. *Profane Play, Ritual, and Jean Genet: A Study of His Drama*, Studies in the Humanities Literature. University: University of Alabama Press, 1974. Cetta draws a portrait of Genet and his protagonists through the use of the Taoist symbol *yang/yin*. The polarities male/female, good/evil, and reality/illusion help demonstrate how and why Genet chose evil and illusion in his exploration of the relationship between the Self and the Other. The major themes are the "play of illusion" and the "illusion of play" and it is in that realm that Genet's characters liberate themselves from the constraints of society to return to the sexless origins of life in childhood.

Coe, Richard, N. "The Plays," in *The Vision of Jean Genet*. New York: Grove Press, 1968, pp. 213-307. One of the soundest and best balanced appreciations of Genet's theater according to which the playwright questions values and arrives at tentative negative conclusions while discovering new dimensions of meaning.

Driver, Tom F., *Jean Genet*. Columbia Essays on Modern Writers No. 20. New York: Columbia University Press, 1966, pp. 25-45. Genet attempts to transform accident into necessity by reconciling reality with illusion and illusion with noth-ingness in order to realize a spiritual triumph of the dispossessed.

Knapp, Bettina, "The Theater," in *Jean Genet*. New York: Twayne, 1968, pp. 87-155. Analysis in depth of the plays which serves as a good introduction to Genet's theater.

McMahon, Joseph H. "Genet and the Theatre," in *The Imagination of Jean Genet*. Yale Romanic Studies, Second Series, 10. New Haven: Yale University Press, 1963, pp. 108-240. Solid analysis of Genet's theater according to which the actors become forces revealing the existence of internal-external tensions, thus creating connections between dissimilar phenomena through the presentation of these juxtaposed forces.

Naish, Camille, "The Dramatist," in *A Genetic Approach to Structures in the Work of Jean Genet*. Cambridge: Harvard University Press, 1978, pp. 129-169. Within the dual structure of the plays Genet's characters search for identity through crime. This surrealist view of reality reveals an oneiric state of mind in which parody and travesty combine the sacred and profane in an erotic universe where image and reflection are one.

Sartre, Jean-Paul, *Saint Genet, actor and martyr*, tr. Bernard Frechtman. New York: George Braziller, 1963. Few writers have been accorded so early in their career an analysis of such depth. Praised and denounced, the book appeared when only *The Maids* and *Deathwatch* had been performed and the latter published. Much of what Sartre wrote is, nevertheless, pertinent to Genet's later theater.

Savona, Jeannette L. *Jean Genet*, Grove Press Modern Dramatists. New York: Grove Press, 1983. Savona provides necessary biographical background as well as illuminating references to the novels while concentrating on the two specific features of the plays which animate their structure, the political and the aesthetic. By relating these two elements to the ideas of the political thinkers and dramatic theorists of the period, Savona offers a clear introduction to Genet's theater.

Thody, Philip, "The Plays," in *Jean Genet: A Study of His Novels and Plays*. New York: Stein and Day, 1968, pp. 155-225. These are carefully balanced analyses according to which Genet succeeds in imposing his terms on the audience "only because his subject-matter mirrors [their] concerns at the same time as his attitudes towards it constitute a complete defiance of their values."

Other Sources

Abel, Lionel, "Genet and Metatheatre," in *Metatheatre: A New View of Dramatic Form*. New York: Hill and Wang, 1963, pp. 76-83. *The Balcony* belongs to the tradition of Western dramaturgy or Metatheatre, that is, plays about life seen as already theatricalized.

Brustein, Robert, "Antonin Artaud and Jean Genet," in *The Theatre of Revolt: An Approach to the Modern Drama*. Boston: Little, Brown, 1964, pp. 361-411. Genet's plays do not belong to the theater of the absurd but realize Artaud's concept of the theater of revolt as the theater of cruelty.

Esslin, Martin, "Jean Genet: A hall of mirrors," in *The Theatre of the Absurd*, Revised Updated Edition. Woodstock, NY: Overlook Press, 1973, pp. 166-197. As Genet progresses from a subjective to a more objective point of view he succeeds in breaking through the spiral of daydreams and illusion by putting his fantasies on the stage and thereby making an impact on the world.

Fowlie, Wallace, "Genet," in *Dionysus in Paris, A Guide to Contemporary French Theater*. New York: Meridian Books, 1960, pp. 218-22. Through the revelation of moral distress in *The Maids* and the depiction of the self-contained world of damnation in *Deathwatch*, Genet attempts to transcend the pretense of Western theater in order to create absolute disorder within a counterfeit society where "the fatal drama of alienation" plays itself out.

Goldmann, Lucien, "The Theater of Jean Genet: A Sociological Study," in *The Drama Review* T-38, (Winter 1968): 51-61. Analysis in the light of structural sociology according to which the spectator witnesses in Genet's theater the encounter between a radical rejection of society and the problems of the intellectual hostile to capitalism.

_____, "Sociology and Cultural Denunciation," in *Essays on Method in the Sociology of Literature*. tr. and ed. William Q. Boelhower. St. Louis: Telos Press, 1980, pp. 117-140. Marxist analysis of Genet's theater as works of cultural denunciation of social life through the exploration of the relationship between the real and the possible within the structure of society and man's relationship to it.

Grossvogel, David T. "Jean Genet: The Difficulty of Defining," in *Four Playwrights and a Postscript: Brecht, Ionesco, Beckett, Genet*. Ithaca: Cornell University Press, 1962, pp. 133-174. The theater as ritual whose effects are achieved through interreflecting mirrors. Genet's scenic imagination proves to be sterile with the result that he has "magnificently" duped his audiences.

Guicharnaud, Jacques, in collaboration with June Guicharnaud, "The Glory of Annihilation: Jean Genet," in *Modern French Theatre from Giraudoux to Genet*, Yale Romanic Studies, Second Series, 7, rev. ed. New Haven: Yale University Press, 1967, pp. 259-77. Among the best analyses of Genet's theater in which the "frenzied plunge into annihilation" is revealed as ceremony become symbol and realism become metaphor. Paradoxically, although the search has an abstract philosophical depth, Genet integrates individual drama into a concrete reality which is the illusion of the theater.

Jacobsen, Josephine, and William R. Mueller, *Ionesco and Genet: Playwrights of Silence*. New York: Hill and Wang, 1968, pp. 126-235. Although Genet's characters display a willing bondage to their fate, there is a metamorphosis of their condition in space and time into an ethereal, abstract absence or nothingness which liberates them while remaining, paradoxically, faithful to the reality of the human condition.

Peyre, Henri, "The Man and His Theatre," in *The Balcony*. New York: The Theatre Recording Society, 1967, pp. 5-6. Discounts the existentialist Sartre and the Marxist Goldmann as critics of Genet and finds *The Balcony* to be the most complex, striking, and objective of Genet's plays. His theater is not one of social protest or political revolt but that of a moralist who through the avoidance of realism dethrones the text to elicit a vision of universality.

Pronko, Leonard C. "Jean Genet: Theater as Ritual," in *Avant-Garde: The Experimental Theater in France*. Berkeley: University of California Press, 1962, pp. 140-53. Within this theater of ritual and ceremony the characters are metaphors performing the religious celebration of an inverted rite in which good becomes evil and faith is replaced by the love of beauty.

St. Aubyn, F.C., "Jean Genet: a scandalous success," in *The Hopkins Review*, 5:1 (Fall 1951): 45-62. Makes only passing reference to *Deathwatch* but recreates in this first essay in English on Genet what was known about his life and works in America by analyzing *Our Lady of the Flowers, Funeral Rites,* and *The Thief's Journal*.

Sherrell, Richard E. "Jean Genet," in *The Human Image: Avant-Garde and Christian*. Richmond, VA: John Knox Press, 1969, pp. 89-109. Genet's metaphysical quest for an understanding of being in *The Maids* and *The Blacks* is a failure because his vision does not succeed in placing his audience in contact with life.

F. C. St. Aubyn
University of Pittsburgh

MICHEL DE GHELDERODE
1898-1962

Author's Chronology

Born April 3, 1898, in Elsene (suburb of Brussels), Belgium, the last of four children of an archives clerk; baptised as Adolphe-Adhemar-Louis-Michel Martens; *1906-1914* attends Jesuit-run school, achieving "very feeble" marks in all subjects but French literature; *1918* begins to use "Michel de Ghelderode" as a pen name; first play produced, *La Mort Regarde a la Fenêtre; 1919* joins Belgian army; *1920* transfers to Belgian navy; January *1921* demobilized, returns to Schaerbeek; *1923* employed by Schaerbeek local government; *1924* marries; *1926* receives Prix Triennal de Litterature Dramatique; *1927-1930* associated with Flemish Popular Theatre; *1936* because of serious asthma, which would be chronic for the rest of his life, begins taking narcotics; *1939* receives second Prix Triennal; *1945* fired from Schaerbeek government job because of collaboration with Germans during World War II; *1945-1953* writer for *Journal de Bruges; 1949* production of *Fastes d'Infer (The Chronicles of Hell)* is a scandalous hit in Paris, igniting several years of "Ghelderode fever" in France and Belgium; *1951* gives the *Ostende Interviews,* a series of radio interviews about himself and works; *1960* translation of *Pantagleize* produced in New York; *1962* dies in Brussels April 1.

Author's Bibliography (selected)

Piet Bouteille, 1918 (play); *The Strange Rider,* 1920 (play); *The Death of Doctor Faust,* 1926 (play); *Chronicles of Hell,* 1929 (play); *Pantagleize,* 1929 (play); *Christopher Columbus,* 1929 (play); *Miss Jaire,* 1934 (play); *Lord Halewyn,* 1934 (play); *Theatre,* 1950-1957 (plays; 5 vols.); *Seven Plays,* 1960 (English translation; 2 vols. with 14 plays plus "Ostende Interviews.")

Overview of Biographical Sources

Ghelderode lived recently enough that many people can write about him from personal memory or from interviews with those who knew him. All published biographical essays are based upon such sources. Additionally, about 5,000 letters to 200 different addressees are extant, though not published. Like most of Ghelderode's published works, most Ghelderode biography and criticism is available only in French.

Evaluation of Selected Biographies

Beyen, Roland, *Michel de Ghelderode.* Brussels: Palais des Academies, 1971. Untranslated. This copious, thorough critical biography is the best single source of detailed information about Ghelderode. It contains a lengthy and closely documented biography, followed by a series of critical chapters on such topics as "Ghelderode and Women," "Ghelderode and Society," and "Ghelderode, God and Religion."

Castro, Nadine Berthe, *Un Moyen-Age Contemporaine: La Theâtre de Michel de Ghelderode*. Lausanne: Editions de l'Age d'Homme, 1976. This PhD dissertation from the City Universities of New York contains a good introductory biography. In French.

Jans, Adrien, *La Vie de Ghelderode*. Untranslated. Paris: Hachette, 1972. Based upon conversations with Ghelderode's wife and friends, and interviews with Ghelderode himself, Jans traces Ghelderode's life from birth to death, with attention to chief works, influences and interests.

Autobiographical Sources
The only significant published autobiographical item is *"Entretiens d'Ostende,"* (published in English as "The Ostende Interviews"). This is an edited transcript of a series of radio interviews Ghelderode made with Roger Iglesias and Alain Trutat in 1951, published in 1956 in French and in an English redaction in 1959 (in the *Tulane Drama Review*, reprinted 1960 in *Seven Plays*). Also available in English is an interview with Samuel Draper published in *Tulane Drama Review*, VIII (1963); 39-50. Ghelderode began work on memoirs before World War II, and in 1960 commented that he was then working on memoirs to be published after his death. No memoirs have been published to date; presumably they remain among his papers.

Overview of Critical Sources
Roland Beyen estimated in 1978 that some 1500 works of review and criticism had been published on Ghelderode and his works. Nearly all of this material is in French and was published in France and Belgium. Critics generally agree that Ghelderode's works consistently share certain themes and motifs that make it possible to speak of a "world of Ghelderode," which resembles late-medieval Flanders. Ghelderode's favorite painters were Bosch and Breughel, and he was very fond of the English Elizabethan playwrights; one critic called him "our man in the sixteenth century." There is a fascination with death, and frequent use of elements from such theatrical forms as the puppet theatre, farce, and carnival revelry. Grotesque characters take part in violent events in an atmosphere often charged with scatology and a deeply Catholic concern for matters of sin and salvation. Much criticism has been devoted to defining this world of Ghelderode, and to analyzing its relationship to its roots in Breughel and other artists, the marionette theatre, or Ghelderode's life. Critics have also drawn comparisons between

Ghelderode and other contemporary dramatists. Though Ghelderode wrote in French, he and a number of critics have stressed his Flemish heritage. The student who reads only English would do best to obtain the McGraw-Hill article described below; Volume VIII (1963) of *TDR* (formerly *Tulane Drama Review*), containing six items on Ghelderode; and the works of Grossvogel and Pronko, described below.

Evaluation of Selected Criticism

Abel, Lionel, "Our Man in the Sixteenth Century," in *TDR*, i (1963): 62-71. In this reply to Weiss (see listing below) Abel asserts that Weiss' main objection to Ghelderode is the playwright's fixation on the sixteenth century. Abel suggests that Ghelderode can validly deal with universal truths in "his chosen century."

Beyen, Roland, *et al. Michel de Ghelderode et le Théâtre Contemporaine.* Brussels: Societe Int. des Etudes sur Michel de Ghelderode, 1979. Untranslated. This volume contains 31 papers on Ghelderode given at a meeting in late 1978. Topics include various themes in Ghelderode's works, studies of individual plays, and reports on Ghelderode's works and reputation in Poland, Spain, Hungary and Russia.

Corrigan, Robert W. *The Theatre in Search of a Fix.* New York: Delacorte, 1973. Corrigan devotes four pages to analyzing *Pantagleize* as a drama of Everyman; the essay appeared earlier in *Tulane Drama Review*.

Francis, Jan. *L'Eternal Aujourd'hui de Michel de Ghelderode.* Brussels: Louis Musin, 1968. Untranslated. Francis, who worked closely with Ghelderode for eight years, provides in the first half of this lavishly illustrated volume a species of literary biography which includes a number of curious anecdotes about the playwright; the last part of the book is composed of chapters on such topics as Ghelderode and Bosch and Ghelderode and Surrealism.

Grossvogel, David. I. *Twentieth-Century French Drama.* New York: Gordian Press, 1967. This book was originally published as *The Self-Conscious Stage in Modern French Drama* in 1958. Guicharnaud credits this book, wherein Ghelderode is given "primary importance," with stimulating American productions of Ghelderode's works by off-Broadway and university theatre companies. This study stresses Ghelderode's theatricality, calling him "a man of the theatre," and tracing his interest in Flemish marionette drama, the influence of that theatre on Ghelderode's works, and his affinities for various other dramatists. Other issues include the influence of painters and engravers; Ghelderode's use of sound effects, both vocal and non-vocal; his preoccupation with death; his humor; and his qualities as a neo-romantic.

Guicharmaud, Jacques, *Modern French Theatre.* New Haven: Yale University Press, 1967. In this volume wherein Ghelderode is noticed in the context of other contemporary dramatists who wrote in French, the playwright's baroque and macabre qualities are examined, and useful emphasis laid on the way material objects are overabundantly forced upon the audience. There is a brief bibliography.

Pronko, Leonard Cabell, *Avant-Garde: The Experimental Theater in France.* Berkeley: University of California Press, 1962, pp. 165-180. Calling Ghelderode a "modern romantic with a Medieval and Renaissance soul" who "sees man in Manichean terms," Pronko celebrates the playwright's non-rational emphases and compares him to other contemporary writers while commenting on a dozen of the more important plays.

Weiss, Aurelieu, "The Theatrical World of Michel de Ghelderode." trans. Ruby Cohn. *TDR,* VIII, i (1963), pp. 51-61, Claiming that Ghelderode's best talents are narrative and pictorial, rather than philosophical or dramatic, Weiss presents perhaps the most strongly negative view in print of Ghelderode's works, concluding that they contain "nothing new in thought or art," and probably will not last.

Wellwarth, George, "Ghelderode's Theatre of the Grotesque," in *TDR,* VIII, i (1963): 11-23. Defining the fictional medieval Flemish world in which most of Ghelderode's work is set, Wellwarth compares it to the worlds of Bosch, Ben Jonson, and especially Breughel (whose works directly inspired several Ghelderode plays) and concludes that for all the grotesquerie, vulgarity, and pessimism, the works show a "completely orthodox Pauline Christian religious feeling."

_____, *The Theater of Protest and Paradox.* New York: NYU Press, 1971. First published in 1964, this book contains a chapter on Ghelderode which is a revised version of Wellwarth's article in *TDR,* listed above. There is also a bibliography of 13 Ghelderode studies, most in English.

Other Sources
Beyen, Roland, *Bibliographie de Michel de Ghelderode.* Leuven: Univ. Uitgaven, 1971. This is Beyen's "exhaustive" bibliography; he noted in 1978 that he had by then found 950 works by Ghelderode and 1500 about him and his works.

_____, *Michel de Ghelderode: ou la Comedie des Apparences.* Brussels: Bibliotheque Royale, 1980. This illustrated volume catalogs an exhibit of photographs, letters, prints, and other Ghelderodiana, held at the Pompidou Center in Paris and later at the Bibliotheque Royale in Brussels in 1980.

Draper, Samuel, "An Interview with Michel de Ghelderode," in *TDR,,* VIII i (1963), pp. 39-50. This interview conducted in 1960 contains comments on writers who influenced Ghelderode, ranging from the Elizabethans to Maeterlinck and Strindberg. There are also comments on individual plays, including *Barabbas, Escurial, Chronicles of Hell, The Women at the Tomb,* and others.

_____, "Michel de Ghelderode: A Personal Statement," in *TDR*, VIII, i (1963): 33-38. Draper spent a year in Brussels studying Ghelderode and his drama. This brief article describes Ghelderode's views on friendship and death, his qualities as a practical joker, and the ambience of the extraordinary "living-room museum" wherein he wrote.

Ghelderode, Michel de, *Seven Plays*. tr./intro. by George Hauger. New York: Hill and Wang, 1960. Volume I contains 24 pages in English translation of selected material from the Ostend Interviews, wherein Ghelderode discusses his life, thought, and works.

Hauger, George, "Dispatches from the Prince of Ostrelande," in *TDR*, VIII, i (1963): 25-32. Prefaced with Hauger's description of Ghelderode's unusual letter-writing habits, this article publishes excerpts from Ghelderode's correspondence with Hauger during 1957-1962. Ghelderode comments on his views of life and death, literary interests and influences, The Brussels World Fair, and other matters.

Marginales: Revue Bimestrelle des Ideés et des Lettres, No. 112/113 (May 1967). This special issue of a Belgian literary journal is devoted to Ghelderode. It contains a variety of reminiscences by those who knew him, a number of excellent photos, drawings, and excerpts from letters, and a previously unpublished three-act play, *La Sommeil de la Raison* (1930).

Selected Dictionaries and Encyclopedias

Contemporary Authors 85, Gale Research, 1980. Brief analysis of life and work, with listing of important works.

Encyclopedia of World Drama, McGraw-Hill, 1984. The most complete single analysis of the life and work available in English, with a meticulous bibliography of the works giving production dates, dates of composition, and dates of publication. Provides a general analysis of Ghelderode's works plus specific comments about 26 individual plays. Also gives a brief listing of criticism.

Encyclopedia of World Literature in the 20th Century, Frederick Ungar, 1982. Surveys Ghelderode's life and works, providing useful critical comments. Includes a bibliography of criticism.

C. Herbert Gilliland
Virginia Military Institute

ANDRÉ GIDE
1869-1951

Author's Chronology

Born André Paul Guillaume Gide November 22, 1869, Paris; *1875* receives private lessons; *1877* enters the Ecole alsacienne, is expelled for three months for "bad habits", threatened with castration, experiences anxiety and guilt; *1880* father dies; *1891* attends salons of Mallarmé, Hérédia, publishes his first book, *The Notebooks of André Walter*, anonymously; *1893-1895* travels in North Africa, spends time with Oscar Wilde, Lord Alfred Douglas, acknowledges homosexuality; *1895* mother dies; marries his cousin Madeleine Rondeaux; *1909* becomes one of the founders of the Nouvelle Revue Française, publishes *Strait Is the Gate*; *1914* publishes *Lafcadio's Adventures*; *1923* birth of Catherine, daughter of Gide and Elizabeth van Rysselberghe; *1925* travels in Congo and Tchad; *1926* publishes *The Counterfeiters*; *1932-1936* becomes politically active, writes antifascist articles, visits Russia, delivers funeral oration for Gorky in Red Square, finally becomes disillusioned with Russia and Communism; *1938* wife Madeleine dies; *1940-1945* retires to South of France, resigns from NRF, visits Tunis and Algiers; *1947* receives honorary degree at Oxford, then the Nobel Prize for literature, awarded him in recognition of his "intrepid love for truth;" *1947-1949* publishes *Théâtre complet* (8 vols.); *1950* his adaptation of *Les Caves du Vatican* is produced at the Comédie Française; February 19, 1951 dies in Paris.

Author's Bibliography (selected)

The Notebooks of André Walter, 1891, tr. 1965 (narrative prose, largely autobiographical); *The Fruits of the Earth*, 1897, tr. 1965 (narrative prose); *Saul*, 1896, tr. 1952 (drama); *El Hadj*, 1899 (drama); *Philoctetes*, 1899, tr. 1952 (drama); *King Candaules*, 1900, tr. 1952 (drama); *Strait Is the Gate*, 1906, tr. 1924 (narrative fiction); *Bathsheba*, 1912, tr. 1952 (drama); *The Vatican Swindle*, 1914, tr. 1925 (narrative fiction, also available as *Lafcadio's Adventures*, 1927 and *The Vatican Cellars*, 1952); *The Pastoral Symphony*, 1919, tr. 1931 (narrative fiction); *Dostoïevsky*, 1923, tr. 1925 (essay); *The Counterfeiters*, 1926, tr. 1927 (novel, also available as *The Coiners*, 1927, 1950); *Oedipus*, 1931, tr. 1958 (drama); *Persephone*, 1933, tr. 1952 (drama); *Theseus*, 1946, tr. 1958 (narrative fiction); *Le Retour de l'enfant prodigue*, 1947 (drama); *Le Procès*, 1947 (drama, adaptation from Kafka by Gide and Jean-Louis Barrault).

The translations by Dorothy Bussy, one of Gide's intimate friends, and those by Justin O'Brien are generally considered the best.

Overview of Biographical Sources

Numerous and very diverse, the biographical accounts of Gide available to date can be viewed in two distinct categories: 1) accounts that attempt to explain the man by studying his literary accomplishments as well as his socio-political activism and his stature as a moralist. Usually, these are relatively detached, or sympathetic and free of concerns for conventional morality or socio-political responsibility. They tend to be thorough and balanced, offering assessments of well-researched facts. 2) accounts motivated by a strong sense of advocacy, focusing on ethical issues and attempting to promote either a totally positive image of the author or a position hostile to him. Studies by accredited experts who dwell specifically in the area of Gide's sexuality and psychopathology generally fall into one of those categories.

Evaluation of Selected Biographies

Delay, Jean, *The Youth of André Gide*. Chicago: University of Chicago Press, 1963; original edition 1956-57, abridged and translated by June Guicharnaud. This is perhaps the most thorough and the most penetrating psychological study of Gide's childhood and youth made by a member of the Académie Française, a distinguished psychiatrist who was also a friend and who observed Gide in the last years of his life. His "case history" is often documented with rare pieces of correspondence which were unpublished at the time, and offers blunt, straightforward descriptions of the facts relating to Gide's early struggle to overcome nervous disorders, a brief bout with tuberculosis, narcissistic homosexuality, guilt, remorse, emotional inhibitions and attempts at liberation. The main conclusions in this study are that the causes of Gide's sexual inhibitions were not physical and that the drama of his life was essentially spiritual.

Fowlie, Wallace, *André Gide his Life and Art*. New York: Macmillan, 1965. A simple, straightforward exposé of known facts of Gide's life and works written in a very readable, inviting style, in a language that is unassuming as much as it is uncomplicated and rid of ambiguous or inflated rhetoric. It offers assessments of biographical accounts made by others and, in a concluding chapter, an assessment of Gide's stature and importance as a man of letters of world-wide appeal. Being succinct and all-embracing, Fowlie's book is particularly valuable as a first, general introduction to Gide.

O'Brien, Justin, *Portrait of André Gide: A Critical Biography*. New York: Alfred A. Knopf, 1953. A combination of critical study and biography, this is the most erudite and far-reaching analysis of Gide the man, brilliantly documented and drawing extensively on Gide's critical writings. The critic convincingly demonstrates that the important moments in Gide's life can be accurately assessed by the portraits of the heroes he created, Narcissus, Prometheus, Philoctetes, Oedipus, Theseus. He also demonstrates that for Gide, esthetic considerations were always more important than ethical ones, and that his personal interpretations of myths were intended to interrogate the fable in such a way as to bring out its psychological significance. In his concluding chapter, the critic articulates a series of strikingly pertinent reflections on Gide's prose style and his very special brand of rigorous classicism.

Painter, George D. *André Gide, a Critical Biography*. New York: Atheneum, 1968. This is an admiring, generally praising assessment of Gide the man and the writer. The critic takes the view that Gide cannot be judged on moral grounds, that everything in his "joy in youth" and "serenity in old age" is legitimate, as it becomes part of one of the "great allegorical lives," a life which is itself a work of art and as such "immortal," inspiring people to live in courage and hope and to achieve liberation and virtue.

Schlumberger, Jean, *Madeleine et André Gide: leur vrai visage*. Paris: Gallimard, 1956. Untranslated. One of the closest friends of André and Madeleine Gide, the critic wrote this book primarily to defend their memories against virulent attacks by Gide's adversaries who, on the occasion of *Et Nunc manet in te*, found new grounds to attack his cruelty to his wife. The critic claims that Gide's marriage was, given the idiosyncrasies of the spouses, not at all a mistake, and could be considered even successful. Schlumberger's account is favorable to both spouses but inclined to favor Madeleine, in whom he sees only the qualities of the spiritual perfection of a saint.

Autobiographical Sources

There is very little in Gide's drama and narrative fiction that can be neatly categorized in terms of genre. Moreover, by the very nature of his creative impulse, fiction and autobiography are consistently blended together, one being an extention of the other, in most of the author's books, even in his stunningly voluminous correspondence. *The Journals of André Gide* (1889-1949), in four volumes admirably translated by Justin O'Brien, provide both factual information and insights on practically every aspect of Gide's life and personality, though somewhat less focused on the ordeal of his secret drama. Some of the larger segments of the *Journals* had appeared separately earlier: *If It Die*, more in the style of memoirs, more explicitly autobiographical and very reminiscent of Rousseau's *Confessions*, opens with the author's earliest recollections of his childhood and ends with the death of his mother and his engagement to Madeleine Rondeaux. It tells the story of his emancipation through his "rebirth," presumed as attained at Biskra, at the time of his liberation from his mother's burdensome influence, and the chains of a moralism he considered a regime of starvation. The story of this evolution from the timid Huguenot to the daring immoralist is written with an openness that at times is almost indiscreet; *Madeleine (Et Nunc manet in te)*, is an equally open, intimate account of a specific drama of his life: his married life and the intensity of remorse he felt for having destroyed the happiness of the only woman he ever loved, his wife Madeleine; *Travels in the Congo* relates his observations during a journey he undertook presumably in search of "new landscapes," but which also induced him to report a documented account of the inhuman treatment of African laborers in the colonies. *Return from the U.S.S.R.* and *Afterthoughts on the U.S.S.R.* offer another illustration of his passion for truth and authenticity. On the eve of his journey to Russia he was full of hope. On his return, rather than confirm the advent of the "new man," in the Marxist utopia he had read so much about, he had to upset both friends and adversaries by pointing out, next to the successes, some of its bitter truths.

Overview of Critical Sources

Countless articles, doctoral dissertations and about a hundred book-length essays and monographs have already been devoted to Gide. Many of them are highly specialized, or reflecting critical approaches inspired by the most recent avant-garde in literary criticism. Gide's drama being a small part of his total production of creative works, the critical literature dealing with it specifically is relatively limited in volume. As of this date only one book-length study dealing with Gide's theater is available. However, practically every other comprehensive study of the author's life and works includes chapters or sections dealing extensively with most dramatic works, particularly *Saul*, *El Hadj*, *King Candaules*, *Philoctetes*, and *Oedipus*.

Evaluation of Selected Criticism

Brée, Germaine, *Gide*. New Brunswick, NJ: Rutgers University Press, 1963. This is a thorough, well documented, perceptive study of the entire body of Gide's creative writings. It includes a large section on Gide's drama which Brée finds "arresting and original" though "more literary than dramatic," suggesting a Gide precursor of Camus' and Sartre's theater. While interested primarily in Gide's art and evaluations of forms and composition devices, Germaine Brée is also credited with some brilliant interpretations of key works (*Saul*, *Les Caves du Vatican*, among others) and her chapter on *Oedipus* is considered by many as the most incisive analysis of the play to date.

Hytier, Jean, *André Gide*. Garden City, NY: Doubleday, 1962. One of the best early studies on Gide's works, it attracted effusive expressions of gratitude from the author. It contains a chapter on Gide's drama. Hytier's judgments of Gide's plays are typically generous. He finds it "regrettable that his efforts were not better rewarded, for Gide evidently had the makings of a dramatist if not powerful, at least original and ingenious." Hytier's analysis concerns itself with Gide the es-thete and not at all with the tormented, contradictory, confused immoral or amoral man. Despite its being dated (the text of the book is the unaltered text of lectures delivered in 1938) it is still valid and admirable.

Ireland, George William, *André Gide: A Study of his Creative Writings*. Oxford: Clarendon Press, 1970. The critic analyzes Gide's most important works in a rather lengthy, almost all-inclusive survey of Gide's achievements, in a presumably objective approach, focusing in on titles that Gide himself classified as creative or "artistic" works, aspiring "to allow Gide to speak for himself." The book includes chapters on most of Gide's more substantial dramatic works, offering detailed analyses of *Saul, Philoctetes, King Candaules, El Hadj, The Return of the Prodigal, Oedipus*.

Lafille, Pierre, *André Gide romancier*. Paris: Hachette, 1954. A relatively early but important study of Gide's approach to writing fiction, a spin-off from a voluminous doctoral thesis successfully defended at the Sorbonne in 1953. The critic's principal argument is that although many of Gide's themes may appear to be immoralisms or dangerous poisons, they are treated in such a way as to be transmuted into "serums of wisdom" and "medicines" for humanity.

McLaren, James C. *The Theater of André Gide: Evolution of a Moral Philosopher*. Baltimore: The Johns Hopkins Press, 1953. The critic offers a wealth of information on the contents and circumstances of composition of Gide's theater, including the latter's less known dramatic texts, translations and adaptations from Shakespeare, Tagore, Kafka. Particularly valuable is an abundance of excerpts from reviews of stage productions which appeared in the Parisian press.

Martin, Claude, *La Maturité d'André Gide. De Paludes à L'Immoraliste (1895-1902)*. Paris: Editions Klincksieck, 1977. Untranslated. Though intended as a "biographical essay," this lengthy, meticulously documented account of an important period of Gide's life contains major sections surveying the circumstances of composition and production of several plays, notably, *Saul, El Hadj*, and *King Candaules*. The author also offers a considerable amount of critical commentary on the contents of the plays themselves, contributing insightful interpretations and useful elucidations of the meaning of Gide's message and philosophical posture at the time.

Other Sources

Cocteau, Jean, *Gide vivant*. Paris: Amiot-Dumont, 1952. A very subjective view on Gide's personality, very critical of Gide, assessing his persistent self-analysis and soul searching as the calculated posture of an exhibitionist very much like Jean-Jacques Rousseau.

Cordle, Thomas, *André Gide*. New York: Twayne, 1969. A very helpful, succinctly presented exposé on Gide's life and works with apt assessments of the psychoanalytical implications of the "Gidian Personality," and considerable focus on several of Gide's plays (*Philoctetes, Saul King Candaules, El Hadj, Oedipus*).

Guérard, Albert, *André Gide*. New York, E.P. Duton, 1963. One of the most important books on Gide's life and works written by academics, focusing on the meaning of Gide's individualism and his importance as a European writer.

Knowles, Dorothy, *French Drama of the Inter-War Years 1918-1939*. London: George G. Harrap, 1967. A brief discussion of Gide's theater viewed as representative of the "literary play" category, in the context of a chronological survey of French drama in the inter-war years.

Lerner, Anne Lapidus, *Passing the Love of Women: a Study of Gide's* Saül *and Its Biblical Roots*. Lanham, MD: University Press of America, 1980. A scholarly probe into the biblical sources of Gide's *Saul* and an account of the desacralization of anecdotal biblical elements in Gide's attempt to develop personal interpretations of biblical themes.

March, Harold, *Gide and the Hound of Heaven*. Philadelphia: University of Pennsylvania Press, 1952. A study of Gide as self-revealed through his obsessive moral preoccupations.

Planche, Henri, *Le Problème de Gide*. Paris: Téqui, 1952. Untranslated. A scientific study of Gide's physical health and his psychological disfunctions focusing on the relation between his "impotence" and his homosexuality.

Watson-Williams, Helen, *André Gide and the Greek Myth: A Critical Study*. Oxford: Clarendon Press, 1967. A scholarly treatment of Gide's debt to classical Greek literature and his use of myth as an "intimate means towards self-understanding." Includes extensive discussions of *Oedipus, King Candaules, Saul*.

Constantin Toloudis
University of Rhode Island

WILLIAM SCHWENCK GILBERT
1836-1911

Author's Chronology

Born November 18, 1836, London; *1838* kidnapped at Naples, ransomed for twenty-five Pounds; *1855-1857* attends Kings College, London, BA 1857; *1858* begins literary career with translation of laughing song from "Manon Lescaut"; *1861* begins regular contributions to *Fun*; *1863* called to the bar; *1866* "The Yarn of the Nancy Bell" appears in *Fun*; Christmas *1866* first play, *Dulcamara*, produced; *1871* meets Sir Arthur Sullivan; *1875 Trial by Jury*, first Gilbert and Sullivan operetta; formation of D'Oyly Carte Company; *1890* feud with Sullivan, withdrawal from D'Oyly Carte; *1896 The Grand Duke*, last play in collaboration with Sullivan, produced; *1911* last play, *The Hooligan*, produced; May 29, 1911 dies of heart failure attempting to rescue drowning girl.

Author's Bibliography (drama)

Dulcamara, or The Little Duck and the Great Quack, 1866; *The Princess*, 1870 (parody of Tennyson, later adapted as *Princess Ida); Thespis*, 1871 (burlesque); *Pygmalion and Galatea, 1873; Trial by Jury*, 1875; *The Sorcerer*, 1877; *HMS Pinafore*, 1878; *The Pirates of Penzance*, 1879; *Patience*, 1881; *Iolanthe*, 1882; *Princess Ida*, 1884; *The Mikado*, 1885; *Ruddigore*, 1887; *The Yeoman of the Guard*, 1888; *Gondoliers*, 1889; *The Grand Duke*, 1896; *The Hooligan*, 1911. Publications: *Bab Ballads*, 1869; *Original Plays*, four series, 1876-1911; *Original Comic Operas*, *Songs of a Savoyard*, with G's illustrations, 1890; *Foggerty's Fairy and Other Tales*, 1890.

Overview of Biographical Sources

Through the years, the Gilbert and Sullivan operettas have been such a popular success that little serious critical attention has been forthcoming on either man, though during their lifetimes both fervently desired to be taken more seriously. To date, no truly scholarly biography of Gilbert exists, though several more popularly oriented attempts deserve some attention. Edith Browne's *W.S. Gilbert* (1907), published four years before her subject's death, capitalizes on the popularity of Gilbert's librettos. Sidney Dark and Robert Gray's *W.S. Gilbert: His Life and Letters* (1924), while more objective, is still a very *public* life, not a thorough assessment of Gilbert's life or work. Even Hesketh Pearson's *Gilbert: His Life and Strife* (1957), while the most objective and thorough of the biographies, is of little help in dealing with the critical issues underlying the operettas, much less the substantial body of drama, verse, and fiction published by Gilbert independent of his collaboration with Sullivan. Most critics and biographers are interested in the partnership only, as was Caryl Brahms in *Gilbert and Sullivan: Lost Chords and Discords* (1975).

Overview of Biographical Sources

Brahms, Caryl, *Gilbert and Sullivan: Lost Chords and Discords*. London: Little, 1975. Brahms' work attests to the focus of interest in Gilbert. This work, like most that deal with this man, centers around his partnership with Arthur Sullivan and the details of that rather stormy relationship. Brahms' treatment is uneven, though the book amounts to a fairly sympathetic treatment of Gilbert's frustrations over his being taken lightly as a dramatist, Sullivan's anger over the public's ignoring of his oratorios, and D'Oyly Carte's previously underestimated role in keeping the collaboration alive. Perhaps this work's real value lies in the more than one hundred illustrations that trace the full history of this famous team, from *Trial by Jury* to *The Grand Duke*.

Browne, Edith A. *W.S. Gilbert*. London: Lane, 1907. While Browne's biography is too sentimental and too favorably biased to be considered authoritative, it is useful as a contemporary response to Gilbert's popularity. Browne does, however, deal with Gilbert's unsuccessful attempts at careers in the army, the law, and the civil service and the material those experiences provided for his librettos.

Dark, Sidney and Robert Grey, *W.S. Gilbert: His Life and Letters*. London: Methuen, 1924. This work is the first that might be called a true biography. Dark and Grey are objective, and while the book lacks the thoroughness of modern scholarship, it is useful as an overview of Gilbert's public life. The authors are not overtly interested in pleasing an adoring public nor in flattering a living author; rather, they deal effectively with the general details of their subject's life.

Pearson, Hesketh, *Gilbert: His Life and Strife*. London: Methuen, 1957. Pearson is a very competent biographer, and his life of Gilbert represents the only fully useful work in the lot. Pearson uses private papers and previously unpublished letters to draw a thorough portrait of his subject. Even this biography, though, is generously sprinkled with anecdotes, and despite Pearson's obvious orientation toward objective, scholarly biography, the portrait which emerges is of a temperamental, irascible Gilbert who capriciously feuded with almost everyone with whom he came into contact. While Gilbert was indeed argumentative and litigious, Pearson does little to explain the biographical reasons behind his abrasive oversensitivity. Like his famous collaborator, W.S. Gilbert wanted to be taken seriously, wanted desperately to be considered a serious dramatist. His failure in this endeavor rankled him all his life, affording him little joy in his purely popular success.

Autobiographical Sources

The only autobiographical source is "Gilbert, An Autobiography," in *The Theater* (April 2, 1883), a brief but revealing self-portrait of a man who was frustrated in his atempts to achieve fame in ways he considered important but who succeeded in a field, comic opera, which even he could not take completely seriously. The autobiography—implicitly—gives greater insight into Gilbert's feistiness than any of the biographies do.

Overview of Critical Sources

As with biography, the critical work on Gilbert is colored by the fact that the operettas receive most of the attention and even then the attention comes principally from those stalwart Savoyards who value the works primarily for the entertainment they provide. A great deal of what might be called popular culture criticism exists, therefore, but Gilbert's role in reforming the way plays were staged and his transformation of Victorian drama from moribund melodrama to a forum for the consideration of ideas that mattered to his society goes largely ignored. While one hesitates to draw a line and label some criticism "serious" and some not, much if not most of what has been written about Gilbert is of little use to the specialist interested in issues of literary and theater history, genre, and so forth. What follows is a sampling of criticism that tends to be more useful to the scholar than to the popular journalist.

Evaluation of Selected Criticism

Helyar, James, ed. *Gilbert and Sullivan.* Lawrence, KS: University of Kansas Press, 1972. This collection of papers presented at a 1970 Gilbert and Sullivan conference offers a somewhat eclectic selection of essays, but one that covers a good deal of territory. At about the time this conference was held, Gilbert and Sullivan's operettas had begun to be taken more seriously as political and social commentary, and the essays preserved in this collection provide a good overview of that beginning.

Jones, John Bush, ed. *W.S. Gilbert: A Centenary of Scholarship and Commentary.* New York: New York University Press, 1970. Jones' collection of essays covers the period from 1868, before Gilbert had even met Sullivan, to 1968, when the movement to take Gilbert more seriously had just begun. Thus, the volume provides a healthy sampling of a century of Gilbert's reception, public and critical. The entries are judiciously chosen, making this book an excellent place to start. Some of the more recent essays, particularly the one by Jane Stedman, are particularly valuable in gaining insight into the impact Gilbert had on the theater and the literary world of his day.

——, Jones, John Bush, "W.S. Gilbert's Contributions to *Fun*, 1865-74," in *Bulletin of The New York Public Library* 73 (1969): 253-266. Gilbert's first literary success was as a regular contributor of both copy and drawings to the magazine *Fun*. Most of the Bab Ballads first appeared there, and the magazine supplied

Gilbert with both emotional and financial support early in his career. Jones' examination of these writings, which extend into the early period of Gilbert's partnership with Sullivan, is a valuable tool in understanding the development of Gilbert's wit and the extent of his creative talents.

_____, "Gilbertian Humor: Pulling Together a Definition," in *Victorian Newsletter* 33 (Spring 1968): 28-31. Jones and Stedman are the major proponents in Gilbert's resurrection. While Gilbert has always had a strong popular reception, Jones' work established strong critical reasons for treating Gilbert's work more seriously than had been the case until the late 1960s. This article by Jones deals with the charisteristic nature of Gilbert's humor, which is more sophisticated and more satiric than most people think.

_____, "Gilbert and Sullivan's Serious Satire: More Fact Than Fancy," in *Western Humanities Review* 21 (1967): 211-224. For many years, while the comic nature of the operettas was, obviously, appreciated, relatively little attention was paid to the serious side of Gilbert's librettos, which were often so scathing as to make him *persona non grata* at court. Indeed, his knighthood was withheld until 1907, primarily because the satire, even in such seemingly innocuous shows as *H.M.S. Pinafore*, hit hard at court, in the cabinet, and in several departments of government. Jones' article looks at that satire as the serious social and political criticism it really was.

Lawrence, Elwood P. " 'The Happy Land': W.S. Gilbert as Political Satirist," in *Victorian Studies* 15 (1971): 161-183. Lawrence's is another in a series of articles that pioneered the reconsideration of Gilbert's librettos. As the title indicates, this article examines the political intentions and impact of several of the operettas.

Stedman, Jane W. ed. *Gilbert Before Sullivan: Six Comic Plays*. Chicago: University of Chicago Press, 1967. While the inclusion of six one-act plays staged between 1869 and 1875 would be of enough interest to make this book important, Stedman's long introductory essay is a fine addition to Gilbert criticism. Stedman deals reasonably and convincingly with Gilbert's position as a dramatist in his own right, and she discusses at some length his contribution to theater in general as well as his impact on conventional notions of staging.

Other Sources

Dictionary of National Biography, Supplement, v.1 (1901-1911). London: Oxford University Press, 1912. This entry, written shortly after Gilbert's death, presents an excellent summary of the central facts about Gilbert's life, together with a complete, if somewhat hard to follow, catalog of his works, both with and without Arthur Sullivan. The *DNB* does provide some insight into the man, in addition to the purely factual report of his life.

Godwin, A.H. *Gilbert and Sullivan: A Critical Appreciation of the Savoy Operas*. London: J.M. Dent, 1926. This early, rather uncritical look at the operettas is nevertheless useful to the researcher just beginning in Gilbert and Sullivan, for it provides an overview of the entire Gilbert and Sullivan canon, and it raises most of the critical issues that are still alive in today's criticism.

Moore, Frank L. ed. *The Handbook of Gilbert and Sullivan*. New York: Thomas Y. Crowell, 1972. This encyclopedic aid answers most of the factual questions one might have about the operettas and about the D'Oyly Carte company. While most of this information is available in greater depth elsewhere, its easy accessibility in Moore's book is an advantage not to be taken for granted.

William Condon
Arkansas Tech University

(HIPPOLYTE) JEAN GIRAUDOUX
1882-1944

Author's Chronology

Born October 29, 1882, Bellac, France, to Léger and Anne Giraudoux; attends local primary schools and secondary schools; *1903-1905* École Normale Supérieure in Paris; *1905-1907* studies at Munich and Harvard; *1914-1917* service in World War I; wounded twice and cited for gallantry in combat (Legion of Honor); enters the French Foreign Service during the war and remains in government service until his death; *1918* marries Suzanne Boland—one son, Jean-Pierre; first publications, largely in autobiographical prose, beginning 1918 with *Simon le pathetique* and 1921 *Suzanne and the Pacific*; *1928* first play, *Siegfried*, based on an earlier novel, establishes Giraudoux as the leading French playwright between the world wars; begins a life-long collaboration with actor-director Louis Jouvet; many of his plays produced and published after his death in Paris, January 31, 1944.

Author's Bibliography

There is no complete collection of Giraudoux's plays in English, although many of his plays have been translated or produced in English adaptions. *Théâtre complèt*, 16 vols., 1945-1953, is the only complete collection of his writings for the theater; most of his prose and his non-fiction writing remains unavailable in English.

Fiction in English: *Suzanne and the Pacific*, 1921; *Bella*, 1926; *Lying Woman*, 1972; *My Friend from Limousin*, 1922.

Plays in English: *Siegfried*, 1928; *Amphitryon 38*, 1929; *Judith*, 1931; *Intermezzo* (also *The Enchanted*), 1933; *The Virtuous Island*, 1935; *Tiger at the Gates* (also *The Trojan War Will Not Take Place*), 1935; *Electra*, 1937; *Ondine*, 1939; *The Apollo of Bellac*, 1942; *The Madwoman of Chaillot*, 1945; *Duel of Angels*, 1954.

Overview of Biographical Sources

A definitive biography of Giraudoux has not yet been written, even in French. Any research into the playwright's life is hampered by the fact that the French government still considers much information about his life in the French Foreign Service a secret; furthermore, many of the playwright's friends were and still are reluctant to make available correspondence and other materials of interest to the biographer. The information which is available thus has been gathered from official documents, writings and statements made by his wife and his son after his death, a small collection of published letters, and deductions made from his autobiographical writings.

The student of Giraudoux will find a wealth of biographical material in the critical studies of Donald Inskip, *Jean Giraudoux: The Making of A Dramatist* (London: Oxford University Press, 1958); Laurent LeSage, *Jean Giraudoux: His Life and Works* (University Park: Penn State University Press, 1959); Georges Lemaître, *Jean Giraudoux: The Writer and His Work* (New York: Frederick Ungar, 1971); and John H. Reilly, *Jean Giraudoux* (Boston: Twayne, 1978). Most of these works concentrate on biographical facts related to the development of Giraudoux as a writer and on data and events which appear to have significance with regard to the thematic content of the plays. The best source for the study of Giraudoux the man is by his son, Jean-Pierre Giraudoux, *Le fils* (Paris: Grasset, 1967. Untranslated).

Autobiographical Sources

Giraudoux was not a prolific writer of personal letters; he preferred to communicate with his friends by telephone or by dropping in on them unexpectedly. His letters have been published in French as *Jean Giraudoux: Lettres* (Paris: Editions Klincksieck, 1975). This collection omits the important correspondence between Giraudoux and Louis Jouvet, which is preserved, as yet unpublished, in the Bibliothcque de l'Arsenal in Paris. Much autobiographical material is contained in the author's early fiction and non-fiction prose and in the posthumously published *Souvenir de deux existences*, 1975. Another collection of autobiographical material in French is *Giraudoux par lui-même* (Paris: Editions du Seuil, 1952).

Overview of Critical Sources

Giraudoux has been the subject of a large number of critical studies, particularly during the 1960s and early 1970s; recently, however, critical interest in the playwright has diminished, probably because many of his plays make reference to political events and ideas which are no longer topical. All the critical material up to 1973 is listed in Laurent LeSage's *L'Oeuvre de Jean Giraudoux: Essai de bibliographie chronologigue* (University Park: Penn State University Press, 1956); and *Supplément* (to the LeSage bibliography) (Bellac, 1974). The following is a critical listing of the main scholarly studies published in English.

Evaluation of Selected Criticism in English

Cohen, Robert, *Giraudoux: Three Faces of Destiny*. Chicago: University of Chicago Press, 1968. Cohen arranges Giraudoux's plays into three distinct thematic groupings: sexual, metaphysical, and political. He links the plays closely to existentialist thought and to the Theatre of the Absurd, not always convincingly. In a closing chapter on Giraudoux's style, the author emphasizes the predominance of form over content in the plays. Quotations are given in the original and in English translation.

Inskip, Donald, *Jean Giraudoux: The Making of a Dramatist*. London: Oxford University Press, 1958. The first comprehensive study of Giraudoux in the English language. This book contains a good biographical section with amusing details of the playwright's early years. There is a good but not very exhaustive analysis of the plays, and a sympathetic but opinionated evaluation of the dramatic work, with little attention given to the prose. Good final section on the artistic and personal relationship with Louis Jouvet.

Lemaitre, Georges, *Jean Giraudoux: The Writer and His Work*. New York: Frederick Ungar, 1971. A good introduction to the work of Giraudoux, examines the various genres (plays, prose fiction, essays, political polemics, etc.) in seven chapters. It is a useful book for students, as it provides a good biographical survey and detailed plot summaries. Lemaitre separates his early prose work and his dramatic work too strictly, neglecting the substantial cross-influences.

LeSage, Laurent, *Jean Giraudoux: His Life and Works*. University Park: Pennsylvania State University Press, 1959. One of the earliest studies in English of Giraudoux by the foremost American Giraudoux scholar, LeSage makes use of biographical information to analyze the works. He sees a steady development in Giraudoux's work from a preoccupation with stylistic matters to a predominance of theme in the later works. Commendable lack of jargon. No bibliography.

Reilly, John H. *Jean Giraudoux*. Boston: Twayne, 1978. This is a good introductory survey without the depth of LeSage and Lemaitre. Reilly concentrates on the conflict between the "real" and the "ideal" in Giraudoux's works; groups the plays similar to Cohen's method. He espouses mainly an autobiographical interpretation: Giraudoux's "pessimism" is stimulated mainly by negative events in his personal life. Includes a useful chronology and a good bibliography. Comprehensive without many new insights.

Other Sources

LeSage, Laurent, *Giraudoux, Surrealism and the German Romantic Ideal*. Urbana: University of Illinois Press, 1952. Intriguing study of the influence of the surrealist school and of the German writers of the Romantic period on the playwright.

Mankin, Paul A. *Precious Irony: The Theatre of Jean Giraudoux*. The Hague: Mouton, 1971. Deals with Giraudoux's use of "irony", claiming that it is more a "Weltanschauung" than a rhetorical device for the playwright. Good bibliography.

Raymond, Agnes G. *Jean Giraudoux: The Theatre of Victory and Defeat.* Amherst: University of Massachusetts Press, 1966. Claims that Giraudoux's dramatic work reflects the victory of World War I and the defeat of World War II. The author claims that theme of the 'tiger-men' is a carefully perpetrated hoax by the playwright. Interesting focus on "woman as a political symbol".

Franz G. Blaha
University of Nebraska

JOHANN WOLFGANG GOETHE
1749-1832

Author's Chronology

Born August 28, 1749, Frankfurt/Main, Germany, son of a cultured but idle lawyer and grandson, on his mother's side, of a mayor of Frankfurt; *1765* enrolls as a student of law at the University of Leipzig yet returns to Frankfurt three years later without having completed his degree; *1770* continues his studies at the University of Strasbourg, befriends the innovative critic and poet Johann Gottfried Herder, and composes his first important poetry under the influence of Herder's ideas; *1771* begins to practice law in Frankfurt but quickly becomes famous as the author of the historical drama *Götz von Berlichingen*; *1772* assumes the position of legal councillor at the imperial law court in Wetzlar; *1773* returns to Frankfurt and lives the life of a young celebrity among a circle of literary friends; *1774* publishes his first novel, *The Sufferings of Young Werther*, which becomes an immediate bestseller; *1775* is invited by Duke Karl August of Sachsen-Weimar to move to Weimar; *1776-1785* assumes various important positions in the government of the duchy; *1782* is granted the diploma of nobility; *1786-1788* escapes professional and personal restrictions in Weimar and embarks on an educational journey through Italy; *1788* upon his return to Weimar, starts to live with Christiane Vulpius, a girl whose social status makes her unacceptable at court; *1791* becomes director of the Weimar Court Theater; *1794* begins his friendship and close collaboration with Friedrich Schiller; *1806* marries Christiane Vulpius; *1808* publishes *Faust*, Part I; *1817* resigns as director of the Weimar Court Theater; *1826* starts preparations for a final edition of his works in forty volumes; *1831* finishes *Faust*, Part II; March 22, 1832 dies after a brief illness and four days later is buried in the Princes' Vault in Weimar.

Author's Bibliography (selected)

Götz von Berlichingen, 1773, tr. 1965 (play); *The Sufferings of Young Werther*, 1774, tr. 1957 (novel); *Iphigenia in Tauris*, 1787, tr. 1963 (play); *Egmont*, 1788, tr. 1960 (play); *Torquato Tasso*, 1790, tr. 1966 (play); *Roman Elegies*, 1793, tr. 1974 (poetry); *Wilhelm Meister's Apprenticeship*, 1795-1796, tr. 1824, reissued 1965 (novel); *Hermann and Dorothea*, 1797, tr. 1966 (epic poem); *Faust*, Part I, 1808, tr. 1965 (play); *Elective Affinities*, 1809, tr. 1963 (novel); *Truth and Poetry: From My Own Life*, 1811-1833, tr. 1848-1849, reissued 1969 as *The Autobiography of Johann Wolfgang von Goethe* (autobiography); *Italian Journey 1786-1788*, 1817-1817, tr. 1962 (autobiographical travelogue); *The West-Eastern Divan*, 1819, tr. 1914 (poetry); *Wilhelm Meister's Travels*, 1821-1829, tr. in incomplete form 1824, reissued 1965 (novel); *Faust*, Part II, published posthumously, 1833, tr. 1965 (play).

Overview of Biographical Sources

Though comparatively few of Goethe's works had been translated at the time of his death, recognition abroad of this last "universal man," as Thomas Carlyle called him, established itself quickly and with surprising ease. In Germany, on the other hand, a whole generation of writers and critics could hardly wait to step out of the shadow of their seemingly immortal father figure. It is, therefore, no accident that it took over twenty years and the efforts of an Englishman to produce the first full-scale biography of Goethe, George H. Lewes' *The Life and Works of Goethe* (1855), an account which remained authoritative for two decades and is considered by many to be still unsurpassed.

Only when the unification of Germany in 1871 brought a noticeable change in literary tastes and values, did Goethe and his work finally gain in his own country the undisputed stature of its culture's exemplary classic. Hermann Grimm's *The Life and Times of Goethe* (Boston: Little, Brown, 1880) opened a new field for literary research which by the turn of the century churned out its results at the rate of one major biography every two years. Of all these efforts, Albert Bielschowsky's *The Life of Goethe*, 3 vols. (New York: Putnam, 1905-1908) has proven to be the most enduring. The 1920s saw the translation into English of the Danish philosopher and critic Georg Brandes' ambitious *Wolfgang Goethe*, 2 vols. (New York: Frank-Maurice, 1925) while the hundreth anniversary of Goethe's death brought the publication of John G. Robertson's still solid and readable *The Life and Work of Goethe* (London: Routledge, 1932). The most popular biography of the first half of the twentieth century, however, was doubtlessly the rather sensational account by Emil Ludwig, *Goethe: The History of a Man* (New York: Blue Ribbon Books, 1928). With the rise of Nazism in Germany, Goethe's reputation was quickly enlisted in the service of ideologies on left and right. The Hungarian Marxist George Lukács' *Goethe and His Age* (London: Merlin Press, 1968) is generally regarded the only lasting contribution of this phase. Since World War II, Goethe scholarship has grown rather leary of previous attempts at constructing Goethe's life and work into one all-encompassing synthesis. Richard Friedenthal's *Goethe: His Life and Times* (1965) is now widely acclaimed as the outstanding example of a new-found modesty of biographical purpose.

Evaluation of Selected Biographies

Eissler, Kurt R. *Goethe: A Psychoanalytic Study. 1775-1786.* 2 vols. Detroit: Wayne State University Press, 1963. One of America's leading Freudians, Eissler unfolds with epic breadth the case history of the poet's incestuous love for his sister and the self-applied psychotherapy through which in mid-life Goethe regained his creative momentum. Though directly concerned with only ten years of a long life, Eissler's approach in fact, includes Goethe's youth and even sheds light on the older man. In spite of its discouraging length, this is a fascinating journey into the unconscious of one of the world's greatest minds.

Fairley, Barker, *A Study of Goethe*. Oxford: Clarendon Press, 1947; rpt. Oxford Paperback, 1961. Written as a biography of the inner man, this account delineates Goethe's growth from the troubled individualism of his youth to the calm mastery of his life in later years. Fairley views the poet's early self-absorption against the background of a whole generation's preoccupation with subjectivity and praises Goethe for the critical example he set by resisting its destructive appeal. Perceptively and convincingly argued, this compact study will be of greatest advantage to those who intend to proceed from it to a reading of Goethe's works.

Friedenthal, Richard, *Goethe: His Life and Times*. Cleveland: World Publishing, 1965. For many, this work continues to be the best modern biography of Goethe. It depicts a great personality sharing in ample measure the contradictions of its historical time and place. Friedenthal communicates his astounding welter of biographical, socio-political, and cultural information in a vigorous and lively style which is free from scholarly pedantry without becoming facile about facts. Where the author spurns his own injuction not to analyze Goethe's individual works, he occasionally drifts into the commonplace. While this study is clearly not an introduction to Goethe's work, it can be recommended as a biography without reservations.

Lewes, George H. *The Life and Works of Goethe*. London: D. Nutt, 1855; rpt. *The Life of Goethe*. New York: Frederick Ungar, 1965. After one hundred and thirty years, Lewes' work is still considered one of the best biographies of any man in any language. It is well researched and elegantly written, clear-sighted in its admiration and reasonable in its criticism. These strong recommendations notwithstanding, Lewes' literary judgments have clearly begun to show their venerable age. The author's almost total neglect of the older Goethe is certainly the most serious flaw. For those who nevertheless intend to turn to this proven biographical classic, the reprint contains an introductory essay by Victor Lange on the historical limitations of Lewes' treatment.

Autobiographical Sources
No other great writer has left to posterity as much autobiographical material as has Goethe during his long life as an international celebrity. Though the implicit vanity of these efforts has often been censured, Goethe's diligent observations of himself ought to be regarded as more than the expression of a self-satisfied egotism. His immense productivity in a variety of intellectual endeavors, his enormous circle of friends and admirers, the many personal and professional obligations that inevitably accompany fame had to require of him repeated reflections on the personal unity behind the centrifugal stress of so many divergent activities. Four of the autobiographical sources distinguish themselves by their literary quality as well as their importance for an understanding of Goethe's personality.

Truth and Poetry: From My Own Life, 2 vols., tr. by John Oxenford (London: Bohn, 1848-1849); rpt. as *The Autobiography of Johann Wolfgang von Goethe* (New York: Horizon Press, 1969) contains an account of Goethe's life from his birth to 1775, the year in which he accepted the invitation of Duke Karl August to come to Weimar. Writing almost a lifetime after the events, Goethe employs a style of dispassionate, frequently ironic understatement as he depicts himself in his relations with the lively urban world of his bourgeois upbringing. His escape from Weimar's confinements and his stay in Italy are evoked in the vivid descriptions of the *Italian Journey 1786-1788*, tr. by W.H. Auden and Elizabeth Mayer (New York: Pantheon Books, 1962). Based on the poet's diaries but not identical with them, this travelogue tells the story of his spiritual and sensual liberation under the sunny skies of a country whose infectuous joy of life made a lasting impression on him. Upon his return to Weimar, Goethe's legendary friendship with Friedrich Schiller resulted in a correspondence which belongs to the most revered documents of Germany's golden age of letters. *The Correspondence between Schiller and Goethe*, 2 vols., tr. by L. Dora Schmitz (London: Bell, 1877-1879) shows these two acknowledged classics of German literature in a remarkably open exchange of ideas that proved to be of major consequence for the works of both men. During his last nine years, Goethe encouraged his young secretary Johann Peter Eckermann to write down the poet's conversations. Though Eckermann's fawning servility has made him the easy target of much supercilious criticism, his *Conversations with Eckermann*, 2 vols., tr. by John Oxenford (London: Smith and Elder, 1850; rpt. in 1 vol. San Francisco: North Point Press, 1984) constitutes an invaluable record of Goethe's consciously stylized wisdom of old age. A selection of letters from and to Goethe which reveal how long the poet had to struggle before he achieved calm mastery of his life has been edited by Berthold Biermann in *Goethe's World as Seen in Letters and Memoirs* (New York: New Directions, 1949).

Overview of Critical Sources

Hermann Grimm's provocative assertion in the 1870s that there was to be a new science called Goethe has proven prophetic as a small army of industrious scholars set about their business. Soon the developments within the resulting criticism became themselves a new branch of Goethe scholarship which has produced more than fifty assessments over the last one hundred years. In English the most accessible and readable survey is Wolfgang Leppmann's *The German Image of Goethe* (Oxford: Clarendon Press, 1961). During the first forty years after Goethe's death, German critics showed an open hostility towards Goethe because of the apolitical aloofness and pedantic egoism of his old age. The years between 1870 and 1920, then, saw the meteoric rise of his fame as writers from all fields of knowledge embarked on ever more recondite and lofty interpretations of Goethe's life and work. Friedrich Gundolf's *Goethe* (Berlin: Bondi, 1916) has frequently been judged exemplary among these efforts. From 1920 onwards, an increasing need was felt to disentangle the poetic works from the overpowering presence of the man. Especially after 1945, a greater emphasis on close textual readings enabled scholars to portray a new sense of structural and symbolic unity in and among Goethe's works. In German important studies along these lines are Emil Staiger's *Goethe*, 3 vols. (Zurich: Atlantis, 1952-1959) and Wilhelm Emrich's *Die Symbolik von Faust II* (Frankfurt/Main: Athenäum, 1957); in English, important works include: Ilse Graham's *Goethe: Portrait of the Artist* (Berlin: de Gruyter, 1977) and Harold Jantz' *The Form of 'Faust'* (Baltimore: Johns Hopkins University Press, 1978). For the last twenty years, a generation of younger scholars has, however, begun to rebel against the perceived manipulation of Goethe's fame at the hands of many Germanists as well as the social and political escapism of their textual criticism. A manifesto of these concerns is *Die Klassik-Legende*, Second Wisconsin Workshop, ed. by Reinhold Grimm and Jost Hermand (Frankfurt/Main: Athenäum, 1971). Among English-speaking critics, this latest trend has not yet aroused a noticeable response. An excellent account of the socio-cultural milieu of Goethe's Weimar, nevertheless, exists in Walter H. Bruford's *Culture and Society in Classical Weimar* (Cambridge: Cambridge University Press, 1962).

Evaluation of Selected Criticism

Atkins, Stuart, *Goethe's 'Faust': A Literary Analysis*. Cambridge: Harvard University Press, 1964. Realizing that mountains of information on this tragedy have begun to make a literary appreciation nearly impossible, the author offers an interpretation of *Faust* which focuses on the details of its dramatic progression. Allegorical and speculative readings of characters and events are shunned as Atkins traces line by line the development of thoughts and actions. Since he prefaces his analysis with only the briefest of introductions on the genesis, background, and reputation of *Faust*, the interpretative paraphrase tends to be dense and hard to absorb. Atkins efforts, nevertheless, constitute an indispensible guide for all who want to advance from a reading about to a reading of Goethe's most famous play.

Carlson, Marvin A. *Goethe and the Weimar Theatre*. Ithaca, NY: Cornell University Press, 1978. Carlson traces in chronological sequence Goethe's career as an actor in the amateur theatricals of his youth, his efforts to reorganize the theater in Weimar, his collaboration with Schiller in the staging of several of that dramatist's plays, his education of audiences and actors, as well as the reasons for his final disenchantment. Richly furnished with illustrations, this study is not only a fascinating source of information on actors, repertory, physical facilities, and the politics of productions, it can also be read as an unusual biography of Goethe's involvement of fifty years with one of Germany's influential cultural institutions.

Dieckmann, Liselotte, *Johann Wolfgang Goethe*. New York: Twayne, 1974. Addressed to readers unfamiliar with Goethe, this study gives a balanced assessment of his many achievements. Dieckmann does not proceed chronologically but groups Goethe's works by genre and treats them, from the autobiographical writings to *Faust*, as ever-widening circles of creativity around the personality of their author. Formal and biographical concerns are thus ingeniously related. Weary of the personality cult that has surrounded Goethe for so long, Dieckmann seems anxious not to appear uncritical and occasionally judges Goethe's dramatic genius too harshly. This is, nevertheless, an excellent introduction which should be the logical starting point for most beginners.

Graham, Ilse, *Goethe: Portrait of the Artist*. Berlin: de Gruyter, 1977. The author is convinced that the nature of Goethe's artistry was centered around his exact sensual fantasy. Graham, therefore, pursues this fantasy as a structuring principle in a variety of Goethe's writings, among them the plays *Iphigenia in Tauris*, *Torquato Tasso*, and *Faust*. Close textual readings probe how Goethe's modes of perception are reflected in his choice of syntax, vocabulary, and symbol. A highly complex approach is made even less accessible by the fact that quotes are not translated. The bibliography announced in the table of contents has been omitted. The work does, however, contain a helpful index of themes and images.

Hatfield, Henry, *Goethe: A Critical Introduction*. New York: New Directions, 1963. A compact chronological survey, Hatfield's treatment concentrates on Goethe's achievements in the genres of lyrical and epic poetry, novel, drama, and autobiography but excludes a discussion of the scientific writings. Against a biographical and cultural background, major works in each category are briefly outlined and evaluated. The mature and older Goethe receive the lion's share of Hatfield's attention. Almost one third of the book is devoted to *Faust*. The author's straightforward style and organization make this an eminently suitable study for readers with no previous knowledge of the poet.

Peacock, Ronald, *Goethe's Major Plays*. Manchester: University Press, 1959; rpt. New York: Barnes and Noble, 1966. Peacock interprets the essentially subjective moral and philosophical dilemmas of Goethe's seven major plays while discussing their unorthodox dramatic qualities. Though he does not consider Goethe a born dramatist, the author stresses that Goethe developed an original form of drama which in spite of its episodic plots achieves a symbolic presentation of the universal problems surrounding man's induction into experience. This unassuming introduction continues to be one of the most important and readable books on Goethe's plays in the English language.

Other Sources

Dieckmann, Liselotte, *Goethe's 'Faust': A Critical Reading*. Englewood Cliffs, NJ: Prentice-Hall, 1972. An introduction to the philosophical presuppositions, the forms of poetic presentation as well as the plot of the tragedy.

Gearey, John, *Goethe's 'Faust': The Making of Part I*. New Haven: Yale University Press, 1981. Describes stages in the conception and composition of Goethe's most famous plays.

Gray, Ronald, *Goethe: A Critical Introduction*, Cambridge: Cambridge University Press, 1967. A General introduction with emphasis on Goethe's poetic genius.

Haile, Harry G. *Invitation to Goethe's 'Faust'*. University, AL: University of Alabama Press, 1978. Interpretative forays which seek to make some of the most complex scenes of Part I and II accessible to modern readers.

Lange, Victor, ed. *Goethe*. Englewood Cliffs, NJ: Prentice-Hall, 1968. Twelve essays by renowned scholars on aspects of Goethe's life and work.

Lukács, Georg, *Goethe and His Age*. trans. Robert Anchor. London: Merlin Press, 1968. Contains five studies of *Faust* from a Marxist perspective.

Reed, Terence J. *The Classical Centre: Goethe and Weimar 1775-1832*. New York: Barnes and Noble, 1980. Places Goethe's achievements within the context of the cultural florescence associated with the court of Duke Karl August.

Selected Dictionaries and Encyclopedias

Encyclopaedia Britannica, 1984. Biographical information, assessment of literary and scientific achievements, extensive bibliographies of primary and secondary literature.

Encyclopedia of World Drama, McGraw-Hill, 1984. Introduction, plot summaries of major plays, chronological listing of all plays, and bibliography of secondary literature.

Joachim J. Scholz
Washington College

NIKOLAI GOGOL
1809-1852

Author's Chronology

Born April 1, 1809 in Sorochintsy, Province of Poltava, in the Ukraine; his father who dies in 1825 was a small landowner and amateur playwright; *1821-1828* high school; upon graduation goes to St. Petersburg to look for a job; starts writing; *1830* contributes stories of Ukrainian life to literary reviews; *1831* he is an unsatisfactory teacher of history at a young ladies' institute; September, *1831* collects stories of Ukrainian life into *Evenings on a Farm near Dikanka*; March, *1832* appointed professor of World History at the University of St. Petersburg, a post for which he is totally unsuited; *1835* publishes his famous collection *Mirgorod* and the less successful "epic" *Taras Bulba*; January 30, *1836* first public reading of *Inspector General* which is first performed on May 1, 1836; *1836-1848* continual travels abroad, in Russia for only short periods of time; flirts with religion, conversion and mysticism; May, *1839* brief romantic friendship with a dying young prince; *1841* completes *Overcoat*; *1841-1842* Part I of *Dead Souls*; *1842-1848* travels, possibly for reasons of health; *1847* publishes *Selected Passages from Correspondence with Friends*, which he expected to be accepted as a great moral treatise and example; *1848-1852* returns to Russia for good, visits monasteries, churches; has become a religious fanatic; March 4, *1852* dies, a famous writer and (in his eyes) a misunderstood and unappreciated philosopher-prophet.

Author's Bibliography (selected)

Evenings on a Farm near Dikanka, 1831-1832, tr. 1926 (short fiction); *Mirgorod*, 1835, tr. 1928 (short fiction); *The Inspector General*, 1836, tr. 1892 (drama); *Marriage*, 1842, tr. 1927 (drama); *Taras Bulba*, 1842, tr. 1855 (novel); *Dead Souls*, 1842-1855, tr. 1887 (novel).

All of Gogol's works appeared in his lifetime. Only the second part of *Dead Souls*, which Gogol attempted to burn immediately before his death, can be considered posthumous. There is a complete Russian edition of his work (1937-1952) and numerous other multi-volume collections. Translations have appeared in great quantity since the 1900s: Constance Garnett, in the early part of the century, and David Magarshack, more recently, have translated all the fiction, published by Penguin Books.

Overview of Biographical Sources

Nikolai Gogol is one of the strangest writers in Russian literature, and his biography is full of unresolved mysteries. Because of his reclusiveness and secretiveness, as well as his penchant for camouflage, there is no first-hand source and guide to his personal life. He seems never to have developed any love relationship with anyone. His comic and grotesque sense of vision has invited strange interpretations: some (i.e. the unimaginative and plodding social critic Belinsky, a Gogol contemporary) consider him a master of "realism"—that is, one who gives a believable and understandable picture of the world around him; others (Viktor Shklovsky, Vladimir Nabokov) consider him the exact opposite, one who distorts and exaggerates and totally blurs reality. These two views are not reconcilable. Gogol's vision, like no other writer, changes dramatically from one reader to another. Vsevolod Setschkareff's *Gogol: His Life and Works* (New York, 1965) provides a panorama of this divisive debate and also contains a solid biographical sketch.

To a reader of Gogol, his drama means *Inspector General* (Gogol's other plays, notably *The Gamblers* and *Marriage*, are much less read and performed). It is said that its lead is the most demanding and varied role of any Russian play. All the surveys of Gogol discuss it at length. It has been translated many times and is available in anthologies of Russian plays (Noyes, republished in 1960; Reeve, 1961-63).

Evaluation of Selected Biographies

Karlinsky, Simon, *The Sexual Labyrinth of Nikolay Gogol*. Cambridge: Harvard University Press, 1976. This is a controversial interpretation of Gogol and his human contacts, heavily reliant on Freudian insights and the implication that Gogol was a homosexual.

Nabokov, Vladimir V. *Gogol*. New York: New Directions, 1944. A tremendously amusing and brilliantly written distortion, Nabokov spanks those who disagree with him, and while he gives a perfectly good biographical sketch of Gogol, he denigrates those who find biography important or helpful. An example: the book begins with the date of Gogol's death and ends with the date of his birth.

Peace, Richard Arthur, *The Enigma of Gogol*. Cambridge: Cambridge University Press, 1981. Peace makes a strange attempt to relate Gogol's strange life to the unusual effect of his work.

Troyat, Henri, *Divided Soul*. Garden City, NY: Doubleday, 1965. Although flowery and semi-fictional like all the Troyat biographies, this book is nicely written and uncontroversial.

Autobiographical Sources

Gogol's correspondence (not translated into English) must be approached with care and read as if it were part of his creative opus. The only contemporary sources of any reliability are the recollections of his friends, such as Pavel Annenkov's *The Extraordinary Decade* (Ardis: Ann Arbor, 1968), which is not very personal.

Overview of Critical Sources

Gogol scholarship is tremendous. His work has been studied seriously since his lifetime. The early leftist critics viewed him as a social critic. The "formalists" in the early part of this century (Boris Eikhenbaum, Viktor Shklovsky) changed the perspective entirely, and treated him strictly as a craftsman. Gogol is solid enough to stand up to either view.

Evaluation of Selected Criticism

Erlich, Victor, *Gogol*. New Haven: Yale University Press, 1969. This is an excellent and well-written short presentation in a formalist vein. Erlich, who is America's leading expert on the formalist school, shows Gogol's preoccupation with words and structure—an especially important consideration in any analysis of *Inspector General.*

Fanger, Donald, *The Creation of Nikolai Gogol*. Cambridge: Harvard University Press, 1979. A good, well-written survey, Fanger describes the major critical views of Gogol.

Gippius, V.V. *Gogol*. Ann Arbor: Ardis, 1981. In this, the best short survey, Gippius successfully blends the various approaches to Gogol. In his discussion of the plays, for example, he points out Gogol's debt to comedy writers of the past, to the comic tradition of the boastful fool and liar, and also carefully analyzes the structural originality of plot and scene.

Maguire, Robert A. ed. *Gogol from the Twentieth Century*. Princeton: Princeton University Press, 1975-5. This is an invaluable source book, containing Gippius' brilliant study of *Inspector General*, and V.I. Wanov's study of the same play. There are good translations and excellent editing.

Nabokov, Vladimir V. *Gogol*. New York: New Directions, 1944, and *Lectures on Russian Literature*. New York: Harcourt, Brace, 1981. Nabokov provides the unique experience of one great writer on another. As with Nabokov's fiction, this criticism must be read with care: To Nabokov, Gogol is a pure wordsman, uninterested in "reality". Nabokov's remarks have become a polemic with the leftist Gogolians of the past. It is brilliantly written, intellectually seductive, and provides countless provocative ideas for the sophisticated reader.

Rahv, Philip, "Gogol as a Modern Instance" in *Literature and the Sixth Sense*. New York: Houghton, Mifflin, 1969. One of the best leftist and political literary critics, a Russian by birth, Rahv relates Gogol to twentieth-century world culture.

Wilson, Edmund, "Gogol: The Demon in the Overgrown Garden," in *A Window on Russia"*. New York: Farrar, Straus & Giroux, 1972. Wilson, a leading man of letters, in opposition to his friend Nabokov, offers a view of Gogol in which every event and character comes from some reality. It is impressionistic in the best sense.

Philippe D. Radley
New York

MAXIM GORKY
1868-1936

Author's Chronology

Born Alexey Maximovich Peshkov, March 28, 1868, to Maxim Savvatievich Peshkov and Varvara Vasilievna; *1873* father dies; *1878* mother dies; little formal education; works as manual laborer, errand boy, cook; wanders the countryside as a tramp; *1892* publishes his first story; *1895* first literary success with stories based on his travels; *1902* becomes director of the publishing house Znanie and is active in assisting young Russian writers; *1905* briefly imprisoned for his part in the December uprising. leaves for western Europe and the United States; *1917-1918* after initial opposition to the Bolsheviks, reaches an understanding with Lenin and heads several societies and associations; *1921-1933* lives abroad; *1934* becomes chairman of the first All Union Congress of Soviet writers and propounds the idea of "Socialist realism," that literature must have social significance; *1936* dies in circumstances still in dispute, a victim of tuberculosis or of Stalin's death warrant.

Author's Bibliography

Drama: *The Lower Depths*, 1902, tr. 1912; *Yegor Bulychov and Others*, 1932, tr. 1937; *Dostigaev and Others*, 1933, tr. 1937.

Novels: *Mat*, 1906; *Mother*, 1906, tr. 1907; *A Confession*, 1908, tr. 1909; *The Life of Matvei Kozhemyakin*, 1910, tr. 1919; *The Artamonov Business*, 1928, tr. 1948; *Zhizn Klima Samgin*, 1927-1936 (4 vols.); *The Life of Klim Samgin: The Bystander*, tr. 1930; *The Magnet*, tr. 1931; *Other Fires*, tr. 1933; *The Spectre*, tr. 1938;

Memoirs and essays: *My Childhood*, 1913, tr. 1914; *In the World,* 1914, tr. 1919; *My Universities*, 1922, tr. 1922; *Reminiscences of Leo Nikolaevich Tolstoy*, 1919, tr. 1920; *Days with Lenin*, 1924, tr. 1932; *Fragments from My Diary*, 1924, tr. 1940;

Collections: *Polnoe sobranie sochineniy*, 1949-1955 (30 vols.); *The Last Plays*, 1937, tr. by Gibson-Cowan; *Seven Plays*, 1946, tr. by A. Bakshy and P. Nathan; *The Lower Depths and Other Plays*, 1959, tr. by A. Bakshy and P. Nathan; *Selected Stories of Maxim Gorky*, 1959, tr. by B. Isaacs; *Letters of Gorky and Andreev 1899-1912*, 1958, tr. by Lydia Weston and ed. by Peter Yershov; *Letters*, 1966, tr. by V. Dutt and ed. by P. Cockerell.

Overview of Biographical Sources

Alexander Kaun's *Maxim Gorky and his Russia* (1931), based in part on his friendship with Gorky, has been the standard full-length biography. Dan Levin,

Stormy Petrel: The Life and Work of Maxim Gorky (1965) provides another comprehensive life. Certain critical studies also contain perceptive biographical analysis. Richard Hare, *Maxim Gorky: Romantic Realist and Conservative Revolutionary* (New York: Oxford University Press, 1962) carefully connects Gorky's life and work, includes a chapter on "legend competes with fact" in the writer's life, and is particularly acute on Gorky's last years. F.M. Borras, *Maxim Gorky, The Writer: An Interpretation* (New York: Oxford University Press, 1967) includes a concise "biographical chronicle," an introductory chapter setting Gorky into the context of pre-Revolutionary Russia, and a chapter clearly summarizing his "ideas and outlook."

Evaluation of Selected Biographies

Kaun, Alexander, *Maxim Gorky and his Russia*. New York: Jonathan Cape and Harrison Smith, 1931. A traditional life and times biography published when Gorky was sixty, Kaun's work derives from a thorough knowledge of Russian sources, from interviews with Gorky and his friends, and from a careful study of Gorky's autobiographical writings. Extensive quotations from Gorky's work give the flavor of his style, although Kaun does not engage in literary analysis. Occasionally Gorky's fiction is used to understand his character. Kaun usually trusts Gorky's own statements, although he identifies facts the autobiographer does not supply and sometimes questions Gorky's version of events.

Levin, Dan, *Stormy Petrel: The Life and Work of Maxim Gorky*. New York: Appleton-Century, 1965. This full-length biography follows Kaun's life and times approach but presents a sharper picture of the quality of Gorky's literary output. Levin, writing thirty years after Gorky's death, is able to be more candid about his subject's relationship with the Soviet government than Kaun, who to some extent was obliged to protect Gorky and his friends. Indeed, the treatment of Gorky's last six years, which are not covered by Kaun, contains a probing analysis of the author's psychology. Did Gorky realize the monstrous brutality of Stalin's regime? Levin, in part relying on sources unavailable to Kaun and on Gorky's own writing, believes Gorky did know about and tried to ameliorate the worst aspects of totalitarianism.

Autobiographical Sources

Gorky's letters, diaries, and memoirs provide a very rich commentary on his life and work, on his times, and on writers who were his contemporaries. His three volume autobiography, *My Childhood* (1913), *In The World* (1917), and *My Universities* (1922) has been hailed for its psychological insights and its vivid presentation of human character. The first volume covers his life from the ages of three to eleven. The second volume picks up his story in 1879 and continues to 1884. The third volume concentrates on the crucial years, 1884-1888, when Gorky, growing into manhood, attempted suicide and gradually recovered his robust constitution. He is not an introspective writer; rather his character is revealed by the way he describes others. Aspects of his life and work after the 1917 revolution are not addressed directly in his autobiographical trilogy, but his ambivalent relationship with Lenin led him on several occasions to rewrite his views of the founder of the Soviet state (See *Days with Lenin*. New York: International Publishers, 1932). The *Letters of Gorky and Andreev 1899-1912* tr. by Lydia Weston and ed. by Peter Yershov (New York: Columbia University Press, 1958) provide significant insights into Gorky's epistolary style and are a valuable source for charting his involvement in revolutionary politics and literary life in Russia and in the West.

Overview of Critical Sources

Because Gorky's works were made available in translation early in his career, a significant body of scholarship exists on all aspects of his writing. Much of his best work is autobiographical, and perhaps for that reason criticism has usually included a significant concern with his life. Most critics agree that Gorky's novels and plays vary considerably in quality and that even his successful fiction and drama are heavily didactic. At the same time, critics are reluctant to judge him on esthetic grounds alone, and point to the tremendous influence of his writing in shaping public opinion in the Soviet Union. Russian emigré scholars have sometimes dismissed him because of his service to the Stalinist state, and some Soviet scholars tend to exaggerate his achievements. Western scholars rate him below Tolstoy and Chekhov but continue to see him as a major presence in Russian literature and a problematic figure in Soviet letters whose precise relationship to the State has still to be determined.

Evaluation of Selected Criticism

Borras, F.M. *Maxim Gorky, The Writer: An Interpretation*. London: Oxford University Press, 1967. Perhaps the best single critical source on Gorky in English, this book covers Gorky's short stories, novels, plays, and memoirs. The distinctiveness of Gorky's achievement in each literary genre is succinctly discussed in the context of both his life and of his culture. The only drawback to this approach is that Gorky's simultaneous work in different genres is not given the emphasis it deserves.

Hare, Richard, *Maxim Gorky: Romantic Realist and Conservative Revolutionary*. New York: Oxford University Press, 1962. The author makes good use of Kaun's biography, discusses Gorky's reputation in both the Soviet Union and in the West, and subjects his style to considerable scrutiny. There is also a careful discussion of what Gorky meant by the term "socialist realism." Hare evaluates Gorky's view of himself as a missionary and critic of Soviet society. In discussing Gorky's last years, Hare emphasizes, in contrast to Dan Levin's biography, Gorky's blindness to Stalinist terror because of his privileged position.

Weil, Irwin, *Gorky: His Literary Development and Influence on Soviet Intellectual Life*. New York: Random House, 1966. Contrary to some Western critics, Weil believes Gorky's involvement in politics was the lifeblood of his writing. Particularly concerned with how Gorky arrived at his mature style, this critic concentrates on the use of first person in the autobiographies which helped Gorky solve problems of narration and characterization in his later fiction. Gorky's "literary persona," his conflicts with Soviet critics, and his impact on his own and subsequent generations of Soviet writers, are subjected to careful study.

Wolfe, Bertram D. *The Bridge and the Abyss: The Troubled Friendship of Maxim Gorky and V.I. Lenin*. New York: Praeger, 1967. Wolfe astutely reconstructs the relationship between Lenin and Gorky that has been obscured and falsified by Soviet sources. The critic seeks to debunk the Stalinist line that Gorky advocated "party control of literature." Exceptionally well informed on the psychology of the man and the artist, Wolfe shows how Gorky was caught between his belief in truth and the "salutary lie." Literary and political analysis are skillfully combined, especially in the discussion of Gorky's three versions of his memoir of Lenin.

Other Sources

Bunin, I. *Memoirs and Portraits*. New York: Country Life Press, 1951. A hostile reminiscence of Gorky.

Clark, Barrett H. *Intimate Portraits*. New York: Dramatists Play Service, 1951. An important reminiscence of Gorky by one of America's most distinguished drama critics.

Dillon, E.J. *Maxim Gorky: His Life and Writings*. London: Isbister, 1902. This early and largely out-of-date biography is nevertheless useful for an understanding of Gorky's sudden, enormous popularity in both Russia and the West.

Gourfinkel, Nina, *Gorky*. New York: Grove Press, 1960. A concise biography including comment on Gorky's style and literary development. Several photographs, chronology, bibliography, and extracts from Gorky's writing make this a useful introductory work.

Gouzenko, I. *The Fall of a Titan*. New York: W.W. Norton, 1954. This novel written by a Soviet defector is difficult to judge for its accuracy, but it is often cited as an informative source on Gorky's death and on the mid-1930s in the Soviet Union.

Habermann, Gerhard, *Maksim Gorki*. New York: Frederick Ungar, 1971. A part of the "Modern Literature Monographs" series, this brief, introductory work takes a chronological approach to Gorky's life and provides a selected bibliography and index.

Holtzman, F. *The Young Maxim Gorky 1868-1902*. New York: Columbia University Press, 1948. A thorough study with excellent sources on Gorky's early life.

Mirsky, D. *A History of Russian Literature*. New York: Alfred A. Knopf, 1955. A highly critical but intelligent study of Gorky from the emigré perspective.

Sorokin, P. *Leaves from a Russian Diary*. Boston: Beacon Press, 1950. Concentrates on Gorky during the revolutionary years.

Roskin, Alexander, *From the Banks of the Volga: The Life of Maxim Gorky*. tr. from the Russian by D.L. Fromberg. New York: Philosophical Library, 1946. The Stalinist version of Gorky's life, emphasizing his pre-revolutionary years, and replete with official photographs, illustrations, and encomiums to Lenin and Stalin.

Carl E. Rollyson Jr.
Wayne State University

ROBERT GREENE
1558-1592

Author's Chronology

Born in Norwich, England, the son of a lower middle-class family (his father was a saddler), and baptized on July 11, 1558; attends Norwich Free Grammar School before matriculating at Corpus Christi College, Cambridge, in 1573 as a sizar, or early work-study student; *1575* transfers to St. John's College where he is awarded a B.A. in 1579-80; *1583* receives his first M.A. from Clare Hall, Cambridge; after marrying, he moves permanently to London where he deserts his wife and young son Fortunatus for the sister of a London criminal; *1588* receives what is evidently an honorary M.A. from Oxford; *1588-1592* enjoys an increasingly popular, if not profitable, career as a writer of romances, plays, and cony-catching pamphlets for which he draws both on his university education and his association with the London underworld; becomes the self-proclaimed leader of the "University Wits," a group of writers that includes Marlowe, Lodge, Nash, and Peele; August *1592* contracts a fatal illness after a banquet of Rhenish wine and pickled herring; lives long enough to repent of his wasted life and talent in the posthumously published *Greene's Groatsworth of Wit Bought with a Million of Repentance*, write his wife to beg her forgiveness, and commend his mistress and illegitimate son to the care of his landlord; September 3 dies in the presence of his landlady who crowns him with a garland of bay leaves.

Author's Bibliography (selected)

Mamillia: A Mirror or Looking Glass for the Ladies of England, 1583, 1593 (fiction); *Morando: The Tritameron of Love*, 1584, 1587 (fiction); *Pandosto: the Triumph of Time*, 1588 (fiction); with Thomas Lodge *A Looking Glass for London and England*, c. 1588 (drama); *Menaphon*, 1589 (fiction); *Alphonsus, King of Arragon*, c. 1588-1589 (drama); *Orlando Furiouso*, c. 1588-1589 (drama); *Friar Bacon and Friar Bungay*, c. 1588-1589, published 1594 (drama); *Greene's Mourning Garment*, 1590 (fiction); *Greene's Never Too Late*, 1590 (fiction); *James the Fourth*, c. 1590-1591, published 1598 (drama); *A Maiden's Dream*, 1591 (poetry); *Greene's Farewell to Folly*, 1591 (fiction); *A Notable Discovery of Cozenage*, 1591 (nonfiction); *The Second Part of Conny-Catching*, 1591 (nonfiction); *The Third and Last Part of Conney-Catching*, 1592 (nonfiction); *Greene's Vision*, 1592 (fiction); *Greene's Groatsworth of Wit Bought with a Million of Repentance*, 1592 (nonfiction); *The Repentance of Robert Greene*,1592 (nonfiction).

Overview of Biographical Sources

Ironically, since Robert Greene was undoubtedly one of the most colorful writers who ever lived, no satisfactory modern biography of the dramatist exists. Anyone attempting to write Greene's life faces innumerable difficulties, the greatest being the playwright's great propensity for presenting fiction as autobiography and fact as fiction in his own work. Potential biographers cannot be blamed for being daunted by the task of untangling the two. In what remains the only complete edition of Greene's works, *The Life and Complete Works of Robert Greene* (1881-6), A.B. Grosart was one of the first scholars to present Greene's complex character with any accuracy. His treatment is flawed, however, because he too often accepts the fictional "Roberto" of Greene's plays and pamphlets as a truthful representation of Greene's own character. J. Churton Collins in the first volume of his edition of *The Plays and Poems of Robert Greene* (Oxford: The Clarendon Press, 1905) has written the definitive biographical study although his treatment of Greene's life covers less than thirty pages. R. Pruvost's *Robert Greene et ses romans* (1938) is an accurate and more extensive study of Greene's life but unfortunately is not available in English. Finally, there are two fictionalized biographies: Carl S. Downes' *Robin Redbeard: Being a Fictional Biography of Robert Greene, Author of Tales, Pamphlets and Plays, Describing the Varying Fortunes of His Life from the Year 1579, When He Returned, Bachelor of Arts from Cambridge to His Home in Norwich, till the Year of His Untimely Death, 1592* (1938), and Gwyn Jones' *Garland of Bays* (1938). Based on actual details, these treatments are not without interest. Downes attempts to reproduce the style and structure of Greene's own romances with realistic Elizabethan vocabulary. The Jones novel is a more straightforward effort to examine Greene's character in the context of fiction.

Evaluation of Selected Biographies

Collins, J. Churton, ed. *The Plays and Poems of Robert Greene*. 2 vols. Oxford: The Clarendon Press, 1905. In spite of its early date, Collins' general introduction in Vol. 1 remains the definitive, and indeed only accessible, treatment of Greene's life. Collins reviews the autobiographical elements in Greene's novels in an attempt to distinguish fact from fiction, reminding his readers that while these references are often analogous to the known facts of Greene's life, they must still be looked on with some measure of scepticism. He then presents the extant records of the dramatist's life and reviews contemporary references to him. The biographical section concludes with an assessment of Greene's contemporary reputation. Given the absence of other biographical treatments, Collins remains the standard resource.

Autobiographical Sources

Compared with the lack of biographies, there is an overwhelming amount of autobiographical material on Greene. In addition to obvious autobiographical references throughout his novels and romances, much of Greene's nonfiction is based on his own experiences. Especially important here are his cony-catching pamphlets which show his intimate knowledge of the tricks and scams practiced in the criminal underworld of sixteenth-century London. The most important autobiographical sources, however, are the two so-called "deathbed" pamphlets, *Greene's Groatsworth of Wit Bought with a Million of Repentance* and *The Repentance of Robert Greene*, both published posthumously in 1592. The *Groatsworth of Wit* has long been famous for its inflammatory references to Marlowe and Shakespeare ("an upstart Crow"). Although some modern critics question the authenticity of these pamphlets, Greene's contemporaries accepted them as being, at least for the most part, his own work. Marlowe and Shakespeare certainly reacted strongly enough to the libels in the *Groatsworth of Wit* to cause its publisher Henry Chettle to bring out an exculpatory retraction. Chettle may indeed have had a hand in polishing or expanding upon Greene's deathbed writings, but the pamphlets are in character with much of Greene's late writings, so much so that the traditional attribution of them probably should not be too highly questioned.

Overview of Critical Sources

Like Ben Jonson and a number of other Renaissance playwrights, Greene has suffered for the crime of not being Shakespeare. Critical attention frequently has been focused on his relationship to his younger and greater contemporary rather than on Greene himself. Indeed, critics have tended to look at Greene only for the light his career and writings could shed on that of Shakespeare instead of concentrating on Greene's role in the development of Elizabethan drama in its earliest years.

Those critics who study Greene's work for its own sake generally concern themselves with one play *Friar Bacon and Friar Bungay*, relegating his other dramas, not without justification, to the roles of historical curiosities. Although *Friar Bacon and Friar Bungay* is almost an anomaly among Greene's work, it is by far his best play, and, as such, has been examined for its influence on the development of English comedy. A number of critical studies trace the relationship of *Friar Bacon and Friar Bungay* to Shakespeare's early comedies.

Evaluation of Selected Criticism

Bevington, David, *Tudor Drama and Politics*. Cambridge: Harvard University Press, 1968. Bevington treats Greene's entire canon within the context of the public and polemic aims of public theater in the sixteenth century. In doing so, he indicates the importance of Greene in the development of Elizabethan drama. He suggests a dichotomy in Greene's dramatic intent—catering to popular taste while presenting a didactic message acceptable to the government—which lends an ambiguity to Greene's drama. Yet Bevington clearly establishes in this study that Greene was a careful craftsman whose plays reflect more than just the current government "line"; any apparent confusion in thought accurately echoes the wild shifts in public opinion typical of this era.

Dean, James Seay, *Robert Greene: A Reference Guide*. Boston: G.K. Hall, 1984. Dean brings to this book a long-established familiarity with Greene's works since he has edited two of Greene's prose romances for the projected critical old-spelling edition of the playwright's complete works by the Shakespeare Institute of the University of Birmingham, England. The book is an exhaustive, and sometimes exhausting, review of all of Greene's publications and almost every critical article or book ever written about him (Dean's bibliography begins with the listings for 1675 and continues through the present). The introduction is especially important as it carefully delineates all the critical issues which have been raised about Greene and also attempts to deal objectively with the issue of the authorship of the so-called "deathbed" pamphlets. This study builds upon, and indeed replaces, Samuel Tannenbaum's *Robert Greene (A Concise Bibliography)* (1939, 1950).

Ellis-Fermor, Una, "Marlowe and Greene: A Note on Their Relations as Dramatic Artists," in *Studies in Honor of T.W. Baldwin*, ed. Don C. Allen. Urbana: University of Illinois Press, 1958. Ellis-Fermor argues from her dating of the plays of Marlowe and Greene that in the writing of *Alphonsus, King of Arragon*, Greene not only imitates Marlowe's *Tamburlaine the Great* but "slavishly" subdues his imagination to the genius of the other playwright. She traces Greene's debt to Marlowe through *Orlando Furioso* but claims that in his later plays Greene's inherent genius had overcome a dramatic influence that was inimical to his own talent. The article is especially important in that Ellis-Fermor sees Greene in the last years of his life on the verge of a greatness as a dramatist that would rival that of Marlowe whose early works Greene so badly imitated.

Sanders, Norman, "The Comedy of Greene and Shakespeare," in *Early Shakespeare: A Reading and Playing Guide*. London: E. Arnold, 1961; New York: Schocken, 1966. Sanders rejects the terms "debt" and "influence" for the relationship between the two playwrights, choosing instead to demonstrate a "kinship" between their early comedies. This distinction serves to allow him to sidestep the issue of who influenced or was influenced by whom. In spite of this, Sanders demonstrates that the relationship between Greene and Shakespeare was an important factor in Greene's development as an artist, allowing him to put aside his unfortunate imitation of Marlowe's bombastic *Tamburlaine the Great*, which heavily influenced his earlier style. Sanders agrees with Ellis-Fermor's judgment that Greene is by far too unappreciated an artist for his real merits. Sanders claims that the major similarities between Greene and Shakespeare lie in their explorations of the nature of love in their comedies. The article contains cogent and useful analyses of all of Greene's undisputed plays.

Senn, Werner, *Studies in the Dramatic Construction of Robert Greene and George Peele*. Swiss Studies in English 74. Berne: Francke, 1973. One of the few recent book-length studies to deal primarily with Greene, this is a careful, if didactic, study of the plot construction in the plays of Greene and Peele. Senn's purpose in his lengthy examination of the dramatic techniques of the two men is to demonstrate that Greene is by far the better playwright than Peele, a point few readers would argue with even before picking up the book. The study is important, however, in that it deals with structural rather than stylistic considerations. As such, it can be a useful adjunct to studies such as those by Ellis-Fermor and Sanders.

Other Sources

Bentley, Gerald Eades, *The Profession of Dramatist in Shakespeare's Time, 1590-1642*. Princeton: Princeton University Press, 1971. Sees Greene and the "University Wits" among one main segment of the numerous individuals who wrote for the Elizabethan stage. Useful for historical materials concerning the actual theaters for which Greene wrote and for knowledge of his theatrical milieu.

Cohen, Walter, *Drama of a Nation: Public Theater in Renaissance England and Spain*. Ithaca: Cornell University Press, 1985. Attempts to include Greene's work in a study which identifies, or at least claims to discover, close similarities in the didactic aims of the theater in sixteenth-century England and Spain. Has an admitted Marxist perspective but is thoroughly and carefully researched.

Doran, Madeleine, *Endeavors of Art: A Study in the Form of Elizabethan Drama*. Madison: University of Wisconsin Press, 1954. Classic study which dismisses Greene as a "lesser" artist than Marlowe and Shakespeare in a discussion of the relationship between "nature" and "art" in Elizabethan drama.

Feldman, Sylvia D. *The Morality-Patterned Comedy of the Renaissance*. The Hague: Mouton, 1970. A not particularly convincing attempt to include Greene in a hitherto "unrecognized" category of English drama. Useful, however, in that it treats *A Looking Glasse for London and England*, the play Greene co-authored with Thomas Lodge, which is usually overlooked by critics for just that reason.

Harrison, G.B. *Elizabethan Plays and Players*. Ann Arbor, MI: Ann Arbor Books, 1956. Extremely useful study which includes much biographical material on Greene and his contemporaries as it looks at the personalities of Elizabethan playwrights and actors and the fortunes of the different acting companies and playhouses of sixteenth-century London. Extremely interesting and readable treatment by a sound scholar.

Klein, David, *Elizabethan Dramatists as Critics*. Westport, CT: Greenwood Press, 1968. Approaches Greene and his fellow playwrights not as dramatists but as literary critics. Provides a valuable look at the critical principles which their plays are based upon.

Symonds, John Addington, *Shakespeare's Predecessors in the English Drama*. Westport, CT: Greenwood Press, 1969. Modern reprinting of a classic study of the earliest Elizabethan dramatists. Helpful for the wealth of detail concerning the everyday workings of the Elizabethan playhouses where Greene's plays were produced.

Mary Anne Hutchinson
Utica College of Syracuse University

LADY AUGUSTA GREGORY
1852-1932

Author's Chronology

Born March 15, 1852, Galway Ireland; *1880* marries Sir William Gregory of Coole Park, Galway; *1881* son, Robert born; *1893* publishes *A Phantom's Pilgrimage: or Home Ruin*, pamphlet against Home Rule for Ireland; *1894* edits Sir William Gregory's *Autobiography*; meets William Butler Yeats in London; *1896* invites Yeats to Coole for the first of twenty yearly visits; *1897* writes first play, *Colman and Guaire*; *1899* founds with Yeats, George Moore and Douglas Hyde the Irish Literary Theatre, later to be called the Abbey Theatre; production of the first two plays including *The Countess Cathleen*; *1901* writes *Cathleen ni Houlihan* and *The Pot of Broth* with Yeats; edits collection of essays on Irish literary movement, *Ideals in Ireland*; *1902* publishes *Cuchulain of Muirthemne*, a retelling of the Irish epics; *1903* publishes collection of Irish folklore, *Poets and Dreamers*; first play produced under her name, *Twenty-Five*; *1904* publishes second book of Irish epics, *Gods and Fighting Men*; writes *The Rising of the Moon, Spreading the News*, and *Kincora*; *1909* publishes *Seven Short Plays*; defies British censor and produces Bernard Shaw's *The Shewing-Up of Blanco Posnet*; *1911* travels to America to produce Synge's *Playboy of the Western World* with Abbey players; *1912* publishes *Irish Folk-History Plays*; *1913* publishes a history of the Abbey, *Our Irish Theatre*; *1915* son killed over enemy lines in Italy; publishes translations of Gaelic poetry, *The Kiltartan Poetry Book*; *1919* acts role of Cathleen in *Cathleen ni Houlihan* at Abbey; directs at Abbey Shaw's *John Bull's Other Ireland*; *1920* publishes collection of folklore, *Visions and Beliefs in the West of Ireland*; *1921* lectures to save the declining Abbey Theatre; publishes biography of nephew: *Hugh Lane's Life and Achievement*; begins friendship with Sean O'Casey; *1928 Three Last Plays* published; 1932 dies of cancer at Coole.

Author's Bibliography

Drama: *Spreading the News*, 1904; *Kincora*, 1905; *The White Cockade*, 1905; *Hyacinth Halvey*, 1906; *The Rising of the Moon*, 1906; *The Unicorn from the Stars and Other Plays*, 1908 (with W.B. Yeats); *The Image*, 1910; *The Full Moon*, 1911; *Irish Folk-history Plays*, 1912; *New Comedies*, 1913; *Three Wonder Plays*, 1922; *The Story Brought by Brigit*, 1924; *On the Racecourse*, 1926.

Misc: *A Book of Saints and Wonders*, 1906 (folklore); *The Kiltartan History Book*, 1909 (history); *The Kiltartan Wonder Book*, 1910 (folklore); *Our Irish Theatre*, 1913 (autobiography).

Standard editions: *The Coole Edition of the Works of Lady Gregory*, ed. T.R. Henn and Colin Smythe. New York: Oxford University Press, 1970. *A Book of Saints and Wonders*. New York: Oxford University Press, 1971. *Lady Gregory,*

Selected Plays. New York: Hill and Wang, 1963. *Gods and Fighting Men*. New York: Charles Scribner's sons, 1904. *The Kiltartan Wonder Book*. Dublin: Maunsel, 1910. *Lady Gregory's Journals*, 1916-1930, ed. Lennox Robinson. New York: The Macmillan Company, 1947. *Seventy Years*, ed. Colin Smythe. New York: Macmillan, 1974.

Overview of Biographical Sources

Biographers of Lady Gregory have found it necessary to discuss her life in the context of both the Irish Literary Renaissance in general and her own works of drama in particular. Most of the biographies focus on her later life after her marriage to Sir William Gregory, when she became mistress of the estate at Coole. All discuss her work in reviving interest in Irish literature and folklore. The earlier biographical discussions are embedded in histories of the Irish Theatre such as Ernest Boyd's *Ireland's Literary Renaissance* (New York: John Lane, 1916) and Peter Kavanaugh's *The Story of the Abbey Theatre, from Its Origins in 1899 to the Present* (New York: Devin-Adair, 1950). Useful for the historical and political contexts they provide, books such as these inadequately present Lady Gregory's life and work, especially her enormous contributions to Irish Literature. Two more recent books are noteworthy: Elizabeth Coxhead's *Lady Gregory, A Literary Portrait* 2nd ed. (London: Secker and Warburg, 1966), which amply demonstrates Lady Gregory's importance as a literary personality; and Mary Lou Kohfeldt's important recent study, *Lady Gregory: The Woman Behind the Irish Renaissance* (1985), which is the best and fullest account of her life.

Evaluation of Selected Biographies

Kohfeldt, Mary Lou, *Lady Gregory: the Woman Behind the Irish Renaissance*. New York: Atheneum, 1985. A carefully researched and gracefully written biography that amply covers Lady Gregory's life before her marriage and her involvement with the Abbey Theatre after the death of her husband. This readable work provides the necessary social context for understanding the Irish literary scene at the turn of the century. It describes Lady Gregory's relationships with a number of important figures both personally and professionally. In the process it provides a lucid analysis of her character and a sensible guide to her mind. In addition, the book includes plot summaries of Lady Gregory's major plays along with insightful criticism, usually biographically oriented.

Kopper, Edward A. Jr. *Lady Isabella Persse Gregory*. Boston: G.K. Hall, 1976. An introductory volume that mixes biography and criticism in about equal measure. The biographical material focuses almost exclusively on Lady Gregory's literary career. Kopper provides brief, helpful accounts of the intellectual, literary and historical background of her work as well as a useful discussion of the rise and fall of the Abbey Theatre. His book is less strictly biographical than Kohfeldt's. Like hers, however, it contains an extensive bibliography of important primary and secondary sources.

Autobiographical Sources

Lady Gregory left a wealth of autobiographical material, some published, some not yet published. The published sources include *Seventy Years: 1852-1922: Being the Autobiography of Lady Gregory* (New York: Oxford University Press, 1974), which while not as personally revealing as one might hope, nonetheless does provide useful contextual background. Another important source of her personal life is *Lady Gregory's Journals*. Vol. I, ed. Daniel Murphy (New York: Oxford University Press, 1978), which covers the years 1916-1925, and an earlier edition *Lady Gregory's Journals: 1916-1930*, ed. Lennox Robinson (New York: Macmillan, 1947). Equally important is her book *Our Irish Theatre: A Chapter of Autobiography*, a volume contained in *The Coole Edition of the Works of Lady Gregory*, ed. T.R. Henn and Colin Smythe (New York: Oxford University Press, 1978). Not to be overlooked are the memoirs, journals, notebooks, diaries, and letters held by the New York Public Library in the Lady Gregory Archives of the Berg Collection. The letters to W.B. Yeats, 1898-1932 occupy 957 Folders in 19 Boxes. Those to Bernard Shaw appeared in selection in an article by Daniel J. Murphy, "The Lady Gregory Letters to G.B. Shaw," *Modern Drama* 16 (19 February 1968), 331-345.

Overview of Critical Sources

Lady Gregory's plays have received a modest amount of critical attention. Nearly all who have written extensively on her work have treated it in relation to the drama of William Butler Yeats, with whom she collaborated on a number of plays. These critics have also discussed her art largely in terms of its social and political context as part of the flowering of Irish literature during the period of the Irish Literary Renaissance.

Evaluation of Selected Criticism

Adams, Hazard, *Lady Gregory*. Lewisburg: Bucknell University Press, 1973. This intelligent work is primarily an introduction to Lady Gregory's art. Adams presents brief analyses of a number of works, making important connections among them. A lucid and insightful book.

Kopper, Edward A. Jr. *Lady Isabella Persse Gregory*. Boston: G.K. Hall, 1976. This is an introductory biographical-critical discussion. Kopper discusses Lady Gregory's work in Irish folklore and myth as well as providing critical analysis of many plays. His book is written partly as a corrective to an earlier view that neglects her literary achievements and disparages her contribution to the Irish

Literary Renaissance. Concise, readable, lucid, and well informed, Kopper's book is a helpful overall guide.

Saddlemyer, Ann, *In Defense of Lady Gregory, Playwright*. Dublin: The Dolmen Press, 1966. This work views Lady Gregory's works through a series of interrelated themes and motifs. The book is useful for its guidance to Lady Gregory's thematic preoccupations and for its perceptive analysis of individual plays.

Other Sources

Bushrui, S.B. *Yeat's Verse-Plays: The Revisions, 1900-1910*. Oxford: Clarendon Press, 1965. A scholarly discussion of the textual revisions which reveal Lady Gregory's influence on Yeats's dramas.

Ellis-Fermor, Una, *The Irish Dramatic Movement*. 2nd ed. London: Methuen, 1954. Perceptive analysis of the range and variety of Irish drama with provocative discussions of individual plays.

Gregory, Anne, *Me and Nu: Childhood at Coole*. Gerrards Cross: Colin Smythe, 1970. Recollections by Lady Gregory's granddaughter.

Gregory, Augusta, *Lady Gregory, Interviews and Recollections*. ed. E.H. Mikhail. London: Macmillan, 1977. A miscellany of biographical, historical, and theatrical material.

Mikhail, E.H. ed. *Lady Gregory: an Annotated Bibliography of Criticism*. Troy, NY: Whitsun, 1982. An important and extensive checklist of criticism.

Murphy, Daniel J. "Lady Gregory, Co-Author and Sometimes Author of the Plays of W.B. Yeats," in *Modern Irish Literature: Essays in Honor of William York Tindall*. eds. Raymond J. Porter and James D. Brophy. New Rochelle, NY: Iona College Press, 1972, pp. 43-52. A lucid and informative discussion of the controversy surrounding the Yeats-Gregory collaborations.

Yeats, William Butler, *Autobiographies*. London: Macmillan, 1956. Includes a record of Lady Gregory's familial relationships and acknowledges her managerial talents, though it neglects her literary abilities and contributions.

Selected Dictionaries and Encyclopedias

British Writers, Vol VI, Charles Scribner's Sons, 1983. An overview of Lady Gregory's life and works tied in with a discussion of the plays of John Synge.

Dictionary of Literary Biography, Gale, 1983. Concise overview of Lady Gregory's life and a discussion of her principal dramatic works.

Great Writers of the English Language: Dramatists. St, Martin's, 1979. Brief commentary on a few of the major works; biographical and bibliographical data.

McGraw Hill Encyclopedia of World Drama, Vol III, 2nd ed. McGraw Hill, 1984. An excellent sketch of Lady Gregory's career, including a portrait and a useful bibliography.

Robert DiYanni
Pace University

ALEXANDER GRIBOEDOV
1795-1829

Author's Chronology

Born January 15, 1795, Moscow, Russia, to aristocratic parents Sergei Ivanovich and Natasha Fedorovna Griboedov; enters Moscow University at age eleven after studying with several foreign-born tutors; *1806-1812* specializes in law, literature, mathematics, and physics; Napoleon's invasion interrupts his intention to proceed to doctorate; joins Hussars and becomes responsible for recruiting and training cavalry reinforcements; *1816* discharged from the military and enrolls in the College of Foreign Affairs; *1818-1822* serves in Iran as Secretary of Foreign Affairs; *1823-1824* writes his dramatic masterpiece *Woe from Wit* in St. Petersburg; *1825* sent to the Caucasus where he hears of the Decembrist Uprising in St. Petersburg (December 14, 1825); *1826* arrested and accused of conspiring with the "Decembrists;" released after a four month investigation; *1827* becomes chief negotiator of Russian relations with Turkey and Iran; *1828* works out Turkmanchai Peace Treaty ending Russo-Iranian War; promoted to Brigadier and awarded order of St. Anne; appointed Russian Minister to Iran which he views as political exile; on the way to Iran marries Nina Chavchavadze (the daughter of a well-known Georgian poet) in Tbilisi; February 11, 1829 Griboedov is killed in Teheran when an angry mob attacks the Russian Legation and tears his body to pieces.

Author's Bibliography

Since Griboedov was killed at the age of thirty-four, his collected works never exceed three or four volumes, regardless of the edition cited. The canonic Russian edition of his work [*Polnoe sobranie sochinenii*, vols. 1-3 (*The Complete Collected Works*)] appeared in St. Petersburg (Leningrad) during the years 1911-1917. More recent editions of his works have been published under the titles [*Sochineniya v dvukh tomakh* (*Works in Two Volumes*), "Pravda," Moscow, 1971], and [(*Izbrannoe* (*Collected Works*), "Khudozh. lit., Moscow, 1978]. With the exception of his famous comedy *Woe from Wit*, Griboedov remains virtually inaccessible to the reader of English. This comedy may be found in the following English translations: "The Misfortune of Being Clever," translated by S. Pring, London, 1914; "The Mischief of Being Clever," translated by B. Pares, London, 1925, reprinted as "Wit Works Woe" in *Masterpieces of Russian Drama*, vol. 1, ed. by G. R. Noyes, New York, 1933, 1960; and "The Misfortune of Being Clever," translated by F.D. Reeve in *Anthology of Russian Plays*, vol. 1, New York, 1961.

Overview of Biographical Sources

The main query of Griboedov's biographers is whether or not his untimely death was provoked by Nicholas I's repressive regime which exiled him to Teheran because of his suspected collusion with the Decembrists. For this reason the major works on Griboedov's life deal with the theme of punishment and death. For example, Yuri Tynyanov's *The Death of Vazir Mukhtar*, 1929 (translated by Alec Brown as *Death and Diplomacy in Persia*. Boriswood, London, 1938) treats the idea of the perennial persecution of Russia's poets by those in power. Other Soviet biographers—N. K. Piksanov (*Griboedov*, Leningrad, 1934), M. Nechkina, *Griboedov i Dekabristy* (*Griboedov and the Decembrists*. Moscow, 1947) and A. Lebedev, *Griboedov: Fakty i gipotezy* (*Griboedov: Facts and Hypotheses*. Moscow, 1980)—strive to promote the theme of Griboedov as a collaborator with the Decembrists.

Evaluation of Selected Biographies

Tynyanov, Yuri, *The Death of Vazir Mukhtar*. 1927-1928; separate edition, 1929; translated into English by Alec Brown with the title *Death and Diplomacy in Persia*. London: Boriswood, 1938. This study is not a biography in the narrow, factual sense of the word, but a fictional psychological novel that has itself become a classic of Soviet historical prose. Tynyanov analyzes the inner conflicts and frustrations which Griboedov (Vazir Mukhtar was his diplomatic name) undoubtedly suffered given his contradictory role as both a faithful servant to the autocratic regime and a liberal target of its paranoia. Because of this dichotomy, Tynyanov views Griboedov as a hidden tragic hero whose psychological make-up is splintered among the masks of the various characters. The prevailing theme of this fictional biography is historical necessity which demands Griboedov's demise so that his fate should not differ from that of the other Decembrists. However, history decrees that Griboedov be granted a few extra years to contemplate his fate as a tragic figure before he, too, is to be eliminated by the onslaught of reaction.

Autobiographical Sources

Just as the magnificent comedy of manners *Woe from Wit* reveals the profound imaginative powers of Griboedov the writer, so the as yet untranslated personal letters (see vol. 2, *Sochineniya v dvukh tomakh*, pp. 179-335), display the multifaceted talents of Griboedov the man. Considered among the best in the Russian language, these letters depict Griboedov as a carefree youth leading the life of a Petersburg dandy similar to that literary example presented in the first chapter of Pushkin's *Eugene Onegin*. However, Griboedov also differs from Onegin in that he is more of an intellectual and less of a dilettante. The letters betray a sincere interest in music (Griboedov was regarded as one of the best pianists in Russia), foreign languages (he studied Greek and Arabic to go along with his firm foundation in French, German, Italian, and English) and literature. In the later years of his correspondence, Griboedov is clearly most occupied with his travels which took him away from his beloved St. Petersburg to the Caucasus and Iran. When absent from the capital, he writes often about his homesickness for both friends and favorite landmarks.

Overview of Critical Sources

Griboedov scholarship in English remains almost nonexistent. As a writer with as yet only one well-known work—the outstanding comedy *Woe from Wit*, Griboedov represents an untapped source for future scholars. Not only has there never been a definitive study of his work in English, but even in Russian secondary literature is sparse and quite modest in comparison with what has been written on other important Russian writers of the nineteenth century.

Griboedov has, indeed, suffered such neglect that Ivan Goncharov's critical study of *Woe from Wit*, written a century ago, has still not been eclipsed by more recent scholarship. Titled "Mil'on terzanii" ("A Million Torments") (see I. A. Goncharov, *Sobranie sochinenii*, vol. 8, Moscow, 1952), Goncharov's article alludes to the unsurpassed vitality of Griboedov's comedy. The hero Chatsky is ranked above both Pushkin's Onegin and Lermontov's Pechorin, since unlike these sickly figures, he is active and most capable of falling in love. According to Goncharov, Chatsky heralds a new age, in which characters who vigorously oppose social stagnation will come forward. Goncharov also lauds the sparkling language of the drama (some 61 phrases or aphorisms from it's dialogue have now become proverbial), and the brilliant depiction of characters typical of the era.

In Soviet Criticism the name N. K. Piksanov is the one most frequently associated with secondary literature on Griboedov. Among his best known works are these two studies: *Tvorcheskaya istoriya "Gorya ot uma,"* Moscow, 1928 (*The Creative History of "Woe from Wit"*), and *A. S. Griboedov v vospominaniyakh sovremennikov*, Moscow, 1929 (*A. S. Griboedov as Remembered by His Contemporaries*).

Evaluation of Selected Criticism

Costello, D. P. "The Murder of Griboedov," in *Oxford Slavonic Papers*, Vol. VIII (1958): 66-89. The author attempts to shift the guilt for Griboedov's murder from English agents who allegedly incited the mob, to leading members of the Persian government who formed a conspiracy against the Russian Legation in Teheran.

Giergelewicz, Mieczylaw, "Structural Footnotes to Griboedov's *Woe from Wit*," in *Polish Review*, 24 (1979): 3-21. Proposes a concentric structure to Griboedov's *Woe from Wit*. At the center of the primary circle stands Chatsky. The second circle represents all persons directly participating in the farcical plot; the third circle includes those guests attending the reception at Famusov's house; the fourth circle embraces all other persons mentioned individually in the test; and finally, the fifth circle focuses on the different social strata groups. The writer attributes to Griboedov an ingenious sense of structure in developing the various layers of his drama.

Hoover, Marjorie L. "Classic Meyerhold: *Woe to Wit* by Griboedov," in *Russian Triquarterly*, No. 7 (Fall 1973): 285-298. This study discusses the timeless influence of Griboedov's play *Woe from Wit*. The innovative director of the Soviet period Vsevolod Meyerhold is linked to Griboedov's play which pleased his taste for avant-garde stylistics even more so than Gogol's *The Inspector General*. Like Griboedov, Meyerhold was committed to the theme of satirizing the ruling class and found the plot of *Woe from Wit* (significantly, he changed the title of his production to *Woe to Wit*) just as apropos for the Moscovite society of the 1930s as it had been for this very same urban milieu a century earlier.

Janecek, Gerald, "A Defense of Sof'ja in *Woe from Wit*," in *Slavic and East European Journal*, Vol. 21, No. 3 (1977): 318-331. One of the only works in any language to treat a subject other than Griboedov's mysterious death or the role of Chatsky in *Woe from Wit*. This critic shows with some justification that Sof'ja (Chatsky's principal lover in the drama) merits further study because as a complex and ambiguous figure, she adds a still unexplored dimension to the work.

Other Sources

Mirsky, D. S. *A History of Russian Literature*. New York: Alfred A. Knopf, 1949, pp. 108-113. In this general essay, Griboedov is viewed as a literary descendant of Moliere since both writers succeeded in creating characters who are at once both types and individuals.

Slonim, Marc, *Russian Theater from the Empire to the Soviets*. New York: Collier Books, 1962, pp. 41-44. Interprets *Woe from Wit* as a dramatic conflict between the progressive intellectual Chatsky and his stagnant environment. However, since Chatsky's intellectual prowess is wasted on his retrograde fellow Moscovites, he prefigures a long line of "Superfluous men," as described in the works of Pushkin, Lermontov, Turgenev, Goncharov, Leskov and Chekhov. Perhaps this is too simplistic a thesis, owing to the fact that Chatsky comes across as a more positive figure than the literary creations of these other writers.

Sokolsky, Anatole A. *Russian Literature XI-XX Centuries*. Madrid, 1970, pp. 85-87. Mentions some of the many aphorisms and expressions in *Woe from Wit* that have emerged as proverbs and folk sayings: e.g., "The happy do not pay attention to the hours," "He who is poor is not a match for you," "The smoke of the fatherland is sweet and pleasant to us," and "Well, whose mouth isn't shut by dinner, supper, and dances."

Harold Schefski

FRANZ SERAFIKUS GRILLPARZER
1791-1872

Author's Chronology

Born January 15, 1791, Vienna, Austria, to Dr. Wenzel and Anna Franziska Sonnleithner Grillparzer; *1801-1804* attends St. Anna-Gymnasium; *1805* meets Beethoven at Sonnleithner residence; *1806* writes *Die Unglücklichen Liebhaber* (*The Unlucky Lovers*), a drama first published in the standard edition of his works; *1807-1811* attends and receives a law degree from the University of Vienna; *1807-1809* writes *Die Schreibfeder* (*The Pen*) and *Blanka von Kastilien* (*Blanche of Castile*), neither published until 1887; *1809* father dies; *1811* writes *Wer Ist Schuldig?* (*Who Is Guilty?*); *1812* assumes tutorial position in Count von Seilern's home and reads Shakespeare in the original and in Schlegel's translations; *1813* secures an unsalaried position in the Vienna *Hofbibliothek* (Court Library) and avidly reads Calderon, Tirso de Molina, and Lope de Vega; at the end of *1813* enters Civil Service; *1817 Die Ahnfrau* (*The Ancestress*) first performed and establishes his dramatic reputation; his brother Adolph drowns himself in the Danube after leaving an ominous note: "If Franz should ever marry and have children, he should warn them that they should not resemble me"; *1818 Sappho* first performed and Grillparzer appointed by Count Stadion as salaried *Theaterdichter* (dramatist) at the Hofburghtheater; also begins an affair with his cousin's wife, Charlotte von Paumgarten; *1819* mother hangs herself in a fit of religious mania; journeys to Italy to escape effect of mother's suicide and guilt from his affair with Charlotte whom he felt he was psychologically exploiting to gain material for his *Das Goldene Vlies* (*The Golden Fleece*); *1820* begins a chaste relationship and eventual engagement to Katharina Fröhlich although they never marry; *1821 Das Goldene Vlies* first performed; *1823* begins an affair with Marie von Smolenitz who becomes a model for his Erny, Hero, and Esther; *1832* becomes Archive Director of the Court Chamber; *1833* opera *Melusina* first performed; although Kruetzer composed this opera's music, its text was completed in 1823 for Beethoven who never set it to music; *1836* brother Karl, temporarily insane, accuses himself of embezzlement and murder; Grillparzer journeys to Paris and London; *1838* failure of *Weh dem, der Lügt* (*Woe to the Liar*) prompts him to lock away his last three plays: *Libussa*, *Ein Bruderzwist in Hapsburg* (*Family Strife in Hapsburg*), and *Die Jüdin von Toledo* (*The Jewess of Toledo*), all performed posthumously; about *1842* completes *Der arme Spielmann* ("The Poor Fiddler") but not published until 1847; *1843* travels to Turkey and Greece; *1850* Grillparzer's dramas revived by Heinrich Laube, the Burgtheater director; *1853* begins *Selbstbiographie* (autobiography) in January but discontinues it in May; *1856* pensioned from Civil Service with honorary title of *Hofrat*; *1861* brother Karl dies; January 21, 1872 dies honored and esteemed.

Author's Bibliography

Although numerous editions of Grillparzer's works exist, the accepted standard edition is the forty-three-volumed *Sämtliche Werke: Historisch-kritische Gesamtausgabe* (Vienna: Gerlach, 1909-1948) edited by August Sauer and Reinhold Backmann. Equally important is the four-volumed *Sämtliche Werke, Ausgewählte Briefe, Gespräche, Berichte* (Munich: Hanser, 1960-1964) edited by Peter Frank and Karl Pörnbacher and based on the Sauer/Backmann edition but with revisions. Pörnbacher also edited *Franz Grillparzer* (Munich: Heimeran, 1970) that contains Grillparzer's notes and comments about his works. Sauer also edited the seven-volumed *Grillparzers Gespräche und die Charakteristiken seiner Persönlichkeit durch die Zeitgenossen* (Vienna: Verlag des Literarischen Vereins, 1904-1941). Grillparzer's dramas and stories have been translated into English. For the Register Press (Yarmouthport, MA), Arthur Burkhard's translations include: *Family Strife in Hapsburg* (1940); *A Faithful Servant to His Master* (1941); *The Golden Fleece* (1942); *Sappho* (1953); *The Jewess of Toledo* (1953); *Hero and Leander* (1962, the title changed from *The Waves of Sea and Love*); *King Ottocar, His Rise and Fall* (1962). English translations of *The Poor Fiddler* (*The Poor Musician*) include Alexander and Elizabeth Henderson's version (Frederick Ungar, 1967) and J.F. Hargreaves and J.G. Cumming's version in *German Narrative Prose* (London: Wolff, 1965). For a more comprehensive view of Grillparzer translations see Arthur Burkhard's *Franz Grillparzer In England and America* (Vienna: Bergland, 1961) and *Grillparzer In Ausland* (Cambridge, MA: The University Press, 1969).

Overview of Biographical Sources

In German, the most comprehensive biography is Josef Nadler's *Franz Grillparzer* (1952). Isle Münch's *Die Tragik in Drama und Persönlichkeit Franz Grillparzers* (Berlin: Junker, 1931) examines the relationship between his works and his own ambivalent attitude about the active and the contemplative life. Hans Hoff and Ida Cermak discuss Grillparzer's problematic personality in *Grillparzer: Versuch einer Pathographie* (Vienna: Bergland, 1961). Gerhard Baumann's Franz *Grillparzer: Dichtung und österreichische Geistesverfassung* (Frankfurt: Athenaum, 1966), a revision of the 1954 work, presents an interesting and comprehensive discussion of Grillparzer's Austrian heritage and its influence on his personality and works. Hein Politzer also examines Grillparzer's personality and works in *Franz Grillparzer oder das abgrundige Biedemeir* (Vienna: Molden, 1972).

In English, the earliest critical biography is Douglas Yate's *Franz Grillparzer: A Critical Biography* (1964) which examines Grillparzer's life, his personal problems, and his works to and including *Des Merres und der Liebe Wellen*; the second volume of Yate's study was not completed. W.E. Yate's *Grillparzer: A Critical Introduction* is not an interpretive biography but rather a purely factual, chronological account of Grillparzer's life and an informative discussion of the thematic links between the works.

Evaluation of Selected Biographies

Nadler, Josef. *Franz Grillparzer*. Vienna: Bergland, 1952. According to most Grillparzer scholars, this is the most comprehensive and intellectual critical biography. Since it is in German, its discussion would be lost to many English-speaking readers and scholars.

Yates, Douglas, *Franz Grillparzer: A Critical Biography*, vol. 1. Oxford: Basil Blackwood, 1946. This was the first critical biography in English and thus provided the English-speaking reader and scholar valuable insights into Grillparzer's private and personal life, both of which contributed to his works. Some of the notes and quoted passages are in German, but the discussion and interpretations are insightful.

Yates, W.E. *Grillparzer: A Critical Introduction*. Cambridge: Cambridge University Press, 1972. Yate's critical biography is indeed a boon for the English-speaking reader and scholar in that it presents an in-depth, chronological account of Grillparzer's life—the dates are highlighted in the margins—, and it provides perceptive readings of Grillparzer's dramas, the dramatic fragment *Esther*, "*Der arme Spielmann*," and a select number of lyrical poems and epigrams.

Autobiographical Sources

Except for certain passages quoted in English by some critics, Grillparzer's autobiographical material is in German and included in the standard Vienna and Munich editions, *Sämtliche Werke*, edited by Sauer/Backmann and Frank/Pörnbacher *respectively*. In addition, *Grillparzers Gespräch und die Charakteristiken seiner Persönlichkeit*, edited by August Sauer, contains Grillparzer's conversations and memoirs.

Overview of Critical Sources

Grillparzer scholarship is voluminous and continues to expand as his works are translated into various languages which provide scholars with easier access to his works. Within the body of Grillparzer scholarship, critics and scholars examine Grillparzer's contributions to and place in Austrian and German literature, his innovative literary techniques, symbols, imagery, and themes. Containing both English and German sources, the following criticism has been selected because the sources are easily accessible and because they indicate the variety of scholarly approaches.

Evaluation of Selected Criticism

DeWalsh, Faust Charles, *Grillparzer As a Poet of Nature*. New York: AMS Press, 1960. Using Grillparzer's poems and plays, DeWalsh analyzes the various aspects of Nature that Grillparzer uses—his descriptions of nature, his definition of nature, and the realationship between man and nature.

Fulleborn, Ulrich, *Das dramatische Geschehen im Werk Franz Grillparzers: Ein Beitrag zur Epochenbestimmung der deutschen Dictung im 19. Jahrhundert.* Using the complex relationships between deeds and events in Grillparzer's works, Fulleborn argues that Grillparzer was an early Realist.

Hock, Erich, *Das Schmerzerlebnis und sein Ausdruck in Grillparzers Lyrik.* Nendeln/Liechtenstein, 1967. Included in this study are interesting interpretations of most of Grillparzer's lyric poems as well as a discussion of the construction of the cycle.

Thompson, Bruce and Mark G. Ward, eds. *Essays on Grillparzer.* New German Studies Monographs, No. 5. Hull: New German Studies, 1978. As its title suggests, this collection assembles informative essays about Grillparzer's *König Ottokar, Des Meeres und die Liebe Wellen, Der Traum eine Leben,* and *Weh dem, der lügt.*

_____, *Franz Grillparzer.* Boston: G.K. Hall, 1981. Thompson's Twayne series is an excellent general introduction for the non-specialist, English-speaking reader. The study emphasizes the more prominent features of Grillparzer's works including his exploitation of drama's visual side, his subtle characterizations, and his skeptical analysis of ideals and institutions. Copious notes and an excellent bibliography enhance the study.

Wells, George Albert, *The Plays of Grillparzer.* Elmsford, New York: Pergamon, 1969. Using Grillparzer's completed dramas, Wells discussed Grillparzer's characterizations and dramatic techniques in terms of the theory of tragedy.

Other Sources
Atkinson, Margaret E. "Grillparzer's Use of Symbol and Image in *Des Meeres und der Liebe Wellen*," in *German Life and Letters* NS 4 (1950-1951): 261-277. As the title indicates, Atkinson's is an interesting analysis of symbol and imagery in this particular Grillparzer drama.

Baker, Christa Suttner, "Structure and Imagery in Grillparzer's *Sappho*," in *Germanic Review*, 48 (1973): 44-55. By analyzing the close interrelationships of the drama's acts, Baker provides an insight into Sappho's character.

Fricke, Gerhard, "Wesen und Wandel des Tragischen bei Grillparzer," in *Studien und Interpretatioinem.* Frankfort: M. Menck, 1956, pp. 264-184. Fricke's philosophical study emphasizes that Grillparzer's works represent life's inevitable destructive forces and thus reflect a disillusionment of the age.

Fuerst, Norbert, *Grillparzer auf der Bühne. Eine fragmentarishe Geschichte.* Vienna: 1958. Fuerst provides a history of the interpretation and reception of Grillparzer's plays in the theater.

Klarmann, Adolf D. "Grillparzer und die Moderne," in *Die Neue Rindschau*, 67 (1956): 137-152. Because of Grillparzer's interest in both psychological detail and his characters' complex personalities, Klarmann argues that Grillparzer is more of a modern author with affinities to Freud, Bahr, and Schnitzler.

Papst, E.E. ed. *Der Arme Spielmann and Prose Selections.* London: Nelson, 1960. Papst's informative introduction and insights into the story regarding the artist's choice between the real and the ideal make this a valuable source.

_____. "Franz Grillparzer," in *German Men of Letters: Twelve Literary Essays*, edited by Alex Nation. London: Wolff, 1961, pp. 99-120. Using the duality of *Sammlung* and *Leben*, Papst's study is a sound introduction to Grillparzer's works; also contains a brief annotated bibliography and English translations of quoted German passages.

Rommel, Otto, *Die Alt-Wiener Vokskömodie Ihre Geschichte vom barochen Welt-Theater biz zum Tode Nestroys.* Vienna: 1912. This is an authoritative history of the drama of the popular theaters in Vienna and an excellent background source.

Edward C. Reilly
Arkansas State University

PETER HANDKE
1942

Author's Chronology

Born December 6, 1942, in Griffen, province of Carinthia, Austria; *1944-1948* lives in Berlin; *1948-1954* attends school in Griffen; *1954-1959* attends Marianum, a Catholic boys school, in Tanzenberg bei Klagenfurt; *1959-1961* attends and graduates from Klagenfurter Gymnasium; *1961-1965* studies law at the University of Graz; involved with the influential literary organization Graz Group; *1964* publishes first short story entitled "The Flood" in *manuskripte*; *1966* publishes first novel; early plays *Offending the Audience, Self-Accusation* and *Prophecy* performed; marries Libgart Schwarz, an actress; leaves Austria for Germany; delivers notorious speech critical of other German writers at the Group 47 meeting in Princeton; *1967* publishes second novel and first full-length play entitled *Kaspar*; awarded the Gerhart Hauptmann Prize; *1968* first performance of *Kaspar*; *1969* daughter Amina born in Berlin; establishes collaborative publishing house Verlag der Autoren with ten other writers; *1970* publishes *The Ride Across Lake Constance*; *1971* visits the United States on a university lecture tour; *1972* first English-language production of *The Ride Across Lake Constance* at the Forum, Lincoln Center, New York; separates from wife; *1973* publishes *They Are Dying Out*; awarded the Georg Büchner Prize; moves to Clamart, a suburb of Paris; *1975* publishes *A Moment of True Feeling*; *1979* publishes *Slow Homecoming*; awarded but declines Austria's Franz Kafka Prize; returns to Austria with daughter to live in Salzburg; continues to write.

Author's Bibliography (selected)

Kaspar and Other Plays, includes *Offending the Audience* and *Self-Accusation*, 1969; *The Goalie's Anxiety at the Penalty Kick*, 1972 (novel); *Short Letter, Long Farewell*, 1974 (novel); *The Innerworld of the Outerworld of the Innerworld*, 1974 (poems); *A Sorrow Beyond Dreams*, 1975 (novel); *The Ride Across Lake Constance and Other Plays*, includes *Prophecy, Calling for Help, My Foot My Tutor, Quodlibet*, and *They Are Dying Out*, 1976; *Nonsense and Happiness*, 1976 (poems); *A Moment of True Feeling*, 1977 (novel); *The Left-Handed Woman*, 1978 (novel); *The Weight of the World*, 1984 (journal); *Slow Homecoming*, 1985 (novel).

Overview of Biographical Sources

At the forefront of a new generation of postwar European writers, Peter Handke is clearly one of the most original and independent figures in contemporary literature. An extremely versatile writer, Handke has achieved the most impact as a dramatist, often hailed as a significant if not exemplary member of the avant-garde

296

theatre. Austrian by birth, Handke is identified as a German-speaking author and in that capacity has achieved both notoriety and international recognition. Appalled by what he considered the complacency of existing literary trends, Handke early in his career launched a campaign designed to challenge the conventional elements of form in both fiction and drama. Breaking from the mainstream of German authors including the more prominent Günter Grass, Heinrich Böll, and Siegfried Lenz, Handke rejected concern for analyzing the aftermath of the Nazi era in favor of provoking an awareness of present day "reality."

As a playwright, Handke has systematically utilized the theatre as a means to explore the nature of language as well as the theatrical process itself. Handke's early plays referred to as *Sprechstücke* or speech plays, written and first produced between 1966-1967, reject inherited rhetoric and traditional aspects of drama. Stripping away plot, character, and dramatic construction, Handke has attempted to revitalize the theatre, demanding both an autonomy of language and an intellectual response from the audience.

Although Handke represents an interesting subject for biography, a full-length biographical treatment has to date yet to appear in English. Considerably more popular in Europe than in the United States, Handke is still a relatively young author, having emerged simultaneously on the literary and theatrical scenes in 1966 at the age of twenty-four. A complex and controversial personality, Handke has distinguished himself as an experimental dramatist and continues to enhance his literary reputation with his fiction. In addition, Handke offers biographers a unique perspective from which to assess the transition and development of German literature and society.

Autobiographical Sources

Although Handke has not written a formal autobiography, most critics agree that autobiographical elements appear throughout Handke's work, most notably in his more recent fiction. An adherent to the therapeutic and cathartic nature of literature, Handke has created several protagonists clearly recognizable if not interchangeable with Handke himself. This seems especially true in *Short Letter, Long Farewell* and *Slow Homecoming*. Representing a departure or perhaps a future literary genre for Handke was his work entitled *The Weight of the World*, first published in Austria in 1977 and subsequently in the United States in 1984. Structured as a combined journal and writer's notebook, covering a period from November 1975 through March 1977 when Handke was living in Paris with his young daughter, this seems at first appearance to be autobiographical but Handke considers it a novel, recognizing "no contradiction between 'journal' and 'fiction.' " Of additional interest is Handke's *A Sorrow Beyond Dreams*, a first-person narrative providing a uniquely sensitive account of his mother's life, which ended in suicide.

As part of a calculated effort to focus attention on himself and his work, Handke is by design a visible and opportunistic author. Having written several autobiographical but as yet untranslated essays including the significant piece entitled "1957," Handke has also consented to numerous interviews offering autobiographical information and insight into Handke's dramatic works. Those available in English translation include "Nauseated by Language: From an Interview with Artur Joseph," *The Drama Review*, 15 (Fall 1970), pp. 56-61; June Schlueter's "An Interview with Peter Handke (July 23, 1979)," *Studies in Twentieth Century Literature*, 4, 1 (Fall 1979), pp. 63-73; and Jack Zipes' "Contrary Position: An Interview with Peter Handke," *Performance*, 1, 4 (1972), pp. 63-65, 68.

Overview of Critical Sources

Rejecting the conventional literary techniques of description, illusion, symbolism, subjectivity, and empathy, Handke has become identified with a clinical, often nonsequential, and formalistic style of writing where one is left with words, which Handke "entrusts with absolute meaning." Attempting to purge literature of its impurities, Handke offers in its place a form of aesthetic anarchy. Consequently, a tremendous disparity exists in the critical interpretation of Handke's work in all genres. Considered by a select but noteworthy coalition as the most important dramatist since Samuel Beckett, Handke has been adversely accused of being self-indulgent, nonsensical, and inaccessible as a writer. The critical debate, undoubtedly spawned with Handke's approval, is likely to continue without resolution: Innovator or trickster? Prophet of the avant-garde or charlatan in the disguise of genius?

Evaluation of Selected Criticism

Hern, Nicholas, *Peter Handke*. New York: Frederick Ungar, 1972. Included in the Modern Literature Monographs series, this was the first substantial critical study on Handke to appear in English, representing an early attempt to assess Handke's literary and aesthetic theories and their practical application in the written form. Although outdated in respect to Handke's current body of work, Hern's text serves as a valuable introduction to Handke, incorporating biographical information and a useful analysis of Handke's *Sprechstücke* and full-length plays *Kaspar* and *The Ride Across Lake Constance*. Sensitive to Handke's objectives as a writer, Hern is most effective in accurately depicting Handke's emerging role as an avant-garde dramatist.

Klinkowitz, Jerome and James Knowlton, *Peter Handke and the Postmodern Transformation: The Goalie's Journey Home*. Columbia: University of Missouri Press, 1983. Emphasizing Handke's role in shaping a postmodern aesthetic in literature, Klinkowitz and Knowlton offer an informative assessment of Handke's fiction with a brief section devoted to the drama. The text is especially valuable for its analysis of Handke's most recent work which previous studies do not include. Attempting to explore Handke's use of the novel as "process," the authors examine Handke's increasing employment of literature as a means of self-discovery. Lacking in development, the text suggests the likelihood and necessity of a future study providing a more comprehensive treatment of Handke's body of work.

Schlueter, June, *The Plays and Novels of Peter Handke*. Pittsburgh: University of Pittsburgh Press, 1981. Intended primarily for an American audience with limited access to Handke's work or critical studies published in German, Schlueter presents an informative and well-documented account of Handke's life and literary career. Incorporating biographical information with literary analysis, Schlueter focuses on Handke's individual achievement as a writer. The most comprehensive treatment of Handke to date, the text is most successful in confronting the critical questions concerning Handke's talent and providing a convincing argument in support of his importance in contemporary literature. Included in the text is a detailed bibliography and Schlueter's previously published interview with Handke conducted shortly after the Austrian publication of *Slow Homecoming*.

Other Sources

Calandra, Denis, *New German Dramatists*. New York: Grove Press, 1983. Calandra offers a valuable resource for comparison of Handke with other contemporary dramatists from Germany. Calandra allocates a significant portion of his text to Handke, providing selective biographical information and an insightful overview of Handke's plays.

Gilman, Richard, *The Making of Modern Drama*. New York: Farrar, Straus and Giroux, 1974. Emphasizing Handke's contribution as a dramatist, Gilman devotes a chapter of his text to an assessment of Handke's plays. In evaluating Handke's unconventional use of language, Gilman discusses the influence on Handke's work of Beckett, Jerzy Grotowski, and the philosopher Ludwig Wittgenstein.

Hayman, Ronald, *Theatre and Anti-Theatre*. New York: Oxford University Press, 1979. In a section of the text entitled "Peter Handke and the Sentence," Hayman provides an interesting assessment of Handke's plays. Using the term "anti-theatre" to emphasize "the negative, destructive, revolutionary, reductionist and abstractionist tendencies" in contemporary drama, Hayman identifies Handke with Beckett, Eugene Ionesco, and Jean Genet as the prime innovators of an artistic transformation of the contemporary theatre.

Hays, Michael, "Peter Handke and the End of the 'Modern,' " in *Modern Drama*, 23 (January 1981): 346-366. Observing Handke not only as a playwright but as a literary critic and theoretician, Hays examines Handke's dramatic ideology which he considers to be in opposition to the traditional concept of "modern" in postwar dramatic literature.

Innes, Christopher, *Modern German Drama: A Study in Form*. London: Cambridge University Press, 1979. Referring to Handke's plays as "linguistic" drama, Innes provides an overview of Handke's work while accurately depicting Handke's confrontational position in contemporary German drama.

Nägele, Rainer, "Peter Handke: The Staging of Language," in *Modern Drama*, 23 (January 1981): 327-338. Brief but informative assessment of Handke's plays from the early *Sprechstücke* to *The Ride Across Lake Constance* emphasizing Handke's exploration of language.

Peymann, Chris, "Directing Handke," in *The Drama Review*, 16 (June 1972): 48-54. Interesting perspective of Handke as playwright from the director of the premier productions of Handke's plays. Peymann explores the psychological depth of Handke's work and comments on the theatrical process of orchestrating aesthetic theory into practice.

Weber, Carl, "Handke's Stage is a Laboratory," in *The Drama Review*, 16 (June 1972): 55-62. A companion piece to Peymann's "Directing Handke," Weber's article assesses the author's experience of staging the Lincoln Center Repertory production of Handke's *The Ride Across Lake Constance*.

Selected Dictionaries and Encyclopedias

Contemporary Authors, Gale Research, 1979. An informative overview of Handke's career providing biographical information and useful analyses of the plays.

Handbook of Austrian Literature, Frederick Ungar, 1973. Biographical information and a critical assessment of Handke's plays through *The Ride Across Lake Constance*. In addition, the text includes entries on Ödön von Horvath and Ludwig Wittgenstein, both extremely significant in influencing Handke's vision of the theatre.

Modern German Literature: A Library of Literary Criticism, Frederick Ungar, 1972. Excerpts of criticism stemming from both Handke's plays and novels. Of interest in providing a sampling of German criticism in English translation.

World Authors: 1970-1975, H.W. Wilson, 1980. Informative, concise overview of Handke's life and career as an avant-garde playwright and novelist.

Steven Serafin
Long Island University

LORRAINE HANSBERRY
1930-1965

Author's Chronology

Born May 19, 1930, in Chicago, to Carl Augustus and Nannie Perry Hansberry; *1945* father dies after winning a Supreme Court case involving the family's move to an all-white Chicago neighborhood; *1948-1950* attends the University of Wisconsin for two years, and also studies art at the Art Institute of Chicago, at Roosevelt College, and in Guadalajara, Mexico; *1950* moves to New York, where she studies African history under W. E. B. DuBois and works as reporter and editor for Paul Robeson's monthly *Freedom* as well as writing plays; *1953* marries Robert Nemiroff, songwriter and producer; *1959* wins New York Drama Critics Circle Award for *A Raisin in the Sun*; March, *1964* Hansberry and Nemiroff are divorced, though this was not made public until after her death; *1964* her second play, *The Sign in Sidney Brustein's Window* opened on Broadway; January 12, 1965, dies of cancer in New York City.

Author's Bibliography

Because of her untimely death at the age of 34, much of Lorraine Hansberry's work was published or produced posthumously, primarily through the efforts of her ex-husband and literary executor, Robert Nemiroff. *A Raisin in the Sun*, 1959 (film version 1960, musical *Raisin* 1978); *The Drinking Gourd*, 1960 (television drama commissioned and then canceled by NBC); *The Movement: A Documentary of a Struggle for Equality*, 1964 (text for photographic essay); *The Sign in Sidney Brustein's Window*, 1964; *To Be Young, Gifted and Black*, 1969 (adapted by Robert Nemiroff and published in book form the same year with the subtitle *Lorraine Hansberry in Her Own Words*); *Les Blancs: The Collected Last Plays of Lorraine Hansberry*, 1972. ed. Robert Nemiroff (includes *The Drinking Gourd* and *What Use are Flowers?*)

Overview of Biographical Sources

No full-length biography of Lorraine Hansberry exists, a fact that is particularly surprising in light of the enormous interest that critics and the public have shown in her life as well as her plays. Though her life was short, it was extremely active, and Hansberry commands a place in the history of both black civil rights and the American theatre. She was closely associated with the major black intellectuals of her day, and was the youngest American—and the only black woman—to win the New York Drama Critics Circle Award. Biographical information is, however, available in several sources. Anne Cheney's *Lorraine Hansberry* (1984) devotes two chapters to the playwright's life and provides a chronology of major events in her life. (Cheney also notes that Margaret B. Wilkerson is working on a critical biography of Hansberry.) Basic facts about Hansberry's life are contained in the entry about her in the *Dictionary of Literary Biography*, Vol. 7: Twentieth-Century American Dramatists, Part I. A warm personal account of Hansberry's final illness is part of Robert Nemiroff's long introduction to the Random House edition of *The Sign in Sidney Br*·*tein's Window* (1965). Hansberry's letters, journals, and papers are in the possession of Nemiroff, whom she named her literary executor.

Evaluation of Selected Biographies

Cheney, Anne, *Lorraine Hansberry*. Boston: Twayne, 1984. Although Cheney's book is not primarily a biography, it does provide more biographical information than does any other single work currently available on Hansberry. Based on careful study of available materials as well as conversations with Robert Nemiroff and Hansberry's sister, Mamie, the first two chapters of Cheney's book present a sympathetic account of Hansberry's childhood in Chicago, her move to New York, and her marriage to Nemiroff. Later chapters provide an overview of Hansberry's work and incorporate some biographical details.

Autobiographical Sources

Few of Hansberry's autobiographical writings have been published, although they have been used as the basis of some biographical and critical studies, such as Anne Cheney's *Lorraine Hansberry*. In addition to letters and journals, Hansberry completed part of a draft of an autobiographical novel to be titled *All the Dark and Beautiful Warriors*. The major autobiographical source at present is *To Be Young, Gifted and Black: Lorraine Hansberry in Her Own Words*, a collection of scenes from her plays, letters, and excerpts from her journals and her autobiographical novel, compiled by Robert Nemiroff. *To Be Young, Gifted and Black* was both published as a book (Englewood Cliffs, New Jersey: Prentice-Hall, 1969) and presented as a play, opening in January 1969. The book includes a number of photographs of Hansberry and some of her drawings. *To Be Young, Gifted and Black* is organized chronologically, with pieces from letters and journals interspersed with scenes and speeches from Hansberry's published and unpublished plays to form a partial record of the playwright's intellectual and personal history from her graduation from high school to shortly before her death. Both the book and the play are highly evocative of Hansberry's life and thought, even for those unfamiliar with her biography or her plays.

Overview of Critical Sources

Although Hansberry has not precisely suffered critical neglect, assessments of her work have tended to regard her as something of an oddity: a realistic playwright in an era of absurdity, a black playwright who did not always write about the black experience, a gifted young woman whose career was cut short by early death. She has been scolded by blacks who do not find her work sufficiently socially-conscious and who point to her middle-class upbringing as a barrier to full understanding of the plight of blacks in mid-century America; she has also been praised for her courage in pursuing a career in a medium—theatre—that did not usually welcome women and certainly not black women. It seems likely that Hansberry, like other women writers, is on the verge of benefitting from the feminist literary revival, and that soon she will be seen not as an anomaly but as a highly-skilled writer.

Evaluation of Selected Criticism

Bigsby, C. W. E. *Confrontation and Commitment: A Study of Contemporary American Drama, 1959-66.* Columbia: University of Missouri Press, 1968, pp. 156-173. As an historian of American drama, Bigsby places Hansberry in the context of the 1950s and 1960s, commenting on her realistic rebuttal to the Theater of the Absurd and on the fact that, unlike James Baldwin and LeRoi Jones, she transcends the anger of racism to comment on all humanity. Bigsby discusses *A Raisin in the Sun* and *The Sign in Sidney Brustein's Window*, preferring the latter because of its optimism and compassion.

Cheney, Anne, *Lorraine Hansberry.* Boston: Twayne, 1984. Cheney's study is an overview of the life and work of the playwright. Cheney takes pains to place Hansberry within a tradition of black intellectuals and reformers in America, and devotes one chapter to brief biographical sketches of some of those who influenced her social thought, including Frederick Douglass and Paul Robeson. Discussions of Hansberry's life and works are deeply sympathetic and clearly written.

Freedomways, Vol. 19, No. 4 (1979). This special issue of *Freedomways* is devoted entirely to essays about Hansberry, and is the best single source of multiple commentary about her work. The eighteen essays range from personal reminiscence, such as the one by James Baldwin, to evaluations of her art, such as "Lorraine Hansberry as Prose Stylist" by Jewell Handy Gresham, to lyrical commentary on her significance, such as Adrienne Rich's "The Problem With Lorraine Hansberry." The final piece in the issue is a complete (to that date) bibliography of works by and about Hansberry.

Miller, Jordan Y. "Lorraine Hansberry," in *The Black American Writer: Vol. II: Poetry and Drama*, ed. C. W. E. Bigsby. Baltimore: Penguin Books, 1969. Miller first summarizes briefly the history of American drama about blacks to make the point that Hansberry wrote *A Raisin in the Sun* at a time of rapid social change, but he prefers to comment on this play and *The Sign in Sidney Brustein's Window* as plays rather than as social commentary, and he focuses on her creation of realistic characters in a "well-made" play as the key to her lasting importance.

Wilkerson, Margaret B. "The Sighted Eyes and Feeling Heart of Lorraine Hansberry," in *Black American Literature Forum*, 17, 1 (Spring 1983): 8-13. A later version of this essay serves as the introduction to the New American Library edition of Hansberry's plays. Wilkerson counters those who contend that Hansberry's middle-class origins obscured her vision of lower-class blacks, and in fact believes that her work presaged the Black Arts Movement of the 1960s. The article treats each of Hansberry's five published plays, with the thesis that although all art makes a social statement, Hansberry's plays have the power to engage the reader or viewer, not merely to serve a political purpose.

Other Sources

Abramson, Doris E. *Negro Playwrights in the American Theatre, 1925-1959*. New York: Columbia University Press, 1969, pp. 239-254, 263-266. Abramson provides a detailed commentary on *A Raisin in the Sun* and a summary of critical reactions to it.

Cruse, Harold, *The Crisis of the Negro Intellectual*. New York: William Morrow, 1967, pp. 267-284. Cruse sharply criticizes Hansberry for adopting the values of the white middle class and failing to come to terms in her plays with the social realities of American blacks.

Malpede, Karen, "Lorraine Hansberry," in *Women in Theatre: Compassion and Hope*. New York: Drama Book Publishers, 1983. This is a compilation of a strongly feminist introductory note, a review of *A Raisin in the Sun* from the *Village Voice*, and two letters by Hansberry, one attacking Arthur Miller for the sexism of *After the Fall*.

Nemiroff, Robert, "The One Hundred and One 'Final' Performances of *Sidney Brustein*,: in *The Sign in Sidney Brustein's Window*. New York: Random House, 1965, pp. xiii-lxi. As an introduction to this edition of Hansberry's play, Nemiroff provides a detailed description of the efforts to keep *The Sign in Sidney Brustein's Window* running while Hansberry was dying of cancer.

Selected Dictionaries and Encyclopedias

American Women Writers, Vol. 2. This reference article provides a brief summary of Hansberry's life and works, accompanied by a list of her published works and selected references.

Dictionary of Literary Biography, Vol. 7: Twentieth-Century American Dramatists, Part I. A somewhat longer reference article that includes brief assessments of the five published plays and of Hansberry's stature in American drama.

Nancy Walker
Stephens College

GERHART HAUPTMANN
1862-1946

Author's Chronology

Born in Ober-Salzbrunn in Silesia, Germany, now part of Poland, on November 15, 1862, son of a hotel manager; given little formal education; *1878* takes a job as a farm worker on his uncle's estate; *1880* attends the Königliche Kunst und Gewerbeschule in Breslau to study sculpture; *1882* studies one semester at the University of Jena; *1883* travels to Italy; *1883-1884* spends the winter in Rome to establish himself as a sculptor, but contracts typhoid and returns home; *1884* attends Königliche Akademie der Künste in Dresden, then the University of Berlin; May 5, *1885* marries Marie Thienemann (who bears three sons) and moves first to Berlin, then to the suburb of Erkner; after publishing several well-received novellas (*Fasching*, 1887; *Flagman Thiel*, 1888), becomes famous overnight with the turbulent premier of *Before Daybreak* on October 20, 1889, performed by the avant-garde company *Verein Freie Bühne* in Berlin, and establishes himself as a herald of German naturalism; writes a series of plays, including *The Weavers* (1892), the dream-play *Hannele* (1893), the social-critical comedy *The Beaver Coat* (1893), the historical *Florian Geyer* (1896), and the neo-Romantic fairy-tale play, *The Sunken Bell* (1896); *1894* visits America and attends the New York premier of *Hannele's Assumption;* wins Grillparzer Prize in 1896, 1899 and 1905; *1901* moves to Agnetendorf in Silesia, his principal residence for the remainder of his life; *1904* divorces Marie Thienemann and marries Margarete Marschalk, a young actress (with whom he has two sons); *1905* is awarded honorary doctorate from Oxford University; *1907* travels to Greece, receiving inspiration for the autobiographical *Griechischer Frühling* (1908) and later neo-Classical works: *The Bow of Odysseus* (1914), and a tetralogy on the House of Atreus, *Iphigenie in Delphi* (1941), *Iphigenie in Aulis* (1943), *Agamemnons Tod* (1948), and *Elektra* (1948); is awarded honorary doctorates from Leipzig and Prague universities (1909 and 1921), and in 1912 the Nobel Prize for Literature; *1920s* receives various honors from the Weimar Republic and enjoys his greatest popularity; *1932* makes second trip, this time in triumph, to America; receives honorary doctorate from Columbia University; early *1930s* refuses to leave his country when Hitler comes to power; *1945* witnesses destruction of Dresden; June 6, *1946* dies in Agnetendorf during the Russian occupation; is buried in Kloster on the island of Hiddensee.

Author's Bibliography (selected)

Poetry, epic, and lyric: *Das bunte Buch* (1888); *Anna* (1921); *Till Eulenspiegel* (1928); *Ährenlese* (1939); *Der grosse Traum* (1942; fragment); *Neue Gedichte* (1946).

Dramas (unless otherwise noted, translations of the plays listed are found in the Ludwig Lewisohn edition listed below): *Before Daybreak* (1889, tr. by Peter Bauland, 1978); *Lonely Lives* (1891); *The Weavers* (pub. 1892, perf. 1893); *Colleague Crampton* (1892); *The Beaver Coat* (1893); *The Assumption of Hannele* (orig. title: *Hannele,* 1893); *The Assumption of Hannele* (orig. title: *Hannele,* perf. 1893, pub. 1894); *Florian Geyer* (1896); *The Sunken Bell* (perf. 1896, pub. 1897); *Drayman Henschel* (1898); *Schluck and Jau* (1900); *The Conflagration* (1901); *Henry of Auë* (1902); *Rose Bernd* (1903); *Elga* (1905); *And Pippa Dances!* (1906); *Charlemagne's Hostage* (1908); *Griselda* (1909); *The Rats* (1911); *Gabriel Schilling's Flight* (1912); *Commemoration Masque* (1913); *The Bow of Odysseus* (1914); *Winter Ballad* (1917); *The White Savior* (1920); *Indipohdi* (pub. 1920; perf. 1922); *Veland* (1925); *Vor Sonnenuntergang* (1932); *Hamlet in Wittenberg* (1935); *Die Tochter der Kathedrale* (1939); *Die Atridentetralogie: Iphigenie in Delphi* (1941); *Iphigenie in Aulis* (1943); *Agamemnons Tod* (perf. 1947, pub. 1948); *Electra* (perf. 1947, pub. 1948).

Prose: *Fasching* (1887); *Flagman Thiel* (1888, tr. by Adele S. Seltzer in *Great German Short Novels and Stories,* 1952); *Der Apostel* (1890); *The Fool in Christ, Emanuel Quint* (1910, tr. Thomas Seltzer, 1911); *Atlantis* (1912, tr. by Adele and Thomas Seltzer, 1912); *The Heretic of Soana* (1918, tr. by B.Q. Morgan, 1923); *Phantom* (1922, tr. by B.Q. Morgan, 1922); *The Island of the Great Mother* (1924, tr. by Willa and Edwin Muir, 1925); *Wanda* (1928); *Die Hochzeit auf Buchenhorst* (1932); *Das Meerwunder* (1934); *Das Märchen* (1941); *Des Schuss im Park* (1942); *Der neue Christophorus* (1943; fragment); *Mignon* (1947).

Collected Works: In German: *Das Gesammelte Werk. Ausgabe letzter Hand zum 80. Geburtstag des Dichters am 15. November 1942,* 17 vols. Berlin: Fischer, 1942. Last edition overseen by author.

Sämtliche Werke. Centenar-Ausgabe zum 100. Geburtstag des Dichters, 15. November 1962, 11 vols. eds. Hans-Egon Hass and Martin Machatzke. Frankfurt-on-the-Main, Berlin and Vienna: Propyläen, 1966-74. Standard, although not a critical edition.

Das dramatische Werk. 4 vols. Berlin and Vienna: Propyläen, 1974. Includes all complete dramas.

In English: *The Dramatic Works of Gerhart Hauptmann.* tr. Ludwig Lewisohn et. al. New York: Huebsch, 1912-29.

The Weavers, Rose Bernd, Drayman Henschel, The Beaver Coat, Hannele: Five Plays by Gerhart Hauptmann. tr. Theodore H. Lustig. New York: Bantam Books, 1961.

Overview of Biographical Sources

The best early biographies of Hauptmann were written by friends and acquaintances or were based on information furnished by his older brother Carl. Often these were reverential in tone. Because Hauptmann chose to remain in Germany during the Nazi era instead of going into exile, many subsequent biographers treat the later years of his life with considerable emotional distance. Hauptmann's popularity reached a zenith during the years of the Weimar Republic, but his plays are performed today in Germany with a frequency that suggests he will remain one of his country's foremost dramatists.

Most of the standard biographies are in German and have not been translated. By 1922, only one critically recognized biography had appeared: Paul Schlenther's *Gerhart Hauptmann: Sein Lebensgang und seine Dichtung.* 2nd. ed. (Berlin: Fischer, 1922). This work remains valuable today for Hauptmann's early years, although full biographic treatments after his death added to the early record. Joseph Gregor's *Gerhart Hauptmann: Das Werk und Unsere Zeit* (Vienna: Diana, 1951), should be used cautiously, as it contains some factual errors. More valuable are the later specialist treatments of Hauptmann's life and works by C.F.W. Behl and Felix A. Voigt, *Chronik von Gerhart Hauptmanns Leben und Schaffen* (Munich: Bergstadt, 1957); Karl S. Guthke, *Gerhart Hauptmann: Weltbild im Werk* (Göttingen: Vandenhoeck and Ruprecht, 1961); Eberhard Hilscher, *Gerhart Hauptmann* (Berlin: Verlag der Nationen, 1969); and Hans Daiber, *Gerhart Hauptmann oder der letzter Klassiker* (Vienna: Molden, 1971). Reliable biographies in English have been slow to appear.

Evaluation of Selected Biographies

Behl, C. F. W. *Gerhart Hauptmann: His Life and His Work.* tr. Helen Taubert. Würzburg: Holzner, 1956. Even today this brief biography by a man who was close to Hauptmann remains valuable, treating his mission, *oeuvre,* and place in literary history. This book offers no substantial analyses of the works, bibliography or notes; nonetheless it is a useful introduction.

Farner, Dorothy C. "Hauptmann at Hiddensee," in *American German Review* 29 (1962): 14-18. An account of Hauptmann's funeral and burial on the Baltic island of Hiddensee, this article includes pictures of the writer and his wife, of his house on Hiddensee, and of his grave.

Garten, Hugh F. *Gerhart Hauptmann.* New Haven: Yale University Press, 1954. The best early critical assessment in English, Garten's study of the author and his works is arranged around literary periods. The appendix includes biographical data, a list of Hauptmann's published works and translations, and a short bibliography.

Gousie, Laurent, "Gerhart Hauptmann: The Natural-Naturalist," in *Germanic Review* 55 (1980): 9-13. Analyzing Hauptmann's ancestry, youth and early schooling, Gousie shows how the writer came quite naturally to his naturalistic themes of the force of heredity and environment. The study discusses Hauptmann's work up to 1892.

Guthke, Karl S. "The King of the Weimar Republic. Gerhart Hauptmann's Role in Political Life, 1919-1933," in *Probleme der Moderne: Studien zur deutschen Literatur von Nietzsche bis Brecht, Festschrift für Walter Sokel.* Tübingen: Niemeyer, 1983, pp. 369-87. An historical account of the writer's political views, as documented by public speeches, statements in newspapers and journals, and diary materials published in the *Centenar Ausgabe.* The most detailed review in English of Hauptmann's politics, this study best explains the lionized poet's public role during the Weimar Republic and his unfortunately ambivalent public and privately expressed opinions during the Hitler era.

Heuser, F.W.J. "Early Influences on the Intellectual Development of Gerhart Hauptmann," in *Germanic Review* 5 (1930): 38-57. This biographical study treats the period from the writer's schooling in Breslau to the summer of 1888 in Zurich and offers descriptions of the individuals and ideas that influenced Hauptmann's childhood and youth. Heuser asserts that Hauptmann was not an orthodox Christian, pagan or socialist.

_____. "Gerhart Hauptmann's Trip to America in 1894," in *Germanic Review* 13 (1938): 3-31. Factual account of the writer's first visit, including detailed descriptions of his impressions of America, places he stayed, newspaper reports, and interviews. Heuser also describes the background, controversy, and reviews of the New York production of *The Assumption of Hannele.*

Maurer, Warren R. *Gerhart Hauptmann.* Boston: Twayne, 1982. Primarily a discussion of Hauptmann's principal works, this valuable monograph successfully integrates biography with critical interpretation. Maurer includes a chronology of the author's life, scholarly notes, and a bibliography. This is the best critical introduction to Hauptmann in English.

Muller, Siegfried, "Gerhart Hauptmann's Relation to American Literature and His Concept of America," in *Monatshefte* 44 (1952): 333-339. Muller reviews the influence of several American authors, including Cooper, Whitman, and Emerson, on Hauptmann, and describes his two trips to America, concentrating on the second in 1932.

Pohl, Gerhart, *Gerhart Hauptmann and Silesia: A Report on the Dramatist's Last Days in his Occupied Homeland.* tr. by W.J. Morgan. Grand Forks: University of North Dakota Press, 1962. A friend's description of Hauptmann's last two and one-half years, including his stay in Dresden and Wiesenstein. As a witness to Hauptmann's last years, Pohl offers an intimate account of events and conversations in Hauptmann's inner circle and of exchanges with the Russians and Poles who entered Silesia at the end of the war. Pohl depicts Hauptmann as much beloved by his countrymen and against Hitler, and cites the writer's anti-facist private remarks as evidence of his real beliefs. Text includes pictures from Hauptmann's last years.

Reichart, Walter A. "Gerhart Hauptmann: His Work in America," in *American German Review* 29 (1962-63): 4-7, 31. Traces Hauptmann's visits to America from obscurity to fame and recognition. Includes excerpts from contemporary reviews.

――――――. "Gerhart Hauptmann and His British Friends: Documented in Some of Their Correspondence," in *German Quarterly* 50 (1977): 424-451. Reprints many letters, from the Hauptmann archives in Berlin and from the Houghton Library of Harvard University, exchanged between the poet and Sir William Rothenstein and others.

Reicke, Ilse, "Reminiscences of Gerhart Hauptmann," in *American German Review* 29 (1962): 11-13. Recollections of Hauptmann's final days by the daughter of a personal friend, including observations about the writer's brothers and Agnetendorf.

Seidlin, Oskar, "Taking Leave of Gerhart Hauptmann," in *South Atlantic Quarterly* 46 (1947): 359-364. Negative assessment of Hauptmann's decision not to leave Germany during the Nazi era, and positive view of his literary accomplishments.

Autobiographical Sources

Hauptmann was very clear about the autobiographical nature of all his works. F.A. Voigt reported that Hauptmann told him that everything he ever wrote, even each line, was in some manner taken from his life. Although this statement is an exageration, scholars believe Hauptmann did draw heavily on personal experiences for his art. Three directly autobiographical works, none of which has been translated into English, are *Griechischer Frühling* (1908), a travel diary of his trip to Greece in 1907; *Buch der Leidenschaft* (1929), a novelistic account of Hauptmann's marital problems and eventual divorce; and *Das Abenteuer meiner Jugend* (1937), a revealing narration of his difficult childhood and youth, covering the first 25 years of his life. The Hauptmann archives, containing manuscripts, letters, notebooks and diaries, are located in West Berlin at the Staatsbibliothek der Stiftung Preussischer Kulturbesitz.

Overview of Critical Sources

The leading German dramatist of his day, Hauptmann owes his popularity in large degree to his compassionate portrayal of people, their suffering and frailty. Although claimed by devotees of many literary movements and political philosophies, Hauptmann was a proponent of no single ideology or literary style. Perhaps because his earliest works were hailed as landmarks of naturalism, that label continued to be applied to the writer even though his styles never stopped evolving. He was widely read in world religions and showed in his work an ironic distance from

Christianity and a mélange of symbolisms borrowed from other cultures. Haupt-mann came to fame as a critic of late nineteenth-century German society, taking up in his famous play *The Weavers,* for example, the plight and exploitation of labor-ers; but his late reputation was marred by the septuagenarian's decision to remain in his native Silesia during the Hitler era, his public statements in support of the government, and his unwillingness to speak out against the Nazis. Sympathetic observers attribute his behavior to political naiveté, while others speak of his fear. Recent criticism has re-focused on the social views and philosophy evident in the works themselves.

By far the majority of scholarship on Hauptmann is written in German and concerns his plays, of which he wrote more than fifty. Recently, Hauptmann's novels and short stories, as well as his late works, have begun to receive more critical attention. More has been written about Hauptmann than almost any other German author; hence any brief listing of critical sources will necessarily be inade-quate. The reader is advised to consult the bibliographies listed at the end of this section, especially for treatments of individual works. Only comprehensive critical works in English are surveyed here.

Evaluation of Selected Criticism

Knight, K.G. and F. Norman, eds. *Hauptmann Centenary Lectures.* London: University of London Press, 1964. Composed of six different studies, this excellent collection of essays covers a wide range of topics. Especially valuable are W.F. Mainland's "The Literary Personality of Gerhart Hauptmann," pp. 9-30; J.W. Mc-Farlane's "Hauptmann, Ibsen, and the Concept of Naturalism," pp. 31-60; and "The 'Active' Hero in Gerhart Hauptmann's Drama," by E. O. H. McInnes, pp. 61-94.

Marschall, Alan, *The German Naturalists and Gerhart Hauptmann. Reception and Influence.* Frankfurt-on-the-Main: Lang, 1982. In this lengthy study, Mars-chall brings forth a wealth of quotations and reviews to establish the definitions and views of naturalism held by writers and scholars of Hauptmann's day. Then follow documents on the critical reception of Hauptmann's works and reactions of fellow authors. Most useful for the specialist in naturalism, this book has copious notes and a large bibliography.

Mellen, Philip, *Gerhart Hauptmann: Religious Syncretism and Eastern Reli-gions.* Bern: Lang, 1984. A vital contribution to Hauptmann scholarship, this book makes use of the Hauptmann archives in West Berlin to reveal his extensive reading and knowledge of Buddhism, Hinduism, Taoism-Confucionism, and gnosticism. Mellen's indispensable study is well documented and makes use of the archival discoveries to shed new light on *Michael Kramer, Indipohdi,* and *Der Neue Chris-tophorus.*

Shaw, Leroy R. *Witness of Deceit: Gerhart Hauptmann as Critic of Society.* Berkeley: University of California Press, 1958. Although it focuses on interpreting one aspect of Hauptmann's early work, this valuable study also examines some biographical aspects of his early life as a playwright. The appendix includes a chronology of Hauptmann's life and works up to 1896, and a short bibliography.

Sinden, Margaret, *Gerhart Hauptmann: The Prose Plays.* Toronto: University of Toronto Press, 1957. Although limited to fifteen of Hauptmann's prose plays, Sinden's study is a useful introduction for the generalist reader. For each play, Sinden gives a summary of the plot followed by a critical discussion that includes comparisons with other works of world literature. The plays are divided into groups: early, historical, middle class, and plays of the common people. Although there are some factual errors and no bibliography, the index of world authors and works to which Sinden compares Hauptmann and his plays is helpful.

Other Sources

Campbell, T.M. "Gerhart Hauptmann: Christian or Pagan?" in *Modern Language Journal* 8 (1924): 353-361. Campbell undertakes to answer the question of Hauptmann's beliefs through a study of *Emanuel Quint, The Heretic of Soana,* and *Griechischer Frühling. Quint* is depicted as a fusion of Christian and pagan elements.

Cast, Gottlob Charles, "The Religious Views of Gerhart Hauptmann as Reflected in His Works," in *Studies in German Literature: In Honor of Alexander Rudolf Hohlfeld.* University of Wisconsin Studies in German Literature 22. Madison: University of Wisconsin Press, 1925, pp. 78-96. Useful introduction to Hauptmann's atypical religious views. Superseded by later scholarship (i.e. Mellen, *Eastern Religions*).

Dussère, Carolyn Thomas, *The Image of the Primitive Giant in the Works of Gerhart Hauptmann.* Stuttgart: Heinz, 1979. Dussère discusses the giant in various periods of Hauptmann's creativity and in various roles (device for humor, as artisan, artist and others).

Gousie, Laurent, "Gerhart Hauptmann and Surrealism," in *Germanic Review* 53 (1978): 156-165. Based on C.J. Jung's definitions of archetypal images, this study demonstrates Hauptmann's development beyond naturalism to surrealism in *Drayman Henschel* and some earlier works.

Guthke, Karl S. "Nihilism and Modern Literature: The Case of Gerhart Hauptmann," in *Forum* (Houston) 5 (1967): 4-13. Guthke discusses the concept of nihilism in Hauptmann's works with reference to Nietzsche, and concludes that Hauptmann's God was a paradox of both diabolical and benevolent intents.

Heuser, Frederick W.J. "The Mystical Hauptmann," in *Germanic Review* 7 (1932): 32-44. Heuser begins with a definition of mysticism, then traces the early influence on Hauptmann of mystics such as Jakob Böhme and Angelus Silesius. The study discusses mystical elements in Hauptmann's works from *Der Apostel* and *The Island of the Great Mother*.

Keefer, L.B. "Woman's Mission in Hauptmann's Dramas," in *Germanic Review* 9 (1934): 35-52. Keefer suggests that love of women, especially of central woman-mother figures, is the source of the principal conflicts in Hauptmann's plays.

Klemm, Frederick A. "Genesis-Thanatos in Gerhart Hauptmann," *Germanic Review* 17 (1942): 273-281. A good study of the death motif in Hauptmann's works.

Maurer, Warren R. "Gerhart Hauptmann's Character Names," in *German Quarterly* 52 (1979): 457-471. An informative discussion of Hauptmann's choice of names and their implications for his characters and works.

McInnes, Edward, "The Domestic Dramas of Gerhart Hauptmann: Tragedy or Sentimental Pathos?" in *German Life and Letters* 20 (1966): 53-60. A study of the significance of the spiritual experience attained through suffering and moral discovery by Hauptmann's protagonists in his domestic plays.

Mellen, Philip, *Gerhart Hauptmann and Utopia*. Stuttgart: Heinz, 1976. A thorough study of Hauptmann's interest in and works about utopian concepts. Especially significant to Americans in view of Hauptmann's interest in a utopian community in Iowa. Mellen focuses primarily on *The Island of the Great Mother* and *Der Neue Christophorus*.

_____, "Gerhart Hauptmann's 'Other Reality'," in *Germanic Notes* 7 (1976): 33-36. A brief introduction to this key concept in Hauptmann's mysticism.

Muller, Siegfried, *Gerhart Hauptmann and Goethe*. New York: King's Crown Press, 1949. A factual survey documenting Haputmann's admitted debt to Goethe by comparing the two authors' works. Appendix contains a list of quotes from Goethe's works used by Hauptmann. Good introduction to a complex subject.

Nabholz, Johannes, *"The Clergyman in Gerhart Hauptmann's Contemporary Plays,"* in *Monatshefte* 39 (1947): 463-476. Nabholz treats seven plays in which clergymen appear, and finds that this figure is portrayed as smug and superior.

Osborne, John, "Hauptmann's Later Naturalist Dramas: Suffering and Tragic Vision," in *Modern Language Review* 63 (1968): 628-635. Osborne emphasizes naturalistic rather than symbolic interpretations for *Drayman Henschel, Michael Kramer, Rose Bernd,* and *The Rats*. He depicts these works as forming a bridge between Hauptmann's early and late works through their emphasis on suffering.

Reichart, Walter A. "The Totality of Hauptmann's Work," in *Germanic Review* 21 (1946): 143-149. An excellent general introduction to the range and scope of Hauptmann's *oeuvre*.

_____. "Gerhart Hauptmann's Dramas on the American Stage," in *Maske und Kothurn* 8 (1962): 223-232. An insightful discussion of the stage performances of Hauptmann's plays in America, their reception, and the controversies that surrounded them.

Steinhauer, Harry, "Gerhart Hauptmann," in *University of Toronto Quarterly* 23 (1963): 247-265. An erudite and eloquent appraisal of the man and his works, including a brief assessment of his behavior during the Nazi period.

_____, "Hauptmann's Vision of Christ," in *Monatshefte* 29 (1937): 331-340. Steinhauer surveys the writer's interest in Christ's life and describes the influence of Albert Dulk's account of Christ on Hauptmann's *Der Apostel* and *The Fool in Christ, Emanuel Quint.*

Stirk, S.D. "Gerhart Hauptmann and Goethe: A Contrast," in *Publications of the English Goethe Society* 14 (1938-39): 101-111. While most commentators note similarities, Stirk offers a penetrating assessment of the differences between Hauptmann and Goethe.

Wahr, F.B. "Gerhart Hauptmann's Shorter Poems," in *Germanic Review* 21 (1946): 215-229. Brief generalist introduction to Hauptmann's poetry.

_____. "The Art of Hauptmann's Shorter Stories," in *Germanic Review* 24 (1949): 52-64. A general introduction to Hauptmann's novellas, beginning with *Fasching* and including several later prose works.

Webb, Karl E. "Islands, Maidens, and the Life Force: Gerhart Hauptmann's Literary *Jugendstil,*" in *Theatrum Mundi: Essays on German Drama and German Literature Dedicated to Harold Lenz on his Seventieth Birthday, September 11, 1978.* ed. Edward R. Haymes. Munich: Fink, 1980. A study of the influence of the *Jugendstil* movement in Germany from 1890 to 1910 and its influence on Hauptmann. Webb treats primarily *The Assumption of Hannele, The Sunken Bell,* and *And Pippa Dances!*

Weigard, Hermann J. "Gerhart Hauptmann's Range as a Dramatist," in *Monatshefte* 44 (1952): 317-332. Excellent study of the diversity of Hauptmann's drama as exemplary of many literary movements.

Weisert, John J. *The Dream in Gerhart Hauptmann.* New York: King's Crown Press, 1949. Although there has been a great deal written since Weisert on Hauptmann's use of the dream, this book still serves as a good introduction to the subject.

Ziolkowski, Theodore, "Gerhart Hauptmann and the Problem of Language," in *Germanic Review* 38 (1963): 295-306. A fresh look at certain aspects of Hauptmann's dramas through an examination of his language.

Selected Bibliographies
In English:

Heuser, F.W.J. "Stages in Hauptmann Criticism," in *Germanic Review* 12 (1937): 106-112. Reviews more than two dozen early critical works through 1936.

Hutchins, W.J. and Ann C. Weaver, "Hauptmann in England: A Bibliography," in *Hauptmann Centenary Lectures,* pp. 142-167 (see above). Valuable guide to criticism and to translations of Hautpmann in English.

Reichart, Walter A. "Fifty Years of Hauptmann Study in America (1894-1944): A Bibliography," in *Monatshefte* 37 (1945): 1-31; and "Hauptmann Study in America: A Continuation Bibliography," in *Monatshefte* 54 (1962): 297-310. The most complete bibliography in English.

In German (but including English entries):

Ludwig, Viktor, *Gerhart Hauptmann: Werke von ihm und über ihn (1881-1931),* Neustadt: n. p., 1932. This expanded edition of a 1922 work of the same title is valuable for early critical reaction.

Reichart, Walter A. *Gerhart-Hauptmann-Bibliographie.* Bad Homburg: Gehlen, 1969. A standard work.

Tschörtner, H.D. *Gerhart-Hauptmann-Bibliographie.* Berlin: Deutsche Staatsbibliothek, 1971. A standard work, but contains few English entries, which are grouped at the end.

Robin A. Clouser
Ursinus College

VACLAV HAVEL
1936

Author's Chronology

Born in Prague, Czechoslovakia on October 5, 1936 to Vaclav M. Havel and Bozena (Vavreckova) Havel; *1955-1957* attends Technical College; *1959-1961* progresses from scene shifter to literary manager at Prague's Theatre ABC and Balustrade Theatre; *1961* co-authors first play, *Autostop*, with Ivan Vyskocil; *1962-1968* student of dramaturgy at Prague's Academy of Visual Arts and resident playwright at Balustrade; *1963 The Garden Party* gains Havel international recognition; *1968* New York critics vote *The Memorandum* (1965) best foreign drama; *1969* forbidden work in Czech theatre and banned from Czech stages following Russian invasion; *1977* co-authors the manifesto *Charter '77*, making Havel one of the most prominent dissidents in Eastern Europe; he has been jailed repeatedly since then.

Author's Bibliography (drama)

Autostop, 1961 (co-written with Ivan Vyskocil); *The Garden Party*, 1963; *The Memorandum*, 1965; *The Increased Difficulty of Concentration*, 1968; *The Conspirators*, 1971; *The Mountain Hotel*, 1971; *The Beggar's Opera*, 1972; *The Audience*, 1975; *Preview to an Exhibit*, 1975; *Protest*, 1978; *The Castle*, 1981; *Letters to Olga*, 1984 (personal correspondence).

Overview of Biographical Sources

Unfortunately, no book or even a separate chapter within a book currently exists about Havel's life. The best that a scholar can do is to turn to an encyclopedia or dictionary of world drama.

Autobiographical Sources

Havel's plays were banned from Czech stages in 1969, when a ban on publishing his works was also imposed. As a result, Havel's immediate reaction was to turn to subjects and techniques of a less-distinctly Czech nature in an attempt to appeal to international audiences. For example, he used John Gay's *The Beggar's Opera* as the basis for his own non-musical production of the same name (1972). These works, however, did not gain the attention that *The Garden Party* and *The Memorandum* did, and, since 1976, much of Havel's writing has been based on his personal experiences and has been critically successful.

Havel's pair of one-act plays, *The Audience* and *Preview to an Exhibit* (published as *Sorry . . . Two Plays: "Audience" and "Private View."* London: Eyre Methuen, 1978) have strong autobiographical overtones. The first discusses ideological and economic pressures on a nonconformist artist working in a totalitarian regime. The second focuses on the artist's isolation resulting from his defiance. *Protest* (1978) also clearly reflects Havel's life. The full text does not seem to be available in English, but Marketa Goetz-Stankiewicz provides a description of it in *The Silenced Theatre: Czech Playwrights Without a Stage* (1979). In this one-act play, a politically ostracized playwright meets with a colleague who has remained on good terms with the ruling regime. The accepted writer makes a long argument about how he can help dissidents most by not joining them.

In 1986, Alfred A. Knopf will publish Havel's *Letters to Olga*, a book of prison letters written to his wife. It was published in 1984 by a West German Company, Rowohlt Verlag.

Overview of Critical Sources

Scholars searching for biographical material about Havel will find most of it included in the sketchy outlines provided along with most critical sources. Havel's life has greatly affected his work. The absurdity of his experiences begins with his being denied a formal education because his father was a wealthy landowner before the Communist takeover of Czechoslovakia. Thus, bureaucracy and meaningless ideology have dominated Havel all his life and, not surprisingly, become the most powerful forces in his plays. When Jan Grossman took control of the Balustrade Theatre in 1963 and oriented it towards the theatre of the absurd, he provided Havel with the proper form for which his ideas were waiting. Since then, Havel has used his powerful satire to try to enlighten Czechs about the nature of their situation, and his work is strongly attached to his country. He tries, as he says, to produce freedom where there is none. Even in recent years, when he has been frequently imprisoned, Havel has refused opportunities to go to the West.

The most important critics, therefore, always discuss Havel within the contexts of both his personal history and the major characteristics of the theatre of the absurd. All of them agree that Havel is one of the most important and innovative dramatists in the world today. There is some disagreement about the quality of his work from 1969 through 1976, but no doubt that *The Garden Party* and *The Memorandum* are great plays in the tradition of Beckett and Ionesco. Walter Schamschula's "Vaclav Havel: Between the Theatre of the Absurd and Engaged Theatre" (1980) gives the fullest analysis of Havel's plays in relation to other absurdist works. Schamschula describes a number of techniques Havel uses to create both partial and total destruction of the action: two characteristic devices of absurdist theatre. At the same time, Havel presents man in the existentialist condition of being alone and unsheltered in a hostile world. Schamschula also sees the post-1969 period of Havel's career as being one of increased experimentation and greater evolution than the early part.

Marketa Goetz-Stankiewicz, in *The Silenced Theatre: Czech Playwrights Without a Stage* (1979), sees all of Havel's career as a gradual evolution. She finds that as he has turned inward, focusing on specifically Czech situations, his work has, nevertheless, become increasingly universal. She also provides a valuable description of one of Havel's later plays, *Protest* (1978), otherwise unavailable elsewhere. Paul I. Trensky, in *Czech Drama Since World War II* (1978), expresses less admiration for *The Increased Difficulty of Concentration (1968) and The Mountain Hotel* (1971) than most other critics for their artistic merits, though he believes that they do reveal new intellectual depth. On the whole, no doubt exists that Vaclav Havel is Czechoslovakia's greatest playwright since Karel Capek and, possibly, its greatest ever.

Evaluation of Selected Criticism

Goetz-Stankiewicz, Marketa. *The Silenced Theatre: Czech Playwrights Without a Stage*. Toronto: University of Toronto Press, 1979. Goetz-Stankiewicz analyzes how Havel uses language to produce not only comedy but also a horrific picture of how mechanistic, cliché-ridden language has come to dominate man. The outcome is a hollow man who goes through life acting on the basis of perverted rational thinking. Goetz-Stankiewicz finds a logical development of both techniques and themes in Havel's plays, producing an increasingly dark vision of the world. She also analyzes how Havel creates universal messages by exploring his own country's problems at their deepest level. In all modern mass society, the corruption of language is a key to man's loss of humanity.

Schamschula, Walter, "Vaclav Havel: Between the Theatre of the Absurd and Engaged Theatre," in *Fiction and Drama in Eastern and Southeastern Europe: Evolution and Experiment in the Postwar Period*. ed. Henrik Birnbaum and Thomas Eekman. Columbus, OH: Slavica Publishers, 1980: 337-348. Schamschula analyzes Havel's major techniques such as gags, mimetic devices, pseudo-proverbs, the parody of rhetorical style, cyclical structure, and spirals of recurrent replicas, producing an avalanche of absurdity. Schamschula finds Havel very innovative because he goes beyond the traditional context of the theatre of the absurd by exploiting arrangements of large units of dialogue and abolishing semantic continuums. Another important point is that since the Russian invasion in 1968, Havel has limited the number of devices he employs, producing a clear expression of anguish and depressing atmosphere. Havel's later plays focus on man's descent into absurdity as a universal threat.

Trensky, Paul I. *Czech Drama Since World War II*. White Plains, NY: M.E. Sharpe, 1978. Trensky provides plot summaries and examples of Havel's use of absurd dialogue, disunified characters, random repetition, and circular structure to criticize man's subordination to the vices of idealism, consummerism, and power. Trensky finds a decline in Havel's work after *The Memorandum* until 1975, when *The Audience* and *Preview to an Exhibit* indicated an artistic resurgence. Trensky also helps explain Havel's development by discussing the growth of the Balustrade Theatre.

"Havel's *The Garden Party* Revisited," *Czech Literature Since 1956: A Symposium*. eds. William E. Harkins and Paul I. Trensky. New York: Bohemia, 1980: 103-118. This essay is material reprinted from Trensky's *Czech Drama Since World War II* (1978). Trensky focuses on *The Garden Party* because, despite the fact that it is Havel's greatest work, it has rarely been performed in the West. Trensky explains the dominance of language in the play as a sign of man's vacuity and corruption of intellect. The first act is a parody of the family drama. Havel uses clichés and nonsense proverbs to reveal the emptiness of middle-class life. The second act is an allegory on the institutionalization of private life in Czechoslovakia while the third act lampoons the country's large bureaucracy.

Dictionaries and Selected Encyclopedias

Contemporary Authors, Vol. 104, Gale Research, 1982. Andrea Geffner briefly discusses Havel's life and difficulties with Czechoslovakia's Communist regime. She reveals how the absurdity of Havel's plays is grounded in the realities of everyday Czech life and cites several American critics of his works.

Contemporary Literary Criticism, Vol. 25, Gale Research, 1983. This entry provides excerpts from several critical essays, a brief biography, and the complete text of Samuel Beckett's play "Catastrophe," written for Vaclav Havel.

McGraw-Hill Encyclopedia of World Drama, Vol. 2, McGraw-Hill, 1984. In this brief entry, Paul I. Trensky provides comments about Havel's life and first three plays. He makes a very brief mention of each of Havel's later works.

Thomas J. Slater
Northwest Missouri State University

FRIEDRICH HEBBEL
1813-1863

Author's Chronology

Born March 18, 1813, Wesselburen, Germany; *1835* moves to Hamburg, begins formal studies; acquaintance with Elise Lensing; *1836* studies jurisprudence for a brief period at the University of Heidelberg; moves to Munich; *1838* death of his mother; *1839* returns on foot to Hamburg; acquaintance with Emma Schröder; in November Elise Lensing gives birth to son Max; *1842* first audience with King Christian VIII of Denmark; *1843* The king grants him a travel stipend; travels to Paris; death of son Max; *1844* travels in Italy; Elise Lensing gives birth to second son Ernst; *1845* moves to Vienna; *1846* marriage to actress Christine Enghaus; establishes reputation as a widely recognized playwright; *1863* appointed Private Librarian to Grand Duke of Weimar; various public honors; December 13, 1863 Friedrich Hebbel dies.

Author's Bibliography (selected)

Judith, 1841 (play); *Genoveva*, 1843 (play); *Maria Magdalena*, 1844 (play); *Herod and Mariamne*, 1850 (play); *Agnes Bernauer*, 1852 (play); *The Niebelungs*, 1862 (play).

The best translations of Hebbel's drama are: *Agnes Bernauer*, in *German Plays of the Nineteenth Century*. New York: Crofts, 1930; *Herod and Mariamne*, University of North Carolina Studies in Germanic Languages and Literatures No. 3, 1950; *Maria Magdalena*, in *The Modern Theatre*. New York: Macmillan, 1964 (also in *Masterpieces of Modern Theatre*. New York: Collier/Macmillan, 1967, 1975); *The Niebelungs*. London: A. Siegle, 1903.

Overview of Biographical Sources

The oldest biographical study about Hebbel is Emil Kuh's, *Biographie Friedrich Hebbels* (2 vols. Wien/Leipzig: Braumüller, 1877, 2nd ed. 1907). Because Kuh knew Hebbel personally, this book which combines the presentation of biographical facts with an evaluation of Hebbel's works is somewhat outdated and not entirely reliable. It is furthermore flawed by its uncritical admiration of Hebbel and by its flowery style. T.M. Campbell's *The Life and Works of Friedrich Hebbel* (Boston: The Gorham Press, 1919) also blends biography and analysis of Hebbel's plays. It is based on a careful scrutiny of Hebbel's diaries and letters (many of which were not yet published at the time the book was written). Special emphasis is placed on the role of women in Hebbel's works. The book is eminently readable and may still be regarded as a valuable biographical source. A useful biographical study which traces Hebbel's intellectual and artistic development is Hayo Matthiesen's *Friedrich Hebbel in Selbstzeugnissen und Bilddokumenten* (Hamburg: Rowohlt, 1970, untranslated). It contains many pictures, a chronological table, and a selected bibliography. The best and most recent biography of Hebbel written in English is Edna Purdie's *Friedrich Hebbel: A Study of his Life and Work* (Oxford: Oxford University Press, 1932; rpt. 1969).

Evaluation of Selected Biographies

Purdie, Edna, *Friedrich Hebbel: A Study of his Life and Work.* Oxford: Oxford University Press, 1932; rpt. 1969. An excellent and penetrating study by one of the foremost Hebbel scholars writing in English. The book offers both a full account of Hebbel's life and an in-depth analysis of his works. The last chapter deals with Hebbel's conception of the tragedy. Purdie focuses especially on the question of tragic guilt and cautions against the practice of interpreting the plays only in the light of Hebbel's metaphysical speculation.

Autobiographical Sources

Hebbel's diaries contain a wealth of autobiographical facts, comments about the genesis of his plays, explanatory remarks about his works, and many philosophical aphorisms. The diaries are available in the German critical Hebbel edition edited by R.M. Werner, *Sämtliche Werke. Historisch-kritische Ausgabe, Abt. 2: Tagebücher*, 4 vols. (Berlin: Behr, 1904 ff.; Centenary Edition, 1911 ff.). The diaries have also appeared in a recent reprint of the Centenary Edition: Berne: Lang, 1970. This centenary edition contains 1004 letters by Hebbel. For letters written by Hebbel also consult: Henry U. Gerlach, *Friedrich Hebbel: Briefe* (Heidelberg: Winter, 1975). Letters written to Hebbel can be found in the following German editions: Enzinger, Moriz and Elisabeth Bruck, eds., *Briefe an Friedrich Hebbel, Teil I: 1840-60* (Wien: Verlag der Österreichischen Akademie der Wissenschaften, 1973, Teil II: 1861-63; rpt. 1975). Part II contains a commentary, biographies of the correspondents, and an index. For letters both from and to Hebbel consult Henry U. Gerlach, *Briefe von und an Friedrich Hebbel* (Heidelberg: Winter, 1978).

Overview of Critical Sources

Hebbel's work has been studied by numerous scholars most of whom wrote in German, but there are also several important book-length studies in English. Among the more recent German studies the following ought to be mentioned: Herbert Kraft's *Poesie der Idee: die tragische Dichtung Friedrich Hebbels* (Tübingen: Niemeyer, 1971); Helmut Kreuzer's *Hebbel in neuer Sicht* (Stuttgart: Metzler, 1963). These are essays on the major plays, on the essence of tragedy, on Hebbel's religion, on tragic guilt. Anni Meetz's *Friedrich Hebbel* (Tübingen:

Metzler, 1962; 2nd ed. 1965) offers a concise presentation of biographical and bibliographical data plus brief critical analyses of his works. Benno von Wiese's *Die deutsche Tragödie von Lessing bis Hebbel* (Hamburg: Hoffmann & Campe, 1948) studies Hebbel's tragedies from the perspective of secularization and nihilism. Other standard sources are Wolfgang Wittkowski, *Der junge Hebbel: Zur Entstehung und zum Wesen der Tragödie Hebbels* (Berlin: de Gruyter, 1969) and Klaus Ziegler, *Mensch und Welt in der Tragödie Friedrich Hebbels* (Berlin, 1938; rpt. Darmstadt: Wissenschaftliche Buchgesellschaft, 1966). Ziegler's book marks a turning point in Hebbel scholarship since it shifts the focus to the text of the plays and away from Hebbel's own comments in the diaries and letters. More recently, though, the pendulum has swung back towards a greater measure of attention given to Hebbel's own dicta.

Evaluation of Selected Criticism

Flygt, Sten G., *Friedrich Hebbel's Conception of Movement in the Absolute and in History*. New York: AMS Press, 1966. Flygt studies Hebbel's thought about historical and social progress pointing out his oscillation between a progressive and a conservative stance.

———, *Friedrich Hebbel*. New York: Twayne, 1968. Offering a clear and concise overview of Hebbel's life and interpretations of his plays in the light of his philosophical ideas, Flygt intentionally avoids discussion of controversial issues. This book is valuable for the student who wishes to acquaint himself with Hebbel's work.

Garland, Mary, "Friedrich Hebbel," in *German Men of Letters*, Vol. I. London: Wolff, 1965, pp. 123-145. A condensed but excellent overview of Hebbel's literary achievement.

———, *Hebbel's Prose Tragedies: An Investigation of the Aesthetic Aspect of Hebbel's Dramatic Language*. Cambridge: Cambridge University Press, 1973. Combines the genetic approach with an analysis of the philosophical content of *Judith*, *Maria Magdalena*, and *Agnes Bernauer*. At the same time, the book offers a careful and penetrating study of the setting, of the central motifs, images, and themes in those plays.

Gerlach, U. Henry, *Hebbel as a critic of his own Works*. Göppingen: Kümmerle, 1972. The book's focus is deliberately narrow. It asks the question: to what extent can Hebbel's statements about his work (both evaluative and explanatory) be used to shed light on his plays? Relevant statements from Hebbel's diaries and letters are carefully checked against the texts of the plays to show that Hebbel's comments often correspond with the text and that they can indeed be used for a better understanding of the plays.

Oehler, William F. *Motivation in the Drama of Friedrich Hebbel*. Glencoe, IL: The Free Press, 1948. Focuses on the major characters in Hebbel's plays, their action, and its movivation. Hebbel's characters are viewed both as symbols (representing historical forces, the "Idea") and as realistic, psychologically motivated human beings. The book demonstrates convincingly that Hebbel succeeds in most instances in achieving a congruent blending of both symbolical and psychological motivation.

Other Sources

Bornstein, Paul, *Friedrich Hebbels Persönlichkeit: Gespräche, Urteile, Erinnerungen*. Berlin, 1924. Recollections and other statements about Hebbel by persons who knew the playwright.

Gerlach, U. Henry, *Hebbel-Bibliographie 1910-1970*. Heidelberg: Winter, 1970.

The *Hebbel-Jahrbuch* (1949/50 ff.) contains essays on Hebbel's work, documents, bibliographical essays, and reports about the annual meetings of the Hebbel Society (all in German).

Wütschke, H., *Hebbel-Bibliographie*. Berlin, 1910.

Christoph Eykman
Boston College

LILLIAN HELLMAN
1905-1984

Author's Chronology

Born June 20, 1905, in New Orleans to Max Bernard Hellman and Julia Newhouse Hellman; *1912* moves with family to New York and spends six months of year in New Orleans, attending school in both cities; *1922-1924* attends New York University; *1924-1932* works as manuscript reader at Horace Liveright; *1925* marries Arthur Kober; *1932* divorces Kober and begins life with Dashiell Hammett; *1934 The Children's Hour* opens to a long successful run; *1952* appears before the House Un-American Activities Committee; *1961* teaches at Harvard; *1969* publishes *An Unfinished Woman*, the first of three volumes of memoirs; dies on June 30, 1984.

Author's Bibliography

The Collected Plays, published in 1972 by Little, Brown and Co., is the definitive text of the eight original plays and four adaptations, with Hellman's revisions and emendations. The volume includes *The Children's Hour* (1934), *Days to Come* (1936), *The Little Foxes* (1939), *Watch on the Rhine* (1941), *The Searching Wind* (1944), *Another Part of the Forest* (1947), *Montserrat* (1950), *The Autumn Garden* (1951), *The Lark* (1955), *Candide* (1957), *Toys in the Attic* (1960), *My Mother, My Father, and Me* (1963). Her prose works include three volumes of memoirs: *An Unfinished Woman: A Memoir* (1969), *Pentimento: A Book of Portraits* (1973), and *Scoundrel Time* (1976). In 1980 she published a long short story, *Maybe: A Story*.

Overview of Biographical Sources

Critical material about Lillian Hellman's drama and prose frequently contains biographical information and speculation, probably because the person of Lillian Hellman looms almost as large as the canon of Lillian Hellman. Lillian Hellman's controversial life and convictions, from her alcoholic binges to her time with Hammett to her appearance before the House Committee on Un-American Activities, have prompted critics to view the morality of her plays through the morality of her life. The first book-length biography, Richard Moody's *Lillian Hellman: Playwright* (1972) addresses this relationship as does Doris Falk's book *Lillian Hellman* (1978). Other books, including Katherine Lederer's *Lillian Hellman* (1979), contain biographical information which explores the relationship between Hellman's life and works while focusing on the works themselves.

Evaluation of Selected Biographies

Falk, Doris V. *Lillian Hellman*. New York: Frederick Ungar, 1978. A biography that relies upon Hellman's works and draws from interviews and Hellman's memoirs, this book summarizes the plays and discusses them briefly. Falk also includes chapters on Hellman's three autobiographical volumes.

Lederer, Katherine, *Lillian Hellman*. Boston: Twayne, 1979. Like Falk, Katherine Lederer begins her book with a chapter that is exclusively biographical and then proceeds to examine, chronologically, Hellman's plays and nonfiction. A major difference between these two books, however, is Lederer's critical stance: she views Hellman as an ironist and evaluates her works according to their success as ironic visions.

Moody, Richard, *Lillian Hellman, Playwright*. New York: Pegasus, Bobbs-Merrill, 1972. Most of the biographical information in this book comes from Hellman's memoir, *An Unfinished Woman*, which limits the value of this first book-length study. In addition to the material about Hellman, the volume includes analyses of manuscript versions of the plays and details about their Broadway productions.

Autobiographical Sources

Lillian Hellman's three volumes of autobiography provide a rich source of information about her as a person and as a playwright. *An Unfinished Woman: A Memoir* (Boston: Little, Brown, 1969), which won the National Book Award, introduces Hellman's family and early influences. *Pentimento: A Book of Portraits* (Boston: Little, Brown, 1973) covers some of the same territory as the earlier volume but devotes more attention to Hellman's career as a dramatist. Commenting on each play chronologically, Hellman has a chapter in this memoir entitled "Theater" in which she writes of her instinct as a playwright. The last autobiographical work, *Scoundrel Time* (Boston: Little, Brown, 1976), is the most limited in focus and also the most controversial, for it explores Hellman's response to the McCarthy witchhunt trials, her moral position in the late 1940s and 1950s, and connections she sees between those times and the era of Vietnam and Watergate.

Overview of Critical Sources

There are not as many full-length studies of Hellman's plays as one might expect, and the scholarship has alternated between scathing criticism and almost unqualified praise. The negative evaluations frequently criticize the plays as being too well-made or melodramatic. Hellman herself responds to these charges in her introduction to *Six Plays* (1960), admitting that she is "a moral writer, often too moral a writer." This admission has, in turn, prompted critics to examine her technique and success as a playwright in light of her moral stance. However her work is finally evaluated, most critics agree that Lillian Hellman is an important American playwright, not only because she is one of the few women to attain prominence but also because she was the country's first important dramatist of the 1930s.

Evaluation of Selected Criticism

Adler, Jacob H. *Lillian Hellman—Southern Writers Series*, Number 4. Austin, TX: Steck, Vaughan, 1969. A brief pamphlet, this study includes biographical information, comments on Hellman's plays, and a lengthy discussion of *The Children's Hour*.

Downer, Alan S. *Fifty Years of American Drama 1900-1950*. Chicago: Henry Regnery, 1951, pp. 60-61, 139-141. In a brief and general discussion of Hellman's plays, Downer criticizes the structure of her dramas while praising *The Autumn Garden* as "the most promising play of the year."

Heilman, R. B. *The Iceman, the Arsonist and the Troubled Agent*. Seattle: University of Washington, 1973. In the section "Dramas of Money," Heilman discusses *The Little Foxes*.

Holmin, Lorena Ross, *The Dramatic Works of Lillian Hellman*. Stockholm: Acta Universitatis Upsaliensis, Studia Anglistica Upsaliensis, 1973. Holmin's book considers Hellman's plays in detail, analyzing characterization, plot, and dialogue. She also includes biographical notes about Hellman, production information about the plays, a list of productions in Nordic countries, and a bibliography of works by and about Hellman.

Weales, Gerald, *American Drama Since World War II*. New York: Harcourt, Brace, and World, 1962, pp. 89-92, 151-152. In his comments about Hellman's dramas, Weales shows the connections between Hellman's early and later plays.

Other Sources

Bills, Steven H. *Lillian Hellman: An Annotated Bibliography*. New York & London: Garland, 1979. This checklist is particularly useful because of its division into eight sections: biographical material; interviews, previews, news concerning Hellman's plays and books; reviews of Hellman's plays; scholarly articles, books, and surveys of Hellman's works; reviews of drama in book form; reviews of Hellman screenplays; reviews of Hellman autobiographies; and graduate studies. The annotations are concise and precise.

Estrin, Mark, *Lillian Hellman Plays, Films, Memoirs: A Reference Guide*. Boston: G. K. Hall, 1980. Chronologically arranged from 1934 through 1979, this is a bibliographical record of writings about Hellman's life and work. The introduction is an especially helpful overview of the critical reception her work has received.

Modern World Drama. New York: E.P. Dutton, 1972, pp. 350-351. Though necessarily brief, the entry in this volume provides both biographical and critical information, succinctly evaluating Hellman's plays and techniques.

Riordan, Mary M. *Lillian Hellman: A Bibliography, 1926-1978*. Like Bills' checklist, this bibliography is arranged, not chronologically, but according to the type of work written by and about Lillian Hellman. Some citations are not annotated, and others are too brief or vague to be particularly helpful.

Rogers, Katharine, "Lillian Hellman," in *American Women Writers*. New York: Frederick Ungar, 1979, pp. 303-305. A brief but useful overview of Hellman's prose and drama, as well as a bibliography of primary and secondary sources.

Triesch, Manfred, ed. *The Lillian Hellman Collection at the University of Texas*. Austin: The University of Texas, 1966. Despite some inaccuracies, this is a useful description of the collection at the University of Texas which includes autographed manuscripts and typescripts, contributions, and letters. The volume also lists secondary sources about Lillian Hellman.

Marjorie Smelstor
The University of Texas at San Antonio

THOMAS HEYWOOD
1572/1575-1641

Author's Chronology

Born 1572-1575, Lincolnshire, England; *1589* entered Emmanuel College, Cambridge; *1593* hired by Henslowe as an actor for Admiral's Men; *1599* first printed work, *The Seige of London*, appeared; *1601* joins Worcester's Men; *1603* marries Ann Butler; *1603* writes his masterpiece, *A Woman Kilde with Kindness*; *1609* publishes *Troia Britannica*; *1612* publishes *An Apology for Actors*; *1619* joins Lady Elizabeth's Men; *1624* publishes *Gunaikeion or Nine Books of Various History Concerning Women*; 1625 joins Queen Henrietta's Company; *1631* begins writing city pageants; *1632* marries Jane Span; *1636* publishes "Curtain Lecture"; 1641 dies, London, England.

Author's Bibliography (selected)

The Foure Prentices of London, c. 1594; *Edward IV, Parts I and II*, 1599; *A Woman Kilde with Kindness*, 1603; *The Wise Woman of Hogdsdon*, c. 1604; *Fortune by Land and Sea*, c. 1607; *The Fair Maid of the West: Or, A Girl Worth Gold, Part I*, before 1610; *Part II*, c. 1630; *An Apology for Actors*, 1612; *Gunaikeion*, 1624; *The Captives: Or, The Lost Recovered*, 1634; *The English Traveller*, c. 1627; *England's Elizabeth*, 1631; *The Late Lancashire Witches*, 1634; *The Life of Merlin, Surnamed Ambrosius*, 1641.

Overview of Biographical Sources

Although Thomas Heywood was one of the most prolific dramatists of the English Renaissance theatre who also wrote numerous other works of prose and poetry, only one book-length biographical study of this important figure exists, that being Arthur Melville Clark's *Thomas Heywood: Playwright and Miscellanist* (1931). Other studies of Heywood do include biographical sketches, especially Barbara Baines' *Thomas Heywood* (1984) which is a superior and much needed addition to the scholarly material on this interesting Renaissance figure. Otherwise, the student of Heywood must turn to the specialized reference volumes on English drama. For detailed biographical study, Clark's volume remains the standard, however, while a more limited investigation would be well served by Baines' text.

Evaluation of Selected Biographies

Baines, Barbara J. *Thomas Heywood*. Boston: Twayne, 1984. Baines' brief biographical sketch of Thomas Heywood serves one distinct purpose. It places Heywood's voluminous literary output into a chronological order that includes as well the major events of his professional life. Otherwise, the sketch adds nothing to that included in Clark's volume and is in fact too limited to provide an understanding of Heywood's life.

Clark, Herman Melville, *Thomas Heywood: Playwright and Miscellanist*. Oxford: Basil Blackwell, 1931. Clark cites the purpose of his study in the Preface: "I have tried to reconstruct the life of Thomas Heywood more fully than has been done before, and to correct many old errors about him and about his work." To that end, Clark clarifies such matters as Heywood's relationship with other writers, the dating of his works, works improperly attributed to him, his stage activities, and his satire of the Puritans. An extremely well-written study, Clark's biography interweaves significant events in Heywood's life and his literary career. The study looks closely at Heywood's apprenticeship and journeyman years, his years of success, and that final period of his life when he turned his hand to pageants and moral prose tracts. The final chapter presents a sober but helpful evaluation of Heywood's achievements.

Autobiographical Sources
Heywood left no autobiographical material. However, many of his literary works seem to have an autobiographical orientation. His *Apology for Actors* is no doubt a reflection of his life in the theatre and his attitude about his profession. His later conservative prose tracts such as "Curtain Lecture" reflect to some extent the moral direction of his thought, shaped as early in life as during his days at Emmanuel College, Cambridge, a stronghold of Puritan thinking.

Overview of Critical Sources
For such a prolific playwright, Heywood has not received the attention one might imagine. Clark's *Thomas Heywood: Playwright and Miscellanist* does give significant account of the dramatist's plays. The most recent study to date is Baines' *Thomas Heywood* which is a much needed study. It gives a more detailed and satisfactory account of the major contributions to English Renaissance drama than does Otelia Cromwell's *Thomas Heywood: A Study in the Elizabethan Drama of Everyday Life* (1928; rpt. 1969) or Mowbry Velte's *The Bourgeois Elements in the Dramas of Thomas Heywood* (1966).

Evaluation of Selected Criticism
Baines, Barbara J. *Thomas Heywood*. Boston: Twayne, 1984. The especial merit of this study is that it treats essentially the entire canon of Heywood's dramas, not just a few major works, *A Woman Kilde with Kindness* in particular. Baines categorizes Heywood's plays in greater detail than has been done before and reviews the characteristics that each group demonstrates. The result is that the student of

Heywood's work begins to see the variety of modes which he controlled and the extent to which his work responded to the many faceted society, thus literary tastes, of his day.

Cromwell, Otelia, *Thomas Heywood: A Study in the Elizabethan Drama of Everyday Life*. Hamden, CT: Archon Books, rpt. 1969. As do most studies of Heywood, this work focuses its attention on the domestic elements in his plays. In particular, Cromwell seems to feel that because Heywood chose to give literary treatment to everyday matters, that his skills were equally pedestrian. The work does not, therefore, recognize the accomplishments of Heywood or his dramatic instincts.

Velte, Mowbray, *The Bourgeois Elements in the Dramas of Thomas Heywood*. New York: Haskell House, 1966. Velte's analysis of the Heywood canon is orthodox, focusing specifically on him as a writer of domestic drama. Although the study does classify the plays and discuss them first as histories, romances, classical plays, and plays of contemporary life, the final chapter seeks the common thread that runs throughout, that being Heywood's bourgeois morality. The general thesis does not, therefore, suggest the diversity of Heywood's interests or the range of his skill.

Other Sources

Boas, Frederick S. *Thomas Heywood*. New York: Phaeton Press, 1975. Treats Heywood's poetry and prose.

Eliot, T. S. *Elizabethan Essays*. New York: Haskell House, 1964. An excellent evaluation of Heywood's dramatic skills.

Grivelet, Michel, *Thomas Heywood et le Drame Domestique Elizabethan*. Paris: Didiet, 1957. Excellent analysis of selected plays with appendix material on the facts of Heywood's career.

Parrott, Thomas Marc and Robert Hamilton Ball, *A Short View of Elizabethan Drama*. New York: Charles Scribner's Sons, 1943. General review of Heywood's contributions to Elizabethan theatre.

Selected Dictionaries and Encyclopedias

A Biography Chronicle of the English Drama, Burt Franklin, 1891. Short biographical sketch.

Critical Survey of Drama, Salem Press, 1985. Review of selected plays.

Critical Survey of Poetry, Salem Press, 1983. Excellent analysis of Heywood's narrative poetry.

Dictionary of National Biography, Oxford University Press, 1917. Short biographical sketch.

Great Writers of the English Language, St. Martin's Press, 1979. Primarily helpful as a bibliographical source.

Gerald W. Morton
Auburn University
Montgomery

HUGO VON HOFMANNSTHAL
1874-1929

Author's Chronology

Born Hugo Laurenz August Hofmann Edler von Hofmannsthal on 1 February 1874 in Vienna, to Doctor of Law Hugo von Hofmannsthal and his wife Anna Maria, formerly Fohleutner; wrote his first poems at age 16 (pseudonyms: Theophil Morren, Loris, Loris Melikow); studies Law, then Romance Languages and Literatures with PhD 1898; *1901* marries Gertrud Schlesinger; *1902* daughter Christiane born; *1903* son Franz born; occasional European travels; *1906* son Raimund born, beginning of collaboration with composer Richard Strauss; *1914-1917* serves in Austrian War Ministry, travels on secret diplomatic missions; *1917* founding of Salzburg Festival; *13 July 1929* son Franz commits suicide; 15 July 1929 Hugo von Hofmannsthal dies of a cerebral hemorrhage in Rodaun near Vienna.

Author's Bibliography

Hofmannsthal gained recognition first as a poetic wunderkind, as accomplished poets were astounded by the polished verses of this precocious teenager. But a language crisis, expounded in 1902 by means of "A Letter" purportedly written by Lord Chandos, halted all poetic production and led Hofmannsthal to the world of the stage. Since that time his dramatical development can be traced from early lyrical playlets like *Death and the Fool*, 1900, tr. 1913, later libretti such as *Electra*, 1904, tr. 1908 and *The Cavalier of the Rose*, 1911, tr. 1912, to the festival plays *Everyman*, 1911, tr. 1917 and *The Salzburg Great Theatre of the World*, 1922, tr. 1963. Fifteen volumes of collected works appeared in German between 1946 and 1960 as his *Gesammelte Werke*, with nearly nine volumes devoted to lyrical plays, comedies, and dramas. While Hofmannsthal's works can be found in numerous anthologies, translations of separate titles are also currently available. The standard collection of Hofmannsthal's writings in English was published under the auspices of the Bollingen Series and the Princeton University Press, edited by Michael Hamburger; appearing as *Selected Writings*, Volume II presents Poems & Verse Plays (1961), while Volume III offers Selected Plays & Libretti (1963).

Overview of Biographical Sources

Hofmannsthal occupies a precarious position in the history of German drama. On the one hand he has been castigated for being an aesthetic recluse, an apolitical man, thus an anachronism in the turmoil of modern European developments; on the other, he is defended as an idealist, misunderstood and unrecognized by his public—all this in the face of Hofmannsthal's enduring popularity: his libretti are

331

among the most performed in all of opera, and his plays remain the backbone of the internationally acclaimed Salzburg Festival. Thus it is understandable that his person has become the object of intense scrutiny, with almost a dozen biographies extant in German. An extensive, scholarly, and credible biography does not, however, exist in English. The curious reader would do well to peruse both of the brief works listed below, for in style they are complementary. Nevertheless, both also share the same weakness: in their brevity they do not attempt to familiarize the reader with the considerable critical literature surrounding their subject.

Evaluation of Selected Biographies

Bangerter, Lowell A. *Hugo von Hofmannsthal*. New York: Frederick Ungar, 1977. A chronology and initial chapter provide basic details concerning Hofmannsthal's life. Succeeding chapters illuminate the developments in his art, highlighting his early poetic fame, the linguistic "crisis" at the turn of the century, and the extended apprenticeship to the stage which resulted in dramatic and operatic successes in later years. Bangerter charts as well the philosophical transformations, depicting the early influence of Stefen George with his aesthetic elite and the mature collaboration with Richard Strauss on significant works in the European cultural tradition. The book concludes with end notes and a bibliography, useful mainly for its list of English translations; since Bangerter does not attempt a summary of Hofmannsthal scholarship-to-date, the reader may be disappointed in this regard. Concise and well-ordered, this brief volume may be considered the standard introduction in English to Hofmannsthal and his works.

Hammelmann, H.A. *Hugo von Hofmannsthal*. New Haven: Yale University Press, 1957. Though not as clearly organized as Bangerter's biography, this book is nevertheless of great value for its refreshing commentary and lucid style. Eschewing a chronological presentation, the author writes authoritatively about Hofmannsthal's milieu and his life, proferring an "inner biography" rather than one defined by names, places, and dates; using correspondence and diary entries, Hammelmann recreates the artist's experiences and resulting insights. The dramatic works themselves are covered succinctly. Though a chronology, list of Hofmannsthal's works, and English translations are appended, their cursory nature renders them useless.

Autobiographical Sources

Fortunately, a great amount of autobiographical material exists and has been made public in the original German. His collected works include one volume of *Aufzeichnungen* or "Notebooks," which complement various editions of diaries, essays and speeches, and letters. Indeed, Hugo von Hofmannsthal was a prolific letter-writer, as witnessed by nearly twenty separate correspondences with such partners as Stefan George, Arthur Schnitzler, and Richard Strauss. This last-named correspondence, one of the most extensive and significant, is available in English under the title *A Working Friendship: The Correspondence between Richard Strauss and Hugo von Hofmannsthal*, tr. Hanns Hammelmann & Ewald Osers (New York: Random House, 1961). These letters (over 530 pages in the present edition) mirror the development of their collaboration over nearly 25 years in six major operas, including *Electra*, *The Cavalier of the Rose*, *The Woman without a Shadow*, and others. Taken in their totality, the epistles illuminate the clash of personalities, Hofmannsthal's ideas and ideals, his perseverence in the face of adversity—often stemming from Strauss—and are useful for an in-depth understanding of the poet and his aesthetic principles.

Overview of Critical Sources

Though the great bulk and variety of Hofmannsthal criticism is written in German, sufficient literature in the form of books and articles exists in English. The following selection offers a good impression of the variety and extent of present Hofmannsthal criticism, centering on such recurring themes as the artist's role in society (often recast as the interrelationship between language and reality), external influences on Hofmannsthal's works, his language "crisis," and further development into the areas of opera and film. Curiously, there seems to be general agreement on the interpretation of Hofmannsthal's works; since a canon has been established, only the "why" and "how" appear to be of interest.

Evaluation of Selected Criticism

Broch, Hermann, *Hugo von Hofmannsthal and his Time: The European Imagination, 1860-1920*. tr. Michael P. Steinberg. Chicago: University of Chicago Press, 1984. This study by the famous Austrian novelist was written between 1947 and 1950 as "a major synthetic examination of the 'end' of the European world—its politics, its art, and, above all, its values," according to Steinberg. In his intellectual history of Europe, Broch delineates the relationship between art and ethics, portraying Hofmannsthal as an exemplary aesthete who ultimately rejects aestheticism. This brilliant, vital essay will prove more useful in comprehending Hofmannsthal and his time than in elucidating the dramatic works themselves.

Coghlan, Brian, *Hofmannsthal's Festival Dramas*. Cambridge: Cambridge University Press, 1964. This seminal study concentrates on the three plays written specifically for the Salzberg Festival: *Everyman*, *The Great World Theatre*, and *The Tower*. Background and plot, structure and meaning are thoroughly discussed, with special emphasis on the enigmatic fragment of *The Tower*. Coghlan masterfully plots the significance of these plays for Hofmannsthal's development as a dramatist, but also for his ethical concerns as a "Kulturpolitiker." This volume will prove invaluable for serious students of Hofmannsthal's mature dramatic art.

Hamburger, Michael, *Hofmannsthal: Three Essays*. Bollingen Series. Princeton: Princeton University Press, 1971. This volume brings together three valuable essays which had previously been published separately. The first details the earliest phase of Hofmannsthal's development discussing "Poems and Verse Plays." "Plays and Libretti" traces his abrupt transition to drama and to the collaboration with Richard Strauss. The final essay, a revised version of the piece appearing in Norman's book (below), "Hofmannsthal's Debt to the English-speaking World," attempts to correct the prevailing view that the dramatist wrote mainly from Catholic-Baroque influences emanating from European traditions. This book represents a well-written, authoritative critique, invaluable as a basic introduction.

Norman, F. ed. *Hofmannsthal: Studies in Commemoration*. London: University of London, 1963. Of the six essays reproduced here, three may prove useful in a consideration of the dramatic works. An essay by J.B. Bednall describes the change in Hofmannsthal's use of language "From High Language to Dialect" in the transition from poetry to stage works such as the comedies and lyrical plays. Considering Hofmannsthal more than just "a good European," Michael Hamburger traces the considerable impact of English literature and culture on the Austrian's works. The volume concludes with a bibliography of Hofmannsthal in England and America, complete through 1961, including translations and critical literature.

Sondrup, Steven P. *Hofmannsthal and the French Symbolist Tradition*. Bern: Herbert Lang, 1976. Concentrating on Hofmannsthal's early works, i.e., those written between 1890 and 1900, Sondrup illuminates the writer's "interest in and application of symbolist techniques and conventions." Following introductory chapters on French symbolism and symbolism in Vienna in the 1890s, Sondrup devotes the final section of this book to the dramatic works conceived during the period; he concludes that despite formalistic and stylistic affinities, Hofmannsthal's moral concerns "stand in marked contrast to the posture of the French symbolists." A more recent volume by Thomas A. Kovach, entitled *Hofmannsthal and Symbolism: Art and Life in the Work of a Modern Poet* (New York: Peter Lang, 1985), posits this attitude as a life-long concern, not specifically limited to the early works.

Yuill, W.E. and Howe, Patricia, eds. *Hugo von Hofmannsthal: Commemorative Essays*. London: University of London, 1981. Of the thirteen symposium papers reprinted here, roughly half will be of interest to students of Hofmannsthal's drama. Relationships between Hofmannsthal and Wilde, Musset, and France are explored. While admitting the writer's greatness in poetry and drama, D.E. Jenkinson demonstrates the romantic-conservative traits in "Hofmannsthal's Social and Political Attitudes" which alienated him from modern life. Yet another essay comments on the sources of the opera librettos, while two other critics discuss Hofmannsthal's comedy, maintaining its dependence on production aspects such as the staging and direction; in addition, the "Theatrum mundi" is seen as conservative and anachronistic in the 20th century when compared with the criticism of Hofmannsthal's contemporary, Karl Kraus.

Other Sources

Bennett, Benjamin, "Hofmannsthal's Return," in *Germanic Review*, 51 (1976): 28-40. Bennett investigates Hofmannsthal's language crisis, estrangement from poetry, and "return" to literary production after the Chandos-letter. Following years of perceived isolation, the Austrian ultimately discovered a social function for his literature.

Clark, Georgina A. "Max Reinhardt and the Genesis of Hugo von Hofmannsthal's *Der Turm*," in *Modern Austrian Literature*, 17 (1984): 1-32. This essay highlights Hofmannsthal's relationship with Reinhardt, Germany's leading theatre director, from 1903 to Hofmannsthal's death in 1929. Their friendship and mutual respect is especially evident in the development of the stage version of Hofmannsthal's last play, *The Tower*.

Daviau, Donald G. and Buelow, George J. *The 'Ariadne auf Naxos' of Hugo von Hofmannsthal and Richard Strauss*. Chapel Hill: University of North Carolina Press, 1975. This nearly 300-page collaborative effort of a Germanist and musicologist offers rare insights into the genesis of the first operatic effort by Hofmannsthal and Strauss. Questions of production and interpretation, revisions, illustrations, and many other facets of the libretto and score are authoritatively clarified by Daviau and Buelow.

Faber, Marion, "Hofmannsthal and the Film," in *German Life & Letters*, 32 (1979): 187-195. Faber's stimulating article surveys Hofmannsthal's essay on film and the three screenplays dating from 1913 to 1926. His understanding of and affinity for this modern medium is apparent; for Hofmannsthal silent film possessed a "dream nature" which was "pre-rational" or non-intellectual.

Mommsen, Katharina, "Hofmannsthal's Theatrical Work as His Life's Calling," in *Modern Austrian Literature*, 28 (1985): 3-20. This scholar observes the development in Hofmannsthal's writing, as he rejected the poetic expression of his youth for a language more easily comprehended by the theatre public of his day. Ironically, as Mommsen points out, his mature efforts also were misunderstood or unrecognized by his contemporaries.

Schorske, Carl E. *"Politics and the Psyche in Fin de siècle*. Vienna: Schnitzler and Hofmannsthal," in *American Historical Review*, LXVI (1960-61): 930-946. During the cultural crisis at the turn of the century, Austrian intellectuals were preoccupied with "the nature of the individual in a disintegrating society," as Schorske writes; the historian is knowledgable and provocative in describing the impact of socio-political events on these two major Austrian figures. According to

Schorske, Schnitzler depicted the cultural decay from a moral-scientific tradition, resulting in a pessimistic world-view, while Hofmannsthal sought to revitalize his society through art and is thus frequently labeled an anachronism.

Schwarz, Egon, "Hofmannsthal and the Problem of Reality," in *Wisconsin Studies in Contemporary Literature*, 8 (1967): 484-504. Schwarz here examines one of the major criticisms of Hofmannsthal's aesthetics; i.e., that they are not relevant to the chaos that is life in the modern world. Yet according to Schwarz, in Hofmannsthal's works mystical traditions of the Catholic Baroque are to be reconciled with the demands of contemporary reality. For this dramatist eternal values did exist, and social or political reality "is meant to be regarded as a task" with which each individual must become involved.

Winkler, Michael, "How to Write Hofmannsthal's Life: Annals, Biography of his Work, or the Poet in his Time?" in *Modern Austrian Literature*, 7 (1974): 113-116. An interesting essay for the knowledgable reader, Winkler outlines the basic difficulties inherent in writing Hofmannsthal's biography. Here the reader is reminded of the conflicting views of the man and his work, as mentioned in the "Overview of Biographical Sources" above.

Todd C. Hanlin
University of Arkansas

VICTOR HUGO
1802-1885

Author's Chronology

Born 26 February, 1802, in Besançon, France, third son of a career officer in Napoleon's army; *1822* publishes first collection of poems, *Odes*, for which he is awarded a pension by the king, and marries Adèle Foucher after a three-year engagement; *1827* publishes a play, *Cromwell*, the preface to which is adopted as the manifesto of the Romantic movement, of which Hugo was promptly declared the leader; *1830* the triumph of Hugo's play *Hernani*, with its unconventional structure, makes the Romantic movement the dominant force in the Paris literary scene; *1848-1851* active in politics, elected Deputy to the Constituent Assembly of the Republic, he flees into exile (Belgium, then the Channel Islands) when Napoleon III becomes Emperor; *1870* returns from exile to Paris in September upon the surrender of Napoleon III to the Prussians; *1885* Hugo's death in May is the occasion for an unprecendented State funeral.

Author's Bibliography

Although principally celebrated as a poet and novelist, Hugo used his writings for the theatre as a means of publicity, to extend the influence of the Romantic movement. His first important play, *Hernani* (1830, tr. 1830) caused a near-riot on its opening night but marked the triumph of the Romantic aesthetic. Later that decade, he published *Le Roi s'amuse* (1832) which became the basis for Verdi's opera *Rigoletto*, and *Ruy Blas* (1838, tr. 1850), regarded as his finest work for the theatre. The failure of his play *Les Burgraves* (1843) ended Hugo's active role in the theatre, and is thought also to mark the end of the Romantic movement's domination of the Paris literary world. During the 1860's Hugo returned to the dramatic form, writing a small group of plays intended to be read but not acted, and eventually published under the title *Théâtre en liberté*. The most reliable edition of Hugo's collected drama is the two-volume *Théâtre complet* which is part of the Pléïade edition of Hugo's complete works, published by Gallimard (1963-64).

Overview of Biographical and Autobiographical Sources

Victor Hugo never himself attempted to record his exceptionally long and full life as a writer and public figure. Instead of an autobiography, there are only autobiographical fragments, in the form of diaries, private notebooks, and some personalized journalism collected under the title *Choses vues* (*Things Seen*), none of which covers any extended period of his life in detail. His voluminous correspondence must be consulted in scattered collections, there being no really complete edition of all the extant letters. His poetry, often highly personal, is a source of autobiographical information but must be used with caution because Hugo was known to put poetic effect ahead of truth even in his most subjective writings. Because the information available from his own hand is so piecemeal and questionable, and because his career was so active and so long, and the public record so diffuse, the problems of a full-dress and comprehensive biography have always seemed daunting, and the task has rarely been attempted. Indeed, except for the massively-researched biography published by André Maurois in 1954, no account of Hugo's life has claimed the status of a complete biography. Each has instead chosen to emphasize one aspect of the life—his literary career, his public role, his turbulent private life—and given the rest minimal attention. Moreover, a truly complete and accurate biography, even if desirable, may never be possible because of the absence, or unreliability, of documentation for so many events. Even the Maurois biography, which is still the best available, was forced to be speculative, rather than authoritative, on many matters.

Evaluation of Selected Biographies

Edwards, Samuel, *Victor Hugo: A Tumultous Life*. New York: David McKay Co., 1971. This popular biography emphasizes the personal over the political or artistic aspects, and makes a fairly exciting narrative of the poet's existence. The writing is somewhat highly charged and overly dramatic at times, but it is never dull.

Grant, Elliott M. *The Career of Victor Hugo*. Cambridge: Harvard University Press, 1945. Clear, and well-researched, this scholarly biography is entirely dependable as to the facts, but it is deliberately limited to an account of Hugo's literary career. The details of his private family life are not given, except as those directly influenced Hugo's creative writings. The style is precise, straightforward and factual. For reliable information on Hugo's life as a writer, this biography remains the best source to consult.

Josephson, Matthew, *Victor Hugo: A Realistic Biography of the Great Romantic*. Garden City, NJ: Doubleday, Doran and Co., 1942. This substantial biography, intended for the general reader, focuses primarily on Hugo's public actions, both in the literary and the political domains, and makes a serious effort to recreate the color and atmosphere of the Paris in which these events took place. The author's highly readable style makes this biography pleasant reading, but his lack of advanced training in French studies makes it less than fully authoritative.

Maurois, André, *Olympio: The Life of Victor Hugo*. tr. Gerard Hopkins. New York: Harper and Brothers, 1956. Maurois is the justifiably renowned biographer of a number of the outstanding English and French writers of the Romantic era, and his account of Hugo's life is one of his best. The research has been painstaking and thorough, and the author's background knowledge of the Parisian literary world is extensive. The intense writing style is a great help to the reader who might otherwise get bogged down in the intricacies of the complex and varied activities in which Hugo was involved all his life. As always in Maurois, the fundamental approach to his subject is through a subtle and penetrating analysis of his psychology as a creative artist. In his Hugo biography, Maurois achieves the best balance available between the needs of the scholar and the interests of the general reader.

Richardson, Joanna, *Victor Hugo*. New York: St. Martin's Press, 1976. The most recent attempt to tame the Hugolian jungle into an orderly biography, this volume takes certain well-known events, such as the "battle" of *Hernani*, more or less for granted and avoids retelling them in detail as unnecessary. The biographical effort here is concentrated instead on seizing the essence of the writer, at each major phase of his life, as the titles of the three-part work indicate: "The Man," "The Prophet," "The Legend." Much of the standard material of biography is sacrificed in the process, but a pleasantly readable style and responsible, well-informed research yield a satisfactory narrative of the essential events of Hugo's life in just three hundred pages, and accomplish the author's stated objective of producing "a comprehensive account of Hugo's life and work, in the context of his times," in order to explain why Hugo was "the dominant figure in nineteenth-century French literature."

Overview of Critical Sources

The accumulated scholarship on Victor Hugo is now tremendous in volume, in spite of the fact that, for at least a generation in the mid-twentieth century, Hugo's works were out of favor, with academic critics especially, even in France. Since 1960, interest in Hugo has revived strongly, but the bulk of the attention has gone to the poetry of his mature years, and most recently, to his novels. On the whole, Hugo's drama has received comparatively little attention as a separate body of work. A characteristic of all Hugo scholarship has been its tendency to be narrowly analytical, focused on individual poems, or specific themes or images. Synthesizing studies have been rare, perhaps because the copiousness and variety of his literary production discourages attempts to find unity or patterned coherence therein. The paucity of work on his dramas, however, whether analysis or synthesis, seems to be based more on the perception that his plays were historically important but of mediocre artistic quality.

Evaluation of Selected Criticism

Affron, Charles, *A Stage for Poets*. Studies in the Theatre of Hugo and Musset. Princeton: Princeton University Press, 1971. This collection of essays discusses the poetic elements in the theatrical writing of two Romantics who were primarily renowned for their poetry. Hugo's dramas are discussed in chapters 2, 3, and 4.

Analyses of two plays are offered: *Hernani* and *Les Burgraves*, with particular attention to the way time is handled, and to the dramatic uses of poetic diction. Chapter 4 offers one of the few available commentaries on Hugo's late closet dramas, *Théâtre en liberté*, singling out *Torquemada* and *Mangeront-ils?* as the most worthy of analysis.

Howarth, W.D. *Sublime and Grotesque*. A Study of French Romantic Drama. London: G.G. Harrap, 1975. A general survey and evaluation of Romantic drama in France, this study gives appropriate pride of place to Hugo's contributions, and his key role in formulating its aesthetic principles and conquering the public for this new style of theatre. All of chapters 5 and 7 are devoted to an excellent summary of Hugo's achievements, both in verse drama and plays in prose, organized around Hugo's characteristic love of juxtaposing sublime and grotesque elements, because he believed such antitheses to have special dramatic power.

Pendell, William D. *Victor Hugo's Acted Dramas and the Contemporary Press*. Baltimore: The Johns Hopkins Press, 1947. A doctoral dissertation, in somewhat ponderous prose, this study does not discuss the individual plays, but does give a scrupulously fair and careful account of the contemporary critical reaction to each of Hugo's plays that had a public performance.

Other Sources

Doyle, Ruth L. *Victor Hugo's Drama: An Annotated Bibliography, 1900-1980*. Westport, CT: Greenwood Press, 1981. The best bibliographical source available, because it is devoted exclusively to Hugo as dramatist.

Grant, Elliott M. *Victor Hugo: A Select and Critical Bibliography*. Chapel Hill: University of North Carolina Press, 1967. Comprehensive in scope, sound and well-informed selection and evaluation of bibliographical items.

Houston, John Porter, *Victor Hugo*. Boston: Twayne, 1974. A basic "life and works" study, in the Twayne format, but done with care and readably written. The drama, however, gets little detailed analysis because of space limitations.

Wren, Keith, *Hugo: "Hernani" and "Ruy Blas"*. (Critical Guides to French Literature, No. 14). London: Grant and Cutler, 1982. A guide to the critical literature on Hugo's two best plays.

Murray Sachs
Brandeis University

HENRIK IBSEN
1828-1906

Author's Chronology

Born March 20, 1828, Skein, Norway to Knud and Marichen Ibsen; *1835* family suffers financial ruin; *1843* leaves school, confirmed in the church; *1844* departs for Grimstad where he is apprenticed to an apothecary; *1846* begets illegitimate son by a servant girl; *1848* inspired by European revolutions, espouses republicanism as the only form of government; *1850 Catiline* published, moves to Christiania (Oslo) to prepare for entrance examination to the university, meets Bjørnstjerne Bjørnson, fails to matriculate but attends some classes; *1851 edits student magazine, writes on dramatic and political topics; 1852* takes position as stage manager at National Theater in Bergen, travels to Denmark and Germany to study the theater; *1853 Saint John's Night* fails on the Bergen stage; *1853* falls in love with Rikke Holst but is rejected by her father; *1856* meets Suzannah Thoresen; *1857* appointed artistic director at the Norwegian Theater in Christiania; *1858* marries Suzannah Thoresen; *1859* establishes The Norwegian Society with Bjørnson; son Sigurd is born; associates with The Learned Holland; *1862 Love's Comedy* published; *1864* after failure of the Norwegian Theater and dismayed by Norwegian politics takes up residence in Rome; *1866* publication of *Brand* relieves financial straits; *1867 Peer Gynt* published; *1868* settles in Dresden; *1869* visits Sweden, represents Norway at opening of Suez Canal; *1870* visits Copenhagan; *1871 Poems* published; 1875 moves to Munich; *1877* receives honorary doctorate from Uppsala University; *The Pillars of Society* published; *1878* moves to Rome; *1879* publication of *A Doll's House* brings international celebrity; *1881* scandal caused by publication of *Ghosts*; *1884 The Wild Duck* published; *1885* leaves Rome to settle in Munich; *1889* meets Emilie Bardach and Helene Raff on summer vacation; *1890 Hedda Gabler* published; *1891* returns to Norway to live; *1894 Little Eyolf* published; *1898 Collected Works* begin to appear in Denmark and Germany; *1899 When We Dead Awaken* published; *1901* suffers first stroke; 1906 dies on May 23 in Christiania.

Author's Bibliography (selected)

Catiline, 1850 (historical tragedy); *The Vikings at Helgeland*, 1858 (folk drama); *Love's Comedy*, 1862 (dramatic poem); *Brand*, 1866 (poetic drama); *Peer Gynt*, 1867 (poetic drama); *Poems*, 1871; *Emperor and Galilean*, 1873 (epic drama); *The Pillars of Society*, 1877 (social drama); *A Doll's House*, 1879 (social drama); *Ghosts*, 1881 (tragedy); *An Enemy of the People*, 1882 (social drama); *The Wild Duck*, 1884 (tragedy); *Rosmersholm*, 1886 (tragedy); *Hedda Gabler*, 1890 (tragedy); *When We Dead Awaken*, 1899 (philosophical drama).

Overview of Biographical Sources

For a writer whose life was so thoroughly subsumed by his work, Ibsen has been the subject of a surprising number of biographies. His reputation was so exalted in his later years that biographies began to appear before his death. Henrik Jaeger's *Henrik Ibsen A Critical Biography*, trans. William Morton Payne (Chicago: A. C. McClung and Company, 1901) is the best of the early lives. It was written with Ibsen's cooperation and was originally published in 1888 for the dramatist's sixtieth birthday. The English translation was reissued by Benjamin Blom in 1972. Edmund Gosse's appreciative life (1907) still contains some sensitive insights, if also some misinformation. Gerhard Gran's biography (1918) tried to present a more personal picture of the man behind the works. Halvdan Koht's *Life of Ibsen* came out in 1928-29, issued to commemorate the centennial of Ibsen's birth. The English translation was published in two volumes in 1931 and for many years was the standard life. In 1954 Koht revised his biography, which appeared in English in 1971. This life and Michael Meyer's monumental *Ibsen* (1971) have completely superseded the earlier lives, which today have only an archaeological interest. For readers desiring a briefer treatment of Ibsen, Hans Heiberg's modest *Ibsen A Portrait of the Artist*, trans. Joan Tate (Coral Gables: University of Miami Press, 1969) can be recommended.

Evaluation of Selected Biographies

Ibsen, Bergliot, *The Three Ibsens*. trans. Gerik Schjelderup. New York: The American-Scandinavian Foundation, 1952. This book by Ibsen's daughter-in-law is the most intimate account available of the dramatist and it is a valuable supplement to the biographies. Beginning with Ibsen's marriage to Suzannah Thoresen in 1858 and concluding with the death of his son Sigurd in 1930, the book relies heavily on the correspondence of the three Ibsens to each other to draw an indelible picture of a close-knit family living for years in self-imposed exile wary of outsiders. Though all three are clearly delineated, the focus is on Henrik, who emerges as a real person whose life was made up in large measure of compensations. He effectively severed all ties with his parents before his sixteenth birthday, but was a devoted husband and father for over forty years. Having been unsuccessful in his university entrance examination years earlier, he took great pride in his son's academic accomplishments, even moving the family from Dresden to Munich for better schools. He was embarrassed by poverty and shabbiness for a good part of his life, but later he was an astute businessman and meticulous dresser. A complex and contradictory personality, Ibsen was not given to open displays of feeling but his hands trembled with emotion when he opened letters from his son; he called his wife by affectionate names and he was filled with anxiety that they would fall victim to illness or accident. Suzannah is characterized as the perfect wife, inspiring Ibsen in his work and shielding him from distractions. Beneath the outward austerity there was a strong and enduring love among the three Ibsens for each other.

This book is made especially interesting by the fact that Bergliot Ibsen was the daughter of Bjørnstjerne Bjørnson, Ibsen's great friend and rival. She sheds considerable light on the vicissitudes of the relations between her father and father-in-law over the years.

Koht, Halvdan, *Life of Ibsen*. trans. Einar Haugen and A. E. Santaniello. New York: Benjamin Blom, 1971. Halvdan Koht, a Norwegian historian of international stature, was already a longtime student of Ibsen when he published his life in 1928-29. The present volume is a translation of Koht's 1954 revision done with the cooperation of Koht and his literary executor. Though the revision, according to the translators, shifts the focus from Ibsen's historical contribution to the drama to his consummate psychological insight and craftsmanship, one of the great strengths of this biography is its sense of historical background. Koht's discussion of Ibsen's political poems of 1863-64 in the context of the failure of Scandinavian solidarity to oppose Germany's aggression against Denmark and his review of the agitation for women's rights in his consideration of *A Doll's House* are especially illuminating.

Following a strict chronology, this biography consists of numerous short chapters, each focusing on a particular work or seminal experience in Ibsen's life. Throughout, much attention is paid to the poems and all citations from them are accompanied by the original text, a unique feature which is of interest only to readers who know Norwegian. Although Koht provides useful insights into Ibsen the man—particularly his relationship with Herman Laading at the Norwegian Theater in Bergen, his early love for Rikke Holst, his terrible depression during 1860 when he was refused travel funds by his government, and his long ambivalent feelings for his country—little attention is paid to his family life and the influence of his wife on his work. The real emphasis is on Ibsen's development as a dramatist. The considerations of the major plays, their gestation in Ibsen's imagination, critical reception, and theatrical history are very valuable indeed. Koht regards *Brand* as Ibsen's most powerful play, a life achievement that marked a watershed in Ibsen's life, freeing him forever from financial worries and establishing him in the forefront of Norway's cultural life. The two chapters devoted to this play rank with the most helpful treatment of it to be found anywhere. The chapters on the other plays from *Saint John's Niàght* to *When We Dead Awaken* all contain valuable information and insights. Koht's biography, the result of a lifetime of study, displays a profound understanding of Ibsen and remains indispensable.

Meyer, Michael, *Ibsen A Biography*. Garden City, NY: Doubleday, 1971. This life by Michael Meyer, an experienced translator of Ibsen, is meticulously researched and encyclopedic in scope. Its thirty-seven chapters are divided into six parts beginning with Ibsen's long apprenticeship as a dramatist in Christiania and Bergen, continuing with his periods in Italy and Germany and his development as a social critic and explorer of the unconscious and concluding with a moving account of his death. Rainer Maria Rilke's beautiful tribute ends the book. Using previously untapped materials, Meyer more successfully than any other biographer conveys a sense of the complex wholeness of Ibsen the man and the writer. He comes to grips forthrightly with the less attractive aspects of Ibsen's character including his physical cowardice, his intermittent problems with alcohol, his irascible quarrels with colleagues throughout his long career, his inordinate pride in medals. But the treatment is judicious and the more positive characteristics of the man come through clearly: his deep affection for his wife and son, his abiding love for his country in spite of everything, and perhaps most important of all his single-minded commitment to his art, which triumphed over poverty, indifference and hostile criticism, and which was nothing short of heroic. In addition to members of his family, others close to Ibsen, people like Bjørnstjerne Bjørnson, Georg Brandes, and Frederick Hegel, are richly characterized.

This book provides a thorough consideration of all of Ibsen's plays. Of special interest is Meyer's account of the symbolism of *The Wild Duck* and the critical receptions of *A Doll's House* and *Ghosts* in Scandinavia and elsewhere. The analyses of the plays are always helpful and full plot summaries of many of them are given. Meyer's extensive knowledge of nineteenth-century literature informs his work throughout, creating a strong sense of Ibsen's intellectual milieu and giving this biography a cosmopolitanism that others lack. The opinions of a host of notable writers such as Henry James, James Joyce, Emile Zola, Anton Chekov, and Leo Tolstoy about Ibsen's work are one of the most interesting features of this massive study, as are the period photographs and caricatures. The bibliography is of only limited help to readers who do not know Norwegian, but the detailed and superbly organized index is of immense value. This should remain the definitive life of Ibsen for the foreseeable future.

Autobiographical Sources

The most reticent of great writers, Ibsen wrote no formal autobiography. His early experiences were apparently too painful to be systemically recorded; so much did he value his privacy that he broke with John Paulsen for writing a novel based on his life. Ibsen sublimated his life in his work, as he more than once indicated. His poems are often intensely personal, and many scholars regard Brand and Peer Gynt as representing antithetical aspects of Ibsen's character. Specific autobiographical elements in his writings have been clearly pointed out by Halvdan Koht, Michael Meyer, and others. Ibsen's letters, translated by John Nilsen Laurvik and Mary Morison (New York: Duffield and Company, 1908) are another source of autobiographical material.

Overview of Critical Sources

It was Ibsen's misfortune in his lifetime to be the subject of much critical excess, either of praise or abuse, and often for the wrong reasons. The production of *Ghosts* in London in 1891 unleashed a period of personal vilification seldom equalled in literary history. In the British press Ibsen was damned as obscene and profane and the subverter of all civilized values. George Saintsbury dismissed him as parochial, D. H. Lawrence regarded him as an effete intellectual, and W. B. Yeats was ambivalent. George Bernard Shaw's vigorous defense, *The Quintessence of Ibsenism* unwittingly reduced the plays to social programs. Only in this century, with time and perspective, has criticism risen to the demands made by this writer. M. C. Bradbook and G. Wilson Knight among many others have written incisively on Ibsen, affirming him as the foremost dramatist of the nineteenth century. Ronald Gray's 1977 dissenting view shows the continuing hold that Ibsen has on contemporary criticism. Today the richness and variety of Ibsen criticism equals that of virtually any other writer.

Evaluation of Selected Criticism

Bradbrook, M. C. *Ibsen the Norwegian.* 1946; new ed. Hamden, CT: Archon Books, 1966. Though first published forty years ago, Muriel Bradbrook's remains one of the best studies of Ibsen. The book is aptly titled, as it is written on the assumption that a knowledge of the nature of the Norwegian character and language is necessary to understand Ibsen. In elegant and witty prose Bradbrook explores Ibsen's work in the context of his "Norwegianness." Her incisive remarks on Ibsen's language could only have come from one who knows Norse. Her treatment of the social plays is of great value, particularly of *A Doll's House*, which is analyzed as a uniquely Norwegian version of the sufferings of women in a male world and which "stands in relation to modern drama as Queen Victoria to the royal families of Europe." Bradbrook's wide knowledge and deep understanding of literature lead to frequent comparisons of Ibsen with other writers, but nowhere with more telling effect than when comparing Ibsen's stern devotion to art and exposure of fraud to Dante or the quality of Ibsen's mature construction of drama through the interplay of details to Jane Austen's plots. The book contains an appendix of twelve of Ibsen's poems, which shed light on his plays and life.

Gray, Ronald, *Ibsen—A Dissenting View.* Cambridge: Cambridge University Press, 1977. In this revisionist study Gray perceives the plays as closely connected with what he regards as Ibsen's personal Faustian aspirations. He makes his case more convincingly in regard to the earlier plays, treated as dramatizing the conflict between self-assertiveness and self-denial, although the focus of the book is on the last twelve. Gray argues that they are rife with one-dimensional characters, rigid character relationships, murky motivations, contrivances of plot, and uninspired flatness of language. Ambiguity is seen as artistic inadequacy instead of real-life fullness and the imprecise symbolism as making for a bogus universality. Gray believes that Ibsen was more interested in creating stage effects than flesh and blood characters. That the plays provide for a variety of stage interpretations in no way raises their value as drama in Gray's view. The book contains interesting comparisons with Chekov and Tolstoy.

Knight, G. Wilson, *Ibsen*. Edinburgh and London: Oliver and Boyd, 1962. This short book is rich in information and insights. Drawing heavily on Koht's life and Ibsen's letters, Knight cuts through the thicket of Ibsen's various political positions to clarify that Ibsen's highest goal of self-realization goes beyond politics. Knight sees all of Ibsen's plays, which he believes rank in power and authority with those of ancient Greece and Shakespeare, as stages in the quest for the total realization of self that Ibsen in *Emperor and Galilean* called the third empire. Relying mainly on theme, image and symbol, Knight provides provocative readings of a number of plays, particularly of *Brand* as "a protest against nineteenth-century humanism," of *Peer Gynt* as a probing of the nature of the self and the redeeming power of love, and of *Emperor and Galilean* as Ibsen's fullest attempt to resolve the conflict between Christ and Dionysus. Knight uncovers thematic and symbolic correspondences throughout Ibsen's corpus, but his readings of the social plays are not uniformly compelling.

McFarlane, James Walter, *Ibsen and the Temper of Norwegian Literature*. London: Oxford University Press, 1960. In this book McFarlane devotes only one chapter to Ibsen, but it is a valuable one in several ways: it gives a synoptic overview of Ibsen's career, details Ibsen's introduction in England through the efforts of Edmund Gosse and William Archer, and communicates a sense of the elusive complexity of the plays. It contains a fine analysis of the nature of Ibsen's fatally flawed characters.

Northam, John, *Ibsen, A Critical Study*. Cambridge: Cambridge University Press, 1973. Northam believes that all of Ibsen's plays possess a significant continuity as an organically developing search for the right form to express what he considers Ibsen's enduring concern: man's capacity for heroism. After the earlier historical plays, according to him, Ibsen sought to define the nature of heroism in contemporary life. *Brand* and *Peer Gynt* are viewed as experiments in finding a suitable vehicle for exploring man's potential for heroic action in the modern world, but not until *The Pillars of Society* did Ibsen find the form that suited him— the prose play. Claiming that all of Ibsen's plays are a form of poetry, Northam argues that in the mature ones the essential experience is conveyed through complex, highly structured patterns of imagery even though Ibsen came to rely increasingly on visual rather than verbal images as he left more and more up to the imagination. Northam gives close readings of six of the later plays analyzing just how character and theme are conveyed through the resources of language. Since Ibsen cannot be translated without losing much of the original, Northam's ambitious study cannot be wholly successful, but his approach is interesting and his readings of *Brand* and *The Wild Duck* are particularly rewarding. Northam's claim that Ibsen's prose is a form of poetry is disputed by Ronald Gray. The book contains a useful biographical table.

Valency, Maurice, *The Flower and the Castle*. New York: Macmillan, 1963. This is a study of Ibsen and Strindberg against the background of nineteenth-century developments in the drama. The chapter on Ibsen, a critical treatment of the plays from *Brand* to *When We Dead Awaken*, emphasizes characterization. The approach is predominately psychological, many of the characters being seen as projections of the playwright's psyche. The book provides illuminating insights into Ibsen's characteristic method of composition, which resulted in such rich ambiguousness of characterization. Valency's methodology and conclusions differ widely from Knight's, and a comparison of the two studies would be worthwhile.

Other Sources

Fjelde, Rolf, ed. *Ibsen: A Collection of Critical Essays*. Englewood Cliffs, NJ: 1965. Excellent collection of fifteen essays, including Eric Bentley's "Henrik Ibsen: A Personal Statement" and Halvdan Koht's "Shakespeare and Ibsen."

Haakonsen, Daniel, ed. *Contemporary Approaches to Ibsen*. Oslo: Universitetsforlaget, 1966. Seven monographs of varying degrees of usefulness.

Lyons, Charles R. *Henrik Ibsen The Divided Consciousness*. Carbondale and Edwardsville: Southern Illinois University Press, 1972. Fresh readings of seven plays as highly complex examinations of the nature of consciousness.

McFarlane, James Walter, gen. ed. *The Oxford Ibsen*. 8 vols. London: Oxford University Press, 1960-1977. Contains helpful critical introductions and appendices by a major Ibsen scholar.

Tennant, P. F. D. *Ibsen's Dramatic Technique*. 1948; rpt. New York: Humanities Press, 1965. Extensive examination of Ibsen's dramaturgy.

Dictionaries and Encyclopedias

An Ibsen Companion A Dictionary-Guide to the Life, Works, and Critical Reception of Henrik Ibsen. Greenwood Press, 1984. Contains brief identifications of Ibsen's characters and people associated with him, synopses and stage histories of the plays.

Robert G. Blake
Elon College

EUGÈNE IONESCO
1912

Author's Chronology

Born November 26, 1912, Slatina Rumania; *1913* family moves to Paris; *1921* taken to Chapelle-Anthenaise for his health, an experience and locale which figures heavily in his mythology, as noted in his essays and several plays; *1925* returns to Rumania and is traumatized by its depersonalized totalitarianism; *1929* takes degree in French from the University of Budapest; *1934* writes *Na* ("No"), his first significant essay which brilliantly argues both sides of a complex issue without resolution; *1937* teaches French in Budapest; *1939* returns to Paris; *1949* writes *The Bald Soprano*; *1950* writes *Jack, or the Submission* and acts in *The Possessed* at the Théâtre de l'Oeuvre, resulting in a new love for the theatre; *1951* writes *The Chairs* which fails commercially but is defended by Beckett, Adamov, Queneau and other noted playwrights and critics; *1956 The Chairs* revived with great success; *1957* writes *The Killers*, his first full-length play; *1958* writes *Rhinoceros*; *1960 Rhinoceros* produced at the Théâtre de France, directed by Jean-Louis Barrault, and in London, directed by Orson Welles, starring Laurence Olivier; *1962* writes *Notes and Counter-Notes*; *1967* writes *Fragments of a Journal*; *1971* elected to the Académie Francaise; *1973* publishes *Macbett*; *1973* writes *What a Hell of a Mess!*; *1974* writes *Exit the King*.

Author's Bibliography (selected)

Four Plays, tr. Donald M. Allen, 1958; *Three Plays*, tr. Donald Watson, 1958; *The Killer and Other Plays*, tr. Donald Watson, 1960; *Rhinoceros and Other Plays*, tr. Derek Prouse, 1960; *Notes and Counter Notes: Writings on the Theater*, tr. Donald Watson, 1964; *Fragments of a Journal*, tr. Jean Pace, 1968.

Overview of Biographical Sources

Ionesco's life is one of creative, intellectual, and critical endeavor, and the secondary source material reflects that mix. No full-length biography exists; few sources in English treat his creative work in the context of his life. Martin Esslin's chapter on Ionesco in *The Theatre of the Absurd* (revised and updated edition, New York: Anchor, 1969), traces the influence of early experiences before Ionesco's career came to full fruition.

Autobiographical Sources

Ionesco has produced a steady stream of essays and manifestos throughout his career. He has always freely discussed his work in the context of his ideas and the state of theatrical and intellectual history of his times. His thoughts about his life and work have been collected in *Notes and Counter Notes* (1964), in which Ionesco discusses his views of the theatre, and his role in a number of public intellectual controversies which pitted him against critics such as Kenneth Tynan, and playwrights such as Bertolt Brecht. Ionesco discusses *The Bald Soprano*; *The Chairs*; *Jack, or The Submission*; and *Rhinoceros*; and relates numerous anecdotes about significant figures of his artistic and intellectual community. Claude Bonnefoy's transcribed interviews, *Conversations with Eugène Ionesco*, tr. Jan Dawson (New York: Holt, Rinehart and Winston, 1966), explores the playwright's views on his work, the ideas of his time, aspects of his life, and his place in modern letters. Little note is taken of Ionesco's life as event, but the origins of his ideas as they affected his creative output are examined. *Fragments of a Journal* (1968), continues the approach of *Notes and Counter-Notes*. Both books combine to form a discursive and fragmentary "intellectual autobiography." Finally, Ronald Hayman's *Eugène Ionesco* (1976), a critical study of his work, begins with a revealing short interview in which the playwright discusses early influences, the role of dreams in his creative process, and the political implications of his philosophical and creative writings.

Overview of Critical Sources

Since Ionesco is at the center of modern French letters and, with Beckett, the most important of the Absurdist playwrights, literally thousands of books, monographs, theses, dissertations, and articles have been produced, in many languages. Ionesco himself has added to the total, with dozens of critical essays dealing with his and others' work. Of the critics who write in English, Martin Esslin, Richard N. Coe, and Rosette C. Lamont have produced some of the clearest and most trenchant discussions of Ionesco's work. In addition, Lamont has edited two collections of critical essays. In addition, Ionesco has been widely discussed in context of other authors and movements, as exemplified by Julian H. Wulbern's *Brecht and Ionesco: Commitment in Context* (Urbana, Illinois, University of Illinois Press, 1971) and Jaques Guicharnaud's *Modern French Theatre from Giraudoux to Beckett* (New Haven: Yale University Press, 1961).

Evaluation of Selected Criticism

Coe, Richard N. *Eugène Ionesco: A Study of his Work*, 2nd. ed. rev. New York: Grove Press, 1968. This brief and succinct study by one of the most noted critics of modern theatre covers the background of the New Theater, and the dominant characteristics of Ionesco's drama. It is organized by topic, rather than by play, and discusses Ionesco's use of coincidence, dissolution, language games, banality and cliché. It also discusses Ionesco's thematic use of death, void, despair, and his radical mix of humor and tragedy. There is an extensive, though unannotated bibliography, but no index, which makes tracing discussions of individual plays difficult—a fault somewhat mitigated by the book's brevity.

Hayman, Ronald, *Eugène Ionesco*. New York: Frederick Ungar, 1976. Unlike Coe's book (above), Hayman organizes his traversal of Ionesco's *oeuvre* by play. The book opens with a revealing interview with the playwright, and then discusses each play in chronological order. Each analysis contains a clear and accurate plot synopsis, critical commentary, and production details. Hayman quotes extensively from the works discussed, allowing the reader to sample the tone and flavor of the play under discussion. The book concludes with Hayman's appraisal of Ionesco's total achievement and place in modern letters. The book contains a detailed catalogue of major stage and broadcast productions, a chronology, a bibliography, and index.

Lamont, Rosette C., ed. *Ionesco, A Collection of Critical Essays*. Englewood Cliffs, NJ: Prentice Hall, 1973. One of the *Twentieth Century Views* series, this is a collection of representative essays on Ionesco, written by significant critics. Several of the essays are excerpted from longer studies by their authors. Included are essays by Lamont herself, one of the most noted Ionesco scholars, Richard Schechner, Jaques Guicharnaud, and Richard Coe. Lamont's introduction is one of the best short pieces on Ionesco's life and work extant, tying his complex web of ideas together with admirable clarity. The collection, ideally suited for advance undergraduate readers, provides a representative cross-section of Ionesco scholarship.

_____ and Melvin J. Friedman, eds. *The Two Faces of Ionesco*. Troy, NY: Whitson, 1978. What Lamont's collection does for undergraduates, this volume does for the advanced student. This collection of essays by critics including Lamont, Bruce Morrissette, Alaxandre Rainof, Roy Arthur Swanson, and John Fletcher, explores Ionesco's techniques, themes, and relationships to the work of other contemporary playwrights. The essays are often difficult, but never opaque. Lamont has contributed several essays which are models of sound and insightful scholarship. The book's utility is marred by the absence of a table of contents or index, but contains a selective and wide-ranging bibliography.

Lewis, Allan, *Ionesco*. New York: Twayne, 1972. Lewis's book begins with a chronology and an introductory chapter, then discusses the major works, grouped chronologically, but cross-referenced thematically. The study concludes with a chapter discussing "the paradox of the illogical." Allan's study is well suited to the undergraduate reader. He cites many of the significant scholars, and integrates plot synopses into the critical discussion of the plays. In addition to notes and references and a selected bibliography, the book contains two appendices dealing with intellectual and political controversies in which Ionesco was actively engaged. This book, along with Hayman's (see above) provide ideal starting places for any student research into Ionesco's work.

Other Sources

Esslin, Martin, *The Theatre of the Absurd*, revised and updated. New York: Anchor Books, 1969. This classic work is indispensable for understanding the movement of which Ionesco was a part. Esslin's chapter on Ionesco should be read with the entire book; but even taken alone, provides one of the best explications of the major themes and concerns. Ionesco is quoted extensively. Esslin's judgments, while obviously not the last word on so rich and complex an artist, have stood the test of time.

Guicharnaud, Jaques, with June Beckelman, *Modern French Theatre from Giraudoux to Beckett*. New Haven: Yale University Press, 1961. While Esslin's discussion is limited to the absurdist movement, Guicharnaud's book discusses all modern French theatre, absurdism (and Ionesco) being only a part of the total picture. This provides a different but equally valid perspective from Esslin's book; and like it, has become a standard critical text, noted both for its lucidity, and its incisiveness.

David Sadkin
Niagra University

BEN JONSON
1572?-1637

Author's Chronology

Born in either 1572 or 1573, probably in or near London, one month after the death of his father, a minister; within several years his mother remarries a master-bricklayer; as a boy Jonson studies under William Camden at Westminster School; *1588?* withdrawn from school and apprenticed as a bricklayer; early *1590s* perhaps working as a bricklayer; serves briefly as a military volunteer in Flanders; *1594* marries Anne Lewis; *1597* acts in a company of transient players; employed as a playwright; imprisoned for part authorship of allegedly seditious play; *1598* kills a fellow actor in a duel; is imprisoned; converts to Catholicism; freed after pleading benefit of clergy; *1599-1601* feuds with John Marston and Thomas Dekker in the "War of the Theatres"; *1603* begins writing aristocratic entertainments; *1604-1625* becomes chief masque-writer for the Jacobean court; *1605* imprisoned, with Marston and George Chapman, for anti-Scottish satire detected in their play *Eastward Ho!*; *1612-1613* travels in France as tutor; *1616* publishes folio *Workes*; pensioned by King James; *1618-1619* tours Scotland on foot; *1619* receives honorary Oxford M.A.; *1623* manuscripts destroyed in fire; *1628* suffers paralytic stroke; appointed Chronologer of London; *1630* receives increased pension from Charles I; *1631* resumes long-standing feud with Inigo Jones; 1637 dies in August.

Author's Bibliography (selected)

Every Man in His Humour, 1598 (comedy); *Sejanus his Fall*, 1603 (tragedy); *Masque of Blackness*, 1605; *Volpone*, 1606 (comedy); *Epicoene*, 1609 (comedy); *The Alchemist*, 1610 (comedy); *Bartholomew Fair*, 1614 (comedy); folio *Workes*, 1616, including *Epigrammes* and *The Forrest* (poems); *Chloridia*, 1631 (final masque); *A Tale of a Tub*, 1633 (final play); *Love's Welcome at Bolsover*, 1634 (final entertainment); second folio *Workes*, 1640-41, including *The Under-wood* (poems), *The English Grammar*, and *Timber, or Discoveries* (prose notes).

Overview of Biographical Sources

Writing Jonson's life is no easy task. His early years are obscure, and his suppression of some early writings makes them obscurer. The later loss of important manuscripts further distorts the record, and much of the surviving evidence is fragmentary, vague, or questionable. His complex relations with superiors, rivals, colleagues, and the law are not always easy to interpret, while his frequent concern with self-presentation complicates matters even more. Still, numerous data about Jonson *do* exist, although no completely satisfying biography has yet been built from them. Many materials are collected in the 11-volume standard edition of his works, *Ben Jonson*, ed. C. H. Herford and Percy and Evelyn Simpson (1925-1952). Volume I includes a short biography; although usually reliable, its effectiveness is limited by its brevity. However, other biographical discussions are dispersed throughout the edition in introductions, commentaries, and appendices. Marchette Chute's *Ben Jonson of Westminster* (1953) is lively, comprehensive, and well-researched, but unfortunately lacks documentation.

Documentation abounds in Barbara De Luna's *Jonson's Romish Plot: A Study of "Catiline" and Its Historical Context* (Oxford: Clarendon Press, 1967). De Luna argues that Jonson's play parallels aspects of the 1605 Gunpowder Plot. The book surveys much of Jonson's career, but its evidence and arguments are not always convincing. Although valuable, it illustrates the pitfalls and difficulties involved in writing about Jonson's life. Eric Linklater's *Ben Jonson and King James: Biography and Portrait* (London: Jonathan Cape, 1931) is a popular, undocumented account that has been criticized for stylistic flaws and factual errors. John Palmer's *Ben Jonson* (London: George Routledge, 1934) is similarly vulnerable. While not strictly biographical, Richard Helgerson's *Self-Crowned Laureates: Spenser, Jonson, Milton and the Literary System* (Berkeley: Univ. of California Press, 1983) does contain an intriguing discussion of Jonson's career.

Evaluation of Selected Biographies

Chute, Marchette, *Ben Jonson of Westminster*. New York: E. P. Dutton, 1953. Written for a popular audience, Chute's book is generally a reliable, sensible account of Jonson's life and times. It effectively blends background discussion with personal information, and sets Jonson's works—especially the plays—in a clear context. Some of its critical judgments have been questioned; although the absence of notes is a defect, the index is helpfully full.

Herford, C. H. and Percy and Evelyn Simpson, eds. *Ben Jonson*, 11 vols. Oxford: Clarendon Press, 1925-1952. A brief biography in volume I surveys the entire life; appendices include contemporary notes and records, Jonson's letters, legal and offficial documents, and books in Jonson's library. Volume II introduces his works and their biographical contexts. Introductions in subsequent volumes concentrate on textual matters but often supply added biographical facts. The commentary in vols. IX-XI is often biographically pertinent. Vol. X includes an appendix on Jonson's relations with George Chapman and Inigo Jones. Vol. XI prints contemporary and later reactions to Jonson; additional notes on his life, masques, and library; and a very full index.

Autobiographical Sources

William Drummond of Hawthornden's fragmentary notes of his 1618/19 conversations with Jonson constitute a crucial but controversial source of information about Jonson's life and mind. Jonson apparently did not know that Drummond was keeping a record of their talks: this fact either enhances the notes' revelatory interest or makes them suspect, depending upon one's point of view. Drummond's portrait of Jonson is sometimes unflattering; some later writers have accused him of various deficiencies that supposedly made him an unreliable witness to his guest's character. But the notes remain a uniquely valuable catalogue of biographical data by one of Jonson's contemporaries. Valuable for different reasons are the twenty-two surviving letters to various patrons and acquaintances that Jonson wrote over a number of years; they provide important glimpses of his character, his opinions, and the milieu in which he operated. Drummond's notes, as well as the letters, are printed in Vol. I of the Herford and Simpson *Ben Jonson*.

Autobiographical elements figure prominently in many of Jonson's creative works, especially in the non-dramatic poems, in the dedications, prologues, inductions, and epilogues of the plays, and in the introductions and marginalia to the masques. Jonson was very concerned with effective self-presentation, and he shaped public images of himself repeatedly during his career. His critical views are reflected in many of these pronouncements, but a good collection of the ideas and ideals—not all literary—that he found congenial is his commonplace book, *Timber, or Discoveries* (printed in Vol. VIII of the Herford and Simpson *Ben Jonson*). James D. Redwine, Jr. has helpfully culled and edited *Ben Jonson's Literary Criticism* (Lincoln: University of Nebraska Press, 1970).

Overview of Critical Sources

Jonson's reputation as a dramatist is perhaps at a higher point today than at any time since the seventeenth century; he is usually regarded as one of the two or three most significant playwrights of the English Renaissance. Even in his own time he was frequently compared with Shakespeare, but by the eighteenth and nineteenth centuries he was often treated as a foil whose limitations helped highlight Shakespeare's greater brilliance. Critics in the twentieth century have therefore stressed Jonson's distinctive purposes, characteristics, and strengths, but more recent writers have begun to argue that the differences between the two dramatists can easily be over-emphasized. Recent criticism has attempted to situate Jonson's works in their relevant literary and historical contexts; to provide detailed readings of specific plays; to explore the significance of such previously neglected works as the masques, the tragedies, and the late plays; to relate the dramas to Jonson's works in other genres; and to emphasize the ambiguities and tensions implicit in much of his best writing.

Evaluation of Selected Criticism

Barish, Jonas A. *Ben Jonson and the Language of Prose Comedy*. Cambridge: Harvard University Press, 1960. Barish offers insightful, detailed explorations of

Jonson's "baroque" style (with its "broken rhythms and perilous balances") and provides sensitive readings of the major plays. "Jonson anticipates the importance attached by Freud to trifling verbal gestures as an index of psychic disturbance, and also the textual 'close reading' to which recent criticism has accustomed us, where every grain, every atom of discourse, is weighed for its expressive substance."

Barton, Anne, *Ben Jonson, Dramatist*. Cambridge: Cambridge University Press, 1984. This important play-by-play survey argues that the "rage for order which shapes [Jonson's] work is almost always met and, in a way, substantiated by an equally powerful impulse towards chaos and license." It also argues that the differences between Jonson and Shakespeare have been exaggerated, and it makes a case for the "substance and delight" of the late plays. Among the themes examined are "Jonson's treatment of women, trust among individuals, father and son relationships, and proper names." Barton also disputes a number of points made in the standard Oxford edition.

Leggatt, Alexander, *Ben Jonson: His Vision and His Art*. London: Methuen, 1981. Because this book groups Jonson's works "not by chronology or genre but according to the ideas they consider and the experiences they explore," it helps place the dramas in the total context of his writings. It emphasizes various ambiguities and tensions in his art, such as the tensions between the delights and potential corruptions of creativity; between his lofty principles and "his awareness of the world's imperfection"; and in general between "an ideal vision and a realistic one." It examines Jonson's notions of the function of art and explores his "depiction of the good struggling against not only the opposition of the world but the weakness of their own natures."

Orgel, Stephen, *The Jonsonian Masque*. Cambridge: Harvard University Press, 1965. This path-breaking re-assessment fulfills its aim to take "Jonson's court masques as seriously as Jonson took them, and to read them in the light of his insistence that the soul of the form was poetry." Although it attempts to "touch on [their] every aspect," it discusses at length six masques that "represent crucial moments in Jonson's development of his own idea of the form."

Parfitt, George, *Ben Jonson: Public Poet and Private Man*. London: J. M. Dent, 1976. This study of Jonson's works in a variety of genres includes discussion of his "Personality and Early Life"; of the tensions between his public persona and private self; of "Self-Projections and Teacher Figures" in his writings; of various periods in his career; of his attitudes towards language, classicism, and society; of his reputation; and of the "theatricality" of his drama.

Summers, Claude J. and Ted-Larry Pebworth, *Ben Jonson*. Boston: Twayne, 1979. This superb introduction sums up the best insights of modern Jonson studies while charting new approaches of its own. An opening chapter on "The Man and His Age" is followed by sections on the comedies, tragedies, and masques. There is a long and substantial discussion of the non-dramatic poems, then a survey of "Jonson's Reputation." The book sensibly explicates the major plays, although its reading of *Epicoene* is provocative.

Other Sources

Arnold, Judd, *A Grace Peculiar: Ben Jonson's Cavalier Heroes.* Pennsylvania State University Studies, 35. University Park: Pennsylvania State University Press, 1972. Argues that Jonson's "comedy depends upon our being able to indulge at least the idea of the inevitable triumph of the cavalierly aloof, intellectual aristocrat over the hopeless, helpless mass of fools."

Bamborough, J. B. *Ben Jonson.* London: Hutchinson, 1970. A sensible survey.

Barish, Jonas A., ed. *Ben Jonson: A Collection of Critical Essays.* Englewood Cliffs, NJ: Prentice Hall, 1963. Includes general essays by Barish, T. S. Eliot, L. C. Knights, Harry Levin, and Edmund Wilson. Plays specifically discussed in other essays include *Every Man In, Every Man Out, Volpone, The Alchemist, Epicoene,* and *Catiline.* Also prints essays on unifying symbols in Jonson's comedy and on the Jonsonian masque.

Beaurline, L.A. *Jonson and Elizabethan Comedy: Essays in Dramatic Rhetoric.* San Marino, CA: Huntington Library, 1978. Emphasizes "Jonson's attempts to speak to, to fool, or to enlighten his audiences."

Blisset, William, *et al.* eds. *A Celebration of Ben Jonson.* An important collection, including pieces on "incredibility" in Jonson's comedy; on his contempt for the stage; on his depiction of "human nature"; on the late plays; on "wit" in his poetry; and on "Public Attitudes and Social Poetry."

Brock, D. Heyward, *A Ben Jonson Companion.* Bloomington: Indiana University Press, 1983. An encyclopedic reference work on Jonson's writings, life, and times.

Bryant, J. A., Jr. *The Compassionate Satirist: Ben Jonson and His Imperfect World.* Athens: University of Georgia Press, 1972. Argues that the plays explore the poet's public roles of "moralist, literary critic, and satirist."

Champion, Larry S. *Ben Jonson's "Dotages": A Reconsideration of the Late Plays.* Lexington: University of Kentucky Press, 1967. Argues that in intent and method, Jonson's late plays are continuous with his early ones and that they deserve more critical respect than they have received.

Dessen, Alan C. *Jonson's Moral Comedy.* Evanston: Northwestern University Press, 1971. Argues that the native English tradition of morality plays was an important influence on Jonson's comedies.

Dick, Aliki L. *Paedeia Through Laughter: Jonson's Aristophanic Appeal to Human Intelligence*. The Hague: Mouton, 1974. Claims Jonson and Aristophanes both emphasize the restorative power of laughter and share similar views of their audiences, of alchemy and sophistry, of satire, and of distortion, exaggeration, and obscenity as satiric techniques.

Duncan, Douglas J. M. *Ben Jonson and the Lucianic Tradition*. Cambridge: Cambridge University Press, 1979. Relates "the serio-comic balance and teasing rhetoric" of Jonson's middle comedies to the ironic writings of Erasmus, More, and Lucian.

Dutton, Richard, *Ben Jonson: To the First Folio*. Cambridge: Cambridge University Press, 1983. Includes chapters on the early plays; on *Sejanus* and *Volpone*; on the *Epigrammes*; on the masques and *Epicoene*; on *The Forrest*, *The Alchemist*, and *Catiline*; on "covert allusions"; and on *Bartholomew Fair*.

Enck, John Jacob, *Jonson and the Comic Truth*. Madison: University of Wisconsin Press, 1957. A comprehensive chronological survey.

Helgerson, Richard, *Self-Crowned Laureates: Spenser, Jonson, Milton and the Literary System*. Berkeley: University of California Press, 1983. A richly stimulating chapter discusses Jonson's conception—and creation—of a distinctive social role.

Hibbard, G. R. ed. *The Elizabethan Theatre IV*. Toronto: Macmillan, 1974. Contains essays on Jonsonian humor; on his elegy on Shakespeare; on *Bartholomew Fair*; on tensions between realism and idealism; on "A Celebration of Charis"; and on: "Jonson's Large and Unique View of Life."

Jackson, Gabrielle Bernhard, *Vision and Judgment in Ben Jonson's Drama*. New Haven: Yale University Press, 1968. Traces the distinction between vision and judgment "from [Jonson's] poetic theory through his structural practice to his choice of specific dramatic actions and his use of language." Attempts to reevaluate the meanings of Jonson's "didacticism," "realism," and "classicism."

Kernan, Alvin, *The Cankered Muse: Satire of the English Renaissance*. New Haven: Yale University Press, 1959. Jonson figures prominently in this important study, which emphasizes his use of satiric *personae*.

Kernan, Alvin, ed. *Two Renaissance Mythmakers: Christopher Marlowe and Ben Jonson*. Baltimore: Johns Hopkins University Press, 1977. Includes essays on "Structural Interplay" in the dramas; on "Jonson and the Moralists"; and on "The Poet in the Poems."

Knights, L. C. *Drama and Society in the Age of Jonson*. New York: George W. Steward, 1937. Although some of its arguments recently have been challenged, this remains an important study.

Knoll, Robert E. *Ben Jonson's Plays: An Introduction.* Lincoln: University of Nebraska Press, 1964. Argues that the plays are "more indigenous than classical" and that dramatic action "is not Jonson's chief interest." Emphasizes his Christian humanism.

Lehrman, Walter D. *et al. The Plays of Ben Jonson: A Reference Guide.* Boston: G. K. Hall, 1980. An annotated bibliography of criticism from 1911 to 1975.

Loewenstein, Joseph, *Responsive Readings: Versions of Echo in Pastoral, Epic, and the Jonsonian Masque.* New Haven: Yale University Press, 1984. Argues that "the myth of Echo is a myth of cultural memory." Using the myth helps Jonson demonstrate the coherence of his work, helps him "create a closure resistant to the extra-literary contraints" of masque occasions, and helps him display the "acoustic power" of his works.

Maus, Katherine Eisaman, *Ben Jonson and the Roman Frame of Mind.* Princeton: Princeton University Press, 1984. Emphasizes Jonson's debt to such "Roman moralists" as "Seneca, Horace, Tacitus, Cicero, Juvenal, Quintilian, and a few others." Includes chapters on "Characterization in the Early Plays"; on "Profit, Delight, and Imitation" in the middle comedies; on the impact of Roman "Moral Psychology" and "Social Ethos" on Jonson's writing; and on his late works.

Meagher, John C. *Method and Meaning in Jonson's Masques.* Notre Dame: University of Notre Dame Press, 1966. A thorough introduction, with chapters on the immediate historical background; on the purpose and general features of the masques; on their use of music, dance, and light; and on such themes as beauty and love, virtue and fame, and order and the king.

Orgel, Stephen, *The Illusion of Power: Political Theater in the English Renaissance.* Berkeley: University of California Press, 1975. An important "essay about theater at court."

Partridge, Edward B. *The Broken Compass: A Study of the Major Comedies of Ben Jonson.* New York: Columbia University Press, 1958. An important study of Jonsonian imagery, of "how metaphorical language helps to create comic effect in *Volpone, The Alchemist, Epicoene* and the last plays."

Randall, Dale B. J. *Jonson's Gypsies Unmasked: Background and Theme of The Gypsies Metamorphos'd.* Durham, NC: Duke University Press, 1975. Contends that Jonson's masque implicitly mocks courtly corruption and satirizes King James' favorite, "the lighthearted Marquess of Buckingham."

Sweeney, John Gordon III. *Jonson and the Psychology of Public Theater: To Coin the Spirit, Spend the Soul.* Princeton: Princeton University Press, 1985. Argues that Jonson's plays deal with the conflict between author and audience over "who determines the nature of experience in the theater."

Thomas, Mary Olive, ed. *Ben Jonson: Quadricentennial Essays. Studies in the Literary Imagination* 6 (April, 1973): 1-271. Includes essays on such topics as alchemy and acting; virtue and pessimism; political imperatives in *Sejanus*; gorgeous speech in *Volpone*; stage adaptations of *Volpone*; new readings of *The Alchemist*; the evolution of the masques; the Cary-Morison ode; naming in the *Epigrammes*; "To Heaven"; and "A Celebration of Charis."

Robert C. Evans
Auburn University at Montgomery

HEINRICH VON KLEIST
1777-1811

Author's Chronology

Born October 18, 1777 in Frankfurt-on-the-Oder, Germany, the son of a retired major and the descendant of a long line of Prussian officers; *1788* father dies; *1792* joins Prussian army; *1793* mother dies; *1797* promoted to second lieutenant; *1799* resigns his commission and enters University of Frankfurt-on-the-Oder to study physics and philosophy; *1800* becomes engaged to Wilhelmine von Zenge; *1801* experiences a crisis over Kantan philosohy which seems to make his studies futile; *1802* travels to Switzerland where he works on such plays as *The Family Schroffenstein*, *Robert Guiscard*, and *The Broken Jug*; *1802* breaks with Wilhelmine von Zenge; *1803* plans to join Napoleon's planned invasion of England, suffers nervous collapse; *1805* employed by Ministery of Finance; *1807* arrested by the French as a suspected spy, but released, returns to Dresden and publishes *Amphitryon*; *1810* completes *Michael Kohlhaas*, meets Henriette Vogel, completes *The Prince Of Homburg*; *1811*, November 21, in a suicide pact, shoots the fatally ill Henriette Vogel and then shoots himself.

Author's Bibliography (selected)

The Family Schroffenstein, 1803 (play); *Amphitryon*, 1807 (play); *Penthesilea*, 1808 (play); *The Battle of Arminius*, 1808 (play); *The Broken Jug*, 1808 (play); *Robert Guiscard*, 1808 (play); *Michael Kohlhaas*, 1808 (novella); *The Marquise of O-*, 1808 (novella); *Kate of Heilbronn*, 1810 (play); *Tales Vol. I*, 1810 (short stories); *Prince Frederick of Homburg*, 1811 (play); *Tales Vol. II*, 1811 (short stories); *Collected Works*, 1905.

Overview of Biographical Sources

There are no standard English-language biographies of Kleist's life, nor have such 19th-century biographies as Otto Brahm's *Das Leben Heinrichs von Kleist* (1884) been translated. Gunter Blocker in his 1960 study, *Heinrich von Kleist* (also not translated), has called him a writer without a biography. The best source of information about the most important aspects of Kleist's life—the Kant crisis, his love affair with Wilhelmine von Zenge, and his suicide can be found in *An Abyss Deep Enough: Letters of Heinrich von Kleist*, edited and translated by Philip B. Miller (New York: E.P. Dutton, 1982).

For other biographical information, one must consult the scattered remarks in the many critical studies of Kleist, most of which get their information from the letters. The best general introduction is the brief study by Richard March, *Heinrich von Kleist* (New Haven: Yale University Press, 1954), a short chronological study which deals with the major works. Other brief biographical accounts can be found in Robert E. Helbling's *The Major Works of Heinrich von Kleist* (New York: New Directions, 1975); John Gearey's *Heinrich von Kleist: A Study in Tragedy and Anxiety* (Philadelphia: University of Pennsylvania Press, 1968); and John G. Blankengagel, *The Dramas of Heinrich von Kleist: A Biographical and Critical Study* (Chapel Hill: University of North Carolina Press, 1931). Walter Silz's *Heinrich von Kleist: Studies in His Works and Literary Character* (Philadelphia: University of Pennsylvania Press, 1961), includes a chapter speculating on the many motives for Kleist's suicide, such as his life-long affinity for death, his professional disappointments, and the fusion of love and death indicated in his letters. However, the problem remains that Kleist is a mysterious figure in German literature, a writer who seems not entirely of this world. Moreover, because his family was so ashamed of the scandal of his death that they burned many of his papers and letters, and because he himself destroyed many others, little is left on which to base a detailed and authoritative biography.

Autobiographical Sources

Autobiographical material by Kleist is sparse. There is no evidence that he kept a diary or journal, and before his suicide he burned all of the papers that he had in his own possession. The letters that have survived are primarily those to his sister, Ulrike von Kleist, and his fiancé Wilhelmine von Zenge, the most important of which are those he wrote in 1801 recounting his so-called Kantian crisis—a disenchantment which has been called the most notorious emotional crisis in German literary history. The central letter in this series is one dated March 22, 1801, in which he tells his fiancé that he has come to the realization that Truth is nowhere to be known on earth. Other important letters are those he wrote to Marie von Kleist, his cousin by marriage and a close friend who interceded for him in court, concerning his suicide with Henriette Vogel who was terminally ill with cancer. These letters recount how joyous he is that he will soon die a most glorious and sensual death.

The one other article written by Kleist which has been of widespread importance to critics attempting to understand his aesthetic and philosophic point of view is a short piece entitled "On the Puppet Theater," published in 1810, which deals with the human tension between the desire to know and the desire to retreat into the primitive. All of these letters, the puppet theater essay, as well as various other essays, fragments, and bits of Kleist's journalism are included in *An Abyss Deep Enough: Letters of Heinrich von Kleist*, translated and edited by Philip B. Miller (New York: E.P. Dutton, 1982), an extremely valuable collection essential for anyone desiring knowledge about Kleist's life and views.

Overview of Critical Sources

There is a tremendous amount of criticism on Kleist; however, most of it is in German and remains untranslated. A good summary of this material can be found in R.E. Helbling's *The Major Works of Heinrich von Kleist* (1975) and James M. McGlathery's *Desire's Sway: The Plays and Stories of Heinrich von Kleist* (1983). The major focus of Kleist criticism has been on the philosophical content of his works and the generic characteristics of his fiction. More recently the focus has shifted to structural and textual analyses, although the primary emphasis is still on the mysterious tension in Kleist's work between the nature of consciousness and the nature of external reality. An analysis of recent criticism can be found in John M. Ellis's *Heinrich von Kleist: Studies in the Character and Meaning of His Writings* (1979).

Evaluation of Selected Criticism

Ellis, John M. *Heinrich von Kleist: Studies in the Character and Meaning of His Writings*. Chapel Hill: University of North Carolina Press, 1979. Ellis presents detailed discussions of six of Kleist's most mature works, primarily novellen *The Marquise of O-*, *The Earthquake in Chili*, and *Michael Kohlhass*, although he does offer a discussion of *Prince Frederick of Homburg* based on his earlier study of that work. Moreover, based on these several analyses, Ellis includes a chapter on the general character of Kleist's work, primarily typical thematic structures, as well as a carping chapter on his reservations about previous Kleist criticism.

Gearey, John, *Heinrich von Kleist: A Study in Tragedy and Anxiety*. Philadelphia: University of Pennsylvania Press, 1968. A good general study of the major novellas and plays, including a long chapter on *Prince Frederick of Homburg*. Gearey's central thesis is that the major conflict in Kleist's work is not simply between the rational and the emotional nor self-consciousness and external reality, but rather that the works must be seen in terms of the nature of opposition as such.

Graham, Ilse, *Heinrich von Kleist: Word Into Flesh, A Poet's Quest for the Symbol*. Berlin, New York: Walter de Gruyter, 1977. Basing her arguments primarily on Kleist's "On the Puppet Theater," Graham tries to show that his work is dominated by "a deeply regressive model of the act of knowing." The structure of Kleist's works, according to Graham, always tends toward facticity; e.g. the metaphoric becomes real, the general tends toward the specific. This is a dense and often self-indulgent and self-consciously written book, certainly not one to be tackled until the more general studies have been read first.

Helbling, Robert E. *The Major Works of Heinrich von Kleist*. New York: New Directions Books, 1975. This is a good general introduction, more detailed than the study by March listed below. Helbling surveys previous Kleist criticism, presents a brief biographical sketch, and then develops his argument that Kleist's is a tragic vision, not simply a pathological one deriving from his personality. The focus is on Kleist's interest in human subjectivity and what Helbling calls the central theme in his works—the confrontation between the individual consciousness and the unresponsive world.

March, Richard, *Heinrich von Kleist*. New Haven: Yale University Press, 1954. This is perhaps the best "first" book for the student to read to gain a basic framework for understanding Kleist's life and art. It is a brief (50 pages) general introduction to Kleist's life and a sketchy introduction to the basic themes in his work. March argues that Kleist's celebrated Kantian crisis is based on a misunderstanding of Kant's *Critique of Pure Reason*.

McGlathery, James M. *Desire's Sway: The Plays and Stories of Heinrich von Kleist*. Detroit: Wayne State University Press, 1983. This is actually a brief study, for almost half of its 250-page length is taken up with notes and bibliography. McGlathery's primary focus is on the tension in Kleist's characters between their typical devotion to lofty and chaste ideas and their frequent outbursts of passion—a tension that suggests a basic affinity to the spirit of comedy.

Silz, Walter, *Heinrich von Kleist: Studies in His Works and Literary Characters*. Philadelphia: University of Pennsylvania Press, 1961. Silz's book is a pasted-together collection of various essays and lectures published in scholarly journals and presented at academic conferences. However, Silz is a well-known American expert on Kleist in particular and the German novelle in general, and thus his ideas, although somewhat unorthodox, especially on the puppet theater essay, are not to be ignored. Of particular interest to those looking for biographical information about Kleist's death is Silz's final speculative chapter about the motives for his suicide.

Other Sources

Blankenagel, John G. *The Dramas of Heinrich von Kleist: A Biographical and Critical Study*. Chapel Hill: University of North Carolina Press, 1931. The first study of the dramas in the U.S. A good introduction to the tension between reason and feeling in Kleist's plays; it also offers some biographical background.

Dyer, Denys, *The Stories of Kleist: A Critical Study*. New York and London, 1977. Not a strikingly original study, but a good introduction for the general reader to Kleist's stories and the criticism that has clustered about them.

Ellis, John M. *Kleist's "Prinz Friedrich von Homburg": A Critical Study*. Berkeley and Los Angeles: University of California Press, 1970. An analysis of the imagistic structure of the play.

Garland, Mary, *Kleist's "Prinz Friedrich von Homborg": An Interpretation Through Word Pattern*. The Hague: Mouton Press, 1968. A textual analysis of the word pattern in the play.

Richardson, F.C. *Kleist in France*. Chapel Hill: University of North Carolina Press, 1962. This revision of Richardson's dissertation is really only a survey of criticism of Kleist's work in France from 1807 to 1961.

Stahl, Ernst Leopold, *Heinrich von Kleist's Dramas*. Oxford: B. Blackwell, 1948. A study of the development of Kleist's plays from *Guiscard* to *Prince Fredrick of Homburg*.

Selected Dictionaries and Encyclopedias
Cassell's Encyclopedia of World Literature, William Morrow, 1954. Very brief biographical sketch and bibliography.

Cyclopedia of World Authors, rev. ed. 1974. A brief biographical and critical sketch, with a bibliography of primary and secondary materials.

The Reader's Encyclopedia of World Drama, Thomas Crowell, 1969. Brief discussion of the themes and background of the plays.

Charles E. May
California State University
Long Beach

THOMAS KYD
1558-1594

Author's Chronology

Born London, England, 1558, son of scrivener father; *1565* attends Merchant Taylors School, London (Edmund Spenser enrolled at same time); *1585* begins period of literary activity including translations of Tasso's *The Householders Philosophie* from Italian and Robert Garnier's *Cornelia* from French, *Soliman and Perseda, The Spanish Tragedy*, and possibly an early (now lost) version of *Hamlet*; *1587* serves a lord who was patron of a group of players; *1590-1591* shares writing quarters and possibly lodgings with Christopher Marlowe; *1593* accused with Marlowe of heresy and atheism by reason of papers found in his belongings; writes to Lord Keeper to deny charges and argue that incriminating papers were Marlowe's; possibly tortured; *1594* dies, buried 15 August; 30 December Kyd's mother, Anna Kyd, renounces right to administer son's estate, presumably because Kyd left nothing but debts.

Author's Bibliography

The only extant work known to be definitely by Kyd is his translation of Robert Garnier's *Cornelia*, 1594, the year of his death. Accepted as Kyd's by virtue of Thomas Heywood's 1612 statement as well as by stylistic evidence is *The Spanish Tragedy*, late 1580s. Other works probably by Kyd: *Soliman and Perseda*, translation of Tasso's *The Householders Philosophie*; works sometimes attributed to Kyd but more recently disproved: *Arden of Feversham, The Murder of John Bremen, The First Part of Ieronimo*. As noted above, an early and now lost version of *Hamlet* may have been Kyd's. All works are agreed to be after 1585; no work except Cornelia can be dated exactly.

Overview of Biographical Sources

The small amount of biographical material extant on Kyd is at best tentative and difficult to date. Frederick Boas' *The Works of Thomas Kyd* (Oxford: The Clarendon Press, 1901) is the major source for biographical material on Kyd, although many of Boas' conjectures, including those on Kyd's authorship of several works included in the edition, are no longer accepted. The book is nevertheless valuable for the background Boas has uncovered and for a good treatment of the difficulties of exploring the relationship and influence among works by Kyd, Marlowe, Shakespeare, and their contemporaries. Philip Edwards, whose *Thomas Kyd and Early Elizabethan Tragedy* (London: Longmans, Green, 1966) complements his Revels edition of *The Spanish Tragedy* (Cambridge: Harvard, 1959), compiles the definitive contemporary scholarship on Kyd; these works should be used by every student of this period. There is no book-length biographical study of Kyd nor, given the dearth of material, is there likely to be.

Autobiographical Sources

The single autobiographical source for Kyd is his "Letter to Sir John Puckering, the Lord Keeper" (1593, reprinted in Boas), in which Kyd argues that the papers found in his possession and used in the charges of atheism were not in fact his writings but "were shuffled with some of myne" by Christopher Marlowe, with whom Kyd shared writing quarters and possibly lodging. Kyd's dedication to *Cornelia*, published the following year, makes reference to the "sufferings" of this experience but there is no further information on this episode or any other facet of Kyd's life.

Overview of Critical Sources

All criticism of Thomas Kyd is directed at *The Spanish Tragedy*, its enormous popularity, its Senecan elements, and its influence on subsequent dramatists, including of course Shakespeare. It is generally agreed that the play is original with Kyd; no sources have been found. Early criticism has as its focus exploration of the elements of Senecan tragedy; recent criticism is more psychological and treats motivation and the questions of revenge. A good deal of Kyd scholarship concerns itself with questions of authorship, although of late these questions are simply left unresolved.

Evaluation of Selected Criticism

Bowers, Fredson Thayer, *Elizabethan Revenge Tragedy 1587-1642*. Gloucester: Peter Smith, 1959, originally published 1940. A classic study of the rise of renaissance tragedy; excellent treatment of Senecan influences on Kyd together with his influences on later writers. Dates *The Spanish Tragedy* 1587-1589 and suggests the existence of the unpublished pre-Shakespearian *Hamlet* (*Ur-Hamlet*) as early as 1587.

Clemen, Wolfgang, *English Tragedy before Shakespeare*. London: Methuen, 1961. Subtitle, "Development of Dramatic Speech," indicates major focus of this excellent study. Convincingly shows Kyd working to merge the classical and native strains of drama, consciously experimenting with language and rhetoric. Pays close attention to soliloquies as vital for character development. Brief mention of *Soliman and Perseda* and *Cornelia*, commenting that these works add nothing to the study of Kyd.

Hallett, Charles A. and Elaine S. *The Revenger's Madness*. Lincoln: University of Nebraska, 1980. An important study of the revenge theme in four major tragedies, beginning with *The Spanish Tragedy*, in an attempt to understand the experience of madness; uses renaissance psychological theory to explore the audience's sympathy for the revenger and his mission, even in the face of moral disapproval. Sees Kyd as greatly concerned with questions of justice, civil and spiritual.

Justice, Steven, "Spain, Tragedy, and *The Spanish Tragedy*," *Studies in English Literature 1500-1900* (Spring 1985): 271-288. Explores the reasons for audience sympathy for Hieronimo despite moral strictures of the time regarding revenge; and shows total futility of revenge by the end of the play, even though the act has been accomplished.

Murray, Peter, *Thomas Kyd*. New York: Twayne, 1969. The principal full-length study of *The Spanish Tragedy*, with excellent treatment of Senecan elements, character development, language, moral issues, and lasting influence of the play on English dramatists. Good annotated bibliography through 1969 and careful chronology at the beginning. The most helpful single work for the student.

Sacks, Peter, "Where Words Prevail Not: Grief, Revenge, and Language in Kyd and *The Spanish Tragedy*," *ELH* 49 (Fall 1982): 576-601. A very sensitive reading of the play, with attention to the characters' realization that words count for very little; hence action, even if it does not satisfy, is necessary.

Selected Dictionaries and Encyclopedias
The McGraw-Hill Encyclopedia of World Drama, 1972, 1984. Volume 3, pp. 192-3. A good brief overview with helpful comments of *The Spanish Tragedy* and its popularity. Includes *The Murder of John Bremen* in Kyd's writings, an attribution no longer made by most scholars.

Moulton's Library of Literary Criticism of English and American Authors. Volume 1, pp. 138-40. A helpful collection of some major nineteenth-century comments on Kyd and *The Spanish Tragedy*; useful for the student wanting to trace the reception of the play in earlier centuries.

Katherine Hanley, CSJ
The College of Saint Rose

EUGÈNE MARIN LABICHE
1815-1888

Author's Chronology

Born May 6, 1815, Paris, France, son of Jacques Philippe Marin Labiche; attends Collège Bourbon; *1834* travels to Switzerland, Italy and Sicily; in September he enrolls in law school but also begins publishing theatre reviews and literary miscellanea; *1837* has his first play performed; *1842* marries Adèle Hubert whose family suggests he give up writing; *1844* becomes regular contributor to the Palais-Royal Theatre; *1848* unsuccessful candidature for the Constituent Assembly; *1851* his first great critical success; *1852-1860* writes 60 plays; *1852* uses royalties to buy estate at Souvigny, where he will begin to spend a part of each year personally overseeing the farming operations; *1856* birth of his only son, André-Marin; *1861* named Chevalier of the Legion of Honor; *1864* has distinction of having a play performed by the Comédie Française; *1877* retires from active authorship after four successive failures; *1878* at urging of friend and collaborator Emile Augier, Labiche selects his best plays which are published as his *Théâtre complet;* *1879* the *Théâtre complet* becomes a best-seller; *1880* is elected to the French Academy; *1885* suffers from heart ailment; January 22, 1888 Labiche dies quietly at home in Paris, a respected and popular figure; at the time of his death there were five revivals of his plays on the Paris stage.

Author's Bibliography

Of the 173 plays Labiche wrote, 159 were printed during his lifetime, mostly in individual editions. A description of these is given in *Bibliographie des auteurs modernes de langue fran*çaise 1801-1949 by H. Talvart and J. Place (Paris: Chronique des lettres françaises, 1928-54). Labiche chose only 57 plays to be published in his 1878 *Théâtre complet*, 10 vols. This selection formed the basis of later editions. Gilbert Sigaux has edited the majority of collections of Labiche plays: 1960 *Nouveau théâtre choisi*; 1964-67 *Théâtre*, 3 vols.; 1966-68 *Oeuvres complètes*, 8 vols. (the most complete collection of all Labiche's known works); 1979 *Théâtre*, 2 vols. Numerous editions of *The Italian Straw Hat* and *Mr. Perrichon's Holiday* were available during the early twentieth century because they were popular pedagogical texts for teaching French in the U.S.

Only nine plays are available in English, *Celimare* (1863; trans. Lynn and Theodore Hoffman in *Let's Get a Divorce and Other Plays*. New York: Hill and Wang, 1958); *Dust in Your Eyes* (1861; trans. Emmanuel Wax, New York: Dramatists Play Service, 1962); *The Spelling Mistakes* (1867; trans. Frederick Davies, New York: Theatre Arts Books, 1967); *The Happiest of Three* (1870; trans. Frederick Davies in *Three French Farces*. London: Penguin, 1973); *An Italian Straw Hat* (1851; trans. Frederick Davies, New York: Theatre Arts Books, 1967); *The Man*

Who Set Fire to a Lady (1856; trans. Fred Partridge in *The Tulane Drama Review*, 4 (Dec. 1959)); *Mr. Perrichon's Holiday* (1860; trans. R. H. Ward in *Let's Get a Divorce and Other Plays*. New York: Hill and Wang, 1958); *90° in the Shade* (1873; trans. Emmanuel Wax, New York: Dramatists Play Service, 1962); *Pots of Money* (1864; trans. John Yeoman, London: Ginn, 1971).

Overview of Biographical Sources

In a letter to a friend Eugène Labiche wrote that his life had been too happy for his biography to be interesting. Rich, famous, and contentedly married, this amiable playwright led a tranquil life, dividing his time between Paris and his farm. No biographer has yet been inspired to write an extensive account of such an uneventful existence. Labiche's contemporaries occasionally recorded anecdotes which illustrated his playful wit, such as Eugène de Mirecourt's *Eugène Labiche— Clairville* (Paris: Librairie des Contemporains, 1869), A. Carel's *Histoire anecdotique des contemporaines* (Paris: Valier-Marescq, 1885), and Jules Clarétie's *Eugène Labiche* (Paris: Quentin, 1883). Ernest Legouvé furnished an interesting testimony to Labiche's method of working with collaborators, "Labiche intime" (1888; reprinted in *Le Crapouillot: Hommage à Labiche*, spec. no., July 1929). Labiche's grandson, G. P. Labiche, contributed a number of details in his short biography-study, *Eugène Labiche, sa vie, son oeuvre* (Paris: Jouve, 1938). The basic facts of Labiche's biography have been repeated by each of the scholars to study his work. Zina Gordon's doctoral thesis, *Labiche et son oeuvre* (Toulouse: Imprimerie Toulousaine, 1932) contains a carefully compiled section on the playwright's life. Philippe Soupault's *Eugène Labiche, sa vie, son oeuvre* (1945, 1964); Jacqueline Autrusseau's *Labiche et son théâtre* (1971), and Leonard C. Pronko's *Eugène Labiche and Georges Feydeau* (1982) all begin with a short biographical chapter which, due to the lack of other facts available, is more an account of Labiche's plays than it is of his life.

Evaluation of Selected Biographies

Autrusseau, Jacqueline, Chapter 1 "Eugène Labiche" in *Labiche et son théâtre*. Paris: L'Arche, 1971. This biographical sketch had the advantage of being able to use not only the standard nineteenth-century sources but also the major synthesis of Soupault and the notable compilations of Gilbert Sigaux, chief Labiche editor since 1957. Autrusseau quotes extensively from letters, plays and Labiche's 1834 travel journal. She tends to portray Labiche as being a calculating individual, concerned with financial solvency and personal glory. This unorthodox depiction contrasts sharply with the usual image of him as a modest person who took neither himself nor his plays too seriously.

Pronko, Leonard C. "Eugène Labiche and the Second Empire," in *Eugène Labiche and Georges Feydeau*. New York: Grove Press, 1982. Pronko has followed the lead of previous biographical sketches and has included many of the popular anecdotes about Labiche. His account of Labiche's life is concise and has the strength that it situates the playwright within the major historical currents of his time. Pronko's style bears hints of the humor and rapid rhythm for which his subject was so famed, and is very readable.

Soupault, Philippe, "Chapter 1" in *Eugène Labiche, sa vie, son oeuvre*. Paris: Sagittaire, 1945; Mercure de France, 1964. Given the paucity of noteworthy events in Labiche's private life, Soupault concentrates on the success or failure of the plays. He has included many of the anecdotes and critiques reported by Labiche's contemporaries: Eugène de Mirecourt, Emile Augier, Francisque Sarcey. The result is a leisurely biographical sketch which succeeds in adding plausible color and substance to an otherwise shadowy figure.

Autobiographical Sources

Biographers have frequently cited an entry in Labiche's journal in order to suggest his rather curious attitude toward his childhood and his family life. A year after his mother died, the young Eugène briefly recorded that the year before at that hour he still had a mother, and that the sun that day had been the last to light her life and the first to shine on his sorrow. No other mention of either his mother or his sorrow has ever been found. Whether from reticence or modesty, Labiche rarely spoke or wrote about his private life in any revealing way. Neither the journal of his 1834 travels nor his surviving correspondence (both published by Sigaux in the 1966-68 *Oeuvres complètes*) contains any particularly enlightening details.

Overview of Critical Sources

Labiche criticism presents several difficulties. There are four book-length studies of a general nature, but two are French doctoral theses and not generally available: Zina Gordon, *Labiche et son oeuvre*, Toulouse: Imprimerie Toulousaine, 1932; Jacques Gilardeau, "Eugène Labiche, histoire d'une synthèse comique inespérée," 1967. The majority of studies and critiques are in the form of articles that have appeared widely scattered in time and space. One notable but difficult to find collection of representative articles is the special July 1929 issue of *Le Crapouillot*. Labiche's theatre itself is difficult to approach because of its voluminous size and its unevenness, and because Labiche never made any significant pronouncements about his plays. Consequently, critics and scholars have never been too certain how to treat Labiche. They often begin by dividing the plays into comedy and farce, those with a philosophical or literary side and those which merely entertain. Yet the line of division is not clear, and most critics remain uncomfortable with the possibility that an author who wrote seriously could also have written simply to amuse, or vice versa. Some critics avoid this paradoxical situation in favor of analyzing the mechanisms which produced the gaiety and humor which Labiche's contemporaries valued in his works. Others have concentrated on the image of bourgeois society and attitudes in the plays. Still others have endeavored to explain Labiche as a moralist, going so far as to compare him to Molière.

Evaluation of Selected Criticism

Autrusseau, Jacqueline, *Labiche et son thèâtre*. Paris: L'Arche, 1971. This is the most recent book-length study in French. Struck by the contrast between the detached, calm, predictable manner in which Labiche lived out his life and the permanent frenzy of the stage characters he created, Autrusseau attempts to reconstruct a more life-like character for the playwright through close analysis of his works. She concludes that Labiche was caught in the ultimate bourgeois contradiction: a wish to succeed coupled simultaneously with a fear of accepting the consequences of success. Labiche was bored with the bourgeois morality yet afraid to criticize it openly. Autrusseau offers a unique solution to the puzzle created by lack of definite biographical information.

Haffter, Pierre, "Labiche et la rhétorique," in *Revue d'Histoire du Théâtre*, 24 (Jan.-Mar. 1972): 46-57. Well-versed in previous criticism, this author takes issue with the traditional judgment that much of Labiche's greatness and claim to posterity lies in the portrait of bourgeois society which he bequeathed us. Haffter suggests rhetoric as his source of originality. Labiche's characters speak in the literary past tense (*passé simple*) in order to lend credibility to their explanations and to create a more illustrious, but false, past for themselves. This rhetorically invented past, however, usually turns against them by creating disagreeable situations. This essay represents an attempt to bring a new perspective to Labiche criticism.

Pronko, Leonard C. *Eugène Labiche and Georges Feydeau*. New York: Grove Press, 1982. A welcome addition to the criticism in English. Although somewhat restricted by the manual format, Pronko does an excellent job of blending the important previous work on Labiche. He emphasizes Labiche's realist tendencies, such as his keen powers of observation. As one of the critics who see a serious underside to many of the plays, Pronko praises Labiche for maintaining the equilibrium between satire and friendly fun, exaggeration and deformation. The chapter "Labiche on Stage" is unique in considering the various staging manners which have been applied to the plays.

Sarvey, Francisque, *Quarante ans de théâtre*, vol. 4. Paris: Annales Politiques et Littéraires, 1901. The review-essays reprinted in this series by the dogen of French theatre critics represent some of the most important ones to have created Labiche's reputation during his lifetime. When revival is contrasted to premiere, the evolving opinion of Labiche as more than a skillful vaudevilliste stands out clearly.

Soupault, Philippe, *Eugène Labiche, sa vie, son oeuvre*. Paris: Sagittaire 1945; Mercure de France, 1964. This is the best general study. Soupault especially emphasizes Labiche's talent as an observer, examining themes, characters, and what the plays reflect of the bourgeois world they depict. He examines the role of Labiche's collaborators, compares the plays to the theatrical standards of their time, and ends by tracing the evolutions of Labiche's reputation. The appendices contain a chronological list of all the plays and a synopsis of Labiche's only attempt at a novel.

Zola, Emile, "Eugène Labiche," in *Nos Auteurs dramatiques*. Paris: Charpentier, 1881. One of the first critics to point out the serious aspects of many Labiche plays. The two essay-reviews which comprise the chapter on Labiche compliment him for having had the ability to present the caricaturable side of life's cruelties without becoming overly serious, for having played with fire without getting burned and without having frightened the audience.

Other Sources

Augier, Emile, Preface to *Théâtre complet de Eugène Labiche*, vol. 1. Paris: Calmann-Levy, 1878; trans. Mary Douglas Dirks, *The Tulane Drama Review*, 4 (Dec. 1959): 163-165. Celebrated preface which pronounced Labiche a master and an imminently readable playwright.

Bergson, Henri, *Laughter*. 1900; trans. in *Comedy*. ed. Wylie Sypher. Garden City: Doubleday Anchor, 1956. A classic analysis of laughter which is based to a great extent on Labiche.

Brunetière, Ferdinand, "Le Théâtre de M. Labiche," in *La Revue des Deux Mondes*, 35 (15 Sept. 1879): 433-444. In an influential, establishment journal, Brunetière opposed Labiche's nomination to the French Academy. He acknowledged Labiche's talent for provoking laughter, but raised questions about the plays' literary and artistic merits and about the "legion" of collaborators.

Chesley, Clair Vincent, "Eugène Labiche, Vaudevillist Member of the Academy," in *Poet Lore*, 28, no. 1 (1917): 55-64. Appreciates Labiche's plays but does not take him seriously.

Doumic, René, *De Scribe à Ibsen: Causeries sur le théâtre contemporain*. Paris: Perrin, 1896. Contains succinct essay which illustrates most commonly held critical opinion of Labiche shortly after his death.

Lemaître, Jules, *Theatrical Impressions*. 1892; trans. Frederic Whyte, 1924; rpt. Port Washington, NY: Kennikat Press, 1970, pp. 21-31. Includes review of the 1890 revival of Labiche's *Les Petits Oiseaux*. Perceptive comments on reasons for Labiche's popularity.

Matthews, J. Brander, "A French Comic Dramatist," in *The Atlantic Monthly*, 46 (July 1880): 48-55. Venerable analysis which is still useful. Later included in

Matthews' seminal *French Dramatists of the Nineteenth Century*, New York: Blom, 1881; 3rd. ed. of 1901 reissued in 1968.

Miller, Judith G. "The Theatrics of Triangular Trysts, or Variations on a Form; Labiche, Vitrac, Beckett," in *Modern Drama*, 26 (December 1983): 447-454.

Smith, Hugh Allison, *Main Currents of Modern French Drama*. New York: Holt, 1925, pp. 171-177. Essay which places highest value on plays containing a vein of philosophy.

Joan M. West
University of Idaho

NATHANIEL LEE
c.1648-1692

Author's Chronology

c.1648 born in Bishops-Hatfield, Hampshire or in Walthamstow, Essex, the son of the controversial clergyman, Richard Lee; *1658* admitted to Charterhouse Grammer School; *1665* enters Trinity College, Cambridge; *1669* receives B.A.; *1669-1671* lives as fellow of Trinity College (?); *1670* publishes his first poem, in a Cambridge collection of elegies on the death of George Monck, Duke of Albemarle; *c.1671* moves to London; appears briefly as an actor with the Duke's Company; *1674* performance of his first play, *Nero,* the first of a series of five produced by the King's Company at Drury Lane; may have received for a time the patronage of the Earl of Rochester; *1667* his poem in praise of John Dryden's *The State of Innocence* initiated the literary relationship of the two authors; *1678* the production of *Oedipus* by the Duke's Company at Dorset Garden marks the end of his contractual arrangement with the King's Company; *1679 The Massacre of Paris* is banned for political reasons; *1680* production of *Lucius Junius Brutus* is banned after several performances; *1684-1688* inmated as insane in Bethlem Hospital; *1689* publishes some occasional poems; *The Massacre of Paris* is produced; dies and is buried in London, May 1692.

Author's Bibliography (with dates of first production and first publication)

The Tragedy of Nero (1674; 1675) *Sophonsiba* (1675; 1676); *Gloriana* (1676; 1676); *The Rival Queens* (1677; 1677); *Mithridates* (1678; 1678); (with John Dryden) *Oedipus* (1678; 1679); *Caesar Borgia* (1679; 1680); *The Princess of Cleve* (1680 (?); 1689); *Theodosius* (1680; 1680); *Lucius Junius Brutus* (1680; 1681); (with Dryden) *The Duke of Guise* (1682; 1683); *Constantine the Great* (1683; 1684); *The Massacre of Paris* (1689; 1690).

Overview of Biographical Sources

The materials of Lee's biography are few, marginal, and, often, secondhand. The date and place of his birth are uncertain, the circumstances of his death reported only in unreliable and contradictory anecdotes. It is known that, during an era of notorious clinical imprecision, he was institutionalized for madness, and that fact has served to license critics to question the lucidity of plays written before his commital. It seems to be a fact that he wrote 13 plays, all before 1684, but their chronology is a matter of dispute and some expectations of the plays rumoured to have been written during his period of madness are still voiced in current criticism. That the most substantially documented treatment of Lee's biography, William Van Lennep's 1931 Harvard dissertation, should have remained unpublished seems somehow appropriate. Instead, in Roswell Ham's "dual biography" of Lee and Thomas Otway appeared in 1933, a book in which Lee's life is regarded only intermittently.

We should not expect the significant details of Lee's life to be extended much beyond those presented in the introduction to Stroup and Cooke's modern critical edition or the somewhat more lengthy introductory chapter in Armistead's volume in Twayne's English Author's Series (in which updated genealogical evidence and more extended consideration of the career of Richard Lee are complemented by a fuller reference to anecdotal material). That the recoverable reality of his life should be sought in his work is perhaps less than a cliché in the case of Lee. Both works, therefore, have important claims as biographical sources: Stroup and Cooke's edition because it supplies so much basic information about Lee's literary productions; Armistead's study because it so consciously attempts to examine Lee's drama as a coherent development of his thought.

Evaluation of Selected Biographies

Armistead, J.M. *Nathaniel Lee*. Boston: Twayne, 1979. Armistead's examination of the author's work is supplemented by a chronology, an introductory biographical chapter, and a selected bibliography. Two sources of continuity are identified in Lee's plays: an interest in exploring "the mental pathology of political leadership" and a concern for demonstrating the actions of providence, the existence of a "cosmic order." It is Armistead's attempt to establish a coherent intellectual development in Lee's dramaturgy which marks his book as more a critical biography than a purely critical work. Although he often introduces his discussion of the individual plays with plot summaries, the dramatic facts of the plays seem at times to be interpreted to fit the thematizing approach which Armistead favors.

Armistead's study is totally coherent, but it is less than comprehensive. There is perhaps good reason for ignoring Lee's poetry, but not for failing to consider his two dramatic collaborations with Dryden. Moreover, while considerable attention is devoted to Lee's sources, very little of the discussion is given to Lee's dramatic language.

Ham, Roswell Gray, *Otway and Lee: Biography From a Baroque Age*. New Haven: Yale University Press, 1933. Reference is still made in current criticism to parts of Ham's biographical and critical treatment of Lee. However, the book's title clearly indicates Ham's priorities: at times, dozens of pages of this relatively short book go by without significant reference to Lee. Moreover, his view of the two playwrights as Restoration "type-figures" was apparently sufficient license for Ham to range beyond biographical facts to discursive considerations of theatrical, social, cultural, and political history. Consequently, readers primarily concerned with Lee might find the book exasperating, unless its index is used judiciously.

Stroup, Thomas B. and Arthur L. Cooke, ed. *The Works of Nathaniel Lee.* 2 vols. New Brunswick, NJ: Scarecrow Press, 1954. The introductory "Life of Nathaniel Lee" may be read without reservation. Each of the critical texts of the plays is prefaced by a discussion of textual and stage history, sources, and criticism.

Overview of Critical Sources

Although most of the significant critical work on Lee's drama has appeared in the last two decades, only one book devoted to Lee has been published. However, two critical tendencies should be identified. One is to be found most conspicuously in books designed as general treatments of Restoration drama. Laura Brown, Eric Rothstien, and Geoffrey Marshall all examine Lee with some particularity, but not so much for his intrinsic merit as for the evidence he supplies for their cases. For Brown and Rothstien, Lee's drama manifests the changes in Restoration dramatic form; for Marshall, Lee's language epitomizes Restoration dramatic diction. The key texts for these books are *Sophonsiba, The Rival Queens,* and *Lucius Junius Brutus.*

Lucius Junius Brutus is perhaps the key text of the criticism representative of the second tendency. This criticism's point of departure is the play's apparently strident Whiggish sentiments. While starting from a problem more of political than purely dramatic history, the attempt to make fuller sense of this play has served to focus attention more closely upon those of Lee's plays which are either politically or dramatically relevant to *Brutus.*

While Robert Hume has shown that these two critical tendencies are not antithetical, the argument of J.M. Armistead's book on Lee (discussed in the previous section) represents a development of neither tendency so much as an attempt to discover thematic coherence in Lee's dramatic career.

Evaluation of Selected Criticism

Brown, Laura, *English Dramatic Form, 1660-1760: An Essay in Generic History.* New Haven: Yale University Press, 1981. Brown's examination of *Sophonsiba, The Rival Queens,* and *Lucius Junius Brutus* is part of a densely and provocatively argued consideration of the interaction of ideology and dramatic form in the transformation of Restoration serious drama. Lee is represented as a key figure in the dramatic (and ideological) shift from the "evaluative hierarchies" of heroic action to the pathetic effects of affective drama on the Restoration stage. Some readers may find her analyses of the plays more convincing than the thesis they are used to support.

Brown, Richard E. "Heroics Satirized by 'Mad Nat Lee.'" in *Papers on Language and Literature* 19 (1983): 385-401. Reacting to the "critical myth" which associates the ranting language of Lee's early plays with his later madness, Brown suggests that the plays Lee produced between 1680 and 1682 should be viewed as a group remarkable for their discipline. He persuasively argues that in these plays the language of passion is sometimes treated ironically and self-control is idealized, and that this tendency finds its fullest dramatic realization in *Lucius Junius Brutus*. However, the notion that the heroic self-control of Brutus is the dramatic core of the play is open to question.

Hume, Robert D. "The Satiric Design of Nat. Lee's *The Princess of Cleve*" in *Journal of English and Germanic Philology* 75 (1976): 117-138. rpt. in Robert D. Hume, *The Rakish Stage: Studies in English Drama, 1660-1800*. Carbondale: Southern Illinois University Press, 1983. Critics have usually found this play repulsive. Hume doesn't simply analyze the play to confirm its nastiness nor is he satisfied to reexamine the chronology of Lee's plays to supply a motivation for Lee's nihilistic attitude—the author's "bow to political expedience" after the banning of *Lucius Junius Brutus*. Hume proposes some dramatic models for the play and identifies the "extrinsic targets" of its satiric attack.

Marshall, Geoffrey, *Restoration Serious Drama*. Norman: University of Oklahoma Press, 1975. The major part of Marshall's study is devoted to examining the conventions of Restoration serious drama. In his chapter on dramatic diction, almost all of his illustrative examples are drawn from *Lucius Junius Brutus*. Consequently, Marshall has done something uncommon in the criticism of Lee—examined closely the use of language in extended passages from one of his plays. His poetic and rhetorical readings of the passages are enlightening, but the passages themselves were chosen as representative of Restoration dramatic practice, not as representative of Lee's most typical style.

Rothstien, Eric, *Restoration Tragedy: Form and the Process of Change*. Madison: University of Wisconsin Press, 1967. Rothstien's chapter on the late heroic play has been influential—one instance is Laura Brown's study. In it, Rothstien offers perhaps the best analysis of *Sophonsiba*. This chapter is followed by one which focuses in part upon Lee in charting the development of tragedy after 1675. Since so much of the recent criticism of Lee has been devoted to *Lucius Junius Brutus*, Rothstien's remarks may not have the freshness they once possessed, but his rigorous analysis of the play's opening speech is still remarkable.

Vieth, David M. "Psychological Myth as Tragedy: Nathaniel Lee's *Lucius Junius Brutus*" in *Huntington Library Quarterly* 39 (1975): 57-76. Vieth begins by identifying three approaches to the play—as Whig propaganda, as Aristotelian tragedy, as affective tragedy—which have gone only part way toward a fully satisfactory reading of the play. Vieth proposes the term "psychological myth" to describe the organizing principle he feels most adequately explains critics' enthusiastic responses to the play. Indeed, Vieth's is a powerfully argued thesis which does much to explain the dramatic dynamics of the play.

Other Sources

Armistead, J.M. *Four Restoration Playwrights: A Reference Guide to Thomas Shadwell, Aphra Behn, Nathaniel Lee, and Thomas Otway.* Boston: G.K. Hall and Co., 1984.

Hagstrum, Jean H. *Sex and Sensibility: Ideal and Erotic Love from Milton to Mozart.* Chicago: University of Chicago Press, 1980.

Hume, Robert D. *The Development of English Drama in the Late Seventeenth Century.* Oxford: Clarendon Press, 1976.

Kastan, David S. "*Nero* and the Politics of Nathaniel Lee" in *Papers on Language and Literature* 13 (1977): 125-35.

Parsons, Philip, "Restoration Tragedy as Total Theatre" in *Restoration Literature: Critical Approaches.* ed. Harold Love. London: Methuen, 1972, pp. 59-64.

Sutherland, James. *English Literature in the Late Seventeenth Century.* New York: Oxford University Press, 1969.

Waith, Eugene M. *Ideas of Greatness: Heroic Drama in England.* New York: Barnes and Noble, 1971.

James Maloney
Ryerson Polytechnical Institute
Ontario, Canada

GOTTHOLD EPHRAIM LESSING
1729-1781

Author's Chronology

Born, 1729, Kamenz, Saxony; *1741* enters St. Afra, Prince's School, Meissen; *1746* enters University of Leipzig; *1751* enters University of Wittenberg; *1752* receives M.A.; *1755 Sara Sampson* performed and published; *1753* begins friendship with Mendelssohn; *1756* begins European tour; *1767* publishes *Hamburgische Dramaturgie*; *1772 Emilia Galotti* performed and published; *1776* marries Eva König; *1778* wife dies; 1781 dies in Braunschweig.

Author's Bibliography (selected)

The Young Scholar, 1748, tr. 1878 (comedy); *The Jews*, 1749, tr. 1801 (comedy); *The Freethinker*, 1749, tr. 1838 (comedy); *Miss Sara Sampson*, 1755, tr. 1878 (domestic tragedy); *Lacoön, or the Limits of Painting and Poetry*, 1766, tr. 1836 (criticism); *Hamburg Dramaturgy*, 1767, tr. 1836 (criticism); *Minna von Barnhelm, or the Soldier's Fortune*, 1769, tr. 1858 (comedy); *Emilia Galotti, A Tragedy in Five Acts*, 1772, tr. 1786; *Nathan, the Wise*, 1779, tr. 1781 (dramatic poem in blank verse); *The Education of the Human Race*, 1780, tr. 1858 (essay).

Overview of Biographical Sources

Limiting the discussion of biographical sources on Lessing to those available in English eliminates many significant studies of this major figure's life; for it does not account for such excellent works as Karl S. Guthke and Heinrich Schneider's *Gotthold Ephraim Lessing* (Stuttgart, 1967). In fact, the student of Lessing's life is left with the dated and sometimes awkwardly written volume, T.W. Rolleston's *Life of Gotthold Ephraim Lessing* (1889). Rolleston's work has merit, but better, although more limited, discussions of Lessing's biography appear in works primarily interested in his drama and criticism such as F. Andrew Brown's *Gotthold Ephraim Lessing* (New York: Twayne, 1971) and H.B. Garland's *Lessing: The Founder of Modern German Literature* (London: Macmillan, 1962).

Evaluation of Selected Biographies

Rolleston, T.W. *Life of Gotthold Ephraim Lessing*. London: Walter Scott, 1889. This source is of little value as a critical tool, in part because it was written before the full impact of Lessing's criticism could be appreciated. It does, however, provide the essential information on Lessing's life. In particular, it discusses in great detail the effect the events of the time had on Lessing and his thought, from the wars he lived through to the theological discussions in vogue. Also, and helpful indeed, is the attention Rolleston gives to discussing the relationship Lessing had with other notable writers such as Goethe and Voltaire. The source is dated, but this fact does not inhibit its primary focus on Lessing's life.

Autobiographical Sources

In large part, autobiographical sources are not available. However, Lessing's correspondence is gathered in *Sämtliche Schriften*, 23 vols. 3rd ed. Franz Muncker. Leipzig: G.J. Goschen' sche Verlagsbuchhandlung, 1886-1924. The collected letters includes both those written by and to Lessing.

Overview of Critical Sources

Several studies of Lessing's work as a dramatist, critic and theologian have been written in English. J.G. Robertson's *Lessing's Dramatic Theory: Being an Introduction to and Commentary on his Hamburgische Dramaturgie* (1939) is perhaps the most important. Also necessary for a complete study would be F.J. Lamport's *Lessing and the Drama* (1981) and F. Andrew Brown's *Gotthold Ephraim Lessing* (1971). For a detailed bibliography that includes materials written in German, the student should consult Karl S. Guthke and Heinrich Schneider's *Gotthold Ephraim Lessing* (Stuttgart, 1967).

Evaluation of Selected Criticism

Brown, F. Andrew, *Gotthold Ephraim Lessing*. New York: Twayne, 1971. This is an excellent Twayne edition as it touches all bases important to an understanding of Lessing's career as a playwright, critic, dramaturg, and theologian. As well, Brown illustrates Lessing's maturing intellect as he moved through several distinct phases in his creative and scholarly career. There are gaps, which Brown acknowledges, and a tendency to eulogize Lessing a bit excessively; however, the study is excellent for the student seeking an accurate overview of Lessing's life and contributions to the German theatre.

Garland, H.B. *Lessing: The Founder of Modern German Literature*. London: Macmillan, 1962. The primary focus of this study is on Lessing the thinker and scholar, not the playwright. Garland provides excellent discussions of Lessing's criticism and theological position. In particular, the volume strives to establish the validity of the author's claim that Lessing was "unsurpassed in his versatility." Garland defends the proposition through this approach that Lessing deserves credit for shaping a chaotic German literary tradition into a major force in European literature. Notable, also, is the ease with which this work reads, making its excellent points accessible to the student.

Lamport, F.J. *Lessing and the Drama*. Oxford: Clarendon Press, 1981. Perhaps the best study on Lessing available, this volume provides the necessary detail on

Lessing's life to explain much of his later thinking. The especial merit, however, is the excellent discussions of Lessing's two major tragedies, *Sara Sampson* and *Emilia Galotti*. Lamport also gives solid discussion to Lessing's role in the development of a national German theatre. The study is extremely well written and deserves especial attention in any study of Lessing.

Robertson, J.G. *Lessing's Dramatic Theory: Being an Introduction to and Commentary on his Hamburgische Dramaturgie*. Cambridge: Cambridge University Press, 1939. Robertson's lengthy and detailed study of Lessing's critical theory is necessary reading. It establishes the link between Lessing's work at the Hamburg Theatre and his theory of the drama. In particular, Robertson notes the influence of the dramas of other countries on Lessing's thought. The result is a full and detailed account of Lessing's major critical work.

Other Sources
Allison, Henry E., *Lessing and the Enlightenment: His Philosophy of Religion and its Relation to Eighteenth-Century Thought*. Ann Arbor: University of Michigan Press, 1966. Study of Lessing's thought aside from his influence on the drama.

Selected Dictionaries and Encyclopedias
McGraw-Hill Encyclopedia of World Drama, McGraw-Hill, 1972. Biography and discussion of major dramas.

The Oxford Companion to the Theatre, Oxford University Press, 1967. Biographical sketch.

The Reader's Encyclopedia of World Drama, Thomas Y. Crowell, 1969. Biographical sketch.

Gerald W. Morton
Auburn University
Montgomery

GEORGE LILLO
1693-1739

Author's Chronology
Born February 4, 1693, Moorfields, London, England; works in family jewelry business in London; *1730 Silvia* produced at Drury Lane; *1731 The Merchant* (later called *The London Merchant*) opens to public acclaim at Drury Lane; September 3, 1739, dies in London.

Author's Bibliography (selected)
Silvia, 1730 (drama); *The London Merchant*, 1731 (drama); *The Christian Hero*, 1735 (drama); *Fatal Curiosity*, 1737 (drama); *Marina*, 1738 (drama); *Elmerick: or Justice Triumphant*, 1740 (drama); *Britannia and Batavia*, 1740 (drama); *Arden of Faversham*, 1762 (drama); *Works*, 1740, 1775.

Overview of Biographical Sources
In his brief article in *Philological Quarterly* (XLVI, 3, July, 1967), C.F. Burgess accurately remarks that "Lillo must be ranked as the least documented and most elusive of figures in the annals of English literary history." Very little is known of the playwright's life. The precise date of his birth is disputed, and even somewhat more significant facts, such as his personal religious persuasion, were held in error until Burgess's discoveries in 1967. Thomas Davies' edition of *The Works of Mr. George Lillo; With Some Account of his Life* (London, 1775, 1810) and Theophilus Cibber's entry in his *Lives of the Poets of Great Britain and Ireland* (London, 1753) are the principal early biographies by authors personally acquainted with Lillo. While interesting for their glimpses of Augustan life and times, they must be used with caution by the student seeking sound information on the life.

Evaluation of Selected Biographies
Burgess, C.F. "Further Notes for a Biography of George Lillo," in *Philological Quarterly*, XLVI (1967): 424-428. Burgess's most important discovery is that Lillo probably was not a religious dissenter as earlier biographers had claimed. This biographical error had long been used to support the view of Lillo's works as vehicles of puritan reform. The evidence obtained from family marriage records strongly supports Burgess's conclusion that Lillo's "religious orientation was, in fact, orthodox and Anglican."

Cibber, Theophilus, *The Lives of the Poets of Great Britain and Ireland*. London, 1753. Cibber was manager of the Drury Lane theatre when Lillo's most famous play, *The London Merchant*, was introduced; Cibber himself played the lead, George Barnwell. The accounts, then, of Lillo's literary career are most likely accurate. The accounts of the personal life, however, are probably less reliable. While Cibber certainly knew Lillo, it is questionable how intimate their relationship was, and since other authors contributed to the production of the biographies, it is not even certain that Cibber authored the Lillo entry.

Pallette, Drew B. "Notes for a Biography of George Lillo," in *Philological Quarterly*, XIX (1940): 261-267. In this brief article, Pallette provides the first new insights into Lillo's life since the biographies of the eighteenth century. Several inaccuracies in the earlier accounts are revealed, and through examination of original records and documents, Pallette discovers that the traditional birth date of the author may be incorrect and sheds light on Lillo's family ties.

Overview of Critical Sources

The London Merchant is among the most frequently authologized British plays. Any biographical-critical account of Lillo will note that the play was praised by Pope, Diderot, and Rousseau, used as a model by Lessing, and lauded by Schiller and Goethe. Now the play survives—to the extent it has survived—as a piece unimportant in itself but of considerable importance as an influence in the history of the European drama. In his *History of English Drama, 1660-1900* (Cambridge: Cambridge University Press, 1952). Allardyce Nicoll calls Lillo a "father of Ibsen," and William H. McBurney in the introduction to the Regents edition of *The London Merchant* (1965) remarks that Millwood sounds "an Ibsenesque note." Still, Lillo has attracted very little critical attention, and this is not surprising. His major play is far too didactic for the modern taste, and his elevated prose works against effective characterization of the middle and lower classes. Indeed, Ernest Bernbaum in *The Drama of Sensibility* (1958) suggests that even in the eighteenth century the play was so often performed due to the urging of the upper class who, not necessarily enjoying it themselves, deemed it a good lesson for the lower classes.

Evaluation of Selected Criticism

Bernbaum, Ernest, *The Drama of Sensibility: A Sketch of the History of English Sentimental Comedy and Domestic Tragedy, 1696-1780*. Gloucester, MA: Peter Smith, 1958. Bernbaum includes a chapter on "The Rise of George Lillo: 1729-1732," which fairly acknowledges his influence but mainly treats him as a product of the already established sentimental tradition. Like most critics, Bernbaum deals almost entirely with *The London Merchant*, but his comparison of the play to its old ballad source and the conventions of sentimental literature finally reveal a work less innovative than has usually been supposed.

Hudson, William Henry, *A Quiet Corner in a Library*. Chicago: Rand McNally, 1915. Hudson's chapter on Lillo includes a thoughtful analysis of *The London Merchant*, which considers both its particular faults as a play and the reasons for its important place in the history of European drama. Lillo, it is argued, was a better playwright than his most famous play would indicate; *Fatal Curiousity* is in all respects a superior tragedy. *The London Merchant* became a classic due to the accident of its unique subject matter appearing at the right time in the social and literary history of Europe to exercise a significant influence on the development of middle class, domestic themes in the literature to follow.

McBurney, William H. ed. *The London Merchant*. Lincoln: University of Nebraska Press, 1965. McBurney's introduction to this Regents Restoration Drama Series edition of *The London Merchant* provides a fine critical overview. The reactions, both positive and negative, of Lillo's contemporaries are discussed with scholarly objectivity before McBurney proceeds to a consideration of the theme against the background of the author's dissenting religious views. McBurney asserts that some of Lillo's characterizations, principally Millwood, go beyond the narrow approach of a morality play and that, in at least some respects, the author was quite effective in his craft.

Other Sources
Baugh, Albert C. ed. *A Literary History of England*. New York: Appleton-Century-Crofts, 1948. George Sherburn's history of the eighteenth century briefly treats Lillo as a greater influence than playwright.

Day, Martin S. *History of English Literature 1660-1837*. Garden City: Doubleday, 1963. A general look at *The London Merchant* intended for students unfamiliar with Lillo and his masterpiece.

Selected Dictionaries and Encyclopedias
The Cambridge Guide to English Literature, Cambridge University Press, 1983. A brief biographical and critical overview.

Great Writers of the English Language: Dramatists, St. Martin's Press, 1979. Lillo's place in the development of domestic tragedy.

The Library of Literary Criticism of English and American Authors, Peter Smith, 1959. An anthology of brief biographical and critical comments on Lillo by eighteenth- and nineteenth-century authors.

William J. Heim
University of South Florida

THOMAS LODGE
1558-1625

Author's Chronology

Born 1558, London, son of Sir Thomas Lodge, sometime Lord Mayor of London; *1571* student at the Merchant Taylor's School; *1573* enters Oxford; *1578* awarded a Bachelor of Arts degree at Trinity College, Oxford; *1578* proceeds to Master of Arts, accepted as a law student at Lincoln's Inn; *1579 A Reply to Gosson's 'Schoole of Abuse'* published; mother dies, leaves Lodge a landed estate; *1584 An Alarum Against Usurers* published; father dies, disinherits Lodge; *1586?* *The Wounds of Civil War* composed; *1587* voyages with Captain Clarke to the Canary Islands and the Azores, approximate composition date of *A Looking Glasse, for London and Englande*, with Robert Greene; *1597* enrolls at the University of Avignon; *1598* awarded M.D. degree from Avignon; *1601* a Latin translation, *The Flowers of Lodowicke of Granado* published; *1602 The Famous and Memorable Works of Josephus* published, becomes Doctor of Medicine at Oxford; *1604* marries Joan Aldred, leaves England after being rejected for a medical license in London, to practice in Belgium; *1610* admitted to College of Physicians at London; *1623* approximate composition date of *The Poor Mans Talentt*, a collection of medical remedies; September *1625* dies of the plague (?) in London—burial place unknown.

Author's Bibliography (selected)

A Reply to Stephen Gosson's 'Schoole of Abuse', 1579(?); *An Alarum Against Usurers*, 1584; *Scillaes Metamorphosis*, 1589; *Rosalynde. Euphues Golden Legacie*, 1590; *The Famous, True and Historicall Life of Robert Second Duke of Normandy, Surnamed for His Monstrous Birth and Behaviour, Robin the Divell*, 1591; *Euphues Shadow, the Battaile of the Sences*, 1592; *Phillis: Honoured with Pastorall Sonnets, Elegies, And Amorous Delights. Whereunto is Annexed, the Tragicall Complaynt of Elstred*, 1593; *A Looking Glasse for London and Englande*, 1594; *The Wounds of Civil War: Lively Set Forth in the True Tragedies of Marcus and Scilla*, 1594; *A Fig for Momus*, 1595; *A Margarite of America*, 1596; *Wits Miserie and the Worldes Madnesse: Discovering the Devills Incarnat of this Age*, 1596; *The Famous and Memorable Workes of Josephus, A Man of Much Honour and Learning Among the Jewes*, 1602; *The Workes both Morrall and Natural of Lucius Annaeus Seneca*, 1614.

Collections: *A Select Collection of Old Plays*, Vol. 8, ed. Robert Dodsley, 1825; *The Complete Works of Thomas Lodge*, 4 vols., ed. Edmund Gosse, 1883; *'Menaphon' by Robert Greene and 'A Margarite of America' by Thomas Lodge*, ed. G.B. Harrison, 1927; *'Rosalynde,' Being the Original of Shakespeare's 'As You Like It,'* ed. W.W. Greg, 1931; *Elizabethan Minor Epics*, ed. Elizabeth Story

Donno, 1963; *Elizabethan Narrative Verse,* ed. Nigel Alexander, 1967; *The Wounds of Civil War,* ed. Joseph W. Houppert, 1970; *An Old-Spelling Critical Edition of Thomas Lodge's 'A Margarite of America,'* ed. James Clyde Addison, Jr., 1980; *'A Looking Glasse for London and England' by Thomas Lodge and Robert Greene: A Critical Edition,* ed. George Alan Clugston, 1980.

Overview of Biographical Sources

Lodge's diverse activities as critic, recusant, novelist, poet, translator, dramatist, man of letters, man of business, sailor, and physician, have made it difficult for biographers to develop a coherent account of his life. Early biographies by Anthony à Wood, *Athenae Oxonienses,* 1813-20, and Sidney Lee, *Dictionary of National Biography,* 1893, depict Lodge as a restless, competent writer who fell just short of greatness. In the 1930s, the use of court records by Charles J. Sisson, *Thomas Lodge and Other Elizabethans,* 1933, provided considerable detail about Lodge's relationship with his father and other members of his family, and also helped future biographers to track Lodge's movements around London and the continent. In 1936, the Historical Manuscripts Commission published some hitherto unknown letters of Lodge, which are discussed in Joseph W. Houppert's "Thomas Lodge's Letters to William Trumbull," in *Renaissance News,* 18 (1965): 117-23. James George made further significant use of archival material in his "Additional Materials on the Life of Thomas Lodge Between 1604 and 1613," in *Papers Mainly Shakespearean,* compiled by George L. Duthie, 1964. Sisson's romantic view of Lodge as an egocentric wanderer is challenged by both Houppert and George, who emphasize Lodge's resourcefulness in meeting his difficulties as a recusant and his commitment to medicine toward the end of his life. N. Burton Paradise's 1931 *Thomas Lodge: The History of an Elizabethan* is a substantial study of Lodge's life and works. There is no standard biography.

Evaluation of Selected Biographies

Paradise, N. Burton, *Thomas Lodge: The History of an Elizabethan.* New Haven, CT: Yale University Press, 1931; rpt. Archon Books, 1970. One of the first and best of the biographical and critical studies of Lodge.

Rae, Wesley D. *Thomas Lodge.* New York: Twayne, 1967. A good general study of Lodge, flawed by some careless errors in discussing his literary output.

Sisson, Charles J. ed., *Thomas Lodge and Other Elizabethans.* Cambridge: Harvard University Press, 1933; esp. Sisson, "Thomas Lodge and his Family;" pp. 1-165. Leans heavily on court documents, but sometimes makes unwarranted assumptions about Lodge's character on the basis of the legal evidence.

Tenney, Edward A. *Thomas Lodge.* Ithaca, NY: Cornell University Press, 1935. A careful but at times speculative study of Lodge's life and work.

Autobiographical Sources

There are autobiographical references in the very first work that Lodge prepared for publication, his *A Reply to Stephen Gosson's School of Abuse*. Additional biographical references appear in his last word on the subject of stage censorship, his preface to *An Alarum Against Usurers*. This latter work, which also satirizes money-lenders, no doubt refers to Lodge's own difficulties in locating money out of season, and is particularly effective in exposing the sharp financial practices then current in London. Usurers are also attacked, again reflecting Lodge's personal experience, in the play he co-authored with Robert Greene, *A Looking Glass for London and England*. *Wits Miserie and the Worlds Madnesse* conveys Lodge's attitude toward contemporary mores, and *A Margarite of America* his pessimistic view of New World explorations. His difficulties with inheritances (the independence his mother left him and his father's decision to disinherit him) form the subject matter of *Rosalynde*. And his last treatise, *The Poor Mans Talentt*, is an amalgam of remedies drawn from his personal experience as a physician.

Critical Sources

The first critic to take Lodge seriously as a literary artist was Edmond Gosse, who discussed him in relation to the other great Elizabethans in the preface to his edition of Lodge (1883), particularly his influence on Sidney and Shakespeare. Aside from general criticism, much of the material about Lodge has focused on his sources, and how he himself has functioned as a source for other, greater writers, usually (according to many critics) in a negative or inferior way. Shakespeare scholars in particular have mined *Rosalynde*, Shakespeare's source for *As You Like It*, for invidious comparisons to Shakespeare's comedy. Robert B. Pierce, in his "The Moral Languages of *Rosalynde* and *As You Like It*," *Studies in Philology*, 68 (1971): 167-76, states that Shakespeare's moral vision is infinitely superior to Lodge's, while Nancy R. Lindheim, in "Lyly's Golden Legacy: *Rosalynde* and *Pandosto*," *Studies in English Literature*, 15 (1975): 3-20, suggests that scholars look backward to Lyly rather than forward to Shakespeare in evaluating Lodge. In contrast, Sylvan Barnet, in "Strange Events: Improbability in *As You Like It*," *Shakespeare Studies*, 4 (1968): 119-131, observes that Shakespeare made Lodge's plot even more implausible than it was originally, and lessened the degree of motivation among the characters, in order to depict a strange and magical world. For Edward Berry, in his "Rosalynde and Rosalind," *Shakespeare Quarterly*, 31 (1980): 42-52, Lodge's female protagonist is useful only as a method of highlighting the superior qualities of Shakespeare's play. Marco Mincoff, in "What Shakespeare Did to Rosalynde," *Shakespeare-Jahrbuch*. 96 (1960): 78-89, casts doubt on the extent of Shakespeare's indebtedness to Lodge's *Rosalynde*. Even Lodge's own drama, *The Wounds of Civil War*, is discussed in Shakespearean terms in Wolfgang Clemen's *English Tragedy Before Shakespeare: The Development of Dramatic Speech*, trans. T.S. Dorsch, NY: Barnes & Noble, 1961. F.L. Beaty, in "Lodge's

Fobronius and Prisceria and Sidney's *Arcadia*," *English Studies*, 45(1968): 38-45, speculates that Lodge read Sidney's *Arcadia* in manuscript. Esther Gurke, in *The Use of Songs in Elizabethan Prose Fiction* (Bern: Francke, 1972), discusses the use of songs within the narrative framework of Lodge's fiction. Lodge's fiction is discussed in its own right in both Claudette Pollack's "Romance and Realism in Lodge's *Robin the Devil*,: *Studies in Short Fiction*, 13 (1976): 491-497, and in Walter R. Davis, "Masking in Arden: The Histrionomics of Lodge's *Rosalynde*," *Studies in English Literature*, 5 (1965):151-163. The most recent full-length study, with an extensive bibliography, is Eliane Cuvelier's *Thomas Lodge Témoin de son Temps* (Paris: the Sorbonne, 1984).

Evaluation of Selected Criticism

Armstrong, W.A. "*Tamburlaine* and *The Wounds of Civil War*," in *Notes & Queries*, 5 (1958): 381-383. Asserts that Lodge's play is indebted to Marlowe's *Tamburlaine* rather than the reverse.

Davis, Walter R. *Idea and Act in Elizabethan Fiction*. Princeton: Princeton University Press, 1981. Emphasizes the strain of idealism in Lodge's fiction, and the testing of that idealism through experience.

Hayashi, Tetsumaro, *A Textual Study of 'A Looking Glasse for London and England' by Thomas Lodge and Robert Greene*. Muncie, IN: Ball State University, 1969. One of the few textual studies of Lodge's work.

Hulse, Clark, *Metamorphic Verse: The Elizabethan Minor Epic*. Princeton: Princeton University Press, 1981. Very detailed on the stylistic and generic traits of Lodge's *Rosalynde, Scillaes Metamorphosis*, and *A Fig for Momus*.

Keach, William, *Elizabethan Erotic Narratives*. New Brunswick, NJ: Rutgers University Press, 1977. Sees the epyllion or minor epic, exemplified in Lodge's *Glaucus and Scylla*, as a serious form.

Larson, Charles, "Lodge's Rosalind: Decorum in Arden," in *Studies in Short Fiction*, 14 (1977): 117-127. Views Shakespeare as altering, for dramatic purposes, the stately and decorous form of Lodge's romance.

Pollack, Claudette, "Lodge's *A Margarite of America*: An Elizabethan Medley," in *Renaissance and Reformation*, 12(1976): 1-11. Stresses the importance of Italian sources for Lodge's work.

Roberts, Josephine A. "*A Margarite of America*: A Dystopian Vision of the New World," in *Studies in Short Fiction*, 17 (1980): 407-414. Observes that Lodge, one of the first transcontinental writers in England, takes a surprisingly negative view of the New World.

Whitworth, Charles, Jr. "*Rosalynde: As You Like It* and as Lodge Wrote It," in *English Studies*, 58 (1977): 114-117. Points out the surprising number of errors Shakespeare critics make in referring to Lodge's romance, often "remembering" it in such a way that the differences in plot and character between Lodge's tale and Shakespeare's play are obliterated.

Other Sources

A Bibliography of the English Printed Drama to the Restoration, The Bibliographical Society (London), 1957-1962. Bibliographical descriptions of Lodge's two plays.

The Elizabethan Stage, Clarendon Press, 1923. A brief biography, descriptions of the plays, and list of doubtful plays.

The History of the English Novel, Barnes & Noble, 1950. Places Lodge's fiction within the tradition of the novel, summarizes it, and analyzes the euphuistic and Arcadian features of the style.

The Predecessors of Shakespeare: A Survey and Bibliography of Recent Studies in English Renaissance Drama, University of Nebraska Press, 1973. A general bibliography of Lodge's life and works, with some annotations.

John Mulryan
St. Bonaventure University

LOPE DE VEGA
1562-1635

Author's Chronology

Born November 25, 1562 in Madrid, Spain, to Félix de Vega Carpio, a poet of modest means and his wife Francisca Fernández Flores; christened Lope Félix de Vega Carpio; *1577-1582* he attends the University of Alcalá; *1588* participates in the failed naval expedition of the Spanish Armada to England, and marries his first wife Isabel de Urbina, daughter of a prosperous Madrid official; found guilty of libel against a well-known theater personality and his family and exiled from Madrid for seven years; *1590s* becomes one of the most popular dramatists of his time and a consummate womanizer; serves as secretary to a succession of important nobles; *1595* Isabel dies; *1598* marries Juana de Guardo (d. 1613), following a passionate liaison with comic actress Micaela de Luján; *1614* takes holy orders, remaining a priest, in name only, until his death in Madrid August 25, 1632.

Author's Bibliography

Perhaps the most prolific of all Spanish writers, Lope is known to have authored an impressive number of plays—of which four hundred have survived—several pastoral novels, serious and burlesque epics, narrative poems, short stories, and a variety of poetic compositions. He is best known, however, for his plays, most of which were performed (and many published) during his lifetime. Historians of literature have attempted to authenticate and catalogue Lope's vast production; partial results appear in Hugo Albert Rennert, "Bibliography of the Dramatic works of Lope de Vega Carpio", *Revue Hispanique* XXXIII (1915): 1-282; and in 1969 ed. of Américo Castro and H. A. Rennert, *Vida de Lope de Vega (1562-1635)*: 433-507; 1916-1930 the Spanish Royal Academy undertook the reediting and publication of the most comprehensive list of Lope's works, the thirteen-volume *Obras de Lope de Vega*, and 1935-1943 the four-volume *Epistolario de Lope de Vega y Carpio*, ed. by Agustín G. de Amezúa.

Overview of Biographical Sources

Lope's professional accomplishments have generated enormous interest among scholars and critics since the sixteenth century. His life, however, has received much less attention in spite of the fact that it was always colorful and at times quite scandalous. Lope's first biographer was his young contemporary and admirer Juan Pérez de Montalbán. In his *Fama póstuma a la vida y muerte del doctor Frey Lope Félix de Vega y Carpio* . . . (17th century), Montalbán emphasizes the genius of his friend while ignoring his more unsavory qualities; the work contains numerous errors in fact and a number of statements other scholars have been unable to substantiate. The first critical modern biography of Lope is C. A. de la Barrera, *Nueva biografía* (Madrid: Sucesores de Rivadeneyra, 1890), and following it closely H. A. Rennert, *The Life of Lope de Vega* (1562-1635), amplified and translated into Spanish by A. Castro with the title *Vida de Lope de Vega* (1918, 1969). This last work is the most definitive biography to date. A useful account of Lope's life is given in Francis C. Hayes, *Lope de Vega* (1967).

Evaluation of Selected Biographies

Astrana Marín, Luis, *Lope de Vega*. New York: Las Américas, 1963. An excellent thorough narrative, in Spanish, of the life of Lope, both detailed and readable. The biographer is careful in his use of the source materials and displays good judgment in assessing Lope's virtues and vices.

Flores, Angel, *Lope de Vega, Monster of Nature*. (1930); rpt. New York: Greenwood Press, 1969. This is a popular and entertaining dramatized account of several episodes in the life of Lope. The work is of little interest to serious students of Lope and his works.

Hayes, Francis C. *Lope de Vega*. New York: Twayne Publishers, 1967. This is a brief and clearly written account of the life and career of Lope, based on some of his writings and on serious secondary sources. The first fifty pages provide a useful summary of the writer's life, although too much emphasis is placed on Lope's romantic attachments.

Rennert, H.A. *The Life of Lope de Vega (1562-1635)*. Glasgow: Gowans and Gray, 1904. This is a thorough, careful and erudite attempt to recreate the life of Lope based on contemporary documentary material, the findings of La Barrera, and ample references from Lope's own work. Castro's additions contribute to a better understanding of the highly autobiographical nature of Lope's *La Dorotea* (1632) and its relationship to the libel episode in Lope's early career (the transcripts of which had been published in 1880s); he also clarifies and establishes decisively the facts surrounding Lope's relationship with Micaela Juján, and uses Lope's ample correspondence to support the view that toward the end of his life, and in spite of his fame, Lope became increasingly unhappy and melancholic.

Autobiographical Sources

Historians of literature have found autobiographical references in Lope's plays, in particular, *La Dorotea, La Arcadia* (1598), and *Belardo el furioso* (1588) and in his poetry and other creative writings. It is in his extensive correspondence, however, that many of the details of his private and creative life are contained. Although many individual letters have been published separately, most of Lope's correspondence appears in vols. 3 and 4 of *Epistolario de Lope de Vega Carpio*, ed. by Agustín G. de Amezúa (Madrid: Artes Gráficas "Aldus", 1941, 1943). The first two volumes of this work contain no letters and serve as a critical introduction to the correspondence. Several letters are addressed to Lope's employers, Spanish aristocrats for whom he worked as secretary; these are useful sources of information regarding Lope's reaction to contemporary events, and they offer details of his family life and his experiences as a writer and theater personality. A second important source of material, in this case a sort of intellectual autobiography, is Lope's *The New Art of Writing Plays* (1609, *Arte nuevo de hacer comedias en este tiempo*), trans. T. Brewster, in *Papers on Playmaking*, ed. Brander Matthews, (New York: Dramabooks, 1957). In this work Lope explains that the esthetic principles he follows in his plays are aimed at pleasing the public rather than the scholars and seek to entertain rather than conform to classical models. His innovations and contributions to stagecraft have earned Lope the title of creator of the national theater of Spain.

Overview of Critical Sources

Lope's creative genius has been of interest to scholars throughout the world for several centuries; there is an impressive number of books and articles in all the major languages devoted to him, and several academic journals in which Lope is the main theme. Part of this voluminous scholarship has been catalogued in Jack H. Parker and Arthur M. Fox, *Lope de Vega Studies. 1937-1962). A Critical Survey and Annotated Bibliography*, (Toronto: University of Toronto Press, 1964) and R.L. Grismer, *Bibliography of Lope de Vega*, 2 vols. (Minneapolis: 1965). Given the vastness of the secondary literature, the selection that follows is intended to offer a small sample of the types of works that English speaking scholars have been writing about Lope de Vega in the last few years.

Evaluation of Selected Criticism

Kossofff, David, A. and J. Amor y Vásquez. eds. *Homenaje a William L. Fichter*. Madrid: Castalia, 1971. This book is comprised of articles on literary criticism, many devoted to Lope, and many by English speaking scholars of the Spanish Golden Age, in honor of a distinguished colleague.

Larson, Donald R. *The Honor Plays of Lope de Vega*. Cambridge: Harvard University Press, 1977. The author defines an honor play as one where the action is centered on a protagonist who attempts to regain his honor after having lost it to a woman or to an antagonist. At the core of the nineteen plays he selected for study is the resolution of this conflict. The theme of honor is a central one in the development of Spanish civilization, and the author, by selecting plays from three separate periods of Lope's career—some of which are his most famous—shows how the playwright has addressed the subject.

McKendrick, Malveena, *Woman and Society in the Spanish Drama of the Golden Age*. Although this work is not exclusively devoted to Lope (it includes many references to Tirso de Molina and Calderón de la Barca, for example), it deals with a subject of great interest to historians of the theater, the 'mujer varonil' (the independent woman) as a character type, a role written for and played by women. The author traces the development of this character, which becomes prominent in plays of the 1580s, in a clear and informed fashion.

Trueblood, Allan S. *Experience and Artistic Expression in Lope de Vega*. Cambridge: Harvard University Press, 1974. In this serious, erudite, and detailed work the author seeks to show how one of Lopoe's best plays, *La Dorotea*, reflects but cannot be reduced to its heavy autobiographical content.

Umpierre, Gustavo, *Songs in the Plays of Lope de Vega*. London: Támesis Books, 1975. An interesting study that attempts to analyze the dramatic function of songs and music in the theater of Lope. Given the fact that most of Lope's plays included at least one song, this work contributes to the understanding of Lope's dramatic technique.

Zuckerman-Ingber, Alix, *El bien más alto. A Reconsideration of Lope de Vega's Honor Plays*. Gainesville: University Presses of Florida, 1984. Concentrating on a definition of honor which includes conjugal honor only, the author studies forty three plays and concludes that Lope sets forth a view of honor quite different from that of his Spanish contemporaries. In this way, the author argues, Lope's plays transcend their original goal—to entertain popular audiences—by challenging the traditional beliefs of his spectators. Given this fact, Lope's works must be considered important literary documents with impact on attitudes in Golden Age Spain.

Other Sources

Allen, John J. *The Reconstruction of a Spanish Golden Age Playhouse*. Gainesville: University Presses of Florida, 1983. A thorough and authentic description of the physical spaces where many of Lope's plays were originally performed.

Fitzmaurice-Kelly, James, *Lope de Vega and the Spanish Drama*. Rep. ed. (1902); rpt. New York: Haskell House, 1971. A reissue of the classic treatment.

McCrary, W. C. *The Goldfinch and the Hawk. A Study of Lope de Vega's Tragedy "El Caballero de Olmedo."* Chapel HIll: University of North Carolina Press, 1966. Informative study of the function of dreams as a dramatic device.

Morley, S. Griswold and Courtney, Bruerton, *The Chronology of Lope de Vega's 'Comedias.'* Rep. ed. (1940); rpt. New York: The Modern Language Association of America, 1966. The Pioneer dating and authenticating study of Lope's plays; a highly technical work.

Shergold, N. D. *A History of the Spanish Stage from Medieval Times to the End of the Seventeenth Century*. Oxford: Oxford University Press, 1967. A good panoramic study.

Templin, Ernst Hall, *Money in the Plays of Lope de Vega*. Berkeley: University of California Press, 1952. An analysis of wealth as a motivating force in several of Lope's works.

Wilson, E. M. & D. Moir, *The Golden Age: Drama 1492-1700*, Vol. III of *A Literary History of Spain*. ed. R. O. Jones. London-New York, 1971. An excellent historical treatment of Lope and the development of Spanish theater.

Clara Estow
University of Massachusetts
Harbor Campus

JOHN LYLY
1553?-1606

Author's Chronology

Born 1553 or 1554, son of Peter Lyly of Canterbury and Jane Burgh, grandson of grammarian William Lily; *1569* enters Magdalen College, Oxford; *1573* receives B.A. from Oxford; *1575* M.A. Oxford; *1578* resides in the Savoy in London; *1579* M.A. (by incorporation) Cambridge; *1580* until at least 1587 is a "servant" to the Earl of Oxford, probably his private secretary; *1583* receives the lease for the Blackfriars Theatre from Oxford; marries Beatric Browne of Mexborough, Yorkshire; *1584* payee for court performances by Oxford's servants, but Blackfriars Theatre is closed and Children of the Chapel, who performed his plays, stop acting at court until 1600; *1585* lends theatrical apparel to Christ Church, Oxford; *1589* enters Martin Marprelate controversy, to support the bishops, by writing *Pappe with a Hatchet*; becomes M.P. for Hindon; *1591* Paul's Boys, whom he writes for, are inhibited until 1599 for taking part in the Marprelate controversy; *1592* moves to Mexborough; *1593* M.P. for Aylesbury; *1596* returns to London and resides in St. Bartholomew; *1597* M.P. for Appleby, but is denied Mastership of Revels, which he desired; *1598* petitions Queen Elizabeth for aid, because of poverty; *1601* M.P. for Aylesbury; *1606* dies and is buried on November 30 at St. Bartholomew the Less.

Author's Bibliography (selected)

Euphues: The Anatomy of Wit, 1578 (prose); *Euphues and His England*, 1580 (prose); *Campaspe* and *Sappho and Phao*, 1583-1584 (plays); *Endimion* and *Gallathea*, 1588? (plays); *Love's Metamorphosis* and *Midas*, 1590? (plays); *Mother Bombie*, 1594 (play); *The Man in the Moon*, 1595 (play).

Overview of Biographical Sources

Knowledge of Lyly's biography and omissions from the record have remained fairly constant over the years. One authoritative treatment appears in the introduction to the standard works: R.W. Bond's *The Complete Works of John Lyly* (Oxford: Clarendon Press, 1902). A more recent assessment, George Hunter's *John Lyly, The Humanist as Courtier* (1962), is an outstanding attempt to reconstruct the social world in which the dramatist functioned. One of the ironies of Lyly studies is that the most exhaustive analysis of the writer's career is in French and has not been translated, Albert Feuillerat's *John Lyly: Contribution à l'histoire dela renaissance en Angleterre* (Cambridge: Cambridge University Press, 1910).

Evaluation of Selected Biographies

Houppert, Joseph, *John Lyly*. Boston: Twayne, 1975. This volume is a good general introduction to Lyly. It is based on the premise that his principal theme concerns the distinction between appearance and reality. Experience teaches how to distinguish the two from each other. Most of the volume concentrates on Lyly as a dramatist and follows his work, often paraphrasing plot, through early, middle, and late phases of his career. The work ends with comments on critical reception and Lyly's reputation and influence. Houppert concludes that Lyly constructed plays with a sophisticated delicacy and was a master in the delineation of plot and character.

Hunter, George, *John Lyly: The Humanist as Courtier*. Cambridge: Harvard University Press, 1962. Hunter places Lyly in the context of an Elizabethan courtly milieu, to show how he merged his literary skills with an attempt to serve the interests of the court. Hunter's work is also one of the most comprehensive treatments of Lyly's comedies. He argues that Lyly wrote for a coterie audience that shaped his aesthetic attitudes and that determined to a large measure the nature of his dramaturgy. Consequently, Hunter does not accept the theory that Lyly independently critiqued the court in his plays. This volume has a wealth of detail that rewards anyone wanting a more penetrating analysis of Lyly's place in Elizabethan society.

Wilson, John Dover, *John Lyly*. Cambridge: Macmillan and Bowers, 1905. This is the first full-length study of Lyly's place in the creation of English romantic drama. He is seen as the father of this comic form, who excelled in the creation of female character, but whose work is overwhelmed by Shakespeare.

Autobiographical Sources

Euphues is not an autobiography, but it can be read as a kind of autobiographical fantasy, in which the protagonist succeeds in every way the author fails. The work's dichotomy of Athens and Naples mirrors Lyly's worlds of the University and London. Euphues has both domains at his feet, as Lyly did not in life, and he achieves this all through his splendid wit. Lucilla, the charming heiress, falls in love with the hero—at first sight. He becomes a reader at the University, despite the fact that Lyly did not gain this position, although he tried. Lyly's hopes for an Oxford fellowship had been crushed. It appears that there are many direct parallels between Euphues and Lyly, but this reflection has been heightened by idealization and wish-fulfillment.

Lyly's letters to Queen Elizabeth, preserved in the Petyt Manuscripts of the Inner Temple tell a truer tale. Virtually bankrupt and in need of assistance, Lyly here implores the Queen, who had formerly encouraged him, to aid him, as he reveals the details of his unfortunate condition (these letters are reprinted in Hunter's *John Lyly*, pp. 85-87, which is listed above).

Overview of Critical Sources

Perhaps the most central question in all of Lyly scholarship is what constitutes the "Euphuistic" style. Ever since Croll defined it as being related to sound rather than sense, fundamentally grounded in the rhetorical effects pleasing to the ear, objections and qualifications have been raised. Critics have also been involved in searching for the sources of this extremely artificial style that became a major literary fashion in the 1580s and early 1590s in England. Aside from this, attention is devoted to the extreme care with which Lyly constructs the plots of both his prose fictions and his dramas. The critical focus in recent years has been shifted to the comedies, by scholars interested in defining a "courtly aesthetic." This has involved an attempt to judge the plays on their own terms, taking them out from the shadow of the more "realistic" drama that they inspired in the early comedies of Shakespeare.

Evaluation of Selected Criticism

Barish, Jonas, "The Prose Style of John Lyly," in *English Literary History* XXIII (1956): 14-35. Barish qualifies Croll's thesis by stressing the importance of "thought" and "sense" in Lyly's prose.

Croll, Morris and Harry Clemons, eds. *Euphues and Euphues and His England*. London: Routledge & Sons, 1916. Croll's introduction, an attempt to define the Euphusitic style, is perhaps the most widely influential criticism on Lyly. Croll maintains that Lyly's prose is held together by rhetorical effects of sound rather than sense.

Davis, Walter, *Idea and Act in Elizabethan Fiction*. Princeton: Princeton University Press, 1969. Chapter 4, "Courtly Fiction: Gascoigne and Lyly," centers on an explication of how the works of these authors test ideas of order by submitting them to experience. Humanist concepts of the value of courtly love or Platonic love, or ethical imperatives, such as self-control, prudence, education, and the Aristotelian mean are explored through the literary technique which appears in both fiction and drama.

Jeffery, Violet, *John Lyly and the Italian Renaissance*. Paris: H. Champion, 1928. This is an early study of Lyly's debt to his Italian predecessors, one that places him in the context of continental sources.

Olson, Paul, "*A Midsummer Night's Dream* and the Meaning of Court Marriage," in *English Literary History*, XXIV (1957): 95-119. This essay links Lyly and Shakespeare in the celebration of aristocratic marriage, indicating the social context that influenced the production of their plays.

Ringler, William, "The Immediate Source of Euphuism," in *Publications of the Modern Language Association* LIII (1938): 678-686. Ringler demonstrates the influence of lectures by John Rainolds of Oxford on Lyly's style.

Saccio, Peter, *The Court Comedies of John Lyly: A Study in Allegorical Dramaturgy*. Princeton: Princeton University Press, 1969. Saccio argues that Lyly's style is superbly fitted for the exploration of a complex world and that the plays are organized to reveal a static but rich world order, conveyed through allegory. The approach is extremely sophisticated and aimed at specialists.

Other Sources

Chambers, E.K. *The Elizabethan Stage*. Vol. 3. Oxford: Clarendon Press, 1923. In a section called "Plays and Playwrights," Chambers provides a condensed biography and a judicious commentary on performance and publication dates of Lyly's plays. This book is a classic, especially because it remains extremely reliable as a stage history.

Johnson, Robert, *Elizabethan Bibliographies, Supplements*. Vol. 5. London: Nether Press, 1968. This volume updates the record of scholarship from 1939-1965.

Tannenbaum, Samuel, *John Lyly (A Concise Bibliography)*. New York: S.A. Tannenbaum, 1940. The bibliography lists relevant books and articles until 1939.

Ward, A.W. and A.R. Waller, *The Cambridge History of English Literature*. Vol. 3. Cambridge: Cambridge University Press, 1909. This has a helpful biography and places the writer's work in the historical, cultural, and literary developments of the period. Particular attention is paid to the study of genre and style in Lyly's prose.

Selected Dictionaries and Encyclopedias

Dictionary of National Biography, Smith, Elder, 1893. Lee's article offers an accurate survey of Lyly's life, career, and contemporary reputation as a wit.

James P. Bednarz
Long Island University

IMRE MADÁCH
1823-1864

Author's Chronology
Born January 21, 1823, Alsó-Sztregova, Hungary; descendant of a prosperous aristocratic family; is educated at the Piarist Gymnasium, a secondary school in Vác; studied philosophy and law at the University in Pest; *1838* edits at age fifteen *Literatúrai Kevercs* (Literary Mixture), a weekly journal featuring short essays; *1838* first writes poetry, later dramas; after a successful bar examination accepts appointment of Deputy Clerk; *1843* becomes Honorary County Notary and 1844 County Court Judge; *1845* marries Erzsébet Fráter; writes reports, articles, essays, short stories, and several dramas; *1846* elected Chief Commissioner of Nográd County but forced to resign due to poor health; a serious and sensitive person with a weak constitution was plagued with health problems (pneumonia, cardiac troubles) all his life; illness prevented him from participation in the 1848 War of Independence; depressed due to collapse of political and family life (brutal murder of his sister Mari and death of his brother Pál during the war in 1849); imprisoned for helping János Rákoczy, secretary of Lajos Kossuth, to escape; *1853* released in May; *1854* divorced; *1859* begins to write his masterpiece *The Tragedy of Man*; *1861* elected to the Hungarian Parliament; *1862* becomes member of the renowned Kisfaludy Society; *1863* elected as corresponding member to the Academy of Sciences; hardly aware of fame dies at age of forty-one of heart trouble on October 5, 1864 in Alsó-Sztregova, Hungary; first performance of his masterpiece in 1883 at the National Theater in Budapest.

Author's Bibliography (selected)
Az anya gyermeke sirján, 1839 (The Mother at Her Child's Grave), (poem); *Lantvirágok*, 1840 (Lyre Flowers), (collection of twenty-six poems); *Commodus*, 1841 (drama); *Nápolyi Endre*, 1841 (Andrew of Naples), (drama); *Müvészeti érte-kezés*, 1842 (Discourse on Art), (essay); *Férfi és nó*, 1843 (Man and Woman), (drama); *Csak tréfa*, 1843 (Just a Joke), (drama); *Az ecce homo*, 1845 (The Ecce Homo), (story); *Krónika két pénzdarab sorsáról*, 1845 (Chronicle of the Fate of Two Coins), (story); *Nógrádi képcsarnok*, 1844 (Picture Gallery of Nográd), (satirical epigram); *Mária királynö, 1855* (Queen Mary), (drama); *A civilizátor*, 1859 (The Civilizer), (drama); *Mózes*, 1860 (Moses), (drama); *Csák végnapjai*, 1861 (The Last Days of Csák), (drama); *Az ember tragédiája*, 1861 (*The Tragedy of Man*, tr. 1908), (drama); *A Kolozsiak*, 1864 (The Kolozsi Family), (drama).

Összes müvei (Collected Works), ed. by Pál Gyulai, 3 vols., 1880; second edition by Gábor Halász, 2 vols., 1942; *Válogatott munkái* (Selected Works), ed. by Menyhért Palágyi, 1902; another edition by István Sötér, 1958; *Összes levelei* (Letters), ed. by Géza Staud, 2 vols., 1942. No critical ed. as yet available.

Individual editions: *A civilizátor*, 1938; *Az ember tragédiája*, 1861; first critical edition 1924; popular standard edition 1954; facsimile edition 1973; *Csák végnapjai*, 1972; *Mária királynö*, 1972; *Mózes*, 1966.

English translations: *The Tragedy of Man*, tr. by William N. Loew, 1908; tr. by Charles Henry Meltzer and Paul Vajda, 1933; tr. by Charles Percy Sanger, 1933; tr. by J.C.W. Horne, 1963; tr. by Joseph Grosz, 1965.

Overview of Biographical Sources

No monographic biography in English has yet appeared. However, Dieter P. Lotze's *Imre Madách* (Boston: G.K. Hall, Twayne, 1981), a primer in English, covers in great detail his life as well as his works and gives insight into the complexity of the poet and his creation. Although the emphasis is on *The Tragedy of Man*, his single outstanding literary work, brief interpretations of all important works are included. His personal life shaped by historical events is also stressed and references to parallel events in other European countries are mentioned.

Evaluation of Selected Biographies (Hungarian)

Balogh, Károly, *Madách, az ember és a kóltö*. Budapest: Vajna, 1934. This biography stresses the connection between his life and creativity. An interpretation of his essays, poems, aphorisms is included; here again great emphasis is placed on his masterpiece. Documented with bibliographical footnotes.

Barta, János, *Madách Imre*. Budapest: Franklin, 1942. Emphasizing his character and the literary quality of his writing, Barta shows his growth of reputation in Hungary and abroad. Includes bibliographical notes.

Palágyi, Menyhért, *Madách Imre élete és költészete*. Budapest: Athenaeum, 1900. This is an extensive biography and analysis of his writings with particular emphasis on his masterpiece *The Tragedy of Man*. Includes documents, letters; illustrated.

Overview of Critical Sources

Madách's masterpiece, *The Tragedy of Man*, a philosophical and poetic drama of fifteen scenes, written in regular iambic pentameters with short-lined rhyming stanzas, conceived on a vast scale (Lucifer escorts Adam and Eve from the Garden of Eden through historical events up to modern times), received the most attention in critical sources. The studies tend to emphasize the universal aspect of the drama and often compare it to works by Goethe, Byron, and Ibsen.

Evaluation of Selected Criticism (English)

Hevesi, Alexander, "Madách and 'The Tragedy of Man'," *The Slavonic and East European Review*, 9 (1930): 391-402. An analysis of his major work; stressing that it is without antecedent in Hungarian literature.

Mark, Thomas R. " 'Tragedy of Man': Salvation or Tragedy?" *Acta Literaria Academiae Scientiarum Hungaricae*, 15 (1973): 291-308. A brief review of major trends is followed by a detailed interpretation of Madách's philosophical concept of tragedy and salvation. See also in the same issue pp. 337-46 an article by Mihály Szegedy-Marzsák, "Life-Conception and Structure in 'The Tragedy of Man'."

Reményi, Joseph, "Imre Madách," *Bulletin of the National Theater Conference*, 12 (1950): 6-26. A critical examination of his masterpiece in the framework of literary movements of the 19th century; includes synopsis. Reprinted in his *Hungarian Writers in Literature*, ed. by A. Molnár. (New Brunswick, N.J.: Rutgers University Press, 1964; pp. 127-45.)

Roheim, Géza, "Psychology and History, or 'The Tragedy of Man'," in his *Psychoanalysis and Anthropology*. (New York: International University Press, 1968; pp. 461-87). Available also in several paperback reprints. A unique interpretation of Madách's masterpiece with emphasis on the psychological aspect of the drama.

Evaluation of Selected Criticism (Hungarian)

Mezei, József, *Madách: az élet értelme*. Budapest: Magvetö, 1977. An up-to-date comprehensive study; a philosophical interpretation of his major drama.

Németh, Antal, *'Az ember tragédiája' a szinpadon*. Budapest: Székesföváros, 1933. On the stage presentation in Hungary and abroad of *The Tragedy of Man*. A fifty years history since its premiere. Includes bibliographies, illustrations of stage sets and summaries in English, French and German.

Voinovich, Géza, *Madách Imre és 'Az ember tragédiája.'* Budapest: Franklin, 1922. Major attention is given to his writings particularly to his masterpiece. See also extensive bibliography on pp. 569-96.

Other Sources

Basa, Enikö Molnár, *The Tragedy of Man as an Example of the Poème d'Humanité*. Diss. University of North Carolina 1972. An analysis of Madách's ambitious poetic drama as well as a comparison with Shelley, Byron, Lamartine and Hugo.

Farnek, Marie Csonka, *Imre Madách's 'The Tragedy of Man' and Wilhelm Jordan's 'Demiurgos': A Comparison*. Diss. State University of New York in Buffalo, 1970. An interpretation and comparison of both works.

Horváth, Károly, *Madách Imre*. Budapest: Gonodolat, 1984. The most up-to-date study of his life and writings. For bibliography see pp. 291-7.

Krizsán, László, *Dokumentumok Madách Imre élettörténetéhez*. Balassagyarmat: Bács Kiskunm. Nyomda, 1964. Document collection covering his life up to 1861, stressing influences on *The Tragedy of Man*.

Selected Dictionaries and Encyclopedias

European Authors 1000-1900. A Biographical Dictionary of European Literature, Wilson, 1967. A short essay on his life with references to translations of his masterpiece in English. Includes a portrait of Madách. pp. 384-385.

Hungarian Authors. A Bibliographical Handbook, Harvard University Belknap Press, 1970. Among others includes brief references to life, editions, biographies and criticism. See particularly pp. 370-377; gives symbols of U.S. libraries where most of the titles listed here can be located.

The Oxford History of Hungarian Literature, Clarendon Press, 1984, pp. 211-216. A compact study referring briefly to his life but most of all to his "single masterpiece out of pessimism." For selected secondary sources see p. 501.

Elizabeth Molnár Rajec
The City College of the
City University of New York

MAURICE MAETERLINCK
1862-1949

Author's Chronology

Born on 29 August, 1862, in Ghent, Belgium, to a well-to-do family of francophone and Catholic tradition, and christened Mauritius Polydorus Maria Bernardus Maeterlinck, which eventually was shortened simply to Maurice Maeterlinck; *1874-1885* educated in a Jesuit College, and in the law school of Ghent University; *1885* first sojourn in Paris, where he meets leading young Symbolist writers; *1889* the success of Maeterlinck's first play, *La Princesse Maleine*, persuades him to give up his law practice in favor of a literary career; *1893* production of his most famous Symbolist play, *Pelléas et Mélisande*; *1901* publication of *The Life of the Bee*, his first scientifically accurate essay on a subject taken from the natural world; *1909* his most famous play, *The Blue Bird*, receives its first production by The Moscow Art Theatre, directed by Stanislavski, and is seen thereafter in London and Paris, to wide acclaim; *1911* awarded the Nobel Prize for Literature; *1940-1947* having fled the Nazis, Maeterlinck takes refuge in the United States during World War II; *1947-1949* returns to his home in Southern France, where he dies on 6 May 1949, in his eighty-seventh year.

Author's Bibliography

Maeterlinck began his literary career as a poet, and in his middle years, published numerous book-length studies on entomology and other aspects of nature, as well as essays on philosophical questions, on mysticism, metaphysics and the occult. Nevertheless, his lasting fame has been that of a dramatist, first in the Symbolist vein, and then in a more realistic manner. His first success came in 1889 with *La Princesse Maleine* (tr. *Princess Maleine*, 1911), and was followed the next year by a play about death called *L'Intruse* (tr. *The Intruder*, 1918). His most enduring triumph from his Symbolist period is the haunting tragedy of *Pelléas et Mélisande*, written in 1892 (tr. *Pelléas and Mélisande*, 1920). As he entered the twentieth century, Maeterlinck moved from unworldly Symbolism to dramas of psychological realism, in recognizable settings of time and place. The best-known of these new-style plays was the historical drama, *Monna Vanna*, of 1902 (tr. 1905). Harking back to his Symbolist style and the themes of childhood, Maeterlinck scored his greatest triumph with *L'Oiseau bleu*, written in 1905 and first performed in 1909 (tr. *The Blue Bird*, 1910). While he continued to write for the theatre, in brief bursts of activity, over the rest of his long life, it is generally considered that the success of *The Blue Bird* marked the end of his career as a famous dramatist, for nothing he produced thereafter added anything to his reputation or his lustre.

Overview of Biographical and Autobiographical Sources

Maeterlinck was a very private man, who mingled little in the literary and theatrical world in which he was famous. As a result, the most usual sorts of biographical information, in the form of letters, memoirs, reminiscences, and public records are all in short supply, and what there is is relatively uninformative. Even with friends, Maeterlinck was not very forthcoming about himself. It is startling indeed that no collection of his letters has ever been published, and only a very few individuals in the theatre who knew Maeterlinck have written much about him in their souvenirs or personal reminiscences, precisely because he was hard to get to know. The only autobiographical writing he did was a volume of memoirs written about two years before his death, and entitled *Bulles Bleues* (Monaco: Editions du Rocher, 1948). The title, which means "Blue Bubbles," suggests the light and informal tone of these memoirs, and the author's intention not to take himself too seriously. While there have been biographies, Maeterlinck is a peculiarly difficult subject for the biographer, since his life was relatively uneventful and went largely unrecorded. The award of the Nobel Prize for Literature in 1911 stimulated considerable interest in the man, for a time, but it was satisfied with relatively perfunctory accounts of his life and work up to the date of writing. As yet, no one has undertaken a thorough and complete biography of Maeterlinck, and it may be that no one ever will, since the sources are so skimpy.

Evaluation of Selected Biographies

Bithell, Jethroe, *Life and Writings of Maurice Maeterlinck*. New York: Charles Scribner's Sons, 1913. The biographical information is thin and perfunctory, but some of the comments, both on his life and his work, still have some value.

Halls, W.D. *Maurice Maeterlinck: A Study of His Life and Thought*. Oxford: Clarendon Press, 1960. Perhaps the best of the "life and works" volumes, giving a clear and reliable account of what is known of the life, and offering a thoughtful commentary on the work as well.

Knapp, Bettina L. *Maurice Maeterlinck*. Boston: Twayne, 1975. Within the two-hundred-page limits of Twayne's World Authors Series, Professor Knapp has given a most lucid and reliable account of the author's life, and an analysis of the works which is enriched considerably by Professor Knapp's expertise in Jungian psychology and the study of mysticism and the occult.

Mahony, Patrick, *Maurice Maeterlinck, Mystic and Dramatist*. A Reminiscent Biography of the Man and his Ideas. Washington: The Institute for the Study of Man, 1984. Written by a man who served as Maeterlinck's secretary during his American sojourn to escape World War II, this biography leans a bit heavily on personal reminiscence, but does provide the essential facts of the life, and a helpful, though somewhat subjective, account of the work.

Overview of Critical Sources

Even among European scholars, Maeterlinck has not been a very popular subject for the last two generations. Neither books nor articles have been numerous, and those that have written about his work have been mainly interested in elucidating that period of European drama when writers turned to the mystical, the poetic, and the surreal as a reaction against the starkness of Naturalist theatre. Maeterlinck had of course been a leader in that movement. Critical commentary has therefore tended to stress Maeterlinck's use of fantasy and of vague and unreal settings, as a period phenomenon, always with the implied acknowledgement that his dramas have dated and no longer speak to our modern world. Practitioners of semiotic and deconstructionist criticism have shown no interest in Maeterlinck, even though his work would lend itself well to those modes of analysis which are so heavily concerned with the way language is used. Since Maeterlinck's plays are not often performed these days, either, it is understandable that his work is not much studied for itself, but only as a historically significant theatrical style.

Evaluation of Selected Criticism

Clark, Macdonald, *Maurice Maeterlinck, Poet and Philosopher*. New York: Frederick Stokes, 1916. A study which is particularly strong on the philosophical elements in Maeterlinck's work, both the plays and the essays, up to the time of the awarding of the Nobel Prize for Literature.

Donneux, Guy, *Maurice Maeterlinck*. Brussels: Palais des Académies, 1961. Written in French by a Belgian, this study is perhaps the best study of Maeterlinck's work to have come from his native land.

Halls, W.D., *Maurice Maeterlinck: A Study of His Life and Thought*. Oxford: Clarendon Press, 1960. Good as a biography, this study is even better as a critical study, particularly in addressing Maeterlinck's philosophy-based ideas as expressed in his varied works.

Knapp, Bettina L., *Maurice Maeterlinck*. Boston: Twayne Publishers, 1975. Perhaps the best and most knowledgeable study of the plays of Maeterlinck, by a scholar who has been a close student of the theatre in the early twentieth century in France and who understands Maeterlinck's contributions both to dramaturgy and to mystical thought.

Postic, Marcel, *Maeterlinck et le symbolisme*. Paris: Nizet, 1970. The first study limited to Maeterlinck's participation in the Symbolist movement, both as a poet and as a dramatist.

Other Sources

Harry, Gérard, *Maurice Maeterlinck*. Brussels: Charles Carrington, 1909. Interesting and helpful early study by a Belgian who was a personal friend of Maeterlinck.

Mahony, Patrick, *The Magic of Maeterlinck*. Hollywood, CA: House-Warven, 1951. A pamphlet in praise of Maeterlinck's evocative skill with words in the theatre, by his American secretary. Excessively worshipful, and therefore to be used with caution.

Taylor, Una, *Maurice Maeterlinck*. London: Martin Secker, 1914. An early study in English, with a strong philosophical orientation.

Murray Sachs
Brandeis University

CHRISTOPHER MARLOWE
1564-1593

Author's Chronology

Born the son of a shoemaker in Canterbury and baptized on February 26, 1564; attends King's School on scholarship and then at age seventeen receives Archbishop Parker scholarship to Corpus Christi College, Cambridge, to prepare for the clergy; *1584* receives his B.A.; *1586* is finally granted his M.A. after the Privy Council, in the name of the Queen, persuades the University to grant it—quite possibly because Marlowe had been employed as a secret agent for Elizabeth; is thus certified as a proper candidate for the ministry; moves to London where he apparently associates with Robert Greene, Thomas Nashe and George Peele; *1587-1593* all his plays probably written and performed in London; *Tamburlaine,* perhaps the first, performed by the Lord Admiral's Men with Edward Alleyn in the lead; *The Jew of Malta* performed by Lord Strange's Men, and subsequently *Edward II* and perhaps *Dr. Faustus* performed by Lord Pembroke's Men; *1589* Marlowe is involved in a fight in which his opponent is killed by a friend of Marlowe's; after five months in prison obtains the Queen's pardon; *1592* charged to keep the peace toward a constable; *1588* and again in 1592 Robert Greene infers in print that Marlowe is an "atheist," meaning not orthodox in his beliefs; during these years associated with Sir Walter Raleigh's "school of night," a group of intellectuals who supposedly questioned orthodox Christian dogma; *1593* Thomas Kyd, who had earlier shared a room with Marlowe, is arrested on suspicion of atheism and under torture declares that a heretical paper found in his room belongs to Marlowe; a few days later a warrant for Marlowe's arrest issued by the Queen's Privy Council; instead of being arrested Marlowe is ordered to be available to the Council for testimony; at this point Richard Baines, a professional informer, describes in detail to the Council Marlowe's alleged heresies; ten days later on May 30, 1593, at a tavern in Deptford Marlowe is stabbed to death in mysterious circumstances by a gentleman named Ingram Frizer; according to the coroner's inquest Frizer invited Marlowe to dinner, a quarrel broke out, Marlowe attacked Frizer, and Frizer in self-defense killed Marlowe.

Author's Bibliography

Marlowe's reputation rests almost exclusively on four plays. The first, *Tamburlaine,* was actually a play and a sequel; probably first staged in 1587 and published in 1590. Next written and performed was most likely *The Jew of Malta.* Finally between 1591 and 1593 *Edward II* and *Dr. Faustus* were written and performed. *Dr. Faustus* was probably last, but *Edward II* may have been. *Edward II* was first published in 1594, the year after Marlowe's death. *Dr. Faustus* was published in two radically different editions, one in 1604 and one in 1616; both very likely contain extensive portions written by a collaborator. Besides the four major plays, Marlowe wrote two lesser plays—*Dido Queen of Carthage* and *The Massacre of Paris*—as well as the unfinished narrative poem *Hero and Leander,* some lyric poems and some translations.

The standard edition of Marlowe's works today remains R.H. Case's six-volume study, *Works and Life of Christopher Marlowe* (1933; rpt. 1966). This modern-spelling edition is fully annotated and has critical appraisals of the works and discussion of their sources. A recent reliable old-spelling edition is that by Fredson Bowers (1973). For *Dr. Faustus* an important source is W.W. Greg's parallel text edition (1950), which asserts the authority of the 1616 quarto over the 1604 version. Irving Ribner's modern-spelling edition of the plays (1963) is an authoritative, practical edition.

Overview of Biographical Sources

Marlowe's life remains a subject of fascination because it appears to have been so flamboyant. Ever since his re-discovery in the Romantic era he has held the reputation of being one of the early prototypes of the "romantic artist." The small amount of evidence about his life does point to several sensational stereotypes: the brawler, the sensualist, the secret agent, the atheist. The plain truth is that there are few reliable facts and few certain conclusions. Almost every detail of his life in clouded by speculation.

A major impetus to our understanding of Marlowe's life occurred in 1925 when Leslie Hotson in *The Death of Christopher Marlowe* first published his discoveries of the records surrounding Marlowe's violent and mysterious death. This information was important in the excellent life by C.F. Tucker Brooke, published in Case's *Works and Life of Christopher Marlowe* (1933). In 1934 Mark Eccles' *Christopher Marlowe in London* uncovered more records showing Marlowe's run-ins with the law. Subsequent biographical studies have often been combined with critical studies—for example, in the works of Boas, Levin, and Cole.

Evaluation of Selected Biographies

Bakeless, John, *The Tragical History of Christopher Marlowe.* 2 vols. Cambridge: Cambridge University Press, 1942. Bakeless' study, although written in a turgid prose, provides the most thorough biography of Marlowe available. It includes a detailed restatement of the biographical discoveries made in the 1920s and 1930s and speculates freely on the various possible interpretations of the facts. Bakeless believes that Marlowe was probably involved in an international web of the secret service and that his death has the appearance of an assassination.

Boas, F.S. *Christopher Marlowe: A Biographical and Critical Study.* Oxford: Oxford University Press, 1940. Boas's book, sometimes considered the standard biography, provides judicious and readable coverage of the life and works. A hallmark of his modesty and restraint in interpreting the scanty evidence is the title of his final chapter, "An Attempt at a Summing-Up."

Kocher, Paul H. *Christopher Marlowe: A Study of His Thought, Learning and Character.* Chapel Hill: University of North Carolina Press, 1946. Kocher's biography argues a thesis: Marlowe was a man of broad learning, a serious thinker who wrote a carefully designed attack on Christian dogma. Starting from contemporary evidence, especially Richard Baines' testimony, Kocher argues that the biographical evidence reveals Marlowe as a fierce individualist fighting the strangulating, tyrannical power of the church; he was, in short, a revolutionary atheist. Kocher then moves from this to the works, arguing that the views of the author, who was "one of the most highly subjective playwrights of his age," are consistently promulgated in his creations. Kocher brings forward evidence to demonstrate Marlowe's substantial learning, above all in the field of divinity. In other fields Marlowe was an amateur but an accomplished one: he was an excellent Latinist, he was a very knowledgeable scholar on witchcraft and on military science, and he had a respectable knowledge of such areas as astronomy, psychology and medicine.

Overview of Critical Sources

Two views have predominated in Marlowe criticism. Through the first half of this century critics continued to see Marlowe as fostering a heroic revolutionary spirit, rejecting all that is orthodox and traditional. In the last three decades, however, this view has been replaced by that of Marlowe as ironist, Marlowe as a questioning, skeptical playwright often ambivalent in his point-of-view. There is a tendency in recent years to see him as a lost and guilt-ridden, and possibly amoral, figure. Recent critics have often focussed exclusively on the structure of the plays and on their potential as theatrical performances. Some critics have blamed weaknesses in the plays on the flawed transmission of the texts, assuming polished originals behind them; others, however, conclude that Marlowe was weak in developing and constructing his dramas. Much criticism continues to see Marlowe, fairly or unfairly, in relation to Shakespeare. Many critics also continue to move from the man to the work: they make assumptions based on the scant evidence of his life and then use these to interpret his plays.

Evaluation of Selected Criticism

Cole, Douglas, *Suffering and Evil in the Plays of Christopher Marlowe.* Princeton, NJ: Princeton University Press, 1962. Written in a clear, plain-spoken style, Cole's book is essentially thematic. It traces the main concerns of medieval and Tudor drama, placing Marlowe directly in the tradition of his English forebears and making clear how deeply he was indebted to the theology which he studied at Cambridge. Cole points out how persistently Marlowe dramatizes themes that are fundamentally Christian. He argues that except for Faustus Marlowe's protagonists do not feel guilt for their actions, that in fact they typically lack human fear and they don't feel pity. What they do feel is a sense of loss which, Cole argues, is deeply painful because it "represents the alienation of the creature from the Creator," man's loss of faith. Cole says that Marlowe is essentially ironic—that his characters fail to see that they bring on their own retribution and suffer as much as man can suffer. The image they project is of fallen man enduring internal hell on earth.

Levin, Harry, *The Overreacher: A Study of Christopher Marlowe*. Cambridge, MA: Harvard University Press, 1952. Whereas Cole sees Marlowe's world as gloom, Levin sees it as glow. His brilliant analysis is dense with wide-ranging insights into Marlowe's mind and all his works. Levin's study, which begins with Marlowe's image among his contemporaries as an Atheist, a Machiavellian, and an Epicurean, extends and generalizes these terms to the epithet, "overreacher." Both Marlowe's style, with its frequent hyperbole, and his subject matter, with its focus on a character's rapid rise to great power, wealth or knowledge, illustrate this impetus toward 'overreaching,' which Levin also refers to as the "Icarus complex." Levin is particularly adept at finding those many small threads that connect the life to the works, one work to another, and both to the literary and intellectual background. There is close stylistic analysis, much of it supported by statistical studies, and there is provocative psychological and psychoanalytical criticism, blended in this extraordinary, stimulating study.

Sanders, Wilbur, *The Dramatist and the Received Idea; Studies in the Plays of Marlowe and Shakespeare*. Cambridge: Cambridge University Press, 1968. Placing Marlowe in relation to the ideas of his time, Sanders emphasizes the difficulty of stating concisely the shifting nature of Elizabethans' religious beliefs, their notions of kingship, or their conceptions of the Machiavellian. Sanders presents Marlowe as a foil to Shakespeare within the parameters of the "received ideas": unlike his great successor, Marlowe did not have a resolute moral sense with which to judge the ideas. In Sanders' judgement *Edward II* "is amoral, not by intention, but by default." In *Dr. Faustus* Marlowe expresses an inability to love a God whom he sees as perenially wrathful toward him. He is frozen in an ineffectual position, "locked in a death embrace with the agonizing God he can neither reject nor love." Sanders admits to the power of this but believes that it falls short of greatness and succeeds only fitfully as art.

Steane, J.B. *Marlowe: A Critical Study*. Cambridge: Cambridge University Press, 1964. In contrast to Levin, Steane manages to neutralize somewhat the impact of biographical criticism and examine the works more independently. While not as brilliant as Levin, Steane does take us closer to the actual reading experience of the works and remains willing to raise questions that he only tentatively answers. In fact, just as Levin is so confident in his understanding of Marlowe's fixed views, Steane is equally frank in exploring what he sees as Marlowe's questioning mind and uncertain conclusions.

Other Sources

Battenhouse, Roy W. *Marlowe's "Tamburlaine": A Study in Renaissance Moral Philosophy.* Nashville: Vanderbilt University Press, 1941. Study that presents a radically conservative picture of Marlowe.

Bevington, David M. *From "Mankind" to Marlowe: Growth of Structure in the Popular Drama of Tudor England.* Cambridge: Harvard University Press, 1962. An examination of the features of Marlowe's plays that stem from theatrical practices of the Tudor era.

Eccles, Mark, *Christopher Marlowe in London.* Cambridge: Harvard University Press, 1934. Biographical study that adds important material about Marlowe's run-ins with the authorities.

Ellis-Fermor, Una M. *Christopher Marlowe.* London: Methuen, 1927. Early study that paints a consistent portrait of Marlowe as a frustrated idealist.

Hotson, J. Leslie, *The Death of Christopher Marlowe.* New York: Russell & Russell, 1925. Seminal work that presents Hotson's discovery of the coroner's report on Marlowe's death.

Henderson, Philip, *Christopher Marlowe.* London: Longmans, Green, 1952. Accessible biography and overview of the works.

Leech, Clifford, ed. *Marlowe: A Collection of Critical Essays.* Englewood Cliffs, NJ: Prentice-Hall, 1964. Selections from most of the major critics and focused primarily on the four major plays.

Logan, Terence P. and Denzell S. Smith, *The Predecessors of Shakespeare: A Survey and Bibliography of Recent Studies in English Renaissance Drama.* Lincoln, NB: University of Nebraska Press, 1973. Contains an excellent fifty-five page survey of Marlowe studies written by Robert Kimbrough.

Elliott Denniston
Missouri Southern State College

JOHN MARSTON
1576-1634

Author's Chronology

Christened October 7, 1576, Wardington, Oxfordshire, England, his father a Coventry lawyer and his mother the daughter of an Italian physician; *1580s* probably attends school in Coventry; *1594* receives bachelor's degree from Brasenose College, Oxford; *1598* first publication, *The Metamorphosis of Pigmalian's Image* and *Certaine Satyres*; *1599* father dies; *1599* first play, *Histriomastix*, published; *1604* buys share of the acting company Children of the Queen's Revels; *1605* possibly imprisoned for collaborating with Ben Jonson and George Chapman on *Eastward Hoe!*, which may have offended the king; also *1605* probably the year he marries Mary Wilkes, daughter of a rector; *1608* imprisoned by the Privy Council for unknown reasons, possibly because a performance of *The Fawne* was deemed an attack on King James and his court; *1608* sells share in Children of the Queen's Revels; *1606-1609* studies philosophy intently, possible leading to a profound religious experience; *1609* becomes church deacon in Stanton Harcourt, Oxfordshire; also *1609* ordained as priest; *1616* victim of strong-arm robbery; also *1616* resident of Christchurch, Hamshire; *1621* mother dies; *1624* only son dies in infancy; *1631* leaves Christchurch; *1633* collected works issued without permission by William Sheares, and he has Sheares remove his name from the collection; dies June 25, 1634, London, England. His epitaph reads *"Oblivioni Sacrum"* (Sacred to Oblivion); wife Mary dies in July 1657 and is buried beside her husband.

Author's Bibliography (selected)

The Metamorphosis of Pygmalions Image and *Certaine Satyres*, 1598 (poetic satire); *The Scourge of Villanie*, 1598 (poetic satire); *Histriomastix*, 1599 (comedy); *The History of Antonio and Mellida*, 1599 (comedy); *Jacke Drum's Entertainment*, 1600 (comedy); *Antonio's Revenge*, 1602 (tragedy); *The Malcontent*, 1604 (tragicomedy); *Parasitaster, or The Fawne* (usually known as *The Fawne),* *1604* (comedy); *The Dutch Curtezan*, 1605 (comedy); *Eastward Hoe!*, with Ben Jonson and George Chapman, 1605 (comedy); *City Spectacle*, 1606 (pageant); *Sophonisba*, 1606 (tragedy); *What You Will*, 1607 (comedy); *Entertainment of the Dowager-Countess of Derby*, 1607 (masque); *The Insatiate Countess*, with William Barksted, 1607 (tragicomedy); *The Plays of John Marston*, edited by H. Harvey Wood, 1934-1939; *The Poems of John Marston*, edited by Arnold Davenport, 1961.

Overview of Biographical Sources

Although John Marston has interested scholars since the seventeenth century, little is known about his life. Only in the past one hundred years have even the bare facts been uncovered, such as the year of his birth; even the place of his birth is a matter of controversy, with many scholars arguing for Coventry, although recent research supports Wardington. The dates for his plays remain uncertain, although those listed above are the most generally accepted ones. For instance, the dating of *What You Will* is still debated, with some scholars arguing that it preceded William Shakespeare's *Twelfth Night, or What You Will* and therefore influenced Shakespeare's play, and other scholars arguing that it followed Shakespeare's play and was therefore influenced by Shakespeare. Many other important aspects of Marston's life are unexplained. For instance, after pursuing fame as an author during his youth, Marston abandoned his literary efforts in 1608 and spent the rest of his life seeking privacy and anonymity. His change of heart may have been encouraged by his imprisonment for writing a play deemed offensive to the king, or by a profound religious experience, or both. The nature of his change of heart has not been explained.

Modern students of literature are primarily interested in Marston for his work as a playwright. Thus, biographical research has emphasized his youth at the expense of his later years as a priest. In addition, some critics have maintained that Marston's work is unworthy of any in-depth study. The almost exclusive interest in his play-writing years combined with the hostility of many critics have discouraged the writing of full-length biographies. The most complete study of Marston's life is Philip J. Finkelpearl's *John Marston of the Middle Temple* (1969). Morse S. Allen's *The Satire of John Marston*, (New York: Haskell House, 1965) and R. W. Ingram's *John Marston*, (Boston: G. K. Hall, 1979), both contain short biographical summaries that could give high school and college students the basic background of the playwright's life.

Evaluation of Selected Biographies

Finkelpearl, Philip J. *John Marston of the Middle Temple: An Elizabethan Dramatist in His Social Setting*. Cambridge, MA: Harvard University Press, 1969. This is a biocritical study of Marston's years as a playwright. It is biocritical because in addition to discussing Marston's life, it illuminates Marston's achievement in his plays by using the background of his life and times to explain what he does with his subject matter, characters, and themes. Finkelpearl takes an approach to his topic similar to that used by many other biographers of sixteenth and seventeenth-century authors for whom there is little solid information, such as diaries, letters, and legal records. He uses a vast amount of historical background to fill in what Marston's life must have been like, explaining social customs, laws, and how English dramatists plied their trade. *John Marston of the Middle Temple* is one of those rare scholarly books that is written so clearly that college students could read it for researching their term papers and with such detail that advanced scholars would profit from reading it. It thoroughly explains the many difficulties in dating the plays and provides a good background on their textual difficulties. Finkelpearl's examination of Marston's personality is the most complete and believable as yet published. The book is divided into two parts: The first provides historical and social background for Marston and his plays. The second applies the background to individual plays; students researching an individual play would find this second part particularly helpful. Seven of the plays have specific chapters devoted to them, providing excellent backgrounds from which to begin research for class papers.

Autobiographical Sources

One of the difficulties in researching John Marston's life is the lack of autobiographical materials. Most of those researchers who have been interested in Marston's biography have sought out autobiographical references in the playwright's writings. They have enjoyed their greatest success in finding such references in the poetic satires, which have allusions to friends and other contemporary personalities. Even so, most discussions of the autobiographical contents of Marston's works are speculative and not to be trusted. In *John Marston of the Middle Temple*, Finkelpearl provides the best evidence that Marston included autobiographical references in poems and plays, and he makes good use of the information to explicate passages and scenes.

Also of interest for anyone who wishes to make a detailed study of Marston's life are the following articles by R. E. Brettle: "John Marston, Dramatist at Oxford: (*Review of English Studies*, 3 [1927], 398-405); "John Marston, Dramatist: Some New Facts about His Life" (*Modern Language Review*, 22 [1927], 7-14); "Notes on John Marston" (*Review of English Studies*, 13 [1962], 309-393); and "Everard Guilpin and John Marston (1576-1634)" (*Review of English Studies*, 16 [1965], 396-399). Brettle has done more than anyone else to clarify the facts of Marston's life.

Overview of Critical Sources

Although many critics have recognized the importance of John Marston's work, from the seventeenth century to the present, only in the last twenty to twenty-five years have his plays been widely accepted as part of the basic canon of important Renaissance English drama. Many critics have maintained that Marston's writings are at best second-rate and unworthy of careful study. In spite of such unsympathetic responses to his work, Marston has become the object of much interest. The mixture of comedy and tragedy in his plays reminds many modern readers of American playwrights, such as Tennessee Williams and Arthur Miller. His plays have a strongly modern appeal and have found audiences sympathetic with his offbeat views of human relationships. *The Malcontent*, in particular, has become a common part of the college curriculum. Excellent editions of *Antonio and Mellida* (edited by George K. Hunter), *Antonio's Revenge* (edited by George K. Hunter), *The Dutch Courtesan* (edited by Martin Wise), and *The Fawn* (edited by Gerald A.

Smith), as well as *The Malcontent* (edited by Martin Wine), from the University of Nebraska Press as part of the Regents Renaissance Drama series have made Marston's plays a readily accessible part of classroom study; increased attention to Marston in the classroom has sparked much of the upsurge of critical publication on his writings.

Critical views of Marston generally fall into two camps. One sees Marston as essentially as satirist who moved from writing poetic satires to writing dramatic ones. This camp explains the problems with Marston's characterizations and plots by asserting that his satire took precedence over dramatic technique, thus subordinating character and plot to the detriment of both. The other main camp sees Marston as primarily a dramatist who was unsuccessful as a poet but found his medium in drama. This point of view portrays Marston's plays as largely successful satiric studies of human relationships and explains weaknesses of the dramas in conventional analyses of characterization, theme, and plotting.

Evaluation of Selected Criticism

Allen, Morse S. *The Satire of John Marston*. Columbus, OH: F. H. Heer, 1920. New York: Haskell House, 1965. Allen's book belongs to the critical view that Marston was primarily a satirist and that Marston's satirical themes were essentially incompatible with the dramatic form. He analyses Marston's satire as an outgrowth of a quarrelsome personality that became bitter over setbacks and disappointments until his writings degenerated from satire into hatefulness, especially toward women. Several of Marston's plays are evaluated as parts of a dramatic dispute with Ben Jonson and others in which the plays are responses to other plays by other dramatists. Brief summaries of the satirical themes of Marston's plays are provided; these may be of some help to students. The rest of the book is for graduate students and scholars.

Caputi, Anthony, *John Marston, Satirist*. Ithaca, NY: Cornell University Press, 1961 and New York: Octagon Books, 1976. Caputi asserts, "The key to the unusual integrity of Marston's work is, I am convinced, his seriocomic view of the Renaissance world." Although he does not rank Marston as a great dramatist, Caputi provides a sympathetic analysis of the plays. He examines how Marston used theme and technique to present a seriocomic view of society, and he argues that Marston can teach modern readers much about his time. Caputi traces Marston's intellectual development, declaring that "most problems concerning him trace back, almost inevitably, to his beliefs, and it bears repeating that his work derives its unity from these beliefs." Chief among the beliefs were Neo-Stoicism and Christianity. This is a fine, sensible evaluation of the merits of Marston's writings; its discussion is clear and accessible to college students.

Colley, John Scott, *John Marston's Theatrical Drama*. Salzburg, Austria: Institut für Englische Sprache und Literatur, Universität Salzburg, 1974. (Jacobean Drama Studies, no. 33.) This book would be particularly useful for anyone interested in studying how Marston's plays would work on the stage. The emphasis is on how Marston used the stage of his day to enhance his dramas and on his role as a theatrical innovator. Colley begins, "Marston's drama is 'theatrical' in every sense. He is constantly preoccupied with the dramatic profession in his plays, and his characters speak of themselves as actors, feigners, tragedians." Colley views Marston as an immature playwright who even in his masterpiece, *The Malcontent*, was unable "to assess the uneasy union of the divine and the profane in human nature." This is an excellent source book for anyone who wishes to stage one of Marston's plays; it is useful both for those who wish to teach the plays strictly as literature, as well as for those who wish to teach them as drama. Non-professional acting students will find this book helpful if they are to participate in the production of one of Marston's plays.

Geckle, George L. *John Marston's Drama: Themes, Images, Sources*. Cranbury, NJ: Associated University Presses (Fairleigh Dickinson University Press), 1980. According to Geckle, "This book is primarily a work of historical criticism designed to offer its readers new interpretations of each of those plays generally acknowledged to be written soley by John Marston." He also declares that he is "primarily concerned with themes and images in the plays of John Marston." The advantage of Geckle's book is the thoroughness of its analyses; few other resources are as detailed in thought and example. Written with high seriousness, students may find this book tough to read, although it provides excellent illustrations of how to analyze the plays. Teachers and scholars will find this book a useful reference for preparing lectures and for researching articles.

Scott, Michael, *John Marston's Plays: Theme, Structure and Performance*. London: Macmillan Press, 1978. Like Colley's *John Marston's Theatrical Drama*, this book examines Marston's plays as works meant for performance and emphasizes their theatricality. Marston is portrayed as an experimenter who tested the limitations of the dramatic form. Like Geckle's *John Marston's Drama*, this book explicates the plays through detailed discussions of their themes; it also shows how their structure would affect performances. Although the tone is too defensive throughout, as though there were some shame in devoting a book to Marston, the interpretations are insightful. Marston is portrayed as an absurdist who mixed dreams and reality, possibly confusing some members of his audience and thus accounting for much of the hostile criticism of the past few hundred years. Writing of Marston's "black vision," Scott notes, "For the vicious and the virtuous, Marston's world of illusions is indeed a bitter place." This book is concise and clear enough to be useful for researching term papers and ought to be of great interest to anyone seriously studying Marston's dramatic achievement.

Other Sources

Ingram, R. W. *John Marston*. Boston: G. K. Hall, 1978. In a general overview of Marston's writings, Ingram summarizes the major critical aspects of the poetry and plays while emphasizing Marston's intelligence and creativity. A good general introduction.

Tucker, Kenneth, *John Marston: A Reference Guide*. Boston: G. K. Hall, 1985. Tucker summarizes the major critical views of Marston in an introduction, then lists editions of the dramatist's works, and follows that list with another of works about Marston from 1598 to 1981. The citations are generally accurate and well annotated. The index lists names and titles with occasional subjects, such as "Comedy (genre)" and "Revenge plays (genre)." This book is a good reference for anyone interested in researching an aspect of Marston's work in depth.

Selected Dictionaries and Encyclopedias

Cyclopedia of World Authors. Harper and Row, 1958. A brief summary of scholarly thinking about Marston's life and work.

Kirk H. Beetz
National University, Sacramento

MENANDER
c.342 B.C.-c.292 B.C.

Author's Chronology

Born c.342 B.C., son of Diopeithes, of the deme Kephisia, northeast of Athens; is pupil of Theophrastus, who followed Aristotle as the head of the Peripatetic school; serves in the military as ephebe with the philosopher Epicurus; *321 B.C.* produces his first play, *Orge* (Anger), now lost; *316 B.C.* wins first prize at the Lenaean festival with *Dyskolos* (*The Grouch*); in thirty years writes more than one hundred plays, and wins eight victories; *c.292 B.C.* Menander drowns while swimming at the Piraeus.

Author's Bibliography

Although in life he seems to have been less popular than some of his contemporaries, Menander enjoyed great posthumous success. Numerous classical authors and critics praised him, and the Latin dramatists Plautus and Terence each based four plays on his work. By some time in the seventh or eighth century, however, all of Menander's more than one hundred comedies had disappeared. His reputation survived only through chance quotations and the Latin versions of Plautus and Terence until 1907. In that year the Cairo codex, which contained as much as one-half of *Epitrepontes* (*The Arbitrants*), *Samia* (*The Woman of Samos*), and *Perikeiromene* (*She Who Was Shorn*), was published. This first great discovery from the sands of Egypt was followed in 1959 by the publication of the part of the Bodmer codex which contained the complete text of *The Grouch*. Several other newly discovered papyri were published in the 1960s, including the remainder of the Bodmer codex in 1969. The plates of papyri in Eric G. Turner's *New Fragments of the Misoumenos of Menander* (London: University of London, Institute of Classical Studies, 1965) give some idea of the difficulty of establishing the text of Menander.

F. H. Sandbach's *Reliquae Selectae* (Oxford: Clarendon Press, 1972; 2nd ed. 1976) gives the authoritative Greek text of Menander's collected works. The Loeb Classical Text, *Menander: The Principal Fragments* (London: William Heinemann, 1921; rpt. Westport, CT: Greenwood Press, 1970) prints the Greek text with a facing English translation by Francis G. Allinson. W. G. Arnott has completed *Aspis-Epitrepontes*, the first of three volumes of a new Loeb series (Cambridge, MA: and London: Loeb Classical Library, 1979). Among the other English translations of Menander are: W. G. Arnott's *Dyskolos, or The Man Who Didn't Like People* (London: Athlone Press, 1960), a prose version with stage directions; Lionel Casson's *The Plays of Menander* (New York: New York University Press, 1971) in one volume translations into idiomatic prose of *TheGrouch*, *The Woman of Samos*, *The Shield*, *The Arbitration*, and *She Who Was Shorn*; Carroll Moulton's *Dyscolus* (New York: New American Library, 1977), a verse translation using

American idiom and Sandbach's text; Gilbert Murray's *Two Plays of Menander: The Rape of the Locks and The Arbitration* (New York: Oxford University Press, 1945), a translation using a dated text and never indicating which of many passages are conjecture; and Eric G. Turner's *The Girl from Samos, or The In-Laws* (London: Athlone Press, 1972), a translation to blank verse, intended for broadcasting. Even Menander's titles cause translators problems: *Dyskolos*, for example, has been variously rendered *The Man Who Didn't Like People*, *The Angry Old Man*, *The Grouch*, *The Misanthrope*, *The Difficult Man*, *The Bad-Tempered Man*, and *The Curmudgeon*.

Overview of Biographical Sources

What little is known about Menander's life often is veiled in anecdote. The reader might justifiably suspect that the stories tell not what did occur but what ought to have occurred. For example, the letter from Menander to the hetaera Glycera and Glycera's reply were both actually written by Alciphron. Does the fact that the letters are fiction make the story they contain about Menander refusing to leave Glycera and Athens for Ptolemy and Egypt an apocryphal one? Menander's biography is also often difficult to separate from criticism of his work; this is true in both ancient and contemporary writers. Michael Grant's *Greek and Latin Authors, 800 B.C.-A.D. 1000: A Biographical Dictionary* (New York: Wilson, 1980, pp. 279-284) gives both a biographical sketch and critical comments. Carroll Moulton's method is similar in T. James Luce's *Ancient Writers: Greece and Rome* (Vol. 1. New York: Charles Scribners' Sons, 1982, pp. 435-446).Almost every edition or translation of Menander contains some biography; and almost every one of those quotes Aristophanes of Byzantium, who said, "O Menander, and O life! Which of you imitated the other?"

Evaluation of Selected Biographies

Hadas, Moses, *Ancilla to Classical Reading*. New York: Columbia University Press, 1954; rpt. 1961, pp. 199-204. Writing before the major textual discoveries of the 1960s, Hadas surveys Menander's reputation among the ancients. The book is full of quotations, charming and comfortable even for the Greekless reader.

Lefkowitz, Mary R. *The Lives of the Greek Poets*. London: Duckworth, 1981, pp. 112-114, 116. Lefkowitz, who believes that virtually everything known of ancient authors is fiction, nevertheless succinctly retells the stories. She points out that much of what was written about Menander in ancient sources may have simply been inferred from his plays: the Suda, for example, describes Menander as "cross-eyed but keen of mind" and "mad for women."

Russell, D. A. and M. Winterbottom, eds. *Ancient Literary Criticism*. Oxford: Clarendon Press, 1972. This book reprints the major works of Greek and Roman literary criticism. The index lists passages where Menander's life and works are discussed by Demetrius, Cicero, Terence, Ovid, Horace, Quintilian, Plutarch, and others.

Autobiographical Sources

There are extant today one complete play of Menander, substantial sections of nine more, eight Latin comedies based upon his originals, and scattered fragments and quotations. There is no true autobiographical writing of Menander; the daring are free to surmise what they may from his dramas.

Overview of Critical Sources

The study of Menander is made difficult by the fact that there is extant a relatively small amount, certainly less than ten percent, of his complete work. It is also difficult for those who do not read German, Italian, and French because much valuable work has been published in each of these languages. And finally, because of the nature of the significant textual publications of 1907, 1959, and 1969, all criticism must be read with a keen eye to dates. Much good work has been done and, because of the comparative recency of major textual discoveries and the anticipation of additional ones, much will continue to be done.

Evaluation of Selected Criticism

Arnott, W. Geoffrey, "Menander, Plautus, Terence," in *Greece and Rome*. New Surveys in the Classics No. 9. Oxford: Clarendon Press, 1975. The author of numerous articles on Menander and his translator in the new Loeb Classical Library series, Arnott surveys the books "essential" for the study of Menander, only one of which—T. B. L. Webster—is in English. Arnott also discusses the form of the plays, the dramatic techniques, and the influence of tragedy, earlier comedy, and Peripatetic philosophy on Menander.

Goldberg, Sander M. *The Making of Menander's Comedy*. Berkeley: University of California Press, 1980. Goldberg, who quotes the plays in translation, explores how Menander's plays work on the stage as plays. He examines five plays in separate chapters, concluding that Menander found creativity within the tradition by reworking the conventions of comedy.

Gomme, A. W. and F. H. Sandbach. *Menander: A Commentary*. Oxford: Oxford University Press, 1973. This book is a line-by-line commentary on the seventeen plays and numerous fragments in the Oxford Classical Text of Menander. The text is sprinkled with Greek, but contains much specific information that is accessible to a patient Greekless reader.

Turner, E. G. ed. *Entretiens XVI: Ménandre*. Geneva: Fondation Hardt, 1970. This fascinating book reprints seven papers on Menander, each followed by comments from German, French, Italian, and English scholars. Both papers and comments remain in the language of the speaker. The three English language selections are E. W. Handley's "The Conventions of the Comic State and Their Exploitation by Menander," pp. 1-26, "Discussion," pp. 27-42; F. H. Sandbach's "Menander's Manipulation of Language for Dramatic Purposes," pp. 111-136, "Discussion," pp. 137-143; and Christina Dedoussi's "The *Samia*," pp. 157-170; "Discussion," pp. 171-180.

Webster, T. B. L. *An Introduction to Menander*. Manchester: Manchester University Press, 1974. Rather than seeing Menander in terms of creativity within convention, Webster organizes his analysis around the terminology of armature and codes that Claude Lévi-Strauss uses in another context. Also, in Appendix 1 Webster gives an alphabetical list of all the plays "of which anything useful can be said," including summary reconstructions, references to ancient sources, and bibliography.

Other Sources

Arnott, W. Geoffrey, "The Modernity of Menander," in *Greece and Rome* XXII (October 1975): 140-155. An analysis of dramatic and stylistic techniques such as linking devices, echoes, and pattern and parallelism in word and structure.

Bieber, Margarete, *The History of the Greek and Roman Theater*. 2nd ed. Princeton: Princeton University Press, 1961, pp. 87-107. The biographical text is generously supplemented with pictures of ancient mosaics, reliefs, busts, wall paintings, and masks which portray Menander or characters from New Comedy.

Fantham, Elaine, "Roman Experience of Menander in the Late Republic and Early Empire," in *Transactions of the American Philological Association*, 114 (1984): 299-309. An exploration of the discrepancy between Menander's reputation and his direct influence.

Handley, E. W. *The Dyskolos of Menander*. Cambridge: Harvard University Press, 1965. The Greek text and the section on meter will probably be interesting only to the specialist, but the information on Menander's life and age, his survival and rediscovery, theatrical convention, and *Dyskolos* in the theater will be of interest to a much wider audience.

Post, L. A. *From Homer to Menander: Forces in Greek Poetic Fiction*. Berkeley: University of California Press, 1951. Menander seen as the successor to Homer and the tragedians.

Webster, T. B. L. *Studies in Menander*. Manchester: Manchester University Press, 1950; 2nd ed. 1960. An analysis that divides Menander's work into plays of reconciliation, social criticism, and adventure and satire.

Wilamowitz-Moellendorff, Ulrich von. *Das Schiedsgericht*. Berlin: Weidmann, 1925; rpt. 1958. A Greek text and German translation of *The Arbitrants* with a lengthy essay on the art of Menander by one of the great scholars of this century.

Elizabeth A. Holtze

THOMAS MIDDLETON
1580-1627

Author's Chronology

Born April 18, 1580, London; father, William Middleton, prosperous bricklayer and landlord, dies five years later; step-father and sister's husband involve family in recurring court battle over father's legacy, familiarizing Middleton with legal intrigue; *1598* matriculates at Queen's College, Oxford, but leaves two or three years later without a degree, possibly because of financial difficulties: writes poems as undergraduate; between *1601-1603* marries Anne Marbeck or Merbeck, daughter of a Clerk in Chancery and sister of an actor; *1601* lawsuit describes him as "daylie accompaninge the players;" *1602* mentioned in Henslowe's *Diary* as collaborating with Thomas Dekker, Michael Drayton, John Webster, and Anthony Munday; *1603* or 1604 son, Edward, born; *1604-1606* writes city comedies for the Children of Paul's; *1613* begins writing pageants for the City of London; *1613* writes last and major city comedy, *A Chaste Maid in Cheapside,* for the Lady Elizabeth's Men, an adult company that had absorbed the Children of the Queen's Revels; *1611-161* turns to tragicomedies for the public theatres; *1615-1621* writes first tragedy, *Hengist, King of Kent, or The Mayor of Queenborough;* his two chief tragedies, *The Changeling,* 1622, in collaboration with William Rowley, and *Women Beware Women,* of uncertain date, follow; *1620* appointed Chronologer of the City of London; *1624* ends playwriting career with political satire, *A Game at Chess,* the first long run in English drama; buried July 4, 1627, in the same London district where he had lived since 1609.

Author's Bibliography

The canon of Middleton's plays includes several much-disputed items, namely *The Revenger's Tragedy* and *The Second Maiden's Tragedy,* which many critics still ascribe to Cyril Tourneur. Using a statistical versification test, David Lake, in *The Canon of Thomas Middleton's Plays* (London: Cambridge University Press, 1975), claims these for Middleton and identifies the undoubted canon of unassisted plays: *The Phoenix,* 1603-1604 (part allegory, part city comedy); *Michaelmas Term,* 1605 (city comedy); *A Mad World, My Masters,* 1605-1606 (city comedy); *A Trick to Catch the Old One,* 1605-1606 (city comedy); *Your Five Gallants,* 1606-1607 (city comedy); *No Wit, No Help Like a Woman's,* 1612 (tragicomedy); *A Chaste Maid in Cheapside,* 1613 (city comedy); *More Dissemblers Besides Women,* c. 1615 (tragicomedy); *The Witch,* c. 1616 (tragicomedy); *Hengist, King of Kent, or The Mayor of Queenborough,* c. 1616-1620 (tragedy); *Women Beware Women,* c. 1612-1627 (comedy); *The Changeling,* 1622 (with Rowley, tragedy); *A Game at Chess,* 1624 (political satire).

Lake's list of plays Middleton wrote in collaboration contains more disputed items: *The Roaring Girl or Moll Cut-Purse,* c. 1608 (with Dekker, comedy); *Wit at Several Weapons,* 1609 (with Rowley, and possibly John Fletcher, comedy); *A Fair Quarrel,* 1617 (with Rowley, tragicomedy); *The Old Law,* 1618 (with Rowley and one other, possibly Philip Massinger, tragicomedy); *Anything for a Quiet Life,* 1620 (with Webster, comedy). In addition to his plays Middleton wrote three early poems and two satirical pamphlets.

Overview of Biographical Sources

The lack of contemporary comments about Middleton and the fact that few of his plays were printed during his lifetime suggest that his fellow Jacobeans did not regard him as a leading playwright in spite of his prolific output. No autobiographical sources have been found; Middleton evidently considered himself an entertainer rather than an artist with critical convictions. Jonson called him "a base fellow," perhaps because he made no pretensions to classical learning. His biography must be reconstructed from the scantiest records, mainly payments for plays and references in legal litigations. His present reputation as one of the leading popular dramatists of the first part of the seventeenth century was first established by such nineteenth-century critics as Lamb and Swinburne. The fullest account of his life can be found in the first chapter of Richard Barker's *Thomas Middleton* (New York: Columbia University Press, 1958), and in Norman Brittin's *Thomas Middleton* (New York: Twayne, 1972). Some of the biographical material in the first volume of the only collected edition of Middleton's works, A.H. Bullen's eight-volume *The Works of Thomas Middleton* (London: 1885) has been superseded. A new collected edition, edited by George Price and Samuel Schoenbaum, is planned by Yale Press.

Overview of Critical Sources

Known chiefly as the co-author of *The Changeling,* and author of *Women Beware Women* and *A Chaste Maid in Cheapside,* his plays most frequently anthologized, Middleton is attracting a growing volume of criticism. Much of it refutes T.S. Eliot's pronouncement in his *Essays on Elizabethan Drama* (New York: Harcourt, Brace, and World, 1932): "He has no point of view, is neither sentimental nor cynical; he is neither resigned nor disillusioned, nor romantic, he has no message. He is merely the name which associates six or seven great plays." (p. 85) But critics disagree about the particular point of view. Middleton has been labelled a satirist, an ironist, a realist, a moralist, and ranked as the third great Jacobean dramatist after Shakespeare and Jonson. A few book-length studies of his entire work have been made, but the bulk of current scholarship is devoted to his city comedies. His reputation as a writer of two major tragedies is secure, confirmed by one major study. Scholars continue to dispute the canon, however, especially *The*

Revenger's Tragedy. Although excellent arguments have been advanced to attribute it to Middleton, no satisfactory reason has yet been found to explain why Middleton should have written a revenge play for the King's Men while he was the principal playwright of a children's company. The dispute continues.

Evaluation of Selected Criticism

Barker, Richard, *Thomas Middleton.* New York: Columbia University Press, 1958. Barker concludes his judicious study of all Middleton's work by allotting him the rank of third great Jacobean dramatist after Shakespeare and Jonson, and remarking that he is almost as close to Ibsen as to his contemporaries. Although slightly outdated now, (the manuscript was written almost fifteen years before publication and used by Barker's students), this comprehensive overview remains the most useful single study of Middleton's complete work. Barker stresses Middleton's theme of sin bringing its own retribution in ironic reversals. The last quarter of the book is devoted to establishing the chronology of the plays, but many of these dates have since been challenged.

Brittin, Norman A. *Thomas Middleton.* New York: Twayne, 1972. In this readable bio-critical survey of all Middleton's writings Brittin gives detailed plot summaries of the plays and a brief summary of critical assessments. Brittin advances no controversial theories but provides a useful introductory study.

Farr, Dorothy, *Thomas Middleton and the Drama of Realism.* New York: Barnes and Noble, 1973. Farr discusses Middleton's early comedies briefly in order to demonstrate how his fundamental skepticism about the human condition and his expression of that attitude through irony gradually evolved into full dramatic power in the transitional play, *A Fair Quarrel,* and then in *The Changeling, Women Beware Women,* and *A Game at Chess.* She concentrates upon these last three plays and concludes that Middleton's work was essentially unfinished.

Friedenreich, Kenneth, ed. *"Accompaninge the Players," Essays Celebrating Thomas Middleton, 1580-1980.* New York: AMS Press, 1983. This most recent publication on Middleton is a collection of essays celebrating the quadricentenary of his birth. The topics, by noted scholars from Kenneth Muir to David Bergeron, range from Middleton's world, his use of adjectives, an account of a production, to three studies of the tragedies.

Heinemann, Margot, *Puritanism and Theatre, Thomas Middleton and Opposition Drama under the Early Stuarts.* Cambridge: Cambridge University Press, 1980. In this attempt to place Middleton against a political background Heinemann concludes that his portraits are not anti-Puritan but designed to expose the weaknesses of society in general.

Holmes, David, *The Art of Thomas Middleton.* Oxford: Clarendon Press, 1970. Holmes looks closely at Middleton's early non-dramatic work where he finds a clear statement of the author's basic faith in universal justice which he believes underlies the later conceptions of character. He praises Middleton's objectivity in portraying figures who gain self-knowledge through their experiences and tragic characters who never attain that understanding.

Lake, David, *The Canon of Thomas Middleton's Plays*. London: Cambridge University Press, 1975. Lake has made a painstaking analysis of the versification and vocabulary in Middleton's plays and compared them statistically with the style of contemporary dramatists to arrive at a canon which many scholars will accept as proven.

Parker, R.B. "Middleton's Experiments with Comedy and Judgment," in *Jacobean Theatre*, Stratford-upon-Avon Studies I. London: Edward Arnold, 1960. Parker sees a tension between moral judgment and a brilliant depiction of manners at the heart of Middleton's comedy.

Rowe, George, *Thomas Middleton and the New Comedy Tradition*. University of Nebraska Press, 1979. In his analysis of seven comedies and two tragicomedies Row explains why Middleton's world is filled with chaos instead of movement towards comic harmony. The two major conventions of classical New Comedy, celebration of a unified society and belief in man's power to renew himself, are purposely subverted.

Schoenbaum, Samuel, *Middleton's Tragedies*. New York: Columbia University Press, 1955. Schoenbaum, a student of Barker's, worked closely with his mentor. He claims Middleton's tragedies in their psychological realism can arouse terror, but rarely pity; their pervasive irony contributes to the decline of heroism in English drama.

Other Sources

Bradbrook, Muriel C. *The Growth and Structure of Elizabethan Comedy*. London: Chatto and Windus, 1955. Bradbrook describes Middleton's ironic portrayal of a comic world ruled by greed, about which its author offers no moral or artistic theory.

Ellis-Fermor, Una, *The Jacobean Drama*. London: Methuen, 1936. Ellis-Fermor praises Middleton's understanding of women, his ability to combine comic and tragic techniques, his careful observation, and his ironic detachment.

Farley-Hills, David, *The Comic in Renaissance Comedy*. Totowa, NJ: Barnes and Noble, 1981. Farley-Hills stresses the morality play nature of Middleton's comedies beneath their naturalistic form.

Kirsch, Arthur C. *Jacobean Dramatic Perspectives*. Charlottesville: University Press of Virginia, 1972. Kirsch finds a single ironic voice in all Middleton's plays, the strong influence of the morality, accounting for his emphasis on self-deceit and self-defeat.

Leggatt, Alexander, *Citizen Comedy in the Age of Shakespeare.* Toronto: University of Toronto Press, 1973. Leggatt considers Middleton the most active of the coterie writers of city comedy, but points out that he satirizes both citizen and courtier in plays that simultaneously assert and subvert morality.

Levin, Richard, *The Multiple Plot in English Renaissance Drama.* Chicago: University of Chicago Press, 1971. Levin examines the structural coherence of eight of Middleton's plays.

The editions of Middleton's plays in the Regents Renaissance Drama Series, the Revels Plays, the New Mermaids, and the Fountainwell Drama Texts offer useful introductions.

Bibliographies
Ribner, Irving, *Tudor and Stuart Drama.* Goldentree Bibliographies in Language and Literature. Northbrook, IL: AHM Publishing Co., 1973.

Salomon, Brownwell, *Critical Analyses in English Renaissance Drama.* Bowling Green, OH: Bowling Green University Popular Press, 1979.

Wells, Stanely, editor, *English Drama.* London: Oxford University Press, 1975.

Gloria E. Johnaon
University of Oregon

ARTHUR MILLER
1915

Author's Chronology

Born October 17, 1915, New York; *1929* moves with family to Brooklyn; *1934* enters University of Michigan; *1938* receives B.A., University of Michigan; works for Federal Theatre Project; *1940* marries Mary Grace Slattery; *1944* gathers material for film, *The Story of GI Joe*; publishes *Situation Normal*, a prose account of his tour of army camps and has his play, *The Man Who Had All the Luck*, produced in New York; *1945* publishes a novel, *Focus*; *1947 All My Sons* produced in New York; *1949 Death of a Salesman* produced in New York; *1950* adapts Ibsen's *An Enemy of the People* for production in New York; *1953 The Crucible* produced in New York; *1954* refused a passport for the opening of *The Crucible* in Brussels; *1955 A Memory of Two Mondays* and *A View from the Bridge* produced in New York; *1956* divorces Mary Slattery and marries Marilyn Monroe; *1957* publishes *Collected Plays*; refuses to give names of suspected communists to Congress; convicted of contempt of Congress; *1958* Supreme Court overturns his conviction for contempt of Congress; *1960* works on film, *The Misfits*; separates from Marilyn Monroe; *1961* divorces Marilyn Monroe; *1962* marries Ingeborg Morath; publishes *Jane's Blanket*, a children's story; *1964 After the Fall* and *Incident at Vichy* produced in New York; *1968 The Price* produced in New York; *1972* publishes *The Creation of the World and Other Business*; *1974 Up from Paradise* produced at Ann Arbor, Michigan; *1977 The Archbishop's Ceiling* produced in Washington, D.C.; with Ingeborg Morath, publishes *In the Country*; publishes *The Theatre Essays of Arthur Miller*; *1978* visits China; *1979* publishes *American Clock* and *Chinese Encounters*.

Author's Bibliography (selected)

The Man Who Had all the Luck, 1944 (play); *Situation Normal*, 1944 (prose); *Focus*, 1945 (novel); *All My Sons*, 1947 (play); *Death of a Salesman*, 1949 (play); *The Crucible*, 1953 (play); *A Memory of Two Mondays*, 1955 (play); *A View From the Bridge*, 1955 (play); *Collected Plays*, 1957; *The Misfits*, 1961 (novel); *After the Fall*, 1964 (play); *Incident at Vichy*, 1964 (play); *I Don't Need You Any More: Stories*, 1967 (short stories); *The Price*, 1968 (play); *In Russia*, with Ingeborg Morath, 1969 (prose); *The Creation of the World and Other Business*, 1972 (play); *In the Country*, with Ingeborg Morath, 1977 (prose); *The Theatre Essays of Arthur Miller*, 1978.

Overview of Biographical Sources

No definitive biography of Arthur Miller exists, although his various and always controversial aesthetics, politics, and marriages have been chronicled aptly by many journalists and several scholars. An early sketch is Jordan Y. Miller's "Arthur Miller," in *American Dramatic Literature: Ten Plays in Historical Perspective* (New York: McGraw-Hill, 1961). Maurice Zolotow in *Marilyn Monroe* (New York: Bantam, 1961) traces Miller's celebrated relationship with Marilyn Monroe. Joan T. Nourse in Arthur Miller's *"Death of a Salesman" and "All My Sons"* (New York: Monarch Press, 1965) adumbrates Miller's life and work. Jean R. Gould in *Modern American Playwrights* (1966) offers a relatively broad introduction to Miller's life and works, although her intent is mainly critical. Bernard Dekle in *Profiles of Modern American Authors* (1969) also chronicles Miller's life and work through *After the Fall*, while Pat Esslinger in *Barron's Simplified Approach to Arthur Miller* (1972), a study guide, offers yet another brief biographical profile. Moreover, Norman Mailer, like Zolotow before him, treats Miller's marriage to Marilyn Monroe in his *Marilyn* (1973). Here Mailer especially covers well the marriage's deterioration. In *Critical Essays on Arthur Miller* (1979) James A. Martine offers a brief biographical introduction to Miller, and Helene Wickham Koon in *Twentieth Century Interpretations of "Death of a Salesman"* (1983), profiles Miller's life in a similar vein.

Evaluation of Selected Biographies

Dekle, Bernard, *Profiles of Modern American Authors*. Rutland, Vermont: Tuttle, 1969. Dekle offers an abbreviated account of Miller's life and work through *After the Fall* in his chapter entitled "Arthur Miller." However, his work is now dated, although it remains very readable and possibly still useful.

Esslinger, Pat, *Barron's Simplified Approach to Arthur Miller*. Woodbury, New York: Barron's Educational Services, 1972. Essinger offers a biographical sketch as part of her critical survey of Miller's dramas through *The Price*. If her work is now dated, it remains a useful aid to students.

Gould, Jean R. *Modern American Playwrights*. New York: Dodd, Mead, 1966. While Gould offers a good, if dated critical survey here, she also gives a very readable biographical profile of Miller—also dated.

Koon, Helene Wickham, ed. *Twentieth Century Interpretations of Death of a Salesman*. Englewood Cliffs: Prentice-Hall, 1983. Koon's introduction offers a well-drawn, updated sketch of Miller's life. While brief, her account is an excellent place to start.

Mailer, Norman, *Marilyn*. New York: Grossett and Dunlap, 1973. Mailer's chapter entitled "The Jewish Princess" analyzes the gradual deterioration of her marriage to Miller. Mailer argues that the marriage was detrimental to both partners and was especially harmful to Miller's art. Offering several interesting biographical speculations on what he perceives to be the failure of *After the Fall*, Mailer's work complements Zolotow's.

Martine, James J. ed. *Critical Essays on Arthur Miller*. Boston: G. K. Hall, 1979. Martine's introduction, like Koon's, offers a crisp, lucid, concise biographical sketch of Miller the artist.

Miller, Jordan Y. *American Dramatic Literature: Ten Modern Plays in Historical Perspective*. New York: McGraw-Hill, 1961. Miller presents a very general, sketchy, and dated biographical profile in his chapter, "Arthur Miller."

Nourse, Joan T. *Arthur Miller's "Death of a Salesman" and "All My Sons."* New York: Monarch Press, 1965. Nourse's monograph essentially is a study guide to Miller's two plays, including a brief biographical sketch. Although dated, her work is designed well for the student.

_____. *Arthur Miller's "The Crucible," "A Memory of Two Mondays," "A View From the Bridge," "After the Fall," "Incident at Vichy."* New York: Monarch Press, 1965. Like her previous guides to *Death of a Salesman* and *All My Sons*, this monograph includes a very readable biographical profile.

Zolotow, Maurice, *Marilyn Monroe*. New York: Bantam, 1961. While Zolotow's subject is Marilyn Monroe, he devotes adequate space to her celebrated and ill-fated romance with Miller. Tracing Miller's themes of guilt in *The Crucible* and *A View From the Bridge* to his infatuation with Monroe while he was still married to Mary Slattery, Zolotow at times forgets that life does not invariably translate directly into art.

Autobiographical Sources
    Miller has not written his autobiography, but he does make several autobiographical allusions and offers some autobiographical summary in interviews. A very important autobiographical source is his interview with Olga Carlisle and Rose Styron, "The Art of the Theatre: II," *Paris Review*, X (1966), pp. 61-98. Here Miller discusses his origins, his filial relationships, and his affinities with several contemporary dramatists. Other significant interviews include Joseph Gruen, "Portrait of the Playwright at Fifty," *New York* (Oct. 14, 1965), pp. 12-13, in which he discusses his reactions to the Vietnam War; William P. Halstead, ed., "Arthur Miller Talks," *Michigan Quarterly Review*, VI (1967), pp. 153-184; and Robert A. Martin, "Arthur Miller and the Meaning of Tragedy," *Modern Drama*, XIII (1970), pp. 34-39.

Overview of Critical Sources
    Both criticism of and scholarship on Miller began to approach maturity in the 1960s. Much has centered on three major plays—*Death of a Salesman, The Cruci-*

ble, and *After the Fall*—but even these plays have attracted both extreme praise and reservation. Journalistic attention over the years has highlighted the most controversial events of Miller's life, such as his marriage to Marilyn Monroe and his conviction of contempt of Congress, but until the 1960s one finds little comprehensive analysis of Miller the artist. More recent criticism focuses on the evolution of Miller's entire canon and on his growing significance in the history of the American stage. Indeed, the decades of the 1960s and 1970s produced some of the most cogent criticism and detailed scholarship to date.

Evaluation of Selected Criticism

Hayman, Ronald, *Arthur Miller*. New York: Frederick Ungar, 1970. A very thoughtful analysis of Miller's supposed intellectual weaknesses, Hayman's work is a provocative complement to Miller's ardent defenders. Hayman discusses Miller's works through *The Price* and especially is helpful with Miller's theme of the function of memory.

Huftel, Sheila, *Arthur Miller: The Burning Glass*. New York: Citadel, 1965. A very detailed and useful work on Miller's canon through *Incident at Vichy*, *The Burning Glass* is a strong defense of both Miller's aesthetic theories and practices. Huftel especially is helpful with character analysis and quotes several of Miller's letters to her. She also includes useful summaries of European as well as American opinions.

Martine, James J., Jr. ed. *Critical Essays on Arthur Miller*. Boston: G. K. Hall, 1979. Martine's edition of critical essays is an indispensable aid to any study of Miller's drama. Martine offers both contemporary reviews of and seminal essays on each of Miller's plays.

Moss, Leonard, *Arthur Miller*. New York: Twayne, 1967. Moss convincingly argues that Miller's social themes are secondary to his plumbing the psychological depths of extremely assertive behavior. He succeeds most as a social dramatist, states Moss, when he successfully dramatizes the complexities of the human psyche. Moss also is helpful for scholars interested in Miller's style, structure, and symbolism.

Murray, Edward, *Arthur Miller: Dramatist*. New York: Frederick Ungar, 1967. Murray cogently defends Miller as a moral and philosophical dramatist. He offers very detailed analysis of both themes and characters as well as interesting explications of structure and dialogue.

Nelson, Benjamin, *Arthur Miller: Portrait of a Playwright*. New York: McKay, 1970. Nelson defends Miller's sometimes polemical didacticism, arguing that Miller ultimately believes in man's capacity to transcend his political and economic bonds. Nelson offers very useful and detailed explications of Miller's dramatic canon through *The Price*.

Welland, Dennis, *Arthur Miller*. New York: Grove, 1961. In this relatively early and now somewhat dated work, Welland surveys Miller's canon through *The Misfits*. He believes that Miller's creative powers increase with each new work and that his major theme is the wonderful pluralism of the American ethos. Welland himself is perhaps too abstract and too easily given to sweeping generalization.

Other Sources

Cohn, Ruby, *Dialogue in American Drama*. Bloomington: Indiana University Press, 1971. Cohn presents a thorough analysis of dialogue in Miller's major works.

Corrigan, Robert W., ed. *Arthur Miller: A Collection of Critical Essays*. Englewood Cliffs: Prentice-Hall, 1969. Corrigan reprints some very useful and provocative essays on Miller's major works.

Ferres, John H. *Arthur Miller: A Reference Guide*. Boston: G.K. Hall, 1979. An updated, thorough, comprehensive reference guide, Ferres' work offers a meticulously annotated bibliography.

_____. ed. *The Crucible: A Collection of Critical Essays*. Englewood Cliffs: Prentice-Hall, 1972.

Koon, Helene Wickham, ed. *Twentieth Century Interpretations of "Death of a Salesman."* Englewood Cliffs: Prentice-Hall, 1983.

Lunley, Frederick, *New Trends in 20th Century Drama*. New York: Oxford University Press, 1972. Lunley compares and contrasts Miller and Tennessee Williams.

White, Sidney, *Guide to Arthur Miller*. Columbus: Charles E. Merrill, 1970. This readable guide surveys Miller's major works, with special attention to *Death of a Salesman*.

Selected Dictionaries and Encyclopedias

An Index to Author Miller Criticism, Scarecrow, 1976. An index that includes masters theses and doctoral dissertations.

Contemporary Authors, Gale Research, 1967. Brief biographical and critical summaries.

Contemporary Literary Criticism, Gale Research, 1973. Abridged collections of criticism from 1953-1969.

Two Hundred Contemporary Authors, Gale Research, 1969. Concise critical and biographical overviews.

John T. Hiers
Valdosta State College

YUKIO MISHIMA
1925-1970

Author's Chronology

Born January 14, 1925, Tokyo, Japan, as Kimitake Hiraoka; *1931-1944* attends the Peers' School (Gakushūin) where he completes the poem "Evil Things" ("Magagoto") that suggests the nature of subsequent writings; *1944* graduates with highest honors and publishes his first important story, "The Forest in Full Flower" under pen name Yukio Mishima; *1944-1947* attends Tokyo Imperial University where he is in the Law Department; *1947* graduates and works as a bureaucrat in the Ministry of Finance but resigns after one year to support himself by writing; *1949* publishes his first major novel, *Confessions of a Mask*, thereby establishing himself as a writer of the first rank; *1950* publishes *Kantan*, the first of his modern Noh plays; *1956* wins the Yomiuri Prize for literature with *The Temple of the Golden Pavilion*; completes *Dear Cry Pavilion*, one of his greatest stage successes, and joins the leading theatre group in Japan, the Bungaku-za; *1960* acts in his first film, *A Dry Fellow*, playing the part of a gangster; early *1960s* concentrates on writing plays; *1962* states, "Within two or three years I must make a plan for life"; *1963* breaks with Bungaku-za, the theatre company with which he had been associated for nearly a decade, accusing its members of hypocrisy; *1965* is mentioned as candidate for Nobel Prize; *1966* poses for the famous photo of himself as St. Sebastian; *1967* forms a militaristic fraternity, the Shield Society (*Tatenokai*), to lead the way to a more traditional Japan; November 25, *1970*, completes his last work, the tetralogy *Sea of Fertility*; on same day, he goes to Self-Defense Force army post at Ichigaya in Tokyo, and, failing in his attempt to incite troops to turn against the government, commits ritual *harakiri*.

Author's Bibliography

Mishima was a prolific writer whose complete works in Japanese fill some 36 volumes. He wrote more than 20 plays, 12 of which have been translated:

Five Modern Nō Plays, tr. Donald Keene. New York: Knopf, 1957; rpt. New York: Random House, 1973. Includes: *Sotoba Komachi*, *The Damask Drum* (*Aya no tsuzumi*), *Kantan*, *The Lady Aoi* (*Aoi no ue*), and *Hanjo*.

Sunflowers at Night (*Yoru no himawari*), tr. Shigeo Shinozaki and Virgil A. Warren. Tokyo: Hokuseidō, 1958.

Tropical Tree (*Nettaiju*), tr. Kenneth Strong. In *Japan Quarterly* (April-June 1964)11.2:174-210.

Dōjōi, tr. Donald Keene. In *Death in Midsummer and Other Stories*. New York: New Directions, 1966, pp. 119-138. A modern Noh play.

Madame de Sade (*Sado kōshaku fujin*), tr. Donald Keene. New York: Grove Press, 1967.

The Three Primary Colors (San genshoku), tr. Miles K. McElrath. In *Occasional Papers No. 11, Japanese Culture II*. Ann Arbor: University of Michigan, 1969, pp. 175-194.

My Friend Hitler (Waga tomo hittora), tr. Hiroaki Satō. In *St. Andrews Review* (Fall-Winter 1977; Spring-Summer 1978; Special Double Translation Issue) 4.3-4.

Yoroboshi: The Blind Young Man (Yoroboshi), tr. Ted T. Takaya. In *Modern Japanese Drama: An Anthology*. New York: Columbia University Press, 1979, pp. 41-58. A modern Noh play.

Overview of Biographical Sources

There are two biographies of Mishima in English, by John Nathan and Henry Scott-Stokes. Mishima had been friendly with both authors during separate periods in the 1960s—with Nathan in 1964-65 and with Scott-Stokes from 1968 until Mishima died. Given the many close connections between Mishima's life and writings, these two biographies are of more than ordinary interest.

Evaluation of Selected Biographies

Nathan, John, *Mishima: A Biography*. Boston and Toronto: Little, Brown, 1974; rpt. Rutland, VT: Tuttle, 1975. Nathan, scholar and translator, takes a chronological approach to his subject, filling his pages with voluminous details gleaned from Mishima's unpublished writings, interviews with his family, friends, teachers, editors, colleagues, and from Nathan's own brief association with Mishima. Mishima's shocking finale, concludes Nathan, is anchored in Mishima's erotic fascination with death; in short, his last act is, in Nathan's view, more private and personal than public and patriotic.

Scott-Stokes, Henry, *The Life and Death of Yukio Mishima*. New York: Farrar, Straus and Giroux, 1974. A journalist and, to some extent, confidant of Mishima's for the last two years of his life, Scott-Stokes creates an intimate, dramatic picture, if less detailed than Nathan's, of Mishima's life and writings. Just under half of his book reconstructs the chronology of Mishima's life; the rest is given over to an examination of the major themes of Mishima's writings and the tightly interwoven connections between his life and his writings. Scott-Stokes sees Mishima's life as a kind of rehearsal of his death; Mishima, he concludes, was less an exponent of Fascist notions than a novelist—an artist whose final act was calculated to meld his art and his life into an indivisible whole.

Autobiographical Sources

Of Mishima's many autobiographical writings, only one volume has been translated: *Sun and Steel (Taiyō to tetsu)*, tr. John Bester. New York: Grove Press, 1970. This fascinating, well-crafted essay contains Mishima's "personal testament on art, action, and ritual death." One discovers here the major themes and concerns that guided both his life and his writings. Perhaps most salient in this regard is his ceaseless seeking after a means to realize the unification of the Apollonian and Dionysian aspects of life.

Overview and Evaluation of Critical Sources

Mishima scholarship in English is principally concerned with his fiction, but even this is not voluminous. With respect to his plays, there is very little. Donald Keene's brief, 11-page introduction to *Five Modern Nō Plays* sheds some light on the appeal for Mishima of the classical Japanese Noh and on the process by which Mishima transformed aspects of the old plays into a compelling modern idiom. Keene's essay "Mishima Yukio," in Donald Keene, *Landscapes and Portraits: Appreciations of Japanese Culture* (Tokyo and Palo Alto: Kodansha, 1971), alludes briefly (pp. 211-213) to Mishima's theatre and its "classicism."

In his biography, Nathan hardly mentions Mishima's plays; when he does (pp. 117-119, 131-137, 186, 193-194, 251-255), he cites only the external details of writing, production and the like with no attempt at critical analysis. Scott-Stokes gives a little more space to the aesthetic achievement of Mishima's plays (pp. 201-216), placing a revealing perspective on the connections between Mishima's writing for the theatre and his cultural milieu. Scott-Stokes contends, however, that Mishima's plays show him to be more interested in dramatic structure and experimentation than in political matters. For Mishima, theatre should be an aesthetic experience created "to give poeple the illusion of life's noblest moments and the apparition of beauty on earth." But Scott-Stokes' discussion of Mishima's plays is so brief as merely to whet one's appetite.

In his introduction to *Modern Japanese Drama: An Anthology*, Takaya discusses Mishima's theatre for a page and a half (pp. xxix-xxx). He places Mishima squarely within the Japanese classical tradition, despite Mishima's modern idiom and admiration for western theatre. Takaya sees Mishima's theatre as steeped in "neoclassicism."

The only critical evaluation in English of Mishima's work for the stage is found in John K. Gillespie, "Beyond Byzantium: Aesthetic Pessimism in Mishima Yukio's Modern Noh Plays," *Monumenta Nipponica* 37 (Spring 1982): 29-39. The author notes the irony of Mishima's making use of consummate artistry in his attempt to show the insufficiency of aesthetics to fulfill life's deepest needs. In each of the plays cited (*Sotoba Komachi*, *The Damask Drum*, and *Hanjo*), an artist figure constructs a wildly romantic aesthetic theory only to have it crumble when confronted with sober reality; the artists' efforts, in short, bring on not life but death or madness.

John K. Gillespie
St. John's University

MOLIÈRE
Jean Baptiste Poquelin
1622-1673

Author's Chronology

Born in Paris and baptised January 15, 1622, at the church of Saint-Eustache; eldest son of Jean Poquelin, a prosperous upholsterer and furniture maker, and his wife, Marie Cressé; *1631* father becomes one of the King's eight *valet de chambre tappisiers*; May 11, *1632* burial of Molière's mother; May 30, *1633* father remarries; *1636-1642*, Molière attends Jesuit Collége at Clermont and studies law at Orleans; *1642* admitted to bar and serves apprenticeship with father; January 6, *1643* receives 630 livres inheritance from his mother's estate, renounces his right of succession to the Royal Upholsterer and becomes one of the first educated men of good social standing to risk both excommunication from the church and poverty for a career as an actor; June 30, *1643* signs contract with a group of actors to establish "The Illustrious Theatre"; June 18, *1644* signs his name "Molière" for the first time; *1645* posts his own credit for the Company; July and August, *1645* arrested for debt connected with the Company and imprisoned in the Grand Chatelet; August 5, *1645* released under bond; late *1645*-early 1646, leaves Paris with the Company for a twelve year tour of the provinces; *1653-1655* produces *The Blunderer* at Lyons; December 12, *1656* produces *The Love Tiff*, at Beziers; *1658* returns secretly to Paris and secures the protection of Monsieur, the King's Brother; October 24, *1658* returns to Paris as manager of a successful theatrical company and performs for the King at the Old Louvre; February 20, *1661* marries Armande Béjart; December 16, *1662* first performance of *The School for Wives*— Molière as Arnolphe; March 17, *1663* name appears for the first time on the King's pension list; January 19, *1664* Louis, Molière's first son, born; May 12, *1664* performance of the first three acts of *Tartuffe*—Molière as Orgon; November 10, *1664* Molière's son Louis dies; February 15, *1665* first performance of *Don Juan; or The Feast of Stone*—Molière as Sganarelle; August 4, *1665* baptism of daughter Esprit-Madeleine; August 14, *1665* Molière's troupe becomes "The King's Troupe" and receives a pension of 6,000 livres; June 4, *1666* *The Misanthrope* presented at the Palais Royal—Molière as Alceste and Mme. Molière as Celimene; Easter *1667* Molière seriously ill and the Palais Royal closes for over six weeks; January 13, *1668* first performance of *Amphitryon at the Palais Royal*— Molière as Sosié; February 25, *1669* death of Molière's father; February 4, *1670* first performance of *The Magnificent Lovers* the subject of which is suggested by the King; September 15, *1672* Pierre-J.B.-Armand, Molière's third child, born— dies October 10; February 17, *1673* Molière dies of hemorrhage at 10:00 P.M. at his home in the Rue de Richelieu; February 18, *1673* as an excommunicated actor, cannot have a Christian burial until Mme. Molière petitions the King; permission is given and on February 21, 1673, burial is performed, secretly, at 9:00 P.M. in St. Joseph Cemetery.

Author's Bibliography

Molière's plays include: *The Blunderer*, 1655; *The Love Tiff*, 1656; *The Romantic Ladies*, 1659; *Sganarelle*, 1660; *The School for Husbands*, 1661; *The School for Wives*, 1662; *Tartuffe*, 1664, *Don Juan*, 1665, *The Doctor in Spite of Himself*, 1665 (a ballet-comedy); *The Misanthrope*, 1666; *Georges Dandin*, 1668; *Psyche*, 1673 (ballet-tragedy, in collaboration with Corneille, Quinault, and Lulli); and *The Hypochrondriac*, 1673,

The standard edition of the works of Molière is that contained in the collection of the *Grands-Ecrivains de la France*, edited by Mm. Eugene Despois and Paul Mesnard, (Paris, Hachette et Cie; 14 vols., 1873-1927). This collection contains a bibliography which is complete up to 1893 (Vol. XI). Other bibliographies worth noting are Madeleine Jurgens and Elizabeth Maxfield-Miller, *Cent Ans de Recherches sur Molière* (Paris: Archives Nationales, 1963); Paul Saintange and Robert W. Christ's *Fifty Years of Molière Studies, a Bibliography*, 1892-1941 (Baltimore: The Johns Hopkins Press, 1942); Author unknown, "Omissions and Additions to *Fifty Years of Molière's studies*"; Modern Language Notes, LIX (1944), pp. 282, 285; Bert Edwards Young and Grace Philputt Young, eds., *Le Registre de La Grange*, (1659-1685) (two vols., Droz, 1947), Facismile reproduction with note on LaGrange; edited by Nathan Edelman; *The Seventeenth Century* ("Moliere," pp. 226-243); and Vol. III of *A Critical Bibliography of French Literature*, edited by David Cabeen and Jules Brody (Syracuse: Syracuse University Press, 1961).

While translators of Molière's work are too numerous to list, fairly complete translations of his work have been made by the following: H. Baker and J. Miller (1729; rpt. Everyman Library, 1919); J. Watts (1748); H. Van Laun (1875-76); C.H. Wall translations (1910); A.R. Waller (8 vols., 1926) in which the French texts are also given; Richard Wilbur, the poet, published a rhymed verse translation of *The Misanthrope* in 1955. *The Plays of Molière in French and English*, edited by A.R. Waller, 1907, with an introduction by George Saintsbury, is an excellent collected edition in translation. A good single volume of selected plays with an introduction by Waldo Frank is *Plays by Molière*, Modern Library edition, 1924.

Overview of Biographical Sources

Although Molière's private life is complicated and virtually unrecorded, his genius and complete devotion to the career of actor, director, playwright and manager have initiated and maintained scholars' interest in his biography. The belief that no great genius was ever more deeply implicated in the life of his times than Molière has encouraged some biographers to incorporate biographical matter, real or assumed, into his achievements. This attempt makes the line between biography and criticism obscure and has helped to produce some biographies that are more exaggerated than true. The earliest biographical study of Molière is a brief preface to the first complete edition of his works entitled *Les Ouvres de Monsieur de Molière* and published by Charles Varlet LaGrange in 1682. LaGrange's reputation appears sound; his rather brief biography is accepted as honest, and the majority of Molière's biographers agree with his presentation. Grimarest, who published a second biography in 1705, obtained most of his information from Baron, a young actor who was for many years in the company of Moliere, but he also accepted material from other suspect sources. Since Grimarest relies upon information taken from persons who may not have been Molière's friends, the critics caution that his statements are not to be accepted without corroboration. They also suggest that the excellent biography of Taschereau (1863) requires careful correction in the light of recent researches. The critics agree that the life prefixed by Ste. Beuve to the edition of 1825 is of more value as criticism than biography, that Paul Mesnard's Volume X, *Ouvres de Molière* is the most scholarly and trustworthy and that next in accuracy is M. Louis Moland's *La Vie de F.-B.P. Molière*. From the human point of view, Gustave Larroumet's *La Comedie de Molière* is acclaimed the most interesting. Among other significant biographies are those of Jules Claretie (1873); J.J. Weiss (1900); Georges Lafenestre (1909); and Maurice Donnay (1911). The contemporary sources may be studied in the documents collected by Edouard Soulié, *Recherches sur Molière et sa Famille* (1863), and the *Collection Molières-que* of Paul Lacroix, a *Nouvelle Collection Molièresque* begun by Paul Lacroix (1863-1884) and continued by Georges Monvall (1884-1890).

Evaluation of Selected Biographies

H.C. Chatfield-Taylor, *Molière A Biography*. London: Chatto & Windus, 1906. This author pursued his study in Paris, the home of Molière, and collected valuable information which results in a scholarly and popular life of the dramatists. While referring to many original French sources, Chatfield-Taylor interprets Molière's life by his plays and his plays by his life. He also includes an informative chronology and extensive bibliography, as well as illustrations by M. George Monval. T.F. Crane, Professor of the Romance Languages at Cornell University, introduces this work and, while making many informative comments of his own, compliments Chatfield-Taylor on his ability to accomplish the difficult task of rendering a vivid and correct picture of Molière, the man, the actor and the dramatist.

Matthews, Brander, *Molière, His Life and His Works*. New York: Charles Scribner & Sons, 1916. A favorite of several critics, Matthews is able to blend biography and criticism in a manner that illuminates Molière's life and works without following a narrow critical approach. This biography is often referred to as the standard critical study of Molière in English. It is of manageable size, and Matthews' style is clear and readable.

Palmer, John, *Moliere*. New York: Brewer and Warren, 1930. Palmer offers an excellent study with a selected bibliography. Ths comprehensive biography consists of twenty-two chapters and presents a straight forward account of the major events of Molière's life. It places him within the context of his times, his career and his family and draws upon all available sources of information to present a thorough and objective portrait. Palmer also discusses several of Molière's plays including *Tartuffe*.

Tilley, Arthur, *Moli*ère. Cambridge: At the University Press, 1921. Tilley centers on the dramatist as a writer of comedy. He sees Molière as both a true humorist and an apostle of common sense who looks at life from the point of view of the average man. Tilley presents Molière as a dramatist who, unlike the intellectual and high-brow, takes the verdict of a community over that of a few superior persons, and rather than making claims on behalf of human nature, feels kindly for its shortcomings as one who is conscious of his own frailty. In this biography, Molière appears a healthy moralist, unsparing of the grasping, the insolent and the self-opinionated but tolerant towards ignorance, folly and crudility.

Autobiographical Sources

In the sixteenth and seventeenth centuries, the actor's profession was under a social ban and neither Molière nor his contemporaries thought to preserve his memories. Consequently, there are in Molière's life unfortunate gaps, especially during his early life, his education, and his first theatrical ventures. The long years spent in the provinces are recorded by civil and notarial documents and after Molière's return to Paris in 1658, there is a profusion of materials dealing almost exclusively with management of the Company and the literary life so inseparately connected with it. Although Molière left no journals, no letters, and no autobiographical materials from which to gather information for a study, he did leave his plays from which authors draw much understanding of the dramatist.

Overview of Critical Sources

Molière's plays have been the object of various modes of criticism down through the centuries. Since the beginning of the twentieth century, there has been a "re-theatricalization" of Molière's works. Several critics point to director Louis Jouvet's lectures as proving particularly instrumental in this endeavor. In 1901, Gustave Lanson contributed to Molière's popularity by publishing an article in which he recalls various sources of Molière's art. At the period of the First World War Jacques Copeau, in his productions and explanations, rediscovered the playwright and the actor of farce by concentrating on *Scapin* which he brought back into esteem. Because of the many brilliant and serious studies made, the following is only a sampling of the myriad critical approaches to his work. Other critical studies of Molière and his plays will be found in *Impressions de Theatre* by Jules Lemaitre (1888-1890), *Etudeset Portraits* by Paul Bourget (1889), *Epoques du Theatre Francais* (1892) and *Etudes Critiques sur l'Histoire* de la *Literature Francaise* (1895-1908) by Brunetiere.

Evaluation of Selected Criticism

Chapman, Percy Addison, *The Spirit of Molière, an Interpretation*. Princeton: Princeton University Press, 1940. In this sensitive but unfinished work edited by M. Bede and introduced by Mr. Gauss, Chapman defends Molière's picture of society "in which character is shown as more important than station in the relations of men with each other." Although part of the book is fragmentary, Chapman discusses Molière's comedies through the *Ecole des femmes* in detail, and compares *Don Garcie* with *Le Misanthrope*. These discussions, as well as references found in "Molière and His Public," add a dimension to the understanding of the playwright.

Fellows, Otis E. *French Opinion of Molière, 1800-1850*. Providence, RI: *Brown University Studies*. Vol. III, 1937. Dr. Fellows traces Molière's popularity from information he gathers in newspapers, periodicals, correspondence and other works. The critic believes that the lowest ebb occurred in the Revolutionary period, but that interest in Molière's plays takes a surge at the beginning of the second half of the nineteenth century. Once again, Molière is considered one of the greatest dramatic writers and the playwright's position gains strength throughout the Romantic period. Fellows further believes Molière was the only classical author consistently exempted from the general condemnation of seventeenth-century literature. While the introduction may assume too readily that the eighteenth century failed to appreciate Molière, Fellows has brought to light a significant, if minor, aspect of Romanticism.

Guicharnaud, Jacques, ed. *Molière, A Collection of Critical Essays*. Englewood Cliffs, NJ: Prentice-Hall, 1964. This is a collection of critical essays by leading scholars setting forth twentieth century views of Molière's work. While he recognizes each essay that appears in this collection, Guicharnaud points to Gustave Lanson, Rene Bray, and Alfred Simon, on the one hand, and Copeau and Dullin, on the other, as representing the artisans who concentrate on the "retheatricalization" of Molière.

Hubert, Judd D. *Molière and The Comedy of Intellect*. Berkeley and Los Angeles: University of California Press, 1962. Herbert presents an interval analysis of the plays in which he explains the unity in terms of a theme, an idea, a dramatic or satirical presupposition.

Lancaster, H.C. *A History of French Dramatic Literature in the Seventeenth Century, Part III, The Period*, 1652-1672, 2 vols., 1936. This work is an outstanding scholarly treatment of each play by Molière and an excellent reference book for plays by his contemporaries. Lancaster includes an analysis of structure from the point of view of unities as well as a good evaluation of critics' interpretations.

Moore, Will G. *Molière, A New Criticism.* Oxford: The Clarendon Press, 1949; rpt. Doubleday, 1962, with an additional "Post-Script." The author introduces a fresh look at Molière through internal analysis that reveals many ideas that were lost before in the overwhelming amount of accumulated material. Through this approach which revolutionizes the study of Molière, the unity of the plays and the very essence of comedy are brought to the surface and made clear to the reader.

Turnell, Martin, *Molière.* Scriveners, 11: 242-258. In this penetrating study, Turnell sees Molière's "Natural Man" as standing between the Cornelian Man of Honor and the Racinian Man of Passion. The critic insists that Molière's vision should be given breadth as well as variety insofar as man and society is concerned, particularly when man's fundamental sanity is concerned. Turnell further believes the theory of the comic is based on the use of masks as its symbol.

Villiers, Andre, *Le Dom Juan de Molière, un probleme de mise en scene.* Paris: "Masques," 1947. Several critics believe that Villiers presents the first serious attempt to rehabilitate the play on both the dramatic and the ideological level. His focus on an analysis of the play, of Don Juan's psychology, and of his possible relation to the heroes of today's theater is astute as well as enlightening.

Wilcox, John, *The Relation of Molière to Restoration Comedy.* New York: Columbia University Press; London: H. Milford, Oxford University Press, 1938. This critic answers the question "What is the real relationship between Molière and the English Comedy of Manners?" by assembling, classifying and applying an excellent critical judgment to the material. Wilcox concludes that while Molière's work is pillaged for characters and situations, his Spirit, Matter and Form were wholly alien to the English Theatre of the Restoration period and did not influence its English writers except for Wycherley who, in his two last plays, experienced a reaction of mind to Molière's art that ultimately afforded greatness to the English playwright. This book should prove valuable to both specialists in seventeenth-century drama and students of comparative literature. Included in this work is a useful chronology of Molière, a good index and valuable bibliographies.

Other Sources

Chapelle, Claude-Emmanuel Luillieu, Extract of a letter written by Chapelle to Molière; vol. V of the *Recueil des plus belles.* Paris: Chez Claude Barbin, 1691.

Fournier, Edouard, *Etudes sur la Vie de Molière* and *Le Roman de Molière.* 1885; New York: B. Franklin, 1965. Fournier is a French biographer who investigates the problems of Molière's marriage and family relationships.

Lane, William Coolidge, ed. Bibliographical Contributions, No. 57, Catalogue of the Molière Collection in the Harvard University Library. Cambridge, 1906.

Loiseleur, Jules, *Les Points Obscurs de la Vie de Molière*. Paris: Liseux, 1877. This French author explores the problems of the marriage and family relations of Molière.

Mantzius, Karl, *A History of Theatrical Art in Ancient and Modern Times*. trans. Louise von Cossel. Vol. IV, *Molière and His Times*. London: Duckworth, 1903-1921. Mantzius concentrates on the theater in France in the seventeenth century and lends a backdrop which places Molière as an actor and playwright in this fashionable period of the theater.

Michaut, Gustave, *La Jeunesse de Molière*. Paris: Hachette, 1925; rpt. Geneva: Skathine, 1968. This is one of the more searching and authoritative modern studies in the biography of Molière. Michaut critically reviews much of the previous evidence and sets forth the results of his investigations in a scholarly but easily readable style.

Monval, Georges, ed. *Le Molieriste*. Paris: Flâmmarion, 1897. This is a monthly magazine devoted to the study of Molière and published during ten years in Paris from 1879 to 1889. Ten volumes.

Waller, A.R. and George Saintsbury, *Molière, Jean Baptiste Poquelin*. Edinburgh: J. Grant, 1926. The plays of Molière are in French with an English translation and notes by A.R. Waller and an introduction by George Saintsbury. Illustrations with thirty-one etchings after Leloir.

Wanda LaFaye Seay
Oklahoma State University

FERENC MOLNÁR
1878-1952

Author's Chronology

Born January 12, 1878, Budapest, Hungary, to Dr. Móric Neumann, a noted physician and Jozefa Wallfisch; attends local high school in Budapest; *1895-1896* studies law in Budapest and Geneva, travels to Paris, returns to Hungary and changes his name to Molnár; *1901* publication of first novel, *Az éhes város* (Hungry City); *1902* opening of first play, *A doctor úr* (The Lawyer); *1906* works as a journalist, marries his editor's daughter, Margit Vészi; *1907* daughter Márta is born, publication of *The Paul's Street Boys*, opening of *The Devil* in Budapest; *1908* death of father; *The Devil* is performed all over Europe and in New York; *1910* divorces M. Vészi; *The Guardsman* opens; *1912* publication of two short story collections and two new plays; *1914-1915* war correspondent on the Galician Front; *1916 The White Cloud* wins the Academy's Voinits Award, war diary is awarded the Franz Joseph Order; *1917-1922* release and performance of one new play each year, publication of two collections of essays and feuilletons as well as several volumes of play translations from French; *1921* opening of *Liliom* in New York; *1922* marries the celebrated prima donna, Sári Fedák; *1926* after divorcing Fedák, marries actress Lili Darvas; *The Play's the Thing* opens in Budapest and New York; *1927* is awarded Legion of Honor after the Paris premiere of *The Swan*; first trip to USA, President Coolidge receives him in the White House; *1928-1930* publication of his play collection in English; *1931-1939* after his separation from Darvas travels with Wanda Bartha; five new plays open in Budapest; *1940* arrives at New York on January 12, moves to the Hotel Plaza where he stays till his death; *1943* suffers a massive heart attack; *1945* publication of three books in English; *1947* becomes an American citizen; Wanda Bartha commits suicide causing his final depression; *1950* opening of two new plays written in English; April 1, *1952*, Ferenc Molnár, the entertainer of the world, the widely popular Hungarian hedonist dies of cancer as a rootless, forlorn American, in New York City.

Author's Bibliography

This prolific, internationally celebrated playwright was also a distinguished essayist, novelist and short story writer authoring 72 books (42 plays), most of them translated into all major languages, including English. Thus, only a selective bibliography is listed here arranged by genres. Among the plays, collections are cited first followed by titles of individual dramas that had long-running, successful performances in America.

1928 the plays are collected in 20 volumes in Hungary; 1929 the English version of his dramatic output is published in New York: *The Plays of Molnár* (reprinted as *All the Plays of Ferenc Molnár*, in 1937); 1950 *Stories for Two* (collection of one-act plays); 1952 *Romantic Comedies: Eight Plays by Ferenc Molnár; Az ördög*, 1907 (*The Devil*, 1908); *Liliom*, 1910 (the first and best trans. by Benjamin Glazer, New York: Boni & Liveright, 1921); *A testör*, 1910 (*The Guardsman*, 1923); *Farsang*, 1917 (*Carnival*, 1924); *Úri divat*, 1917 (*Fashions for Men*, 1922); *A hattyú*, 1921 (*The Swan*, 1929); *A vörös malom*, 1923 (*The Red Mill*, 1928); *Az üvegcipó*, 1924 (*The Glass Slipper*, 1925); *Olympia*, 1928 (Eng. 1928); *A jó tündér*, 1930 (*The Good Fairy*, 1932); *Csoda a hegyek közt*, 1933 (*Miracle in the Mountain*, 1939); *A cukrászné*, 1935 (*Delicate Story*, 1941); *The Emperor*, 1942 (originally written in English).

Novels: *Andor*, 1918; *Prisoners*, 1924; *The Paul Street's Boys*, 1927; *Angel-Making Music*, 1935; *Farewell My Heart*, 1945; *Companion in Exile: Notes for an Autobiography*, 1950.

Short stories: *Husbands and Lovers*, 1924; *The Captain of St. Margaret's: Twenty-five Chapters of Memoirs*, 1945.

Non-fiction: *Diary of a War Correspondent, 1914-1915*, 1916.

Overview of Biographical Sources

Molnár, already a legend in his lifetime, epitomized all the virtues and defects of his art. His paradoxical personality and his works evoked extreme emotions. Throughout his career, he was besieged by ardent admirers and fanatical enemies. He split the camps of critics both in Hungary and abroad; at the summit of his success, each Molnár play or novel was greeted with sound and fury with panegyrics and scorn. His friends and foes were equally vocal and passionate in their attempts to explain the author's unprecedented popularity, but their temporary evaluation was always charged with emotions and often motivated by social and political reasons, subject to changes, in accordance with the intellectual climates of the successive micro-eras. As a result, no comprehensive biography (or objective, scholarly critical analysis) of Molnár has been written so far in Hungarian and only one exists in English: Clara Györgyey's *Ferenc Molnár*. This critical biography was researched on locales and completed by interviews with still surviving contemporaries of literary significance. In addition to Györgyey's solo, full-length, reliable biography, a great deal of gossipy information can be found in dramatic portraits printed in popular magazines and periodicals, in biographical sketches covering a certain period in the author's life, or in drama textbooks where superficial overviews of Molnár's career is provided to introduce one of his play selections. Minor biographical details, often embellished, can also be obtained from the massive amount of reviews and feature stories written about Molnár during his halcyon years. A rather poorly catalogued collection of such material is in the Molnár-deposit at the Beinecke Rare Book Library of Yale University, and an even larger and better arranged selection at the New York Public Library Drama Annex at the Lincoln Center.

Evaluation of Selected Biographies

Györgyey, Clara, *Ferenc Molnár*. Boston: Twayne, 1980. A comprehensive biography placing Molnár in the context of his era, milieu, and family, drawing upon all available sources of information to present a thorough and objective portrait of this controversial author. All his works are presented closely intertwined with historical and biographical comments. Molnár's final years in America, first time described fully in print, also warrants special attention. The book includes a chronology of Molnár's life, extensive references, bibliography and an index.

Halasz, George, *Ferenc Molnar: The Man Behind the Monocle*. New York: n.p., 1929. This fragmented, gossipy biography covering Molnár's early years is penned by one of his contemporaries, a fellow journalist, eager to "throw light" on the complex love relationships of the playwright and to reveal the real identity of numerous characters in the early plays. Though utterly unscholarly, the book is fascinating reading.

Halmi, Bódog, *Molnár Ferenc, az író és az ember*. (Molnár Ferenc, the Writer and the Man). Budapest: published by the author, 1929. Unfavorably biased study of Molnár's place in Hungarian literature with brief, unresearched biographical chapters covering his life between 1900-1927. So scarce were longer biographies of Molnár that this inferior Hungarian text has for long served as basis for several scholars of drama in other countries.

Vécsei, Irén, *Molnár Ferenc*. Budapest: Gondolat, 1966. This unevenly composed monograph is the first detailed Marxist analysis of Molnár's art. The authoress is long-winded on the historical background of the plays and highly critical of their apolitical nature. Although the book gives a fairly complete biographical summary, there are grave errors in the second part dealing with Molnár's itinerant life spent outside of Hungary. Otherwise, it is a clear and readable biography presently being translated into English.

Autobiographical Sources

Always regarded as an autobiographical author, it was generally assumed that Molnár's life was public property: its details either discussed or joked about in the cafés or revealed in the tabloids. In reality, little was known of his childhood or youth, and for decades he refused to write directly about himself.

During his stay in America, as his life reached its nadir and the nostalgic longing for his homeland and the past reached its zenith, Molnár no longer made any conscious effort to disguise the autobiographical elements in his work. On the contrary, he seemed anxious to disclose long-concealed events of his life, and to expose his emotions and views more sincerely than ever before. Thus, all his late works are blatant self reverations. Unfortunately, they were written at a time when his artistry and reputation alike were in a decline.

His formal, loosely constructed autobiography, *Companion in Exile*, is his most dolorous and depressing work. Composed as a final tribute to his companion, Wanda Bartha, immediately after her suicide in 1947, the book in fact is a pathetic story of an old man's tragic love and a swansong of remorse. It contains brief episodes from their life in America, explains their work routine, lists their friends and acquaintances, includes daily logs she had kept of festive Molnár openings, luxurious travels and encounters with famous people. This odd memoir, despite its several artistic flaws, is a valuable literary evidence of the profound changes Molnár and his art had undergone after World War II. Though traveling a lot, Molnár was not an ardent letter-writer; very few epistles are included in the Molnár memorabilias and none has ever been published.

Overview of Critical Sources

In his native land and in the United States, Molnár scholarship is virtually non-existent yet, essays, studies, portraits, interviews, book and play reviews (mostly superficial) are voluminous: a briefly annotated bibliography of the English materials alone covers over 200 pages. (Reasons for why Molnár's art has not been studied seriously are expanded upon in the "Overview of Biographical Sources"). The publication of Györgyey's volume in 1980 made the first objective critical analysis of the entire Molnár *oeuvre* readily available to scholars. This study also redressed the inordinate subjectivity of previous critics and at least partially filled the lack of critical evaluation of the writer.

The renewal of interest in Molnár is manifest not only in the numerous revivals of both his popular and lesser known plays across North America, but also in the emergence of valid judgments of his art in the subsequent drama reviews. The true impact and the real accomplishments of Molnár, the Hungarian "King of Entertainment," albeit worthy of listing in the annals of world literature, have still not been mapped out adequately.

Evaluation of Selected Criticism

Behrman, S. N. "Playwright: Ferenc Molnár," in *The Suspended Drawingroom*. New York: Stein & Day, 1965, pp. 191-253. Based on the author's admiration for and intimate friendship with Molnár during the first decades of the century, the study offers an amusing, tender biographical sketch filled with Molnár anecdotes and noted ripostes. It also provides short but perceptive analyses of *The Devil, The Liliom, The Guardsman, The Wolf, Carnival, The Swan* and *Olympia*.

Chandler, Frank W. "Hungarian and Czech Innovators: Molnár and the Ĉapeks," in *Modern Continental Playwrights*. New York: Harper & Brothers, 1931, pp. 438-453. Useful, clear critique of the first ten plays of Molnár. The approaches to the dramas include the linguistic, the thematic and the biographical.

Gassner, John, "Molnár and the Hungarians," in *Masters of the Drama*. New York: Dover Publications, 1945, pp. 468-481. Very brief but extremely sensitive, scholarly account of Molnár's contribution to the world of drama, with special emphasis on the relevance and universality of *Liliom*.

Gergely, Emro J. *Hungarian Drama in New York: American Adaptations 1908-1940*. Philadelphia: University of Pennsylvania Press, 1947. This massive volume gives outstanding analyses and critical commentaries of sixteen plays which had been performed on Broadway.

Györgyey, Clara, *Ferenc Molnár*. Boston: Twayne, 1980. The first critic to benefit from access to the complete works of Molnár, Györgyey presents each work, chronologically arranged by genres, in the framework of events both historical and personal. The critical comments provide the Hungarian and American views alternately. *Liliom* and the last plays are discussed in separate chapters. A useful resource book offering a general exposition to the complete art of Molnár.

Reményi, József, "Ferenc Molnár, the Hungarian Playwright," in *Hungarian Writers and Literature*. New Brunswick: Rutgers University Press, 1964, pp. 348-362. Scholarly study of Molnár's achievement in Hungary and abroad; a highly critical account of the author's major works in every genre. It contains detailed biographical and historical background and an impressive bibliography.

Other Sources
Klaniczay, Tibor, *History of Hungarian Literature*. Budapest: Corvina Press, 1964. Provides good background material and fine summary of Hungary's literary climate during Molnár's early career.

Liliom. trans. and int. by Benjamin Glazer. New York: Boni & Liveright, 1921. Poignant analysis of the play, its sources and reception in Hungary and abroad.

Middleton, George, *These Things are Mine*. New York: The Macmillan Co., 1947, pp. 363-369. An intimate portrait of Molnár in the 1920s with an entertaining explanation of his extraordinary appeal as a dramatist in Europe and elsewhere.

Molnár, Erzsébet, *Testvérek voltunk*. (We Were Siblings). Budapest: Magvetö, 1958, (untranslated). Personal memoirs of Molnár's only sister about their family and their relationship while growing up in Budapest at the turn of the century. It merely describes their lives without contributing any particular insights.

Molnár, Ferenc, *Husband and Lovers*. trans. and int. by Benjamin Glazer. New York: Boni & Liveright, 1924. Glazer's sensitive introduction gives a detailed interpretation of Molnár's one-act plays tracing the omni-presence of the battle of the sexes in each.

Nagy, George L. *The Plays of Ferenc Molnár and their Performances in German*. Albany: State University of New York Press, 1982. Fine biographical and critical account of the complete Molnár art with special emphasis on the reception and staging of his plays in Germany and Austria. The book provides scholarly charts, statistics, bibliography and a handy index. Useful reference book.

Nagy, Péter, "Molnár Ferencröl," in *Irodalomtörténet*, 48 (1960), pp. 377-392. Erudite, sober critical interpretation of some of Molnár's short stories and *Companion in Exile*.

Rajec, Elizabeth, *Molnár Bibliography*. Wien: Böhlau, 1986. A monumental, comprehensive, almost complete bibliography of primary and secondary sources in Hungarian, German and English, including thousands of variegated articles and reviews by and about Molnár.

Wilson, Edmund, "Hungary," *New Yorker*, June 4, 1966, pp. 110-139. A handy survey of Molnár's popularity in New York with detailed critical commentaries about *The Devil* and *Fashions for Men* which incorporate summaries of contemporary American reviews of the two plays.

Clara Györgyey
Yale University

LEANDRO FERNÁNDEZ DE MORATÍN
1760-1828

Author's Chronology

Born March 10, 1760, Madrid, Spain, to Nicolás Fernández de Moratín (a Neoclassical poet and playwright) and Isidora Cabo Conde; *1779* in the contest of the Royal Academy, young Leandro receives an honorable mention for his narrative poem, "The Conquest of Granada;" *1780-1786* works in a silversmith shop in Madrid; *1780* his father dies prematurely at the age of 42; his mother dies in 1785; Leandro's *Lección poética* (A Literary Lesson), a satire on literary vices in contemporary poetry, wins second honorable mention from the Royal Academy; *1786* his first play, *El viejo y la niña* (The Old Man and the Girl) is read to the dramatic company of Manuel Martínez; *1787* becomes secretary of the Count of Cabarrús, director of the San Carlos Bank, and accompanies him on a trip to France; composes the musical play, *The Baron*; *1789* in France, he becomes an *abbé* (secular ecclesiastic); publishes his prose satire, *La derrota de los pedantes* (The Defeat of the Pedants); *1790* theatrical career is launched with the premiere of *El viejo y la niña* at Madrid's Principe Theater; *1792* obliged to leave Paris because of the French Revolution, he goes to London where he learns English and attends the theater; travels to Italy, Germany and Switzerland, returning in 1796 to Spain where he is appointed Secretary of the Interpretation of Languages; *1798* published his translation of *Hamlet*; *1806* his greatest theatrical success, *El sí de las niñas* (*When a Girl Says Yes*) is produced; *1812* flees Madrid with the retreating French forces; lives in Barcelona; *1814* fear of the Inquisition motivates his move to France and Italy; *1820-1821* his brief return to Barcelona is terminated by an outbreak of pestilence; flees to Bordeaux, never again to live in Spain; *1827* moves to Paris, where he dies on June 21, 1828; 1830-1831 Spanish Academy of History published his collected works.

Author's Bibliography

The most accessible works of Moratín are those published in the twentieth century. The majority are in Spanish, with very few translations. The following list limits itself to the collected works and translations of individual works. *Teatro*, edited by F. Ruiz Morcuende in the standard Clásicos Castellanos collection (no. 58; Madrid: Ediciones de la Lectura, 1924). *La comedia nueva. El sí de las niñas.* Ediciones, introducciones y notas de John Dowliny y René Andioc (Madrid: Clásicos Castalia, 1968). *La derrota de los pedantes. Lección poética.* Edición con introducción, notas y glosario de John Dowling (Barcelona: Editorial Labor, 1971). *El viejo y la niña.* Edited, with introduction, notes, bibliography by Leslie Bannister Walton (Manchester: The University Press, 1921).

Overview of Biographical Sources
There is little available in English about Moratín's life. What is accessible is limited to highlights of his career and dates of publications. There is no definitive biography or full-length study of the Spanish dramatist's life in any language. Among the relevant and accessible material is a *Diario* (Journal) from 1780-1808 which has been edited and annotated by René and Mireille Andioc (Madrid: Editorial Castalia, 1967). It gives the best perspective of Moratín's adult life and his theatrical activities. The volume in the Twayne World Authors Series by John Dowling (1971) also has perceptive information on Moratín's life. Leslie Bannister Walton in his edition for English-speaking students of *El viejo y la niña* (1921) likewise provides relevant biographical information in addition to some historical background and notes on the culture of the times.

Evaluation of Selected Biographies
Andioc, René and Mireille Andioc, *Diario*. Madrid: Editorial Castalia, 1967, Untranslated. In this annotated journal, these authors have made available to researchers what is probably the best extant source on Moratín's life in any language. These authors managed to decipher the diaries (composed in the writer's personal shorthand and at one time considered a cipher), augmenting the material so that the scholar now has accessible a very good perspective of the dramatist's life and principal theatrical activities.

Dowling, John, *Leandro Fernández de Moratín*. New York: Twayne, 1971. Dowling introduces biographical commentary and information in the course of his examination of the different works. This volume includes a chronology of Moratíín's life, extensive references and bibliography in a very clear and readable style with solid scholarly judgment.

Walton, Leslie Bannister, *El viejo y la niña*. Manchester: University Press, 1921. Walton provides limited but interesting background information concerning Moratín and his times.

Autobiographical Sources
Moratín travelled extensively in Europe, and he recorded his experiences and observations in letters, his diary and occasionally in indirect fashion in his more strictly literary works. It should be noted that he utilized a number of pseudonyms, in some instances to avoid reprisal for his collaboration with the occupying French forces. Among his pen names are Inarco Celenio; Efrén de Lardinaz y Morante (an obvious anagram); Melitón Fernández (the first name was one of his four baptismal names), used while in hiding in Barcelona, 1814-17; and Ginés de Posadilla, the pseudonym used for republishing the *Auto de fe*. The best autobiographical source available is Moratín's journal, *Diario* which covers the period from May of 1780 to

March of 1808 and comprises the composition of his most significant works. This has been made available with annotation and expansion by René and Mireille Andioc (Madrid: Editorial Castalia, 1967). John Dowling's *Leandro Fernández de Moratín* (New York: Twayne, 1971) is extremely valuable for its references both to the *Diario* and to Moratín's correspondence.

Overview of Critical Sources

Although very little has been written in English about Moratín, a not inconsiderable amount of scholarship does exist in Spanish in a number of journals and books available in any university library. Moratín's literary reputation has suffered for two important reasons: the first was a result of his collaboration with the French forces of occupation following the Napoleonic invasion, resulting in his classification as an *afrancesado* or French sympathizer (actually, as the son of a Neoclassicist and himself a Neoclassical writer, he was both by upbringing and culture a Francophile). The second reason is that Moratín was not prolific, due to a tendency to polish his works, perhaps excessively (another result of his Neoclassical formation). Nonetheless, he is an unquestioned master of the Spanish language, thanks especially to his versatility, eloquence and wealth of vocabulary. His place in the history of Spanish theater is secure for two reason, first his usage of an entirely new approach to writing plays, and second, his pioneering work of historical scholarship on the early development of the genre in Spain. Although a Neoclassicist, Moratín did not limit himself to the imitation of Classical sources, nor did he simply follow the dramatic patterns of Spain's Golden Age writers employed by traditionalists of his day. His personal theatrical formulas make him the most modern Spanish playwright of his period.

Evaluation of Selected Criticism

Cook, John A. *Neo-Classic Drama in Spain: Theory and Practice*. Dallas: Southern Methodist University Press, 1959. A useful overview is provided by Cook, who traces the development of Neoclassic drama from the time of the first enunciation of principles in Luzán's *Poetics* during the 1730s across approximately a century, spanning both the life and works of Moratín's father, Nicolás, and his own production, as well as that of those influenced by the younger Moratín.

Dowling, John, *Leandro Fernández de Moratín* New York: Twayne, 1971. Perhaps the best and most detailed study of Moratín available, and certainly the outstanding source in English, Dowling not only studies Moratín's works but also gives biographical information and background relevant to each. His monograph provides the reader with an initial chronology which is most useful in summarizing, as well as in relating overall literary output to important events in Moratín's life and contemporary history.

Ferreres, Rafael, *Moratín en Valencia (1812-1814)*. Valencia: Centro de Cultura Valencia, 1962. Untranslated. A monograph of some interest for its study of an obscure period in Moratín's life, this work also publishes some newspaper articles possibly attributable to the author.

Lázaro Carreter, Fernando, *Moratín en su teatro*. Cuadernos de la Cátedra de Feijóo, No. 9 (Oviedo: Universidad de Oviedo, 1961). Untranslated. In a distinguished series emphasizing Neoclassicism in Spain, this well-known Spanish scholar evaluates the place of Moratín and his theater within the context and history of the Neoclassic movement.

Melón R. de Gordejuela, Santiago, *Moratín por dentro*. Cuadernos de la Cátedra Feijóo, No. 16 (Oviedo: Universidad de Oviedo, 1964). Untranslated. One of the only sources to attempt a study of the personality and psychology of Moratín and its relevance to his theater.

Ruiz Morcuende, Federico, *Vocabulario de D. Leandro Fernández de Moratín*. Madrid: Real Academia Española, 1945. Untranslated. Although somewhat ponderous by reason of its very thoroughness, this work defines and illustrates every word used in Moratín's writings, and can be particularly useful for close textual interpretation.

Shergold, N.D. *A History of Spanish Stage from Medieval Times Until the End of the Seventeenth Century*. Oxford: The Clarendon Press, 1967. This is a fundamental work with sound scholarly treatment of Spanish theater and its development, which traces evolution of the stage in Spain up to the beginnings of the Neoclassical period.

Walton, Leslie Bannister, introduction and notes to Leandro Fernández de Moratín's *El viejo y la niña*. Manchester: The University Press, 1921. Walton provides an excellent introduction to the state of Spanish literature under the Bourbons, as well as to Moratín's life and works.

Other Sources

Andioc, René, *Sum la querelle du théâtre au temps de Leandro Fernández de Moratín*. Tarbes: Imprimerie Saint-Joseph, 1970. Very scholarly and slow-moving study of problems and disputes in the theatre during the lifetime of Moratín.

_____. "A propos d'une reprise de *La comedia nueva* de Leandro Fernández de Moratín," in *Bulletin Hispanique*, LXIII (1961): 54-61. A recapitulation of the documentary evidence drawn from his correspondence, journal and other sources of Moratín's insistence of painstaking care in the production of his works.

Casalduero, Joaquín, "Forma y sentido de *El sí de las niñas*," in *Nueva Revista de Filología Hispánica*, XI (1957): 36-56. A well-known critic investigates Moratín's masterpiece and produces an excellent analysis of form and meaning.

Díaz-Plaja, Guillermo, "Perfil del teatro romántico español," in *Estudios Escénicos*, No. 8 (1963): 29-56. Identifies Moratín as a precursor of the nascent Romantic theater in Spain through analysis of the emphasis on sentiment and freedom of choice in *El sí de las niñas*.

Flores, Angel, ed. *Spanish Drama*. New York: Bantam, 1962. Contains an English version of *El sí de las niñas* (*When a Girl Says Yes*), translated by William M. Davis.

Helman, Edith F. "The Younger Moratín and Goya on *Duendes* and *Brujas*," in *Hispanic Review*, XXVII (1959): 103-22. This article provides insightful comparisons between Moratín's re-edition of *Auto de fe* and Goya's *Caprichos*, illuminating a little-known liberal aspect of the writer.

Insula, XV, No. 161 (April 1960). A special number of the well-known Madrid literary periodical with articles on Moratín by Azorín, José Luis Cano, John Dowling, Nigel Glendinning, Edith Helman, Fernando Lázaro Carreter, Vicente Llorens, Julián Marías, Antonio Odriozola.

Moratín y la sociedad española de su tiempo, *Revista de la Universidad de Madrid*, IX (1960), No. 35: 567-808. Devoted to articles on Moratín by Antonio Domínguez Ortiz, Juan Antonio Gaya Nuño, Luis S. Granjel, Edith Helman, Angela Mariutti de Sánchez Rivero, Paul Merimée, Antonio Oliver and Luis Sánchez Agesta.

Rooney, Sister St. Dominic, "Realism in the Original Comedies of Leandro Fernandez de Moratín" (Ph.D. Dissertation, University of Minnesota, 1963). Establishes Moratín's place as a link between the Golden Age dramatist Ruiz de Alarcón and the Nineteenth-Century problem play.

Spaulding, Robert K. "The Text of Moratín's *Orígenes del Teatro Español*," in *PMLA*, XLVII (1932): 981-991. Provides an interesting account of how Spanish censorship affected the first edition of Moratín's history of the Spanish theater.

Genaro J. Pérez
The University of Texas
Permian Basin

KAJ MUNK
1898-1944

Author's Chronology

Born January 13, 1898, Maribo, Denmark, to Carl Immanuel and Ane Mathilde Petersen; *1916* adopted by Peder and Marie Munk; *1917* university entrance exam; *1917-1924* attends University of Copenhagen; *1924* receives a degree in divinity and is ordained as a minister; the same year Munk becomes pastor of Vedersø in western Jutland, where he lives until the time of his arrest and murder by the Gestapo in 1944; *1929* marries Elise Marie Jørgensen; January 4, 1944 Munk is executed outside the town of Silkeborg.

Author's Bibliography

Beginning his career shortly after World War I, Munk wrote close to sixty plays, as well as numerous poems, essays and sermons. A selection of his work, *Mindeudgave*, 9 vols., ed. Niels Nøjgaard and Knud Bruun-Rasmussen, 1948-1949, includes his most important dramas. Available in English in *Five Plays by Kaj Munk*, 1953, 2nd ed. 1964, tr. by R.P. Keigwin, *Herod the King*, 1928; *Cant*, 1931; *The Word*, 1932; *He Sits at the Melting-Pot*, 1938; and *Before Cannae*, 1943; *Niels Ebbesen*, 1942 (in *Scandinavian Plays of the Twentieth Century. Second Series*, 1944, tr. by R.P. Keigwin). Additional publications in English are the two volumes *Four Sermons*, 1944 and *By the Rivers of Babylon: Fifteen Sermons*, 1945.

Overview of Biographical Sources

Initially showing some sympathy for Fascist ideology, Munk became one of the most prominent and outspoken critics of the German occupational forces during World War II. His political involvement caused him to become one of the most discussed—criticized and glorified—cultural personalities in post-war Denmark. Gradually, however, the aura of his martyrdom has faded and given way to a more analytical approach to his authorship. This shift away from biography towards literary analysis has thrown his real contribution to Danish literature in relief: a revitalization of the country's drama replacing a bloodless, derivative naturalistic tradition with a—technically perfect—powerfull, Shakespearean mode of expression strongly advocating ethical values. Studies such as H.H. Siegumfeldt's *Kaj Munk. En Mand og hans Daad* (Aalborg: F. and L.C. Lauritzen, 1945) and Niels Nøjgaard's *Ordets Dyst og Daad* (Copenhagen: Nyt Nordisk Forlag, 1946) are predominantly biographical focusing on the World War II-period. The monographs by Alf Henriques: *Kaj Munk* (Copenhagen: Athenaeum, 1945) and Gudrun Cavin:

Kaj Munk. Dramaturge, prophete et martyr (Genève: Editions Labor et fides, 1946) combine biography with some text analysis, while later works such as Søren Holm's *Kaj Munk. Den religiøse* Problematik i hans Dramaer (Copenhagen: Nyt Nordisk Forlag, 1961) and Alfred Otto Schwede's *Verankert im Unsichtbaren. Das Leben Kaj Munks* (Berlin: Evangelische Verlagsanstalt, 1970) explore the theological dimension of Munk's authorship. Only two biographical sources are available in English, one being a review article, the other an essay exclusively based on secondary material.

Evaluation of Selected Biographies

Bang, Carol K. "Kaj Munk's Autobiography," in *The American-Scandinavian Review*, 33 (1945): 45-50. Taking her point-of-departure in a review of Munk's autobiography, *Foraaret saa sagte kommer*, 1942, Bang retells certain episodes from his life, almost totally ignoring Munk as an artist.

Harcourt, Melville, "Kaj Munk," in *Portraits of Destiny*. New York: Sheed and Ward, 1966, pp. 1-47. Harcourt's anecdotic, occasionally chatty essay deals extensively with historical and political events during the German occupation of Denmark frequently without much relevance to Munk's life. Too much emphasis is put on Munk's childhood, youthful religious questionings and his "Christo-centric" theology in general. Only a few of his plays are even listed. At times, Harcourt's treatment—although generally reliable—takes on a hagiographic tone.

Overview of Critical Sources

Danish Munk scholarship is primarily biographical and comprises numerous book-length works. Critical approaches to his plays are rather rare and frequently limited to shorter articles. No definitive monograph has yet been written. On the other hand, major contributions to the study of Munk as a playwright can be found in American scholarship.

Evaluation of Selected Criticism

Arestad, Sverre, "Kaj Munk as a Dramatist," in *Scandinavian Studies*, 26 (1954): 151-176. Undoubtedly Arestad's study is the most significant treatment of Munk's plays making extensively use of Danish sources and criticism. After showing Munk's relation to dramatic tradition Arestad discusses with great poise his use of history in the historical dramas and his religious philosophy as the source of his concept of tragedy. The study concludes with thorough analyses of the plays *The Word, He Sits at the Melting-Pot* and *Herod the King*.

Schmidt, Robert, "Kaj Munk: A New Danish Dramatist," in *The American-Scandinavian Review*, 21 (1933): 227-232. Drawing certain parallels to the uncompromising individualism of Søren Kierkegaard, Schmidt analyses *The Word, Herod the King* and *Cant* as fierce attacks on superficiality, hypocrisy and the compromise seeking spirit of the times in general. The article—subjective as it may be in its judgments—serves as a sketchy but thought-provoking introduction to Munk the artist.

Thompson, Lawrence, "The Actuality of Kaj Munk's Dramas," in *Books Abroad*, 15, (1941): 267-272. With great expertise Thompson places Munk in the European dramatic tradition. His article contains brief but succinct analyses concluding with a gripping prediction of the likely killing of Munk by the Gestapo.

Sven H. Rossel
University of Washington

THOMAS NASHE
1567-1601?

Author's Chronology

Born in the autumn of 1567, in Lowestoft, Suffolk, to William Nashe and Margaret, his second wife; October 13, *1582* enters St. John's College, Cambridge University; November, *1584* becomes scholar of Lady Margaret Foundation; March, *1586* receives Bachelor of Arts and continues studying toward Master of Arts; *1587* father dies; *1588* moves to London and begins a journalistic career; December 2, *1589* mother dies; *1589-1590* joins the Martin Marprelate controversy and attacks Puritanism; *1592*, September or October, may have composed *A Pleasant Comedie, Called Summer's Last Will and Testament* while living at Archbishop Whitgift's palace at Croydon; *1592* attends banquet of pickled herring and Rhenish wine hosted by Robert Greene, who dies on September 2 or 3, 1592; *1592-1596* engages in a pamphlet war with Richard and Gabriel Harvey in part over their censure of Robert Greene; *1593* composes *Strange Newes of the Intercepting Certaine Letters* in response to Gabriel Harvey's attack on him in *Foure Letters*; February, *1593* may have visited the home of Robert Cotton at Conington near Huntingdon; March-June, *1593* works for printer John Danter; late *1593*-early 1594 lives with family of Sir George Carey, governor of the Isle of Wight; spring and summer 1597 works on the play *The Isle of Dogs*; *1597* pamphlet entitled *The Trimming of Thomas Nashe, Gentleman* satirizes Nashe after the uproar over *The Isle of Dogs*; late *1597* escapes to Yarmouth after suppression of *The Isle of Dogs* and writes *Lenten Stuffe* during Lent of 1598; June 1, *1599* Archbishop Whitgift and Bishop Bancroft order the satires by Nashe and Harvey called in and specify that no more are to be printed; *1601* Nashe described as deceased in Charles Fitzgeffrey's *Affaniae*.

Author's Bibliography

Nashe's bibliography is complicated because his love of controversy, satire, and topical allusions rendered his work susceptible to censorship by the authorities. Early in his career as a pamphleteer and spokesman for the Anglican establishment against the Puritans, his pamphlets also appeared anonymously and under pseudonyms. Even so, there has been little controversy over the canon and text since the appearance of the five-volume edition of his works prepared by Ronald B. McKerrow in 1903-1910 and revised by F.P. Wilson in 1958.

Summer's Last Will and Testament is the only surviving play attributed to Nashe that is believed to have been entirely his work. Modern critics have followed McKerrow in assuming that the play was composed for immediate performance at the home of Archbishop Whitgift in September or October, 1592, even though it did not appear in print until 1600.

Nashe may have collaborated with Christopher Marlowe in writing *The Tragedie of Dido, Queene of Carthage*; *Dido* was not published until 1594, but must have been written prior to Marlowe's death on May 30, 1593. Nashe claims to have written only the induction and first act of the *The Isle of Dogs* (1597); the play may have been completed by Ben Jonson who was imprisoned for writing and possibly acting in the play. No copy of *The Isle of Dogs* has survived.

Overview of Biographical Sources

Materials for Nashe's life are drawn principally from three sources: official registers, autobiographical statements in his works, and comments in the works of his adversaries and contemporaries. The major sources for Nashe's life were identified in Ronald B. McKerrow's *The Works of Thomas Nashe*, (1904-1910, rpt. 1958). The chronology has been corrected in a series of articles by C.G. Harlow appearing in *The Review of English Studies* in 1961 and 1963. The known facts are summarized judiciously in a recent overview by Donald J. McGinn, *Thomas Nashe* (1981).

Since even the circumstances of Nashe's death are not known and much biographical information has been gleaned from analysis of his and his opponent's controversial pamphlets, his biographers have sometimes conflated fictional surmise with fact. Authors interested in connecting Nashe with William Shakespeare or Francis Bacon have been especially eager to fill in the factual gaps in Nashe's life with conjectures. In *Gabriel Harvey and Thomas Nashe* (1923, rpt. 1974) Edward George Harman argues that Francis Bacon and Thomas Nashe were the same person, and, more recently, Charles Nichol, in *A Cup of News* (1984), has connected Nashe with a number of Shakespearean plays and the *Sonnets*.

Evaluation of Selected Biographies

Harlow, C.G. "Nashe's Visit to the Isle of Wight and his Publications of 1592-4," in *Review of English Studies*, XIV (1963); 224-142. Harlow corrects McKerrow's dating of Nashe's visit to the home of Sir George Carey and his family in the Isle of Wight from 1592 to late 1593.

_____. "Thomas Nashe, Robert Cotton the Antiquary, and *The Terrors of the Night*," in *Review of English Studies*, XII (1961): 7-23. Harlow convincingly argues that Nashe was the guest of Robert Cotton, the antiquary, in February, 1593. This argument corrects McKerror's dates of composition and publication for *The Terrors of the Night*.

_____. "Thomas Nashe and William Cotton, M.P." *Notes and Queries*, VIII (1961): 424-425. Harlow presents biographical evidence that William Cotton, from whom Nashe sought patronage, was a man of some prominence.

Harmon, Edward George, *Gabriel Harvey and Thomas Nashe*. London: J.M. Ouseley, 1923; rpt. Folcroft, PA: Folcroft Library Editions, 1974. Harmon painstakingly examines the extant materials to argue that Nashe and Francis Bacon are the same person.

McGinn, Donald J. *Thomas Nashe*. Boston: G.K. Hall, 1981. McGinn offers a factual summary of Nashe's life. He accepts the basic outline established by McKerrow, as corrected by Harlow.

McKerrow, Ronald B. *The Works of Thomas Nashe*. London: A.H. Bullen, 1904-1910, rpt. Oxford: Blackwell, 1958. 5 vols. This standard edition of Nashe's works was corrected by F.P. Wilson in 1958 and remains definitive.

Nicholl, Charles, *A Cup of News: The Life of Thomas Nashe*. London: Routledge & Kegan Paul, 1984. Nicholl uses the facts of Nashe's life and passages from his works as a springboard for speculation.

Schrickx, W. *Shakespeare's Early Contemporaries: The Background of the Harvey-Nashe Polemic and* Love's Labour's Lost. Antwerpen: De Nederlandsche Boekhandel, 1956; rpt. New York: AMS Press, 1972. Schrickx describes a *School of Night* led by Sir Walter Raleigh and its background to Shakespeare's *Love's Labour's Lost* and George Chapman's *Hymn of Night*. Although he draws conclusions for which there is little evidence, Schrickx presents some interesting arguments.

Autobiographical Sources

All autobiographical sources regarding Nashe's life appear as asides in his prefaces or digressions in his works. He typically prefaces his early works with dedications or epistles that comment upon the contemporary literary scene. In *The Antatomie of Absurditie* Nashe launches into a diatribe against romantic fiction and then turns evenhandedly to an attack on Puritan pamphleteers. *Pierce Penilesse, His Supplication to the Divell* (1592), Nashe's first literary success, begins with Pierce's lament over his poverty. Observing that wealthy young upstarts waste their patrimonies while scholars starve, Pierce decides to send a supplication to the devil asking for aid and in the process digresses upon a series of Elizabethan counterparts to the Seven Deadly Sins. *Pierce Penilesse* contains a digression in which Nashe makes his first satiric thrust at Gabriel Harvey. Allusions in his more serious pamphlets, *The Terrors of the Night* (1593) and *Christ's Teares Over Jerusalem* (1594), identify Nashe's patrons as Sir Robert Cotton and Sir George Carey, respectively.

Nashe's first sustained attack on Richard and Gabriel Harvey occurs in *Strange Newes*. The scatalogical puns which appear in the full title of this pamphlet suggest the tone of Nashe's outrageous satire: *Strange Newes of the Intercepting Certaine Letters, and a Convoy of Verses, as they were going Privilie to victuall the Low Countries*.

His battle with Harvey continues in several more pamphlets, climaxing in his final reply, *Have With You to Saffron-Walden* (1596). Nashe tells the reader that he began his final pamphlet, *Lenten Stuffe* during Lent, 1598. In this work, which appeared in 1599, Nashe acknowledges that he was forced to leave London because of the uproar over *The Isle of Dogs*. He admits only to having written the induction and the first act. Having learned that his escapade can be appealed and possibly pardoned, he says that he decided to write *Lenten Stuffe* in praise of Yarmouth, the city that sheltered him during his banishment.

Overview of Critical Sources

Noted for his satirical wit, Nashe in his own time was compared with the satirist Juvenal rather than the more genial Horace. Twentieth-century criticism has paid more attention to Nashe's picaresque novel, *The Unfortunate Traveller* (1594), than to his satirical pamphlets or his dramatic compositions. His brief lyric, "Adieu, Farewell Earth's Bliss," which appears in *Summer's Last Will and Testament*, has received an extraordinary amount of critical attention, much of it having to do with a famous crux in the poem, the line "Brightness falls from the air." Since *Summer's Last Will and Testament* is included in the first volume of the new two-volume anthology entitled *Drama of the English Renaissance: The Tudor Period*, edited by Russell A. Fraser and Norman Rabkin (1976), it may well receive more attention in the future.

Critical studies of Nashe's works, particularly of *The Unfortunate Traveller*, are described in two recent and informative bibliographical articles by Robert J. Fehrenbach: "Thomas Nashe," *The Predecessors of Shakespeare*, ed. Terence P. Logan and Denzell S. Smith, Lincoln: University of Nebraska Press, 1973, pp. 114-117; "Recent Studies in Nashe (1968-1979)," *English Literary Renaissance*, 3 (1981), 344-350.

Evaluation of Selected Criticism

Auberlen, Eckhard, *The Commonwealth of Wit: The Writer's Image and His Strategies of Self-Representation in Elizabethan Literature*. Studies & Texts in English. Tubingen: Gunter Narr, 1984. Correcting the view that Nashe was content to regard himself as a journalist, Auberlen demonstrates that Nashe began by presenting himself as a scholar writing for a select audience. This study is the best recent critical discussion of Nashe.

Best, Michael R. "Nashe, Lyly, and *Summer's Last Will and Testament*," in *Philological Quarterly*, XL (1969): 1-11. Best argues that the play's structure may have resulted from Nashe's having reworked an entertainment originally written by John Lyly.

Cook, Elizabeth, "'Death proves them all but toyes': Nashe's unidealizing show," in *The Court Masque*. ed. David Lindley. Manchester: Manchester University Press, 1984, pp. 17-32. Cook assumes exclusively on the basis of internal compliments to Queen Elizabeth that she personally attended the performance. Since even the precise date of the performance has not been established, Cook's assumption is strongly inferential. In an otherwise perceptive and insightful essay, Cook shows that Nashe combines the idealizing elements of the masque and the realistic or anti-idealizing elements of the antimasque in one work.

Crewe, Jonathan V. *Unredeemed Rhetoric: Thomas Nashe and the Scandal of Authorship*. Baltimore and London: The Johns Hopkins University Press, 1982. Crewe interprets *Summer's Last Will and Testament* as the enactment of the loss of poetic order and argues that Nashe believed that the poetic order or brightness could only be experienced in the moment of loss.

Drew, Philip, "Was Greene's 'Young Juvenal' Nashe or Lodge?" in *Studies in English Literature 1500-1900*, VII (1967): 55-56. Drew argues that Robert Greene alluded not to Nashe but to Thomas Lodge by the epithet, "Young Juvenal."

Empson, William, *Seven Types of Ambiguity*. London: Meridian, 1950. Empson examines the line, "Brightness falls from the air," in Nashe's song, "Adieu, Farewell Earth's Bliss."

Hibbard, G.R. *Thomas Nashe: A Critical Introduction*. Cambridge: Harvard University Press, 1962. This is the only critical study of all of Nashe's work, but its chronology should be corrected by the two articles published by C.G. Harlow in *Review of English Studies* (1961, 1963). Hibbard describes *Summer's Last Will and Testament* as plaintive in tone and identifies mutability as its principal theme.

McGinn, D.J. *Thomas Nashe*. Boston: G.K. Hall, 1981, esp. pp. 48-56. Expanding Harlow's theory that *Summer's Last Will and Testament* was written for a particular audience on a particular occasion, McGinn suggests that the play was performed during the last hours of summer preceding the autumnal equinox. McGinn provides an excellent overview and judicious summary of critical analyses of Nashe's work.

Other Sources
Born, Hanspeter, *The Rare Wit and the Rude Groom: The Authorship of 'A Knack to Know a Knave' in Relation to Greene, Nashe, and Shakespeare*. Swiss Studies in English, 64. Bern: Francke, 1971. Born argues that Nashe collaborated with Greene on this play, but that Nashe's contribution was very small.

Carlson, Leland H. *Martin Marprelate, Gentleman: Master Job Throkmorton Laid Open in His Colors*. San Marino, CA: Huntington Library Press, 1981. Carlson attacks McGinn (1966 below) and convincingly argues that Job Throckmorton was the author of the anonymously published Martin Marprelate tracts.

Davis, Walter R. *Idea and Act in Elizabethan Fiction*. Princeton: Princeton University Press, 1969. Davis disputes Nashe's claim to have written the first historical novel.

Gardette, Raymond, "Satire et gueuserie: *Summer's Last Will and Testament* (1600) de Thomas Nashe," in *Misere et gueuserie au temps de la Renaissance*. ed. Marie-Therese Jones-Davies. Paris: Univ. de Paris-Sorbonne, Inst. de Recherches sur les Civilisations de l'Occident Mod., 1976, pp. 35-49.

Helgerson, Richard, *The Elizabethan Prodigals*. Berkeley: University of California Press, 1976. Helgerson views Nashe's *Anatomy of Absurdity* as an attack on Greene and other authors of romantic fiction.

Lewis, C.S. *English Literature in the Sixteenth Century Excluding Drama*. London: Oxford University Press, 1954. Useful discussion of Nashe's pamphlets and brilliant analysis of his style.

McGinn, D.J. *John Penry and the Marprelate Controversy*. New Brunswick: Rutgers University Press, 1966. McGinn presents a comparison of Penry's signed writings with the Martinist pamphlets and claims that their similarity in style demonstrates that Penry was Martin Marprelate.

Percy, Walker, "Metaphor as Mistake," in *Sewanee Review*, LXVI (1958): 79-99. Discusses the aptness of the line "Brightnesse falls from ayre" in Nashe's "Adieu, Farewell Earth's Bliss."

Stern, Virginia F. "The *Bibliotheca* of Gabriel Harvey," in *Renaissance Quarterly*, XXV (1972): 1-62. Stern provides a helpful bibliographical study of Harvey's library.

Trimpi, Wesley, "The Practice of Historical Interpretation and Nashe's 'Brightnesse falls from the ayre,' " in *Journal of English and Germanic Philology*, LXVI (1967): 501-518. Using classical discussions of astronomy, Trimpi argues that "lightning" is an appropriate synonym for "brightnesse."

Jeanie R. Brink
Arizona State University
Tempe

JOHANN NESTROY
1801—1862

Author's Chronology

Born December 7, 1801, Vienna, Austria, the son of a wealthy lawyer; *1820* enrolls as a student of law at the University of Vienna but soon decides to pursue a career as singer instead; *1822* makes a successful debut at the Viennese Court Theater in the role of Sarastro in Mozart's *The Magic Flute*; *1823* marries Wilhelmine von Nespiesni; *1823-1831* works as an opera singer, and increasingly also as an actor of comical roles, in Amsterdam (Holland), Brünn (in today's Czechoslovakia) and Graz (Austria); *1827* starts his career as a satirical dramatist with the production of his first farce, *Der Zettelträger Papp* (*Papp: The Bill Distributor*); this same year his wife leaves him for another man; *1828* enters into an unofficial union with the actress Marie Weiler; *1831* signs contract with Karl Carl, director of the *Theater an der Wien* and returns to Vienna; *1832* is engaged by Carl to write comical plays in which Nestroy regularly plays one of the leading roles; *1835* is convicted of libelous ad-libbing on the stage and sentenced to five days in prison; *1845* divorces his wife Wilhelmine; *1848* his political satire *Die Freiheit in Krähwinkel* (*Freedom Comes to Krähwinkel*) is received by audiences with enthusiasm but suppressed the same year by the authorities; *1854* takes over, after Carl's death, as the new director of the Carl-Theater; *1860* retires as director and moves to Graz; May 25, 1862 dies after having suffered a stroke.

Author's Bibliography (selected)

Der böse Geist Lumpazivagabundus oder Das liederliche Kleeblatt, 1833 (The Evil Spirit Lumpazivagabundus or The Trio of Tramps), (farce); *Zu ebener Erde und erster Stock oder Die Launen des Glücks*, 1835 (Downstairs and Upstairs or The Whims of Fortune), (farce); *The Talisman*, 1840, tr. 1967 (farce); *Einen Jux will er sich machen*, 1842 (He Intends to Have a Fling), (farce); (adapted by Thornton Wilder as *The Merchant of Yonkers*, 1938, and *The Matchmaker*, 1954, which in turn served as the basis for the musical comedy, *Hello, Dolly!*, 1964, music and lyrics by Jerry Herman, and for the movie of the same title, directed by Gene Kelly in 1969; a new adaptation of Nestroy's play is Tom Stoppard's *On the Razzle*, 1981); *Love Affairs and Wedding Bells*, 1843, tr. 1967 (farce); *A Man Full of Nothing*, 1845, tr. 1967 (farce); *Freedom Comes to Krähwinkel*, 1848, tr. 1961 (political satire); *Judith und Holofernes*, 1849 (Judith and Holofernes), (parody of Friedrich Hebbel's *Judith*, 1840).

Overview of Biographical Sources

To the day of his death, Nestroy thought of himself not as a playwright, in spite of the eighty-three plays which by then he had to his credit, but as an actor who simply had been forced to write so many plays because he seemed forever short of the comical roles he so eagerly wanted to project. During the course of a long career, he stood on stage in the masks of no less than 879 characters, and whether his audiences delighted in the demonic passion of his comic talent or whether they felt outraged by the often bawdy aggressiveness of its satire, they did not seem particularly eager to look for the man behind those many masks. Thus well hidden by the camouflage of a series of popular characters, much of Nestroy's own personality remained a mystery. The facts of his life are clear and rather undramatic. The few reports by contemporaries about Nestroy the man describe an amiable, modest, even shy individual whose charming awkwardness offstage seems to have enhanced the affection and esteem which the Viennese felt for their most popular comedian. Modern biographers have generally tried to narrow the gap between the extroverted actor and the introverted man by descovering in Nestroy's life many of the grotesquely comical tensions which distinguish his art: tensions between the henpecked husband who also was a great ladies man, the industrious actor and director who could be as punctilious as he could be disorganized, the spendthrift unable to manage his own money, the timidly lewd, the pedantic bohemian.

There exists no biography of Nestroy in English, and even in German biographical studies are not abundant. A great welter of information on Nestroy's life and times is contained in *Johann Nestroy: Sämtliche Werke*, 15 vols., ed. by Fritz Brukner and Otto Rommel (Vienna: Schroll, 1924-1930). A biographical account which stresses the inner conflicts of Nestroy's life and career is Otto Forst de Battaglia's *Johann Nestroy* (Munich: Langen-Müller, 1962). Otto Basil's *Johann Nestroy* (Reinbeck: Rowohlt, 1967) provides a more factual delineation. This biography can be recommended even to those unable to read German because it contains a good number of old photos which show Nestroy in a variety of his most famous roles and thus gives the viewer an amazingly vivid sense of Nestroy's comic presence on the stage. In the absence of a full-scale biography in English, two brief, introductory assessments of Nestroy's life, times, and artistic achievements are especially valuable: Thornton Wilder's "Foreword" and Max Knight's and Joseph Fabry's "Introduction" to *Three Comedies by Johann Nestroy*, translated by Max Knight and Joseph Fabry (New York: Frederick Ungar, 1967).

Autobiographical Sources

Almost no autobiographical material is available in printed form, and none of it has been translated into English. The first collection of Nestroy's plays, Johann Nestroy, *Gesammelte Werke*, 12 vols., ed. by Vinzenz Chiavecci and Ludwig Ganghofer (Stuttgart: Bonz, 1891), includes a diary Nestroy kept as a young opera singer in Amsterdam. In addition, a small volume of Nestroy's correspondences, containing about one third of all letters still extant, has been edited by Fritz Brukner in *Johann Nestroys gesammelte Briefe und Revolutionsdokumente 1831-1862* (Vienna: Wallishausser, 1938). As Nestroy was an infrequent and reluctant letter writer, these correspondences divulge little about his personal and next to nothing about his artistic life. Nestroy's will, published as an appendix in Rio Preisner's *Johann Nepomuk Nestroy: Der Schöpfer der tragischen Posse* (Munich: Hanser, 1968), reveals a man in whom an unrealistic fear of being buried alive and a very realistic disposition of his property are both curiously mocked by flashes of an indomitable sense for the comical in even this most serious of all human situations.

Overview of Critical Sources

For most of his contemporaries, Nestroy was an overwhelmingly funny comedian whose roles, tailor-made as they were for the actor Nestroy, could not be expected to survive the death of their gifted creator. Though almost all of Nestroy's eighty-three plays had been performed many times during his life, they disappeared so quickly and so completely from the stage after 1862 that the texts of no less than seven have been lost ever since. This total neglect lasted for nearly twenty years and only came to an end with the sensationally successful revival of twenty of Nestroy's plays at the Carl-Theater in early 1881. So powerful was the impression of the cycle on the Viennese public that barely one month afterwards Nestroy received a new graveside among Austria's most famous artists in the *Zentralfriedhof*. Exactly ten years later, his literary reputation was put on a sound footing with a first complete edition of his plays, only fourteen of which had been published during his lifetime. Though Nestroy's star continued to rise, his fame remained that of a remarkable Austrian dialect poet with a peculiarly Viennese appeal until another great Austrian master of the German language, the critic and moralist of linguistic purity Karl Kraus, heralded Nestroy in "Nestroy und die Nachwelt" (*Die Fackel*, no. 349-50., May 1912, 1-23) as one of the greatest satirists of the German-speaking world. With the historical-critical edition of his complete works, *Sämtliche Werke*, 15 vols., ed. by Fritz Brukner and Otto Rommel (Vienna: Schroll, 1924-1930), Nestroy ascended to the undisputed position of an Austrian classic. Volume XV of this edition contains Rommel's *Johann Nestroy. Ein Beitrag zur Geschichte der Wiener Volkskomik*, the first detailed and comprehensive assessment of Nestroy's artistic achievements. A steady flow of monographs and scholarly articles on all aspects of Nestroy's work continue to use Rommel's pioneering study as an indispensable starting point.

In spite of Kraus' decided advocacy of Nestroy as a satirist in and of the German language, Nestroy's international reputation continues to suffer from the loving possessiveness with which Austrian scholars have treated his art. From Leopold Liegler's pedantic attempt in the 1920s to improve Nestroy's texts by translating them into a properly Viennese dialect to more recent assertions that Nestroy's plays are simply untranslatable into any language, standard German not excluded, such partisan support has managed to perpetuate the mistaken notion that Nestroy must have written in broad dialect and that his genius is therefore destined to remain the exclusive property of a parochial clientele. The fact that experienced playwrights like Thornton Wilder in *The Matchmaker* (1954) and Tom Stoppard in *On the Razzle* (1981) have shown how effectively Nestroy's comical verve can be transposed into English has apparently made few converts among Nestroy's native admirers. Though the 1970s have seen a noticeable increase of Nestroy scholarship in English, the most immediate task still seems to be that of providing the English-speaking world with more and better translations of Nestroy's satirical comedies.

Evaluation of Selected Criticism

Evenden, Mike, "Nestroy on Stage," *Theater*, XII (Spring 1981): 66-71. Though Nestroy combined foolish farce, social satire, and elaborate wit in his comedies, Evenden points out that Nestroy's plays have generally been staged by stressing only one of these three distinct comic devices. For each of the resulting one-dimensional readings, Evenden cites typical examples from the history of theatrical productions and lists their conspicuous shortcomings. He concludes with several suggestions on how Nestroy's works could be staged and acted so as to approximate their original impact. Clearly intended as a brief foray into some weighty problems of theatrical technique, Evenden's approach is surprisingly fresh and insightful. It should prove helpful to those who have never seen a Nestroy production but would like to form a first impression of its appropriate theatricality.

Harding, Laurence V. *The Dramatic Art of Ferdinand Raimund and Johann Nestroy*. The Hague: Mouton, 1974. Fighting a prevalent trend which disassociates the literary qualities of Austrian folk plays from the theatrical tradition out of which they arose, Harding studies the theatrical techniques used by its two most accomplished practitioners. An opening chapter on the history of the Austrian popular theater is followed by discussions of plot, characterization, language, staging, music and choreography. Each chapter is divided into two parts, allowing those interested in Nestroy to read only the sections devoted to him. A readable and important study, Harding's focus makes it of only limited value to those for whom the literary text remains at present the only avenue towards an appreciation of Nestroy's art. Considerable knowledge of German is required as none of the quotations has been translated.

Seidmann, Gertrud, "Johann Nestroy," in *German Men of Letters*, vol. V. London: O. Wolff, 1969, pp. 275-99. Starting with a succinct biography of Nestroy, Seidmann briefly discusses the dramatist's controversial role in the history of Austria's popular theater and then proceeds to delineate the main stages in the artistic development of his comedies. For each of these stages, Seidmann selects at least one play, of which she presents a brief summary and interpretation. Though written in the condensed style demanded by the format of the essay and at times unnecessarily interrupted by references to secondary literature within the text, this is a helpful survey whose value is greatly enhanced by the fact that all quotations are translated in endnotes.

Yates, W. Edgar, "Let's Translate Nestroy," in *Forum of Modern Language Studies*, XVIII (July 1982): 247-257. Considerable mystification surrounds the claim that Nestroy's comedies defy translation. Yates offers, first of all, a most welcome evaluation of existing translations and adaptations. In addition, he tries to assess why translators in the past have erred and, even more importantly, where the problems of translating Nestroy are largely imaginary and where they are truly insurmountable. At times somewhat technical, this essay sheds much needed light on the question of Nestroy's language and its adequate rendition in English.

Yates, W. Edgar, *Nestroy: Satire and Parody in Viennese Popular Comedy*. Cambridge: Cambridge University Press, 1972. Yates, who has probably done more than anyone else to advance the scholarly reception of Nestroy's works in the English-speaking world, analyzes in this study the dominant elements of Nestroy's comic genius. Prefacing his interpretations with excellent chapters on Nestroy's Vienna, the tradition of its popular theater and Nestroy's career within it, Yates proceeds to close readings of five of Nestroy's most popular and important comedies. He shows how the artist in each case transformed existing plays into parodies or farces through a satirical attack on their literary, social, and political conventions. Yates concludes with a summary chapter on Nestroy's radicalism and his battle with censorship. Demanding a good knowledge of German to take full advantage of Yates' textual analyses, this study is indispensable for any serious acquaintance with the magic of Nestroy's comic wit. An extensive glossary of Austrian dialect terms greatly facilitates the understanding of Yates' argument.

Other Sources

Corriher, Kurt, "The Conflict Between Dignity and Hope in the Works of Johann Nestroy," in *South Atlantic Review* XLVI (May, 1981): 27-42. Sees Nestroy's dignified pessimism about human fate strike a compromise with hope in an effort to avoid despair.

Esslin, Martin, "Nestroy: Between Hanswurst and Horváth," in *Theater*, XII (Spring 1981): 62-65. Views Nestroy as the dramatist who transformed Austria's popular theater into a creative influence on modern playwrights.

Walker, Colin, "Nestroy's *Judith und Holofernes* and Antisemitism in Vienna," in *Oxford German Studies* XII (1981): 85-110. Convincingly argues that Nestroy's most famous parody was perceived as antisemitic at the time of its first performance.

Yates, W. Edgar, "Editing Nestroy," in *German Life and Letters*, XXXVI (July 1983): 281-293. A report on the history of previous Nestroy editions and on the reasons for a new one.

Selected Dictionaries and Encyclopedias

Encyclopedia of World Drama, McGraw-Hill, 1984. Brief introduction, plot summaries of five Nestroy comedies, as well as a chronological listing of all his plays and their sources.

The Oxford Companion to German Literature, Clarendon Press, 1976. Concise overview of Nestroy's life, work, and reputation.

Joachim J. Scholz
Washington College

SEAN O'CASEY
1880-1964

Author's Chronology

Born John Casey, March 30, 1880, Dublin, the youngest of thirteen children, five of whom survived childhood; his parents were devout Protestants; *1886* Michael Casey dies at forty nine, leaving the family in poverty; *1891* attends theater for the first time with his older brother, Isaac, an actor; *1894* takes first job as a stock clerk in a wholesale chandlers; plays Fr. Dolan in Boucicault's *The Shanghraun* at the Mechanic's Theatre, later to become The Abbey; *1906* learns Irish language; becomes secretary of the Drumcondra Branch of The Gaelic League; *1907* publishes first article, "Sound the Loud Trumpet," in *The Peasant and Irish Ireland*; *1909* Jim Larkin founds The Irish Transport and General Workers Union; O'Casey joins two years later; *1914* Secretary for the Irish Citizen Army, resigns because of dispute with the executive council; *1916* Easter Rebellion takes place; provides background for *The Plough and the Stars*; *1918* death of his mother, Susan Casey; *1919-1921* The Anglo-Irish War, provides background for *The Shadow of a Gunman*; *1923 The Shadow of a Gunman* accepted by The Abbey; *1924* The Abbey produces *Juno and the Paycock*; O'Casey begins full-time career as a writer; *1924* visits Lady Gregory at Coole Park; *1926* receives the Hawthornden Prize in London for *Juno*; *1927* marries Eileen Carey Reynolds, an actress; *1928* birth of son Breon; *The Silver Tassie* rejected by Abbey; *1929 The Silver Tassie* produced in London; *1932* Shaw and Yeats form The Irish Academy, but O'Casey and Joyce declined to join; *1934* makes his only visit to the United States; *1936* birth of son Niall; *1939* birth of daughter Shivaun; O'Caseys move to Totnes, Devon; *1956* death of Niall O'Casey of leukemia; *1958* The Archbishop of Dublin disapproves of *The Drums of Father Ned* as well as a dramatization of Joyce's *Bloomsday*; Beckett withdraws his plays in support of O'Casey and Joyce; O'Casey bans all professional production of his plays in Ireland which he maintains until 1964; *1964* dies of a heart attack in Torquay, Devon.

Author's Bibliography (selected)

Songs of the Wren, 1918, 1st and 2nd series (verse); *More Wren Songs* (verse); *The Story of Thomas Ashe* (pamphlet); *The Sacrifice of Thomas Ashe* (pamphlet); *The Story of the Irish Citizen Army*, 1919 (history); *The Shadow of a Gunman*, 1923 (play); *Juno and the Paycock*, 1924 (play); *The Plough and the Stars*, 1926 (play); *The Silver Tassie*, 1928 (play); *Within the Gates*, 1933 (play); *Windfalls*, 1934 (essays, verses, short stories, and two one-act plays); *The Flying Wasp*, 1937 (essays); *I Knock at the Door*, 1939 (first volume of autobiography); *The Star Turns Red*, 1940 (play); *Red Roses for Me*, 1942 (play); *Drums Under the Windows*, 1945 (third volume of autobiography); *Rose and Crown*, 1952 (fifth volume of autobiography); *Sunset and Evening Star*, 1954 (sixth volume of autobiography); *The Green Crow*, 1956 (essays, with stories from *Windfalls* and articles from *The Flying Wasp*); *The Drums of Father Ned*, 1960 (play); *Feathers From the Green Crow*, 1962 (stories, essays, songs and short plays); *Under a Colored Cap*, 1963 ("Articles Merry and Mournful with Comments and a Song")' *Blasts and Benedictions*, 1967 (articles and stories selected and introduced by Ronald Ayling).

Overview of Biographical Sources

O'Casey had a long, productive, and on the whole a happy life. At birth, he seemed to have everything against him. Born in the poorest of Dublin slums, he was the youngest of thirteen children five of whom survived. His father died when he was six leaving the family virtually destitute. O'Casey had little formal education and his eyesight was poor. Yet he was able to learn Gaelic, and he eventually read all the Irish and English writers. He wrote in every genre but the novel. The theater became his passion. He was forty before he gained recognition in Ireland and it is on the basis of the Dublin trilogy that his fame spread to England. It is on these three plays and the *Autobiographies* that his reputation rests today. *The Shadow of a Gunman* (1923), *Juno and the Paycock* (1924), and *The Plough and the Stars* (1926) were all produced by The Abbey. In 1926 he went to London and spent the rest of his long life in England as an expatriate, who like Joyce continued to write largely about Ireland. E.H. Mikhail and John O'Riordan's, *The Sting and the Twinkle* (London: Macmillan, 1974) is the earliest collection of interviews with O'Casey and contains much insightful biographical material. Gabriel Fallon's *Sean O'Casey: The Man I Knew*, (London: Routledge, 1965) is the first full-length biography. Fallon provides much inside information about O'Casey's relation to The Abbey. His criticism is sometimes eccentric. Martin Margulies' *The Early Life of Sean O'Casey* (Dublin: Dolman Press, 1970) is based on interviews with those who knew O'Casey, and contains a great deal of information that would be lost were it not for Margulies' work.

Evaluation of Selected Biographies

Armstrong, William A. *Sean O'Casey*. London: Longmans, Green, 1967. This is a judicious balance between the life and the work. The criticism is fine, the life accurate and well told.

Cowasjee, Saros, *O'Casey: The Man Behind the Plays*. Edinburgh and London: Oliver and Boyd, 1964. This is well-researched and readable, although some of the criticism is arcane.

Krause, David, *Sean O'Casey: The Man and His Work*. New York: Macmillan, 1975. The most nearly definitive critical biography; this is a superb, well-researched work.

O'Casey, Eileen, *Sean*. New York: Coward, McCann and Geoghegam, 1972. A personal, loving and intimate portrait of O'Casey from age forty six until his death in 1964. A remarkable book by a remarkable woman.

Autobiographical Sources

Krause, David, ed. *The Letters of Sean O'Casey*, I-II, 1910-1954. New York: Macmillan 1975, 1980. An invaluable resource for a knowledge of the man and the work.

Mirror in My House: The Autobiographies of Sean O'Casey. 2 vols. New York: Macmillan, 1956. These are the collected autobiographies and present a full portrait of the man. Next to his plays these are his great work.

Overview of Critical Sources

From the early reviews of O'Casey's plays in Dublin, London and later New York there has been an abundance of criticism written about O'Casey to the present day. Most of the criticism focuses on the *Autobiographies* and plays.

Evaluation of Selected Criticism

Ayling, Ronald, *Sean O'Casey: Modern Judgements*. London: Macmillan, 1969. An excellent collection on all aspects of O'Casey's work by famous writers.

DaRin, Doris, *Sean O'Casey*. New York: Frederick Ungar, 1976. This book examines twelve plays with useful summaries and critical analysis. It also contains a sympathetic biographical sketch.

Hogan, Robert, *The Experiments of Sean O'Casey*. New York: St. Martin's Press, 1960. A fine analysis of the plays and the autobiographies.

Kilroy, Thomas, *Sean O'Casey: A Collection of Critical Essays*, Englewood Cliffs, NJ: Prentice Hall, 1975. Contains excellent comments on O'Casey from Lady Gregory to Beckett.

Lowery, Robert G. ed. *Brooks Atkinson, Sean O'Casey*. Totowa, NJ: Barnes and Noble, 1982. Atkinson's reviews and writings about O'Casey from the first appearance of *Juno and the Paycock* to O'Casey's obituary in the *New York Times*. Atkinson was a friend and admirer. Lowery also has edited *O'Casey's Annual*, I-IV. London: Macmillan, 1982-1985. This is an ongoing series of first-rate essays on O'Casey which also contains reviews.

Mikhail, E.H. *Sean O'Casey: A Bibliography of Criticism*. Seattle: University of Washington Press, 1972. An excellent listing of the huge number of articles and books on O'Casey by one of the leading O'Casey scholars.

Moya, Carmela, "The Mirror and the Plough," in *The Sean O'Casey Review*, II, 2 (Spring 1976). Shows that O'Casey's dramaturgy in *The Autobiographies* is found in *The Plough and the Stars*.

Rollins, Ronald G. *Sean O'Casey's Drama*. University, AL: University of Alabama Press, 1979. This well written book contains an interesting chapter reproducing letters from O'Casey to the author.

Scrimgeour, James R. *Sean O'Casey*. Boston: Twayne, 1978. An astute, accurate, and insightful treatment of the *Autobiographies* and major plays. It contains a briefly annotated, useful bibliography.

Smith, B.L. *O'Casey's Satiric Vision*. Kent, OH: Kent State University Press, 1978. An analysis of twenty-two plays from the point of view of their satire. This is a limited but valid approach.

Other Sources

Ayling, Ronald and Michael J. Durkin, *Sean O'Casey, A Bibliography*. London: Macmillan, 1978. A useful bibliography by a leading authority on O'Casey.

Lowery, R. ed. *The Sean O'Casey Review*. New York, 1974-1981. During its publication this journal published articles on all aspects of O'Casey.

Selected Dictionaries and Encyclopedias

Anglo-Irish Literature, Modern Language Association, 1976. David Krause has a fine chapter on resources for the study of O'Casey.

British Writers, Charles Scribner's Sons, 1984. Scott-Kilvert has assembled a fine bibliography especially on O'Casey's association with The Abbey. It also contains an excellent sketch of the life.

Dictionary of Irish Literature, Greenwood Press, 1979. Hogan provides an excellent overview of O'Casey's life and work, as well as a bibliography of primary and secondary material.

John J. Dunn
St. John's University

EUGENE O'NEILL
1888-1953

Author's Chronology

Born October 16, 1888 in New York City to Ellen Quinlan O'Neill and James O'Neill, Sr., an actor; *1895-1900* educated at St. Aloysius Academy for Boys in Riverdale, New York; *1900-1902* attends De La Salle Institute in New York City; *1902-1906* attends and graduates from Betts Academy in Stamford, Connecticut; *1906-1907* studies at Princeton University and then is suspended for breaking a window of a railroad stationmaster's house; *1907-1908* works at the New York-Chicago Supply Company; *1909* marries Kathleen Jenkins; goes to Honduras to prospect for gold; *1910-1911* sails as a seaman to South America and South Africa and then serves on several luxury liners; *1912* attempts suicide by taking a drug overdose; becomes divorced; enters a sanitorium to be treated for tuberculosis; decides to become a serious writer; *1914-1915* studies playwriting under George Pierce Baker at Harvard University; *1916* moves to Provincetown, Massachusetts and becomes involved with the Provincetown Players; *1918* marries Agnes Boulton; *1920* receives a Pulitzer Prize for *Beyond the Horizon*; *1922* receives another Pulitzer Prize for *Anna Christie*; *1923* is elected to the National Institute of Arts and Letters; *1928* receives a Pulitzer Prize for *Strange Interlude*; *1929* Agnes divorces him and he marries Carlotta Monterey and resides in France; *1932* serves as editor, along with Theodore Dreiser, George Jean Nathan, and James Branch Cabell, of *The American Spectator*; *1936* is awarded the Nobel Prize for Literature; *1953* dies of pneumonia in Boston on November 27; *1957* receives a Pulitzer Prize and the New York Drama Critics Circle Award for *Long Day's Journey into Night*.

Author's Bibliography (selected)

Thirst and Other One Act Plays, 1914; *The Moon of the Caribbees and Six Other Plays of the Sea*, 1919; *Beyond the Horizon*, 1920 (play); *The Emperor Jones, Diff'rent, The Straw*, 1921 (plays); *The Hairy Ape, Anna Christie, The First Man*, 1922 (plays); *All God's Chillun Got Wings and Welded*, 1924 (plays); *Desire under the Elms*, 1925 (play); *The Great God Brown, The Fountain, The Moon of the Caribbees and Other Plays*, 1925; *Marco Millions*, 1927 (play); *Lazarus Laughed*, 1927 (play); *Strange Interlude*, 1928 (play); *Dynamo*, 1929 (play); *Mourning Becomes Electra*, 1931 (play); *Ah, Wilderness* 1933 (play); *The Iceman Cometh*, 1946 (play); *A Moon for the Misbegotten*, 1952 (play); *Long Day's Journey into Night*, 1956 (play); *More Stately Mansions*, 1964 (play); *Poems 1912-1944*, 1980.

Overview of Biographical Sources

A very private man, Eugene O'Neill discouraged potential biographers. However, since his death in 1953, scholars have devoted themselves, for years in some instances, to examining letters, articles, and papers and to conducting extensive interviews in an attempt to explore O'Neill's past—a past that they believed would illuminate his intensely personal plays. One of the earliest biographical accounts, covering O'Neill's life only from 1917 through 1919, is provided by his second wife, Agnes Boulton, in *Part of a Long Story* (1958). Another biography reflecting the viewpoint of family members is Croswell Bowen's *The Curse of the Misbegotten: A Tale of the House of O'Neill* (1959). This book, written with the assistance of Shane O'Neill, the playwright's second son, benefits from interviews Bowen conducted with O'Neill himself, his third wife Carlotta, and Eugene O'Neill, Jr., his eldest son. In the year 1962 came the publication of two fine O'Neill biographies: Doris Alexander's *The Tempering of Eugene O'Neill* (1962), which covers the playwright's life to 1920, and Arthur and Barbara Gelb's *O'Neill* (New York: Harper, 1962), a lengthy, carefully researched volume. The following year Clifford Leech published *Eugene O'Neill* (New York: Grove, 1963), an effective introduction to O'Neill's life and plays. Clearly the most comprehensive biography is Louis Sheaffer's two volumes—*O'Neill: Son and Playwright* (1968) and *O'Neill: Son and Artist* (1973). Sheaffer's painstaking research process of sixteen years sets a high standard for biographers.

Evaluation of Selected Biographies

Alexander, Doris, *The Tempering of Eugene O'Neill*. New York: Harcourt, Brace, World, 1962. Having spent a decade on research, Alexander succeeds in her goal of providing as objective as possible an account of Eugene O'Neill's life from birth to 1920. Her focus is upon the playwright's intellectual development—the people, ideas, and events that shaped his personality and career. Alexander notes significant changes in O'Neill's political, philosophical, and aesthetic views. However, perhaps the most notable achievement of her book is that it provides the first complete and accurate account of the playwright's father, James O'Neill, Sr.

Boulton, Agnes, *Part of a Long Story*. Garden City, NY: Doubleday, 1958. This highly personal book by Eugene O'Neill's second wife covers the period from her first meeting with the playwright in 1917 to the birth of their child Shane in 1919. Although sometimes sketchy on factual details, Boulton gives an interesting account of O'Neill's first marriage and suicide attempt, as her husband related it to her. She also paints a vivid picture of O'Neill's struggle to achieve artistic recognition in Greenwich and Provincetown and of his problems with alcoholism.

Bowen, Croswell, *The Curse of the Misbegotten: A Tale of the House of O'Neill*. New York: McGraw-Hill, 1959. With the assistance of O'Neill's son Shane, Bowen has written a personal history of the playwright based upon extensive interviews with family friends and acquaintances, as well as O'Neill's third wife Carlotta and O'Neill himself. Bowen treats O'Neill as a gloomy Irishman whose family was cursed with the inability to express deep love. This failure of communication Bowen believes is responsible for O'Neill's emphasis upon man's isolation in his plays.

Gelb, Arthur and Barbara Gelb, *O'Neill*. New York: Harper, 1962. The Gelbs have written a comprehensive study of O'Neill's life and work in this volume of nearly one thousand pages. Meticulous in their research, the authors spent five years interviewing over four hundred people and gathering material from O'Neill's three wives and from the O'Neill Collection at the Yale University Library. Their work represents a major contribution to O'Neill scholarship.

Sheaffer, Louis, *O'Neill: Son and Playwright*. Boston: Little, Brown, 1968. *O'Neill: Son and Artist*. Boston: Little, Brown, 1973. Sheaffer's two volumes deserve to be recognized as the definitive biography of Eugene O'Neill. The author devoted sixteen years to researching his subject, examining letters, published interviews, memoirs of O'Neill's contemporaries, biographical and critical studies, and correspondence with O'Neill's nursemaid, a large number of his classmates, and some of his fellow seamen. Most assuredly, Sheaffer has done the literary world a great service in not only unearthing new information about the playwright but also in correcting past published errors, some of them caused by O'Neill himself, who had a tendency to exaggerate and embroider details of his life. The first volume covers the family background of O'Neill's parents and his life through 1920; the second extends from 1920 to the author's death. The key to understanding O'Neill's personality and his plays, Sheaffer contends, is his relationship with his parents—a relationship that left O'Neill an "emotional hemophiliac," bleeding from wounds that never healed.

Autobiographical Sources

O'Neill did not write autobiography as such; instead he used the medium of the theater to confront his life and attempt self-understanding. The reader or viewer may find autobiographical elements in a number of O'Neill plays, of which the most overtly autobiographical is *Long Day's Journey into Night*. Also illuminating are O'Neill's letters. To date there is not a published edition of his letters; however, a number of them have been reprinted in such works as Barrett H. Clark's *Eugene O'Neill* (New York: Robert M. McBride, 1926), Arthur Hobson Quinn's *A History of the American Drama, from the Beginning to the Civil War* (New York: Harper and Brothers, 1923), and various books by George Jean Nathan.

Overview of Critical Sources

The work of Eugene O'Neill has received much critical attention from reviews—both American and international—of productions of his plays, to general critical studies, to essays and books focusing on specialized topics. Early accounts of his work tend to be evaluative, either dismissing his plays as melodramatic and undisciplined or praising his raw genius. A number of critics have discussed the literary influences upon O'Neill, particularly those of the ancient Greek tragedians, Ibsen, Strindberg, Thoreau, Freud, Jung, and Nietzsche. Psychoanalytic examinations of his plays abound. Some studies link O'Neill to intellectual movements, including romanticism, realism, symbolism, expressionism, and Marxism. Others focus upon the ritualistic aspects of his works, both pagan and Christian. There have also been several interpretations of O'Neills plays based upon his Irish Catholic background. More recent studies of the late 1960s and 1970s have turned to his stage techniques, especially his use of masks and symbolic settings. From the start of O'Neill's career to the present day, probably the most pervasive topic that critics have pursued is the degree to which O'Neill's work is autobiographical.

Evaluation of Selected Criticism

Bogard, Travis, *Contour in Time: The Plays of Eugene O'Neill*. New York: Oxford University Press, 1972. Believing that "O'Neill used the stage as his mirror and the sum of his work comprises an autobiography," Bogard traces the contour of O'Neill's life as portrayed in his art. Appropriate to that purpose, he organizes his book according to the chronological order of composition of the O'Neill canon. Perhaps the most valuable contribution to O'Neill criticism that Bogard makes is the attention he pays to theatrical history, as he explains how O'Neill shaped American drama. Bogard offers interesting comparisons between O'Neill's plays and those of his contemporaries, and notes the influence he exerted upon such playwrights as Edward Albee, Arthur Kopit, and Sam Shepherd. Striking black and white photographs of O'Neill at various stages of his life enhance this book.

Carpenter, Frederic I. *Eugene O'Neill*. Boston: Twayne, 1964. rev. ed. 1979. As is typical of the Twayne series, Carpenter's *Eugene O'Neill* provides a clear and concise overview of the subject's life and work, as well as a bibliography of primary and secondary sources. Carpenter begins with a biographical sketch that emphasizes the relationship of O'Neill's life to his work. He then examines a common pattern in the plays: an emphasis upon the contrast between the dream of ideal beauty and the modern reality of ugliness, alienation, and despair. The central chapters of the book offer insightful discussions of twenty of O'Neill's major plays. Finally in his conclusion, entitled "Greatness and Limitations," Carpenter outlines O'Neill's theory of tragedy and assesses the playwright's achievement.

Clark, Barrett H. *Eugene O'Neill*. New York: Robert M. McBride, 1926. (Subsequent editions were entitled *Eugene O'Neill: The Man and His Plays*.) Clark's book holds a seminal place in O'Neill criticism, for it was the first study to be entirely devoted to Eugene O'Neill's work. Indeed, in its subsequent editions it continued to be the best critical work on O'Neill until the early 1950s. Clark provides a brief biography and short analyses of individual plays, with liberal quotations from letters, the plays themselves, and critical articles. In addition, the volume has interesting illustrations, checklists of first productions and first publications, and a selected bibliography of biographical and critical material.

Engel, Edwin A. *The Haunted Heroes of Eugene O'Neill*. Cambridge: Harvard University Press, 1953. This book represents one of the most intelligent and original critical studies of O'Neill's work. The author examines the entire canon, providing synopses, excerpts, and close analyses. According to Engel, O'Neill's plays reflect his attempt to transmute his personal sufferings into impersonal art. Their central theme is the struggle between life and death, with important secondary themes being the conflicts between love and hate, faith and skepticism, and dream and reality. O'Neill's work, Engel observes, gave scant attention to political and social events. Rather he brought to his audiences an awareness of religious, philosophical, and psychological problems that had not previously been presented in the commercial theater. Although O'Neill's later and lengthier plays, such as *Long Day's Journey into Night*, have received the most critical acclaim, Engel believes that the earlier pieces, such as *The Emperor Jones* and *Desire under the Elms*, are more effective because they are better written, clearer in conception, and more powerful than their successors.

Falk, Doris V. *Eugene O'Neill and the Tragic Tension: An Interpretive Study of the Plays*. New Brunswick, NJ: Rutgers University Press, 1958. Falk analyzes O'Neill's plays in chronological order, tracing in them a single pattern. She states that each play is "an attempt at once to express and to assuage the lifelong torment of a mind in conflict." Thus O'Neill tried to find order and meaning by reconciling opposites; he believed tension produces growth and change. According to Falk, O'Neill's tragedy is classical in its emphasis upon two beliefs: 1) that suffering is the source of significant human action and creativity, and 2) that man is an ultimately free being who often brings grief upon himself through pride. Falk's book is provocative, especially in its discussion of the influence of Jungean psychology upon O'Neill.

Other Sources

Cargill, Oscar, N. Bryllion Fagin, and William J. Fisher, eds. *O'Neill and His Plays: Four Decades of Criticism*. New York: New York University Press, 1961. Brings together material concerning O'Neill's life, the playwright's offstage observations about his works, reviews of his plays, discussions of the international responses to O'Neill's productions, and critical essays.

Chabrowe, Leonard, *Ritual and Pathos—the Theater of O'Neill*. Lewisburg, PA: Bucknell University Press, 1976. Views O'Neill's plays as fulfilling a religious function in demonstrating a Dionysian spirit inspired by ancient Greek tragedy and the philosophy of Nietzsche.

Manheim, Michael. *Eugene O'Neill's New Language of Kinship*. Syracuse: Syracuse University Press, 1982. Proposes that O'Neill's plays assert the importance of kinship, that is, interdependent human relationships, and examines the rhythmic alternations between hostility and affection in the playwright's dialogue.

Raleigh, John Henry, *The Plays of Eugene O'Neill*. Carbondale: Southern Illinois Press, 1965. Evaluates the plays to reveal O'Neill's gradual development into a masterful playwright.

Tiusanen, Timo T. *O'Neill's Scenic Image*. Princeton: Princeton University Press, 1968. Studies the presence of the stage in O'Neill's plays, including the setting, the properties, sound and light effects, music, and the facial expressions, gestures, movements, voice qualities, and make-up of the actors.

Tornqvist, Egil, *A Drama of Souls: Studies in O'Neill's Super-naturalistic Technique*. New Haven: Yale University Press, 1969. Examines the dramatic devices O'Neill uses to transcend realism and project values through super-naturalism, a term O'Neill coined to describe the work of the dramatist August Strindberg.

Selected Dictionaries and Encyclopedias

American Writers: A Collection of Literary Biographies. Charles Scribner's Sons, 1974. An overview of O'Neill's life and plays.

Critical Survey of Drama. Salem Press, 1985. Description of O'Neill's achievements, a brief biography, and analyses of his most important plays.

Dictionary of Literary Biography. Gale Research. 1981. Discussion of O'Neill's life and work and a bibliography of primary and secondary sources.

Lynne P. Shackelford
Furman University

CLIFFORD ODETS
1906-1963

Author's Chronology

Born July 18, 1906 in Philadelphia, to Louis and Pearl Geisinger Odetrs; *1912* family moves to New York City where Odets attends Morris High School from 1921-1923; leaves school short of graduation; *1923-1930* has small roles in Theater Guild productions; *1930* joins the Group Theater as a charter member and continues his association with it until 1941; *1935 Waiting for Lefty* produced and is followed in the same year by *Awake and Sing!*, *Till the Day I Die*, and *Paradise Lost*; *1935* wins the George Pierce Baker Drama Cup of Yale University for *Waiting for Lefty*; *1937* marries actress Luise Rainer; *Golden Boy* produced on Broadway in *1937*, the year Odets goes to Hollywood to write for films; *1937* Odets writes his first film scenario, *The General Dies at Dawn*; *1938-1961* writes numerous plays and film scripts; *1961* receives drama award from the American Academy of Arts and Letters and writes the scenario for *Wild in the Country*; dies on August 14, 1963 following ulcer surgery; was working on a musical version of *Golden Boy* and on scripts for *The Richard Boone Show* in the year of his death.

Author's Bibliography (drama)

Waiting for Lefty, 1935; *Three Plays by Clifford Odets*, 1935 (includes *Waiting for Lefty*, *Awake and Sing!*, and *Till the Day I Die*); *I Can't Sleep: A Monologue*, 1936; *Paradise Lost*, 1936; *Golden Boy*, 1937; *Rocket to the Moon*, 1939; *Six Plays of Clifford Odets*, 1939 (gives the full text of all his produced plays from *Waiting for Lefty* to *Rocket to the Moon*); *Night Music*, 1940; *Clash by Night*, 1942; *The Big Knife*, 1949; *The Country Girl*, 1949 is available only in an acting edition published by Dramatists' Play service. *The Flowering Peach*, 1954 exists only in an abridged version in *The Best Plays of 1954-55* edited by Burns Mantle and Louis Kronenberger.

Overview of Biographical Sources

The best brief biographical treatment of Odets is in Gerald Weales' *Clifford Odets: Playwright* (1971), which is both biographical and critical. R. Baird Shuman's *Clifford Odets* (1962), the first book-length study of Odets, covers similar ground but is less extensive than the Weales book. Certainly the most ambitious biography to date is Margaret Brenman-Gibson's *Clifford Odets: American Playwright, The Years from 1906-1940* (1981), the first volume of a proposed two-volume study. Brenman-Gibson, who as Odets' literary executor has access to all of his unpublished papers, has produced a well-documented biographical study. The author is a professional psychologist and the critical orientation of her book is essentially psychoanalytical. Of particular biographical value also are the frequent allusions to Odets and his relationship to the Group Theater in Harold Clurman's *The Fervent Years* (1945). Excerpts from Arthur Wagner's extensive interview with Odets were published in *Harper's* CCXXXIII (September, 1966) under the title "How A Playwright Triumphs," and Michael Mendelsohn's interview published in "Odets at Center Stage," *Theatre Arts*, XLVII (May and June, 1963) are also useful in understanding Odets' ties to his Jewish-American background, which gives his ethnic writing the high degree of credibility that made it appealing to New York audiences. Harvey Herman's interview with Odets was recorded less than six months before the playwright's death and was aired on KNXT-TV in Los Angeles on February 3, 1963. The published transcript of it is worthwhile for Odets' revealing comments on his early career and for the insights it gives into his plans for future writing projects.

Evaluation of Selected Biographies

Brenman-Gibson, Margaret, *Clifford Odets: American Playwright, The Years from 1906-1940*. New York: Atheneum, 1981. Brenman-Gibson's book is based upon Odets' personal papers, which he left to the author when he died. Even though this first volume of the two-volume set stops at 1940, it covers the most dynamic years of Odets' artistic development. The scholarship is meticulous and thorough. The approach is psychoanalytical. Of particular biographical interest is the thirteen page prologue which goes beyond 1940 and recounts conversations with Odets during his last days. Despite Brenman-Gibson's close friendship with Odets, she remains an objective scholar who permits the facts to speak for themselves. Her knowledge of Odets is encyclopedic. Her book is the most comprehensive study available to date, despite the limitation imposed by its stopping at 1940. The companion volume in progress will, of course, overcome this limitation.

Mendelsohn, Michael J. *Clifford Odets: Humane Dramatist*. Deland, FL: Everett-Edwards, 1969. Mendelsohn presents substantial portions of his interview with Odets shortly before the playwright's death. His study contends that it is an over-simplification to categorize Odets in any way, particularly as a proletarian writer. Mendelsohn's chapter on Odets in Hollywood is instructive, as are the chapters on his style and influences and on his themes and concepts.

Shuman, R. Baird, *Clifford Odets*. New York: Twayne, 1962. This is the earliest book-length study of Odets. It deals individually with each play from *Waiting for Lefty* to *The Flowering Peach*. Its chronological table remains useful, although the book has now been superseded by later books on Odets.

Weales, Gerald, *Clifford Odets: Playwright*. New York: Bobbs-Merrill, 1971; updated and reissued in 1985 by Methuen. This book is the most serviceable brief critical biography of Odets. It is valuable for its insights into Odets' background and into his use of the Jewish-American dialect. The critical analysis of the plays is well focused and the interpretations are sensitive. The new edition of the book is a welcome addition to Odets scholarship.

Autobiographical Sources

Odets wrote no autobiography as such. Although his plays, particularly *Awake and Sing!*, contain strong autobiographical elements, they are not a reliable source for specific autobiographical information. Odets' letters have not yet been edited, although much of the material in Margaret Brenman-Gibson's biography is drawn from Odets' correspondence and notebooks. At present, the most helpful autobiographical sources are two published interviews with Odets, Michael J. Mendelsohn's "Odets at Center Stage," *Theatre Arts*, LXVII (May and June, 1963) and Arthur Wagner's "How a Playwright Triumphs," *Harper's*, CCXXIII (September, 1963). The Wagner typescript was submitted to Odets before it was published, and he corrected details in it. This typescript, containing Odets' corrections, is among the Odets papers that are in Margaret Brenman-Gibson's custody.

Overview of Critical Sources

Odets was somewhat neglected critically until the early 1960s. In the decade after the publication of Shuman's *Clifford Odets* in 1962, Odets was the subject of three more book-length studies, one of which has now been reprinted. Margaret Brenman-Gibson also began writing her comprehensive study in the 1960s, although the first volume of it was not published until 1981. Harold Cantor's *Clifford Odets: Playwright-Poet* was published in 1978. It is likely that Odets' reputation as a proletarian playwright evoked the renewed interest in him during the 1960s, which were times as troubled and as filled with social protest as the 1930s, about which Odets was writing. Articles on Odets' use of the Jewish-American dialect began to appear in the 1960s as well as articles that focused on his ethnicity.

Evaluation of Selected Criticism

Cantor, Harold, *Clifford Odets: Playwright-Poet*. Metuchen, NJ: Scarecrow Press, 1978. Cantor is much interested in Odets' use of language, particularly in the authenticity of the playwright's use of dialect. While it does not compare in scope to Brenman-Gibson's or Weales' studies, it is an interesting approach to Odets.

Mendelsohn, Michael J. *Clifford Odets: Humane Dramatist*. Deland, FL: Everett-Edwards, 1969. Mendelsohn calls Odets "a humanitarian by inclination and a radical by accident." His book, although it does not ignore the proletarian militancy of Odets' early and best known plays, emphasizes the warmth and humanity of Odets' characterizations, particularly in such plays as *Awake and Sing!*

Clifford Odets

and *Paradise Lost*, which depict family life. The book provides the best insights into Odets' career as a Hollywood screen writer.

Murray, Edward, *Clifford Odets: The Thirties and After*. New York: Frederick Ungar, 1968. Murray thinks that *Waiting for Lefty*, Odets' most frequently anthologized play, is not representative of him. He discusses eight plays in depth, focusing particular attention on *The Big Knife*, *The Country Girl*, and *The Flowering Peach*, in his attempt to prove that Odets was concerned with the universal dilemmas that face man more than with the narrow dilemmas upon which a specifically proletarian playwright might focus attention.

Shuman, R. Baird, "Clifford Odets and the Jewish Context," in *From Hester Street to Hollywood: The Jewish-American Stage and Screen*. Bloomington, Indiana: Indiana University Press, 1983. This chapter shows how Odets' Jewish-American background is reflected in all of his plays, not only those that are Jewish-American in their orientation. The author focuses considerable attention on Odets' faithful representation of the Jewish-American dialect.

―――――, "Clifford Odets: From Influence to Affluence," in *Modern American Drama: Essays in Criticism*. Deland, FL: Everett-Edwards, 1968. In this chapter, Shuman shows an Odets who is growing artistically, particularly in his redaction of the Noah story, *The Flowering Peach*, but whose public still listens for the angry voice of the proletarian playwright in his plays and complains when the author tries to move away from proletarian writing.

Weales, Gerald, *Clifford Odets: Playwright*. New York: Bobbs-Merrill, 1971. Weales essentially uses *Awake and Sing!* as the measuring stick for assessing Odets' other plays, showing how the playwright grew and how his dramatic technique changed through the years. The book provides keen insights into the times and social situations about which Odets wrote. He shows an Odets who is torn between preserving his artistic integrity for relatively meager financial gains or selling out by going to Hollywood to write film scripts, a course that Odets reluctantly followed in 1937.

Other Sources

Block, Anita, *The Changing World of Plays and Theatre*. Boston, Little, Brown, 1939. One of the earliest treatments of Odets as a social dramatist, the presentation is balanced and reasonable.

Clurman, Harold, *The Fervent Years*. New York: Alfred A. Knopf, 1945. An indispensable resource for understanding Odets' development as a playwright. The book is a history of the Group Theater, which Odets joined in 1930, and with which he had continuous association as actor and playwright until just before it was disbanded in 1941.

Cohn, Ruby, and Bernard F. Dukore, *Twentieth Century Drama: England, Ireland, and the United States*. New York: Random House, 1966. The treatment of Odets is especially valuable for its insights into his use of language.

Dusenbury, Winifred L. *The Theme of Loneliness in Modern American Drama*. Gainesville: University of Florida Press, 1960. An intelligent discussion of loneliness as a controlling theme in Odets' plays from *Waiting for Lefty* to *Night Music*.

Gibson, William, "Preface," *Golden Boy Musical*. New York: Bantam Books, 1966. This is a deeply felt reminiscence of Odets and provides interesting material about his interest and involvement in turning *Golden Boy* into a musical.

Harvey, Herman, "The Sum and Substance," University of Southern California's *Alumni Review* (Spring) 1963. This transcript of a television interview conducted with Odets six months before his death is useful because it gives some indication of the direction Odets thought his writing would take in the coming years.

Haslam, Gerald W. "Odets' Use of Yiddish English in *Awake and Sing!*", *Research Studies of Washington State University*, XXXIV, 1966. Although it focuses on just one play, Haslam's study can be generalized quite productively to help one understand Odets' use of language in all his plays.

Krutch, Joseph Wood, *American Drama Since 1918: An Informal History*. New York: George Braziller, 1957. Krutch provides valuable comments on the rise of realism in American drama of the 1930s and relates Odets quite convincingly to this movement.

Mersand, Joseph, *The American Drama, 1930-1940: Essays on Playwrights and Plays*. New York: Modern Chapbooks, 1941. Mersand presents one of the fullest early appraisals of Odets and his work.

Shuman, R. Baird, "Clifford Odets: A Playwright and His Jewish Background," *The South Atlantic Quarterly*, LXXI, 1972. This article explores the cultural influences that helped to shape Odets and their manifestations in his work.

_____, "Thematic Consistency in Odets' Early Plays," *Revue des Langues Vivantes*, XXXV, 1969. This article deals with Odets' abhorrence of the economic and social conditions that thwart human beings and make it impossible for them to find personal fulfillment in life. The essay gives special attention to Odets' first six plays.

Willett, Ralph, "Clifford Odets and Popular Culture," *The South Atlantic Quarterly*, LXIX, 1970. Willett shows the early Odets as a mirror to his culture, particularly in his early protest plays.

R. Baird Shuman
University of Illinois
at Urbana-Champaign

ISTVÁN ÖRKÉNY
1912-1979

Author's Chronology

Born April 5, 1912, Budapest, Hungary, to Hugo and Margit Örkény; attends local schools; *1934* earns a diploma in chemical engineering and pharmacy; *1936* begins writing; *1937* marries Flóra Gönczi, joins a liberal magazine and begins a long European study-tour; *1942* is drafted and sent to the Russian Front, is taken prisoner, POW for four years, writes essays and his first play in labor camp; *1946* returns to Hungary, writes in earnest, translates from the French; *1948* marries Angela Nagy, mother of his two children, publishes first short story collection *Budai böjt* (*Lent at Buda*) and play *Voronyezh*; *1950* father dies, releases first novel; *1953* awarded József Attila Prize but soon is blacklisted and stops publishing; *1956* ardently supports the Revolution and after its defeat is silenced again; *1963-1964* novel versions of *Catsplay* and *The Toth Family* appear; *1965* marries Zsuzsa Radnóti, a noted dramaturg who turns him toward the stage; *1967* success of first drama, *The Toth Family*, second J. Attila Prize, becomes known all over Europe, travels to US; *1970* wins Grand Prize of Black Humor in Paris after the play's French premiere; *1972* four-volume collection of his works is published, *Idörendben* (*Chronologically*); *1974* two new plays are staged, the movie version of *Catsplay* scores enormous triumphs; *1977* at the peak of popularity, three new books are published; *1978* publication of complete drama collection *Élöszóval* (*Orally*); *1979* attends premiere of a long rejected play *Pisti a vérzivatarban* (*1969*, *Pisti in the Bloodbath*), becomes ill, on the hospital bed finishes a new drama, *Forgatókönyv* (*Screenplay*), few days before succumbing to cancer in June, 1979.

Author's Bibliography

This prolific, internationally known playwright, one of the most prominent representatives of the East European absurd theater, was also a distinguished essayist, novelist, short story writer and journalist authoring twenty-eight books, many of them translated into major languages, including English. Thus, only a selective bibliography is listed here arranged by genres. Among the plays, collections are cited first, followed by titles of individual plays, only those that had long-running, successful performances not only in Hungary but also abroad.

Plays: *Idörendben—Szinmüvek*, 1972 (*Chronologically*); *Élöszóval*, 1978 (*Orally*); *Drámák*, 3 vols., 1983 (*Dramas*); *Tóték*, 1967 (*The Toth Family*); *Macskajáték*, 1971 (*Catsplay*); *Kulcskeresök*, 1975 (*Keysearchers*); *Forgatókönyv*, 1979 (*Screenplay*).

Novels: *Chronologically, II.*, 1972; *Gloria*, 1957; *Catsplay*, 1963; *The Toth Family*, 1964; *Kisregények* (Short Novels), 1982.

Non-Fiction: *Chronologically, III.*, 1973; *Lágerek népe*, 1981 (*Camp Folk*); *Párbeszéd a groteszkröl*, 1981 (*Dialogue about the Grotesque*); *Önéletrajzom töredékekben*, 1982 (*Autobiography in Fragments*); *Visszanézve—Arcképek, körképek*, 1985 (*Glancing Back—Personal and Period Portraits*).

Overview of Biographical Sources

It was only toward the end of his life that Örkény, this ironic humanist, enjoyed popularity in Hungary and also became an internationally famous playwright. Even though several of his fifteen plays had successful runs in major theaters of Europe and America, in addition, hundreds of analytical Örkény studies and personal interviews had seen print in England and in the US, as of 1985 no English language biography of stature has been released. However, some of the dissertations in drama schools featuring the author may be published soon. Strangely enough, even in Hungary only one comprehensive biography has been written thus far. Örkény's controversial life and literary heritage are under scholarly scrutiny now.

Evaluation of Selected Biographies

Gyorgyey, Clara, "The Ironic Humanist," in *Cross Currents*, No. 5 (Winter, 1986). In this lengthy study Örkény's English translator provides a succinct yet revelatory overview of the author's life as an introduction to a selection of *One-Minute Stories* in English translation. The article places Örkény in the context of his milieu, first as a son of a prosperous, Jewish pharmacist, as a dehumanized POW in the Soviet Union, then either as a celebrated "Communist" writer, or a blacklisted "enemy of the people," and, at last, as the undisputed leader of the Hungarian stage in the 1970s. The style is scholarly but not abstruse.

István, Lázár, *Örkény István*. Budapest: Szépirodalmi, 1979. In this Hungarian biography the prominent drama expert, Mr. Lázár, is capable of blending biography and criticism in a manner that illuminates Örkény's problem-ridden artistic career. Since the book was published in a totalitarian country, political restrictions censored some parts, especially the ones that discuss both Örkény's imprisonment in the Soviet Union and his persecution in his own country during the Stalinist era. Still, this book which also includes rich illustrations, photographs and a detailed chronology of the author's life, is a reliable, well-proportioned reference work. An English version will soon be available to serve as basic resource material in the US.

Vercors, "My Friend, István Örkény," in *New Hungarian Quarterly*, Vol. 77 (Spring, 1980): 89-92. The noted French author gives a few important biographical data in his obituary of Örkény delivered at the French Academy. Though an obvious admirer of the artist—especially his grotesque nature and its manifestation in the late works—Vercors emphasizes the predominant dualities in Örkény's life and dramatic works.

Autobiographical Sources

For the first time Örkény became famous in Budapest during the darkest years of Stalinism; thus, his life was public property and he was often called upon to disclose his life to critics at the time of a new publication of his works or a play's premiere. Numerous details, however, became known only when the political tension had eased in Hungary and when, at the end of his life, he wrote two brilliant, unorthodox autobiographical pieces. Also, Örkény is an autobiographical author whose prose works in particular are quite revelatory. Furthermore, his widow, Ms. Radnóti is in the process of collecting his extensive correspondence in foreign languages. This book containing hundreds of his private communications promises to be a reference work of paramount importance.

Örkény, István, *Önéletrajzom töredékekben* (Autobiography in Fragments). Budapest: Szépirodalmi, 1982. The volume contains four unfinished novels bridging the years of 1953 to 1977; each piece featuring the writer either as a character by his own name or as a narrator thinly disguised. The format varies: straight first person descriptions of events and people, verbatim reproduction of correspondence between himself and some unfortunate, tragic, mistreated men of the street, ruthless party-bureaucrats as well as leading Marxist culture-functionaires; interviews, imaginary dramatic encounters, transcripts of taped telephone conversations and the like. A fascinating reading, almost as absurd as his plays.

_____, *Párbeszéd a groteszkröl* (*Dialogue about the Grotesque*). Budapest: Gondolat, 1981. This similarly autobiographical volume contains over two dozen dialogues between the author and a number of literary historians, TV commentators, drama critics, philosophers and well-known friends, discussing a wide variety of topics, mainly his life and his views of the grotesque. Several of these interviews had also been published in foreign periodicals.

Overview of Critical Sources

Both in Hungary and abroad, the Örkény scholarship is on the rise and a great many studies are currently in preparation. Voluminous as it were, most of the critical pieces so far have been only in the form of essays, studies, prefaces to his English translations, book and play reviews. In Hungary only two books were published dedicated to Örkény but research is being manifested in the notes and references of each newly printed volume of his *Collected Works*.

Evaluation of Selected Criticism

Földes, Anna, *Örkény—Szinház* (*Örkény-Theater*). Budapest: Szépirodalmi, 1985. This richly illustrated, conscientiously researched volume is a well-deserved tribute to Örkény. It comprises many previously published critical studies and reviews of ten Örkény dramas as well as a finely edited overview of the major foreign productions of six of these plays. Also included are a good biographical introduction and a handy index to the interviews. An English version is planned.

Koltai, Tamás, "Bend over to See the World: Örkény the Playwright," in *New Hungarian Quarterly*, Vol. 80 (Winter, 1980), 202-212. A distinguished drama critic provides an erudite analysis of Örkény's dramatic technique, mood-creation and absurdity apparent in six plays. Best documented study on the playwright's place among the East European Absurd dramatists. This is a helpful reference work.

Lázár, István, *Örkény István*. Budapest: Szépirodalmi, 1979. This expansive biography also includes sensitive, scholarly accounts of Örkény's contribution to the world of drama, evaluation of his novels and essays and, finally, numerous photographs.

Other Sources

Földes, Anna, "The Anatomy of Compromise," in *New Hungarian Quarterly*, Vol. 74 (Summer, 1979), 204-211. The critic who went to see almost every premiere of Örkény's productions both in Hungary and in several other countries, offers a brief comparative critique of the various renditions of *Pisti in the Bloodbath*.

Gyorgyey, Clara, "Megkésett Születésnapi Köszöntö" (Belated Birthday Toast), in *Szivárvány*, Vol. 7 (May, 1983): 22-26. An interesting mixture of casual style and significant insights, the essay gives a comparative review of seven American performances of *Catsplay*.

Klaniczay, Tibor, *History of Hungarian Literature*. Budapest: Corvina Press, 1964. The Örkény entry explores his art in general: good background material both for biographical and critical purposes.

Örkény, István, *The Flower Show—The Toth Family*. trans. and int. by Michael Henry Heim and Clara Gyorgyey. New York: New Directions, 1982. "A European with a Hungarian Passport," an analytical introduction to these short novels gives a moving portrait of the artist.

_____, *Catsplay*. trans. and int. by Clara Gyorgyey. New York: Samuel French, 1976. Contains background material and useful production notes to the play.

Clara Gyorgyey
Yale University

JOE ORTON
1933-1967

Author's Chronology

Born John Kingsley Orton on January 1, 1933, in Leicester, England, where he spends the first eighteen years of his life; *1945-1947* attends Clark College, a local private school; leaves to engage in a series of despised jobs to earn his livelihood; *1949* discovers the theatre as a refuge from an "ordinary" existence and begins to perform in local amateur productions; *1951* wins a scholarship to the Royal Academy of Dramatic Art in London where he meets fellow classmate Kenneth Halliwell who becomes a surrogate father, friend, and lover; *1953* graduates from RADA, spends four months with the Ipswich Repertory Theatre; *1954-1961* returns to London to live with Halliwell with whom he forms a noteworthy but unsuccessful literary collaboration; *1962* sentenced with Halliwell to six months in prison for theft and malicious damage, the result of a juvenile prank involving the defacement of library materials; *1963* achieves first professional breakthrough with the acceptance of *The Boy Hairdresser* (later retitled *The Ruffian on the Stair*) as a radio drama for the BBC Third Programme; *1964 Entertaining Mr. Sloane* produced in London, and the following year in New York; relationship with Halliwell begins to deteriorate; *Loot* produced in London; wins the *Evening Standard* Award as best play of the season; *1967* finishes work on a new play entitled *What the Butler Saw*; brutally murdered on August 9 by a despondent Halliwell who then commits suicide.

Author's Bibliography (selected)

Entertaining Mr. Sloane, 1964 (play); *Loot*, 1967 (play); *Crimes of Passion*, (includes the revised *The Ruffian on the Stair* and *The Erpingham Camp*), 1967 (plays); *What the Butler Saw*, 1969 (play); *Head to Toe*, 1971 (novel); *Orton: The Complete Plays*, 1977; *Up Against It*, 1979 (screenplay).

Overview of Biographical Sources

Emerging in the wake of a new wave of postwar British dramatists as diverse as John Osborne and Harold Pinter, Joe Orton is considered today a unique comic talent having the capacity for being at once "mischievous, irreverent, truthful, outrageous, infantile, vulgar, and brilliant." From 1963 to his untimely death in 1967, Orton wrote three critically important and four lesser plays which clearly established him as a playwright of international reputation. Forever trespassing into forbidden literary territory, Orton aimed both an aggressive anger and satirical wit at the social and political conventions of an abhorrent, suffocating, yet curiously tantalizing society.

An interesting subject for biography, Orton was early dubbed an *enfant terrible* by the press, a role willfully accepted and played with unexpected grandeur. As a playwright, Orton both seduced and incensed his audience, bringing to the theatre a mixture of passion, controversy, and creativity. Sparked primarily by the bizarre circumstances surrounding his death, numerous biographical treatments have appeared on Orton in a wide variety of periodical literature. However, the only full-length Orton biography is John Lahr's *Prick Up Your Ears* (New York: Alfred A. Knopf, 1978). Critics disagree whether or not this is the "definitive" biography on Orton, but certainly a strong argument can be made in support of this premise.

Evaluation of Selected Biographies

Lahr, John, *Prick Up Your Ears: The Biography of Joe Orton.* New York: Alfred A. Knopf, 1978. Captivated by Orton's creative vision and artistic temperament, Lahr offers a full, well-documented account of Orton's life and literary career. Supplemented by generous cooperation from Orton's family, friends, and theatrical colleagues, Lahr's study reveals a world clouded with anonymity and explores both the richness of Orton's gift as a playwright and the complexity of his personality. Extremely engaging, often characteristic of fiction rather than non-fiction, *Prick Up Your Ears* (referring to the title of a projected Orton play) intertwines biographical information with a critical analysis of Orton's body of work.

Rigidly unbending in his defense of Orton's talent, Lahr has been criticized for over-sensationalizing the Orton/Halliwell relationship in a disproportionate amount of the book. However, Lahr has unquestionably written the most accurate and complete treatment of Orton to date. Relying heavily on Orton's diaries and letters for insight and perception, Lahr creates with authentic realism the life and death of a remarkably innovative voice in the theatre.

Autobiographical Sources

Deeply aware of the cathartic ability of literature, Orton enlisted the theatre both to vent his rage against society and to serve as an introspective journey into his own nature. No doubt Orton also recognized this potential in other genres, and partly at the suggestion of his literary agent Peggy Ramsey, Orton began keeping a diary to coincide with his blossoming literary career. Comprising two volumes which primarily cover the last six months of Orton's life, the diaries represent an important addition to the Orton canon. An adolescent diary also exists which provides valuable insight into Orton's life prior to his arrival in London. Unfortunately, neither the diaries nor Orton's letters have been published in collected form. Excerpts from the diaries are used extensively in Lahr's *Prick Up Your Ears* and have appeared elsewhere under the titles "Orton on theatre and literature" in *Plays and Players*, November 1978, pp. 12-14 and December 1978, pp. 14-16, and "The Private Diaries of Joe Orton" in *The Village Voice*, November 20, 1978, pp. 1, 112-113.

In addition, several interviews with Orton exist which provide limited but interesting biographical information accentuating Orton's career, particularly "Joe Orton Interviewed by Giles Gordon," *Transatlantic Review*, 24 (Spring 1967), pp. 94-100.

Overview of Critical Sources

Despite a relatively limited literary output, Orton survives as a significant spokesperson for his generation, allowing for the term "Ortonesque" to be generally recognized as an imaginative brand of comedy rich in dramatizing the perverse hypocrisy of conventional morality. The major critical debate concerning Orton questions the depth of his talent as a playwright and the extent of his influence on contemporary drama. Most critics agree that Orton's most important quality rests primarily in his ability to transform his rebellious vision of the world into commercially successful theatre. This is well substantiated in Lahr's study as well as several articles, including Joan F. Dean's "Joe Orton and the redefinition of farce," *Theatre Journal*, 34 (December 1982), pp. 481-492, Keath Fraser's "Joe Orton: His Brief Career," *Modern Drama*, 14 (1971), pp. 413-429, and Leslie Smith's "Democratic Lunacy: The Comedies of Joe Orton," *Adam International Review*, 395-396 (1976), pp. 73-92. Of additional importance is Kimball King's *Twenty Modern British Playwrights: A Bibliography, 1956 to 1976* (New York and London: Garland, 1977), which contains a complete index of works by and about Orton through 1976.

Evaluation of Selected Criticism

Bigsby, C.W.E. *Joe Orton*. New York: Methuen, 1982. Part of a series on contemporary writers, Bigsby offers a brief study which is interesting as a supplement to the more detailed and comprehensive treatment by Lahr. Although limited in scope, Bigsby provides a partly successful analysis of Orton's work divided into chronological stages ranging from an early Pinter-influenced black comedy to a later form of anarchic farce.

Charney, Maurice, *Joe Orton*. New York: Grove Press, 1984. Similar in form and context to Bigsby's study, Charney offers an intelligent overview of Orton's life and literary career. Included in the Grove Press Modern Dramatists Series, the text is most valuable in providing a relatively updated interpretation of Orton's body of literature and clarifying his contribution to contemporary drama.

Other Sources

Esslin, Martin, "Joe Orton: The Comedy of (Ill) Manners," in *Contemporary English Drama*, C.W.E. Bigsby, ed. New York: Halmes and Meier, 1981. Excellent account of Orton's career incorporating selected biographical information with critically sound interpretations of the plays.

Gilliatt, Penelope, "Could-Haves" in *Unholy Fools: Wit, Comics, Disturbers of the Peace—Film and Theatre*. New York: Viking, 1973. Interesting commentary on Orton's career as a writer of comedy, with particular emphasis on Orton's conversion from playwright to screenwriter.

Taylor, John Russell, *The Second Wave: British Drama for the Seventies*. New York: Hill and Wang, 1971. A keen observer of changing theatrical climates, Taylor devotes an entire chapter of this text to Orton, emphasizing Orton's "genuine and extraordinary" talent and his importance in contemporary British drama.

Selected Dictionaries and Encyclopedias
Dictionary of Literary Biography: British Dramatists Since World War II, Gale Research, 1982. Informative overview of Orton's life, literary career, and contribution as a dramatist.

Great Writers of the English Language: Dramatists, St. Martin's Press, 1979. Brief biography and analysis of Orton's plays, offering a limited but accurate account of the playwright's career.

Steven Serafin
Long Island University

JOHN OSBORNE
1929

Author's Chronology

Born December 12, 1929 in Fulham, London of middle-class parents; *1941* father dies; *1946* is expelled from Belmont College and begins to work as a journalist for trade magazines; *1948* acts in *No Room at the Inn* at Sheffield; *1950* his first play, *The Devil Inside Him*, written with Stella Linden, is staged at the Theatre Royal, Huddersfield; June *1951* marries actress Pamela Elizabeth Lane; *1956 Look Back in Anger* is directed by Tony Richardson at the Royal Court, London; becomes an actor in the English Stage Company and acts on the London Stage in *Don Juan;* receives *Evening Standard* award as Most Promising Playwright of the Year; *1957 The Entertainer* is performed; *Look Back in Anger* is produced on Broadway and wins the New York Critics Award for the best foreign play of the year; with Tony Richardson founds Woodfall Film Productions; divorces Pamela Lane and marries Mary Ure, an actress; *1960* television play, *A Subject of Scandal and Concern* is produced; *1961 Luther* opens in the Theatre Royal, Nottingham; *1962* has a son Colin; *1963* film script for *Tom Jones* is produced; marriage to Mary Ure is dissolved; marries Penelope Gilliatt, critic and journalist; *Luther* receives the New York Drama Critics Award and the Tony Award for the best play of 1963; *1964 Inadmissable Evidence* is produced in London; wins Theatre Critics Award for *Inadmissable Evidence* as best play of the year; *1967* Penelope Gilliatt divorces him; *1968* marries actress Jill Bennett; *1971* television play *Very Like a Whale* is published; *1977* divorces Jill Bennett; *1978* marries drama critic, Helen Dawson; *1980 You're Not Watching Me, Mummy* and *Very Like a Whale* are televised; *1981* publishes autobiography, *A Better Class of Person.*

Author's Bibliography (selected drama)

Look Back in Anger, 1957; *The Entertainer*, 1957; *Epitaph for George Dillon*, 1958; *The World of Paul Slickey*, 1959; *A Subject of Scandal and Concern*, 1961; *Luther*, 1961; *Plays for England: The Blood of the Bambergs* and *Under Plain Cover*, 1963; *Tom Jones: A Screenplay*, 1964; *Inadmissable Evidence*, 1965; *A Patriot for Me*, 1956; *A Bond Honoured*, 1966; *Time Present*, 1968; *The Hotel in Amsterdam*, 1968; *The Picture of Dorian Gray*, 1973; *A Better Class of Person: An Autobiography, 1929-1956*, 1981.

Autobiographical Sources

The first volume of Osborne's autobiography, *A Better Class of Person*, contains some of his finest prose. Detailed portraits of his relatives give a vivid impression of his family. Several relatives are identified as models for characters in his plays.

As a child, Osborne was plagued by illness and was conscious of not being loved, except by his father. The rest of his family is portrayed as cold, bitter, and intolerant. School was an ordeal for Osborne. Because of the pain and humiliation he experienced there, he was frequently truant. Osborne narrates his experiences as a regular cinema patron beginning at the age of four.

The chapters on his adolescence include accounts of his father's illness and death, the war years, and Osborne's expulsion from boarding school. Next the book chronicles his early years in the theatre, working as a stage manager and actor. His financial struggles during this period and his marriage to Pamela Lane are also described. Osborne shows how he adapted memories of his marriage to create the stormy marriage between Jimmy Porter and Alison in *Look Back in Anger*.

Throughout the book Osborne uses relevant passages from his plays, nondramatic prose, notebooks, and letters as glosses on the significant people and events in his life. As a result, Osborne's life and art appear closely related. This first volume of his life ends with the English Stage Company's request for an option on *Look Back in Anger*.

Overview of Critical Sources

Studies of Osborne view him as the leading representative of new wave drama and as a spokesman for the fifties generation in England. Critics tend to focus on his domineering protagonists and his skillful use of language to jolt audiences into feeling intensely about his concerns. Critics also examine Osborne's attempts to combine personal drama and social criticism.

Evaluation of Selected Criticism

Banham, Martin, *Osborne*. Edinburgh: Oliver and Boyd, 1969. This short study corrects the popular misconception that Osborne was the leader of "the angry young men writers." Banham analyzes the revolutionary impact that *Look Back in Anger* had on English theatre. The range of Osborne's theatrical forms and anti-establishment themes is explored. This criticism includes both an appreciation of Osborne's honesty, wit, and compassion, as well as comments on the limitations of his plays.

Carter, Alan, *John Osborne*. Edinburgh: Oliver and Boyd, 1969. The first chapter of this criticism is a brief biography of Osborne. Carter's emphasis, however, is on the plays. Osborne is viewed as too much of an individual to be subsumed under labels and clichés. All the plays are analyzed in considerable detail, in particular their criticisms of England's postwar bankrupt society and their concern with the isolation caused by people's failure to communicate effectively. Carter argues convincingly that Osborne's subjectivity prevented him from writing successful satire. Carter examines English society and theatre of the 1950s, to which Osborne was responding in *Look Back in Anger*. One chapter is devoted to a scrutiny of Osborne's innovative use of everyday language. In the final chapter, entitled "Appreciation," Carter credits Osborne with introducing love in its various forms as a problem that can be fruitfully explored in the theatre.

Hayman, Ronald, *John Osborne*. New York: Frederick Ungar, 1972. Hayman maintains that Osborne's larger-than-life heroes represent the condition of England at the time he was writing. Subsequent chapters closely examine these heroes, stressing their isolation and rebelliousness. Hayman discusses each play's flaws in characterization, structure, and style. Hayman regards *The Entertainer* as a more successful play than *Look Back in Anger*, because its music hall monologues are more effective than Jimmy Porter's tirades, and minor characters are more developed than in the later play. In Hayman's opinion, *Inadmissable Evidence* is the most refined of Osborne's one-man plays, the play that could have been a turning point in his development as a dramatist. According to Hayman, Osborne never successfully fused the private and public elements in his plays. Though his plays have brilliant moments, each is marred by inconsistencies in style. At the back of this book, Hayman includes lists of London premieres and New York productions of Osborne's plays.

Hinchliffe, Arnold P. *John Osborne*. Boston: Twayne, 1984. Presently this is the most complete study of Osborne's works. It begins with a brief bioigraphy and ends with discussions of Osborne's television dramas produced between 1970 and 1980. Each chapter provides detailed plot summaries and critical analyses followed with relevant comments by dramatists, actors, and other critics. This re-assessment of Osborne is also important because it refutes other critics' oversimplifications of the plays. Hinchliffe points out that all the themes of the later plays are found in *Look Back in Anger*. Hinchliffe demonstrates that Osborne's best plays are still compelling theatre and that even his weaker plays contain fine moments. Osborne's last play, *A Sense of Detachment*, is discussed as an unplay. An annotated bibliography of books and articles on Osborne are included at the end of the study.

Taylor, John Russell, ed. *Look Back in Anger: A Casebook*. London: Macmillan, 1968. Taylor's introduction is a summary of the play's reputation. Part One consists of twenty reviews of the first performance of the play. The second part is a selection of Osborne's non-dramatic writings. Eight critical essays on *Look Back in Anger* form Part III, the bulk of this casebook. The essays examine the play from various perspectives: Jimmy Porter as an angry young man; the influence of Orwell's essay on Gandhi; comparisons with plays by other modern dramatists; a comparison of *Look Back in Anger* and *Luther*. The essays by John Russell Taylor and George E. Wellwarth discuss Osborne's other plays, comparing them to *Look Back in Anger*. The casebook also includes reviews by foreign critics, a number of brief criticisms of the play, study questions, and an annotated bibliography.

Trussler, Simon, *The Plays of John Osborne*. London: Victor Gollancz, 1969. Trussler states that his purpose is to stimulate critical debate about Osborne's plays. Trussler's approach is dramaturgical, centered on aspects of each script that might interest future directors. Intended as a companion to the plays, this book offers brief plot synopses in each chapter. The autobiographical origins of *Look Back in Anger* are discussed. Trussler finds it a well-made problem play offering significant psychological insights. He examines in detail the lop-sided relationships and lack of communication between characters in *The Entertainer*. Trussler demonstrates that *Luther* is a collection of characteristics connected by the theme of physicality. In Trussler's opinion, *Inadmissable Evidence* is Osborne's play that is most likely to continue attracting audiences. Analyzing Maitland's nostalgia, malaise, and progressive disintegration, Trussler argues that the play must be interpreted metaphorically as a conspiracy of abandonment. Trussler is more positive about *A Patriot for Me* than other critics have been; he considers it Osborne's most successful attempt to socialize his drama. The penultimate chapter assesses Osborne's journalism, especially its vitriolic, intolerant aspects. In Trussler's conclusion he credits Osborne with having transcended the flaws of his early plays. But Trussler asserts that Osborne was never able to balance a dramatist's need to empathize with his central character and his need to be detached from that character. Trussler asserts that Osborne's least developed plays are his best plays.

Other Sources

Anderson, Michael, *Anger and Detachment*. London: Pitman, 1976. A study of the later plays of Osborne, John Arden, and Harold Pinter.

Brown, John Russell, *Theatre Language: A Study of Arden, Osborne, Pinter, and Wesker*. New York: Taplinger, 1972. A lengthy chapter on Osborne that discusses his methods of controlling theatrical reality through words, actions, and time.

Ferrar, Harold, *John Osborne*. New York: Columbia University Press, 1973. A short survey of the plays, from *Look Back in Anger* to *West of Suez*, assessing the achievement and impact of each.

John Osborne: A Symposium, London: Royal Court Theatre, 1966. A collection of essays assessing Osborne's stature as an English dramatist, ten years after the opening of *Look Back in Anger*.

Kennedy, Andrew, K. *Six Dramatists in Search of a Language: Studies in Dramatic Language*. London: Cambridge Universtiy Press, 1975. A study that focuses on Osborne's revitalization of drama through language, and argues that only *The Entertainer* and *Inadmissable Evidence* achieve a fusion of structure and dialogue.

Taylor, John Russell, *Anger and After: A Guide to the New British Drama*. London: Methuen, 1969; New York: Hill and Wang, 1962, as, *The Angry Theatre:*

New British Drama. A chapter on Osborne that begins with an analysis of *Look Back in Anger* viewed through the eyes of its first audience and then briefly discusses the later plays up to *The Hotel in Amsterdam*.

Trussler, Simon, *John Osborne*. Essex: Longmans, Green, 1969. A short study of the plays, with an emphasis on Osborne's repeated use of one central dominant character.

Worth, Katherine J. *Revolutions in Modern English Drama*. London: G. Bell, 1973. An analysis of the influence of Shaw and Coward on Osborne's comic forms, in Chapter 5.

Margaret Schramm
Hartwick College

THOMAS OTWAY
1652-1685

Author's Chronology

Born March 3, 1652, at Woolbeding in Sussex, England, only son of Humphrey Otway, Rector of Woolbeding; *1668* admitted as a commoner to Winchester College; May 27, *1669* matriculates at Christ Church, Oxford; *1670* fails as an actor in the role of the King in Mrs. Aphra Behn's *The Forc'd Marriage*; *1671* leaves Oxford; *1675 Alcibiades* produced; *1676 Don Carlos, Titus and Berenice with The Cheats of Scapin*, produced; *1678* commissioned an ensign in the army; *1678 Friendship in Fashion* produced; *1679 The History and Fall of Caius Marius* is produced; *1679* leaves the army, after the Peace of Nymegen; challenges Jack Churchill to a duel; *1680* awarded honorary M.A. at St. John's College, Cambridge; April 14, 1685, dies on Tower Hill.

Author's Bibliography (selected)

Alcibiades, 1675; *Don Carlos*, 1676; *Titus and Berenice with The Cheats of Scapin*, 1677; *Friendship in Fashion*, 1678; *The History and Fall of Caius Marius*, 1680; *The Orphan*, 1680; *The Poet's Complaint of His Muse*, 1680; *The Soldiers Fortune*, 1681; *Venice Preserv'd*, 1682; *The Atheist*, 1684; *The Works of Mr. Thomas Otway*, 1692; *The Works of Mr. Thomas Otway*, 2 vols., 1712; *Thomas Otway*, ed. R. Noel, 1888; *The Complete Works of Thomas Otway*, ed. Montague Summers, 3 vols. 1967; *The Works of Thomas Otway: Plays, Poems, and Love-Letters*, ed. J.C. Ghosh, 2 vols. 1968; *Venice Preserv'd*, ed. Malcolm Kelsall, 1969; *The Orphan*, ed. Aline Mackenzie Taylor, 1976.

Overview of Biographical Sources

Otway's early death in poverty and (supposedly) on the brink of starvation at thirty-three, encouraged more legendary accounts of his life than true biography. Eighteenth and nineteenth-century biographers also tended to assume that the presumed immorality and sentimentality of his plays reflected the life of a dissolute, hard-drinking Otway overflowing with sentiment and afflicted by the pangs of unrequited love for the actress Mrs. Barry. Anthony à Wood's *Atheniae Oxonienses* (1691) is the most straightforward of the early biographies, while Theophilus Cibber's *Lives of the Poets of Great Britain and Scotland* (1753) and *Spence's Anecdotes* (1820) offer conflicting and highly improbable accounts of Otway's death. Samuel Johnson's life of Otway in his *Lives of the English Poets* (1779-81) is skeptical of the events surrounding his life, but also highly censorious of both Otway's life and work. The account in the *Dictionary of National Biography* (1895) is still useful; there is no definitive biography.

Evaluation of Selected Biographies

Ham, Roswell Gray, *Otway and Lee: Biography From a Baroque Age*. New Haven: Yale University Press, 1931. The biographies of the two great Restoration dramatists run concurrently. Although somewhat pious and moralistic in tone, the biography does cover the major events of Otway's life, and is particularly full on the staging of the plays.

Warner, Kerstin B. *Thomas Otway*. Boston: Twayne, 1982. A sympathetic, scholarly biography that seeks to restore the modern reader's faith in Otway as a great dramatist and a fundamentally decent man.

Autobiographical Sources

First in importance is Otway's lengthy poem, *The Poet's Complaint of his Muse* (1680), in which he chronicles his life, complains of a loss of poetic inspiration, and settles old scores with his enemies. There are also the love letters to Elizabeth Barry (1681-82), some scattered remarks in the prologues and epilogues of his plays, and allusive references to his bitterness toward Mrs. Barry in his play, *Friendship in Fashion*, 1678.

Overview of Critical Sources

Criticism of Otway has centered on the supposed sentimentality, sexual immorality, and pessimism of his plays, his sources, and the influence of his plays on later writers, particularly Byron and Swift. Much of this literature has appeared in article form, e.g. John D. Jump, "A Comparison of *Marino Faliero* with Otway's *Venice Preserved*," *Byron Journal*, 5 (1977): 20-37; James Ogden, "Literary Echoes in Otway's Comedies," *Notes & Queries*, 25 (1978): 26; Robert D. Hume, "Otway and the Comic Muse," *Studies in Philology*, 73 (1976): 87-116; J.A. Downie, "Swift's Dismal," *Notes & Queries*, 25 (1978): 43; Gordon Williams, "The Sex-Death Motive in Otway's *Venice Preserv'd*," *Trivium*, 2 (1967): 59-70; Hazel M. Batzer, "Shakespeare's Influence on Thomas Otway's 'Caius Marius;' " *Revue de l'Université d'Ottawa*, 39 (1969): 533-561.

Evaluation of Selected Criticism

De Porte, Michael, "Otway and the Straits of Venice," in *Papers on Language and Literature*, 18 (Summer 1982): 245-257. Discusses betrayal, politics, and the function of sex roles.

Hughes, Derek W. "A New Look at *Venice Preserv'd*," in *Studies in English Literature*, 11 (1971): 437-457. Stresses the relationship of the sexual and financial imagery in the play.

Marshall, Geoffrey, "The Coherence of *The Orphan*," in *Texas Studies in Language and Literature*, 11 (1969): 931-943. Denies that the play is either morbid or inconsistent.

Rothstein, Eric, *Restoration Tragedy: Form and the Process of Change*. Madison, WI: University of Wisconsin Press, 1967. Why the Restoration tragedies declined in popularity, and what their merits are.

Taylor, Aline Mackenzie, *Next to Shakespeare: Otway's 'Venice Preserved' and 'The Orphan' and Their History on the London Stage*. Durham, NC: University of North Carolina Press, 1950. A scholarly account of the stage history of Otway's best two plays, with a careful account of the rise and fall of Otway's reputation.

Waith, Eugene M. *Ideas of Greatness: Heroic Drama in England*. London: Routledge and Kegan Paul, 1971. Sees the decline in heroic drama and a movement toward domestic sentimental tragedy in Otway's *The Orphan*.

Other Sources

Four Restoration Playwrights: A Reference Guide to Thomas Shadwell, Aphra Behn, Nathaniel Lee, & Thomas Otway. ed. J.M. Armistead. Boston: G.K. Hall, 1984. A comprehensive bibliography of materials relating to Otway's life and work, through 1980.

The London Stage 1660-1800, ed. William Van Lennep. 4 vols. in 8. Carbondale, IL: Southern Illinois University Press, 1965. A calendar of plays and quasi-dramatic performances for the period, with useful commentary on stage history.

John Mulryan
St. Bonaventure University

GEORGE PEELE
1556-1596

Author's Chronology

Born in London, England, where he is baptized July 27, 1556, son of middle-class parents; *1565* begins education at Christ's Hospital School, public institution for indigents and orphans where his father James is administrator and accountant; *1571* enters Pembroke Hall, Oxford; later transfers to Christ Church College where he develops interest in theater with production of college plays, including his Latin translation of Euripides' *Iphigenia*; *1577* takes his B.A., and his M.A. in 1579; *1580* marries Ann Cooke (or Christian), sixteen-year-old Oxfordshire heiress by whom he has at least one daughter; becomes embroiled in years of litigation about her inheritance; early *1580s* returns to London where he begins to write for the public stage and gains reputation as one of the dissolute "University Wits"; writes at least three of the Lord Mayor's annual pageants during this period; *1583* returns to Oxford to direct plays honoring visit of the Count Palatine; *1587(?)* Ann Peele dies; *1591(?)* marries Mary Yates (or Gates), a widow, whose claims against the government for her first husband's death in military service in the Netherlands involve Peele in more futile legal battles; *1595* unsuccessfully appeals to Lord Burghley for patronage because of poverty and ill-health; *1596* dies after a long illness, reportedly syphillis; November 9 buried at St. James, Clerkenwell.

Author's Bibliography (selected)

The Hunting of Cupid (lost), c.1581-1585 (drama); *The Arraignment of Paris*, c.1584 (drama); *The Device of the Pageant Borne Before Woolstone Dixi*, 1585 (pageant); *The Battle of Alcazar*, c.1589 (drama); *A Tale of Troy*, 1589, revised as *The Tale of Troy*, 1604 (narrative poem); *Polyhymnia*, 1590 (poem); *The Famous Chronicle of King Edward the First*, c.1590-1591 (drama); *Descensus Astraeae*, 1591 (pageant); *The Old Wives' Tale*, c.1591-1594 (drama); *The Love of King David and Fair Bethsabe*, c.1593-1594 (drama); *The Turkish Mahomet and Hiren the Fair Greek* (lost), c.1594.

Overview of Biographical Sources

For over three hundred years after his death, Peele's reputation was based on scurrilous references by contemporaries, such as Francis Meres' assertion in *Palladis Tamia: Wit's Treasury* (1598) that "as Anacreon the Poet died by the pot: so George Peele by the pox," guilt by his association with the undoubtedly dissolute Robert Greene whose *Groatsworth of Wit Bought with a Million of Repentance* (1592) contains admonitions to his fellow playwright about his misspent life, and a highly suspect autobiographical source, *The Merry Conceited Jests of George Peele*

500

(1607). Now believed to be mostly fictitious in the usual jestbook tradition, *The Merry Conceited Jests* portrays Peele as a jester, a wastral, a drunkard, a lecher, and the boon companion to the denizens of London's underworld in the late sixteenth century. Although some of Peele's notoriety may have been deserved, the worst of the defamatory material was dispelled by David H. Horne in his biographical and critical study *The Life and Minor Works of George Peele* (1952). Recent biographers, such as Leonard Ashley in *George Peele* (1970) and A.R. Braunmuller in *George Peele* (1983), follow this revisionist tendency, not glossing over Peele's faults of character but concentrating on contemporary references which emphasize his middle-class background and examining his contributions to the development of Elizabethan drama.

Evaluation of Selected Biographies

Ashley, Leonard R.N. *George Peele*. New York: Twayne, 1970. Although intended for general rather than scholarly readers, Ashley's biography is nonetheless a well-documented as well as accessible study of the few known facts of Peele's personal life and a helpful introduction to his major plays. Its value lies in its attempt to study Peele the dramatist for himself rather than to contrast his achievements with those of his more famous contemporaries. It also presents Peele against the background of the Elizabethan theatrical milieu without becoming bogged down in scholarly minutiae.

Braunmuller, A.R. *George Peele*. Boston: Twayne, 1983. Another general biography, Braunmuller's study focuses on Peele as theatrical craftsman rather than as playwright or stylist. It links political, social, and economic issues of his day with Peele's varied literary productions, emphasizing the public and didactic aims of his work. It includes careful studies of the Lord Mayor's pageants and their relationship to serious drama.

Horne, David H. *The Life and Minor Works of George Peele*. New Haven: Yale University Press, 1952. For over thirty years this has remained the standard, if not the definitive, critical study of Peele's life and work. Horne was the first scholar to debunk the more dissolute aspects of Peele's life and to de-emphasize his association with the more notorious of the so-called "University wits." He provides a thorough review of all contemporary references to Peele's life and reputation, and examines the disputed *The Merry Conceited Jests of George Peele* as a collection of popular anecdotes rather than as material worthy of serious biographical consideration.

Autobiographical Sources

The Merry Conceited Jests of George Peele (1607) purports to be a posthumous collection of witty stories with which Peele regaled his drinking companions at the

White Horse Tavern. If it is what it is represented to be, *The Merry Conceited Jests* undoubtedly reinforces the view of Peele as the wild and dissipated individual of questionable morals who enjoyed cheating his friends. Early critics accepted *The Merry Conceited Jests* as factual and used it to bolster their portrait of the wanton and dissolute playwright. Although David Horne's research has shown that all but eight of the thirty-four jests were originally printed elsewhere, their attribution to Peele in this collection, coupled with numerous contemporary references to this wildness, indicates that the characterization of Peele as an impecunious and freckless *bon vivant* with connections to the London underworld may have had some basis in fact.

Overview of Critical Sources

Critical approaches to Peele have focused on a number of related areas. First of all, it has been necessary to establish the canon; at one time or another almost every unattributed play from the 1580s and early 1590s has been assigned to Peele. Another area for critical discussion has been the establishment of Peele's role in the development of Elizabethan drama, especially in his relationship to the other "University Wits": Nashe, Greene, Lodge, Lyly, and Marlowe. Finally, there have been numerous attempts to evaluate Peele's "worth" as a dramatist.

This last area has caused the most disagreement among critics. Opinions range from those who see Peele as a brilliant minor dramatist to those who rank him as an uninspired hack. Peele's earliest plays are undeniably crude but hardly more so than most other extant drama from the period. Most critics now concede that Peele was among the predecessors of Shakespeare who helped revolutionize the theater of their day. They commend Peele for his linguistic virtuosity, his experimentation with varied modes (romance, melodrama, chronicle, pastoral) within the drama, and, in his best play, *The Old Wives' Tale*, with the creation of realistic and believable middle-class characters.

Evaluation of Selected Criticism

Ashley, Leonard R.N. *Authorship and Evidence: A Study of Attribution and the Renaissance Drama Illustrated by the Case of George Peele, 1556-1596.* Geneva: Librairie Droz, 1968. Ashley, later to become Peele's biographer, uses the dramatist as a specific example of the problems of correct attribution of the vast number of "masterless" plays of the late sixteenth-century. He is not interested in this idiosyncratic study in establishing the Peele canon, leaving that to the editors of the Yale edition of Peele's works. Instead, he reviews the numerous misattributions of plays to Peele in order to point out what he considers the shortcomings of the methods of many textual editors. The book is helpful for indicating what Peele is not and does include an extensive bibliography.

Hunter, G.K. *Lyly and Peele*. London: Longmans, Green, 1968. Hunter provides a brief but valuable study of the relationship of two of the "University Wits" who wrote both for the court and the popular stage. He outlines the influence of Lyly's euphuistic style on Peele's dramatic language and demonstrates that Peele's best work moves beyond a preoccupation with linguistic facility into the representation of the direct speech of the common people.

Prouty, Charles T. ed. *The Life and Works of George Peele*. 3 vols. New Haven: Yale University Press, 1952-1970. This definitive edition of Peele's works is invaluable for its discussion of the textual and publication history of all of Peele's work. It includes information on the background and occasion of each piece and cites all contemporary allusions to Peele and his writing.

Senn, Werner, *Studies in the Dramatic Construction of Robert Greene and George Peele*. Swiss Studies in English 74. Berne: Francke, 1973. Senn presents a useful and detailed comparison of the major plays of both playwrights. Although his ultimate goal is to show that Greene is by far the better dramatist, Senn's discussion of Peele's *The Battle of Alcazar*, *David and Bethsabe*, and *Edward I* is balanced and complete.

Other Sources

Axton, Marie, *The Queen's Two Bodies: Drama and the Elizabethan Succession*. Royal Historical Society Studies in History. London: Royal Historical Society, 1977. Contains extremely valuable discussion of *The Battle of Alcazar* and *Edward I* in reference to political motives of Elizabethan drama.

Bergeron, David M. *English Civic Pageantry 1558-1642*. London: Edward Arnold, 1971. Examines Peele's Lord Mayor's pageants in light of the tradition of civic entertainment for propaganda purposes.

Bevington, David, *Tudor Drama and Politics: A Critical Approach to Topical Meaning*. Cambridge: Harvard University Press, 1968. Brief but important discussion of Peele's plays, especially *Edward I* and *The Battle of Alcazar*, as jingoistic devices intended to foster anti-Spanish, anti-Catholic hysteria in the late 1580s.

Boas, Frederick S. *University Drama in the Tudor Age*. Oxford: Clarendon Press, 1914. Dated but still valuable study of the revival of the classical drama in the English universities and its influence on the popular theater; discusses Peele's *Iphigenia* and the role of the "University Wits" in general.

Cheffaud, P.H. *George Peele (1558-1596?)*. Paris: Felix Alcan, 1913. For many years the standard biography. Factual material now unreliable. Critical commentary on Peele's plays excellent.

Clemen, Wolfgang, *English Tragedy Before Shakespeare: The Development of Dramatic Speech*. trans. T.S.Dorsch. London: Methuen, 1961. Comprehensive study of the development of the Elizabethan theater with an entire chapter devoted to Peele's role and the importance of his tragedies.

Doran, Madeleine, *The Endeavors of Art*. Madison: University of Wisconsin Press, 1954. Dismisses Peele as an early and unskilled playwright whose works are shapeless and unselective.

Ewbank, Inga-Stina, "The House of David in Renaissance Drama: A Comparative Study," in *Renaissance Drama* 8 (1965): 3-40. Influential article which sees Peele as a moralist whose *David and Bethsabe* is based on the principle of the destruction of divine order and its ramifications for the kingdom at large, a similar theme to that of Shakespeare's history plays.

Greenfield, Thelma N. *The Induction in Elizabethan Drama*. Eugene: University of Oregon Books, 1969. Contains a discussion of both *The Battle of Alcazar* and *The Old Wives' Tale*; finds the frame structure of the latter a particularly sophisticated treatment of the device of the induction.

Jones, Gwenan, "The Intention of Peele's 'Old Wive's Tale,'" in *Aberystwyth Studies* 7 (1925): 79-93. Influential article which convincingly argues against the traditional view of the play as literary satire, sees it instead as folkloric in nature.

Ribner, Irving, *The English History Play in the Age of Shakespeare*. rev. ed. London: Methuen, 1965. Discusses Peele as one of the originators of the history or chronicle play although he views *Edward I* as one of the crudest extant examples of the genre.

Mary Anne Hutchinson
Utica College of Syracuse University

ARTHUR WING PINERO
1855-1934

Author's Chronology

Born May 24, 1855, London, England; of John Daniel Pinero, a lawyer, and Lucy Daines of old English family (father's family were originally Portuguese Jews who migrated to England early in the eighteenth century); *1874* begins his theatrical career as an actor in the stock company of Mr. and Mrs. R.H. Wyndham, making his first appearance at the Theatre Royal, Edinburgh, on June 22; works and studies law in his father's office, while taking elocution lessons at Birkbeck Institute, London; goes to Liverpool, then back to London, working for R.C. Carton at the Globe and Henry Irving at the Lyceum; *1877* launches his career as a dramatic author at the Globe; *1883* marries actress Myra Holme; *1887* elected to membership in the Garrick Club as a dramatic author; *1909* knighted by King Edward VII; *1919* death of Lady Myra Pinero; *1934* dies on November 23 after an operation at the Marylebone Nursing Home, London.

Author's Bibliography (selected drama)

Two Hundred a Year, 1877; *The Money Spinner*, 1880; *The Squire*, 1881; *The Magistrate*, 1885; *The Schoolmistress*, 1886; *The Hobby Horse*, 1886; *Dandy Dick*, 1887; *Sweet Lavender*, 1888; *The Profligate*, 1889; *The Cabinet Minister*, 1889; *The Times*, 1891; *Lady Bountiful*, 1891; *The Amazons*, 1893; *The Second Mrs. Tanqueray*, 1893; *The Notorious Mrs.Ebbsmith*, 1895; *The Benefit of the Doubt*, 1895; *The Princess and the Butterfly*, 1897; *Trelawny of the Wells*, 1898; *The Gay Lord Quex*, 1889; *Iris*, 1901; *Letty*, 1903; *A Wife without Smile*, 1904; *His House in Order*, 1906; *The Thunderbolt*, 1908; *Mid-Channel*, 1909; *The Mind-the-Paint-Girl*, 1912; *The Widow of Wasdale Head*, 1912; *Playgoers*, 1913; *The Big Drum*, 1915; *The Freaks*, 1918; *The Enchanted Cottage*, 1922.

Overview of Biographical Sources

"The private life of Arthur Wing Pinero," wrote Clayton Hamilton in the general introduction to his 1917 edition of *The Social Plays of Arthur Wing Pinero*, "has been, quite literally, private. Pinero has always avoided the lime-light for himself and reserved it for his plays." Further in that same introductory essay, Hamilton quotes part of a letter from the playwright to him, in which the former declared, "There will be some difficulty about 'biography,' because I have never troubled myself to supply particulars of my early life to any writer." Indeed, Pinero's biographical pickings range from slim to uneventful; the biographical studies tend, eventually, to develop into commentaries upon Pinero's plays. Will W. Massee begins his essay in *Living Dramatists*, ed. Oscar Herman (New York: Brentano's,

1905, pp. 3-62) by filtering Pinero's development as a playwright through his theatrical training with the Lyceum company and Haymarket Theatre, while Camilla Pellizzi, in *English Drama, the Last Great Phase* (London: Macmillan, 1935, pp. 47-52) sees practically the opposite effect. Pellizzi maintains that Pinero's failings as a comic actor produced a bland uniformity in his comic characters. Both J.P. Wearing—in his doctoral dissertation, *The Life and Achievement of Sir Arthur Wing Pinero, 1855-1934* (University of Wales, 1971)—and Walter Lazenby, in *Arthur Wing Pinero* (New York: Twayne, 1972), explore other biographical influences upon Pinero's drama: employment in his father's law office, marriage, neglect of family (but nonetheless love of that family), and the death of his wife.

Evaluation of Selected Biographies

Dunkel, Wilbur Dwight, *Sir Arthur Pinero. A Critical Biography, with Letters.* Chicago: University Press, 1941; rpt. Port Washington, NY: Kennikat Press, 1967. Dunkel's study of Pinero's achievement remains one of the better attempts to relate the life of the playwright to his work. From one point of view, Dunkel seeks reasons for Pinero's status as a minor contributor to the cultural and intellectual history of Victorian-Edwardian England. Essentially, the dramatist remained aloof from the world of fashion, refrained from self-praise, and published no valid critical commentary upon the genre that he developed. His contemporaries (Henry Arthur Jones, Oscar Wilde, George Bernard Shaw, Hendrik Ibsen), on the other hand, assumed opposite positions. Although Dunkel's biographical narrative must necessarily be superficial, an abundance of correspondence placed strategically within each of the eleven chapters allows both Pinero and his correspondents to provide perceptive commentary upon the man and his work. As such, Dunkel's biography serves as an important interim stage between Pinero's death and the 1974 edition of J.P. Wearing's *Collected Letters*.

Autobiographical Sources

Wearing, J.P. *The Collected Letters of Arthur Wing Pinero.* Minneapolis: University of Minnesota Press, 1974; London: Oxford University Press, 1974. Pinero once declared that "the public cannot possibly be interested in me." That may have been so, but at least Wearing's edition of the letters has provided needed biographical details about the playwright and has contributed helpful footnotes to his plays. Those letters have allowed Wearing to construct a useful (and *recent*) biographical sketch and a clear chronology of Pinero's life and works. The edition benefits from careful and thorough documentation.

Overview of Critical Sources

Criticism of Pinero's plays appears in almost every type of critical journal. Both the quality and the viewpoint of that criticism depend not only upon the popular or scholarly journal or book in question, but upon the chronological moment, upon whether the piece appeared during or after Pinero's lifetime. Profesors Jack W. Weaver and Earl J. Wilcox—in "Arthur Wing Pinero, an Annotated Bibliography of Writings about Him," *English Literature in Transition*, 23 (1980), 231-259—have done the scholarly world a considerable favor with their list and comments; further, their two-paragraph introduction does as well as anything to provide an *overview* of critical attitude toward Pinero.

Evaluation of Selected Criticism

Armstrong, Cecil Ferard, *Shakespeare to Shaw. Studies in the Life's Work of Six Dramatists of the English Stage.* London: Mills and Boon, 1913; rpt. Freeport, NY: Books for Libraries Press,1968, pp. 206-245. Armstrong discusses groupings of Pinero's plays: tragi-comedies, sentimental serials, and Gibes ("tilting" comedies). From there, he summarizes the plays and fits them to the various definitions, being attentive to the major themes and the functions and meanings of major characters. The reader of these analyses receives specific details on each piece, but the critical commentator never turns his attention to Pinero's texts, to the sound and the sense of his language. Armstrong concludes on the notion of Pinero as an "ordinary" dramatist—but at least ordinary enough to deserve recognition from literary history.

Cunliffe, John W. *Modern English Playwrights. A Short History of the English Drama from 1825.* New York: Harper and Brothers, 1927; Port Washington, NY: Kennikat Press, 1969, pp. 33-47. Cunliffe emphasizes the versatility of Pinero's early theatrical experiences in London and the provinces as positive contributors to the playwright's overall familiarity with theatrical production. In analyzing *The Profligate, The Second Mrs. Tanqueray, The Notorious Mrs. Ebbsmith, The Benefit of the Doubt, The Gay Lord Quex, The Thunderbolt,* and *Mid-Channel,* Cunliffe remains convinced of Pinero's strength as a skillful craftsman of the stage and an admirable contriver of lively drawingroom comedy. However, this critic sees nothing of value in terms of Pinero's contribution to English dramatic *literature*, and he agrees with those who have severely but "justifiably" attacked the playwright for his moderate applications of passion, intelligence, conviction, and literary style.

Shaw, George Bernard, *Dramatic Opinions and Essays, with an Apology by Bernard Shaw.* London: Constable, 1907, 1:32-40, 90-97, 194-199, 348-356; 2: 228-237, 406-414. The majority of Shaw's critical comments upon Pinero's plays appeared, originally, in the London *Saturday Review* between February 1895 and February 1898. As such, they constitute commentaries upon individual pieces, rather than being overall assessments of the playwright's craft and art. Shaw objects to Pinero's absurdities in Bygones, the lack of reality in *The Princess and the Butterfly, The Notorious Mrs.Ebbsmith,* and *Trelawney of the Wells.* On the positive side, he views *The Second Mrs. Tanqueray* as decent theatrical production containing a certain degree of appeal, even though it fails as a work of dramatic literature. Also, *The Benefit of the Doubt* achieves success because it reflects accurately that which Pinero knew about life. In general, Shaw believed that his own criticisms helped to improve the quality of Pinero's plays.

Other Sources

Hamilton, Clayton, ed. *The Social Plays of Arthur Wing Pinero*. 4 vols. New York: E.P. Dutton, 1917; rpt. New York: AMS Press, 1967. Contains a general introduction to each volume and critical prefaces to all of the plays. Certainly one of the better editions published during Pinero's lifetime.

Morgan, Arthur Eustace, *Tendencies of Modern English Drama*. New York: Charles Scribner's Sons, 1923; rpt. Freeport, NY: Books for Libraries Press, 1969, pp. 35-41. Eustace labels Pinero "the most typical dramatist of the "nineties," and believes his success came from his being truly English. Thus, the playwright took advantage of reality and strong theatrical tradition.

Nicoll, Allardyce, *A History of English Drama, 1660-1900. Volume V. Late Nineteenth-Century Drama, 1850-1900*. Cambridge: At the University Press, 1967, pp. 173-182; 524-525 (Handlist of Plays). Reflects the objectivity and the distance of the serious scholar attempting to fit his subject into the proper context of literary history. Nicoll admits to Pinero's lack of high intellectual ideal, but at the same time recognizes his real contribution to the drama of the period: as a writer of "sneering comedies" that gather inspiration from serious purposes.

Selected Dictionaries and Encyclopedias

Dictionary of National Biography, Oxford University Press, 1949, pp. 699-701. Although generally positive toward Pinero's craftsmanship, St. John Ervine labels the dramatist's dialogue as stilted and maintains that "his mind did not move easily among ideas."

Modern British Dramatists, 1900-1945. Part 2: M-Z, Gale, 1982, pp. 98-110. Thorough entry on Pinero includes a complete list of productions, a critical survey of the major plays, and a full listing of references.

The Reader's Encyclopedia of World Drama, Thomas Y. Crowell, 1969, pp. 655-656. Brief biography, sketchy survey of the major plays, short list of secondary sources.

Samuel J. Rogal
Illinois Valley Community College

HAROLD PINTER
1930

Author's Chronology

Born October 10, 1930 in Hackney, East London, the only son of parents of Jewish descent; *1939* evacuated from London at the outbreak of war; *1944-1947* returns to attend the Hackney Downs Grammar School; performs in school productions; *1948-1949* receives grant to study at the Royal Academy of Dramatic Art but leaves after a short stay; refuses National Service as a conscientious objector for which he is tried and fined on two occasions; begins writing short stories and poems, including the seminal dramatic dialogue "Kullus"; *1950* publishes first poems under the name "Harold Pinta" in *Poetry London*; *1951* resumes training at the Central School of Speech and Drama; tours England and Ireland until the following year playing Shakespeare with Anew McMaster's acting company; *1953* acts in Donald Wolfit's classical season at the King's Theatre, Hammersmith; first meeting with actress Vivian Merchant; *1954* adopts the stage name of David Baron; continues to act with various provincial repertory companies; *1956* marries Merchant; *1957* writes first play, *The Room*, produced by the Drama Department of Bristol University; *1958* birth of son, Daniel; *1959* first production of *The Birthday Party*; *1960 The Caretaker* opens in London and wins the Evening Standard Award for best play; *1962* begins association with the Royal Shakespeare Company; *1964* receives British Screenwriters Guild Award for the screenplay of *The Servant*; *1965* wins British Film Academy Award for the screenplay of *The Pumpkin Eater*; *1967 The Homecoming* opens in New York and receives the New York Drama Critics' Circle Award and Tony Award for the best play of the season; *1971 Old Times* opens in London and New York; directs *Butley* by Simon Gray; *1973* appointed by Peter Hall as an Associate Director at the National Theatre; *1975 No Man's Land* opens in London; first sued for divorce by Merchant; *1978 Betrayal* opens in London; *1980* divorces Merchant; marries Lady Antonia Fraser; continues to write and direct for the theatre.

Author's Bibliography (selected)

The Birthday Party and The Room, 1961 (includes the plays *The Birthday Party, The Room* and *The Dumb Waiter*); *The Caretaker and the Dumb Waiter*, 1961 (plays); *Three Plays: A Slight Ache, The Collection, The Dwarfs*, 1962; *The Homecoming*, 1967 (play); *Landscape and Silence*, 1970 (includes the plays *Landscape, Silence*, and *Night*); *Old Times*, 1973 (play); *The Proust Screenplay*, 1978; *Betrayal*, 1979 (play); *The Hothouse*, 1980 (play); *The French Lieutenant's Woman: A Screenplay*, 1981.

Overview of Biographical Sources

Recognized primarily as a dramatist, Harold Pinter is a prolific and versatile talent, having distinguished himself as an actor, director, and screenwriter. Considered a major literary voice at a relatively early stage of his career, today Pinter is acknowledged as one of the most significant figures in contemporary theatre. Perhaps more than any other living playwright, Pinter is credited with challenging the boundaries of the conventional stage and redefining the essence of dramatic language, action, and character. Although charged with any number of offenses as a dramatist, Pinter has demonstrated in his craft a unique capacity "to surprise, puzzle, tease, and delight." Initially dismissed as a serious writer for being eclectic, obscure, and void of meaning, Pinter has since won both critical recognition and widespread audience acceptance.

An intriguing subject for biography, Pinter to date has presented an elusive target for biographers. Emerging as a theatrical enigma, Pinter has capitalized throughout his career on his ability to possess an air of mystery. Reluctant to disclose biographical detail and to discuss the "meaning" of his dramatic work, Pinter continues to provide a certain validity to Martin Esslin's prophetic statement in the introduction to *The Peopled Wound: The Plays of Harold Pinter* (Garden City, NY: Doubleday, 1970) that the "time, clearly, is not ripe for a biography of Harold Pinter."

Autobiographical Sources

Referring to his earlier plays as comedies of menace, critics generally agree that Pinter has clearly established himself as a master of ambiguity and evasiveness not only in his writing but also in his personal life. Fitting his reputation, Pinter has produced very little in the way of autobiographical material. He prefers instead to let his creativity define his identity. Consequently, despite the attempts by numerous critics to identify autobiographical elements in his plays, Pinter has consistently denied any correlation. Likewise, although Pinter has consented throughout his career to a variety of interviews, the majority serve only to protect his anonymity rather than provide significant insight into his character. Of noteworthy exception, however, are Lawrence M. Bensky's "Harold Pinter: An Interview," *Paris Review*, 39 (Fall 1966): 13-37, reprinted in *Writers at Work: The Paris Review Interviews*, third series (New York: Viking, 1967): 347-368, and Mel Gussow's "A Conversation (Pause) with Harold Pinter," *New York Times Magazine* (5 December 1971): 42-43, 126-136, both of which provide valuable information concerning Pinter's life and techniques of writing.

Overview of Critical Sources

Although critics and audiences alike were generally unprepared for Pinter's emergence as a dramatist, he was early recognized as an original and creative

talent. Primarily as a result of the controversy generating from his plays, a voluminous body of criticism has coincided with the development of his literary career.
Early treatments providing selected biographical information and critical analyses
of the plays include Ronald Hayman's *Harold Pinter* (London: Heinemann Educational Books, 1968), Arnold P. Hinchliffe's *Harold Pinter* (1967), Walter Kerr's
pamphlet-length study *Harold Pinter* (New York and London: Columbia University
Press, 1967), and John Russell Taylor's *Harold Pinter* (London: Longmans,
Green, 1969). Slightly more inclusive, offering an early Freudian interpretation of
Pinter's work, is Lois G. Gordon's *Strategems to Uncover Nakedness* (Columbus:
University of Missouri Press, 1969). Gordon also prepared the first significant
bibliographic treatment of Pinter entitled "Pigeonholing Pinter: A Bibliography,"
Theatre Documentation, Fall 1968.

A pivotal study which semingly unleashed an avalanche of Pinter criticism was
Martin Esslin's *The Peopled Wound*. Other studies appearing in rapid succession
include Katherine H. Burkman's *The Dramatic World of Harold Pinter—Its Basis
in Ritual* (Columbus: Ohio State University Press, 1971), Arlene Sykes' *Harold
Pinter* (New York: Humanities Press, 1971), Simon Trussler's *The Plays of Harold
Pinter* (London: Victor Gollancz Ltd., 1973), and Austin E. Quigley's *The Pinter
Problem* (Princeton: Princeton University Press, 1975). Varied in their interpreta-
tions, with the exception of Trussler, the authors confirm Pinter's increasing maturity and importance as a dramatist. Offering departures from the critical norm are
William Baker and Stephen Ely Tabachnick's *Harold Pinter* (New York: Harper &
Row, 1973) and Lucina Paquet Gabbard's *The Dream Structure of Pinter's Plays: A
Psychoanalytic Approach* (Rutherford, NJ: Fairleigh Dickinson University Press,
1976). Limited in their approach, Baker and Tabachnick examine the Jewish element in Pinter's early writing through *The Homecoming* which the authors claim
lies embedded in Pinter's work. Gabbard, on the other hand, offers a Freudian
interpretation of Pinter's work through *No Man's Land*, exploring the plays in
detail through the mechanism of the dream.

More recent studies continue to probe the "meaning" of Pinter's plays while
emphasizing Pinter's influence on the contemporary theatrical scene. Of scholarly
value are two bibliographical treatments: Herman T. Schroll's *Harold Pinter: A
Study of His Reputation (1958-1969) and a Checklist* (Metuchen, NJ: Scarecrow
Press, 1971) and Steven H. Gale's "Harold Pinter: An Annotated Bibliography
1957-1971," *Bulletin of Bibliography*, 29 (1972): 46-56. It is also noteworthy that
several authors, including Bernard F. Dukore, Martin Esslin, Ronald Hayman, and
Arnold P. Hinchliffe, have been compelled to periodically update earlier studies on
Pinter to incorporate more recent plays and to reevaluate their critical interpreta-
tions of Pinter's career.

Evaluation of Selected Criticism

Almansi, Guido and Simon Henderson, *Harold Pinter*. London and New York:
Methuen, 1983. A brief study published as part of a "Contemporary Writers"

series, this offers general biographical information and critical analyses of the plays through *Other Places* (including *Family Voices*, *A Kind of Alaska*, and *Victoria Station*). Although limited in scope, this serves as an effective introduction to Pinter's work in the theatre.

Dukore, Bernard F. *Harold Pinter*. New York: Grove Press, 1982. Included as part of the Grove Press Modern Dramatists Series, this is a concise and practical study incorporating biographical information with a thematic survey of Pinter's plays as theatre, focusing primarily on matters of performance, character interpretation, and staging.

Esslin, Martin, *Pinter: The Playwright*. London: Methuen, 1984. Originally published as *The Peopled Wound*, this is the fourth, expanded edition of Esslin's critical study on Pinter. Of major importance in establishing Pinter's critical reputation, Esslin's test offers a psychological interpretation of the plays through *Betrayal* and *Other Places*. Most effective in exploring the subtleties of Pinter's use of language, Esslin has produced the most in-depth and complete critical work on Pinter to date.

Gale, Steven H. *Butter's Going Up: A Critical Analyses of Harold Pinter's Work*. Durham, North Carolina: Duke University Press, 1977. Arranging Pinter's work into periods and offering a detailed analysis of the plays through *No Man's Land*, Gale provides a thorough, well-documented study designed to illuminate and clarify Pinter's increasing development and popularity as a dramatist. The text includes a chronology, an annotated bibliography, and complete information concerning first performances of Pinter's plays.

Ganz, Arthur, ed. *Pinter: A Collection of Critical Essays*. Englewood Cliffs, NJ: Prentice-Hall, 1972. An interesting collection of critical essays on diversified topics relating to Pinter with an introduction by Ganz. Most noteworthy are Ruby Cohn's "The World of Harold Pinter," John Lahr's "Pinter and Chekhov: The Bond of Naturalism," and John Russell Taylor's "A Room and Some Views: Harold Pinter." Also included in the text is Lawrence M. Bensky's "Harold Pinter: An Interview."

Hinchliffe, Arnold P. *Harold Pinter*. New York: Twayne, 1967. Considered by Hinchliffe as Britain's most important twentieth-century dramatist, Pinter is viewed in this study with intelligence and perception. Designed for the reader with limited exposure to Pinter's plays, this serves as an informative introduction to Pinter's life and work. Revised from the original study published in 1967, the text provides a valuable assessment of Pinter's plays and also summarizes the various critical approaches to Pinter's body of literature.

Other Sources
Esslin, Martin, *The Theatre of the Absurd*. New York: Doubleday, 1961. A landmark study when it first appeared, Esslin's text identified Pinter as a peripheral

playwright of the "absurd," while providing early insight into Pinter's techniques as a writer and vision of the theatre.

Modern Drama 17 (December 1974). This entire issue is devoted to critical studies incorporating various aspects of Pinter's work. Of exceptional interest are Eric Salmon's "Harold Pinter's Ear" and Anita R. Osherow's "Mother and Whore: The Role of Woman in *The Homecoming*."

Thomson, Peter, "Harold Pinter: A Retrospect," *Critical Quarterly* 20 (Winter 1978): 21-28. Published prior to the production of *Betrayal*, considered by many critics to have rejuvenated Pinter's reputation in the theatre, Thomson's article is of interest primarily as a part of a growing critical response that viewed Pinter with having lost momentum and confidence as a playwright.

Wellwarth, George E. *The Theatre of Protest and Paradox*. New York: New York University Press, 1971. Identifying Pinter as a significant figure in the avant-garde theatre of postwar Britain, Wellwarth devotes a brief but informative section of his text to providing a perceptive analysis of Pinter's plays and his position in contemporary theatre.

Selected Dictionaries and Encyclopedias

Contemporary Dramatists, St. Martin's Press, 1982. Biographical summary and brief but informative analyses of Pinter's plays through *Betrayal*.

Dictionary of Literary Biography: British Dramatists Since World War II, Gale, 1982. A concise overview of Pinter's life and literary career, providing an effective analysis of the plays through *Other Places* as well as an accurate evaluation of Pinter's role in contemporary theatre.

Steven Serafin
Long Island University

LUIGI PIRANDELLO
1867-1936

Author's Chronology

Born in Girgenti, Sicily, 28 June 1867; his father, Stefano, a former soldier under Garibaldi and a rich sulphur mining contractor; publishes his first short story in a Turin newspaper at age seventeen; begins his university studies at Palermo, studying law, later moving to the University of Rome and finally to Bonn University, where he wrote a thesis on the development of the Agrigento dialect; starts his writing career as a poet, publishing *Joyful Pain* in 1889; *1891* publishes his Bonn degree; *1893* settles in Rome; *1894* marries Antonietta Poutulano, the daughter of his father's business partner; the couple has three children, Stefano, born 1895, Lietta, born 1897 and Fausto, born 1899; *1901* appearance of his first novel *The Outcast*; family fortune collapses and Antonietta suffers first signs of psychic illness in 1904; *1904* attains a teaching post at the Instito Feminile di Magisterio, a girl's college, in Rome; *1918* places his wife into an institution; *1921* publishes *Six Characters in Search of an Author*; its first performance in Rome causes pandemonium, and the author has to be rescued from the crowd; *1925* sets up an Arts Theatre in Rome; *1929* becomes a member of the Accademia d'Italia; *1934* awarded the Nobel Prize; dies in Rome, 10 December 1936.

Author's Bibliography (selected)

Fiction: *The Merry-Go-Round of Love*, 1902, tr. 1964 (novel); *The Late Mattia Pascal*, 1904, tr. 1923 (novel); *The Outcast*, 1908 tr. 1925 (novel); *The Old and the Young*, 1913, tr. 1928 (novel); *The Horse in the Moon*, 1932 (stories); *Better Think Twice About It and Twelve Other Stories*,1933; *The Medals and Other Stories*, 1939; *Short Stories*, 1959.

Drama: *Sicilian Limes*, 1910, tr. 1921; *Liola*, 1916, tr. 1952: *Right You Are If You Think So*, 1925, tr. 1952; *The Rules of the Game*, 1918, tr. 1959; *All for the Best*, 1920, tr. 1960; *Six Characters in Search of an Author*, 1921; *Henry IV*, 1922; *The Imbecile*, 1922; *Naked*, 1922, tr. 1962; *The Life I Gave You*, 1923, 1959; *The New Colony*, 1928, tr. 1958; *Lazzara*, 1929, tr. 1952; *Tonight We Improvise*, 1930, tr. 1932.

Overview of Biographical Sources

Since most biographical commentaries about Pirandello are in Italian, the reader of English must rely strongly on material either written in English or translated from the Italian. The seriousness of the problem is particularly noticeable when one considers that even the English version of the most extensive biography of the author available, *Pirandello: A Biography*, by G. Guidice, is neither as extensive nor as complete as the Italian original. Since this problem of adequate translations is insurmountable to those not bilingual, a short summary of the key biographical issues might assist a reader concerned with the relationship of Pirandello's art and life. In the main, three crucial aspects of Pirandello's life give shape to the biographical studies. The first is that Pirandello came to drama only after decades of writing poetry, essays and novels. Since his first effort to have a play performed failed, he vowed to keep away from the theatre. His friend, Angelo Musco, made him reconsider his decision during the years of World War I. Soon afterward, Pirandello met the actress Marta Abba, and she not only inspired him to write further dramas, but also aided in transforming his works into living theatre. The second aspect of biographical importance is that Pirandello was an irreducible Sicilian who, in a sense, achieved for Sicily what Joyce achieved for Ireland: both depicted the problems of a specific country and, by doing so, penetrated the particular deeply enough to become truly universal. Finally, the third important biographical fact is that many of Pirandello's plays and dramas are the result of lived, private experience transformed into art. Italian sources of importance are A. Leonte de Castris, *Storia de Pirandello*. Bari: Laterza, 1962; N. Ciarletta, "Pirandello europeo e siciliano" in *D'Annunzio, Pirandello*. L'Aquila: Japadre, 1967.

Evaluation of Selected Biographies

Bentley, Eric, *Naked Masks*. New York: E.P. Dutton, 1952. The book offers a short but lucid account of the man. It is especially accessible to those reading Pirandello's drama for the first time.

Bishop, Thomas, *Pirandello and the French Theater*. New York: New York University Press, 1960. This work focuses on many of Pirandello's ideas and their importance to the development of French theatre. Although primarily concerned with the historical development of French drama, the opening chapters of the book offer numerous and worthwhile insights into Pirandello's thoughts, ideas and attitudes.

Guidice, Gaspare, *Luigi Pirandello*. Turin: UTET, 1963. Translated as *Pirandello: A Biography*. London: Oxford University Press, 1975. (Note the English version is not as extensive as the Italian). Guidice provides a thorough, scholarly, in-depth biography which considers the great majority of Pirandello's works. This study places the author in his intellectual, philosophical, political, and sociohistoric context. While tracing the life, Guidice refrains from extensive or detailed critical commentary, although he does often give sharp and clear focus to the reasons why Pirandello wrote a particular play, novel or story.

Autobiographical Sources

Only a small portion of Pirandello's correspondence has been published in Italian books and journals, although a substantial number of letters exist. With the exceptions of sections of letters cited or summarized in Gaspare Guidice's biography, and snippets of letters included in some of the critical sources listed later in this article, direct autobiographical analysis will have to wait until an adequate Italian original of the letters is published and translated.

Overview of Critical Sources

Critical scholars of Pirandello have generally agreed that no serious study of twentieth century drama can ignore his works, although these critics differ sharply about where to place the emphasis when dealing with Pirandello's work. He is often seen as anticipating the existentialist anguish of later European, especially French, writing. Furthermore, he is particularly important for his depiction of the disintegration of the personality in conjunction with the isolation of modern man. Finally, his innovation of theatre within theatre makes him a forerunner of so-called experimental drama. In the earlier criticism, the *verism*, the regionalism, of Pirandello's work is stressed. In more recent studies, the emphasis is being placed upon the pessimistic humour, the clash between illusion and reality, and, finally, the techniques of compelling an audience to self-reflection and thought.

Evaluation of Selected Criticism

Bassnet-McGuire, Susan, *Luigi Pirandello*. London: Macmillan, 1983. Although often marred by excessive plot summary, for those reading Pirandello for the first time, this book is a good general introduction to the author's techniques and aims.

Bentley, Eric, *In Search of Theatre*. New York, 1959. The work contains an excellent critical essay, "Pirandello: Joy and Torment" (pp. 179-175).

Budel, Oscar, *Pirandello*. New York: Hillary House, 1966. The book gives a clear indication of the place of Pirandello in modern European literature and thought. The chapters entitled "The Relativist" and "Humour as Pity" are essential reading.

Cambon, Glauco, ed. *Pirandello: A Collection of Critical Essays*. Englewood Cliffs, NJ: Prentice Hall, 1967. This is a useful collection of critical essays, including important pieces by R. Brustein and F. Fergusson, with extracts from A. Tilgher's seminal work on Pirandello. Tilgher offers a metaphysical interpretation of Pirandello's work.

Moestrup, Jörn, *The Structural Pattern of Pirandello's Work*. Odense: Odense Universtiy Press, 1972. Moestrup discusses more stories than any other critic. Since the development of Pirandello's drama comes through his development as a narrative writer, this book offers fruitful approaches to Pirandello's handling of theatre.

Radcliff-Umstead, Douglas, *The Mirror of Our Anguish: A Study of Luigi Pirandello's Narrative Writings*. A necessary work to read for an understanding of the range of Pirandello's art, this book focuses on Pirandello's seven novels and his most typical tales.

Ragusa, Olga, *Pirandello: An Approach to His Literature*. Edinburgh: Edinburgh University Press, 1980. An uneven study of selected plays, the focus is on how the works received their shape.

Ragusa, Olga, *Luigi Pirandello*. New York: Columbia University Press, 1968. This short work places Pirandello as a transitional figure of the late nineteenth-century early twentieth-century.

Starkie, Walter, *Luigi Pirandello*. London: Dent, 1926; 3rd ed. rev. Berkeley: University of California Press, 1965. Although even the revised edition of the original book reveals that it is an early study, the book does give valuable insight into Pirandello as a Sicilian and as a regionalist writer.

Sugliuzzo, A. Richard, *Luigi Pirandello, Director: The Playwright in the Theatre*. Metuchen, NJ: The Scarecrow Press, 1982. The book stresses two aspects of Pirandello's theatre: his role as a director and his specific direction of particular plays. The first part of the book is particularly important for the light it throws on Pirandello's views of stage performance.

Vittorini, Domenico, *The Drama of Luigi Pirandello*. Philadelphia: University of Pennsylvania Press, 1935. This is an excellent study of all 38 plays written between 1918 and 1935. The plays are summarized and analyzed closely and carefully. Most importantly, their cultural background, place in European drama, symbolic techniques and plot structure are examined in relation to the philosophical outlook underlying Pirandello's dramas. The book includes a grateful letter from Pirandello to the author.

Other Sources

MacClintock, Lander, *The Age of Pirandello*. Bloomington: Indiana University Press, 1951. A one-volume survey of twentieth century Italian drama, this work offers a larger context in which to place Pirandello's craft and thought.

May, Frederick, ed. *Pirandello's Short Stories*. London: Oxford University Press, 1965. An especially important work because it contains, in an appendix, a complete list of the author's individual stories.

Selected Dictionaries and Encyclopedias

The Oxford Companion to the Theatre, 1967. The section on Italian drama, entitled "Italy," is the best brief commentary available for a sense of Pirandello's place in his native tradition.

The Penguin Companion to European Literature, 1969. Brief biography, critical introduction, and bibliography.

Ed Jewinski
Wilfrid Laurier University

PLAUTUS
254-184 B.C.(?)

Author's Chronology

Next to nothing is known with certainty about the life of Plautus. His birth and death dates are based only on the doubtful statements of later authorities, and even his full name, Titus Maccius Plautus, has been questioned. This name may be a theatrical joke, a parody of the upper-class Roman *tria nomina* in which each element is a play on theatrical associations—like calling a modern playwright "Thespian Othello Greasepaint." Plautus is said to have come from Sarsina, Umbria, in central Italy. Traditional stories link him firmly with the stage, maintaining, for instance, that he made money in the theater but lost it again in business ventures and was destitute until he returned to writing comedies. Two dates that seem relatively solid are 200 and 191 B.C.—the years when his plays *Stichus* and *Pseudolis*, respectively, were produced in Rome.

What is not in question is Plautus' popularity. One indication of this popularity is the remarkable survival rate of Plautus' comedies. While Plautus is sometimes said to have been a mere adapter of Greek New Comedy and while his work has been unfavorably compared with that of Terence, more Plautus has survived than all extant Greek New Comedy put together, and there are three times as many surviving plays by Plautus as by Terence.

Author's Bibliography (selected)

The standard complete editions of Plautus are those of W. M. Lindsay, *T. Macci Plautae Comoediae*, 2nd edition (Oxford: Oxford University Press, 1963), 2 vols.; and Paul Nixon, *Plautus*, Loeb Classical Library (Cambridge: Harvard University Press, 1916-1938), 5 vols. (with translations). Plautus attracts good translators. Fine recent translations include E. F. Watling's two volumes, *The Rope and Other Plays* (Harmondsworth: Penguin, 1963) and *The Pot of Gold and Other Plays* (Harmondsworth: Penguin, 1965); and also Erich Segal's *Plautus: Three Comedies* (New York: Harper & Row, 1969). Stephen Sondheim's *A Funny Thing Happened on the Way to the Forum* (New York: Dodd, Mead, 1985) also deserves mention. This modern musical comedy based on Plautus' work is faithful to the unbridled spirit of Plautus not only in its characters, situations, and jokes but in its use of music, which was an important ingredient in original Plautine productions.

Overview of Biographical Sources

Most details of Plautus' life are purely conjectural. Aulus Gellius, who based his remarks on now-lost writings of the Roman scholar Varro, relates stories about

Plautus' theatrical career, but these are not widely accepted by modern authorities. Cicero makes a few comments on Plautus, for instance, giving the traditional year of his death; so does Saint Jerome. Scraps like these are all that is left of Plautus' life. Scholars have combed the plays looking for autobiographical references, but so far without clear-cut success.

Evaluation of Selected Biographies

Almost the only thing that Plautus authorities insist on is that little is known about the playwright's life and anyone who says otherwise is not to be trusted.

Duckworth, George E. *The Nature of Roman Comedy: A Study in Popular Entertainment*. Princeton: Princeton University Press, 1952. Duckworth is still regarded as the most careful and scholarly commentator on Plautus in English. His account, pp. 49-51, judiciously explains all that is known and not known about Plautus' life.

Segal, Erich, *Roman Laughter: The Comedy of Plautus*. Cambridge: Harvard University Press, 1968. Segal takes a different line. While he acknowledged that the facts of Plautus' life are lost, he maintains that the plays tell a great deal about the author's habits of thought and the world of values he and his audiences inhabited. Segal's description of Roman society in the age of Cato the Elder and the way in which Plautus' humor upends common assumptions of the day comes as close as presently possible to reconstructing the tone of Plautus' imaginative life.

Autobiographical Sources

Not only are there none, but Plautus' habit of working from Greek originals within the general conventions of comedy up to his time makes attempting to draw details of his life from what goes on in the plays an extremely doubtful enterprise.

Overview of Critical Sources

Earlier critics starting with Horace have been unkind to Plautus. Horace considered the plays vulgar, poorly constructed, and mercenary—designed to appeal to the lowest common denominator—adding that Plautus' vivid and racy language and the uncommon metrical variety of his writings are merely evidence of poor craftsmanship. And these charges have been often repeated. However, even critics who deplored Plautus' popularity could not overlook his influence. It is Plautus—not Terence, or Menander, or Aristophanes—who laid the groundwork for such diverse later forms as Elizabethan comedy (including Shakespeare's *The Comedy of Errors*), the sparkling satires of Moliere, Restoration comedy, the revolutionary farces of Beaumarchais, and even such comic novelists as Waugh, Amis, and Wodehouse. Today every television sit-com shows that Plautine conventions like mistaken identity, wild coincidence, and rapid-fire wisecracks still make effective popular entertainment.

Plautus is popular with researchers and critics. The German scholar Eduard Fraenkel started a Plautus renaissance with his *Plautinsches im Plautus* (Berlin: Weidmann, 1922), a seminal study of Plautus' style. the periodic discovery of new scraps of Greek New Comedy has fueled a continuing debate on Plautus' originality, and technical studies examine his use of poetical meters. Of broader interest, however, is the attempt to define what the comedies meant to their original audiences. Plautus' topical satire and repeated use of comic conventions sum up what the Rome of his time found most amusing, and many critics have found in this a key to unlocking the real character of the age.

Evaluation of Selected Criticism

Arnott, W. Geoffrey, *Menander, Plautus, Terence*. Oxford: Clarendon Press, 1975. Arnott's book is scarcely more than a pamphlet, but it manages to pack a vigorous and readable account of discoveries and trends over three-quarters of a century of Plautus studies into seventeen pages. Equally concise and valuable for Menander and Terence.

Beare, William, *The Roman Stage: A Short History of Latin Drama in the Time of the Republic*. 3rd edition. London: Methuen, 1965. Beare's strong suit is explaining the staging conventions and physical arrangements of the Roman theater.

Duckworth, George E. *The Nature of Roman Comedy: A Study in Popular Entertainment*. Princeton: Princeton University Press, 1952. This is a large, solid, and nicely written survey of all Roman comedy, much of which is now known only at second hand, through the comments of later Roman writers. Duckworth is the most sensible and thorough commentator on Plautus in English, and his description of Roman stage conditions and the festivals in which drama figured adds a useful bonus. Duckworth is interested in Plautus as a Roman writer. His book marks the beginning of Plautus criticism focusing on the plays' social and intellectual background.

Segal, Erich, *Roman Laughter: The Comedy of Plautus*. Cambridge: Harvard University Press, 1968. Segal's book is an engagingly written treatment of the relationship between Plautus and his audience, examining the strategy of Plautus' comic invention to show how the plays systematically subvert the established values of the time. Spectators were thoroughly amused by the "upside-downness" of Plautus—cowardly soldiers, slaves bossing their masters, wives hectoring husbands, sons squandering the wealth of the fathers, *gravitas* taking a back seat to love—and they may have learned some valuable lessons about humanity and compassion to offset the repressive sternness and practicality of their everyday experience.

Other Sources

Handley, E. W. *Menander and Plautus: A Study in Comparison*. London: University of London, 1968. The latest authoritative word on the question of Plautus' debts to the Greeks. Handley scrupulously compares recently discovered fragments of Menander's *Dis Expaton* with relevant portions of Plautus' *Bacchides*, which it inspired. The result is a two-edged conclusion—that Plautus was capable of both faithful translation and extremely free adaptation, depending on his own dramatic purposes.

Segal, Erich, "Scholarship on Plautus 1965-1976," *The Classical World*, 74 (1981): 353-433. This annotated bibliography not only surveys criticism and scholarship on Plautus but gives a detailed account of the critics' findings, an important contribution because much work in the area is in foreign languages and journals or hidden away in doctoral dissertations. Segal's range is enormous, and his article is broken down topically and by play so that relevant entries are easy to find.

Wright, J. *Dancing in Chains: The Stylistic Unity of the Comoedia Palliata*. Rome: The American Academy in Rome, 1974. An attempt to reconstruct the characteristics of such mostly lost authors of Latin comedy in Greek dress as Livius Andronicus, Ennius, and Naevius. If Wright is correct, much of what seems uniquely Plautine is really characteristic of a general style of writing Roman comedy.

Selected Dictionaries and Encyclopedias

McGraw-Hill Encyclopedia of World Drama. 2nd ed. McGraw-Hill, 1984. Separate accounts of all Plautus' plays, along with a general appreciation by Sander M. Goldberg.

The Reader's Encyclopedia of World Drama. Thomas Crowell, 1969. Brief biographical and critical commentary on Plautus.

Joe Glaser
Western Kentucky University

ALEXANDER PUSHKIN
1799-1837

Author's Chronology

Born May 26, 1799, Moscow, to Sergei Lvovich Pushkin, a retired army officer from a 600-year-old noble family, and Nadezhda Osipovna Hannibal, the "beautiful creole" granddaughter of Peter the Great's Abyssinian engineering general; *1811-1817* attends first class of the Tsarskoye Selo Lyceum for gifted noble children; *1815* is praised for poetry by Derzhavin, greatest eighteenth century Russian poet; *1815-1817* belongs to Arzama Society, founded to promote new ideas in Russian literature; *1817* takes minor Foreign Office post and pursues poetry and pleasure in St. Petersburg; *1819* joins the Green Lamp, a literary society devoted to revels, actresses, and forbidden political liberalism; *1817-1820* works on first long narrative poem, *Ruslan and Lyudmila*; *1818-1820* though not a member of secret revolutionary societies, Pushkin writes inflammatory verse in their cause; May *1820* is ordered by tsar to Caucasus to shed liberal tendencies; *1820-1823* drinks, duels, writes Byronic poetry, and begins "novel in verse," *Evgeny Onegin*; *1823-1824* writes "The Gypsies," first genuinely individual poem; *1824* is returned in disgrace to family estate at Mikhailovskoye because of atheistic sentiments, tantamount to treason in tsarist Russia; *1824-1826* under police surveillance produces newly objective lyrics, experiments with folk poetry, and reads Shakespeare; as his progressive liberalism wanes, Pushkin writes historical tragedy *Boris Godunov* and continues *Evgeny Onegin*; December *1825* takes no active part in Decembrist uprising, but writes poems sympathetic to their cause; *1826* impregnates servant girl, the occasion for his unfinished dramatic poem "Rusalka"; September *1826* new tsar Nicholas I promises Pushkin freedoms that soon proved illusory, for Pushkin endured doubled censorship and police surveillance until his death; *1828* writes heroic epic *Poltava*; *1829* runs *Literary Gazette* in St. Petersburg; *1830* is engaged to beautiful but vapid Natalia Goncharov; autumn *1830* completes *Evgeny Onegin*, the blank verse *Little Tragedies*, short lyrics, narrative poems, and his first experiments in short fiction; *1830* is allowed to publish *Boris Godunov* after four-year wait; *1831* after marriage frequents glittering society his wife adores; *1833* writes *The History of Pugachev* and begins his supreme poetic achievement, *The Bronze Horseman*; December *1833* receives minor court post to keep him and his wife close to the tsar; *1834-1837* tormented by debts, Pushkin begs fruitlessly to be released from court duty; *1834* completes only one major work; *1836* finishes novel *The Captain's Daughter*, his finest short story, "The Queen of Spades," and his version of Horace's "Exegi Monumentum"; January 27, *1837* duels with Georges d'Anthès ostensibly over Natalia, is mortally wounded, and dies two days later; February 6, *1837* government buries Pushkin secretly near Mikhailovskoye to avoid civil disruption.

Author's Bibliography

Since Pushkin was primarily a poet, *Boris Godunov* and the *Little Tragedies* ("The Covetous Knight," published anonymously 1836; "Mozart and Salieri," 1830; and "The Stone Guest," published posthumously 1840) comprise a relatively small, though important, part of his work. Authoritative Russian editions are the "large" Academy of Sciences edition, not annotated but thoroughly reliable, and the "small" Academy edition, 1959-1962, with commentary. Scholarly Russian editions of Pushkin's letters to 1833 appeared in three volumes, 1926-1935; the 1834-1837 letters, in 1969. Although Russians claim Pushkin's work is untranslatable, English versions include the widely known *Poems, Prose and Plays of Alexander Pushkin*, ed. Avraham Yarmolinsky, 1936, containing translations of *Boris Godunov* and the *Little Tragedies*. Pushkin considered *Boris Godunov* his greatest production; Philip L. Barbour's 1953 translation supplies both an edited Russian text and useful English notes. Fine poetic translations of "Mozart and Salieri" and "The Stone Guest" appear in *The Bronze Horseman*, tr. D. M. Thomas. No comparable translations yet exist for "Angelo," a dramatic poem Pushkin based on Shakespeare's *Measure for Measure*; the "Scene from Faust," in which Pushkin opposes Goethe's eighteenth century optimism with his own nineteenth century realism; and "Feast in the Time of Plague," the last of Pushkin's 1830 series of dramatic sketches. J. Thomas Shaw's three-volume translation of *The Letters of Alexander Pushkin* appeared in 1963.

Overview of Biographical Sources

Pushkin's martyrdom is the great abiding myth of Russian literature. Shortly after his violent death, the younger poet Lermontov savagely indicted the Imperial court for destroying Pushkin, and in 1880 Dostoevsky declared that Russia's writers must accept the duty of revealing and deciphering the secret of creativity Pushkin had carried to his grave. Thus was born the enduring Russian conviction that Pushkin's life is the stuff of hagiography, to be handled with equal love and precision, a profound devotion that Soviet critics since 1917 have shaped to political purposes. No definitive Pushkin biography yet exists in any language, despite V. Verasaev's painstaking collection of Russian raw material, his two-volume *Pushkin in Real Life*, a reconstruction from all available sources contemporary with Pushkin. The earliest and still most widely respected English biography is Ernest J. Simmons' *Pushkin* (1937). Henri Troyat's French *Pushkin* (1946; published uncut in English, 1970) draws on Verasaev for a dashing Gallic *biographie romancée*. Walter N. Vickery's *Pushkin: Death of a Poet* (1968) soberly and accurately demythologizes Pushkin's last days. Outstanding biographical sketches appear in Walter Arndt's *Alexander Pushkin: Collected Narrative and Lyrical Poetry* (Ann Arbor, MI: Ardis Publishing Co., 1984); *Alexander Pushkin: Complete Prose Fiction*, tr. Paul Debreczeny (Stanford: Stanford University Press, 1984); and *The History of Pugachev*, tr. Earl Sampson (Ann Arbor, MI: Ardis Publishing Co., 1984).

Evaluation of Selected Biographies

Simmons, Ernest J. *Pushkin*. Cambridge: Cambridge University Press, 1937. Simmons' massive and highly readable biography studies Pushkin "as a man, as a poet, and as a historical figure." Simmons incorporates apposite quotations from Pushkin's works to whet the literary appetite, and the book is thoroughly annotated and supported by a comprehensive, though now dated, Russian and English bibliography.

Troyat, Henri, *Pushkin*. tr. Nancy Amphoux. 1946; New York: Doubleday, 1970. Troyat's keynote comes from the early twentieth century Russian poet Alexander Blok, who balanced all of Russia's turbulent history with "one bright sound: Pushkin." Troyat's humanized portrait of Pushkin verges on the novelistic, and only Russian sources appear in Troyat's bibliography.

Vickery, John, *Pushkin: Death of a Poet*. Bloomington: Indiana University Press, 1968. Vickery scrupulously documents the basis upon which the Russian philosopher Vladimir Soloviov reverently challenged the concept of Pushkin as national martyr in 1899 and concludes that the Imperial court probably had little part in an essentially private, though sordid, family tragedy. Vickery also discusses the hint that Pushkin's creativity may have been declining at the time of the fatal duel. His view, now largely accepted in the West, would be considered sacriligious in the Soviet Union.

Autobiographical Sources

Although Pushkin consistently interwove autobiographical elements into all of his work, critics agree in cautioning against assuming even his lyrics are entirely subjective, and after 1826 Pushkin remained altogether outside of his writing. J. Thomas Shaw's translation of *The Letters of Alexander Pushkin* (3 vols. in one; Madison, WI: University of Wisconsin Press, 1967) is the chief English source of autobiographical information left from Pushkin's rudely abbreviated life. The *Letters* supply an engaging and informative panorama of Russia's Golden Age of Poetry, told in astonishing stylistic variety and quintessential candor by a man of letters who knows he is also a man of the world.

Overview of Critical Sources

Forty years after Pushkin's death, Dostoevsky wrote, "Everything we have comes from Pushkin," and a loving familiarity with his works pervades Russian life even today. Pushkin's work has never received appropriate attention from English-speaking audiences, who know him principally as the source of nineteenth century Russian opera librettos. The first English discussion of Pushkin's writings is Maurice Baring's *Landmarks in Russian Literature* (London: Home University Library, 1910); subsequent critics continue to explore Pushkin's marriage of Russian literary tradition to Western classicism, in particular D. S. Mirsky in his *History of Russian Literature* (1949) and John Fennell in *A History of Russian Literature* (London: Faber, 1971). Effective new translations, usually accompanied by valuable biographical and critical introductions, are appearing; John Fennell's skillful Introduction to his *Pushkin* (1964), plain prose translations of a broad range of poems, treats the universality of Pushkin's work, and D. M. Thomas' Introduction to *The Bronze Horseman* (1982) offers valuable insights into the difficult challenge of translating Pushkin. John Bayley's *Pushkin: A Comparative Commentary* (1971) masterfully places the entire spectrum of Pushkin's writings in the context of *Weltliteratur*.

Evaluation of Selected Criticism

Bayley, John, *Pushkin: A Comparative Commentary*. Cambridge: Cambridge University Press, 1971. Bayley investigates Western influences on Pushkin's work and the wide range of literary forms he bequeathed to his successors. In the context of a creativity he calls "Protean," Bayley considers the effects of Byronic and Shakespearean works on Pushkin's dramas and dramatic poetry, concluding that the *Little Tragedies* elevate the dramatic sketch to "a climax of perfection" and "the status of a master genre."

Fennell, John, *Pushkin*. New York: Penguin, 1964. Fennell's Introduction probes Pushkin's aims, his concepts of the poet's role and function, and the nature of his own originality. Fennell lauds *Boris Godunov* as an enormous experiment in "truly Romantic tragedy," and he cites the "intense and highly concentrated psychological analysis" Pushkin achieved in the *Little Tragedies* as the seedbed for Dostoevsky's novels.

Thomas, D. M., tr. *The Bronze Horseman: Selected Poems of Alexander Pushkin*. New York: Viking, 1982. Thomas' warm and intimate Introduction stresses that Pushkin's sexual and creative instincts ran parallel, a germinal viewpoint which animates Thomas' discussions of "Mozart and Salieri" and "The Stone Guest," which Thomas considers "Pushkin's greatest achievements in pure dramatic form."

Other Sources

Debreczeny, Paul, *The Other Pushkin: A Study of Alexander Pushkin's prose fiction*. Stanford: Stanford University Press, 1984. The first detailed study in English of Pushkin's prose fiction, Debreczeny discusses Pushkin's experiments with the form and his literary debts to contemporary novelists Scott and Stendhal.

Johnston, Charles, tr. *Narrative Poems by Alexander Pushkin and Mikhail Lermontov*. New York: Random House, 1983. Kyril FitzLyon's Introduction considers "Mozart and Salieri," brilliantly translated here by Johnston, as Pushkin's answer to critics who felt about him as Salieri had about Mozart: that Pushkin was "too careless of his own gifts, unworthy of himself."

Magarshack, David, *Pushkin: A Biography*. New York: Grove Press, 1968. A pedestrian introduction that drains the excitement from Pushkin's life and times.

Mirsky, D. S. *A History of Russian Literature*. New York: Alfred A. Knopf, 1949. Mirsky's moving discussion incorporates fine, though brief, insights into Pushkin's dramatic works.

Senelick, Laurence, tr. and ed. *Russian Dramatic Theory from Pushkin to the Symbolists*. Austin: University of Texas Press, 1981. Contains Pushkin's "Remarks on the Russian Theater" and "On National-Popular Drama."

Wolff, Tatiana, ed. *Pushkin on Literature*. London: Methuen, 1970. Wolff tries "to catch the man as he works," setting newly translated prefatory material by Pushkin beside excerpts from his letters, and includes a short-title catalog of non-Russian books in Pushkin's library.

Yarmolinsky, Avrahm, ed. *The Poems, Prose and Plays of Alexander Pushkin*. New York: Modern Library, 1936. This collection contains the Alfred Hayes translation of *Boris Godunov* and A. F. B. Clark's translations of the *Little Tragedies*.

Mitzi M. Brunsdale
Mayville State College

JEAN RACINE
1639-1699

Author's Chronology

Jean Racine born at La Ferté-Milon, France, December 22, 1639; *1641* his mother, Jeanne Sconin, dies after the birth of a daughter; *1643* father, Jean, dies; young Jean left in the care of his grandparents; *1649* grandfather dies; grandmother retires to the Jansenist Abbey of Port-Royal; young Racine sent to the Jansenist Collège de Beauvais where he remains for six years; *1655* at the age of 16, goes to school at Les Granges at Port-Royal; receives a good foundation in the classics from M. Hamon; *1658* leaves to study logic at the Collège d'Harcourt in Paris, works in the law office of his cousin Nicolas Vitart; *1600* begins his literary career with "Ode sur la Nymphe de la Seine," in honor of Louis XIV's marriage; goes to his uncle's parish in Uzès because of ill health and in hope of gaining a benefice; *1663* returns to Paris, meets Jean de la Fontaine, Molière, and Boileau; *1664* publishes his first play, *La Thébaïde*, produced by Molière's company; second play, *Alexandre*, moderately successful; *1667* Racine breaks with Molière, falls in love with the actress Mlle du Parc, for whom he writes *Andromaque*, his first great success; breaks with Port- Royal; rivalry of Racine and the Chevalier de Rohan over Mlle du Parc, who dies mysteriously in 1668; produces a successful comedy, *Les Plaideurs*, the same year; rivalry with Corneille grows; *1670* beginning of Racine's six-year liaison with Mlle de Champmeslé; *1673* received into the Académie Française; *1677* last tragedy, *Phèdre*, fails because of the cabale of his enemies, especially Pradon, author of *Phèdre et Hippolyte*; Racine breaks with Champmeslé and with the theater; marries Catherine de Romanet; named historian for the King together with Boileau; at invitation of Mme de Maintenon, writes *Esther*, 1689, and *Athalie*, 1691 for the young ladies at Saint-Cyr; the latter practically a failure, leaves Racine despondent, never to return to the theater; dies on April 21, 1699.

Author's Bibliography

Other than a *Histoire du règne de Louis XIV* (History of the reign of Louis XIV), destroyed by fire in 1726, and an *Abrégé de l'Histoire de Port-Royal* (Résumé of the History of Port-Royal), 1695, several hymns and early poems, the greater part of Racine's literary output consists of his plays. Almost all are on classical subjects, and other than *Les Plaideurs*, 1668, a comedy, they are tragedies. They include *La Thébaïde*, 1664, *Alexandre*, 1665, *Andromaque*, 1667, *Britannicus*, 1669, *Bérénice*, 1670, *Bajazet*, 1672, *Mithridate*, 1673 (of Turkish inspiration), *Iphigénie*, 1674, and *Phèdre*, 1677. The two biblical dramas, *Esther*, 1689, and *Athalie*, 1691, were written at the request of Mme de Maintenon.

The long-time authoritative edition of Racine was *Oeuvres*, ed. P. Mesnard, 8 vols., Hachette, 1865-1873. The most recent and most complete scholarly edition is the Pléiade publication, *Oeuvres complètes*, ed. Raymond Picard, 2 vols., Gallimard, 1950. There are numerous English editions, including paperbacks, the best of which are the Penguin series. *The Complete Plays of Jean Racine*, translated by Samuel Solomon, New York: Random House, 1967, is considered an authoritative edition. Also good is the Princeton University Press edition by Lacy Lockert, 1936, 1952.

Overview of Biographical Sources

In proportion to the number of critical works dealing with Racine's plays, biographies are surprisingly lacking, although Picard cites twenty between 1885-1940. The *Mémoires* by Jean Racine's son Louis, published in 1747, blurred the real Racine for many years and created a widespread "golden legend." A popular contemporary biography is François Mauriac's *La Vie de Racine* (Paris: Plon, 1928), which aims to correct Louis Racine's work, as well as to evaluate some of Racine's masterpieces. Mauriac is criticized for his attempt to "christianize" Racine. Many critical works contain fairly ample and accurate biographical elements, notably those by Raymond Picard, Jean Pommier and René Jasinski, indispensable tools in understanding Racine as a person. One of the most popular and accessible in French is Pierre Moreau's *Racine, l'homme et l'oeuvre* (Paris: Hatier, 1943). The most popular English biography is by Mary Duclaux, *The Life of Racine* (1925). Another is Geoffrey Brereton's *Jean Racine* (London: Cassell, 1951).

Evaluation of Selected Biographies

Duclaux, Mary, *The Life of Racine*. New York: Harper, 1925; reprints: 1971 (Kennikat), 1973 (R. West). Although the author writes in a highly romanticized style, and the 1925 edition contains minor inaccuracies in quotations and dates, the biographical elements are generally accurate. There is an ample treatment of Racine's relationship with Mlle du Parc, including the later accusation of poison, and la Champmeslé. Racine's role as court historian is amply treated. Duclaux gives insights into the society of the seventeenth century and quotes from contemporaries such as Mme de Sévigné. She also uses Racine's later letters as primary sources, relying too heavily on them to develop Racine's personality. The book contains no notes and a rather limited bibliography. For a real understanding of Racine, more recent research, such as that by Picard and Jasinski, should be consulted (refer to Evaluation of Selected Criticism).

Racine, Louis, *Mémoires sur la vie et les ouvrages de Jean Racine*. Pléiade, vol. 1, Paris: Gallimard, 1950. Untranslated. Racine's son Louis was only six years of age at his father's death, and therefore his recollections of his father are not personal. The merits of his biography are edifying rather than historical or even literary. He presents his father as a saintly figure, who after abandoning his early errors, notably the theater, returned to Port-Royal and an exemplary Christian life. Louis was responsible for creating a legend about the great author and a number of dubious anecdotes. In the Pléïade edition, Picard points out the errors in Louis's *Mémoires*, while at the same time noting some few reliable aspects of the work.

Autobiographical Sources

Racine wrote no autobiography nor any reminiscences. The closest material approaching autobiography is his correspondence, of which most letters date from the period after 1678. There are none between 1665-1678. Although the early letters give some insight into Racine, the author and the "bel esprit," the more numerous later ones reveal only the edifying family man. During this period most of Racine's letters were addressed to his eldest son, Jean-Baptiste, with numerous fatherly counsels. The letters are available in the Pléïade edition, with a good introduction by Raymond Picard.

Overview of Critical Sources

In contrast to the paucity of biographies, there is an enormous amount of literary criticism devoted to Racine. The passionate nature of Racine's plays has invited a great deal of psychoanalytical works, of which the best known is Charles Mauron's *L'Inconscient dans l'oeuvre et la vie de Racine*. Lucien Goldmann's *Le Dieu caché* (*Hidden God*) is a sociological study; depth psychology dominates in Georges Poulet and Jean Starobinski's works. Roland Barthes develops Racine's thought from a structuralist viewpoint in *Sur Racine* (*On Racine*). Raymond Picard and Jean Pommier stress the biographical element in Racine's works. Short articles by these authors and other classical critics of Racine are available in English in *Racine: Modern Judgments*, edited by R.C. Knight (London: Macmillan, 1963). Knight is himself the author of an important study on the Greek influence on Racine (*Racine et la Grèce*. Paris: Didier-Boivin, 1951). More recently, English-speaking countries have been attracted by Racine, although the lack of English criticism has repeatedly been noted. An important example of recent scholarly criticism in English is Bettina Knapp, whose *Jean Racine: Mythos and Renewal in Modern Theater*, is a well-documented, Jungian study of Racine's characters. Many classical French critical sources are also available in translation, as noted.

Evaluation of Selected Criticism

Barthes, Roland, *Sur Racine*. Paris: Seuil, 1963; tr. *On Racine*. New York: Performing Arts, 1983. One of the great contemporary classics of literary criticism on Racine, this structuralist study is composed of three parts. The first and longest borders on a psychoanalytical study, but is concerned with the characters of Racine, not the author. Barthes examines the role of place and space in Racine's plays, themes such as Eros and the father, and the fundamental nature of human relationships, which he sees not as love, but authority. The second part is a critique of a representation of *Phèdre* at the TNP in 1958.The third addresses general questions of literary criticism through the works of Racine. This short work, dense and poetic, assumes a thorough knowledge of Racine and his works, and adds unusual insights.

Clark, A.F.B. *Jean Racine*. New York: Octagon Books, 1969. This work is a good English introduction to Racine. The author makes no claim to new discoveries, in the biography and works of Racine, but rather to fill the gap in English criticism. The book examines the age of Racine, the state of drama before Racine, and Racine's contribution to the theater. Clark analyzes the principal plays, gives a résumé of the action, and quotes important lines, both in French and in English. There is an extensive bibliography, which unfortunately was not updated for the 1969 edition, and hence omits the more recent and very significant criticism.

Giraudoux, Jean, *Racine*. 1930; rpt. Cambridge: Gordon Fraser, 1938. This short monograph on a dramatist by a dramatist is frequently quoted and emphasizes the aesthetic side of Racine's plays. Giraudoux examines Racine's relationship with Port-Royal, and finds him more Greek than Christian, more attracted to persons than to ideas. Giraudoux examines the serious, sacrificial nature of Racine's plays and explores his theater as a drama of passion and a portrayal of incest.

Goldmann, Lucien, *Le Dieu caché*. Paris: Gallimard, 1959; tr. *Hidden God*. New York: Humanities Press, 1964, 1976. Influenced by the theories of Marx and Engels, and especially by the literary criticism of Georg Lukàcs, Goldmann aims to present a sociological criticism of Jansensim, Pascal, Kant, and Racine. Based on the idea that human experiences constitute certain significant global structures, Goldmann's study identifies the "tragic vision" as one of these, and explores it in the three authors and in Jansenism. Goldmann sees Racine's tragedies as basically anchored in the absence of God and the refusal of this world and of life, although he admits of one category in which the hero compromises with the world and life. Although Goldmann's study focuses on Racine's plays, he notes the decided influence of Port Royal on Racine.

Jasinski, René, *Vers le vrai Racine*. 2 vol. Paris: Armand Colin, 1958. Untranslated. Not unlike Mauron, but by a different path, Jasinski tries to reconcile Racine the man with the author of passionate tragedies. In contrast to the myth begun by Racine's son Louis of a dispassionate and edifying author, Jasinski identifies an extremely sensitive but generous man, irresistibly drawn to the theater, but paradoxically also to his Jansenist masters; an ambitious author seeking personal glory. He sees a parricidal relationship between Racine and Port-Royal, resulting in a spiritual crisis and dilemma. Jasinski bases his conclusions on numerous documents heretofore unexamined, and on the tragedies themselves. Even for those who question the conclusion, the text is rich in source material and literary analysis.

Knapp, Bettina L. *Jean Racine: Mythos and Renewal in Modern Theater*. University, AL: University of Alabama Press, 1971. This book provides a brief introduction of Racine's life, complete documentation on the genesis and production of Racine's plays, and an analysis of the works. It is a Jungian interpretation of the characters in Racine's plays, without any effort to analyze thereby the character of Racine. Knapp groups the characters into various Jungian categories, archetypes, and concludes with new staging possiblities according to the tenets of the contemporary dramatist Antonin Artaud, thus emphasizing the modernity of Racine's theater.

Mauron, Charles, *L'Inconscient dans l'oeuvre et la vie de Racine*. Gap: Centre National de la Recherche Scientifique, 1957. Untranslated. A contemporary work of psychocriticism, Mauron's study uses Freudian methods of analysis to determine Racine's obsessions. The dramatic situation in which a man oscillates between a virile wife and a tender mistress appears fundamental to Mauron. He also identifies two types of characters: those who are driven by passion, and those who fear it. He examines other images, such as the father, incest, and two types of feminine figures. Mauron seeks to determine the way in which the author reveals himself through the characters he has imagined. Through a systematic examination of Racine's plays, Mauron concludes that Racine was unconsiciously passionate, possessed of an Oedipus complex, projected upon Port-Royal, and he identifies certain neurotic tendencies in Racine. As Mauron himself indicates, his criticism using medical and scientific terminology and methods often reaches the same conclusions as traditional classical literary criticism.

Mourges, Odette de. *Racine or the Triumph of Relevance*. Cambridge; Cambridge University Press, 1967. The author of this brief but well-researched volume aims at an integrated study of Racine, contrary to modern critics who tend to emphasize only one aspect. She takes the various stylistic devices in Racine's theater: time, place, action, tragedy, catharsis, and shows their interdependence in creating and intensifying "tragic emotion." The book is an aesthetic study of Racine's drama, rather than a summary of the plays or a biographical work.

Picard, Raymond, *La Carrière de Jean Racine*. Paris: Gallimard, 1954. Picard, critic and editor of the definitive Pléïade edition of Racine, has assembled a wealth of materials relative to Racine's surprising career, begun as a provincial bourgeois and ending at the Court of Versailles. Picard aims to study the social aspects of Racine's literary career. Although the book seems to take the form of a biography, Picard emphasizes it as literary history, in which he aims to keep adequate distance and objectivity. This work is one of the best documented of all Racinian studies, evaluating criticism from Racine's day to the present, and is indispensable in understanding Racine and his times.

Pommier, Jean, *Aspects de Racine*. Paris: Nizet, 1954. This book by a noted Racinian specialist concentrates on the documentation for lesser known biographical information and uses letters and manuscripts of the period. It includes a study devoted to *Phèdre* and its sources. Pommier's research is important in illuminating new aspects of Racine the man and the author.

Sister Irma M. Kashuba, S.S.J.
Chestnut Hill College

NICHOLAS ROWE
1674-1718

Author's Chronology

Born 1674 at Little Barford, Bedfordshire, the son of John Rowe (1647-1692), a London barrister, and Elizabeth Edward; baptized June 30; attended private school at Highgate; *1688* elected a king's scholar at Westminster, but after a short time enters the Middle Temple and is called to the bar; *1692* father dies leaving him an income of 300 pounds a year; marries Antonia Parsons; *1699* son, John, born; *1700 The Ambitious Stepmother* produced at Lincoln's Inn Fields; *1702 Tamerlane* produced; *1703 The Fair Penitent*, an adaptation of Massinger's *The Fatal Dowry* presented at Lincoln's Inn Fields; *1704* a comedy *The Biter* acted unsuccessfully; *1707 The Royal Convert* presented at the Haymarket; *1706 Ulysses* produced; death of Rowe's wife; *1708* publishes life of Boileau in John Ozell's translation of *Lutrin*; *1709* appointed Undersecretary to the Duke of Queensberry; edits the first modern edition of Shakespeare's *Works* in six volumes; February 2, *1713-1714 Jane Shore* produced at Drury Lane for a run of nineteen nights; *1715 Lady Jane Grey*, Rowe's last tragedy, offered at Drury Lane; succeeds Nahum Tate as Poet Laureate; marries Anne Devenish; appointed Clerk of the Council of the Prince of Wales; *1706-1715* friendship for Pope leads to attacks by Edmund Curll (*Critical Remarks on Mr. Rowe's Last Play, Call'd Ulysses*, 1706), and Charles Gildon (*The New Rehearsal, or Bays the Younger*, 1714; and *Remarks on the Tragedy of Lady Jane Grey*, 1715); *1718* appointed Clerk of the Presentations by the Lord Chancellor; daughter Charlotte born; December 6 dies and is buried at Westminster Abbey; *1719* translation of Lucan's *Pharsalia* published.

Author's Bibliography (selected)

The Ambitious Stepmother, 1701 (tragedy); *Tamerlane*, 1702 (tragedy); *The Fair Penitent*, 1703 (tragedy); *The Biter*, 1704 (comedy); *Ulysses*, 1705 (tragedy); *The Royal Convert*, 1707 (tragedy); *The Golden Verses of Pythagoras*, 1707 (translation); *On the Late Glorious Successes of Her Majesty's Arms*, 1707 (occasional verse); *Poems on Several Occasions*, 1713; *The Tragedy of Jane Shore*, 1714 (tragedy); *The Tragedy of Lady Jane Grey*, 1715 (tragedy); *Lucan's Pharsalia. Translated into English Verse by Nicholas Rowe, Esq.*, 1718 (translation).

Overview of Biographical Sources

Modern scholarship has not produced a definitive biography of Nicholas Rowe, despite the importance of his work in the history of eighteenth-century drama and his appointment as Poet Laureate. A study of his life must rely on Johnson's almost contemporary account in his *Lives of the Poets* (London, 1779-1781), the summary of his life in the *Dictionary of National Biography*, and on a gleaning of information about the dramatist and his work from letters of his contemporaries. Most important among these are those of John Dennis (*Original Letters, Familiar, Moral and Critical*, London, 1721), Alexander Pope (*Correspondence*, ed. George Sherburn, 1956), and Jonathan Swift (*Correspondence*, ed. F.E. Bell, London, 1910-1914). Of considerable importance are the references to Rowe in the autobiography of the actor, playwright, and theatrical manager, Colley Cibber (*An Apology for the Life of Colley Cibber*, ed. B.R.S. Fone, Ann Arbor, 1968). An additional early account of Rowe's life may be found in Theophilus Cibber's, *An Account of the Lives of the Poets* (London, 1753). As poet laureate, a discussion of Rowe's career is included in *The Laureatship: A Study of the Office of Poet Laureate in England* by E.K. Broadus (Oxford, 1921). Most twentieth-century accounts dealing with the drama of the early eighteenth-century, and many biographical studies of Swift and Pope contain important incidental references to Rowe. The extent of his theatrical career may be determined from modern histories of the drama of the time, most notably Allardyce Nicoll's *A History of the Early Eighteenth-Century Drama, 1700-1750* (London, 1929), and *The London Stage*, Part II, Vol. 1, ed. Emmett L. Avery (Carbondale: Illinois State University Press, 1960). A sense of the extent of Rowe's knowledge and interests can be gleaned from the catalogue of the sale of his library in *A Catalogue of the Library of N. Rowe, Esq. Late Poet-Laureat* (London, 1718). Also of importance is Alfred W. Hesse's discussion of biographical records in "Some Neglected Life-Records of Nicholas Rowe," in *Notes and Queries* XX (1975): 248-253; 484-488.

Evaluation of Selected Biographies

Broadus, E.K. *The Laureateship: A Study of the Office of Poet Laureate in England*. Oxford: The Clarendon Press, 1921. A brief account of Rowe's life is included in this volume, with particular emphasis on his work as laureate.

Hesse, Alfred W. "Some Neglected Life-Records of Nicholas Rowe," in *Notes and Queries*, Vol. XXII No. 8 (1975): 348-353; 484-488. The article concerns the contribution to the knowledge of Rowe's life made by a consideration of the previously neglected Rowe Estate Act of 1706, and of the records at the Church of St. Dunstan in the West dealing with Rowe's marriage and children.

Hopkins, Kenneth, *The Poets Laureate*. Carbondale, IL: Southern Illinois University Press, 1954. Hopkins gives a good straight-forward account of Rowe's life that is valuable despite its brevity. He also includes in the second part of the volume a number of Rowe's contributions to the political and occasional poetry of the day, including a selection from *Tamerlane*, the chief character of which was regarded as a portrait of William III, and his politically slanted "Prologue" to Colley Cibber's comedy, *The Non-Juror*.

Jenkins, Annibel, *Nicholas Rowe*. Boston: Twayne, 1977. Jenkins' is the only book-length study of Rowe that is available. Although primarily a critical study, the volume presents the known facts of Rowe's life, setting his dramatic and literary work within that framework. Jenkins' study is the best contemporary approach to a study of the facts of the dramatist's life.

Johnson, Samuel, "Nicholas Rowe," in *Prefaces, Biographical and Critical, to the Works of the English Poets*. London: 1779-1781. Johnson's relatively brief biography of Rowe may be found in a number of modern editions, usually published as *Lives of the English Poets*. In an almost contemporary account, Johnson reveals the then known facts about the dramatist's life, built largely around his dramatic career. It has particular value in providing a portrait and evaluation of Rowe's personality and character.

Overview of Critical Sources
Critical study of Rowe has tended to concentrate on his major "she" dramas, *The Fair Penitent*, *Jane Shore*, and *Lady Jane Grey*, The dramatist's chronological position, as author of dramas between the tragedies written during the Restoration and early eighteenth century, and the later drama of sensibility, has led to discussion of the pathetic and sentimental aspects of his work as representative of the transition between the two eras. Any critical study should begin with the introductory material in James Sutherland's *Nicholas Rowe: Three Plays* (London, 1929). Similarly, there is important introductory material in the editions in the Regents Restoration Drama Series of *The Fair Penitent*, ed. Malcolm Goldstein (Lincoln, Nebraska, 1969), and *The Tragedy of Jane Shore*, ed. Harry W. Pedicord (Lincoln, Nebraska, 1974). A chapter on Rowe is included in Frederick S. Boas, *An Introduction to Eighteenth-Century Drama 1700-1780* (1953). A complete study of Rowe's career has been undertaken by Annibel Jenkins for the Twayne English Authors Series.

Evaluation of Selected Criticism
Boas, Frederick S. *Eighteenth Century Drama, 1700-1780*. Oxford: The Clarendon Press, 1953. This comprehensive study of eighteenth-century drama devotes a substantial portion to Rowe (pp. 1-31), with the criticism concerned particularly with *The Ambitious Stepmother*, *Tamerlane*, *The Fair Penitent*, *Ulysses*, *The Royal Convert*, *Jane Shore*, and *Lady Jane Gray*. After a detailed discussion of the plays, Boas concludes, contrary to most critical opinion, that *Lady Jane Gray* is superior in dramatic technique to *Jane Shore* and *The Fair Penitent*, despite the greater stage success of the latter two dramas.

Clark, Donald B. "An Eighteenth-Century Adaptation of Massinger," in *Modern Language Quarterly*, XIII (1952): 239-258. This is a good study of dramatic adaptation in the eighteenth century. Clark demonstrates how Rowe adapted Massinger and Fields, *The Fatal Dowry*, to have it conform to contemporary taste in fashioning *The Fair Penitent*, and reveals how the dramatist brought the play in line with then current theories of tragedy.

Dussinger, John A. "Richardson and Johnson: Critical Agreement on Rowe's *The Fair Penitent*," in *English Studies*, XLIX (1968): 45-47. Dussinger argues that Samuel Johnson shares Samuel Richardson's conviction that domestic tragedy and novels are popular because they are easily grasped by the imagination and readily identified with common life. He notes that Johnson points out the parallel between Lothario in *The Fair Penitent* and Lovelace in Richardson's *Clarissa*.

Friedman, Arthur, "Aspects of Sentimentalism in Eighteenth-Century Literature," in *The Augustan Milieu*, ed. Henry Knight Miller, Eric Rothstein, and G.S. Rousseau. Oxford: The Clarendon Press, 1970, pp. 245-261. In the third part of his essay, Friedman discusses the sentimental nature of Jane Shore's suffering as reflective of sentimentalism in the period.

Goldstein, Malcolm, "Pathos and Personality in the Tragedies of Nicholas Rowe," in *English Writers of the Eighteenth Century*. ed. John H. Mittendorf. New York and London: Columbia University Press, 1971, pp. 172-185. Goldstein argues that not only Rowe's so-called "she tragedies", but all his tragedies contain substantial parts for women. He emphasizes the use by Rowe of contrasting female characters in his plays.

Jenkins, Annibel, *Nicholas Rowe*. Boston: Twayne, 1977. Ms. Jenkins discusses Rowe's plays within the context of his life, providing the reader with all essential detail regarding their productions. Her criticism gives an excellent picture of the plays discussed, with recognition of their emphasis on pathos, and with understanding of Rowe's special concern for women in his dramas. The study also provides useful primary and secondary bibliographies.

Rowan, D.F. "Rowe's Wife," *Studies in English Literature*, VI (1966): 447-464. The essay traces the historical Jane Shore through the popular literature of England from her own time until her treatment by Rowe, noting that his drama is the last important work devoted to telling of her story.

Wyman, Lindley A. "The Tradition of the Formal Meditation in Rowe's *The Fair Penitent*," in *Philological Quarterly*, XLII (1963): 412-416. The essay relates the final scene of the play to the tradition of meditation in sixteenth and seventeenth-century literature, and demonstrates how it is used by Rowe. He notes the stage directions for the presence of a skull and a spiritual book, and suggests that they provided the required framework for such meditation. He argues that when the final scene is viewed within this tradition Calista's repentance is genuine.

Other Sources
Biographia Dramatica. ed. David Erskine Baker, Isaac Reed, and Stephen Jones. London: Longman and others, 1812 (AMS reprint 1966). Contains a brief account

of Rowe that is of interest because of its proximity to when he lived. The earliest section of the *Biographia* was published in 1764.

The London Stage, Part 2, 1700-1729. ed. Emmett L. Avery. Carbondale, IL: Southern Illinois University Press, 1960. This major reference work contains a Calendar of Plays, a listing of casts, statement of box-office receipts, and specimens of contemporary comment. It is an essential tool for all students of eighteenth-century theatre and drama.

Selected Dictionaries and Encyclopedias

The Revels History of Drama in English (Vol. V. 1660-1750), Methuen, 1976-1981.

The Reader's Encyclopedia of World Drama, Thomas Y. Crowell, 1969.

The Oxford Companion to the Theatre, Fourth Edition, Oxford University Press, 1983.

The McGraw-Hill Encyclopedia of World Drama, four volumes, McGraw-Hill, 1972.

Richard J. Dircks
St. John's University
New York

THOMAS SACKVILLE
1536-1608

Author's Chronology

Born 1536 at Buckhurst, England, the only son of Sir Richard Sackville, first cousin to Anne Boleyn, Queen Elizabeth's mother; *c.1551* attends Oxford; *1555* marries; admitted to the Inner Temple for preparation in law and public affairs; *1561 Gorboduc* performed at the Inner Temple and then before Queen Elizabeth; *1563* visits Rome; "Induction" and "Complaint of Henry, Duke of Buckingham" published; *1563-1566* visits France on the Queen's business; *1567* knighted and named Baron Buckhurst; *1571* again in France, negotiates for Elizabeth's proposed marriage to the Duke of Anjou; *1572* serves as commissioner at the Duke of Norfolk's trial; *1586* purportedly informs Mary, Queen of Scots, of her death sentence; *1587* investigates for the Queen the conduct of the Earl of Leicester in the Netherlands; *1589* elected Knight of the Garter; *1599* appointed Lord High Treasurer (in 1603, under James I, reappointed for life); *1601* is Lord High Steward at the Earl of Essex's trial; *1604* created Earl of Dorset; *1608* dies suddenly, on April 19, at the Council table.

Author's Bibliography

Gorboduc, coauthored with Thomas Norton, 1561 (play); "Induction" and "Complaint of Henry, Duke of Buckingham," in *A Mirror For Magistrates*, 1563 (verse narratives).

Overview of Biographical Sources

Because Sackville led a life of important involvement in public affairs, there are sufficient records in public documents and letters by which a fairly full biography can be told. Sackville wrote nothing literary after the age of twenty-five. Still, commentators have found interesting the relationship between his many public roles and the themes emphasized in his verse narratives and the play *Gorboduc*. There is no book-length biography. Most of the books of literary commentary contain useful sections on the poet's life.

Evaluation of Selected Biographies

Berlin, Normand, *Thomas Sackville*. New York: Twayne, 1974. This general bio-critical introduction begins with a balanced account of how themes in the biography are reflected in the poet's writings. Chapters on each work present detailed readings, with a good survey of the discussions on Senecan influence in the chapter on *Gorboduc*. A very useful chapter on Sackville's literary sources elucidates his typically Elizabethan synthesis, through imitation of classical and native sources, among diverse themes and styles.

Swart, Jacobus, *Thomas Sackville: A Study in Sixteenth-Century Poetry*. Groningen: Wolters, 1949. The first chapter of this book is the most thorough biographical account among recent sources. Swart's study remains influential also in its thorough exposition of the grounding of Sackville's art in contemporary practices in poetic diction and literary rhetoric.

Autobiographical Sources
Sackville left no directly autobiographical sources. Surviving letters are mostly from after his literary period and involve public more than personal affairs. Nevertheless, Sackville's literary works reflect the political, religious, and moral themes by which the poet conducted his life: devotion to Queen and country; a strong sense of public duty and high ethical standards; a subtle awareness of the vicissitude of fortune and public favor. He expresses in *Gorboduc* his own convictions on weighty contemporary public issues involving political stability and the succession.

Overview of Critical Sources
The traditional view that Sackville is the only substantial author of *belles lettres* between Chaucer and Spenser has been substantially qualified. Poets who worked in shorter forms, such as Thomas Wyatt and the Earl of Surrey, and other figures such as George Gascoigne, now have an important place in Elizabethan literary history. In his pieces for the *Mirror for Magistrates* Sackville's epic style, texture of literary allusions, and smooth metrical line are seen as significantly predicting later Elizabethan achievements and as influencing Edmund Spenser. Sackville's two poems and *Gorboduc* are significantly of their time in their evocations of contemporary practices in rhetoric and oratory.

Evaluation of Selected Criticism
Campbell, Lily B., ed. *The Mirror For Magistrates*. Cambridge: Cambridge University Press, 1938; rpt. New York: Barnes & Noble, 1960. Campbell's introduction settles many questions about the planning and execution of this collective literary project. It also valuably characterizes Elizabethan attitudes towards the meaning of history, which are reflected intensively in Sackville's, as well as others', contributions to the work.

Cauthen, Irby B., ed. *Gorboduc or Ferrex and Porrex*. Lincoln: University of Nebraska Press, 1970. This modern-spelling edition is preferable for all but the specialist. Its valuable introduction places the play in a contemporary context and summarizes its political content.

Clemen, Wolfgang, *English Tragedy Before Shakespeare: The Development of Dramatic Speech*. London: Methuen, 1955. A chapter in this book focuses on *Gorboduc*. Clemen finds the play's center in earlier Renaissance developments in rhetoric. Its dramatic set-pieces on contemporary moral and political issues reflect the same literary world as that of the *Mirror For Magistrates*. Norton and Sackville's play stands near the beginning of an evolution in the English drama towards effective expression of dramatic verisimilitude.

Davie, Donald, "Sixteenth-Century Poetry and the Common Reader: The Case of Thomas Sackville," in *Essays in Criticism* 4 (1954): 117-127. For Davie, Sackville's achievement is not well characterized in studies of the influence of sixteenth-century rhetoric, such as Swart's. The distinctive qualities of Sackville's poetry are economy of expression and strength of syntax rather than richness of metaphor.

Hearsey, Marguerite, ed. *The Complaint of Henry, Duke of Buckingham*. New Haven: Yale University Press, 1936. This book presents a scholarly edition of the St. John's College manuscript of Sackville's two narrative poems. This edition allows suggestive glimpses of the poet at work, when the manuscript is compared to the versions in *The Mirror For Magistrates*.

Other Sources

Bacquet, Paul, *Un Contemporain d'Elizabeth I: Thomas Sackville: L'Homme et L'Oeuvre*. Geneva: Librarie Droz, 1966. A comprehensive study, in French, of Sackville's life, poetic style and technique, and literary backgrounds.

Bohlmeyer, Jeannine, "Mythology in Sackville's 'Induction' and 'Complaint'," in *Costerus* 2 (1972): 9-23. An account of Sackville's creative uses of classical mythology in language, theme, and structure.

Ribner, Irving, *The English History Play in the Age Before Shakespeare*. Princeton: Princeton University Press, 1957. The chapter "Emergence of a Genre" places *Gorboduc* in the context of the development of historical drama in the English Renaissance.

Talbert, Ernest William, "The Political Import and First Two Audiences of *Gorboduc*," in *Studies in Honor of De Witt T. Starnes*. Austin: University of Texas Press, 1967. Detailed discussion of the contemporary political import of *Gorboduc*.

Selected Dictionaries and Encyclopedias

Critical Survey of Poetry, Salem Press, 1982. Concise overview of Sackville's life and writings, with interpretations of "Induction" and "The Complaint of Henry, Duke of Buckingham."

Richard J. Panofsky
New Mexico Highlands University

JEAN-PAUL SARTRE
1905-1980

Author's Chronology

Born June 21, 1905 in Paris; *1906* father dies; *1915* enters Lycée Henri IV; *1917* moves to La Rochelle with mother and stepfather; *1920* returns as a boarding pupil to Lycée Henri IV in Paris; *1924* enters Ecole Normale Supérieure; *1929* meets Simone de Beauvoir; *1929-1931* serves in military; *1933-1934* studies at Institut Français in Berlin and works on novel *Nausea; 1938* published; *1940* serves in military, captured and imprisoned in France and Germany; *1941* returns from Germany and settles in Paris; *1943* writes play *The Flies,* ontological study *Being and Nothingness,* and filmscripts; meets Camus; *1944* writes *No Exit; 1951* writes *The Devil and the Good God; 1952* draws close to French communists, writes essay on Cold War, and quarrels with Camus; *1957* criticizes Algerian policy of French government; *1959* experiences fatigue and ill health; *1964* writes autobiography, *The Words,* and refuses Nobel Prize; *1968* actively supports students in May uprisings, associates with Maoist groups, and condemns Soviet invasion of Czechoslovakia; *1973* loses sight and ceases writing; dies April 15, 1980.

Author's Bibliography

Sartre's bibliography is enormous. His works up to 1973, the year of his blindness, can be found in Michel Contat and Michel Rybalka, editors, *The Writings of Jean-Paul Sartre,* vol. 1, *A Bibliographical Life,* and vol. 2, *Selected Prose* (Evanston, IL: Northwestern University Press, 1974), translated by Richard C. McCleary from the one-volume French edition, *Les Ecrits de Sartre* (Paris: Gallimard, 1973). Another useful translation of Sartre's plays is *No Exit and Three Other Plays,* translated by S. Gilbert and L. Abel (New York: Vintage, 1955).

Overview of Biographical Sources

Sartre's life has been chronicled not only by himself but also by his distinguished lifetime companion Simone de Beauvoir. Her five volumes on their lives and activities are an indispensable source of information on Sartre: *Memoirs of a Dutiful Daughter* (tr. James Kirkup, New York: Harper and Row, 1974) recounts her meeting with Sartre at the university, *The Prime of Life* (tr. Peter Green, New York: World Publishing, 1962) details their activities in the 1930s and during the war, *The Force of Circumstances* (tr. Richard Howard, New York: G.P. Putnam; 1964) covers their lives from the Liberation to Algerian independence, *All Said and Done* (tr. Patrick O'Brien, New York: G.P. Putnam, 1974) details their lives in the 1960s, and *La Ceremonie des adieux, suivi de Entretiers avec Jean-Paul Sartre*

(Paris: Gallimard, 1981) includes long interviews which recount the last ten years of their shared lives. In addition to Beuvoir's writings, there are good joint biographies of the two and also good separate biographies of Sartre himself.

Evaluation of Selected Biographies

Jeanson, Francis, *Sartre dans sa vie.* Paris: Editions du Seuil, 1974. Untranslated. Jeanson, a close friend of Sartre's and Beauvoir's in the 1950s, wrote the review of Camus' *The Rebel* which led to the split between Sartre and Camus. He has also authored the important critical study *Sartre and the Problem of Morality* and a flattering biography of Beauvoir. *Sartre dans sa vie* is considered by some to be the best biography of Sartre: it follows the events in Sartre's life yet also offers analysis of Sartre's philosophical thought and literary works. The book is divided into two parts: a chronological survey of Sartre's life followed by a series of interviews granted by Sartre over the years (1947, 1951, 1964, 1965, 1968 and 1973).

Madsen, Axel, *Hearts and Minds: The Common Journey of Jean-Paul Sartre and Simone de Beauvoir.* New York: Morrow, 1977. This very readable biography is based on the writings of both Sartre and Beauvoir and interviews with Sartre. Beginning with their meeting in the summer of 1929 and ending in 1976, it is filled with photographs from various times throughout their lives. Madsen's concern is with telling the story of Sartre's and Beauvoir's lieves rather than assessing the merits of their ideas and actions. He focuses on Sartre's political and social identifications rather than Sartre's philosophical ideas. At times there is evident strain in Madsen's presentation of the two lives as a "common journey."

Autobiographical Sources

Sartre's autobiography, *Les Mots (The Words,* tr. Bernard Frechtman, New York: George Braziller, 1964) was composed mostly from 1954 on, revised and published in 1963 in magazine form and in 1964 in book form. During the 1950s Sartre subjected himself to intense self-questioning, especially about literature as a way of life. His autobiography is an outgrowth of that questioning. It, unfortunately, stops in mid-childhood, though of course it contains insights about Sartre's later life and beliefs. Other important autobiographical materials include *The War Diaries of Jean-Paul Sartre, November 1939-March 1940* (tr. Quintin Hoare, New York: Pantheon Books, 1984), interviews such as the long one published in *Situations* X (Paris: Gallimard, 1976), and the text of the film "Sartre par lui-même," published as *Sartre by Himself* (tr. Richard Seaver, New York: Urizen Books, 1978). There will in the next few years probably be much personal material published, including his letters.

Overview of Critical Sources

Scholarship on Sartre over the last thirty years has been voluminous, both in French and English. There are critical studies of many aspects of Sartre's thought and work—his philosophy, his literature, his biographies, his insights into psycho-analysis, and his politics.

Barnes, Hazel E. *Sartre.* Philadelphia: J.P. Lippincott, 1973. Barnes, translator of Sartre's *Being and Nothingness* and *Search for a Method,* concentrates on the development of Sartre's thought and attempts to demonstrate its essential unity. Barnes argues that Sartre's life offers visible proof that good faith is possible and that Sartre constructed a positive theory of human relations which accords with his first analysis of what it means to be an individual consciousness in the world.

Brossman, Catharine Savage, *Jean-Paul Sartre.* Boston: Twayne, 1983. Directed to a general audience, this work describes and assesses Sartre's chief literary works in relation to the development of Sartre's philosophy. It is based on Sartre's entire production and contains a useful bibliography of Sartre criticism.

Carson, Ronald A. *Jean Paul Sartre.* Valley Forge, PA: Judson Press, 1974. This short examination of Sartre and his works is divided into three sections: Sartre's life, chief ideas, and mature thought. The chief ideas section includes analysis of *The Devil and the Good Lord* and *Dirty Hands* in terms of the development of Sartre's thought.

Champigny, Robert, *Sartre and Drama.* Columbia, SC: French Literature Publications, 1982. One of the few works which deals exclusively with Sartre's drama, this book analyzes Sartre's theory of drama and each of his plays within the perspective of his theory. Champigny also compares Sartre's plays to others published in the 1950's.

Kern, Edith, *Sartre: A Collection of Critical Essays.* Englewood Cliffs, NJ: Prentice-Hall, 1962. This collection includes essays on many aspects of Sartre's work, including five on his plays. These examine the symbolism and themes of *The Flies,* compare the theater of Sartre to that of Camus, describe Sartre's reception in America, see *The Devil and the Good God* as moralizing theater, and assert that *Lés Sequestrés d'Altona* is Sartre's look at torture in France.

Other Sources

Anderson, Thomas, *The Foundations and Structure of Sartrean Ethics.* Lawrence: The Regents Press of Kansas, 1979. Discussion of Sartre's moral theory and its political implications.

Caws, Peter, *Sartre.* London: Routledge and Kegam Paul, 1976. Excellent analysis of Sartre's philosophy, particularly if reader has prior background.

Charlesworth, Max, *The Existentialists and Jean-Paul Sartre.* New York: St. Martin's 1976. Overview of Sartre's thought which contains long interviews with Sartre.

Danto, Arthur, *Jean-Paul Sartre.* New York: Viking, 1975. Helpful analysis of Sartre's philosophy.

Howells, Christina, *Sartre's Theory of Literature.* London: Modern Humanities Research Association, 1979. Study of Sartre's criticism and his study of language and imagination.

Jeanson, Francis, *Sartre and the Problem of Morality.* tr. Robert V. Stone. Bloomington: Indiana University Press, 1980. Originally written in French in 1947 and revised in 1965, this work is still important for its tracing of the evolution of Sartre's ethical thought. Sartre praised it as the best presentation of his ethics.

Mézárox, István, *The Work of Sartre.* Vol. 1: *Search for Freedom.* Atlantic Highlands, NJ: Humanities Press, 1980. Survey of Sartre's philosophic development and analysis of concept of freedom in Sartre's early works.

Sartre on Theatre. ed. Michel Contat and Michel Rybalka. tr. Frank Jellinek. New York: Pantheon Books, 1976. Translation of *Un Théâtre de Situations.* Collection of short texts in which Sartre talks about dramatic art.

Ann W. Engar
University of Utah

FRIEDRICH SCHILLER
1759—1805

Author's Chronology

Born November 10, 1759, Marbach, Germany, the second child of an army surgeon in the service of Karl Eugen, Duke of Württemberg; *1773* is commanded to enter the duke's military academy, where he is forced to prepare himself for a career as army surgeon; *1780* is appointed surgeon to a regiment of grenadiers stationed in Stuttgart; *1781* publishes his first play, *The Robbers*; *1782* deserts the army, after having been told to stop writing for the stage, flees to Mannheim, in the neighboring state of the Palatinate, and finally hides for several months in a small village in Thuringia; *1783* returns to Mannheim, where he is given a contract as playwright in residence at the National Theater; *1785* moves to Leipzig and Dresden at the invitation of a group of literary admirers; *1787* visits Weimar, at that time the cultural capital of the politically disunited Germany; *1788* is nominated by Johann Wolfgang Goethe for a professorship of history at the University of Jena; *1790* marries Charlotte von Lengefeld, with whom he has four children; *1791* suffers from a lung infection, possibly tuberculosis, which is to cost him his life sixteen years later; *1794* begins his close friendship and collaboration with Goethe; *1799* gives up teaching and moves to Weimar; *1802* is elevated to the rank of nobility by Duke Karl August of Sachsen-Weimar; May 9, *1805* dies of an inflammation of the lungs; *1827* his remains are transferred to the Princes' Vault of the Dukes of Sachsen-Weimar.

Author's Bibliography (selected)

The Robbers, 1781, tr. 1792 (tragedy); *Fiesco: or The Genoese Conspiracy*, 1783, tr. 1796 (tragedy); *Intrigue and Love*, 1784, tr. 1971 (middle-class tragedy); *Don Carlos, Infante of Spain*, 1787, tr. 1959 (tragedy); *The Apparitionist*, 1789, tr. 1826 (incomplete novel); *On the Aesthetic Education of Man in a Series of Letters*, 1795, tr. 1967 (philosophical essay); *Naive and Sentimental Poetry*, 1795-96, tr. 1966 (essay on aesthetics); "The Cranes of Ibikus," 1797, tr. 1901 (ballad); "The Hostage," 1798, tr. 1901 (ballad); "The Song of the Bell," 1799, tr. 1901 (ballad); *Wallenstein: A Historical Drama in Three Parts*, 1800, tr. 1960 (tragedy); *Mary Stuart*, 1801, tr. 1961 (tragedy); *The Maid of Orleans*, 1801, tr. 1961 (romantic tragedy); *The Bride of Messina*, 1803, tr. 1962 (tragedy); *William Tell*, 1804, tr. 1962 (historical drama); *Demetrius*, 1805, tr. 1962 (incomplete tragedy).

Overview of Biographical Sources

Almost immediately upon his death, Schiller began to be heralded as someone whose noble sentiments and lofty idealism could show all men of good will new visions of their own inalienable dignity. Yet since his rather uneventful life did not easily lend itself to such heroic posturing, Schiller's personality was soon recast in the image of the sublime characters which he, better than any German before or after him, had so forcefully brought to life on the stage. This trend was firmly established by Schiller's first important biographer in any language, the hero-worshipping Thomas Carlyle, who wrote his *The Life of Friedrich Schiller* (London: Taylor and Hessey, 1825) in no small part to introduce himself favorable to Germany's greatest living author and Schiller's most famous friend, Johann Wolfgang Goethe. While Carlyle still had to compensate his lack of biographical information with the exalted rhetoric of his portrayal, German biographers soon felt justified by such enthusiasm to dig into and display the undramatic events of Schiller's career with an increasingly pompous pedantry. Karl Hoffmeister's monumental *Schillers Leben, Geistesentwicklung und Werke im Zusammenhang*, 5 vols. (Stuttgart: P. Balz, 1838-1842) set standards which apparently failed to daunt future biographers. The Schiller-centennial of 1859 saw the publication of the most popular Schiller biography of the nineteenth century, Emil Palleske's admiring *Schillers Leben und Werk*, 2 vols. (Berlin: Duncker, 1858-1859), immediately translated into English by Grace Wallace as *Schiller's Life and Work* (London: Longman, 1860). Though Schiller's reputation as Germany's foremost classic was eclipsed after 1870 by the rising star of Goethe's fame, biographers of Schiller continued to plow the well-turned ground only to prove that not even the most sophisticated tools of historiographical research could add further meaningful details to the knowledge of Schiller's life. The years after World War I witnessed a general exhaustion among Schiller's biographers which lasted until the publication of Herbert Cysarz' *Schiller* (Halle: Niemeyer, 1934) and Reinhard Buchwald's very readable *Schiller: Leben und Werk*, 2 vols. (Leipzig: Insel, 1937). After World War II, a time when Germans and Germanists felt the need to refocus on what in their culture still proved viable, new interest in Schiller asserted itself. Although Schiller has always been considered a peculiarly German classic, biographies in English certainly kept pace with those in German, and it was precisely during this post-war period that the last important biography in English was published, Henry B. Garland's *Schiller* (London: Harrap, 1949). Today Schiller's life is no longer thought of as a necessary or even particularly helpful key to an understanding of his work. Biographies have finally been relegated to the very modest status which the extremely unassuming and private Schiller would have appreciated.

Evaluation of Selected Biographies

Carlyle, Thomas, *The Life of Friedrich Schiller*. London: Taylor and Hessey, 1825; rpt. of 1899 ed. New York: AMS Press, 1974. The earliest important biography of Schiller in any language, Carlyle's study has stood the test of time amazingly well. The inclusion of long excerpts from Schiller's plays shows that Carlyle still felt the need to acquaint English-speaking readers with the works of Schiller. Considering the low tide of Schiller's fortunes in America today, this aspect of Carlyle's efforts should prove less superfluous than it might have several decades ago. Carlyle's treatment appears most dated not in its rhetorical flourishes nor in its surprising neglect of Schiller's aesthetic theory, but in his stated contention that Schiller's distinguishing genius was moral and intellectual and that he had turned dramatist only by historical chance.

Garland, Henry B. *Schiller*. London: Harrap, 1949; rpt. Westport, CT: Greenwood, 1977. One of the last biographical introductions to appear in English, Garland's study is clearly anxious not to portray Schiller as an unapproachable monument. The author draws a sympathetic picture of a sensitive but troubled young man in his gradual ascent from an almost violent subjectivity to the classical composure of his mature years. In contrast to more recent scholarship, Garland views Schiller's aesthetic theory to be of only minor importance. His treatment of Schiller blurs, as have many before it, the line between biography and critical assessment. Readable and comparatively compact, it can serve as a logical starting point for anyone wanting to become familiar with Schiller's life and work.

Thomas, Calvin, *The Life and Works of Friedrich Schiller*. New York: H. Holt, 1901; rpt. New York: AMS Press, 1970. Written at the height of historical research into Schiller's life, this biography still recommends itself by the modesty with which its American author refrains from competing with his German colleagues in the accumulation of biographical details. As in most biographies of Schiller, the earlier chapters of Thomas' study concentrate on Schiller's life, the later ones on Schiller's work. Freely admitting that his own estimation of Schiller has undergone marked fluctuations, Thomas brings to his treatment an independence of judgment which even today proves refreshingly devoid of partisanship. He concludes with a very informative chapter on the history of Schiller's reputation in the nineteenth century and adds a helpful survey of biographical and critical literature of the same period.

Autobiographical Sources

Schiller's art is of a decidedly non-confessional nature, so it is not surprising that the dramatist also showed an unusual lack of interest in any kind of autobiographical venture of his own. Quite unpreoccupied with himself, he instinctively shied away from anything that might draw the public to his life rather than his art. Schiller's diaries contain only the most factual of entries, and, to the horror of literary scholars and biographers alike, he did not even refrain from burning many of his notes and manuscripts. Schiller did, however, possess a great gift and a great need for establishing and keeping close friendships. A good and diligent letter writer like so many of his contemporaries, he thus left a series of fascinating correspondences which constitute an important aspect of his work. A complete edition of Schiller's letters has been published in *Briefe: Kritische Gesamtausgabe*, 7 vols., ed. by Fritz Jonas (Stuttgart: Deutsche Verlagsanstalt, 1892-1896). Individual correspondences that have proven to be of particularly lasting value are: Schiller's exchanges of letters with his admirer and friend Gottfried Körner, *Briefwechsel zwischen Schiller und Körner*, ed. by Klaus L. Berghahn (Munich: Winkler, 1973), a much earlier edition was translated by Leonard Simpson as *Correspondence of Schiller with Körner* (London: Bentley, 1849); his correspondence with the humanist Wilhelm von Humboldt, *Briefwechsel zwischen Schiller und Wilhelm von Humboldt*, ed. by Albert Leitzmann (Stuttgart: Cotta, 1900); and, of course, the letters to his world famous friend and collaborator, Johann Wolfgang Goethe, *Briefwechsel zwischen Schiller und Goethe*, 2 vols., ed. by Emil Staiger (Frankfurt/Main: Insel, 1966), a translation of an earlier edition was published by L. Dora Schmitz as *The Correspondence between Schiller and Goethe*, 2 vols. (London: Bell, 1877-1879). Schiller's letters reveal a cordial man who devoted himself to intellectual discourse with a passionate, yet polite intensity. They offer not so much a remarkable source of information on Schiller's private life as they constitute an invaluable commentary on the intellectual and artistic concerns of an author and his age.

Overview of Critical Sources

In the years immediately following Schiller's death, it appeared for a while as if the antipathy which many Romantics felt towards Schiller's stiffly rhetorical moralizing might irreparably damage his fame. Yet Romanticism itself rapidly declined, and when by 1820 a politically and morally bankrupt aristocracy restored its repressive regime over Germany, a whole generation of its middle-class intellectuals eagerly embraced Schiller as their prophet of freedom and lofty idealism. By 1850, Schiller was the most respected and popular poet in Germany, the first widely acknowledged classic in its language. What is amazing about this ascent to national glory is the fact that it proceeded almost exclusively on the strength of Schiller's personality and convictions, not on that of his artistic genius. In the flood of critical and biographical explorations which a reverential century dedicated to the memory of Schiller, there exists only one study of his dramas that has proven to be of any lasting value, Ludwig Bellermann's *Schillers Dramen* (Berlin: Weidmann, 1888).

When in 1871 Germany at long last received its political reorganization, Schiller's idealistic fervor soon sounded much less relevant. His fame started its long decline from which it has never fully recovered. The first part of the twentieth century saw the low point of his fortunes. Schiller scholarship, nevertheless, propelled itself for a while by the sheer force of its previous momentum, its emphasis directed towards an analysis of ideas, as in Eliza M. Butler's *The Tyranny of Greece over Germany* (Cambridge: Cambridge University Press, 1935), or of Schiller's philosophy, as in Friedrich W. Kaufmann's *Schiller: Poet of Philosophical Idealism*

(Oberlin, OH: Academy Press, 1942). While the same period showed increasing interest in Schiller's dramatic accomplishments, it is only after World War II that a primarily poetic perspective began to dominate with several sophisticated studies of form, language, and style in Schiller's plays. In English this trend is represented by such works as Henry B. Garland's *Schiller: The Dramatic Writer* (Oxford: Clarendon Press, 1969) and Ilse Graham's *Schiller's Drama: Talent and Integrity* (New York: Barnes and Noble, 1974). An exploration of the historical and socio-political conditions of Schiller's dramatic theory and practice, as it is pursued for example in Dieter Borchmeyer's *Tragödie und Öffentlichkeit: Schillers Dramaturgie* (Munich: Fink, 1973) has not yet found a strong echo in the English-speaking world. A good social history of Schiller's environment is, however, available in Walter H. Bruford's *Culture and Society in Classical Weimar* (Cambridge: Cambridge University Press, 1962). John R. Frey edited a bibliography of Schiller literature in America in *Schiller 1759-1959: Commemorative American Studies* (Urbana, IL: University of Illinois Press, 1959, 203-13); a similar service has been performed for England by Robert Pick with his "Schiller in England 1787-1960: A Bibliography," in *Publications of the English Goethe Society*, XXX (1961): 832-62.

Evaluation of Selected Criticism

Garland, Henry B. *Schiller: The Dramatic Writer*. Oxford: Clarendon Press, 1969. Garland examines Schiller's plays in chronological order by focusing on one of the most neglected aspects of the dramatist's art: his poetic language. As he discusses Schiller's use of metaphors, of vocabulary, rhetoric, and syntax, the author is able to delineate a stylistic individuality for each play while assessing features common to all. This important analysis fills an embarrassing gap in Schiller scholarship. The nature of Garland's undertaking, however, presupposes a good knowledge of German, a fact which unfortunately will limit the usefulness of its fine insights.

Graham, Ilse, *Schiller's Drama: Talent and Integrity*. New York: Barnes and Noble, 1974. By means of a close textual analysis of images and verbal structures, Graham builds up an appreciation of Schiller's dramatic work as an aesthetic totality which proves less divorced from reality and less preoccupied with morality than has often been assumed. The author does not discuss the plays in chronological order but instead groups them in self-contained chapters according to such themes as "Possibility," "Irrevocability," and "Integration." A thorough knowledge of the plays and of the German language seem presupposed. In spite of these forbidding prerequisites, Graham's brilliant insights could prove rewarding, when taken in small portions, to the ambitious beginner.

Passage, Charles E. *Friedrich Schiller*. New York: Frederick Ungar, 1975. Passage opens with a helpful survey of Schiller's life and the state of the theater in his day. He devotes the following nine chapters to Schiller's nine completed plays, giving information on historical background and sources, stages of their composition, as well as long plot summaries. For some of the plays, Passage also provides a selective history of their productions. One of the foremost translators of Schiller's dramas, the author is clearly more concerned with theatrical effectiveness than literary merit. Good for a first acquaintance with Schiller's plays, this introduction cannot be considered complete by itself.

Sharpe, Lesley, *Schiller and the Historical Character*. Oxford: Oxford University Press, 1982. Arguing against a long-standing trend which interpreted Schiller's dramas as the works of a highly abstract idealist, Sharpe analyzes the impact of Schiller's historiographical studies on the development of his art. The author concludes that they influenced the dramatist to proceed from the exploration of contradictions within characters to a portrayal of historical roles in their interactions with historical events. This convincing and well-written study does much to refocus critical attention and could serve even as an introduction for experienced readers, except for the fact that its many quotations are not translated.

Simons, John D. *Friedrich Schiller*. Boston: Twayne, 1981. This book is intended as an introduction for the nonspecialist. Simons views Schiller's poetry and drama in the light of the poet's theoretical writings. While this approach integrates the works rather nicely, it does tend to follow in the footsteps of those who have regarded Schiller's art as an afterthought to his theory. The author's frequent efforts to illustrate Schiller's ideas through references to other well-known writers seems to diffuse rather than focus his argument. It is surprising that this introduction for the beginner is satisfied with a brief chronology and does not contain a chapter on Schiller's life and times. Though Simons' treatment of poetry and dramas is illuminating, the overall design of this study leaves much to be desired. The author's concluding, imaginary interview with his subject represents an unnecessarily forced attempt at making this German classic relevant.

Stahl, Ernest L. *Friedrich Schiller's Drama: Theory and Practice*. Oxford: Clarendon Press, 1954. Stahl proceeds from the conviction that Schiller's dramas can only be assessed adequately against the background of Schiller's philosophy. More aware than many of his predecessors of the charge that such an approach judges art by extraneous standards, Stahl nevertheless traces the connection between Schiller's idealistic doctrines and the conduct of his tragic heroes and finds that they often influenced one another. For Stahl, Schiller's characters enact modes of behavior which have been conceived by the dramatist as ideal symbols of universal conflicts, not as expressions of historical or psychological predicaments. Though an important, informative, and lucidly argued book, Stahl's analysis seems weighed all too heavily in favor of a philosophical perspective and, for this reason, can only be recommended with some reservations as an appropriate introduction to Schiller's plays.

Other Sources

Graham, Isle, *Schiller: A Master of the Tragic Form*. Pittsburgh Duquesne University Press, 1973. Discusses the relationship between Schiller's theory of tragedy and his development as a writer of tragic plays.

Kaufmann, Friedrich W. *Schiller: Poet of Philosophical Idealism*. Oberlin, OH: Academy Press, 1942. General introduction to Schiller's work viewed as the expression of a rigorous moral philosophy.

Mann, Thomas, "On Schiller," in *Last Essays*. New York: Alfred A. Knopf, 1959. Sympathetic assessment of Schiller's achievements by one of Germany's greatest writers.

Norman, Frederick, ed. *Schiller: Bicentenary Lectures*. London: University of London Institute of Germanic Languages and Literatures, 1960. Six essays by leading scholars from Great Britain and Germany.

Willson, Leslie A., ed. *A Schiller Symposium*. Austin: University of Texas Press, 1960. Six essays by leading American and British scholars.

Witte, William, *Schiller*. Oxford: Blackwell, 1949. A general introduction with two interesting chapters on Schiller's correspondence.

Selected Dictionaries and Encyclopedias

Encyclopaedia Britannica, 1984. Succinct introduction to Schiller's life and work together with an extensive bibliography.

Encyclopedia of World Drama, McGraw-Hill, 1984. Brief introduction, plot summaries, chronological bibliography of Schiller's plays as well as of secondary literature in German and English.

Joachim J. Scholz
Washington College

ARTHUR SCHNITZLER
1862-1931

Author's Chronology

Born 15 May 1862 in Vienna to Dr. Johann Schnitzler and his wife Louise, née Markbreiter; *1879* attends medical school at University of Vienna; *1885* becomes doctor of medicine; residency at General Hospital in Vienna, working in internal medicine, psychiatry, dermatology and syphilis; *1888* travels to London, Paris, Copenhagen to study; *1893* begins private practice after death of father; *1893-1894* chooses writing as his profession; *1901* demotion by military court of honor for writing "None but the Brave"; *1902* son Heinrich born; *1903* marries Olga Gussmann; *1909* daughter Lili born; *1921* separation from Olga; *1928* daughter's suicide; 21 October 1931 dies of heart attack in Vienna.

Author's Bibliography

Schnitzler's fame and popularity are due to a score of plays which have gained international recognition, if not notoriety. The cycle of one-act plays entitled *Anatol*, 1893, tr. 1911; *Light-O'-Love*, 1895, tr. 1912; *The Green Cockatoo*, 1898, tr. 1913; and *Hands Around*, 1900, tr. 1929; have become staples of the theatrical repertory and inspired versions for cinema and television as well. A premature edition of Schnitzler's collected works to commemorate his fiftieth birthday appeared 1912-1913, including the dramatic works, *Die Theaterstücke*, in four volumes; on the one-hundreth anniversary of his birth a two-volume edition of plays was published as *Die dramatischen Werke*. While there are several extant anthologies of Schnitzler's plays in English, one can also count nearly twenty separate works of drama and prose currently available in translation. Volume 55 of The German Library (Continuum Publishing, 1983), offers a fine selection of Schnitzler's plays and stories, edited by the literary scholar Egon Schwarz.

Overview of Biographical Sources

Due to the titilating, if not salacious nature of many of his plays, Schnitzler's works have often been a center of attention and even scandal. Frequent bouts with censorship, indeed riots during actual theatrical performances, guaranteed a curious public. However, since Schnitzler himself was reluctant to expose his own life to public scrutiny, early critics were forced to concentrate on his literary production, thus either damning him for his supposed preoccupation with eroticism or attempting to rehabilitate his image through scholarly interpretations of his works. In addition, the friendship with Sigmund Freud and Schnitzler's own knowledge of psychology have proven to be fruitful areas for investigation.

With the posthumous publication of the autobiography of his early years (*Jugend in Wien*) in 1968, as well as the appearance in print of significant correspondence and diary entries in the early 1980s, present Schnitzler biographers now possess a more detailed, accurate picture of the man and the writer; for this reason a major reassessment is long overdue. The biographies in English listed below—concentrating almost exclusively on the plays and their reception—offer a tantalizing yet frustratingly incomplete glimpse of this major dramatist's life.

Evaluation of Selected Biographies

Liptzin, Sol, *Arthur Schnitzler*. New York: Prentice-Hall, 1932. Although Schnitzler had died only shortly before the appearance of Liptzin's book, this authoritative work is remarkably complete in its discussion of the Austrian's *oeuvre*. Despite its size, the book does not present a detailed biography as such, honoring Schnitzler's own abrupt utterance: "I was born in 1862 and was a physician." Instead, Schnitzler's life and works are discussed according to the major recurring themes such as love, marriage, morality, and mortality as they appear in his literature. This volume includes neither critical literature nor a bibliography, yet due to Liptzin's insights and elegant style the reader gains perhaps a greater understanding of the dramatist than could be attained through conventional means.

Swales, Martin, *Arthur Schnitzler: A Critical Study*. Oxford: Clarendon Press, 1971. Following an introduction into the world of Viennese culture at the turn of the century—and thus into Schnitzler's milieu—Swales investigates the social, moral, and existential facets of the author's work. Representative plays are utilized as case studies with which to clarify seven broad themes such as ambiguity, psychoanalysis, language, comedy, and tragedy, among others. While not blind to Schnitzler's shortcomings, Swales ably demonstrates the author's concerns and his artistic successes, thus offering a lengthy, studied commentary on Schnitzler's place in literature. An index and footnotes throughout the text provide the only assistance to the interested reader.

Urbach, Reinhard, *Arthur Schnitzler*. trans. by Donald Daviau. World Dramatists Series. New York: Frederick Ungar, 1973. The detailed chronology and lengthy introduction provide biographical information on Schnitzler's life, though the strength of this book lies elsewhere. Urbach discusses each dramatic work individually, including production history of the major plays, pertinent excerpts from Schnitzler's correspondence, as well as international critical reception over the years; a limited bibliography, including English translations of the major plays, is located at the conclusion. Though the language and style is at times clumsy, this volume can be read profitably, especially when used in conjunction with Liptzin's—the two books are at times complementary, at times divergent in their opinions: where Liptzin sees Schnitzler as a philosopher, for example, Urbach considers the man more a social critic and moralist.

Autobiographical Sources

The bulk of Schnitzler's writings are accessible only in German, including early autobiographical writings published as *Jugend in Wien* and edited by his son Heinrich, diaries from 1909 through 1916 in two volumes, as well as correspondence with Rilke, Hofmannsthal, and other significant writers of his day. Two volumes of Schnitzler's letters are, however, useful to readers seeking information in English:

The Correspondence of Arthur Schnitzler and Raoul Auernheimer. eds. Donald G. Daviau & Jorun B. Johns. Chapel Hill: University of North Carolina Press, 1972. The modest number of letters, encompassing the years from 1906 to 1931, are reproduced in German; however, the thoughtful introduction and the detailed end notes provide insights into the views and attitudes of these two writers of *Jung-Wien*.

The Letters of Arthur Schnitzler to Hermann Bahr. ed. Donald G. Daviau. Chapel Hill: University of North Carolina Press, 1978. Though the correspondence itself (dated 1893-1931) is retained in the original German, the extensive introduction, abundant end notes, and selective bibliography circumscribe both authors' lives and works.

Overview of Critical Sources

While not as extensive as that in German, the critical literature in English concerning Schnitzler's work includes examination of specific works and influences, as well as thoughtful evaluation of his place in German drama and on the world stage. As these books and essays attest, the attempt to rehabilitate Schnitzler's dramatic reputation through scholarly studies and the fascination with the man himself continue unabated.

Evaluation of Selected Criticism

Allen, Richard H. *An Annotated Arthur Schnitzler Bibliography*. Chapel Hill: University of North Carolina Press, 1966. An indispensable work for the serious student, this volume contains a brief survey of Schnitzler's life and works, a chronology of primary works, translations, criticism and reviews in German, English, and French from 1879 to 1965. Allen's bibliography has been supplemented in subsequent issues of *Modern Austrian Literature*.

Daviau, Donald G. ed. *Modern Austrian Literature* (Special Arthur Schnitzler Issue), X, nos. 3/4 (1977). This nearly 350-page issue is devoted to Schnitzleriana, with several illustrations of the dramatist. Of the seventeen contributions, four English-language essays will prove of value to interested readers. Frederick J. Beharriell's piece initially recounts the prevailing opinion that Schnitzler created ideas first and invented characters later to illustrate his literary "case studies"—here the point is convincingly made that many personal experiences and acquaintances may have influenced the outcome of major works. As a supplement to his book of 1971, Martin Swales examines *The Far Land* as one of Schnitzler's finest tragi-comedies. Murray H. Sherman offers psychoanalytic insights into the Austrian's writings by relating Theodor Reik and Sigmund Freud to Schnitzler. On a complementary note, Wolfgang Nehring dismisses the commercialized image of Schnitzler as Freud's *alter ego*.

Reichert, Herbert W. and Herman Salinger, eds. *Studies in Arthur Schnitzler*. Chapel Hill: University of North Carolina Press, 1963. Three essays in this volume prove mildly stimulating: Lore B. Foltin's piece on the meaning of death in Schnitzler's works, i.e., that of purification or of strengthening human bonds; Herbert W. Reichert's attempt to establish Nietzsche's influence on Schnitzler in a provocative if unconvincing article; finally, the most ambitious contribution, Robert A. Kann's exposition on the image of the Austrian in Schnitzler's writings, charting the variety of native types as depicted in representative works.

Other Sources
Alexander, Theodor W. "Olga Waissnix: The Model for the Character of the Married Woman in the Early Works of Arthur Schnitzler," in *Modern Austrian Literature*, 7 (1974): 99-107. Alexander's brief essay offers fascinating insights into Schnitzler's private affairs while tracing these autobiographical elements in the dramatist's early plays.

Beharriell, Frederick J. "Arthur Schnitzler's Range of Theme," in *Monatshefte für deutschen Unterricht*, XXXXIII (1951): 301-311. Beharriell challenges the notion of Schnitzler's preoccupation with love and sex, and that the Austrian portrays only one recurring theme: decadence. In support of Liptzin's monograph, this article enumerates Schnitzler's sociological, medical, and psychological themes, examines the Jewish problem and attempts to come to grips with the eternal enigma of life and death.

Lederer, Herbert, "Arthur Schnitzler before 'Anatol'," in *The Germanic Review*, XXXVI (1961): 269-281. Lederer masterfully describes the first thirty years of Schnitzler's life, prior to his literary "turning point" with *Anatol*. This essay traces his early writings and notes the influences of the theatre, various readings from literature, philosophy, religion, and medicine on Schnitzler's development, eluminating the writer's autobiographical traits in this pivotal drama.

Morse, Margaret, "Decadence and Social Change: Arthur Schnitzler's Works as an Ongoing Process of Deconstruction," in *Modern Austrian Literature*, 10 (1977): 37-52. Morse compares *Light-O'-Love* with a later novella which is thematically related, insisting that Schnitzler does not primarily depict a world in decomposition, but rather attempts to examine existing values in hopes of constructing a new social reality.

Politzer, Heinz, "Arthur Schnitzler: The Poetry of Psychology," in *Modern Language Notes*, 78 (1963): 353-372. This essay outlines the personal relationship between Freud and Schnitzler, denoting their common interest in psychology. Since Freud feared that the dramatist was his "double," he avoided meeting him, yet praised the latter's determinism, skepticism, and depiction of love and death in his tragicomedies.

Schorske, Carl E. "Politics and the Psyche in *Fin de siècle* Vienna: Schnitzler and Hofmannsthal," in *American Historical Review*, LXVI (1960-61): 930-946. During the cultural crisis at the turn of the century, Austrian intellectuals were preoccupied with "the nature of the individual in a disintegrating society," as Schorske's writes; the scholar is knowledgable and provocative in describing the impact of socio-political events on these two major Austrian figures. According to Schorske, Schnitzler depicted the cultural decay from a moral-scientific tradition, resulting in a pessimistic world-view, while Hofmannsthal sought to revitalize his society through art and is thus frequently labeled an anachronism.

Swales, Martin, "Arthur Schnitzler's Occasions: Reflections on the *Tagebuch 1909-1912*," in *German Life & Letters*, 36 (1982-83): 368-373. In contrast to the literary works, Schnitzler's diaries present an unemotional description of the events and personalities in his life. For those who do not read German, this essay may serve as an informative introduction to the autobiographical writings.

Tax, Petrus W. and Richard H. Lawson, eds. *Arthur Schnitzler and His Age: Intellectual and Artistic Currents*. Modern German Studies 13. Bonn: Bouvier, 1984. This volume contains six papers from a 1981 symposium which might prove of tangential value to readers interested in Schnitzler's cultural environment. Three essays treat Sigmund Freud, Hermann Bahr, and abstract art, respectively; the remainder concentrate on Schnitzler's prose and are thus of little relevance to the Austrian's dramatic production.

Todd C. Hanlin
University of Arkansas

LUCIUS ANNAFUS SENECA
c. 4 B.C.-65 A.D.

Author's Chronology

Born at Cordova, Spain, c. 4 B.C., the second of three sons, in a wealthy, cultured family; his father, Seneca the Elder, the well-known Rhetor, and his mother, Helvia; family removes to Rome in his early childhood; is trained by tutors in grammar, literature, rhetoric, and subsequently in philosophy; visits Egypt in his early twenties; *A.D. 31* returns to Rome and commences a public career; *c. 33* becomes quaestor, and perhaps aedile or tribune of the plebs about A.D. 36 or 37; becomes well-known orator and a popular writer; suffers from ill-health, and resigns his oratorical career; develops as a full-fledged Stoic philosopher; *41-49* is sent into exile on Corsica by the Emperor Claudius; *49* is recalled by Agrippina, Claudius' fourth wife, to serve as tutor to her young son, Nero; Seneca also obtains the praetorship and a place in the Roman Senate; *54* Nero becomes Emperor upon Claudius' demise; *54-59* known as the *Quinquennium Neronis*, a five-year period of benign rule by Nero under Seneca's tutelage; *59-62* Nero's excesses multiply, and *62-65* Seneca retreats to seclusion when Nero can no longer be restrained or controlled; these last years are the most productive of Seneca's literary career; *64* the great fire in Rome; *65* Seneca is accused of participating in the Pisonian Conspiracy to overthrow Nero, is ordered by Nero to take his own life, and dies after severing arteries in his arms and legs.

Author's Bibliography

All dates are uncertain. Treatises (mistakenly labelled "Dialogues") published regularly, including 3 Consolations to persons bereaved (c. A.D. 41-43); a discourse *On Anger* (c. 41-49), *On Constancy* (c. 55), *On Tranquillity of Mind* (c. 60), *On Leisure* (c. 62), *On Providence* (c. 64), and others. A satire upon the Emperor Claudius, the *Apocolocyntosis* published (c. 54). Essays *On Clemency* (c. 56) and *On Benefactions* (c. 60); a scientific treatise on geography and weather, the *Natural Questions* (c. 62-64); 124 *Moral Epistles to Lucilius*, his friend (c. 62-65); numerous writings now lost; some poems and epigrams; and seven poetic tragedies (*Agamemnon, Hercules Furens, Medea, Oedipus, Phaedra, Thyestes, Troades*), a fragment of an eighth (*Phoenissae*), and one the *Hercules Oetaeus*, where authorship is doubtful—all composed anywhere between 45-65; *Tragedies*, 1917, 2 vols., ed. & trans. F. J. Miller (Latin and English, Loeb Classical Library series); *Tragoediae*, 1966, 2 vols., ed. Ioannes Carolus Giardina.

Overview of Biographical Sources

Seneca was in fact one of the most renowned figures of Roman civilization—political minister, tutor, philosopher, essayist, scientist, poet, satirist, letter-writer, and tragedian. Yet much information about Seneca is no longer extant. Accounts of Nero and his reign (with references to Seneca) may be found in Tacitus, in Suetonius, and in Dio Cassius; Quintilian discusses Seneca's style, and other authors, such as Martial and Juvenal, allude to Seneca. In the Middle Ages, it was conjectured that there were two younger Senecas—the philosopher and essayist but also a second author, the tragedian. Only in the Renaissance did it become clear that this polymath was but one individual. Not until the present century have large major biographies been published.

Evaluation of Selected Biographies

Griffin, Miriam T. *Seneca: A Philosopher in Politics.* Oxford: Clarendon Press, 1976. The first political biography of Seneca in English, this study provides a detailed treatment of the Philosopher's career in politics and government. Her analysis is cautious, precise, and informed; she carefully weighs all evidence (focusing upon the ancient historical sources) and refuses to be conjectural. She finds Seneca's influence considerable in Nero's court, but overshadowed by the corruption and intrigue of the court. The volume includes lengthy appendices and full bibliography.

Grimal, Pierre, *Sénèque ou la conscience de l'Empire.* Paris: Société d'Edition "Les Belles Lettres," 1979. A large biography, Grimal deals with Seneca the Philosopher's life, philosophy, writings, and style. Considerable attention is paid to the Greek sources of some of Seneca's ideas, and his eclecticism is well-treated. Seneca's fervor to impart Stoic ideals renders him, for Grimal, "la conscience de l'empire." Only a brief section of the book (pp. 424-431) deals with the dramas.

Motto, Anna Lydia, *Seneca.* New York: Twayne, 1973. Motto presents a biography of Seneca, a description of his major ideas and works, and an overview of his influence. One chapter is devoted specifically to the tragedies (Ch. IV), and several stress the Philosopher's skill in deploying irony, wit, and humor. Concludes with a brief annotated bibliography.

Roselaar, Marc, *Seneca. Eine Gesamtdarstellung.* Amsterdam: Adolph Hakkert, 1976. This is a long, careful study of Seneca's life and personality from a psychoanalytical point of view. Rozelaar wishes to explain some of Seneca's ambiguities and contradictions in behavior, but this narrow focus too much stresses a great man's weaknesses and neuroses—his supposed fixation upon the mother, psychosomatic illnesses, *Angst* concerning life and death, &c. The picture is single-mindedly conceived—hardly a fair or full portrait of Seneca—and neglects the times and the literary-philosophical traditions.

Waltz, René, *La vie politique de Sénèque.* Paris: Librairie Académique, 1909. This is an early major biography, scholarly, well-documented and gracefully written, which emphasizes Seneca's key role in politics in the Neronian era. It also presents a broad view of Seneca's environment, social and intellectual, in first-century Rome.

Autobiographical Sources

In his essays and letters, Seneca occasionally refers to himself, but he does so obliquely, and he often refers to events that have occurred at an earlier period of time. He never retails gossip, and is remarkably laconic and reserved about many personal and almost all public affairs. This silence is not surprising in an era of the early empire that had witnessed a series of rulers—Tiberius, Caligula, Claudius, Nero—who were volatile, violent, spiteful, murderous, and deranged. Seneca sometimes lightly mocks himself; at times alludes to his illnesses. Throughout his writings (including his plays) he is concerned with clemency, with the control of fury and violence, and with meditations upon the themes of insecurity and death; such concerns patently reflect the dangers and instabilities of the contemporary milieu. The best Latin edition of his letters is the *Annaei Senecae Ad Lucilium Epistulae Morales*, 2 vols., ed. L. D. Reynolds (Oxford: Clarendon Press, 1965); and the standard Latin/English text is the Loeb edition, *Ad Lucilium Epistulae Morales*, 3 vols., ed. R. M. Gummere (New York: G. P. Putnam's Sons, 1917-1925).

Overview of Critical Sources

Throughout the eighteenth and nineteenth centuries, it became commonplace to disparage Senecan drama. Scholars conceded that his plays, characters, themes, and ideas had exerted a signal influence upon Renaissance drama, but they thought him overrated. He was too often compared minutely with the great Greek playwrights of Fifth-Century Athens—Aeschylus, Sophocles, Euripides—and his work found unlike theirs; it was assumed that he had sought to imitate the Greeks but had done so ineffectually. Hence, Seneca was examined chiefly as a Stoic and a rhetorician; most studies explored, in the plays, his moralizings and his oratory. Increasingly in this century, however, there has been a turnabout. His works are valued because they are the only extant Roman tragedies to come down to us. But most importantly, they have an intrinsic value of their own. T. S. Eliot wrote a pair of essays favoring Seneca in 1927, and more and more critics are coming to recognize his worth, slowly discovering that Seneca has created a species of theatre all his own. Such drama—mannered, melodramatic, taut, expressionist, and grotesque—constitutes a genre in its own right, one that appeals particularly to the twentieth-century sensibility. As a result, appreciation of Senecan theatre is currently enjoying an unprecedented revival.

Evaluation of Selected Criticism

Braden, Gordon, *Renaissance Tragedy and the Senecan Tradition*. New Haven: Yale University Press, 1985. Senecan influence upon Renaissance and Elizabethan tragedy had long been thought to be substantial (see John W. Cunliffe's *The Influence of Seneca on Elizabethan Tragedy*, 1893), but several scholars over the last forty years have been challenging that claim. Braden demonstrates that there was a broad "Senecan tradition" in the Renaissance of the hero, of classical selfhood expressed through the exercise of anger, and of the response of underlings who practice Stoic endurance and withdrawal from such tyranny into the self. All of these attitudes were popular upon the stage in almost every one of the European nations during the Renaissance. His book traces these traditions; well-documented and scholarly; interesting but often largely conjectural.

Henry, Denis, and Elisabeth Henry, *The Mask of Power: Seneca's Tragedies and Imperial Rome*. Chicago: Bolchazy-Carducci, 1985. An interesting study treating Seneca's dramas as meaningful artistic productions. The book focuses upon Seneca's imaginative intensity, especially as he creates striking recurrent images and themes concerned with violence, death, and disintegration. His depressing subjects, the authors feel, reflect the Neronian age, where mad emperors have donned "the mask of power."

Herington, C. J. "Senecan Tragedy," in *Arion* 5 (1966): 422-471. A most influential essay, praising Seneca for his creative image-making and for the fatal power with which his dramas present a protagonist's loss of control until there is an explosion of fury and ire.

Herrmann, Léon, *Le théâtre de Sénèque*. Paris: Sociétè d'Edition "Les Belles Lettres," 1924. The first major study in our era to treat Seneca with respect and to value his dramas. Herrmann discusses general problems relating to Senecan drama, such as the dating of the plays, consideration of whether the plays were acted or not, and evaluation of Greek influence. He is best in treating characters, ideas, *topoi*, but his method of flitting from play to play, from topic to topic, again and again, renders the volume discontinuous and uneven.

Lefèvre, Eckard, ed. *Senecas Tragödien*. Darmstadt: Wissenschaftliche Buchgesellschaft, 1972. A large collection of essays by various hands on Seneca's plays, including nine overviews of all the plays, and several essays on each of the individual plays, together with an apt introduction and an extensive bibliography.

Mendell, Clarence W. *Our Seneca*. New Haven: Yale University Press, 1941. A general but often digressive appreciation, without scholarly annotation. The volume devotes much time to comparisons of Senecan theatre with that of the Greek dramatists. Each chapter studies particular conventions in the Senecan plays, such as prologues, dialogue, choruses, deities, ghosts, and ideas, concluding with verse translations of the *Oedipus* plays of Sophocles and Seneca.

Motto, Anna Lydia and John R. Clark, *Senecan Tragedy*. Las Palmas, Spain: Adolf M. Hakkert, 1986. The authors stress the artistry in Seneca's plays. Each chapter is devoted to the analysis of a given play. A conclusion traces the several major recurrent patterns Seneca employs in shaping the plots and characters of his plays. Particular attention is paid throughout to the anti-heroic world Seneca portrays, where small, furious men run amuck—a far cry from the noble world of mythic heroism. A lengthy bibliography is included.

Regenbogen, Otto, *Schmerz und Tod in den Tragödien Senecas* (1927-1928), 2nd ed. Darmstadt: Wissenschaftliche Buchgesellschaft, 1963. A most notable brief study; Regenbogen explores the imagery and themes of pain, suffering, and death which saturate the plays. He openly concedes the power and effectiveness of the dramas, praising them as significant psychological studies of human characters in torment.

Other Sources

Boyle, A. J. ed. "Seneca Tragicus," in *Ramus* 12 (1983). An entire issue of a journal devoted to 12 essays, by various hands, upon Senecan drama.

Coffey, Michael, "Senecan Tragedies, including pseudo-Senecan Octavia and Epigrams attributed to Seneca. Report for the years 1922-1955," in *Lustrum* 2 (1957): 113-86. A useful annotated bibliography of 34 years of scholarship.

Jacquot, Jean, ed. *Les Tragédies de Sénèque et le théâtre de la Renaissance*. Paris: Editions du Centre national de la recherche scientifique, 1964. Useful essay collection.

Kiefer, Frederick, "Seneca's Influence on Elizabethan Tragedy: An Annotated Bibliography," in *Research Opportunities in Renaissance Drama*, 21 (1978): 17-34. Important bibliography on the question of influence.

Lefèvre, Eckard, ed. *Der Einfluss Senecas auf das europäische Drama*. Darmstadt: Wissenschaftliche Buchgesellschaft, 1978. Convenient collection of essays on Seneca's influence.

Nicoll, Allardyce, *World Drama, from Aeschylus to Anouilh*, rev. ed. Barnes & Noble, 1976. Stresses that Seneca is writing at the "end" of a tradition, and finds his dramas something of a "puzzle," and essentially unworthy of analysis.

Oldfather, Guilielmo Abbott, Arthuro Stanley Pease, Howardo Vernon Canter. *Index Verborum Quae in Senecae Fabulis Necnon in Octavia Praetexta Reperiuntur*. Urbana: University of Illinois Studies in Language and Literature, IV. ii, 1918. Useful word index to all the plays.

Pratt, Norman T., Jr. "Major Systems of Figurative Language in Senecan Melodrama," in *Transactions of the American Philological Association*, 94 (1963): 199-

234. Extremely useful essay listing clusters of recurrent images in each of Seneca's major plays.

Tarrant, R. J. "Senecan Drama and Its Antecedents," in *Harvard Studies in Classical Philology*, 82 (1978): 213-263. Important study of origins of late Roman tragedy. Tarrant emphasizes Seneca's debts to Hellenistic tragedy, to New Comedy, and especially to the Augustan tragic writers—Asinius Pollio, Varius, and Ovid.

Selected Dictionaries and Encyclopedias

The Cambridge History of Classical Literature, II: *Latin Literature*, Cambridge University Press, 1982. Important lengthy critical essay on Seneca's life, thought, style, and works by C. J. Herington.

Magill's Bibliography of Literary Criticism, Salem Press, 1979. Very brief bibliography of criticism of the tragedies in English.

The Oxford Classical Dictionary, 2nd ed. Clarendon Press, 1970. Extensive critical essay on Seneca's life and works, with a brief bibliography.

Anna Lydia Motto
John R. Clark
University of South Florida

WILLIAM SHAKESPEARE
1564-1616

Author's Chronology

Born April 23, 1564, Stratford-upon-Avon, England, of John Shakespeare, a glover, and Mary Arden Shakespeare; *1582* married Anne Hathaway; May 26, *1583*, first child (Susanna) baptized; February 2, *1585*, twins Hamnet and Judith christened; ca. *1590* goes to London; *1592* Greene's attack against "upstart crow"; *1593 Venus and Adonis* published; *1596* coat of arms granted, his son Hamnet dies;*1597* buys New Place in Stratford; *1603 Hamlet* Q1 published; *1612* retires to Stratford; April 23, *1616* dies, buried in Holy Trinity Church, Stratford; *1623* collected plays published (First Folio).

Author's Bibliography (selected)

The Comedy of Errors, 1591 (comedy); *Romeo and Juliet*, 1596 (tragedy); *Henry IV, Parts I and II*, 1597-1598 (history); *Julius Caesar*, 1599 (tragedy); *Twelfth Night*, 1600 (comedy); *Hamlet*, 1601 (tragedy); *Othello*, 1603 (tragedy); *King Lear*, 1605 (tragedy); *Macbeth*, 1606 (tragedy); *The Tempest*, 1612 (romance).

Overview of Biographical Sources

Although actual documents and verifiable facts directly concerning Shakespeare's life are far from abundant—they are totally lacking for the period between 1585 and 1592—biographies of the English National Poet are legion. Initiating a practice that has endured to the present day, Shakespeare's first editor, Nicolas Rowe, prefaced a "Life" of the dramatist to his edition of the plays in 1709. Seventeenth century biographical notices aside, this is the first true biography, and it incorporates some of the traditions, such as Shakespeare's attendance at Stratford Grammar School, that have since been generally accepted. It also incorporates less likely legends, such as the story of young Shakespeare's deer poaching at Charlecote Manor or Queen Elizabeth's asking him to write a play about Falstaff in love (*The Merry Wives of Windsor*). This mixture of fact, tradition, and myth is discernible in almost every biography, as recorded in S. Schoenbaum's extensive and invaluable volume, *Shakespeare's Lives* (Oxford: Clarendon Press, 1970). Schoenbaum's *William Shakespeare: A Documentary Life* (1975), supplemented by *William Shakespeare: Records and Images* (New York: Oxford University Press, 1981), is now the standard biography, although Sir E. K. Chambers, *William Shakespeare: A Study of Facts and Problems* (1930), 2 vols., is still a very useful study. Of the anti-Stratfordians—those who refuse to accept William Shakespeare as the author of the plays and poems—little need be said. Sir Francis Bacon, Christopher

Marlowe, and many others have been put forward as the true author, but all of these various claimants have been answered decisively by scholars such as Frank Wadsworth, whose book, *The Poacher from Stratford* (Berkeley: University of California Press, 1958), exposes the snobbery underlying the views of Baconians and their ilk.

Evaluation of Selected Biographies

Alexander, Peter, *Shakespeare's Life and Art*. New York: New York University Press, 1961. After a brief introduction on life in Shakespeare's Stratford and the publishing history of Shakespeare's plays, Alexander traces the development of the playwright through four main periods, giving the relevant data for each play in chronological order. On the basis of an allusion to Henry of Navarre as heir to the French throne, he dates *The Comedy of Errors* from before 1589, and he carefully considers the circumstances surrounding Shakespeare's departure from the Pembroke's Men in 1592 and his joining the Chamberlain's Men.

Bentley, Gerald Eades, *Shakespeare: A Biographical Handbook*. New Haven: Yale University Press, 1961. This compact volume presents the significant documents relating to Shakespeare's life and career in the context of other similar documents and the background of Elizabethan customs and prejudices to give a fuller understanding of both the documents and Shakespeare's life as it is reflected by them. Bentley reviews Shakespearean biography in the seventeenth and twentieth centuries, then Shakespeare in Stratford, in London as actor, playwright, and poet, and finally his reputation. He chronicles the legends of the "lost years"—Shakespeare as schoolmaster, actor, deer poacher—and carefully analyzes the famous will, explaining the true meaning of the bequest to his wife of the "second best bed."

Bradbrook, Muriel C. *Shakespeare: The Poet in His World*. New York: Columbia University Press, 1978. Bringing a wealth of knowledge about Elizabethan literature and the age to bear, Bradbrook offers a sociological approach in her biography, as her subtitle suggests. For all its great learning, the book is written in a clear and readable style, free of jargon. What emerges is a detailed picture of Shakespeare and his milieu, and yes, still another candidate for the identity of Shakespeare's Dark Lady of the Sonnets, Winifred Burbage, wife of Shakespeare's colleague, Richard Burbage.

Chambers, Sir Edmund Kerchever, *William Shakespeare: A Study of Facts and Problems*. Oxford: Clarendon Press, 1930, 2 vols. This is the culmination of Chambers's earlier work, *The Mediaeval Stage* and *The Elizabethan Stage*, and his still earlier editions of the plays for the Red Letter Shakespeare. The actual biography of the playwright takes only some ninety pages; the rest of the first volume covers the state of the stage in 1592, Shakespeare's company and his part in it as actor, shareholder, etc., the composition and publication history of the plays and the problems of authenticity (for example, in *Pericles*), and the bibliographical and textual information on each composition, including those ascribed to Shakespeare. Volume 2 contains extensive appendices of documents and records, a list of contemporary allusions, discussion of what Chambers calls the "Shakespeare-Mythos," and other data. In 1933 Clarendon Press published an abridged version of this monumental work, *A Short Life of Shakespeare with the Sources* by Charles Williams.

Eccles, Mark, *Shakespeare in Warwickshire*. Madison: University of Wisconsin Press, 1961. A supplement to Chambers's *William Shakespeare*, this study carries objective biography to the extreme, as Schoenbaum notes, refusing to augment the bare record of facts with imaginative speculation or conjecture. But true to its title, it provides the information available concerning Shakespeare's native environment, his ancestors and family members, Stratford's school, Anne Hathaway, Shakespeare's friends in the town, and other items of note.

Reese, M. M. *Shakespeare: His World and His Work*, revised ed. London: Edward Arnold, 1980. This, one of the best of the "popular" biographies, is a somewhat shortened as well as updated version of the first edition of 1953. Reese arranges his material by theme rather than strict chronology, with the avowed intention of offering the general reader acquainted only with the plays the fruits of more erudite scholarship. Largely dependent upon Chambers for his facts, Reese writes in a clear and attractive style, rejecting such myths as the deer-stealing episode on the basis of known facts, namely, that Sir Thomas Lucy of Charlecote had no park and no deer in it, as the scholar J. S. Smart proved.

Rowse, A. L. *William Shakespeare: A Biography*. New York: Harper and Row, 1963. An eminent historian of the Elizabethan age, Rowse has for the last twenty years also busied himself in Shakespearean scholarship and criticism. In this biography, he boasts of bringing new and certain light to problems "hitherto intractable" through "historical investigation, by proper historical method." But he is essentially a popularizer, and his claim to have resolved, for example, all the problems of the Sonnets, except for the identity of the Dark Lady, is inadequately justified, just as his certainty concerning the date and occasion of the first performance of *A Midsummer Night's Dream* is based entirely on circumstantial evidence. A subsequent work, *Shakespeare the Man* (New York: Harper and Row, 1973), proclaims the discovery of the true identity of Shakespeare's Dark Lady, Emilia Bassano Lanier, but other scholars have demonstrated that Rowse misread Dr. Simon Forman's casebooks, the source of the discovery, regarding her physical description.

Schoenbaum, Samuel, *William Shakespeare: A Documentary Life*. New York: Oxford University Press, 1975. Schoenbaum claims to offer "a straightforward account of Shakespeare's life" together with supporting documents in faithful facsimiles in this folio-sized volume, "not shirking vexatious issues like the significance of the marriage records and the second-best bed." He is as good as his word, and his biography is at once as engaging as it is lucid and informative. The narration of events involving the curious circumstances of Shakespeare's marriage, for example, takes the reader to the diocesan court at Worcester for the special license and discusses the reasons for the license without sensationalism but with an honest recognition of the fact that young Will was still a minor, needing his father's approval, and Anne was pregnant. In this discussion as in others, Schoenbaum refers to other biographies, agreeing, amending, or rejecting views as facts and reason dictate. In 1977 Oxford Press published a shorter version, *William Shakespeare: A Compact Documentary Life*, in a smaller and handier format with fewer of the facsimiles and some revisions of the original text, and in 1981 a supplementary volume, *William Shakespeare: Records and Images*, again folio-sized, appeared with sections on Shakespeare's handwriting, the various portraits (none reproduced in color, however), and other materials.

Wilson, John Dover, *The Essential Shakespeare: A Biographical Adventure*. Cambridge: Cambridge University Press, 1933. Well to the other extreme of "objective" biographies such as those by Chambers and Eccles, this one is appropriately subtitled. Wilson gives the reader a frankly subjective appraisal, drawn from a study of the plays, the known facts, and the period, of the kind of man he believes Shakespeare really was. He emphasizes the young Shakespeare, the writer of comedies, as against the Victorian Olympian, the writer of tragedies.

Autobiographical Sources

Many biographers have sought to find in Shakespeare's plays and poems clues or at least hints concerning his private life, since he wrote no autobiography as such. The closest approximation to actual autobiography is his sonnet sequence, published in 1609 by Thomas Thorpe and dedicated "To the Only Begetter . . . Mr. W. H." Most of the sonnets were written at least a decade or more earlier and circulated privately among Shakespeare's friends. Unlike *Venue and Adonis* and *The Rape of Lucrece*, which Shakespeare dedicated to his then patron, the Earl of Southampton, and published in 1593 and 1594 through his friend, the printer Richard Field, the sonnets were not authorized for publication, and the mystery still surrounds the identity of the young man (to whom the majority of them are addressed), "Mr. W. H.," the Dark Lady who appears late in the sequence, and the Rival Poet who competes with the speaker of the sonnets for the young man's affection. Henry Wriothesley, the young Earl of Southampton, has long been the favorite candidate for the identity of the young man, but another young nobleman, William Herbert, the third Earl of Pembroke, has his champions, among them Dover Wilson and E. K. Chambers. In *Mr. W. H.* (New York: Alfred A. Knopf, 1964), Leslie Hotson put forward William Hatcliffe of Grey's Inn, London, but this candidate, born in 1568 in South Kelsey, Lincolnshire, has not won many adherents. It is possible that "Mr. W. H." refers not to the person who inspired the sonnets but the one who procured them for Thorpe, and this possibility has generated still other identifications. Finally, astute critics have reminded biographers that the sonnets, like the poems, might have been written as purely imaginative works, and the stories they tell could simply be products of Shakespeare's invention. But the poet's devotion to his young friend, his arguments persuading him to marry, the emotions generated by rivalry and competition, his feelings about his mistress, all have the ring of something much closer to lived experience, and so the hunt continues for the key to unravel the mystery.

Overview of Critical Sources

Approaches to Shakespeare's work are many and varied, and like everything else wax and wane with the times: to understand Shakespeare better, but also itself, each age discovers new interpretations, or believes it does. For this reason, the articles and books, in addition to the critical introductions that preface editions of the poems and plays, seem endless. A series of book-length bibliographies—one volume for each play, two for *King Lear*, and several for *Hamlet*—have recently begun to appear from Garland Publishing Company with hundreds of annotated entries designed to facilitate research in Shakespearean scholarship and criticism. These volumes supplement and update earlier bibliographies, such as those by Walther Ebisch and L. L. Schücking (Oxford: Clarendon Press, 1931, 1937), or Gordon Ross Smith (Pennsylvania State University Press, 1963), and are more complete than selective bibliographies, like James G. McManaway and Jeanne Addison Roberts' (Charlottesville: University of Virginia Press, 1974) or Stanley Wells's *Select Bibliographical Guides* (London: Oxford U.P., 1973), useful as these are.

Historical criticism of Shakespeare, that is, criticism that attempts to interpret his work in and from the context of the age in which it was written, is a perennial favorite among scholars deeply versed in sources that derive from the late sixteenth and early seventeenth centuries. The works by Hardin Craig, E. M. W. Tillyard, and Virgil Whitaker are notable examples of this approach. A sub-category of historical criticism includes studies of Shakespeare's language—his pronunciation, use of rhetoric, changing meanings of words—as exemplified in Helge Kökeritz's *Shakespeare's Pronunciation* (New Haven: Yale University Press, 1953) and Sister Miriam Joseph's *Shakespeare's Use of the Arts of Language* (New York: Columbia University Press, 1947). Yet another sub-category concentrates on the conditions of Elizabethan theaters and stagecraft as they may have influenced Shakespeare's composition, as in Bernard Beckerman's *Shakespeare at the Globe 1599-1609* (New York: Macmillan, 1962) and John Styan's *Shakespeare's Stagecraft* (Cambridge: Cambridge University Press, 1967).

Character studies is another perennial favorite among critics, for a while falling into disfavor as the New Criticism analyzed the fallacies of the approach, notably in L. C. Knights's landmark essay, "How Many Children Had Lady Macbeth?"

(1933). Although approaches from the standpoint of psychological realism inevitably involve the critic in methodological and other problems, psychoanalytical criticism of Shakespeare's works remains attractive to some scholars and has produced books like Norman Holland's *Psychoanalysis and Shakespeare* (London: Chatto and Windus, 1966). Studies of Shakespeare's use of imagery may also lead to insights about Shakespeare the man, as Caroline Spurgeon's pioneer work, *Shakespeare's Imagery and What It Tells Us* (Cambridge University Press, 1935), claims; but more often investigations of this sort properly limit themselves to showing how image patterns reflect thematic developments or are otherwise involved in Shakespeare's skills as a poet and dramatist, as in Wolfgang Clemen's *The Development of Shakespeare's Imagery* (1936; Harvard University Press, 1951).

Thematic studies have recently been criticized as reductivist, and the call for a more comprehensive approach has gone out, one that includes the experience of both reading and witnessing the plays in the theater. Thus, performance criticism has lately gained in favor, stimulated by the work of Arthur Colby Sprague, John Styan, Marvin Rosenberg, John Russell Brown, and others. As more and more film and television productions of the plays have become available, articles and books on Shakespeare in the media, such as Jack Jorgens' fine survey, *Shakespeare on Film* (Bloomington: University of Indiana Press, 1977), have increased in number. The items listed below emphasize performance criticism.

Social commentaries provide still another approach to Shakespeare and are by no means limited to Marxist studies, like Terence Eagleton's *Shakespeare and Society* (New York and London: Chatto and Windus, 1967) or Robert Weimann's *Shakespeare and the Popular Tradition in the Theater* (1967; English tr., Baltimore: Johns Hopkins Press, 1978). Feminist criticism has increased rapidly in the last two decades, resulting in such impressive work as the collection of essays in *The Woman's Part*, ed. C. R. S. Lenz, Gayle Greene, and C. T. Neely (Urbana: University of Illinois Press, 1980) and Linda Bamber's *Comic Women and Tragic Men: Gender and Genre in Shakespeare* (Stanford: Stanford University Press, 1982). Anthropology has lent its discipline also to Shakespearean scholarship, as in Marjorie Garber's *The Coming of Age in Shakespeare* (London: Methuen, 1981), and for many years studies of myth and ritual have yielded useful insights.

Music and the other arts have not been ignored in Shakespeare studies. As critics have become competent in more than one field, interdisciplinary approaches have gained steadily. Shakespeare loved music and uses it frequently in his plays, both directly and in his imagery. Genre studies—those that focus primarily on the comedies or tragedies or histories—continue to attract attention and have gained in depth from such seminal works as Northrop Frye's *The Anatomy of Criticism* (Princeton University Press, 1957) and C. L. Barber's *Shakespeare's Festive Comedy* (Princeton University Press, 1959). Finally, the important advances made in this century in textual and bibliographical scholarship, as in the work of Alfred W. Pollard, Ronald B. McKerrow, W. W. Greg, Fredson Bowers, and Charlton Hinman, have helped elucidate more clearly what it was that Shakespeare actually wrote and how it came into print in the copies that survived. Some of the most exciting as well as controversial work now going on is in this special area of Shakespeare studies, which quite literally provides the foundation for all other work. A good example of the kind of work that ties together literary criticism, performance, and textual studies are the essays in *The Division of the Kingdoms: Shakespeare's Two Versions of 'King Lear'*, ed. Gary Taylor and Michael Warren (Oxford: Oxford University Press, 1984).

Evaluation of Selected Criticism

Bethell, S. L. *Shakespeare and the Popular Dramatic Tradition*. London: King and Staples, 1944. This is one of the first studies to discuss the self-reflexive aspects of Shakespeare's drama and relate them both to earlier drama and later forms, including films. The analysis of Shakespeare's use of "planes of reality" is enlightening and instructive.

Bradley, A. C. *Shakespearean Tragedy*. 2nd ed. London: Macmillan, 1905. Although sometimes criticized for its character-oriented approach, this landmark of criticism brings the nineteenth-century psychological approach to full fruition. The chapter of "The Substance of Shakespearean Tragedy" contains many useful insights. Bradley treats only *Hamlet*, *Othello*, *King Lear*, and *Macbeth*—the greatest of the tragedies in his view.

Brown, John Russell, *Shakespeare's Plays in Performance*. London: Edward Arnold, 1966. Starting with the text and the actors, Brown discusses the various aspects of Shakespeare's plays that are essential to understand when they are performed. He treats such topics as speaking the verse, subtext, gestures and business, grouping and movement, and draws most of his examples from Shakespeare's "early-middle" period.

David, Richard, *Shakespeare in the Theatre*. Cambridge: Cambridge University Press, 1978. The focus here is on actual performances of Shakespeare's plays (mainly at Stratford-upon-Avon, England) and particularly on different performance styles, the function of the director, staging and set design, individual actors and their interpretations, and other aspects of theater art.

Doran, Madeleine, *Endeavors of Art*. Madison: University of Wisconsin Press, 1954. By no means limited to Shakespeare's achievements though extensively treating them, this essay in historical and esthetic criticism provides a broad context for understanding what Shakespeare and his contemporaries accomplished in drama as an art in all its variety of forms.

Goldman, Michael, *Shakespeare and the Energies of Drama*. Princeton: Princeton University Press, 1972. Approaching the plays from the standpoint of the actors and the audience's reaction to them, Goldman tries to account for "the whole theatrical moment—our entire accumulating reaction to what takes place of stage," that is, the nature and meaning of dramatic. He treats in detail *Romeo and Juliet, Henry V, Hamlet, King Lear, Coriolanus, The Tempest,* and other plays.

Granville-Barker, Harley, *Prefaces to Shakespeare.* Princeton: Princeton University Press, 1946, 2 vols. Originally published as a series beginning in 1930, these "Prefaces" provide detailed studies of the plays *as plays,* not overlooking important considerations such as versification, characterization, and textual problems in addition to the staging, costumes, music, and overall dramatic structure of the works treated.

Sprague, Arthur Colby, and J.C. Trewin, *Shakespeare's Plays Today.* Columbia: Universiity of South Carolina Press, 1970. This little book treats many aspects of Shakespeare's plays in performance, such as stage business, cutting and adding to the text, speaking the lines, and set design. The authors bring to their study a wealth of theatrical experience as scholars, critics, and reviewers of Shakespeare on stage.

Styan, John L. *The Shakespeare Revolution: Criticism and Performance in the Twentieth Century.* Cambridge: Cambridge University Press, 1977. Styan traces the development of Shakespearean productions from the extremely pictorial and realistic traditions of the Victorian age through the experiments of William Poel, Gordon Craig, and Granville-Barker to the achievements of Barry Jackson, Tyrone Guthrie, Peter Brook, and Peter Hall. The importance of critics such as L. C. Knights, Derek Traversi, G. Wilson Knight, and others in this "revolution" is also recorded.

Thomson, Peter, *Shakespeare's Theatre.* London: Routledge & Kegan Paul, 1983. The organization of Shakespeare's company and its activities during its best ten years, 1597-1607, the nature of the Globe Theatre and the plays produced there, and specific analyses of *Twelfth Night, Hamlet,* and *Macbeth* are the subject of this book.

Traversi, Derek A. *An Approach to Shakespeare.* 3rd rev. ed. New York: Doubleday, 1969. Traversi's work, here expanded from the second edition of 1956 to include the entire canon, emphasizes a close reading of the texts. The approach has influenced a whole generation of critics.

Other Sources
Barton, John, *Playing Shakespeare.* London and New York: Methuen, 1984. Actually an edited transcript of taped discussions with and presentations by members of the Royal Shakespeare Company, this book focuses on various aspects of Shakespeare's plays primarily from the point of view of acting them and with special attention to the verse.

Berry, Ralph, *On Directing Shakespeare: Interviews with Contemporary Directors.* London: Croom Helm; New York: Barnes & Noble, 1977. Among the directors interviewed by Berry are Jonathan Miller, Trevor Nunn, and Peter Brook.

Brockbank, Philip, ed. *Players of Shakespeare: Essays in Shakespearean Performance by Twelve Players with the Royal Shakespeare Company.* Cambridge: Cambridge University Press, 1985. Among the contributors are Donald Sinden on Malvolio in *Twelfth Night*, Tony Church on Polonius in *Hamlet*, Sinead Cusack on Portia in *The Merchant of Venice*, and David Suchet on Caliban in *The Tempest*.

Muir, Kenneth, Jay L. Halio, and D. J. Palmer, eds. *Shakespeare, Man of the Theater*. Newark: University of Delaware Press, 1983. Of special note in this collection of papers from the 1981 International Shakespeare Association Congress are Inga-Stina Ewbank's "The Word in the Theater" and Anne Barton's "Shakespeare and Jonson."

Jay L. Halio
University of Delaware

GEORGE BERNARD SHAW
1856-1950

Author's Chronology

Born George Bernard Shaw, 26 July 1856, at Dublin, Ireland, third child and only son of George Carr and Lucinda Elizabeth Gurly Shaw; *1866* his mother's music teacher, George John Vandeleur Lee, becomes fixture in Shaw household; *1871* leaves school to work in office of land agent Charles Uniacke Townshend; *1875* his mother and sisters leave George Carr Shaw in Dublin to follow Lee to London: *1876* moves to London; *1879-1880* works for Edison Telephone Company of London, last non-literary employment; *1879-1883* completes five novels; *1884* joins Fabian Society; *1885-1888* reviews books for the *Pall Mall Gazette*; *1886-1890* writes art criticism for the *World*; *1888-1890* writes column of music criticism for the *Star*; *1890-1894* writes music criticism for the *World*; *1892 Widowers' Houses* performed at the Royalty Theatre, London, by J.T. Grein's Independent Theatre Society; *1893 Mrs Warren's Profession* refused license for performing by the Lord Chamberlain's Office; *1895-1898* writes theater criticism for the *Saturday Review*; *1898* marries Charlotte Payne-Townshend (1 June); *1902 Mrs Warren's Profession* performed at the New Lyric Club, London; *1909* presents evidence to Parliamentary Committee on the licensing of plays after *The Shewing-Up of Blanco Posnet* is banned by the Lord Chamberlain's Office; *1911 Fanny's First Play* begins first run of 622 performances at the Little Theatre; elected to the Academic Committee of the Royal Society of Literature; *1913* his mother dies; *1914* draws international notoriety after publishing *Common Sense About the War* (14 November); is expelled from the Dramatists' Club; *1917* visits the front with the government's approval and publishes report in *The Daily Sketch* in March; *1923* regains public interest and respect due to performance of *Saint Joan*; *1923-1929* compiles collected edition and writes *The Intelligent Woman's Guide to Socialism and Capitalism*; *1925* wins Nobel Prize for Literature but refuses to accept the money; *1931* publishes *What I Really Wrote About the War*; visits Russia and interviews Stalin; *1932* begins round-the-world voyage on *The Empress of Britain*; *1933* stops briefly in California, Florida, and New York, where he lectures at the Metropolitan Opera House; *1938* wins Academy Award for Best Screenplay (*Pygmalion*); *1943* settles permanently at Ayot St. Lawrence (purchased in 1906 as a weekend house) after the death of his wife; *1950* Shaw Society of America founded on Shaw's ninety-fourth birthday; *Far-fetched Fables* becomes his fifty-fourth play produced in his lifetime (two will be performed posthumously); dies 2 November at Ayot St. Lawrence, Hertfordshire.

Author's Bibliography (selected)

Cashel Byron's Profession, 1886 (novel); *An Unsocial Socialist*, 1887 (novel); *The Quintessence of Ibsenism*, 1891 (criticism); *Widowers' Houses*, 1893 (play);

The Perfect Wagnerite, 1898 (criticism); *Plays: Pleasant and Unpleasant*, 1898; *Three Plays for Puritans*, 1901; *Man and Superman*, 1903 (play); *John Bull's Other Island* and *Major Barbara:* also *How He Lied to Her Husband*, 1907 (plays); *The Sanity of Art*, 1908 (criticism); *The Doctor's Dilemma, Getting Married* and *The Shewing-Up of Blanco Posnet*, 1911 (plays); *Androcles and the Lion, Overruled, Pygmalion*, 1916 (plays); *Heartbreak House, Great Catherine,* and *Playlets of the War*, 1919 (plays); *Back to Methuselah*, 1921 (five-play cycle); *Saint Joan*, 1923 (play); *The Intelligent Woman's Guide to Socialism and Capitalism*, 1928 (politics); *The Apple Cart*, 1930 (play); *What I Really Wrote About the War*, 1931 (essays); *Standard Edition of the Works of Bernard Shaw*, 1947-1952; *Sixteen Self Sketches*, 1949 (autobiographical essays); *Platform and Pulpit* (ed. Dan H. Laurence), 1961 (speeches); *The Matter With Ireland* (ed. Dan H. Laurence and David H. Greene), 1962 (essays); *Shaw: An Autobiography. 1856-1898* (ed. Stanley Weintraub), 1969; *Shaw: An Autobiography. 1898-1950. The Playwright Years* (ed. Stanley Weintraub), 1970; *The Bodley Head Bernard Shaw*, 1970-1974; *The Collected Screenplays of Bernard Shaw* (ed. Bernard F. Dukore), 1980; *Early Texts: Play Manuscripts in Facsimile* (ed. Dan H. Laurence), 1981; *Shaw's Music* (ed. Dan H. Laurence), 1981 (criticism); *The Shaw Diaries* ed. Stanley Weintraub), 1986. In progress are the definitive collection of Shaw's dramatic criticism by Bernard F. Dukore, the definitive collection of Shaw's art criticism by Stanley Weintraub, and a facsimile edition of Shaw's novel manuscripts by Dan H. Laurence.

Overview of Biographical Sources

Shaw's influence as a public figure and as the British dramatist second only to Shakespeare has inspired several biographies. Published biographical sources range considerably in quality and focus, including a biography for teenagers and a collection of Shaw's vegetarian recipes. Although several works exploit interest in Shaw without providing much that is reliable or useful, many biographies offer extensive information about Shaw's life.

For biographers who wrote during Shaw's lifetime, his active participation was a mixed blessing. Shaw generously provided information but also exerted control over what others published. The first major biography was Archibald Henderson's *George Bernard Shaw. His Life and Works* (London: Hurst & Blackett, 1911), to which Shaw contributed greatly (at one point writing a letter of more than fifty-four pages to inform and instruct his biographer). Henderson, whose field was mathematics, often accepted Shaw's revisions and contributions uncritically. Although sometimes unreliable, the biography contains a wealth of source material. Frank Harris's *Bernard Shaw. An Unauthorized Biography Based on First-hand Information, with a Postscript by Mr. Shaw* (London: Gollancz, 1931) was edited after Harris's death by Shaw, who apparently was willing to supply the sensational elements in which Harris delighted. Henderson updated his 1911 biography in *Bernard Shaw, Playboy and Prophet* (New York: Appleton, 1932), still accepting Shaw's additions and emendations unquestioningly. Shaw contributed information to and revised Hesketh Pearson's *Bernard Shaw. His Life and Personality* (London: Collins, 1942), which is more an anecdotal memoir than a documented biography. William Irvine's *The Universe of G. B. S.* (New York: Whittlesey House, 1949), although published in Shaw's lifetime, remains the best account of Shaw's intellectual development.

Six years after Shaw's death, Archibald Henderson published *George Bernard Shaw: Man of the Century* (1956), a massive work which contains source material relevant to the full spectrum of Shaw's life and career. St. John Ervine's *Bernard Shaw: His Life, Work and Friends* (London: Constable, 1956), written by an Irish playwright who had been Shaw's close friend for four decades, suffers from Ervine's anti-Fabian bias and from his failure to document his findings. Stanley Weintraub's *Private Shaw and Public Shaw: A Dual Biography of Lawrence of Arabia and Bernard Shaw* (1963), the first biographical analysis of a crucial period of Shaw's career, examines Shaw's life and work from 1922 to 1935 in the context of his friendship with T.E. Lawrence. B.C. Rosset's *Shaw of Dublin. The Formative Years* (1964) explores Shaw's childhood and adolescence in Dublin, examines the effect on Shaw of Vandeleur Lee's presence in the household, and relates Shaw's later work to these early years. Stanley Weintraub's *Journey to Heartbreak. The Crucible Years of Bernard Shaw, 1914-1918* (1971) focuses on Shaw's activities during the war years, with particular reference to *Heartbreak House, Back to Methuselah*, and *Saint Joan*. Margot Peters's *Bernard Shaw and the Actresses* (Garden City, NY: Doubleday, 1980), exploring Shaw's relationships with other women as well as with actresses, provides a reliable view of Shaw's personal life. Stanley Weintraub's *The Unexpected Shaw: Biographical Approaches to G. B. S. and His Work* (New York: Frederick Ungar, 1982) examines Shaw's diverse roles as novelist, critic, pugilist, Fabian, friend, and playwright. Rodelle Weintraub's edition *SHAW 5: Shaw Abroad* (University Park, PA: Penn State University Press, 1985) is the fullest biography extant of Shaw the public man as revealed through his travels over a lifetime, and also is informative about his politics, his amorous life, and his plays.

Other biographical sources include memoirs and reminiscences. One of the most useful, written by Shaw's secretary, is Blanche Patch's *Thirty Years with G. B. S.* (London: Gollancz, 1951). Alan Chappelow has edited two collections which provide helpful source material. *Shaw the Villager and Human Being. A Biographical Symposium* (London: Charles Skilton, 1960) consists of recollections by Shaw's friends and neighbors at Ayot St. Lawrence, and *Shaw—"The Chucker-Out": A Biographical Exposition and Critique* (London: Allen & Unwin, 1969) reprints speeches, newspaper clippings, and other material from obscure sources. Stanley Weintraub has edited *The Shaw Diaries* (University Park, PA: Penn State University Press, 1986), which annotates and indexes Shaw's 1885-1897 diaries.

Since he was a prominent public and literary figure, Shaw's correspondents carefully preserved tens of thousands of his letters. The most complete published collection, projected to include more than 3,000 letters, is Dan H. Laurence's four-volume edition of *Bernard Shaw. Collected Letters. 1874-1897* (New York: Dodd, Mead, 1965); *1898-1910* (New York: Dodd, Mead, 1972); *1911-1925* (New York: Viking, 1985); and *1926-1950* (forthcoming). Laurence has scrupulously annotated the letters, which often differ significantly from versions edited by Shaw for publication elsewhere. Editions of Shaw's correspondence with individuals will continue to supplement Laurence's sampling. Useful collections include *Bernard Shaw and Alfred Douglas: A Correspondence*, ed. Mary Hyde (New York: Tichnor & Fields, 1982); *Bernard Shaw and Mrs. Patrick Campbell: A Correspondence*, ed. Alan Dent (New York: Alfred A. Knopf, 1952); *Bernard Shaw's Letters to Harley Granville Barker*, ed. C.B. Purdom (New York: Crown, 1957); *Ellen Terry and Bernard Shaw: A Correspondence*, ed. Christopher St. John (New York: G.P. Putnam's, 1931); and *The Playwright and the Pirate, Bernard Shaw and Frank Harris, a Correspondence 1898-1930*, ed. Stanley Weintraub (University Park, PA: Penn State University Press, 1982).

In 1970 the Bernard Shaw Trustees appointed Michael Holroyd to write an authorized biography of Shaw. This work will draw from previously unavailable sources but will not appear for some time.

Evaluation of Selected Biographies

Henderson, Archibald, *George Bernard Shaw. Man of the Century*. New York: Appleton-Century, 1956. This was the third biography by Henderson, Shaw's authorized biographer for half a century, but the first without Shaw's control and editing. The biography updates the earlier books, quotes extensively from Shaw's correspondence and other unpublished material, and is an invaluable source of information on the whole of Shaw's life and career.

Rosset, B.C. *Shaw of Dublin. The Formative Years*. University Park, PA: Penn State University Press, 1964. Rosset's biography focuses on Shaw's years in Dublin and on the early London years. The book is thoroughly documented and researched, resolving several contradictions and inconsistencies present in the earlier (and Shaw-dominated) biographies. Rosset focuses on the influence of Lucinda Elizabeth Gurly Shaw and George John Vandeleur Lee's relationship on the young Shaw, tracing the impact of the early years in Shaw's plays, letters, prefaces, and autobiographical writings.

Weintraub, Stanley, *Journey to Heartbreak. The Crucible Years of Bernard Shaw, 1914-1918*. New York: Weybright & Talley, 1971. This is the best biographical examination of Shaw, focusing on his responses to the Great War and on the influence of the war on his masterpieces, most notable *Heartbreak House, Back to*

Methuselah, and *Saint Joan*. In additon to exhaustively following Shaw's activities and development during the period of notoriety which followed publication of *Common Sense About the War*, the book reveals the nature of Shaw's farsightedness and the extent of his personal and political courage when he was virtually alone in his opposition to the war.

_____, *Private Shaw and Public Shaw: A Dual Biography of Lawrence of Arabia and Bernard Shaw*. New York: George Braziller, 1963. Focusing on the 1922-1935 friendship of Shaw and Lawrence, this work examines Shaw's writing and other activities during the period, provides information and insight regarding the composition of *Saint Joan* and *Too True to Be Good*, and reveals the extent of Shaw's role in the preparation of Lawrence's *Seven Pillars of Wisdom*. It also illuminates the nature of Shaw's marriage and his efforts on behalf of Lawrence and others in their literary endeavors.

Autobiographical Sources

Shaw included autobiographical material in his letters, prefaces, essays, interviews, diaries, and even in some of his plays, while his domineering collaboration in several biographies also had an autobiographical dimension. His only overtly autobiographical work, however, is *Sixteen Self Sketches* (New York: Dodd, Mead, 1949), a collection of essays describing his childhood, parents' families, schooling, work in Townshend's land agency, phases as novelist and critic, development as a political speaker, Fabian friends, and religious views. He also devoted several pages to correcting "blunders" of various biographers, including Winston Churchill and Thomas O'Bolger (whose dissertation Shaw barred from publication after providing help during the writing). In a parody of Frank Harris, Shaw also provided a sample of "How Frank Ought To Have Done It."

Combining hundreds of extracts from Shaw's autobiographical writings, Stanley Weintraub compiled a two-volume autobiography: *Shaw: An Autobiography. 1856-1898* (New York: Weybright & Talley, 1969) and *Shaw: An Autobiography. 1898-1950. The Playwright Years* (New York: Weybright & Talley, 1970). Although the selection, arrangement, and annotation are Weintraub's, every word of the text, including the chapter titles, is Shaw's. The two volumes contain significant material not available elsewhere, and the notes are both thorough and enlightening.

Overview of Critical Sources

Criticism on Shaw has been prolific, ranging from general explications of the plays to analyses of various aspects of his art, including his literary relationships with and indebtedness to specific writers, his dramaturgy, and his affinity with numerous schools of philosophical and literary theory. Publications about Shaw have been so extensive that Shaw coverage in the Annotated Secondary Bibliography Series, to be published by Northern Illinois University Press, will run to three volumes.

Among the significant critical studies of Shaw is Eric Bentley's *Bernard Shaw, 1856-1950* (New York: New Directions, 1957), an updated revision of Bentley's earlier books which emphasizes Shaw's theatrical innovations. Richard M. Ohmann's *Shaw: The Style and the Man* (Middletown, CT: Wesleyan University Press, 1962) presents a rhetorical analysis of Shaw's prose style. Martin Meisel's *Shaw and the Nineteenth-Century Theater* (Princeton, NJ: Princeton University Press, 1963), the first reliable criticism of Shaw's plays through their antecedents, places Shaw's work into the context of the dramatic tradition. Fred Mayne's *The Wit and Satire of Bernard Shaw* (New York: St. Martin's Press, 1967) focuses on Shaw's use of paradox and other satirical strategies. Two collections of essays offer useful overviews of Shaw's life and work: *Fabian Feminist: Bernard Shaw and Woman*, ed. Rodelle Weintraub (University Park, PA: Penn State University Press, 1977) and *The Genius of Shaw*, ed. Michael Holroyd (New York: Holt, Rinehart and Winston, 1979). Eldon C. Hill's *George Bernard Shaw* (Boston: Twayne, 1978) provides a useful introduction, critical overview, biographical sketch, and bibliography, but several inconsistencies and inaccuracies missed by the editor detract from Hill's sensible evaluation of Shaw.

Evaluation of Selected Criticism

Berst, Charles A. *Bernard Shaw and the Art of Drama*. Champaign and Urbana: University of Illinois Press, 1973. This book is the best single analysis of Shaw's major plays. Berst devotes chapters to *Mrs Warren's Profession*, *Arms and the Man*, *Candida*, *Caesar and Cleopatra*, *Man and Superman*, *Major Barbara*, *Androcles and the Lion*, *Pygmalion*, *Heartbreak House*, and *Saint Joan*. Many of Berst's conclusions are original and thought-provoking, while penetrating judgments and lively style make his study both valuable and enjoyable.

Crompton, Louis, *Shaw the Dramatist*. Lincoln: University of Nebraska Press, 1969. This explication illuminates the plays' literary, historical, social, and intellectual contexts. Crompton mostly focuses on those plays which have had the greatest success in the theater, including *Arms and the Man*, *Candida*, *The Devil's Disciple*, *Caesar and Cleopatra*, *Man and Superman*, *Major Barbara*, *The Doctor's Dilemma*, *Pygmalion*, *Heartbreak House*, *Back to Methuselah*, and *Saint Joan*. Crompton traces many of Shaw's ideas to their sources, establishes Shaw's place in theatrical tradition, and identifies many historical, literary, and contemporary prototypes of Shaw's characters.

Dukore, Bernard F. *Bernard Shaw, Playwright: Aspects of Shavian Drama*. Columbia: University of Missouri Press, 1973. This study concentrates on the relationship between Shaw's stagecraft and his ideas, analyzing Shaw's rehearsal and staging methods. The book is particularly valuable for its analysis of Shaw's principles and practices as a playwright, revealing the extent of Shaw's attention to problems of staging when he composed his plays. Dukore examines frequently neglected plays and argues that the neglected plays undeniably fit into Shaw's surprisingly coherent canon.

Wisenthal, J.L. *The Marriage of Contraries: Bernard Shaw's Middle Plays.* Cambridge: Harvard University Press, 1974. Wisenthal provides a comprehensive analysis of the period of Shaw's greatest achievement, focusing on *Man and Superman, Major Barbara, John Bull's Other Island, The Doctor's Dilemma, Pygmalion, Misalliance, Heartbreak House, Saint Joan,* and *Back to Methuselah.* By addressing the influence of Ibsen and Blake on these plays and by arranging the plays into a linear progression of ideas, Wisenthal resolves many of the apparent contradictions and paradoxes in Shaw's work. The book brings many original insights to competent and instructive explication of Shaw's more problematic plays.

Other Sources

Bevan, Earle Dean, ed. *A Concordance to the Plays and Prefaces of Bernard Shaw.* Detroit: Gale, 1971. This ten-volume concordance uses the Key-Word-in-Context (KWIC) principle, making it much longer than the plays and prefaces themselves. Although it follows the Constable *Standard Edition,* superseded by the Bodley Head edition, it remains very useful.

Evans, T.F. ed. *Shaw: The Critical Heritage.* London: Routledge & Kegan Paul, 1976. This is a comprehensive bibliography of writings about Shaw, identifying hundreds of secondary sources and offering extracts from 135 pieces to show the evolution of Shaw's reputation.

Laurence, Dan H. *Bernard Shaw: A Bibliography.* New York: Oxford University Press, 1983. This two-volume bibliography of Shaw's writings (1058 pages) lists Shaw's works in their many editions, amply quotes from letters, presents synopses of anonymous and pseudonymous contributions, resolves several disputed attributions, and provides informative and interesting notes and comments. The bibliography is extraordinarily well proofread and also has a very useful index.

Pfeiffer, John R. "A Continuing Checklist of Shaviana," in *SHAW: The Annual of Bernard Shaw Studies.* University Park, PA: Penn State University Press, 1981-. This feature, continued from the *Shaw Review* and *Shaw Bulletin,* is a scrupulously annotated and updated compilation of primary and secondary source references, including doctoral dissertations and works chiefly devoted to contemporaries who knew Shaw.

Weintraub, Stanley, "Bernard Shaw," in *Anglo-Irish Literature: A Review of Research,* ed. Richard J. Finneran. New York: Modern Language Association of America, 1976, pp. 167-215. This extensive bibliographical essay traces book-length Shavian scholarship in the areas of bibliography, editions, biography and autobiography, criticism, and Shaw's influence and reputation, providing succinct and trenchant evaluations of both reliable and unreliable works about Shaw.

_____, "Bernard Shaw," in *Recent Research on Anglo-Irish Writers*. ed. Richard J. Finneran. New York: Modern Language Association of America, 1983, pp. 66-84. This essay updates the 1976 bibliographical essay, evaluating articles as well as book-length studies of Shaw. A revision is in preparation.

_____, ed. *SHAW: The Annual of Bernard Shaw Studies*. University Park, PA: Penn State University Press, 1981-. This annual continues the *Shaw Review* (1959-1980), which itself continued the *Shaw Bulletin* (1951-1958). The annual publishes articles on various subjects pertinent to Shaw and articles on specific themes ("Shaw and Religion," "Shaw's Plays in Performance," "Shaw Abroad") in alternate years. *SHAW* is an invaluable source of continuing bibliography, scholarly articles on Shaw, reviews of significant Shavian publications, and information on the current state of Shavian scholarship.

Selected Dictionaries and Encyclopedias

Dictionary of Literary Biography, Volume 10: Modern British Dramatists, 1900-1945. Detroit: Gale Research, 1982, 129-148. Of scores of reference articles devoted to Shaw, this is by far the most useful. The approximately 15,000-word entry includes a biographical sketch of Shaw, a chronology of performances of his plays, a list of his publications, a reference list of important biographical and critical sources, and a critical review of Shaw's major works.

Fred D. Crawford
University of Oregon

RICHARD BRINSLEY SHERIDAN
1751-1816

Author's Chronology

Born 1751, Dublin, birth registered 4 November; father, Thomas Sheridan, a famous teacher of oratory with theatrical connections; his mother, Francis (dies 1766), a minor dramatist; educated at Harrow; *1770* after some time in France to escape debtors, the family moves to Bath; *1772* elopes with the beautiful singer, Elizabeth Linley (dies 1792); they marry illicitly and then legally in 1773, Sheridan fighting two duels in the process; *1795* remarries Esther Ogle; *1775 The Rivals* is staged, immediately withdrawn then successfully re-presented on 28 January; November *1775 The Duenna*, a musical play is also staged; *1776* takes over management of Drury Lane Theatre from Garrick; builds new theatre (opens 1794 and burns in 1809); *1777 A Trip to Scarborough* and *School for Scandal* are presented; continues his theatre involvement with several minor pieces but writes only one more play after *The Critic*, the enormously successful *Pizarro* (after Kotzebue), 1799; *1780-1812* member of Parliament; Treasurer of the Navy 1806-7; prominent in Trial of Warren Hastings, especially 1788 and 1794; *1813* is arrested for debt and humiliatingly imprisoned; *1816* dies in poverty.

Author's Bibliography (selected)

The Rivals, 1775 (play); *St. Patrick's Day*, 1775 (play); *The Duenna*, 1775 (play); *A Trip to Scarborough*, 1777 (play); *The School for Scandal*, 1777 (play); *The Critic*, 1779 (play); *Pizarro*, 1799 (play).

Many editions exist of Sheridan's plays but easily the best is *The Dramatic Works*, ed. Cecil Price, 2 vols. Oxford: Clarendon Press, 1974. This includes reviews of early productions. Sheridan's speeches deserve more attention than they get but are available only in uncertain reports and nineteenth century editions. See *Speeches of . . . Sheridan*, ed. by A Constitutional Friend, 5 vols. London, 1816; and in *Speeches for the Managers and Counsel in the Trial of Warren Hastings*, 4 vols. ed. E.A. Bond, London, 1859-61.

Overview of Biographical Sources

There is a large number of biographies of Sheridan but many are inadequate, some are unreliable, and none is wholly satisfactory. A good new biography is needed. Probably the best readily available biography is that by R. Crompton Rhodes, *Harlequin Sheridan*, (1933), but that is over a half-century old and written before Price's edition of Sheridan's letters. *Sheridan*, by Walter Sichel, (1909), is even older but much more comprehensive. It is the best source biography but not easy to read. Lewis Gibb's *Sheridan*, (1947), is well-written and organized but short on documentation. Another large-scale biography is W. Fraser Rae, *Sheridan: A Biography*, 2 vols. London: Bentley, 1896. This was a 'family-authorized' study with the benefits (new source material) and drawbacks (family inhibitions) of this approach. Rae also edited Sheridan's plays (London, 1902) in which he included Mrs. Sheridan's unfinished *A Journey to Bath*, touches of which are to be found in Sheridan's work.

Certain other nineteenth century sources are valuable and still readily available. The journal of Sheridan's younger sister, Elizabeth, was published in 1960 as *Betsy Sheridan's Journal*, ed. William LeFanu, London: Eyre & Spottiswoode. The *Reminiscences* (1826) of Michael Kelly (actor, singer, friend of Sheridan and Mozart) is available in a good modern edition, ed. Roger Fiske, Oxford: Oxford University Press, 1975. William Hazlitt's essay, 'On the Want of Money' (1827; available in many editions) contains a vivid account of Sheridan's penury. Though no longer in print, *Memoirs of the Life of . . . Sheridan* by Thomas Moore (1825) is not too difficult to find and is well worth the trouble.

Evaluation of Selected Biographies

Gibbs, Lewis, *Sheridan*. London: Dent, 1947. This is designed for the 'general reader', and has the merit of being eminently readable, culling the main facts with skill. It is not always easy to know which year is being referred to, but it gives the best *impression* of Sheridan, if in an undocumented manner.

Rhodes, R. Crompton, *Harlequin Sheridan: The Man and the Legends, with a Bibliography and Appendices*. Oxford: Basil Blackwell, 1933. Despite Rhodes being editor of Sheridan's *Plays and Poems* (3 vols, Oxford: Basil Blackwell, 1928), his biography is singularly light on the plays—less than ten percent considers the comedies, though there is a short chapter devoted to *Pizarro*. Relatively little attention is paid to Sheridan's managership of Drury Lane Theatre. There is a curiously cursory feel about much that is discussed, such as Sheridan's part in the Trial of Warren Hastings and the fifteen page chapter on Sheridan as Treasurer of the Navy, which devotes just over a page to the topic of its title. This is partly due to Sheridan's multifarious life, but the result is less than satisfactory. Rhodes does include 'The Political Adventurer', a satirical sketch of Sheridan attributed to George III (1784).

Sichel, Walter, *Sheridan: From New and Original Material*. 2 vols. London: Constable, 1909. Sichel's account is extremely full—it has 1200 pages—and is provided with an excellent index, including a chronological index. It is comprehensive, full of detail, and it reprints the Duchess of Devonshire's Diary from the manuscript. It is not an easy book, but an invaluable one for the research scholar.

Despite many attempts (most not even noticed here), there is no satisfactory biography. Whereas Rhodes is probably the most nearly adequate, Gibbs introduces his subject best (and is ideal for the general reader) and Sichel is essential for graduate study. All should be supplemented by Price's editions of the plays and letters (see below).

Autobiographical Sources
Best by far is *The Letters of Richard Brinsley Sheridan*. ed. Cecil Price, 3 vols. Oxford: Clarendon Press, 1966. This is not only reliable but has a first-rate commentary. Note also the *Speeches* from this point of view, but bear in mind they are based on reports not on original manuscript.

Overview of Critical Sources
In sharp contrast to the mass of biographies and the great and continuous success of Sheridan's best comedies on-stage, criticism is thin, especially in book-length form, and many articles are devoted to minutiae and solving tangled textual problems. Sheridan is referred to, sometimes derogatively, in a number of general studies, e.g.: Marvin Mudrick, 'Restoration Comedy and Later' in *English Stage Comedy*, ed. W.K. Wimsatt Jr., New York: Columbia University Press, 1955; Arthur Sherbo, *English Sentimental Drama*, East Lansing: Michigan State University Press, 1957; and A.N. Kaul, *The Action of English Comedy*, New Haven: Yale University Press, 1970. The fullest study is in French and may not be available to many readers: Jean Dulck, *Les Comédies de Richard Brinsley Sheridan*, Paris: Didier, 1962. There are three more recent books, one of which, by John Loftis, is outstanding.

Evaluation of Selected Criticism
Auburn, Mark S. *Sheridan's Comedies; Their Contexts and Achievements*, Lincoln: University of Nebraska Press, 1977. Auburn is overshadowed by Loftis's book but is not without merit. It tries too hard to make its (thoroughly worthwhile) case of relating Sheridan to his time but sometimes lacks conviction.

Durant, J.D. *Sheridan*, New York: Twayne, 1976. This is a modest account designed as a general introduction to Sheridan by the author of the excellent article, 'Prudence, Providence and the Direct Road of Wrong: *The School for Scandal* and Sheridan's Westminster Hall Speech', *Studies in Burke and His Time*, XV (1973): 241-251.

Loftis, John, *Sheridan and the Drama of Georgian England*. Oxford: Basil Blackwell, 1976. This is a first-rate study of Sheridan's drama. It includes an account of *Pizarro* and does not ignore either Sheridan as an orator nor his political activities. Full attention is paid to the context in which he wrote. It is based on wide knowledge of an experienced scholar and is well written.

Other Sources

Charles Lamb's essay, 'On the Artificial Comedy of the Last Century', 1822 (found in many editions) is good on *School for Scandal*; reviews of that play by George Bernard Shaw (1896) and of *The Rivals* by William Hazlitt (1818) and Max Beerbohm (1900) are to be found in their respective collected works and are well worth reading. They are included in the Macmillan (London) Casebook, *Sheridan: Comedies*, ed. Peter Davison (1986). Among other items are: Sir Lawrence Olivier's excellent introduction to his 1948 production of *School for Scandal* (London: Folio, 1949).

Other good sources include:

Schiller, Andrew, '*The School for Scandal*: The Restoration Unrestored', PMLA, 71 (1956): 699-704; Jackson, J.R. 'The Importance of Witty Dialogue in *The School for Scandal*', MLN, 76 (1961): 601-607; Macey, Samuel L. 'Sheridan: The Last of the Great Theatrical Satirists', *Restoration and Eighteenth-Century Theatre Research*, 9 (1970): 35-45; Auburn, Mark S. 'The Pleasures of Sheridan's *The Rivals*: A Critical Study in the Light of Stage History', MP, 72 (1974-75): 256-271; Jason, Philip K. 'A Twentieth-Century Response to *The Critic*', *Theatre Survey*, 15 (1974): 51-58.

Peter Davison
Albany, London, England

JAMES SHIRLEY
1596-1666

Author's Chronology

September 7, 1596 born in London, eldest son of James 'Sharley'; *1608* admitted to the Merchant Taylor's School; *1612* leaves (?) Merchant Taylor's; *1615* matriculates at Cambridge; *1618* marries Elizabeth Gilmet; *1620-1625* Master, St. Alban's Grammar School; *1624/25* first play, *Love Tricks*, or *The School of Compliment* licensed; *1636* departs for Ireland; *ca. 1633* becomes part of the household of Queen Henrietta Maria; *1637-1640* sixteen of his plays published by the London firm, William Cooke and Andrew Crooke; *1640* returns from Ireland, becomes dramatist for King's Men at Blackfriars; *1642* closing of the theaters, Shirley retires from the stage, prepares poems for the press, and teaches school; *1646* *Poems & C.* published; *1647* first folio of Beaumont and Fletcher published, with Shirley's address to the reader; *1666* dies, along with his wife, from injuries sustained in the Great London Fire; both buried 29 October at St. Giles in the Fields, London.

Author's Bibliography (selected)

The Wedding, 1629; *The Grateful Servant*, 1630; *Love Tricks*, or *The School of Compliment*, 1631; *The Changes*, or *Love in a Maze*, 1632; *The Bird in a Cage*, *Contention of Honour and Riches* (an interlude), *The Triumph of Peace* (a masque); *The Witty Fair One*, 1633; *The Traitor*, 1635; *The Example, The Gamester, Hyde Park, The Lady of Pleasure, The Young Admiral*, 1637; *The Duke's Mistress, The Royal Master*, 1638; *The Ball, The Maid's Revenge*, 1639; *The Arcadia, The Constant Maid* or *Love Will Find a Way, The Coronation, The Doubtful Heir, The Humorous Courtier, Love's Cruelty, The Opportunity, St. Patrick for Ireland*, 1640; *Poems & C.*, (including the masque, *The Triumph of Beauty*), 1646; *Grammatica angllatina*, 1649, 1651; *Six New Plays*, 1652/3; *Cupid and Death* (a masque), 1653; *The Gentleman of Venice, The Politician*, 1655; *The Rudiments of Grammar*, 1656, 1660 (as *Manductio*); *Honoria and Mammon . . . with The Contention of Ajax and Ulisses*, 1659.

The Dramatic Works and Poems of James Shirley, ed. William Gifford and Alexander Dyce, 6 vols. 1833; *The Mermaid Series: James Shirley*, ed. Edmund Gosse, 1888; "James Shirley and a Group of Unnoted Poems on the Wedding of Thomas Stanley," *Huntington Library Quarterly*, 2 (1939), 219-231; *The Poems of James Shirley*, ed. Ray Livingstone Armstrong, 1941; *Elizabethan Minor Epics*, ed. Elizabeth Story Donno, 1963; *A Book of Masques: In Honour of Allardyce Nicoll*, ed. T.J.B. Spencer and Stanley W. Wells, 1967; *The Gentleman of Venice*, ed. Wilson F. Engel, 1976; *St. Patrick for Ireland*, ed. John P. Turner, Jr., 1979: *The Young Admiral*, ed. Kenneth J. Ericksen, 1979; *The Bird In a Cage*, ed. Francis Frazier

Senescu, 1980; *The Humorous Courtier,* ed. Marvin Morillo, 1980; *The Lady of Pleasure,* ed. Marilyn J. Thorssen, 1980; *Love's Cruelty,* ed. John Frederick Nims, 1980; *The Maid's Revenge,* ed. Albert Howard Carter, 1980; *The Politician,* ed. Robert J. Felrenbach, 1980; *The Wedding,* ed. Sister Martin Flavin, 1980.

Overview of Biographical Sources

The facts of Shirley's life are more accessible than are those of most other writers of the period, for his education was conventional, and he was a prominent, professional dramatist whose movements and writings were often a matter of public record. Anthony à Wood's *Atheniae Oxonienses* (1691) is the earliest biography, and the one on which all later biographers depend. Most of the corrections and additions to Wood have been in article form. Albert C. Baugh, in "Some New Facts About James Shirley," *Review of English Studies,* 7 (1931): 62-66, tries to pinpoint Shirley's movements during the "lost years" of 1619-1624, on the basis of contemporary documents. He is attacked by George Bas, in "Two Misrepresented Biographical Documents Concerning James Shirley," *Review of English Studies,* n.s., 27 (1976): 303-310. Bas also casts doubt on the traditional claim that Shirley and Izaak Walton were friends: "Thomas Zouch's 'Life of Walton' and the Alleged Friendship between James Shirley and Izaak Walton," *Notes & Queries,* 222; n.s. 24 (1977): 125-126. Stephen J. Radtke makes a claim for Shirley's Catholicism in his *James Shirley: His Catholic Philosophy of Life* (Washington, DC: Catholic University of America, 1929), while Alan H. Stevenson, along with many others, tries to determine the exact dates of Shirley's stay in Ireland: "Shirley's Years in Ireland," *Review of English Studies,* 20 (1944): 19-28. And Marvin Morillo discusses Shirley's treatment at court in "Shirley's 'Preferment' and the Court of Charles I," *Studies in English Literature,* I (1961): 101-117. Arthur Nason's *James Shirley Dramatist* (1915) is the first comprehensive biographical and critical study of Shirley; the most recent is Ben Lucow's *James Shirley* (1981), which is a good summary of previous research on Shirley's life, but the attempts to link Shirley's life to his work are somewhat strained. William D. Wolf's, "Some New Facts and Conclusions About James Shirley: Residence and Religion." *Notes & Queries,* n.s. 29 (1982): 133-134, summarizes most recent research, and claims scholars cannot determine whether or not Shirley was a Catholic.

Evaluation of Selected Biographies

Nason, Arthur, *James Shirley Dramatist.* University Heights, NYC: Arthur Nason, 1915. Although superseded in some details by later research, this is still the standard account of Shirley's life. Besides reflecting on Shirley's life and work, Nason reprints some important contemporary documents, including Shirley's will.

Autobiographical Sources

Most of the autobiographical references are scattered among the various prefaces, introductions, and other ancillary pieces that accompany Shirley's major works. He reveals his loyalty to the king in his encomiastic poem, "Upon the Prince's Birth," 1630, and attacks the Puritan critic of the stage, William Prynne, in his dedication to "The Bird in a Cage," 1633. In the prologue to *The Maid's Revenge* (1639), Shirley claims that he lost court preferment by refusing to engage in the "court sin," flattery. He remarks on his long absence from England and soujourn in Ireland in the prologues to *The Imposture* and *The Sisters* (both 1652/3), and he announces his intention to cease writing for the stage in the preface to his masque *Honoria and Mammon,* 1659.

Overview of Critical Sources

Shirley, who has been one of the most neglected playwrights, suffered a very damaging blow to his reputation when John Dryden attacked him, unjustly but very effectively, in his *Mac Flecknoe* (1682). Thereafter, his reputation went into an eclipse that lasted until the mid-nineteenth century, when some of his plays were collected in various editions. Gebhard Josef Scherrer follows the ebb and flow of Shirley's literary reputation in *James Shirley's Nachruhm* (Zurich: Juris-Verlag, 1951). Since Scherrer's study, there has been much significant criticism of individual plays, poems, and masques, but no overall study of Shirley's works. Such a study must await a new edition of Shirley, for the only complete edition, *The Dramatic Works and Poems of James Shirley,* first appeared in 1833, and is both outdated and inaccurate. Ray Livingstone Armstrong's *The Poems of James Shirley* (1941) is not complete, and must be supplemented by the studies of later scholars.

Evaluation of Selected Criticism

Cogan, Nathan, "James Shirley's *The Example* (1634): Some Reconsiderations," in *Studies in English Literature,* 17 (1977): 317-331. Cogan sees the structure of the play as arising from the contrast between idealized and licentious love.

Levin, Richard, *The Multiple Plot in English Renaissance Drama.* Chicago: University of Chicago Press, 1971. A careful consideration of Shirley plays that contain multiple plots, and their relation to other multiple-plot plays of the period.

Richards, Kenneth, "Satire and Values in James Shirley's *The Lady of Pleasure,*" in *Acta Neophilologica,* 13 (1980): 49-59. Notes that the satire in the play, which is very specific and wide-ranging, traces the destruction of the old order of pre-Caroline England.

Stafford, Tony J. "Shirley's *The Lady of Pleasure:* The Dialectic of Earth and Sky," in *Journal of the Rocky Mountain Medieval and Renaissance Association* 4 (1983): 125-134. Focuses on the characterization and imagery of the play.

Wertheim, Albert, "Games and Courtship in James Shirley's *Hyde Park*," in *Anglia*, 90 (1972): 71-91. Claims that the play is presented as a sport or competition.

Other Sources

A Bibliography of the English Printed Drama to the Restoration. The Bibliographical Society (London), 1957-1962. Bibliographical descriptions of Shirley's plays.

The Jacobean and Caroline Stage. Clarendon Press, 1956. The fifth volume contains a general biography and bibliography of Shirley, with a stage history, in narrative form, of each play.

James Shirley: A Reference Guide. G.K. Hall, 1980. A comprehensive, annotated bibliography of studies on Shirley's life and work to 1978.

The Later Jacobean and Caroline Dramatists. University of Nebraska Press, 1978. A general bibliography of Shirley's life and work, with some annotations.

John Mulryan
St. Bonauenture University

SOPHOCLES
c.496 B.C.-c.406 B.C.

Author's Chronology

Born c.496 B.C. at Colonus, the son of Sophillus; *468 B.C.* first competes in tragic festival and defeats Aeschylus with a tetralogy that included *Triptolemus*, now lost; *440 B.C.* serves with Pericles as *strategos* (general), one of his several public offices; wins, according to the Suda, twenty-four victories and never places lower than second; *c.406 B.C.* outlives Euripides, but dies before the Lenaean festival of 405; Sophocles is posthumously honored as a hero under the name Dexion.

Author's Bibliography

According to the Suda Sophocles wrote 123 tragedies and satyr plays, paeans, and a prose treatis, *On the Chorus*. His great popularity in life was followed by great esteem in later centuries: Ptolemy Euergetes (c.280 B.C.-221 B.C.) borrowed the official Athenian test of his works and returned only a deluxe copy instead of the original. Wilamowitz theorized that the seven tragedies which survived the decline in learning following the Byzantine period did so because they were a standardized selection for schools. The first printed edition of the seven surviving tragedies was done in A.D. 1502 by Aldus Manutius (1449-1515) in Venice. Two standard editions of the Greek text are A. C. Pearson's *Sophocles Fabulae* (Oxford: Oxford University Press, 1924; corr. 1928) and R. D. Dawe's *Ajax, Oedipus Rex, Electra*, and *Trachiniae, Antigone, Philoctetes, Oedipus Coloneus* (2 vols. Leipzig: Teubner, 1975-79). A portion of Sophocles's satyr play, *Ichneutae (Searching Satyrs)*, was among the papyri found from 1897 onwards in the ancient city of Oxyrhynchus in Egypt, and was published by Hunt and Wilamowitz in Volume 9 of *Oxyrhynchus Papyri* (1912).

R. C. Jebb's *Sophocles: The Plays and Fragments* (7 vols. Cambridge: Cambridge University Press, 1883-1896; rpt. Amsterdam: Hakkert, 1962; St. Clair Shores, MI: Scholarly Press, 1972) contains an early translation in a very useful edition of all seven plays. Volume 2 of David Grene and Richmond Lattimore's *The Complete Greek Tragedies* (Chicago: University of Chicago Press, 1959) also contains the seven plays in English translation. Other translations of individual plays include: Robert Fagles and B. M. W. Knox's *The Three Theban Plays* (New York and London: Viking, 1982), for which Fagles did the translation and Knox the introduction and notes; Thomas Gould's *Oedipus the King* (Englewood Cliffs, NJ: Prentice-Hall, 1970), a translation with line-by-line commentary; Kenneth McLeish's *Sophocles: Electra, Antigone, Philoctetes* (Cambridge: Cambridge University Press, 1979), a translation into verse; and Philip Vellacott's *Sophocles and Oedipus* (Ann Arbor: University of Michigan Press, 1971), a literal translation

589

590 *Sophocles*

with notes and a facing verse translation, followed by a lengthy and controversial essay.

Overview of Biographical Sources

What is known about Sophocles's life comes from anecdotes in various ancient writers, an anonymous *Life* found in a thirteenth century manuscript of his plays now in Paris, and information in the Suda lexicon. Gotthold Ephraim Lessing's *Leben des Sophokles* (Berlin, 1790) is an early modern attempt to establish fact and chronology. Gennaro Perrotta's *Sofocle* (Messina: G. Principato 1935; rpt. Rome: Bretschneider, 1963) includes a lengthy "Life" as a preface. Unfortunately the former work is printed only in German, and the latter only in Italian. Moses Hadas's *Ancilla to Classical Reading* (New York: Columbia University Press, 1954; rpt. 1961, pp. 183-190) retells many ancient anecdotes, such as Sophocles' reading of a passage from *Oedipus at Colonus* to successfully defend himself against charges of senility. There are also accounts that combine biography and critical comment, such as Michael Grant's *Greek and Latin Authors, 800 B.C.-A.D. 1000: A Biographical Dictionary* (New York: Wilson, 1980, pp. 397-402). Many editions of Sophocles and books of criticism also include brief biographical surveys.

Evaluation of Selected Biographies

Ehrenberg, Victor, *Sophocles and Pericles*. Oxford: Basil Blackwell, 1954. Ehrenberg discusses Sophocles' involvement in the political life of Athens. The actual and possible interaction of the great dramatist and the great statesman during the years of the Peloponnesian War is intriguing, but some would argue that an approach seeking to learn about Pericles from *Antigone* and *Oedipus Rex* is flawed.

Lefkowitz, Mary R. *The Lives of the Greek Poets*. London: Duckworth, 1981, pp. 75-87, 96-98, 160-163. Lefkowitz has assembled all of the ancient sources. She retells all three accounts of Sophocles' death, and points out that such stories may often be what seems fitting rather than what was. She also prints the complete text of the ancient *Life* of Sophocles (Appendix 4).

Russell, D. A. and M. Winterbottom, eds. *Ancient Literary Criticism*. Oxford: Clarendon Press, 1972. This book reprints the major works of Greek and Roman literary criticism. The index lists passages where Sophocles' life and works are discussed by Plutarch, Aristotle, Horace, Ovid, and others.

Autobiographical Sources

There are extant today seven complete tragedies of Sophocles, part of a satyr play, and fragments. The only things that approach autobiography are quotations found in other authors. For example, Aristotle says, "Sophocles said that he imitated men as they should be but that Euripides imitated them as they are." (*Poetics* 1460b35.) Some critics have also read autobiography into the extant plays, a highly speculative but tempting endeavor.

Overview of Critical Sources

All are in agreement that Sophocles is among the greatest dramatists of all time, but there is no similar concensus about why this is so or what his dramas express. Critics have seen the plays as moral examples of the necessity for piety, as paeans to humanism, or just as plays. The difficulty of making generalizations is compounded by the fact that only seven complete plays out of 123 survive, and even the dating of these is problematic. The selections that follow include the works of both the great scholars of the early twentieth century and some of the many contemporary scholars who continue that work.

Evaluation of Selected Criticism

Bowra, C. M. *Sophoclean Tragedy*. Oxford: Clarendon Press, 1944; rpt. 1967. Bowra devotes a separate chapter to the close analysis of each of the seven plays. His book is a classic argument for the view that Sophocles teaches moral lessons and that each play ends with the harmony of the gods' rule restored.

Jebb, R. C. *Sophocles: The Plays and Fragments*. 7 vols. Cambridge: Cambridge University Press, 1883-96; rpt. Amsterdam: Hakkert, 1962; St. Clair Shores, MI: Scholarly Press, 1972. A great classical scholar, Jebb excelled in exegesis. Although the usefulness of his text and translation is limited by age, the value of his comments in the introduction, appendices, and line-by-line notes are attested to by the fact that his editions continue to be reprinted.

Kitto, H. D. F. *Sophocles: Dramatist and Philosopher*. London: Oxford University Press, 1958. Kitto's urbane, literary approach is very readable and representative of traditional Sophoclean scholarship.

Knox, B. M. W. *Oedipus at Thebes*. New Haven: Yale University Press, 1957; rpt. 1966. Using an historical approach, Knox explores the irreconcilable themes of the greatness of the gods and the greatness of man. Knox is interested in the idea of the hero, an archetype he also considers in *The Heroic Temper* (Berkeley: University of California Press, 1964).

Reinhardt, Karl, *Sophokles*. Frankfort: Klostermann, 1933; 3rd ed. 1947; tr. by Hazel Harvey and Francis Harvey, New York: Harper & Row, 1979. Reinhardt examines the development of structure and character, particularly the tragic protagonist. Despite its early date, this remains an influential book.

Segal, Charles, *Tragedy and Civilization: An Interpretation of Sophocles*. Cambridge: Harvard University Press, 1981. Segal takes a structuralist approach, thinking that the modern reader is more interested in the dissonances in the universe than in its harmony. He explores the paradoxes of human nature and the idea of civilization implicit in the plays.

Whitman, Cedric H. *Sophocles: A Study of Heroic Humanism*. Cambridge: Harvard University Press, 1951. Whitman is the antithesis of Bowra: he sees true divinity only in the indomitable nature of the Sophoclean hero. This hero is responsible not to the gods but to himself, and is himself the example of *arete*.

Other Sources

Burton, R. W. B. *The Chorus in Sophocles' Tragedies*. Oxford: Oxford University Press, 1980. A technical book on one of the elements of Greek tragedy most foreign to the modern reader.

Goheen, Robert F. *The Imagery of Sophocles' Antigone: A Study of Poetic Language and Structure*. Princeton: Princeton University Press, 1951; rpt. 1970. A study of metaphor and related forms that concludes that *Antigone* is a "tragedy of human folly."

Musurillo, Herbert, *The Light and the Darkness: Studies in the Dramatic Poetry of Sophocles*. Leiden: E. J. Brill, 1967. This analysis seeks to establish a chronology for the plays by examining their images; it includes a separate chapter on the fragment *Ichneutae* (*The Tracking Satyrs*).

Scodel, Ruth, *Sophocles*. Boston: Twayne, 1984. A very useful overview that devotes one chapter to Sophocles and Athens, one to each of the extant tragedies, and a final one to general matters including a history of Sophoclean scholarship from the Renaissance to modern times.

Seale, David, *Vision and Stagecraft in Sophocles*. Chicago: University of Chicago Press, 1982. An interpretation of each play scene-by-scene to show the distinctiveness of Sophoclean stagecraft.

Steiner, George, *Antigones*. New York: Oxford University Press, 1984. An exploration of the Western world's fascination with Greek myth, particularly Antigone.

Waldock, A. J. A. *Sophocles the Dramatist*. Cambridge: Cambridge University Press, 1951. Caustic critiques of Bowra and others, concluding that what Sophocles "has to say as a wise man will be incidental to what he is about as a dramatist."

Wilamowitz-Moellendorff, Tycho von. *Die dramatische Technik des Sophokles*. Berlin: Weidmann, 1917. His revolutionary thesis, which has been refined by

Reinhardt and others, that Sophocles made character and consistency of dramatic form subservient to extraordinary, single scenes. In German.

Winnington-Ingram, R.P. *Sophocles: An Interpretation*. Cambridge: Cambridge University Press, 1980. Inquiries about the nature of the hero, of the gods, of piety, with Sophocles seen as the supreme ironist.

Woodward, Thomas, ed. *Sophocles: A Collection of Critical Essays*. Twentieth Century Views. Englewood Cliffs, NJ: Prentice-Hall, 1966. Eleven essays by classical scholars and others, including Nietzche and Virginia Woolf.

Elizabeth A. Holtze

KONSTANTIN STANISLAVSKY
1863-1938

Author's Chronology

Born Konstantin Sergeevich Alexeev on January 5, 1863 in Moscow into an extremely weatlthy merchant family who were devotees of music, ballet and the theatre; *1875* starts attending school at the age of 12; *1877* starts acting in a theatre which was built for him in a village purchased by his father; *1878* enrolls in the Institute for Eastern Languages and is a weak student; *1881* graduates and joins his father's business, but continues his deep involvement with the theatre; *1883* opens a new theatre in Moscow and becomes its translator, director and principal actor; *1884* studies voice with Fedor Komissarzhevsky; *1885* studies at Moscow Theatre School and becomes director and treasurer of the Moscow Section of the Russian Musical Socity; *1888* founds Society for Art and Literature, travels abroad, and receives international acclaim as an actor; *1889* marries leading actress Lilina; *1890* adopts the directing techniques of the Meiningen Theatre Group, acts leading roles at the Maly Theatre and directs his first major play, Gutzkow's *Uriel Acosta*; *1895-1897* directs a number of Shakespeare's plays; *1898* founds Moscow Art Theatre (MAT), with Vladimir Ivanovich Nemirovich-Danchenko; *1898-1904* nearly total preoccupation with Anton Chekhov's plays; *1905* starts the "Theatre Studio" and puts V.S. Meyerhold in charge; *1911* stages *Hamlet* with Gordon Craig; *1912* founds new Art Studio which is followed by a string of other studios primarily for the purpose of teaching the Stanislavsky "Method" of acting and direction; *1914-1917* continues staging plays at MAT throughout the war years; *1917-1923* has constant difficulties with the Soviet authorities and successfully weathers many attempts to close MAT; *1924-1938* writes books and articles concerning staging, production, direction and acting; *1929* starts working with Elizabeth Hapgood, the translator of his major works; *1935* opens School for Opera and Drama; August 7, 1938 dies of a heart ailment.

Author's Bibliography

Although most of his works have been translated into English, the Russian eight-volume collection of his writings is still the definitive one: *Sobranie sochinenii v vosmi tomakh*, edited by M.N. Kedrov and published in Moscow in several identical editions.

Major works on the Stanislavsky "Method" translated by Elizabeth Hapgood include: *An Actor Prepares* (New York: Theatre Arts Books, 1979); *Building a Character* (London: Max Reinhardt, 1969); and *Creating a Role* (New York: Theatre Arts Books, 1980).

A shorter, more general collection of Stanislavsky articles, translated by David Magarshak, is *Stanislavsky on the Art of the Stage* (London: Faber & Faber, 1967).

Overview of Biographical Sources

Because of Stanislavsky's rather long and active life, a countless number of biographies have been written about him in English, German, French, Russian and many other languages. Virtually all are for the most part, based on Stanislavsky's autobiography. Many biographies which were written about him during his lifetime contain major fallacies which infuriated him.

An interesting Soviet work is a collection of articles translated by Vic Schneierson, *Stanislavsky 1863-1963—Man and Actor*. Moscow: Progress Publishers, 1965. This is a "Festschrift" on the occasion of the 100th anniversary of Stanislavsky's birth and is filled with meaningless biographical platitudes. It is, nevertheless, interesting reading since it clearly proclaims the Soviet view of Stanislavsky as pronounced by several orthodox Soviet critics. Much more objective is another collection of comments on Stanislavsky's life and art in Russian, translated by Elizabeth Hapgood, *Stanislavsky's Legacy* (New York: Theatre Arts Books, 1958). One of the very best sources of biographical information on Stanislavsky is the biography of his life-long partner and friend V.I. Nemirovich-Danchenko, *My Life in the Russian Theatre*, translated by John Cournos (New York: 1936).

Evaluation of Selected Biographies

Elena, Polyakova, *Stanislavsky*. Moscow: Progress Publishers, 1982. This book which was translated into English by Liv Tudge has its linguistic faults and is sometimes a bit unclear. Nevertheless it is written by a highly knowledgeable person who obviously feels considerable affection for the subject of her study. Therefore, if one overlooks the required references to Lenin and other Party dignitaries, it is surprisingly objective. It is highly informative, particularly concerning Stanislavsky's problems during the early Soviet period, and plugs informational gaps in the autobiography. The many photographic reproductions are delightful. The major weakness is the absence of an index to list the hundreds of names mentioned in the text.

Magarshak, David, *Stanislavsky: A Life*. Westport, CT: Greenwood Press, 1975. This is most probably the best biography of Stanislavsky written in English by an extremely knowledgeable scholar. It is thorough, objective and highly informative, in addition to being pleasurable reading.

Autobiographical Sources

Stanislavsky's monumental *My Life in Art* has appeared in numerous editions and has been translated into most languages. It is not only an autobiography, but a collection of memoirs which reflect the evolution of the theaatre during major cultural changes in Russia and Western Europe. It is written with love and patience for those less fortunate and talented than the author and with total commitment to the art of theatre. Its reading is a must for anyone interested in the stage. Those editions with a good index are highly recommended. One of the most easily obtainable editions is the J.J. Robbins translation published by Penguin.

Stanislavsky wrote furiously wherever he went. He kept a series of informal diaries and also packets of disorganized notes which he wrote to himself on a daily basis. In addition he was an avid letter writer. During one year alone he wrote some fifty letters to Nemirovich-Danchenko, a number of which were more than twenty pages long. Unfortunately, most of the diary-notes and letters have not yet been definitively collected in Russian and have certainly not been translated into English.

Overview of Critical Sources

Virtually all critical sources discuss Stanislavsky's theories of directing and acting. The best works concern themselves with the following concepts: the director must be in complete control of a production; he must create a theatre ensemble composed of actors who work together repeatedly and know each other's strengths and weaknesses; there must be verisimilitude bordering on naturalism in sets, props, lighting, sound, costuming and, primarily, acting; the audience must be considered the "fourth wall" and should therefore not be "played to;" there can be no "star" system; all phases of a production must be carefuly and thoroughly rehearsed over a lengthy period of time; particular attention must be paid to voice and gestures; all involved must study the individual parts, the entire text and the historical-cultural period of the action; the actor must feel the part rather than simply act to it.

Evaluation of Selected Criticism

The following are a number of the best critical works many of which concern themselves at least in part with the application of the Stanislavsky system to the American stage:

Cole, Toby, *Acting: A Handbook of the Stanislavski Method*. New York: Crown, 1955. A reasonably authoritative though somewhat superficial treatment of the "Method," and a highly interesting introduction by Lee Strasberg.

Hirsch, Foster, *A Method to their Madness*. New York: W.W. Norton, 1984. An excellent, up-to-date history of the "Actors Studio" and "method acting;" the arrival of Stanislavsky's theories and their reception in New York; Lee Strasberg's work and its impact on the legitimate stage and on Hollywood; excellent bibliography and index.

Marowitz, Charles, *Stanislavsky and the Method*. New York: Citadel Press, 1964. A good basic description of some of the most superficial elements of the "Method."

Moore, Sonia, *The Stanislavski System*. New York: Viking Press, 1974. This author is one of the best and most active scholars of the stage and is thoroughly acquainted with Stanislavsky's system.

_____ *Training the Actor: The Stanislavsky System in Class*. New York: Viking Press, 1968. A good text for university theatre courses and actors' workshops.

_____ *Stanislavski Today*. New York: American Center for Stanislavski Theatre Art, 1973. A good update on Stanislavsky in America.

Munk, Erika, ed. *Stanislavsky and America*. Greenwich, CT: Fawcett, 1967. An important collection of articles by foremost scholars on the development of Stanislavsky's critical theories and the American practice.

Rumiantsev, Pavel I. *Stanislavski on Opera*. trans. Elizabeth Hapgood. New York: Theatre Arts Books, 1970. Stanislavsky, from early childhood, was extremely involved with music. This excellent book discusses his directions specifically for opera.

Other Sources

Edwards, Christine, *The Stanislavsky Heritage: Its Contribution to the Russian and American Theatre*. New York University Press, 1965. The first part of this important book discusses the development of Russian theatre before Stanislavsky, the early Stanislavsky and the development of MAT. It then discusses American acting techniques before Stanislavsky and his impact upon the American stage. It also contains a superb bibliography of over 130 books and 100 articles in English, and a good index.

Gorchakov, Nikolai M. *Stanislanvsky Directs*, a new edition of an older work, translated by Miriam Goldina. New York: Funk and Wagnalls, 1954. This work was first published during Stanislavsky's lifetime. He considered it full of misinformation and basically worthless.

Morgan, Joyce Vining, *Stanislavski's Encounter with Shakespeare: The Evolution of a Method*. Ann Arbor: UMI Research Press, 1984. This excellent book discusses Stanislavsky's staging of *Othello*, *Julius Caesar* and *Hamlet*.

Stanislavsky Produces Othello. London: Geoffrey Bles, 1948. This is an invaluable book which was compiled from Stanislavsky's notes which he took in Italy, 1929-30. Stanislavsky procedes scene by scene to give stage directions, draw sketches and indicate the "sub-text," the real meaning of a line which may run counter to its literal meaning.

Selected Dictionaries and Encyclopedias
Dictionary of Russian Literature, Littlefield, Adams, 1959. See the section on "Drama and Theatre."

Encyclopedia of Russia and the Soviet Union, McGraw-Hill, 1961. See entries on "Stanislavsky" and "Nemirovich-Danchenko."

Handbook of Russian Literature, Yale University Press, 1985. See sections on "Theatre" and "Stanislavsky."

Leo Hecht
George Mason University

AUGUST STRINDBERG
1849-1912

Author's Chronology

Born January 22, 1849, Stockholm, Sweden, to steamship agent Carl Oscar Strindberg and former waitress Ulrica Eleonora Norling; *1853* father goes into bankruptcy; *1867* Strindberg graduates eighteenth in high school class of twenty and begins studies at Uppsala University; *1869* fails chemistry examination and acting tryout at the Royal Theater, attempts suicide, then in four days writes first drama; *1872* leaves Uppsala and fails another acting audition; *1875* meets Carl Gustav Wrangel and his wife, née Siri von Essen, whom Strindberg calls "the most beautiful woman in Sweden"; *1876* attempts suicide; Siri is divorced and begins acting career (1876-1883); *1877* Strindberg marries Siri; *1879* bankruptcy despite wide literary recognition of novel *The Red Room*; *1880-1883* writes drama, cultural history, and satire; *1883* self-exile to France; *1884* is tried for blasphemy; *1884-1891* writes fiction during increasing marital discord; *1886-1892* "naturalistic" period of Strindberg's drama; *1886* writes autobiography and dramas, notably *Miss Julie*; *1889* returns to Sweden; *1892* divorced from Siri; *1893* premiere of *Miss Julie* at the *Théatre libre*, Paris, and marriage to Frida Uhl, whom he leaves in 1894 and divorces in 1897; *1894-1897* "Inferno" crisis, pseudo-scientific experimentation, occult experiences, physical and emotional illnesses, and conversion to Swedenborgian syncretism; *1897* resumes creative writing and autobiographical novel *Inferno*; *1899-1901* writes history plays and marital drama; *1901* marries actress Harriet Bosse and divorces her in 1904; *1907-1910* founds and works with his Intimate Theater Group, which closes in 1910; *1912* receives Anti-Nobel Prize of 50,000 crowns through public subscription, and dies May 14 of stomach cancer in Stockholm.

Author's Bibliography

Strindberg's sixty plays comprise almost a third of his prodigious artistic output, which includes nearly a dozen novels, over 150 short stories, three volumes of poetry, scores of essays, and 5600 letters. His literary reputation began in 1879 with the novel *The Red Room*, tr. 1967, and grew steadily more controversial: 1886-1887 *The Son of a Servant*, 1886-1887 (autobiography); *The Father*, 1887 (drama); *Miss Julie*, 1888 (drama); *The Inferno*, 1897 (autobiography); *To Damascus*, 1898-1901 (dramatic triology); 1899 the history plays; *The Dance of Death*, 1900 (drama); *The Chamber Plays*, 1907-1909, including *The Ghost Sonata*. Authoritative English translations of the plays began appearing in the 1950's under the general editorship of Walter Johnson of the University of Washington Press, including Johnson's translation of the history plays and the 1908 *Open Letters to the Intimate Theater*, tr. 1968. Other distinguished translations are: *The Plays of*

599

Strindberg, 2 vols., tr. Michael Meyer, 1964 and 1971; *The Chamber Plays*, tr. Evert Sprinchorn et al., 1962; *To Damascus. A trilogy*, tr. Graham Rawson, 1960. Translations of autobiographical material include *The Son of a Servant*, tr. Evert Sprinchorn, 1966; *A Madman's Defense*, tr. Evert Sprinchorn, 1967; *The Inferno*, tr. Evert Sprinchorn, 1968. Of Strindberg's correspondence, to date only *Letters of Strindberg to Harriet Bosse*, tr. and ed. Arvid Paulson, 1959, have appeared in English.

Overview of Biographical Sources

Strindberg's art and life seem so inextricable that not until the 1980s have biographers attempted to untangle them. Due to the controversial nature of his personality and his writings, research material is difficult to obtain; most of his non-dramatic work has not been translated, and even the uncut text of *Miss Julie* was not published in Swedish until 1984. The earliest biographies, like Elizabeth Sprigge's *The Strange Life of August Strindberg* (London: Chatto and Windus, 1949), could not draw on the scholarly edition of his correspondence, which Torsten Edlund began in 1948, presently covering only half of Strindberg's voluminous letters. Almost all critical studies of his work include biographical sketches, following the example of Martin Lamm's landmark study of 1940-1942, *August Strindberg*; Lamm maintains that childhood and adolescence are the only two periods of Strindberg's life that can be discussed without simultaneous analysis of his writings. In the Biographical Sketch which opens his 1971 translation of Lamm's book, Harry G. Carlson cites the "dual perspective" Strindberg presented in his short story "Evolution," calling himself "the son of two epochs" with two viewpoints on everything, "the monk's and the satyr's." Two comprehensive biographies now are available: Olof Lagercrantz' 1979 Swedish *August Strindberg*, tr. Anselm Hollo (1984) avoids the customary pitfalls—condemning Strindberg's excesses or dismissing them as symptoms of insanity—and objectively accepts his paradoxes of personality in order to create a vital portrait of a complex human being. The British scholar Michael Meyer, in his enormous and painstakingly documented *Strindberg: A Biography* (1985), allows Strindberg and his contemporaries to speak for themselves, conveying a pervasive sense of Strindberg's presence by quotation, with a consequent de-emphasis on literary analysis.

Evaluation of Selected Biographies

Lagercrantz, Olof, *August Strindberg*. tr. Anselm Hollo. New York: Farrar, Straus and Giroux, 1984. Swedish critic and poet Lagercrantz never spares Strindberg in this profound biography, which neither admires or condemns, but consistently searches out the reality behind the multitudinous self-images Strindberg created throughout his work. Only Lagercrantz, of all Strindberg's commentators, refuses to accept his writings as mere thinly veiled versions of his experiences, and thus only Lagercrantz' biography offers convincing answers to the ultimate riddle of Strindberg's life and art: why Ibsen, the consummate modern moralist whom Strindberg hated, kept Strindberg's portrait above his desk.

Meyer, Michael, *Strindberg: A Biography*. New York: Random House, 1985. Meyer, a leading British scholar and translator of Scandinavian literature, treats his difficult subject with restraint, especially in view of Strindberg's violent sexism and antisemitism, providing the greatest amount of documented biographical detail as yet available in English. The critical value of this biography is limited by Meyer's conviction that Strindberg was "only a great writer when he was writing about this obsession the simultaneous love and hatred that infect sexual relationships."

Autobiographical Sources

Critics claim with reason that nearly everything Strindberg wrote is autobiographical, but in several works he deliberately revealed himself more directly than in his drama and fiction, although the Strindberg that emerges may not be the Strindberg the author intended to be seen. The harrowing scenes of marital life he depicted in *Getting Married*, 1884-86, tr. and ed. Mary Sandbach (New York: Viking, 1972), led to a sensational trial for blasphemy in 1884, which, though Strindberg was acquitted, produced the severe mental strain he describes in *The Son of a Servant*, 4 vols., 1886-1887, Part I, tr. Evert Sprinchorn (New York: Doubleday, 1966); Part II, *The Time of Ferment*, tr. Claude Field as *The Growth of a Soul* (London: Rider, 1914). Strindberg further chronicled the bitter shattering of his idealistic marriage to Siri von Essen in *A Madman's Defense*, 1887, tr. Evert Sprinchorn (based on Ellie Schleussner's 1912 translation *Confession of a Fool*) (New York: Doubleday, 1967). *Inferno* is a searing account of Strindberg's 1894-1897 spiritual and creative crisis in Paris; its sequel, *Légendes*, written in French, has not been translated. *Alone*, meditations on the collapse of Strindberg's marriage to Harriet Bosse, appear in *Inferno, Alone, and Other Writings*, tr. Evert Sprinchorn (New York: Doubleday, 1968) and in *From an Occult Diary: Marriage with Harriet Bosse*, tr. Mary Sandbach (New York: Hill and Wang, 1965), as well as in *Letters of Strindberg to Harriet Bosse*, ed. and tr. Arvid Paulson (New York: Nelson, 1959). For the last six years of his life, Strindberg worked on *A Blue Book*, four volumes of aphorisms and short essays, which he called "my life's synthesis"; excerpts appear in *Zones of the Spirit: A Book of Thoughts*, tr. Claude Field (London: Allen, 1913). The ongoing Swedish edition of Strindberg's letters by Torsten Eklund is neither complete nor translated.

Overview of Critical Sources

Although most of Strindberg's commentators, like the writer himself, find it virtually impossible to separate his life from his art, as striking a dichotomy exists between Swedish scholars and those who write in English as the dualities which tormented Strindberg into creation. Swedes acknowledge him as both the exile who drew unflattering attention to his countrymen's shortcomings and the national author whose prose revitalized their language. The rest of the world accepts Strindberg as Ibsen's only rival as the most influential of modern playwrights, while critics fail to define the undeniable power of his drama or pinpoint its sources, its function, and its very nature. Early Swedish opinion of Strindberg's literary merit was adversely affected by the "Strindberg feud," 1910-1912, ignited by his 1910 *Speeches to the Swedish Nation*, supporting the realistic writers of the 1880s and denouncing the romantic partisans of the 1890s and their decadent *fin de siècle* successors. Later Swedish critics see Strindberg primarily as a force for personal and social regeneration. British and American scholars, concentrating upon his dramas, first acclaimed him through Max Reinhardt's work as the father of dramatic expressionism. Since 1970, critical opinion has focused more on Strindberg's literature than his life; recent scholarship is pursuing Strindberg's psychological self-analysis, his mythopoeic impulse, and his function as a forerunner to as diverse dramatists as O'Casey, O'Neill, Tennessee Williams, Sartre, Ionesco, Pinter, and Weiss.

Evaluation of Selected Criticism

Carlson, Harry G. *Strindberg and the Poetry of Myth*. Berkeley: University of California Press, 1982. Carlson believes Strindberg's lifelong preoccupation with myth led to the evolution of his own mythic landscape in his works. Carlson examines the mythic structures of eight major plays in the light of Strindberg's conviction that "his private visions had universal relevance and application," and concludes that Strindberg's use of diverse mythological sources produced a "richness of poetic texture unparalleled in modern drama."

Johnson, Walter, *August Strindberg*. Boston: Twayne, 1976. Johnson, the leading U.S. Strindberg scholar, incorporates a wealth of biographical and bibliographical detail into this general study, analyzing Strindberg's metamorphoses as literary creator from autobiographer, scholar, scientist, poet and storyteller, to the successive stages of Strindberg's development as a dramatist.

Lamm, Martin, *August Strindberg*. tr. and ed. Harry G. Carlson. 1940-1942, rev. ed. 1958; rpt. New York: Benjamin Blom, 1971. Written at the request of the Swedish Academy, Lamm's comprehensive critical study probes Strindberg's turbulent life for the roots of his art and treats the entire enormous range of Strindberg's work, a combination of biography and criticism well suited to this highly subjective author.

Sprinchorn, Evert, *Strindberg as Dramatist*. New Haven: Yale University Press, 1982. This heavily documented study traces the phases of Strindberg's development as a dramatist, focusing on four groups of plays: the "sex tetralogy" of the 1880s; the "dream tetralogy," 1898-1901; the "Vasa trilogy" of history plays, 1872 and 1899; and the *Chamber Plays*, 1907. About half of this book is revision or expansion of material published between 1962 and 1978.

Other Sources

Bentley, Eric, "August Strindberg," in *The Playwright as Thinker*. New York: Reynal and Hitchcock, 1945. Bentley considers Strindberg's plays pivotal to the transition of drama from the nineteenth to the twentieth century.

Brustein, Robert, "August Strindberg," in *The Theater of Revolt*. Boston: Little, Brown, 1964. Brustein believes Strindberg converted psychological and sexual pathology into "penetrating, powerful, and profound drama."

Gilman, Richard, "Strindberg," in *The Making of Modern Drama*. New York: Farrar, Straus and Giroux, 1974. Gilman proposes that Strindberg's author's notes offer "nearly the whole" of the theory behind the avant garde drama of the last fifty years.

Mortensen, Brita M. E. and Brian W. Downs, *Strindberg: An Introduction to his Life and Word*. Cambridge: Cambridge University Press, 1949. A useful but brief early study using Strindberg's life as basis for all of his art.

Ollén, Gunnar, *August Strindberg*. New York: Frederick Ungar, 1972. A general study containing an essay locating Strindberg's work in his times, short discussions of 61 plays, and a record of premieres and unusual performances of each play.

Reinert, Otto, ed. *Strindberg: A Collection of Critical Essays*. Englewood Cliffs, NJ: Prentice-Hall, 1971. A collection of biographical and critical essays and discussions of five major plays by Swedish, American, and British scholars.

Steene, Birgitta, *The Greatest Fire: A Study of August Strindberg*. Carbondale: Southern Illinois University Press, 1973. Steene concentrates on Strindberg's drama and fiction, emphasizing him as a "form-giving" artist.

Valency, Maurice, *The Flower and the Castle*. New York: Macmillan, 1963. Valency discusses Strindberg with Ibsen as shapers of modern drama, considering Strindberg's a highly moral nature that at last found its way to God.

Mitzi M. Brunsdale
Mayville State College

ALEXANDER SUMAROKOV
1717-1777

Author's Chronology

Birth date and place are greatly disputed; many sources list it as June 4, 1718, most recent edition of the *Great Soviet Encyclopedia* cites November 17, 1717; born in Finland into one of the foremost Muscovite families of ancient nobility which was, nevertheless, not particularly wealthy; *1732* enrolls in a cadet academy for higher nobility located in St. Petersburg, where his entire education is patterned after West European standards and French language; attends numerous performances of French School Plays which were presented on the private stage of the academy; *1740* graduates, publishes two odes; begins to believe that his purpose in life was to lay the foundation for a new Russian literature firmly based on West European, particularly French classicism, to be modeled after artistic concepts of Nicolas Boileau-Despereaux. Boileau's influence initially felt in Sumarokov's poetry and songs, but spread to his dramatic works on which his fame eventually rested, became known as the Russian "Racine," "Moliere" and "La Fontaine"; *1750s* becomes the first professional playwright of both comedies and tragedies; *1756* Empress Elizabeth appoints him director of the first permanent theatre in Russia, the Imperial Theatre; his great success, to a considerable degree, is due to the popularity of Fedor Volkov, the finest tragic actor of the period who starred in Sumarokov's plays; *1740s-1770s* writes twelve comedies and ten tragedies; late *1760s* falls out of favor with Catherine the Great and loses his job and sinecure; last years of his life are spent in abject poverty and obscurity; dies on October 1, 1777.

Author's Bibliography (selected)

Comedies include *Tresotinius*, 1750; *Narcissus*, 1750; *A Meaningless Quarrel*, 1750; *The Guardian*, 1764; and *The Usurer*, 1768.

Tragedies *Hamlet*, 1747, tr. 1970; *Khorev*, 1747, tr. 1970; *Sinav and Truvor*, 1750; *Oedipus*, 1750; *Artistona*, 1750; *Semira*, 1751, tr. 1970; *Dimiza*, 1756; *Vysheslav*, 1770; *Dimitry the Impostor*, 1771, tr. 1970; and *Mstislav*, 1774.

Translations into English of Sumarokov's works include the following: Both his "Epistles;" one fable; a major choral song; and a satire in prose may be found in the translation by Harold B. Segel, *The Literature of Eighteenth-Century Russia*, Vol. I (New York: E.P. Dutton, 1967). A translation of *Dimitry the Impostor* may be found in Vol. II of the same set. Also see *Selected Tragedies of A.P. Sumarokov* translated by Richard and Raymond Fortune (Evanston, IL: Northwestern University Press, 1970), which contains the texts of *Khorev*, *Hamlet*, *Semira* and *Dimitry the Impostor*.

The only easily available edition of Sumarokov's works in the original Russian is P.N. Berkov (ed.), *Izbrannye proizvedeniia* (Leningrad: Biblioteka Poeta, 1957).

Overview of Biographical Sources

Other than emperors and empresses, and just a few major figures in the arts and sciences such as Mikhail Lomonosov, little biographical data were either published or collected on other eighteenth century Russians. The relatively few sufficiently literate persons of the period were otherwise occupied; e.g., writing panegyric propaganda for the Romanovs, or composing their own belles lettres. Much of the same is true for the early nineteenth century. The initiators of the "Golden Age" of Russian literature which included the beginnings of Russian drama and modern theatre preferred not to heed what they believed to be the embarrassingly low quality of eighteenth century arts. Therefore there is no biography of Sumarokov which was written during his century, and very little biographical information which was composed later. The few exceptions are all in Russian and are not of a quality worthy of translation.

Evaluation of Selected Biographies

Although there are no books available in English which concern themselves exclusively with the biography of Sumarokov, there are a number of general works which have significant segments allocated to Sumarokov's life and works. Some of the most significant are:

Billington, James H. *The Icon and the Axe: An Interpretive History of Russian Culture*. New York: Random House, 1970. Billington discusses Sumarokov in the context of the period in which he worked.

Brown, William Henry, *A History of 18th Century Russian Literature*. Berkeley: University of California Press, 1980. This book contains numerous, lengthy passages concerned with Sumarokov's life and works. This is the only easily available literary history of the period in the English language and is strongly recommended. Any of the many biographies of Catherine the Great contains entries on her own activity as a playwright and on her view of Sumarokov's plays.

All important general histories of Russian literature, no matter when they were written, do have significant entries on Sumarokov; for example, D.S. Mirsky, *A History of Russian Literature From Its Beginnings to 1900* (New York: Vintage Books, 1958); and Peter Kropotkin, *Russian Literature: Ideals and Realities* (London: Duckworth, 1916). The same is true for all histories of Russian drama and theatre.

Autobiographical Sources

Sumarokov neither wrote a diary nor memoirs. Very little other than a rather limited record of correspondence is available to the researcher, and that only in Russian. Sumarokov exposes his personality virtually exclusively in his own works and in his recorded relations with his contemporaries. With no exception, he was one of the most disliked intellectuals of his age.

Overview of Critical Sources

Sumarokov was an adamant supporter of the classical tradition which observed the unities and established firm laws of high, middle and low styles for the various genres of literature. He was a rigid and uncompromising opponent of any deviation. Virtually all the criticism is therefore divided into three major segments: an attack upon his intolerance and his refusal to consider innovative forms; a low opinion of the quality of his own plays; and the recognition that, despite all his personal and artistic faults, he is truly the father of the Russian drama and theatre.

A number of doctoral dissertations have been written on Sumarokov and his contemporaries during the past two decades. The following two, copies of which may be ordered from University Microfilms, are certainly the best:

Heim, Michael, *Trediakovskij, Sumarokov and Lomonosov as Translators of West European Literature* (Harvard University, 1971).

Dabars, Zita, *The Similies of Sumarokov, Karamzin and Derzhavin* (Indiana University, 1971).

Also see Michael H. Heim, "Two Approaches to Translation: Sumarokov vs. Trediakovskij," in J.T. Baer and N.W. Ingham, eds., *Mnemozina. Studia literaria russica in honorem Vsevolod Setchkarev* (Munich: 1974).

Evaluation of Selected Criticism

Karlinsky, Simon, *Russian Drama from Its Beginnings to the Age of Pushkin.* Berkeley: University of California Press, 1985. Karlinsky allocates a great deal of space to Sumarokov and is quite harsh with him, sometimes unfairly so, even denying him his achievements and importance as the firt professional dramatist and theatrical impressario. Nonetheless, this is a superb critical work.

The two very best critical studies of Sumarokov in a language other that Russian are both in German.

Harder, Hans-Bernd, *Studien zur Geschichte der russischen klassizistischen Tragoedie 1747-1769.* Wiesbaden: Otto Harrassowitz, 1962. This superb piece of research encompasses a careful, thorough analysis of the plot, style and scene-by-scene staging of Sumarokov's first five tragedies.

Vetter, Eveline, *Studien zu Sumarokov.* Berlin: Free University, 1961. This book discusses Sumarokov's style, composition and theories in the utmost critical detail and is highly recommended to those able to do research in German.

Other Sources

All of the books written about Mikhail Lomonosov invariably contain long passages which discuss Sumarokov. Some examples are: Boris N. Menshutkin, *Russia's Lomonosov* (Princeton University Press, 1952); and B.B. Kudryavtsev, *The Life and Work of Mikhail Vasilyevich Lomonosov* (Moscow: Foreign Languages Publishing House, 1954).

Vissarion G. Belinsky, the first and most important Russian literary critic, discusses Sumarokov in many of his writings; for example, in *Selected Philosophical Works* (Moscow: Foreign Languages Publishing House, 1956).

Some anthologies, such as Clarence A. Manning (ed., trans.), *Anthology of Eighteenth Century Russian Literature*, vol. I (New York: King's Crown Press, 1951), have good introductions to Sumarokov's life and works. This specific one also contains the original Russian text of the tragedy *Sinav and Truvor*.

B.V. Varneke, *History of the Russian Theatre, Seventeenth through Nineteenth Century* (New York, 1951), translated by Boris Brasol and edited by B. Martin, also mentions Sumarokov frequently.

Leo Hecht
George Mason University

JOHN MILLINGTON SYNGE
1871-1909

Author's Chronology

Born Edmund John Millington Synge at Rathfarnham, Ireland, on April 16, 1871; *1872* father dies; *1881-1885* attends Classical and English School, Dublin; *1885-1888* tutored at home; *1887* begins study of the violin; *1888* enters Trinity College, Dublin; becomes interested in Irish antiquities and literature; *1889* begins study at Royal Irish Academy of Music; *1891* becomes member of student orchestra at the Academy; *1892* wins prizes in Hebrew and Irish at Trinity; graduates in December from Trinity with Second Class Bachelor of Arts; *1893* travels to Germany to study music; *1894* decides to give up music career; *1895* begins study of literature and languages in Paris; *1896* travels to Italy; meets W.B. Yeats in Paris; *1897* briefly joins Irish League in Paris with Yeats and Maud Gonne; experiences hair loss and lump on neck; operated on for Hodgkin's Disease; *1898* makes first of five visits to Aran Islands; *1902* leaves Paris for Dublin and active involvement in Irish National Theatre Society; *1903 The Shadow of the Glen* produced at Molesworth Hall, Dublin; *1904 Riders to the Sea* produced at Molesworth Hall; *1905 The Well of the Saints* produced at the Abbey Theatre, Dublin; travels with Jack Yeats through the Congested Districts; travels in Kerry; becomes member of the Abbey Theatre Board of Directors; *1906* engaged to Molly Allgood (actress Maire O'Neill); *1907 The Playboy of the Western World* produced at the Abbey Theatre, resulting in riots; *1908* mother dies; undergoes another operation; *1909* dies of Hodgkin's Disease on March 24; *The Tinker's Wedding* produced at His Majesty's Theatre in London; *1910 Deirdre of the Sorrows* produced at the Abbey Theatre.

Author's Bibliography (selected drama)

Riders to the Sea, 1903; *The Shadow of the Glen*, 1904; *The Well of the Saints*, 1905; *The Playboy of the Western World*, 1907; *The Aran Islands*, 1907 (prose); *The Tinker's Wedding*, 1908; *Poems and Translations*, 1909; *Deirdre of the Sorrows*, 1910; *The Works of John M. Synge*, 4 vols., 1910 (includes prose writings, *In Wicklow, In West Kerry, In the Congested Districts*, and *Under Ether*); *J.M. Synge: Collected Works*, 4 vols., Robin Skelton, Alan Price, and Ann Saddlemyer, editors, 1962-1968; *John Millington Synge: Collected Letters*, 2 vols., Ann Saddlemyer, editor, 1983 and 1984.

Overview of Biographical Sources

Several biographical accounts of Synge appeared a few years after his death, though none of any authority. The best of these is *John Millington Synge and the Irish Theatre* by Maurice Bourgeous (London: Constable, 1913), a book that examines Synge's life and works. John Masefield, the English poet and Synge's friend, published *John M. Synge: A Few Personal Recollections with Biographical Notes* (Dublin: Cuala Press, 1915). The official biography, which did not appear until 1959, fifty years after Synge's death, is *J.M. Synge: 1871-1909*, by David H. Greene and Edward M. Stephens. Also of interest is *My Uncle John: Edward Stephens' Life of J.M. Synge*, edited by Andrew Carpenter (London: Oxford University Press, 1974). It contains selections from the typescripts of Stephens' personal recollections of Synge's life. *J.M. Synge and His World* by Robin Skelton (New York: Viking, 1971) is a collection of photographs of Synge and his family, friends and places, accompanied by a biographical sketch based on Greene's biography.

Evaluation of Selected Biographies

Greene, David H. and Edward M. Stephens, *J.M. Synge: 1871- 1909*. New York: Macmillan, 1959. This is the official biography of Synge, written by Greene but with the help of extensive typescripts of Stephens. Stephens, Synge's nephew, had inherited Synge's papers—diaries, journals, letters, and other materials— and had been preparing to write a biography of Synge, based on these papers and his own recollections of Synge, when he died suddenly in 1955. Stephens' widow then asked Greene to write the biography, giving him access to Synge's papers and Stephens' typescripts and asking that Stephens be listed as co-author. The result is a fluent, detailed, valuable account of Synge's life, times, and works.

Autobiographical Sources

Synge did not publish a formal autobiography, though he apparently made several attempts to write one. Alan Price used these drafts (which are among Synge's unpublished writings, catalogued by Ann Saddlemyer) to construct and publish *The Autobiography of J.M. Synge* (Dublin: Dolmen, 1965). Price then included a simplified version of the autobiography in Volume II (1966) of the *Collected Works*. Constructed from three different drafts written by synge between 1896 and 1907, *The Autobiography* treats some of his experiences up to age twenty- two when he left Ireland for musical study in Germany.

In addition to these attempts at formal autobiography, Synge wrote some pieces with veiled autobiographical elements. Several of these pieces, including *Vita Vecchia* and *Etude Morbide* are published with *The Autobiography* in Volume II of *Collected Works* under the heading of "The Man Himself."

Synge's many letters, another good autobiographical source, have been published as *The Collected Letters of John Millington Synge*, 2 volumes, edited by Ann Saddlemyer (Oxford: Clarendon Press, Vol. I, 1983; Vol. II, 1984).

Overview of Critical Sources

Within the first six or seven years after the death of Synge there was a rush of favorable critical commentary on his drama with particular emphasis on its place in the Irish dramatic movement, but then little commentary appeared in the next two decades and much that did appear was negative. Critical interest in Synge was renewed in the late 1930s and it has continued to grow over the years. Commentary in this period has been marked by an overwhelmingly favorable attitude toward Synge, by examination of all of Synge's works, his prose and poems as well as his plays, by an interest in the universal appeal of his themes as well as their Irishness, and by attention to the artistic qualities of his works considered apart from their social commentary on Irish life. There is now such a considerable body of high quality criticism on Synge's works that his reputation as one of the finest twentieth century dramatists is firmly established.

Evaluation of Selected Criticism

Gerstenberger, Donna, *John Millington Synge*. New York: Twayne, 1964. This work offers students a valuable introduction to Synge. Gerstenberger does not attempt, as other critics have, to find thematic unity in Synge's works; instead she presents a mostly chronological study of the works, interjecting biography, history, and Synge's own theories of drama wherever they are helpful in showing Synge's development as a writer.

Grene, Nicholas, *Synge: A Critical Study of the Plays*. Totowa, NJ: Rowman and Littlefield, 1975. Grene's purpose is to demonstrate the distinctive character of each of the plays. It is Grene's belief that critical focus should now be placed almost exclusively on the six major plays that Synge wrote, for they are the works that have secured his literary reputation. The poems and the prose are, for Grene, no longer of major literary concern. He does, however, include some biographical material because an appreciation of Synge's development as a writer is necessary to understand the plays. Grene's interpretations of the plays are clear and perceptive.

Kiberd, Declan, *Synge and the Irish Language*. Totowa, NJ: Rowman and Littlefield, 1979. Kiberd's book is an illuminating study of the relationship of Synge's works to the Irish language and the Gaelic tradition. An Irish scholar, Kiberd argues persuasively that because previous Synge critics have not been Irish scholars they have been unable to explain the full extent of Synge's debt to the Irish tradition. Kiberd attempts to assess the debt, examining Synge's knowledge and use of Irish language, myth, literature, song, saga, and romance. He concludes that Synge fused the Gaelic tradition to the Anglo-Irish tradition and became not only a great Anglo-Irish writer but truly a Gaelic artist as well. Kiberd's study differs from Synge criticism in recent decades (which has been intent on establishing Synge's universal qualities) in that it establishes that much of value in Synge's works is closely related to his Gaelic influences.

Price, Alan, *Synge and Anglo-Irish Drama*. London: Methuen, 1961. Price's thesis is that Synge's central theme is the conflict between dream and reality. He pursues this theme in all of Synge's works, the prose, poems, and translations as well as the plays, though he gives greatest attention to the latter. In the early chapters he discusses such Irish-related issues as Synge's idiom and his presentation of Irish life, but he is concerned ultimately with the broader issue of Synge's place in English literature. Students will find Price's study valuable.

Other Sources

Bushrui, S.B. ed. *Sunshine and the Moon's Delight: A Centenary Tribute to John Millington Synge, 1871-1909.* New York: Barnes & Noble, 1972. A collection of insightful essays ranging over Synge's works, his literary relationships and influences, and the translation and performance of his drama in several foreign countries, including Japan, Germany, France, and the Arab world.

Kopper, Edward A., Jr. *John Millington Synge: A Reference Guide.* Boston: G.K. Hall, 1979.

Levitt, Paul M. *J.M. Synge: A Bibliography of Published Criticism.* New York: Barnes and Noble, 1974.

Mikhail, E.H. *J.M. Synge: A Bibliography of Criticism.* Totowa, NJ: Rowman and Littlefield, 1975.

Selected Dictionaries and Encyclopedias

Critical Survey of Drama, Salem Press, 1985. Brief biography and insightful commentary on Synge's drama.

Dictionary of Irish Literature, Greenwood Press, 1979. Biographical sketch and valuable commentary on Synge's literary influences and characteristics.

Michael L. Storey
College of Notre Dame
of Maryland

RABINDRANATH TAGORE
1861-1941

Author's Chronology

Born May 7, 1861 in Calcutta, fourteenth child of Devindranath Tagore and Sarada Devi; *1868* attends Oriental Seminary and then normal school; *1869* writes first verse at age eight; *1871* attends Bengal Academy; *1873* travels to Himalayas with father for three months; *1874* studies under a tutor at home until admitted to St. Xavier school; *1875* reads his own poetry in public for the first time, publishes first poem, leaves St. Xavier school; *1876* publishes first literary criticism, mother dies; *1877* family literary monthly, *Bharati*, commences, becomes forum for his poems, essays, reviews, short stories; he appears on stage for the first time; *1883* marries and begins management of father's estate in Shelaidaha; is influenced by the natural beauty of the Bengali landscape and the life of country people; *1883-1903* most prolific period of his literary life; *1884* writes first prose drama; *1901* moves family to Santiniketan, founds Indian school; *1902* wife dies; *1905* father dies; *1912* becomes internationally known and begins lecture tour of United States; *1913* finishes lecture tour in April, receives Nobel Prize for Literature in November; *1915* is knighted in England; *1919* resigns knighthood; *1921* adds to his school Visva-bharati, an international university for the study of Eastern civilization and the promotion of East-West relations (the university and travel abroad promoting world unity occupy much of the rest of his life); *1930* delivers Hibbert lectures at Oxford; *1932* accepts university chair of Bengali at Calcutta University; *1940* receives honorary degree of Doctor of Literature from Oxford University in special convocation at Santiniketan; *1941* dies August 7 at Jorasanko, Calcutta.

Author's Bibliography (selected drama)

Chitra, 1913; *The King of the Dark Chamber*, 1914; *The Post Office*, 1914; *Sacrifice, The Ascetic, Malini, The King and the Queen,, The Cycle of Spring*, 1917; *The Curse of Farewell*, 1914; *Red Oleanders*, 1915; *Mukta-Shara, Natir Puja, Chandalika*, 1950.

Overview of Biographical Sources

Study of Tagore's biography illuminates his enormous creative energy and literary genius in its many facets. Each successive phase of his life reveals the ever-opening horizon that was his career. From boy poet, dramatist, and lecturer, Tagore grew to national and international fame as India's voice for peace, Eastern and Western unity, and Indian education. Thus an understanding of the dramatist's personal history is essential not only for a biographical appreciation of his creative works, but also for a sense of the nature of his overall accomplishment. Since the great wave of popular approbation that followed his being awarded the Nobel Prize, many biographies have been written about Tagore, in Bengali and English both; a few of the more important ones are surveyed below.

Evaluation of Selected Biographies

Kripalani, Krishna, *Rabindranath Tagore: A Biography*. London: Oxford University press, 1962. Considered the standard biography of Tagore, Kripalani's book is detailed, accurate, interesting, and readable. The author was well acquainted with the Tagore family, and this position greatly facilitated an insightful analysis of Tagore's life. The volume begins with a lengthy introduction chronicling the political and social atmosphere of the time and provides a helpful account of the history of the influential and celebrated Tagore family. A shorter version of this work is entitled *Tagore: A Life* (Calcutta: Kripalani, 1971).

Ray, Niharranjan, *An Artist in Life: A Commentary on the Life and Works of Rabindranath Tagore*. Trivandrum: University of Kerala, 1967. In a careful study of Tagore's physical and philosophical life, the author divides this unique biography into two parts, hoping to demonstrate clearly the dramatist's genius. In the first part he discusses the cultural and sociopolitical milieu in which Tagore lived and wrote. This section also includes an interpretation of the major ideological and intellectual forces of the day, including the dramatist's reactions to the complex movements within his contemporary India. The second and longer part is a critical biography of Tagore's life and works, broken into six phases.

Tagore, Rathindranath, *On the Edges of Time*. Calcutta; Longmans, 1958. This account is written by Tagore's son about his life with the great dramatist. Although often inaccurate and unsympathetic, this volume does shed light on the personality of Tagore.

Autobiographical Sources

My Boyhood Days. trans. Marjorie Sykes. Calcutta: Visva-Bharati, 1940. This is an interesting, detailed, and often nostalgic knitting together of Tagore's boyhood memories, which includes reminiscences of old Calcutta, servants, and traditional folk beliefs, from the author's earliest recollections to age 18.

My Reminiscences. New York: Macmillan, 1917. Written when the dramatist was fifty, the contents amount to a series of "memory pictures" which reveal "a connected history of his inner life together with that of varying literary forms in which his growing self found successive expression, up to the point at which both his soul and poetry attained maturity" (Tagore's note). He presents a detailed account of his childhood, studies, family, and the progress of his literary career.

A Tagore Testament. trans. Imdu Dutt. London: Meridian Books, 1953. This is a series of autobiographical essays paired with poems selected by the translator, and it offers an unusual and useful source.

Overview of Critical Sources

During his lifetime Tagore enjoyed enormous success both nationally and internationally. His collected works—lectures, essays, short stories, novels, plays, and poems—totaled 103 volumes, only a small selection of which have been translated into English. Tagore was a prolific and active dramatist, producing 41 plays in various genres: comedy, tragedy, social satire, musical comedy, dance-drama, and verse drama. Of this varied dramatic *oeuvre* only nine plays were translated by the author and published in English while he was alive.

Although Tagore is a significant and influential literary figure, his international fame and critical acclaim were relatively short-lived. Analysts attribute this unfortunate fact to the inaccurate Western stereotype of the dramatist as a mystical Indian guru; to the flawed, incomplete, and half-hearted attempts at translation of his works; and to the flooding of the market for Tagore's works in the first half of the twentieth century. Thus, although Tagore's nearly incredible rise to prominence culminated in the award of the Nobel Prize for Literature in 1913, the poet and dramatist too quickly lost public and critical interest for the West.

Tagore's centenary in 1961 revitalized some interest in him and his accomplishments, but contemporary critics still call for the accurate re-translation of his works already in English renderings, the continued translation of works known only in Bengali, and a thorough consideration of the artistic wealth of his drama.

Evaluation of Selected Criticism

Ayyub, Abu Sayyeed, *Tagore's Quest*. Calcuta: Papyrus, 1980. Short interpretive studies of the plays *The Post Office*, *The King of the Dark Chamber*, *Nature's Revenge*, and *Sacrifice* are included.

Chakravorty, B.C. *Rabindranath Tagore: His Mind and Art*. New Delhi: Young India Publications, 1971. Traces the evolution of Tagore's thought through the stages of his literary career. Attempts a conclusive and comprehensive view of his literary genius and overall accomplishment.

Gargi, Balwant, "The Plays of Tagore," in *The Genius of Tagore: Tagore Centenary Volume, Part I*. ed. Mahendra Kulasrestha. Hoshiarpur: Vishveshvaranand V.R. Institute, 1961, 101-106. Gargi discusses the themes of selected dramas as well as description of Tagore as an actor in his own works. This volume also contains numerous articles on Tagore's various artistic endeavors, and thus offers a fine introduction for the student.

Gupta, S.C. Sen. *The Great Sentinel: A Study of Rabindranath Tagore*. Calcutta: A. Mukherjee and Co., 1948. Although this book includes a short biography, it is primarily a critical work which pays lengthy and careful attention to Tagore's dramatic achievements. Gupta divides his career into two phases—non-symbolic and symbolic dramas—and devotes a chapter to each type.

Guhathakurta, P. *The Bengali Drama: Its Origin and Development*. London: K. Paul, Trench, Trubner, 1930. Includes a history of modern Bengali drama and theaters, as well as a detailed account of Tagore in his historical context.

Iyengar, K.R. Srinivasa, "Tagore the Playwright," *Indian Literature*, IV (1961): 51-64. Short discussions of the themes of *The Ascetic*, *The King and the Queen*, *Sacrifice*, *Malini*, *The Cycle of Spring*, *Red Oleander*, *Chitra*, *The Post Office*.

Lago, Mary M. "Restoring Rabindranath Tagore," in *Encounter*, (January 1974): 52-57. Lago discusses the causes of Tagore's fall in public and critical popularity, and offers suggestions for restablishing his reputation in the West, specifically among critics.

_____. *Rabindranath Tagore*. Boston: Twayne, 1976. This is an interesting and well written literary study primarily of the author as poet. It includes short discussions of Tagore as dramatist, novelist, and short story writer, and is an excellent introduction to the scope of Tagore's literary talents. It includes a selected bibliography.

Mukherjee, Sujit, *Passage to America: The Reception of Rabindranath Tagore in the United States, 1912-1914*. Calcutta: Bookland Private Ltd., 1964. Contains a helpful chapter on Tagore's dramatic techniques, influences, and themes, with a short history of his evolution as a dramatist and of the private and public performances of his plays.

Naravane, Vishwanath, *An Introduction to Rabindranath Tagore*. Calcutta: Macmillan of India, 1977. Useful for the beginning student of Tagore, this work includes a short outline of the dramatist's contributions to philosophy and religious thought, poetry, fiction, drama, music, painting, and education. It also includes an informative chapter on Tagore as dramatist.

Sanyal, Hirankumar, "The Plays of Rabindranath Tagore," in *Tagore 1861 to 1961: A Centenary Volume*. New Delhi: Sahitya Akademi, 1961, pp. 233-242. Sanyal presents short discussions and interpretations of the greatest plays in Tagore's dramatic canon and traces the evolution of his dramatic career. He also includes a brief description of Tagore as actor, director, and choreographer. The entire centenary volume in which this article appears is invaluable for the beginning student of Tagore, for it features a wide range of commemorative articles on the various facets of the artist's literary career, an extensive chronology, and an exhaustive bibliography of his works.

Thompson, E.J. *Tagore: Poet and Dramatist*. London: Oxford University Press, 1926. The first and probably the best full-length literary study, Thompson thoroughly discusses Tagore's development as a dramatist as well as closely considers selected plays. This is the indispensable standard source.

Other Sources

Devi, Maitraye, *Tagore by Fireside*. Calcutta: Rupa and Co., 1961. Transcriptions of conversations with the dramatist on his visits to Devi's home.

Tagore, Rabindranath, *Glimpses of Bengal*, trans. Surendranath Tagore. London: Macmillan, 1921. Letters written during Tagore's most prolific period, 1885-1895.

————, *Letters from Abroad*. Madras: S. Ganesan, 1924. Letters to C.F. Andrews, May 1920-July 1921.

————, *Letters to a Friend*. London: Allen and Unwin, 1928. Rev. and enl. of *Letters from Abroad*, 1913-1922.

————, *Rolland and Tagore*. ed. Alex Aronson and Krishna Kripalani. Calcutta: Visva-Bharati, 1945. Letters and transcriptions of conversations from 1919-1930.

————, *Letters from Russia*. Calcutta: Visva-Bharati, 1960. Letters written to his family on his impressions of Russia in 1930.

————, *Imperfect Encounter*. ed. Mary M. Lago. Cambridge: Harvard University Press, 1972. Letters of Rothenstein and Tagore, 1911-1941.

Anne-Marie Foley
University of Missouri

MANUEL TAMAYO Y BAUS
1829-1898

Author's Chronology

Born September 15, 1829 in Madrid to José Tamayo, leading actor and theatre director, and Joaquina Baus, a leading lady of the theatre who encouraged her son to follow a career as a playwright; family moved about frequently so that Tamayo did not receive a formal education but was largely autodidactic (some of his letters suggest he knew French and could read German, which may be inferred from the fact that in 1847 he opened his first play, *Juana de Arco* (Joan of Arc), based on Schiller's *The Maid of Orleans); 1849* marries María Emilia Máiquez, daughter of an impresario, a marriage lasting fifty years; *1847-1856* first period of literary output; *1856* Tamayo writes his last play in verse, *La bola de nieve* (The Snowball); *1858* elected Spain's most prestigious literary institution, The Royal Academy of the Language, an honor motivating a radical change in his writing career and initiating his second literary stage; *1862-1870* his second period shows more concern with moral issues, and the writing of thesis plays becomes fully developed; during this period, Tamayo ceases using his own name, writing under a series of pseudonyms: Joaquín Estébanez, José María García, Don Fulano de Tal, Juan del Peral; *1863* produces *Lances de honor* (Duels of Honor); *1867* produces *Un Drama nuevo* (A New Drama), considered by most critics his masterpiece; *1870* produces his last play *Los hombres de bien* (The Upright Men); *1871* makes an unsuccessful bid for public office as a candidate on the Carlist ticket; *1874* elected Executive Secretary of the Royal Academy; *1884* becomes Director for the National Library; *1898* dies after requesting that all his personal papers be destroyed.

Author's Bibliography

The complete works are available in both Spanish and English. It must be noted, however, that since Tamayo adapted many plays from the French, it is questionable how many are really his. Higher estimates range from thirty-five to fifty, but most critics credit him with twenty-three. *Obras*, 4 volumes (Madrid: Rivadeneyra, 1893-1900) is perhaps the most complete compilation. *Obras completas de Tamayo y Baus* (Madrid: Editorial Pax, 1947) is not complete, despite the title, since it contains only eighteen plays plus Tamayo's speech upon his reception into the Royal Academy. *The Oberlin College Spanish Drama Collection* contains five of Tamayo's plays, and editions of single plays are also available, notably *Una apuesta* and *Huyendo del perejil*, edited by Cony Sturgis and Juanita C. Robinson (New York: Macmillan, 1930), containing notes and a Spanish-English vocabulary. *Un drama nuevo*, edited by R.T. House and A.M. Kaufman (New York: Allyn and Bacon, 1923) is an edition for American students, with notes and a Spanish-English vocabulary, as is another edition of the same work by Clarence King

Moore and J. Horace Nunemaker (New York: Silver Burdett, 1937). *La locura de amor*, edited by Robert M. Ashburn (New York: Prentice-Hall, 1931) provides an introduction with a detailed account of the historical background, bibliography of Tamayo's plays and secondary studies to 1931. *Lo positivo*, edited by Philip Harry and Alfonso de Salvio (New York: Heath, 1908) offers an introduction which attempts to show that Tamayo and his contemporary Adelardo López de Ayala attempted to move Spanish theater away from post-Romantic excess back to the terrain of Realism and common sense. This, too, is a students' edition with notes and Spanish-English vocabulary.

Overview of Biographical Sources

Since Tamayo requested that his personal papers be burned after his death, very little autobiographical material is extant. There are a number of letters and a few papers which have appeared, and the fact that he was very well-known during his lifetime has allowed scholars to compile some facts about his life. Esquer Torres Ramón has edited and published a number of letters which are useful in understanding the life of Tamayo. His "Contribución al epistolario de Tamayo y Baus," *Boletín de la Sociedad Castellonense de Cultura*, Cuaderno IV (1962): 377-397 presents thirteen letters from Tamayo to various recipients, twelve of them belonging to the "silent period" of his last quarter century. The same scholar's "Epistolario de Manuel Tamayo y Baus a Manuel Cañete" *Revista de Literatura*, II (julio-diciembre 1961): 367-405 is the most complete of several letter collections, containing fifty letters from "Manuel #1" (Tamayo) to his best friend and fellow academician, "Manuel #2" (Cañete). Esquer Torres, the leading expert on Tamayo, has also published most of the other extant autobiographical material, Tamayo's correspondence with other friends and intellectuals, which escaped the posthumous destruction of personal papers willed by the playwright and carried out by his nephew: "Para un epistolario Tamayo y Baus—Asenjo Barbieri,: *Boletín de la Real Academia Española, Cuaderno CLXV, Tomo XLII (1962): 121-143* reflects the friendship with a famous composer; *"Para un epistolario Tamayo—Menéndez y Pelayo,"* *Boletín de la Biblioteca de Menéndez y Pelayo*, XXVIII (1962): 153-172 comprises twenty-four letters from Tamayo, then Secretary of the Royal Academy, to its youngest and most erudite scholar. "Para un epistolario Valera—Tamayo y Baus,"*Boletín de la Real Academia Española*, XXXIX (1959): 89-163 comprises thirty-eight letters from Juan Valera while this leading Nineteenth-Century novelist was an ambassador abroad (1882-1896) and also sheds light on Tamayo's silent period. "Tamayo y Baus: sus proyectos literarios inacabados," *Boletín de la Real Academia Española*, XLIII (1963): 151-64 contains Esquer Torres' discussion of a few fragments and notes surviving from Tamayo's papers which he believes to be part of projected plays and other unfinished works. In "Tamayo y Baus y la Real Academia," *Boletín de la Real Academia*, XLIII (mayo-agosto 1962): 299-335, the same scholar provides commentary and letters relating to Tamayo's petition for acceptance into the Academy, his acceptance speech, his pseudonyms, his work as secretary, and his death. Finally, Gerard Flynn's *Manuel Tamayo y Baus* (New York: Twayne, 1973) is a most informative volume with a chronology, biographical information, and numerous letters within the text and appendices.

Evaluation of Selected Biographies

There are no biographies per se, and the only sources on Tamayo's life which are available are found in the introductions to the editions of single plays listed in the Author's Bibliography, in the letters compiled by Esquer Torres in the Overview of Biographical Sources, plus another contribution by this critic, "Tamayo y Baus y la política del siglo XIX," *Segismundo: Revista Hispánica de Teatro*, I (1967): 71-91, which divides Tamayo's political life into four periods, in three of which he held government assignments or a pension. In the fourth, his only politically-active period, following the Revolution of 1868, he became a Carlist for a short time and was an unsuccessful candidate for elective office. Some additional biographical information not found elsewhere is contained in Emilio Cotarelo y Mori, *Discursos leídos en la Real Academia Española el día 27 de octubre de 1929 para celebrar el centenario del nacimiento de Don Manuel Tamayo y Baus* (Madrid: Tipografía de Archivos, 1929), and the same authority contributed a long necrology read before the Academy and published in *Estudios de historia literaria de España* (Madrid: Imprenta de la Revista Española, 1901), pp. 363-403, which contains biographical data and an examination of major plays.

Autobiographical Sources

Tamayo's letters are the only extant autobiographical documents, since other personal papers were destroyed in accord with his request following his death. From his letters and thesis plays, it is possible to reach conclusions about his attitudes and principles, i.e., that Tamayo was a traditionalist who believed in the authoriity of the Catholic Church, and a staunch supporter of family unity. A supporter of the Crown, he also became for a time a member of the reactionary group supporting Carlos de Borbón, the pretender to the throne opposed by liberals and most intellectuals.

Overview of Critical Sources

Scholarship in Spanish on Tamayo is extensive, but that in English is limited to the already-cited Twayne book by Gerard Flynn, the introductions to single plays, and some articles in scholarly journals. However, the information available in United States colleges and universities is substantial enough to provide those with no reading knowledge of Spanish with an excellent overview of this playwright. José Alberich, "El papel de Shakespeare en *Un drama nuevo* de Tamayo," *Filología Moderna*, X, no. 39 (1970): 301-322, points to the character of Shakespeare as a spokesman for the author's theatrical and moral ideas, and argues that Tamayo's dramatic principles here are consistent with those set out in the prologue to *Virginia* and his Academy speech. The leading Tamayo authority, Ramón Esquer Torres, has contributed a very thorough book-length study of his theater, *El teatro de Tamayo y Baus* (Madrid: Consejo superior de Investigaciones Científicas, 1965). Isidro Fernández Florez, "Estudio crítico-biográfico de don Manuel Tamayo y Baus," in Pedro de Novo y Colson, *Autores dramáticos contemporáneos y joyas del arte español del siglo XIX*, II (Madrid, 1886): 451-486, provides some biographical data and discusses Tamayo's major plays one by one, noting the author's exaltation of women and premeditated breaks with his own aesthetic credo. John D. Fitz-Gerald's "*Un drama nuevo* on the American Stage," *Hispania*, VII (1924): 171-176 postulates the existence of two American translations of this play during the 1870s, one by William Dean Howells. Both of these lost translations altered the plot; not so one published by The Hispanic Society of America under the title *A New Drama*. Blance Emma Goodell's "Manuel Tamayo y Baus, Sources and Aesthetics," (Unpublished Doctoral Dissertation, University of Wisconsin, 1950) examines plays reworked from foreign authors in an attempt to derive Tamayo's dramatic creed on the basis of changes he made with regard to the originals. Robert E. Lott's "On Mannerism and Mannered approaches to Realism in *Un drama nuevo*, *Consuelo*, and Earlier Nineteenth-Century Plays," *Hispania*, LIV (1971): 844-855 considers *Un drama nuevo* "an irritatingly mannered play, "and argues that the *alta comedia* of the day did not truly reflect human experience and thought. Guido E. Mazzeo in "Yorick's Covert Motives in *Un drama nuevo*," *Modern Language Notes*, LXXXIII (1968), 175-78 takes a psychoanalytic approach to argue that Yorick suffered a covert desire to enact the role of the betrayed husband, and was suspicious of his wife even before receiving the part of Count Octavio. Peter L. Podol's "The Evolution of the Honor Theme in Modern Spanish Drama," *Hispanic Review*, XL (1972): 53-72 believes that the *alta comedia* anticipates repudiation of traditional concepts of honor as found in Twentieth Century writers, and discusses particularly Tamayo's *Lances de honor* and *Un drama nuevo* as containing antecedents. Charles B. Qualia's "The *Raisonneur* in the Social Drama of Spain from Tamayo to Linares Rivas," *Hispania*, XIX (1936): 407-414 identifies the character who voices moralizing attitudes or messages as the *raisonneur* and considers those of Tamayo to be old-fashioned spokesmen for honor, straitlaced Catholic ethics and resistance to temptation. Paul Patrick Rogers' "Galdós and Tamayo's Letter-Substitution Device," *Romanic Review*, XLV (1954): 115-120 identifies Tamayo as perhaps the only playwright in history to substitute a real letter for the blank stage prop, and argues that Galdós imitated Tamayo's innovation in *La corte de Carlos IV*.

Evaluation of Selected Criticism

Shaw, Donald L. "The Anti-Romantic Reaction in Spain," *Modern Language Review*, LXIII (1968): 606-611. Sees Tamayo as one of those Nineteenth-Century writers who viewed Romanticism as revolutionary and espoused the need for a return to more wholesome doctrines as the basis for literature. The same critic in "Towards the Understanding of Spanish Romanticism," *Modern Language Review*, LXVIII (1963): 190-195 continues to expound a similar thesis, suggesting that many Spaniards in the Nineteenth Century believed that there was no middle ground between orthodoxy and nihilism. This study is helpful to readers who may wonder at Tamayo's championship of orthodoxy in his thesis plays.

Sicars y Salvadó, Narciso, *D. Manuel Tamayo y Baus. Estudio crítico-biográfico*. Barcelona: Tipografía Católica, 1906. Contains some biographical information, but for the most part is a ponderous, lengthy eulogy which considers Tamayo "immortal."

Tayler, Neal H. "Manuel Tamayo y Baus: Some Early Influences," *Hispania*, XXV (1932): 395-398. Studies Tamayo's work in relation to the influences of Schiller and Hugo. The same critic in *Las fuentes del teatro de Tamayo y Baus. Originalidad e influencias* (Madrid: Gráficas Uguina, 1959) investigates sources of Tamayo's work, studies the playwright's theatrical theory, and discusses Tamayo in relation to the German, French, English and Spanish theaters.

Genaro J. Pérez
The University of Texas
Permian Basin

TERENCE
Publius Terentius Afer
195—159 B.C.?

Author's Chronology

Born 195 B.C., Carthage, North Africa; *185* set as the traditional date of birth, probably because of the birthdate of the younger Scipio Africanus, one of Terence's patrons; *c. 185* brought to Rome as slave of Publius Terentius Lucanus, a senator who educates and frees him; *c. 175* enters circle of the younger Scipio; *c. 168* reads *Andria* (*The Woman of Andros*), his first play, for dramatist Caecilius Statius; *166* Caecilius dies; *Andria* is given its first performance; *165* unsuccessful first performance of *Hecyra* (*The Mother-in-Law*); *163* first performance of *Heautonti-morumenos* (*The Self-Tormentor*), successfully received; *161 Eunuchus* (*The Eu-nuch*) and *Phormio* successfully staged; *160 Adelphoe* (*The Brothers*) presented at funeral games for Aemilius Paulus (father of younger Scipio); second performance of *Hecyra*, also unsuccessful; *Hecyra* given third and successful performance, per-haps at Roman Games; Terence leaves Rome for Greece, perhaps for study; *159* all references to Terence cease, is presumed to have died in Greece.

Author's Bibliography

Sidney G. Ashmore, ed., *P. Terenti Afri Comoediae*, 2nd ed. (New York: Oxford University Press, 1908) contains helpful English commentary; J. Sargeaunt, ed., *Terence*, 2 vol., Loeb Classical Library. (Cambridge: Harvard University Press, 1912) provides clear Oxonian translation with Latin text on facing pages; R. Kauer, W. M. Lindsay, O. Skutsch, ed., *P. Terenti Afri Comoediae*, Oxford Classical Text. (Oxford: Clarendon Press, 1926, rev. 1958) contains Latin text based on Ashmore with apparatus but no translation; J. Marouzeau, ed., trans., *Térence: Comédies*, 3 vol. Budé (Paris: Les Belles Lettres, 1942-1947) reprinted with addenda and corri-genda, vol. 1 (1947), vol. 2 (1956), contains Latin text, French translation and commentary; R. H. Martin, ed., *P. Terenti Afri Phormio*. (London: Methuen, 1959) has Latin text, English introduction and commentary; G. Shipp, ed., *P. Terenti Afri Andria* (Melbourne: Oxford University Press, 1960) with Latin text, English introduction and commentary; R. H. Martin, ed., *P. Terenti Afri Adelphoe* (London: Cambridge University Press, 1976) provides Latin text, apparatus, En-glish introduction and commentary, with appendices on Menander as play's source and on Terentian metre. Four good modern translations are: George E. Duckworth, *The Complete Roman Drama* (New York: Random House, 1942); Frank O. Copley, Moses Gadas, *Roman Drama*, Library of Liberal Arts (Indianapolis: Bobbs-Merrill, 1942) prose translation; Palmer Bovie, C. Carier, D. Parker, *The Com-plete Comedies of Terence* (New Brunswick: Rutgers University Press, 1974) verse translation; Betty Radice, *Terence: The Comedies* (New York: Penguin, 1976) prose with good introduction. Two good annotated bibliographies with surveys of Terentian scholarship are: Heinrich Marti, "Terenz 1909-59." *Lustrum* 8 (1963): 5-101 and Sander M. Goldberg, "Scholarship on Terence and the Fragments of Roman Comedy: 1959-80." *Classical World* 75 (1981): 77-115.

Overview of Biographical Sources

Lives of Terence rely on the often problematic *Vita* by C. Suetonius Tranquillus (c. 69-140 A.D.) which has been transmitted as the preface to a commentary on the plays bearing the name "Donatus" though probably in actuality the work of several authors. A modern edition of this life is that edited by P. Wessner: Aelius Donatus, Eugraphius, *Commentum Terenti*, 3 vol. (Leipzig: Teubner, 1902-08). The best modern sources for the little that is known are W. Beare, *The Roman Stage* (London: Methuen 1950, rev. 1964); George E. Duckworth, *The Nature of Roman Comedy* (Princeton: Princeton University Press, 1952); J. Wight Duff, *A Literary History of Rome*, vol. 1 (New York: Barnes & Noble, 1968). These also contain analyses of the plays. Walter E. Forehand, *Terence* (Boston: Twayne, 1985) considers Terence's life, career, the Roman theatre of Terence, and analyzes the plays.

Evaluation of Selected Biographies

No full-length study exists because of the lack of information; still, the Beare and Duckworth volumes cited above are considered standard sources. There are minor differences in their approach. Beare tends to be conservative in the chronology he offers for Terence. He prefers the later birthdate, for example, even though this would make Terence a teenager when his first play was staged. Beare explains that he considers Terence's powerful patrons might have hastened production and that this could explain a debut at nineteen. Duckworth prefers the earlier birthdate (as most have done) and concentrates on what biographical information can be found in Terence's prologues.

Autobiographical Sources

The prologues of the six comedies are Terence's only writings with possible autobiographical elements. Even in these, however, Terence never refers to himself by name, nor does he specifically refer to any of his patrons. Terence, even in his own times as it seems, faced accusations that his plays were written by his wealthy patrons who could not allow themselves to appear as authors. Cicero (*Atticus* 7.3.10) believed that the plays were written by Gaius Laelius; Quintilian (10.1.99) believed that they were by the younger Scipio. It may be (as Beare suggests) that Terence added prologues to his already written plays in order to defend himself against similar charges. (see the good observations in Beare, rev. ed., p. 159.) More information on the prologues and the *didascaliae* (production notes which appear in the manuscripts and in Donatus's commentary) can be found in H. Mattingly, "The Terentian *Didascaliae.*" *Athenaeum*, n.s. 37 (1951): 148-73.

Overview of Critical Sources

Modern criticism focuses on several topics: the prologues (if and when they were added), the relation of Terence to his patrons and to his Greek sources (the question of whether *contaminatio*, the combining of sources to form a new play), the reliability of the *didascaliae*, the production notes of the manuscripts. The Beare and Duckworth surveys discuss these matters and consider staging conventions, costumes, and general theatre history. Marguerite Bieber, *History of the Greek and Roman Theatre* (Princeton: Princeton University Press, 1961) is a standard volume on architecture and theatre history. The Mattingly article, cited above has become an important work. Mattingly uses the *didascaliae* to argue dates for the plays which differ from those traditionally held. Such alternate dates directly bear on problems of Terentian chronology cited above.

Evaluation of Selected Criticism

Büchner, Karl, *Das Theater des Terenz.* Heidelberg: Winter, 1974. Impressive in its depth and thoroughness, Büchner's study is primarily for the specialist. It provides close readings of all the plays and discusses technical questions of interpretation and production.

Forehand, Walter E. *Terence.* Boston: Twayne, 1985. This is a sound introduction designed for the generalist. It provides a brief biographical sketch, examines Terence's relationship to the theatre of his time, and discusses the plays as offshoots of Greek New Comedy and how they influenced the course of Roman drama.

Jachmann, G. "P. Terentius Afer," in *Realencyclopäedie der classischen Altertumswissenschaft.* A. F. Pauly, G. Wissowa, A. Reihe, ed., vol. 5, pt. 1, col. 598-650, Stuttgart: Metzlersche, 1934. This article is a standard. Though technical and specialized it remains an important source on all textual questions and is inevitably cited in serious studies on Terence.

Konstan, David, *Roman Comedy.* Ithaca: Cornell University Press, 1983. Konstan provides a good introduction to Terence. He deals primarily with differences between Plautus and Terence and offers a good analysis of the *Phormio* and the *Hecyra.*

Norwood, Gilbert, *The Art of Terence.* Oxford: Blackwell, 1923. Norwood's has been for many years a standard college study. It seems increasingly dated in style and approach but is still sound and readily available. He is particularly good on questions of Terentian style.

Other Sources

Greenberg, N. A. "Success and Failure in the *Adelphoe*" in *Classical World* 73 (1979-80): 221-26. Greenberg provides a general analysis of the play and focuses on textual problems in its conclusion. This is a particularly good discussion for students.

Harper's Dictionary of Classical Literature and Antiquities. H. T. Peck, ed. New York: Cooper Square, 1963. This easily found reference work provides the best capsulized biography available and has brief plot summaries of the plays. There are also cross references to Plautus, theatre buildings and history, costumes and staging.

Laidlaw, W. A. "Roman Drama," in *Fifty Years (and Twelve) of Classical Scholarship* with an "Appendix on Roman Comedy" by M. M. Willcock. New York: Barnes & Noble, 1968. This widely circulated study contains essays on all the major areas of classical scholarship. They are written clearly and are for those interested in the major scholarship done in classical studies since the beginning of the century.

Lefèvre, E. *Die römische Komödie: Plautus und Terenz*. Darmstadt: Wissenschaftliche Buchgesellschaft, 1973. This study contains a good chapter on the *Heautontimorumenos* and has good notes on Terence's sources and the question of *contaminatio*, the combining of Greek originals to form a new play.

McGarrity, Terry, "Thematic Unity in Terence's *Andria*," in *Transactions of the American Philological Association* 108 (1978): 103-114. Discusses the play and considers questions of unity and theme.

Segal, Erich, and Carroll Moulton, "*Contortor Legum*: The Hero of the *Phormio*," in *Rheinisches Museum* 121 (1978): 276-288. Provides an interpretation of the play, discussing its hero against the background of ancient law.

Segal, Erich, *Roman Laughter*. Cambridge: Harvard University Press, 1968. This popular treatment provides an introduction to the subject and deals with all the extant plays of Plautus and Terence. It avoids technical matters and is intended for the general reader.

Robert J. Forman
St. John's University, New York

TIRSO DE MOLINA
1582?-1648

Author's Chronology

Born Gabriel Tellez; date of birth is unknown and the year debated, now believed to be in the very early 1580s; possibly illegitimate; nothing is known of his life until 1601 and what little is known after that date cannot be known with a great degree of certainty; *1601* professes into the Order of Our Lady of Mercy; *1603-1607* studies theology at Toledo and Guadalajara; *1608-1610* thought to be studying theology at Alcalá; *1610* begins to write for the stage; *1611 El vergonsozo en palacio*, first play that can be dated with any certainty; *1616* begins to use pseudonym Tirso de Molina and departs for two years for Santo Domingo; *1620* returns to Madrid and continues writing plays; March 6, *1625* the Committee for Reform of the Council of Castile puts out an edict forbidding him to write any more plays, although he continues writing, but less frequently; *1630-1632* resides in Toledo and 1632-1639 goes to Barcelona; dies around February 20, 1648, in Almazán.

Author's Bibliography

Tirso wrote some 400 plays, many of which have been lost. During his lifetime, five "Partes" of *Doze comedias nuevas del Maestro Tirso de Molina* were published: 1627, 1635, 1634, 1635, 1636. His plays have been collected in the older and less reliable edition for the Nueva Biblioteca de Autores Españoles (vols. 4 and 9) by Emilio Cotarelo y Mori and the more carefully edited *Obras dramáticas completas* (3 vols.) by Blanca de los Ríos. Tirso's major prose work is *Los cigarrales de Toledo* (1621), a collection of stories where he briefly discusses dramatic theory (2 vols. Madrid: Espasa-Calpe, 1942).

Overview of Biographical Sources

Because of the scant information available on Tirso, no full-length, definitive biography has appeared. The best and most comprehensive information appears in Manuel Penedo's Introduction to his edition of Tirso's *Historia general de la Orden de Nuestra Señora de las Mercedes* (2 vols. Madrid: Provincia de la Merced de Castilla, 1973, 1974). Emilio Cotarely y Mori has the earliest comprehensive study in *Tirso de Molina: Investigaciones bio-bibliográficas* (Madrid: Imprenta de Enrique Rubinos, 1893). Blanca de los Ríos deals with some important biographical issues in *El enigma biográfico de Tirso de Molina* (Madrid: Tipografía de A. Fontana, 1926). Ruth Lee Kennedy has planned a three-volume study of Tirso and his cultural milieu; so far only Vol. I, *The Dramatist and His Competitors*, has appeared (North Carolina Studies in Romance Languages and Literatures, 3; Valencia: Artes Gráficas Soler, 1974).

Evaluation of Selected Biographies

Cotarelo y Mori, Emilio, *Tirso de Molina: Investigaciones bio-bibliográficas.* Madrid: Imprenta de Enrique Rubinos, 1893. Although Cotarelo y Mori devotes a great part of this early study to a discussion of Tirso's canon, this is the best of the early attempts to bring together the little information available on Tirso.

de los Ríos, Blanca, *El enigma biográfico de Tirso de Molina.* Madrid: Tipografía de Alberto Fontana, 1928. The most important and controversial issue of this biographical study is the baptismal certificate which de los Ríos found. After analyzing it, she suggests that it is Tirso's and argues that it points to the influential Duke of Osuna as Tirso's father. De los Ríos arrives at this conclusion after examining some words that have been scratched out in the baptismal certificate.

Kennedy, Ruth Lee, *The Dramatist and His Competitors.* Vol. I of *Studies in Tirso.* North Carolina Studies in Romance Languages and Literatures, 3. Valencia: Artes Gráficas Soler, 1974. Kennedy discusses the rich cultural milieu of Tirso's Madrid, 1610-1620. In this volume, Kennedy focuses on Tirso's early years in Madrid and his personal and professional relationships with Lope de Vega, Miguel de Guevara, and Ruiz de Alarcón. With the completion of this study, Kennedy should give a more complete and accurate understanding of Tirso.

Penedo, Manuel, Introduction to Tirso de Molina's *Historia general de la Orden de Nuestra Señora de las Mercedes.* 2 vols. Madrid: Provincia de la Merced de Castilla, 1973, 1974. This is the latest and most comprehensive biography of Tirso. Penedo argues against de los Ríos' contention that Tirso was the illegitimate son of the Duke of Osuna. In order for a candidate of illegitimate birth to enter the Order, he would have needed a special dispensation, and Penedo points out that there is no record in the Order for a special dispensation given to Gabriel Tellez.

Autobiographical Sources

Like so many of his contemporaries, Tirso did not collect his letters, and, therefore, no autobiographical information is available. Those biographers who argue that Tirso was an illegitimate child point to passages in his plays where he defends those who were born illegitimate.

Overview of Critical Sources

For a dramatist of his stature, Tirso de Molina has received insufficient critical study. Even the publication in 1955 of de los Ríos's edition of his works did not spark the flurry of critical study that usually accompanies such an event. It seems that now, however, this neglect is slowly being remedied. Naturally enough, *El Burlador de Sevilla* has received most of the attention, but these studies have appeared mostly in articles in scholarly journals.

Evaluation of Selected Criticism

Agheana, Ion Tudor, *The Situational Drama of Tirso de Molina*. New York: Plaza Mayor, 1972. Drawing from most of the canon, Agheana focuses on Tirso's characters as the most important aspect of Tirso's artistic individuality. Agheana also points to Tirso's innovative approach to the use of traditional image patterns.

Darst, David H. *The Comic Art of Tirso de Molina*. Estudios de Hispanofíla, 28. Valencia: Artes Gráficas Soler, 1974. This study is limited to plays in which the characters undergo some sort of spiritual growth. Darst very closely reads each act in each of the seven plays he analyzes to suggest the theatricality of the different scenes within the act and to point to details in the process of the characters' development and change.

Hughes, Ann Nickerson, *Religious Imagery in the Theater of Tirso de Molina*. Macon, GA: Mercer University Press, 1984. Hughes concentrates on the types of plays and *autos sacramentales* which almost by definition would be full of religious imagery. For each type of play, she focuses on the image patterns that are most frequently found: verbal, allegorical, and scenic. Although a comprehensive study, it discusses the plays that are least read, with the exception of *El Burlador de Sevilla*.

McClelland, Ivy L. *Tirso de Molina: Studies in Dramatic Realism*. Liverpool Studies in Spanish Literature, Third Series. Liverpool: Institute of Hispanic Studies, 1948. McClelland argues for the realism of Tirso's characters. While discussing most fully *El Burlador de Sevilla*, McClelland covers many of Tirso's serious dramas and historical plays, leaving out the comedies and including some plays of doubtful authorship.

Sullivan, Henry W. *Tirso de Molina and the Drama of the Counter Reformation*. Amsterdam: Rodopi, 1976. During Tirso's lifetime, Spain was in the middle of the Counter Reformation, and neo-Scholastic theology exerted tremendous influence on all aspects of Spanish culture. Sullivan examines Tirso's drama in light of this theological movement but does not focus on any single play.

Vossler, Karl, *Lecciones sobre Tirso de Molina*. Madrid: Taurus, 1965. This is a collection, published posthumously, of six lectures Vossler gave in 1938 to the University of Havana. Although four of the lectures discuss more general issues such as Tirso's life and canon, Vossler devotes one to *Ninfa del cielo* and *El condenado por desconfiado* and another to *El Burlador de Sevilla*. A bit outdated, this collection offers some close readings of plays that are still useful.

Other Sources

Campbell, Roy, tr. *The Trickster of Seville*, in *Masterpieces of the Spanish Golden Age*. ed. Angel Flores. New York: Holt, Rinehart and Winston, 1957. *El*

Burlador de Sevilla is the play by Tirso that has been translated most often into English, and this verse translation is probably the best.

Parker, Alexander A. *The Approach to the Spanish Drama of the Golden Age.* London: Hispanic and Luso-Brazilian Councils, 1957. Although this seminal study does not concentrate on Tirso, it offers an enlightening reading of *El Burlador de Sevilla*. This short essay is a must reading for all students of Golden Age drama.

Poesse, Walter, comp. *An Annotated, Analytical Bibliography of Tirso de Molina Studies, 1627-1977.* Columbia: University of Missouri Press, 1979. This much awaited bibliography definitely is a major work of scholarship. The thorough annotations should be of use to both the beginning and the seasoned Tirso student.

Singer, Armand E. *A Bibliography of the Don Juan Theme, Versions, and Criticism.* West Virginia Bulletin, Series 54, No. 10-11. Morgantown: West Virginia University Press, 1965. Although not a strictly Tirsian bibliography, this work should be helpful to students of *El Burlador de Sevilla*. Now a bit outdated, it offers a lot of useful information on not only sources for Tirso's most famous and memorable character, but for others that evolved from this creation. Its four main parts consist of a bibliography of the origin, versions, criticism of individual works, and general criticism.

Tirso de Molina: Ensayos sobre la biografía y la obra del Padre Maestro Fray Gabriel Tellez. Madrid: Revista Estudios, 1949. This collection of essays is divided into four parts: biographical studies, studies on the dramatic art of Tirso, studies on documents relating to Tirso's life, and a bibliography of Tirso. The strong point of this collection is the section on Tirso's biography; the weakest, the studies on Tirso's artistry.

Gisela Casines
Florida International University

LEO NIKOLAEVICH TOLSTOY
1828-1910

Author's Chronology

Born August 28, 1828, in Yasnaya Polyana, Russia; mother, Marya Nikolaevna Volkonskaya, dies two years later; father, Nikolai Ilyich, dies when author is nine; lives in a household of women; studies at home and later in Moscow, and at Kazan University, but never graduates; *1841-1847* travels and loose living; *1852* enters army in the Caucasus as a cadet; *1852* publishes first work, *Childhood*; *1852* travels to Paris, London, Germany, Italy, until marriage with Sofia Andreyevna Behrs; *1863-1869* settles at Yasnaya Polyana, writes *War and Peace*; *1873-1877 Anna Karenina*; *1879-1881* religious crisis; chooses a simple life style in the country with manual labor, abstinence from meat, alcohol, and tobacco; changes style of writing; tensions with his wife grow as the family increases; renounces property rights in 1892; *1899 Resurrection* published; *1910* excommunicated by the Holy Synod; October 28, *1910* leaves Yasnaya Polyana seeking interior peace and freedom; falls ill at Astapavo Station (now Leo Tolstoy); dies on November 7, 1910, without a reconciliation with his wife or the Church; buried at Yasnaya Polyana, one of the most important literary shrines in the Soviet Union.

Author's Bibliography

Although Tolstoy's plays are not among his most popular works, nor are they his best, since he was principally a story-teller, he did write several. Among the most important are *Zarazhennoye Semeystvo* (*A Contaminated Family*), 1865, published in 1928; *The Nihilist*, 1866; *Vlast' T'mi* (*The Power of Darkness*), 1866, one of Tolstoy's most popular plays and first performed in Paris in 1888; *Plody Prosveshcheniya* (*The Fruits of Enlightenment*), 1890, a comedy, and also one of his more popular plays; *Zhivoy Trup* (*The Live Corpse*), 1900; *I svet vo t'me svetit* (*A Light Shineth in the Darkness*), 1902, unfinished, but staged; *Ot ney vse kachestva* (*The Cause of it All*), 1910; and *The Progressives*, written around 1863, but not published until 1931. In all Tolstoy began sixteen dramas, but not all were completed. The official Russian edition of all of Tolstoy's works is the *Polnoe sobranie sochinenii*, Moscow: Khydozhestvennaya literatura, 1928-1958, in 90 volumes, the so-called Jubilee Edition. *The Centenary Edition of Tolstoy*, in 21 volumes, London: Oxford University Press, 1929-1937, translated by Louise and Aylmer Maude, contains the most important works, including a volume of the *Plays*. The most recent English edition is the *Complete Works of Tolstoy*, edited by Leo Wiener, New York: AMS Press, 1968.

Overview of Biographical Sources

There are numerous biographies of Tolstoy in all languages. Since Tolstoy is very popular in the Soviet Union and is acclaimed as the model of "Socialist Realism," biographies by Soviet authors tend to stress his leanings toward the peasantry, and hail him as a forerunner of the Revolution. The first official Soviet biography is by P.I. Biryukov, *Lev Nikolaevich Tolstoy: Biografiya*, in four volumes, 1911-1923. One of the most popular Soviet biographies is V. Shklovsky's, Lev Tolstoi (Moscow, 1963). English editions include the authoriattive *The Life of Tolstoy*, by Aylmer Maude (1930), and the American biography by Ernest J. Simmons, *Leo Tolstoy* (1960) is extremely readable and reliable. Henri Troyat's biography first published in French and widely available in English (1967), is likewise well-documented and reliable. There are many volumes of reminiscenses of unequal value written by Tolstoy's family, friends, and contemporaries, such as those by his sons and daughters, Ilya, Lev, Sergei, and Alexandra. Alexandra's final volume, *Tolstoy, A Life of My Father*, seems the most objective.

Evaluation of Selected Biographies

Maude, Aylmer, *The Life of Tolstoy: First Fifty Years*. London: Oxford University Press, 1908, 1930; *The Life of Tolstoy: Later Years*. vol. II, 1910, 1930. This two-volume series is still considered by many the definitive English biography of Tolstoy. Written by the translator and publisher of many of Tolstoy's works, and a personal acquaintance of the great writer, it contains records of personal encounters of Maude with Tolstoy. The first volume especially contains numerous and lengthy quotations from Tolstoy's diaries, letters, and reminiscences. The chapter of *Confession* is simply an edited text of Tolstoy's work. Maude is obviously sympathetic to Tolstoy in his conflict with his wife, documenting his work with numerous quotations from Countess Tolstoy's diaries. The book is basically biographical, with little literary analysis, although there is good documentation of Tolstoy's works, with a chronology of the author and a list of sources.

Simmons, Ernest J. *Leo Tolstoy*. Boston: Little, Brown, 1945; New York: Vintage Books, 1960. This is a well-documented, extremely readable, biography, praised by scholars as a definitive work. In addition to detailed biographical information, it contains an analysis of most of Tolstoy's works, and just about all are mentioned and related to his life. Simmons makes ample use of Tolstoy's diaries and letters, and other archival material. He analyzes Tolstoy's tumultuous marriage and the ensuing bursts of hysteria by Tolstoy's wife Sonya with impartiality, and develops Tolstoy's religious crisis and change in behavior from its beginning stages. This is a basic text for the Tolstoy scholar. It has family tables, but no notes, bibliography, or list of works.

Tolstoy, Alexandra L. *Tolstoy, A Life of My Father*. Belmont, MA: Nordland Press, 1953; rpt. 1975. Tolstoy's youngest daughter, totally devoted to her father, is also the author of *Memoirs* and *The Tragedy of Tolstoy*. This sizeable volume is based mainly on personal recollections, letters, and diaries. Alexandra notes, however, that much material, held in the Soviet Union, was unavailable for her use. Alexandra's preference for her father is evident, although she has made every effort to understand her mother, and speaks touchingly of her final reconciliation. There is little literary criticism, although the composition of most works is noted and related to the biography.

Troyat, Henri, *Tolstoy*. New York: Doubleday, 1967. First published in France by the Librairie Arthène Fayard in 1965 as *Tolstoï*, this biography joins those written by the author on Pushkin and Dostoevsky. Since Troyat is mainly an author of fiction, the biography resembles a novel. Troyat makes extensive use of diaries and letters. While the major works are analyzed and related to Tolstoy's biography, especially *Anna Karenina* and *War and Peace*, the plays are simply mentioned. Troyat maintains objectivity in the delicate analysis of Tolstoy's family relations. There is a fairly extensive bibliogrpahy with English, French, and Russian sources.

Autobiographical Sources

Although Tolstoy never wrote an autobiography properly speaking, there are numerous materials that qualify as autobiograhical. Tolstoy's diaries, as well as his wife's, played a very important role in their marital relationship, and caused an initial tension between the two when Tolstoy insisted that his future wife read his diary before their marriage. The standard Russian "Jubilee Edition" devotes about half of the ninety volumes to Tolstoy's diaries, notebooks, and letters. Not all of these are available in English. The reader anxious to discover Tolstoy's personal life should consult *The Diaries of Leo Tolstoy*, 1847-1852, translated by C.J. Hogarth and A. Sirnis (London: Oxford University Press, 1917), and *The Private Diary of Leo Tolstoy*, 1853-1857, translated by Louise and Aylmer Maude, 1927. *The Letters of Tolstoy and His Cousin Countess Alexandra Tolstoy*, 1857-1903, translated by L. Islavin, London, 1929, are also valuable materials. Aylmer Maude also translated a number of works entitled *Recollections and Essays* (London: Oxford University Press, 1937).

Tolstoy, Literary Fragments, edited by René Fülöp-Miller (New York: AMS Press, 1971), contains a good choice of literary fragments, including two unpublished plays, and letters, reminiscences, and entries to diaries by Tolstoy and his family and friends. Most recently, R.F. Christian has selected, edited, and translated the letters of Tolstoy in two volumes: *Tolstoy's Letters*, vol. 1, 1828-1879; vol. II, 1880-1910 (London: Oxford University Press, 1978), an important contribution to Tolstoy scholarship.

Autobiographical elements dominate throughout Tolstoy's works, particularly after 1870. Two important works that relate to his religious struggles are *Confession*, 1879, a record of his extensive inquiry into the purpose of life, and *What I Believe*,

1883, again addressing his relationship to religion. Neither book was published in Russia at that time because of Tolstoy's critical attitude toward the Orthodox Church. The fictional series, *Childhood*, 1852, *Boyhood*, 1856, and *Youth*, 1857, contain much that is autobiographical, with certain passages in Tolstoy's *Recollections* practically duplicating the material. *Childhood* is considered the best in the series, even by Tolstoy himself.

Evaluation of Selected Autobiographies

Confession, 1879. Tolstoy subtitled his *Confession* "An Introduction to a Criticism of Dogmatic Theology and an Investigation of the Christian Teachings." He traces his reflections on the meaning of life for the previous five years, and describes his state as a spiritual malaise. Thoughts of suicide plagued him. He recalls his investigation of various philosophies, religions, and the life of the simple peasants. The work is honest and forthright, and expresses Tolstoy's desire to spend his life as a "seeker after truth." This slim volume is essential to the understanding of Tolstoy's inner life and spiritual evolution.

Recollections. Written between 1902 and 1908, but never prepared for publication, these pages are accessible to the English-speaking reader in the Aylmer Maude edition *Recollections and Essays*. London: Oxford University Press, 1937. They are considered "jottings," and focus mainly on Tolstoy's boyhood days, although there is a significant section in which he recalls his first horror of capital punishment. There are also repeated references by Tolstoy to the "ant brotherhood," showing how it related to his dream of universal human brotherhood.

Overview of Critical Sources

Although the amount of criticism of Tolstoy is voluminous, both in the Soviet union and abroad, most of the works address the novels, considered as the major portion of Tolstoy's literary output. For anyone studying his drama, it is well to consult the general works that deal with art, style, personal and religious beliefs, and his philosophy of history. Among these are Isaiah Berlin's classic *The Hedgehog and the Fox* (New York: New American Library, 1957), dealing with Tolstoy's philosophy of history; Malcolm Jones' *New Essays on Tolstoy* (London: Cambridge University Press, 1978), which in addition to the major novels treats the question of time in an essay by Evgenii Lampert, religion, addressed through Tolstoy's semiautobiographical works, and his Rousseauistic tendencies in an essay by E.B. Greenwood, and an excellent bibliographic survey of works published in Great Britain, 1946-1977. Ralph Matlaw's *Tolstoy, A Collection of Critical Essays* (Englewood Cliffs, NJ: Prentice Hall, 1967), also contains many valuable essays, mainly on the novels. Among the Soviet critics, one of the best known and most reliable is the Tolstoy specialist Boris Eikhenbaum, whose works on Tolstoy are now available in English.

Evaluation of Selected Criticism

Christian, R.F. *Tolstoy: A Critical Introduction*. Cambridge: Cambridge University Press, 1969. Although mainly devoted to a detailed analysis of *War and Peace* and *Anna Karenina*, with a chronological survey of Tolstoy's other major fiction, the book contains a chapter on "Art, Drama, and the People." Christian discusses Tolstoy's dramatic tastes, including his criticism of Shakespeare, and his four major plays. He sees biographical interest rather than character development in the serious plays, whereas the comedies present dramatic interest. He notes also the reaction of Soviet critics and the staging of Tolstoy's plays both in the USSR and abroad. There is also a brief but perceptive analysis of Tolstoy's autobiographical work *Confession*.

Eikhenbaum, Boris, *The Young Tolstoy*. Ann Arbor, MI: Ardis, 1972; (*Molodoi Tolstoy*, 1922); *Tolstoy in the Sixties*, 1982 (*Lev Tolstoi, shestidesiatye gody*, 1931); *Tolstoy in the Seventies*, 1982 (*Lev Tolstoi, semidesiatye gody*, 1960). This three-volume work, only recently available in English, is the classic criticism of Tolstoy and represents the life-work of Boris Eikhenbaum. Eikhenbaum belonged to a literary movement popular in Russia from 1915-1930 called Formalism, which aimed to separate the inner psychological life of the author from his literary production, and to concentrate as far as possible exclusively on the latter. The books contain detailed literary analysis of all of Tolstoy's major works, including his drama, and include detailed notes and references. A knowledge of this work is indispensable to the Tolstoy scholar.

Gibian, George, *Tolstoy and Shakespeare*. The Hague: Mouton, 1957. This short monograph traces Tolstoy's dislike of Shakespeare throughout his career, with particular emphasis on *What is Art* and *On Shakespeare and On Drama*. Gibian analyzes Tolstoy's criticism of *King Lear*, and his proposed work on *Hamlet*. He concludes that Tolstoy found Shakespeare's works deficient in subject, technical beauty, and emotional sincerity, and especially found their moral basis corrupt. He points out that both in practice and theory Tolstoy's dramatic art differed essentially from Shakespeare's, particularly in Tolstoy's emphasis on moral and religious purpose. The scholar of Tolstoy's drama will find here an important critical base.

Gifford, Henry, *Tolstoy*. Oxford/New York: Oxford University Press, 1982. This short book, deeply indebted to Aylmer Maude's *Life of Tolstoy*, and primary sources from Tolstoy's letters, aims to trace the development of Tolstoy's thought and his literary vocation. Gifford studies Tolstoy as related to his times, an expression of nineteenth-century Russia, and analyzes his importance for today, especially for the western world. He sees Tolstoy as an artist and creative writer, and a seeker after truth. Detailed analysis is given to the novels rather than the plays, but the emphasis on Tolstoy's artistic philosophy and moral convictions make it helpful in understanding all of Tolstoy's works.

Lavrin, Janko, *Tolstoy: An Approach*. New York: Macmillan, 1946. This long-time popular book is a good introduction to Tolstoy the author, with some essential biographical references. Very readable, without a great number of quotations, it concentrates on the art and religious views of Tolstoy, concluding with comparisons of Tolstoy with Rousseau and Nietzsche.

Lomunov, K.N. *Dramaturgiya L. N. Tolstogo*. Moskva, 1956. One of the few volumes devoted entirely to Tolstoy as a dramatist, this book is available only to Russian readers. The author incorporates Tolstoy's views on Shakespeare, the French theater, and the Russian stage. He analyzes each play well, and traces its composition. The thrust of the criticism is Marxist-Leninist, emphasizing Tolstoy's portrayal of the people and his dislike of bourgeois capitalism, yet it contains ample analysis and various interpretations of Tolstoy's dramas. There are numerous notes and references to the production of Tolstoy's plays in the USSR and abroad.

Merejkowski, Dmitri, *Tolstoi as Man and Artist*, Westport, CT: Greenwood Press, 1970 (original edition, 1902). This long-time classic of pre-Revolutionary Russia compares Tolstoy and Dostoevsky as persons and as writers, and contrary to the formalist view, seeks to integrate the two. It is mainly a religious study of the two authors, in which Merejkowsky sees Tolstoy as the seer of the body in a Greek and Old Testament sense, and Dostoevsky as a prophet of the spirit in a Christian and New Testament interpretation. The literary criticism is very perceptive, although the biographical and symbolic conclusions have frequently been questioned.

Other Sources

Bailey, L.W. "Tolstoy as a Playwright". *Drama*, CX (Autumn 1973): 50-55.

Countess Tolstoy's Later Diary, 1891-1897, tr. A. Werth. London: Oxford University Press, 1929.

The Diary of Tolstoy's Wife, 1860-1891, tr. A. Werth. London: Oxford University Press, 1928.

Egan, David R. and Egan, Melinda A. *Leo Tolstoy: An Annotated Bibliography of English-Language Sources to 1978*. Scarecrow, 1979.

The Final Struggle, being Countess Tolstoy's Diary for 1910. tr, A. Maude. London: Oxford University Press, 1936. Also contains selections from Tolstoy's diaries, letters, and reminiscences.

Gorki, Maxim, *Reminiscences of Tolstoy, Chekhov, and Andreyev*. London: Oxford University Press, 1934.

The Russian Review, April 1960. Edition devoted to Tolstoy. *Literaturnoe Nasledstvo*, Moscow, 1939. Contains important articles by Lukacs on Tolstoy and the development of realism, and V. Vinogradov on Tolstoy's language; 1960 and 1965: also issues devoted to Tolstoy.

Sister Irma Mercedes Kashuba, S.S.J.
Chestnut Hill College

CYRIL TOURNEUR
1575?-1626

Author's Chronology

Born between 1570 and 1585, possibly to the family of Edward Turnor of Canons, Great Parndon, Essex; *c. 1596* probably begins service as secretary to Sir Francis Vere, perhaps accompanying him on an expedition against the Spanish fleet at Cadiz; *1600* publishes *The Transformed Metamorphosis*; *1607 The Revenger's Tragedy* is recorded on the Stationers' Register; publishes *A Funeral Poem Upon the Death of . . . Sir Francis Vere*, further indicating his association with that family; *1611 The Atheist's Tragedy* entered on the Stationers' Register; *1612* reference made on the Register to Tourneur's lost play *The Nobleman*; *1613* publishes *A Grief on the Death of Prince Henry*; carries diplomatic papers from London to Brussels in connection with the war in the Low Countries; *1617* arrested for unknown reasons at the order of the Privy Council, then released within a month; *1625* joins, as secretary to both Sir Edward Cecil and the Council of War, an abortive naval attack on Cadiz; abandoned, mortally ill, with other casualties at Kinsale, Ireland; *1626* dies, February 18, at Kinsale; *1632* Tourneur's impoverished widow renews a petition to the Council of War for her late husband's back pay.

Author's Bibliography (selected)

The Transformed Metamorphosis, 1600 (allegorical poem); **Laugh and Lie Down*, 1605 (pamphlet); **The Revenger's Tragedy*, c. 1607 (play); *A Funeral Poem Upon the Death of the Most Worthy and True Soldier Sir Francis Vere*, 1609 (elegy); *The Atheist's Tragedy*, c. 1611 (play); "Character of Robert Earl of Salisbury," 1612 (prose "portrait"); **A Grief on the Death of Prince Henry*, 1613 (elegy); ***"On the Death of a Child But One Year Old," 1899 (elegy); ***"Of My Lady Anne Cecil . . . ," 1660 (poem). Entries marked with an asterisk are of uncertain authorship.

Overview of Biographical Sources

Writing in 1878, John Churton Collins, an early Tourneur editor, could find only "a blank" in his search for facts about the playwright's life; exactly one hundred years later, editor George Parfitt confirms that Tourneur is "an almost completely obscure figure." This sketchiness of biographical information is reflected in the above chronology and accounts for the fact that nothing like a full-length biography of Tourneur is (or is likely to be) available. The most detailed account remains Allardyce Nicoll's bio-critical introduction to his *The Works of Cyril Tourneur* (1963). More recent biographical summaries can be found in Peter B. Murray's *A*

Study of Cyril Tourneur (Philadelphia: University of Pennsylvania Press, 1964); Irving Ribner's Revels edition of *The Atheist's Tragedy* (Cambridge: Harvard University Press, 1964); Brian Gibbon's New Mermaid edition of *The Revenger's Tragedy* (1967); and Samuel Schuman's *Cyril Tourneur* (Boston: Twayne, 1977).

Evaluation of Selected Biographies

Nicoll, Allardyce, ed. *The Works of Cyril Tourneur.* London, 1929; rpt. New York: Russell and Russell, 1963. Nicoll's biographical review encompasses some forty-six pages, but the account is padded with explications of the works and Nicoll's defense of Tourneur as the author of *The Revenger's Tragedy.* Further, the lack of solid information about Tourneur's life prompts Nicoll into some ingenious but questionable speculations, including the suggestion that the playwright may be identified with one Captain William Turner (or Turnour), a particularly dissolute spy in the continental service of Robert Cecil. Finally, a bit of biographical material has emerged since Nicoll's work, notably James R. Sutherland's discovery of a reference to Tourneur in a letter, dating form 1614, from James Bathurst to William Trumbull (see Sutherland's "Cyril Turneur," *Times Literary Supplement*, 16 April 1931, p. 307). Nonetheless, Nicoll's account of Tourneur is the most complete, and even his speculations are sharp and illuminating. Nicoll's conservative edition of the works, retaining the original spelling (though not the original punctuation) of the quarto, is the standard research source for Tourneur's plays; it is hampered only by the paucity of its notes.

Schuman, Samuel, *Cyril Tourneur.* Boston: Twayne, 1977. Schuman's book is an especially solid contribution to Tourneur studies. The first chapter reviews what is known of Tourneur's life in a sane, witty, and straightforward manner. The book as a whole provides the reader who is new to Tourneur with the best available overview of the biographical, critical and textual problems that the playwright presents.

Autobiographical Sources

Although the elusive Tourneur left behind no autobiographical information, some scholars, desperate for facts about his life, have sought to discover the background and personality of the author in his works. Accordingly, some critics see Tourneur in the brooding narrator of *The Transformed Metamorphosis* or in the character of Vindice in *The Revenger's Tragedy*, while a reference to the defense of Ostend in *The Atheist's Tragedy* has led others to draw conclusions about Tourneur's military career. Such conjectures, given the difficulties of properly attributing Tourneur's canon, seem especially doubtful. The closest one comes to a dependable source is the petition of Mary Tourneur (see *Chronology*) to the Council of War; only because of this appeal, for example, do we know that Tourneur was a married man.

Overview of Critical Sources

Tourneur's reputation has long resided under a critical cloud. *The Revenger's Tragedy*, a work of compelling appeal, is recognized as one of the signal accomplishments of Shakespeare's contemporaries, and Tourneur's claim to greatness rests chiefly with that play. But the tragedy was registered anonymously in 1607; and although it was attributed to Tourneur as early as 1656, that attribution has been widely challenged since the 1890s. The situation has given rise to some inevitable ironies. For example, the only general book-length treatment of Tourneur (save for Schuman's review, cited above) is Peter B. Murray's *A Study of Cyril Tourneur*, a work which labors hard to "prove" that *The Revenger's Tragedy* was written by Thomas Middleton. Recently, attempts have been made to rehabilitate *The Atheist's Tragedy*, a play which is indisputably Tourneur's but which is still reckoned, on most counts, to be distinctly inferior to *The Revenger's Tragedy*. To generalize, three major areas interest Tourneur scholars today: the authorship of *The Revenger's Tragedy*, the moral position implied by that drama, and the degree to which to character of Vindice reflects the playwright's own world-view. The sampling of critical approaches which follows chiefly addresses those three concerns.

Evaluation of Selected Criticism

Eliot, T. S. "Cyril Tourneur," in *Selected Essays, 1917-1932*. 1932; rpt. London: Faber and Faber, 1950. Eliot seems to identify Tourneur with *The Revenger's Tragedy*'s Vindice, finding in both figures an intense loathing of life and a pathological fascination with death and corruption, so that the play becomes a sort of psychological indictment of the playwright himself. Eliot's view, while commonly derided today, remains germinal and important.

Kernan, Alvin, *The Cankered Muse*. New Haven: Yale University Press, 1959. Kernan argues for the classification of *The Revenger's Tragedy* as a "tragical satire" rather than as a pure example of the revenge tragedy. In this view, Vindice (like Hamlet) is primarily a satirist, an unmasker of pretense and illusion. Ironically, Vindice himself becomes one with the corrupt society he detests, so that his own death is finally necessary to set his fictive world right. Kernan's discussion is immensely valuable, not only with regard to Tourneur but also in terms of the entire tradition of Senecan blood revenge.

Lisca, Peter, "*The Revenger's Tragedy*: A Study in Irony." *Philological Quarterly* 38 (1959): 242-51. Lisca focuses on the technique of ironic reversal in the Ambitioso-Supervacuo episode in *The Revenger's Tragedy*. Indeed, Lisca finds that verbal and dramatic irony abounds in the play, growing out of the discrepancy between the revenger's actions on the one hand and his Calvinistic sensibilities on the other.

Murray, Peter B. *A Study of Cyril Tourneur*. Philadelphia: University of Pennsylvania Press, 1964. Murray deals mainly with *The Transformed Metamorphosis*, *The Atheist's Tragedy*, and *The Revenger's Tragedy*. Against Eliot and others, he sees Vindice not as the dramatist's mouthpiece nor as an inveterate life-hater but—at least initially—as one who occupies Anglican middle moral ground. However, Vindice quickly degenerates within the inverted, corrupt society around him, a declination which can be measured in his attitude toward the dead Gloriana and toward all women generally; his "quest for justice" becomes instead a certain "journey to damnation." Murray expends some thirty pages (complete with charts!) in an attempt to demonstrate Middleton's authorship of the play.

Ribner, Irving, *Jacobean Tragedy: The Quest for Moral Order*. London: Methuen, 1962, pp. 72-96. Ribner views the action of *The Revenger's Tragedy* as a kind of medieval *danse macabre* and sees Tourneur as an advocate of primitive Christianity, championing in the play an exclusive reliance on God and a contempt for the natural world. Ribner's characteristic tendency to perceive Jacobean dramas as didactic object lessons in morality is apparent in his approach to Tourneur.

Other Sources

Bowers, Fredson Thayer, *Elizabethan Revenge Tragedy, 1587-1642*. Princeton: Princeton University Press, 1940, pp. 133-44. *The Revenger's Tragedy* and *The Atheist's Tragedy* viewed in light of the revenge play tradition.

Boyer, Clarence Valentine, *The Villain as Hero in Elizabethan Tragedy*. New York: Russell and Russell, 1964, esp. pp. 145-151, 165-171. Vindice (*The Revenger's Tragedy*) and D'Amville (*The Atheist's Tragedy*) as villainous protagonists.

Forker, Charles R. "Cyril Tourneur," in *The New Intellectuals: A Survey and Bibliography of Recent Studies in English Renaissance Drama*, ed. Terence P. Logan and Denzell S. Smith. Lincoln: University of Nebraska Press, 1977, pp. 248-280. Detailed bibliographic essay on all of Tourneur's works; absolutely essential reading.

Higgins, Michael H. "The Influence of Calvinistic Thought in *The Atheist's Tragedy*." *Review of English Studies* 19 (1943): 255-262. Sees the play as reflecting Calvin's *Christian Institutions*.

Jackson, MacD. P. "Compositional Practices in *The Revenger's Tragedy*, 1607-08," *Papers of the Bibliographical Society of America* 1981; 75 (2): 157-70. Following the lead of George R. Price, David Lake, and others, Jackson argues that holographic similarities between *The Revenger's Tragedy* and Middleton's *A Game of Chess* (1624) indicate a common Middleton authorship.

Ornstein, Robert, *The Moral Vision of Jacobean Tragedy*. Madison: University of Wisconsin Press, 1960, pp. 105-127. Denies any identification between Tourneur and the Italianate Vindice, seeing the revenger as one "whose moral viewpoint is limited and perverse"; affirms Tourneur's authorship.

Peter, John, "*The Revenger's Tragedy* Reconsidered." *Essays in Criticism* 6 (1956): 131-134. Argues, against Eliot, that positive moral standards are implicit throughout the play.

Ribner, Irving, ed. *The Atheist's Tragedy*. The Revels Plays. Cambridge: Harvard University Press, 1964. Traces the influences on the play and discusses the antagonism between D'Amville and Charlemont.

Salingar, L. G. "*The Revenger's Tragedy* and the Morality Tradition," *Scrutiny* 6 (1938): 402-412. Asserts that the play is a natural outgrowth of medieval drama.

Selected Dictionaries and Encyclopedias

Critical Survey of Drama, Vol. 5, Salem Press, 1985. A brief biographical note followed by Arthur Kincaid's admirable critical overview of the two extant tragedies.

Dictionary of National Biography, Vol. 19, Oxford University Press, 1885-1900. Offers a helpful biographical sketch and a decidedly lurid commentary on the plays.

William Ryland Drennan
University of Wisconsin Center-
Baraboo/Sauk County

IVAN TURGENEV
1818-1883

Author's Chronology

Born October 28, 1818, in Oryol, central Russia, to Varvara Petrovna, a wealthy landowner, and Sergey Turgenev, a cavalry officer, and raised on his mother's estate, Spasskoye; *1827* moves to Moscow to attend Moscow University; *1834* transfers to Petersburg University, from which he graduates in 1837; *1838-1841* travels in Europe; *1843* meets Pauline Viardot, a French singer who becomes his lifelong inspiration; *1847-1850* publishes *A Sportsman's Sketches*; *1850* mother dies and he receives large inheritance; *1852-1853* arrested for praising Gogol and exiled to Spasskoye; *1856* publishes *Rudin*; *1860* accused of plagiarism concerning *First Love* but charges are arbitrated; *1862* publishes *Fathers and Sons*; *1863* moves to Baden-Baden, Germany where he lives with the Viardot family until 1871; *1867* publishes *Smoke*; *1870* publishes *A King Lear of the Steppes*; *1872 A Month in the Country* is first performed in Moscow; *1875* buys estate with the Viardots in Bougival near Paris where he lives until his death; *1877* publishes *Virgin Soil*; September 3, 1883 dies in Bougival of cancer.

Author's Bibliography (selected)

The Bachelor, 1849 (play); *A Month in the Country*, 1850 (play); *The Provincial Lady*, 1851 (play); *A Sportsman's Sketches*, 1852 (short stories); *Rudin*, 1855 (novel); *A Nest of Gentlefolk*, 1859 (novel); *On the Eve*, 1860 (novel); "First Love," 1860 (novella); "Hamlet and Quixote," 1860 (essay); *Fathers and Sons*, 1861 (novel); *Smoke*, 1867 (novel); *Reminiscences*, 1869; *Spring Freshets*, 1872 (novel); "Punin and Barburin," 1874 (novella); *Virgin Soil*, 1877 (novel); "Clara Milch," 1883 (novella); *Collected Works*, 1883.

Overview of Biographical Sources

Because Turgenev's fiction was influential in the development of Russian realism, because he was so widely respected as a novelist by such influential writers as Henry James, and finally because he was such a controversial writer in terms of 19th-century Russian intellectual life, particularly in regard to the controversy that surrounded the publication of *Fathers and Sons*; there has always been a great public desire to know about his life. It is fortunate therefore, primarily because Turgenev was such a prolific writer of letters, that a great deal is known about him. It is doubly fortunate that two biographers who know so well the Russian language and Russian culture have written very readable and well-researched studies of the man and his age. There is little doubt that David Magarshack's *Turgenev: A Life* (1954) and Avrahm Yarmolinsky's *Turgenev: The Man, His Art and His Age* (1959) are still the standard biographies—the ones upon which subsequent studies depend the most heavily. However, for those who wish a more popular introduction, perhaps preparatory to the Magarshack and Yarmolinsky studies, V.S. Pritchett's *The Gentle Barbarian* (1977) is the most accessible. On the other hand, the reader desiring the most recent biography, one that makes use of material previously unavailable and one that is highly documented with footnote reference, may wish to consult Leonard Schapiro's *Turgenev: His Life and Times* (1978).

Evaluation of Selected Biographies

Magarshack, David, *Turgenev: A Life*. London: Faber and Faber, 1954. This detailed and readable account of Turgenev's life is one of the two most cited and dependable biographies, rivaled only by the study by Yarmolinsky in giving a complete account of Turgenev's life and its integration into his art. It is more detailed on Turgenev's dramas and the role they played in the development of his art than the biography by Yarmolinsky.

Pritchett, V.S. *The Gentle Barbarian: The Life and Work of Turgenev*. New York: Random House, 1977. This is a very readable, popular study based largely on the biographies of Magarshack and Yarmolinsky and based solely on previous work in translation. Therefore, although there is little new here, the book has Pritchett's lucid style and his own knowledge of the nature of fiction to recommend it. Taking the position that Turgenev was primarily an autobiographical writer, Pritchett attempts to use Turgenev's life to increase our understanding of his works, particularly his novels and short stories.

Schapiro, Leonard, *Turgenev: His Life and Times*. New York: Random House, 1978. This most recent biography, although it does not substantially change the view of Turgenev established by Magarshack and Yarmolinsky, does make use of new material about Turgenev's work available previously only in Russian as well as new material about his relationship to Pauline Viardot available previously in French. It is strictly a study of Turgenev's life and makes no attempts to analyze his art. Heavily documented and quite an extensive study, it is readable and primarily objective in its presentation of the facts of Turgenev's life.

Yarmolinsky, Avrahm, *Turgenev: The Man, His Art and His Age*. New York: Orion Press, 1959. This is a complete revision of Yarmolinsky's 1926 biography, which, based as it was on Russian sources unavailable to the English-speaking reader, was the first authoritative biography of Turgenev for the West. Not only is it a full-developed account of the events of Turgenev's life, it also provides a discussion of his intellectual and artistic development as well as a discussion of his contribution to an understanding of 19th-century Russian culture.

Autobiographical Sources

Turgenev was a prolific letter writer; thus his correspondence, of which over 6,000 letters covering more than fifty years of his life are known, give the reader a first-hand knowledge of his widely diverse interests and his views of events and social movements of his time. The most helpful collections of English translations of Turgenev's letters are the selection translated by A.V. Knowles, *Turgenev's Letters* (London: Athlone Press, 1983); Edgar Lehrman's *Turgenev's Letters: A Selection* (New York: Alfred A. Knopf, 1960); Nora Gottlieb and Raymond Chapman's *Letters to an Actress* (Athens: Ohio University Press, 1974); and the two-volume collection edited and translated by David Lowe, *Turgenev Letters* (Ann Arbor, MI: Ardis, 1983). This last collection contains over 200 letters not previously available in English. In addition to his massive collection of letters, the best source of autobiographical information about Turgenev are within the sketches contained in *Turgenev's Literary Reminiscences*, translated by David Magarshack (New York: Farrar, Straus & Cudahy, 1958). The book contains an apologia for *Fathers and Sons* which clearly states Turgenev's views of the novel form, as well as a series of eight autobiographical fragments that deal with various periods in Turgenev's life.

Overview of Critical Sources

Although there are numerous studies of Turgenev in Russian and a rather large number of brief essay-length studies of individual works in English, there are few full-scale studies of his art. Biographical studies are more predominant and dependable than full-length critical estimates. Moreover, the critical studies which do exist focus almost solely on Turgenev's fiction—the great novels, short stories and novellas. Very little has been done with Turgenev's dramas, with most critics tacitly agreeing that they are early work, a false start before Turgenev found his true vocation in fiction. With the exception of *A Month in the Country*, Turgenev's most famous play, a respected psychological comedy, Turgenev's dramas are not very often taken seriously. In fact, Turgenev himself did not seem to take them seriously, saying that they do not show the slightest dramatic talent, and that he did not even intend *A Month in the Country* for the stage, but rather that he conceived it as a short novel in dramatic form.

Evaluation of Selected Criticism

Freeborn, Richard, *Turgenev: The Novelist's Novelist*. London and New York: Oxford University Press, 1960. A general study of the basic features of the Turgenev novel both in terms of its place in 19th-century Russia and in terms of Henry James's estimate that Turgenev was the "novelist's novelist." The center of the book is an analysis of the structure, ideas, characters and artistic achievement of Turgenev's four major novels: *Rudin*, *A Nest of Gentlefolk*, *On the Eve*, and *Fathers and Sons*.

Garnett, Edward, *Turgenev: A Study*. London: W. Collins Sons, 1917. This early general study, the first in English to evaluate Turgenev's art, is made up primarily of the prefaces that Garnett wrote to the translations of Turgenev by his wife, Constance Garnett. It is less a detailed criticism than it is a fragmented and sketchy appreciation and a defense of Turgenev against the adverse early criticism with which his work was received.

Kagan-Kans, Eva, *Hamlet and Don Quiote: Turgenev's Ambivalent Vision*. The Hague: Mouton, 1975. A study of Turgenev's short stories and novellas from the perspective of their philosophic world view. The emphasis is on Turgenev's technique for conveying his philosophic concepts, which primarily vacillate between faith and doubt. Although the study does not deal with the drama, it is helpful in establishing Turgenev's philosophic position, especially insofar as it informs his male and female characters.

Ledkovsky, Marina, *The Other Turgenev: From Romanticism to Symbolism*. Wurzburg: jal-verlag, 1973. Because Turgenev has been primarily seen as a "realist" author, Ledkovsky argues that his interest in the irrational and the supernatural have been ignored. This study fills a gap in Turgenev criticism by tracing the influence both of German romanticism and of Hegel and Schopenhauer's aesthetics on Turgenev's thought. Ledkovsky surveys the many "non-realist" themes in Turgenev's work and is especially helpful in clarifying many of Turgenev's short stories which do not fit within the definition of realism. The study quite convincingly shows that Turgenev paves the way for Russian Symbolism.

Ripp, Victor, *Turgenev's Russia*. Ithaca, NY: Cornell University Press, 1980. Although this study focuses on Turgenev's fiction between the publication of *A Sportsman's Sketches* and *Fathers and Sons* and therefore does not deal with the drama, it is valuable in delineating Turgenev's place in progressive political thought in 19th-century Russia and in clarifying the important cultural issues that inform Turgenev's work.

Other Sources

Gettman, Royal A. *Turgenev in England and America*. Urbana: University of Illinois Press, 1941. A survey of the reception of Turgenev's novels by English and American critics during the following periods: 1855-1877, 1877-1885, 1885-1900, and 1900-1937.

Mirsky, D.S. *A History of Russian Literature*. New York: Alfred A. Knopf, 1949. This famous general study of Russian Literature includes an important section on Turgenev that analyzes his fiction in terms of the development of Russian realism.

Waddington, Patrick, *Turgenev and England*. New York: New York University Press, 1981. A detailed biographical and historical study of Turgenev's interest in things English and a chronicle of his visits to England and his reactions to what he experienced there.

Waddington, Patrick, *Turgenev and George Sand: An Improbable Entente*. London: Macmillan Press, 1981. A brief study of a neglected aspect of Turgenev's life—his relations with the French novelist George Sand, drawn partially from previously unpublished diaries and letters of Sand. The focus is primarily on the relationship as an attraction of opposites.

Zhitova, V. *The Turgenev Family*. New York: Roy Publishers, 1947. A series of reminiscences published originally in 1884 and told in narrative style.

Selected Dictionaries and Encyclopedias

Cassells's Encyclopedia of World Literature, William Morrow, 1954. Brief biographical sketch, selected bibliography of primary and secondary works.

Cyclopedia of World Authors, rev. ed. Salem Press, 1974. Brief biography and analysis of major themes, bibliography of primary and secondary works.

The Reader's Encyclopedia of World Drama, Thomas Crowell, 1969. Brief discussion of the basic themes and background of the plays.

Charles E. May
California State University
Long Beach

ROYALL TYLER
1757-1826

Author's Chronology

Born William Clark Tyler on July 18, 1757 in Boston, Massachusetts, to Royall and Mary Steele Tyler; following his father's death in 1771, changes his name to Royall Tyler, since his older brother, John Steele had been disinherited and since the entire estate left by his father went to the now legally named Royall Tyler; *1772-1776* attends Harvard College; receives B.A. from Harvard and an honorary B.A. from Yale; *1778* serves as Brigade Major of the Light Corps and probably sees action during General John Sullivan's unsuccessful assault on Newport, Rhode Island; *1779* receives M.A. in law from Harvard; *1780* is admitted to the Massachusetts bar; *1782-1785* practices law in Braintree (Quincy), Massachusetts where he meets and courts Abigail Adams, daughter of John Adams, second President of the U.S.; *1787* while on a negotiating mission to New York City for General Benjamin Lincoln, suppressor of Shay's Rebellion, Tyler writes *The Contrast,* America's first native comedy to be produced professionally (on April 16 at the John Street Theatre); *1790 The Contrast* sees publication under the auspicies of Thomas Wignell, the renowned English actor of comedy, and Tyler transfers his legal practice to Guilford, Vermont; *1794* marries Mary Palmer, becomes State's Attorney for Windham County, Vermont, and starts Colon and Spondee series with Joseph Dennie; *1797* publishes *The Algerine Captive* (a novel) and allows *The Georgia Spec* (a play) to be produced in Boston; *1807* is elected Chief Justice of the Vermont Supreme Court; *1808-1809* publishes leagal tracts and a collection of satirical letters (fiction); *1811* secures appointment as Professor of Jurisprudence at the University of Vermont; *1812* fails to be elected to the U.S. Senate; *1822-1824* his health begins to decline but works on three plays, the autobiographical *The Bay Boy,* several poems and essays; *1826* dies on August 16, of cancer of the face.

Author's Bibliography

Although Royall Tyler is thought to have written some nine or ten plays, he witnessed the performance of only three during his lifetime. These three are the comedy *The Contrast* (April 16, April 18, May 2, May 5 and May 12 of 1787 in New York City, and at the time of Washington's inauguration as first President of the U.S. in 1789, also in New York City, and in several other southern and northern cities of America before 1800); what may well be called the first American comic opera *May Day in Town, or New York in an Uproar* (May 19, 1787 in New York City); and the non-extant drama *The Georgia Spec; Or, Land in the Moon* (October 30, 1797 in Boston and in New York City on December 20 and 23, 1797, and February 12, 1798). Recently (1974), the lyrics for the songs of *May Day in Town* were discovered by Katherine Jarvis; enough of these lyrics, apparently set to once familiar tunes, now exist to reconstruct the plot of the play.

In 1941, Arthur W. Peach and George F. Newbrough published *Four Plays by Royall Tyler* (as Volume XV of Princeton University's series America's Lost Plays), none of which has ever been performed, including one comedy, *The Island of Barrataria* and three biblical dramas, *The Origin of the Feasts of Purim, Joseph and His Brethren* and *The Judgement of Solomon.* Three other plays have, with varying degrees of authority, been attributed to Tyler's authorship: *The Medium, or Happy Tea-Party* (performed at Boston's Federal Street Theatre on March 2, 1795), *The Mock Doctor* (an adaptation of Moliere's *Doctor in Spite of Himself* and performed in Boston on February 3, 1796), and *The Farm House, or The Female Duellists* (produced at Boston's Federal Street Theatre on May 6, 1796).

Overview of Biographical Sources

No book-length study devoted exclusively to Royall Tyler's life has as yet been written. The most thorough biographical study in print remains the fifty or so pages which introduce G. Thomas Tanselle's *Royall Tyler* (1967). One essential source for scholars of Tyler is *Grandmother Tyler's Book,* a collection of memoirs by Mary Palmer Tyler, wife of the playwright; this manuscript was edited by Frederick Tupper and Helen Tyler Brown and printed as early as 1925 by G.P. Putnam's of New York. Another valuable biographical source written by a member of the Tyler family but still available only in manuscript (in the Vermont Historical Society) is "Memoir of Royall Tyler" by Thomas Pickman Tyler, one of Royall's sons.

Evaluation of Selected Biographies

Carson, Ada Lou and Herbert L. Carson, *Royall Tyler.* Boston: G.K. Hall, 1979. In their basic coverage of Tyler's life and works, the Carsons present a comprehensive table of "Chronology" and give a chapter to a succinct consideration of Tyler's entire life, placing emphasis on his career as a man of letters—i.e. as playwright, poet, novelist, and essayist. Appended to the book is a complete list of all Tyler's published writings, including plays, poems, novel, letters (fictionalized), law reports, and essays.

Tanselle, G. Thomas, *Royall Tyler.* Cambridge: Harvard University Press, 1967. With impeccable scholarship, Tanselle traces Tyler's eventful life from his prankish early years at Harvard College, to his unfortunate courtship of Abigail Adams, daughter of John Adams, second President of the United States, to his brief success as acclaimed author of *The Contrast,* and thence to his successful career as practicing attorney, Chief Justice in the state of Vermont and sometime collaborator with Joseph Dennie on the Colon and Spondee essays (Tyler was Spondee). Tanselle's treatment of Tyler's biography (in which he also includes a chronological table) remains the most complete in print.

Autobiographical Sources

Supposedly a sequel to his *Algerine Captive,* Royall Tyler's unfinished, autobiographical novel *The Bay Boy* contains much material which is of great interest to students of the drama in early America. In manuscript until 1972 when it was edited by Marius B. Pédadeau and published by the Vermont Historical Society (Montpelier, Vermont) as part of Péladeau's *The Prose of Royall Tyler, The Bay Boy* details a homespun effort to produce Joseph Addison's *Cato* before the Revolutionary War and describes a performance of a farcical mask by a wandering troop of mummers—this last depiction more nearly bespeaking the Elizabethan countryside rather than Puritan Boston.

Overview of Critical Sources

Tyler scholarship is much less than voluminous; while his poetry, much of it of fine quality, has scarcely received any attention, his prose has not begun to be properly evaluated. Since it is no exaggeration to submit that Tyler is the major American dramatist before the twentieth century, it should follow that his forays in this genre have received extensive consideration. Such is not the case, however. While *The Contrast* has been given some critical treatment, its possibilities for interpretative readings have hardly been exhausted; and the additional four extant plays, three biblical dramas and especially the farce *The Island of Barrataria,* certainly merit more critical consideration. Barrataria could very well make for effective theatre, even today.

Evaluation of Selected Criticism

Carson, Ada Lou and Herbert L. Carson, *Royall Tyler,* Boston: G.K. Hall, 1979. In their chapter on *The Contrast,* the Carsons include, in addition to a basic discussion of the play's "firsts" and its contrasts, sections on the writing of the play and on critical responses to the play. The authors emphasize this play's continuing actability and briefly discuss the positive reception of Anthony Stimac's recent (1972) musical version of *The Contrast.* Of particular importance is the Carson's chapter treating "Tyler's Other Plays." This critical assessment is the only one in print which gives fair analytical attention to Tyler's four other extant plays. While the discussion of *The Island of Barrataria* is comprehensive, equal time is provided for each of the biblical plays: *Joseph and His Brethren, The Judgement of Solomon* and *The Origin of the Feast of Purim.*

Lauber, John, *"The Contrast:* A Study in the Concept of Innocence" in *English Language Notes,* I, No. 1 (Sept. 1963): 33-37. Lauber's brief article is of decisive importance in the history of Tyler's drama criticism because it draws a definite connection between the American characters in *The Contrast* and R.W.B. Lewis's concept of the American Adam, figure of innocence, simplicity and nature. Both

Tyler's American characters, particularly Colonel Manly and Jonathon, and Lewis's Adam stand in stark contrast to European sophistication, corruption and artificiality.

Siebert, Donald T. Jr. "Royall Tyler's 'Bold Example': *The Contrast* and the English Comedy of Manners" in *Early American Literature,* 12 (Spring 1978): 3-11. Siebert attacks the position that *The Contrast* is a comedy of sentiment. Rather, Siebert maintains, the play owes more to Restoration comedy of manners. Finally, however, the play's contrasts are not between Old and New World values but between those Americans such as Manly and Jonathon who are always themselves and those other Americans such as Charlotte who try to be something they are not—hence this last group is not truly American.

Stein, Roger B. "Royall Tyler and the Question of Our Speech" in *The New England Quarterly,* 38 (December 1965): 454-474. As is characteristic of Stein's work, this splendid article informs as it argues. Stein identifies the central critical problem of *The Contrast* as that of language. While critics of the past have concentrated on the question of the play's genre, whether comedy of sentiment or comedy of manners, Stein holds that in *The Contrast* Tyler is attempting to discover, not merely the national morality but the new country's linguistic idiom. Stein finds that Tyler's perhaps inevitable conclusion is to draw a pattern of linguistic ambiguity among the play's American characters. In an admirable conclusion, the author traces this pattern of linguistic ambiguity from Tyler and J.F. Cooper to Hemingway and Faulkner. This essay constitutes a classic examination of *The Contrast* and firmly anchors the play at the beginning of a clearly American drama.

Other Sources

American Writers Before 1800: A Biographical and Critical Dictionary. James A. Levernier and Douglas R. Wilmes, eds. Greenwood Press, 1983. Good general overview of Tyler's life and career.

Brown, Herbert R. "Sensibility in Eighteenth-Century American Drama," in *American Literature,* 4 (March 1932): 47-60. Traces what he calls the "ascendency of the sentimental over the true comic spirit" from the 1750's to 1800 and identifies *The Contrast* as a comedy of sentiment.

Critical Survey of Poetry. Salem Press, 1985. Competent overview of Tyler's dramatic career which draws portions of *The Bay Boy* into the discussion.

Meserve, Walter, J. *An Emerging Entertainment: The Drama of the American People to 1828.* Bloomington: Indiana University Press, 1977. This now standard critical history of early American drama places Tyler's extant works within the context of an evolving art form (pp. 95-102).

Pédadeau, Marius B. "Royal Tyler's *Other* Plays," in *The New England Quarterly,* 40 (March 1967): 48-60. Gives comprehensive coverage of data available when published concerning Tyler's plays exclusive of *The Contrast.*

John C. Shields
Illinois State University

NICHOLAS UDALL
1504-1556

Author's Chronology

Born during the Christmas season of 1504 to a prominent Uvedale (Udall) family in Southhampton, Hampshire, England; *1517* enters Winchester College; *1520-1524* attends Corpus Christi College, Oxford, receiving his Bachelor of Arts in 1524; *1526* becomes full fellow and lecturer in Greek at Oxford; *1529-1533* leaves Oxford and perhaps travels in France and Germany after having been admonished for his participation in the great Protestant movement; *1533* collaborates with his friend John Leland on verses for the coronation of Anne Boleyn; *1534* writes *Floures for Latine Spekynge* and in June is appointed headmaster of Eton; July 13, *1534* awarded Master of Arts from Oxford; *1541* dismissed as headmaster of Eton after being charged with complicity in the theft of "certain images of silver and other plate" and "other felonious trespasses" and sent to Marshalsea, but released in the same year; *1542* publishes *Apophtheges*, a translation of the oral sayings of the ancients collected by Erasmus; *1543* appointed to direct a group of scholars translating *The Paraphrase of Erasmus upon the New Testament*; *1549* appointed tutor to Edward Courtenay, a royal prisoner in the Tower; *1551-1554* serves as canon of St. George's Chapel at Windsor Castle; *1552* presents *Ralph Roister Doister* for the first time; *1555* appointed headmaster of St. Peter's Grammar School, Westminster; December 23, *1556*, buried at Westminster.

Author's Bibliography

Nicholas Udall is known today almost exclusively as the author of the first regular English comedy, *Ralph Roister Doister* (c. 1552). He was better known in his own time, however, as a scholar translator. With the exception of *Roister Doister*, only one other play is credited to Udall with any degree of certainty: *Ezechias* (c. 1545), a nonextant moral allegory instructing Protestants in the dangers encountered when a ruler does not provide responsible counselors for his successor. Two other plays are sometimes thought to be by Udall, but inadequate evidence exists to make such an assertion: *Thersites* (1537), an interlude whose title character is a braggart soldier in the vein of Roister Doister; and *Res Publica* (1554), a piece of dramatic propaganda illustrating how Roman Catholicism is beneficial to a nation. Still two more plays are occasionally mentioned in connection with Udall, mainly because the authors are unknown and because they resemble *Roister Doister* in some ways. In the *Historie of Jacob and Esau* (entered in the Stationer's Register in 1557) the household servants of Esau are reminiscent of those in the household of Dame Christian Custance in *Roister Doister*. In *Jack Juggler* (SR 1562) a Plautine plot is given English dress, again like *Roister Doister*.

Aside from a few occasional verses and a medical book (*Compendiosa totius Anatimiae delineatio*, published in 1552), the balance of Udall's work consists of translations of Latin authors. In 1534 appeared his *Floures for Latine Spekynge*, a translation into idiomatic English selected parts of Terence. Two translations of the great Humanist Erasmus followed, *Apophthegmes* in 1542 and *The Paraphrase of Erasmus* in 1549. Finally in 1550 he published a translation of Peter Martyr's Protestant desputation with Roman opponents, *Tractatie de Sacramente*; Udall's work is entitled *A Discourse of Tractise of Petur Martyr.*

Overview of Biographical Sources

Much of what scholars believe about Udall's biography is based upon speculation. Because his family name was spelled in a number of different ways (Udal, Uvedale, Owdall, Dowdall, Woodall, or Woddell), biographers often have trouble determining in the few sources available which few references are relevant to the author of *Ralph Roister Doister*. Most biographical references appear as parts of introduction to editions of one or another of his works, usually *Ralph Roister Doister*. John S. Farmer's Early English Drama Society edition of *Roister Doister*, for example, discusses the major elements of Udall's life in an introduction, but without much analysis. G. Scheurweghs' edition gives a somewhat more complete discussion. F. S. Boas, in *An Introduction to Tudor Drama* (1933) and in *University Drama in the Tudor Age* (1914), gives not only important background information, but also significant basic discussions of Udall as a dramatist. But it is not until William L. Edgerton published his *Nicholas Udall* in 1965 that we have a thorough review of Udall.

Evaluation of Selected Biographies

Edgerton, William L. *Nicholas Udall.* New York: Twayne, 1965. The only full-length book devoted to Udall, Edgerton gathers accumulated facts from scattered sources to give a chronological account of Udall's life. His purpose is not only to give background to the famous play *Roister Doister*, but also to give a clear picture of what "a typical Protestant humanist contributed to Tudor literature." Edgerton's treatment of Udall is thorough and scholarly.

Farmer, John S. "Introduction," *Ralph Roister Doister.* London: Early English Drama Society, 1907. Much of what Farmer offers in his discussion of Udall is done more thoroughly by Edgerton. Farmer has the advantage, however, of conciseness: he presents a great deal of significant information in brief form without omitting helpful documentation.

Scheurweghs, G. "Introduction," *Nicholas Udall's Roister Doister* (Volume 16 of *Materials for the Study of Old English Drama, Hew Series*). Louvain: Ch. Uystpruyst, 1939. Scheurweghs offers a thoroughly scholarly account of Udall's life and works. Edgerton drew heavily upon the sources and scholarship presented here for his book.

Autobiographical Sources

Nicholas Udall left no autobiographies, no diaries, no notebooks. One may speculate on his tastes and ideas by observing his drama and poetry and from the works he chose to translate; but only occasionally can a scholar find biographical references in Udall's works, and then only by conjecture. His only autobiographical writing, a letter to Sir Thomas Wriothesley, is helpful to some extent in clarifying Udall's complicity in the charges that resulted in his being dismissed in 1541 as headmaster of Eton.

Overview of Critical Sources

Because Udall left only one work of any significant interest to modern audiences, Udall scholarship is not voluminous. *Ralph Roister Doister* is often printed and therefore often discussed: both Farmer and Scheurweghs (discussed above) offer thorough scholarly notes and criticism on the famous play. But his other works draw scant attention. Noteworthy is the fact that no Collected Works of Nicholas Udall, with biography, notes, and analyses, has ever been published. Occasional notes and articles appear in scholarly journals, and standard histories of English literature offer criticism of Udall's major works in passing. Most of Udall's works, excepting *Ralph Roister Doister*, are of interest only to scholars specializing in the English Renaissance.

Evaluation of Selected Criticism

Edgerton, William L. *Nicholas Udall*. New York: Twayne, 1965. Although listed above as a biography, Edgerton's book devotes seven of its seventeen chapters to careful analyses of Udall's literary works, discussing all of Udall's works, including *Ezechias*, *Thersites*, and *Res Publica*, but not *Jack Juggler* or *Historie of Jacob and Esau*.

Wright, Eugene P. "The Drama of Nicholas Udall," in *Critical Survey of Drama*, 1985, pp. 1955-1964. Offers both biographical and critical discussions of Udall.

Other Sources

Baldwin, T. W. *Shakespeare's Five-Act Structure*. Urbana: University of Illinois Press, 1947. A clear and specific discussion of the structure of Latin comedy that Udall used in *Roister Doister*.

Boas, Frederik S. *An Introduction to Tudor Drama*. Oxford: The Clarendon Press, 1933. Presents Udall's famous play in the context of early English drama.

Edgerton, William L. "The Apostasy of Nicholas Udall," in *Notes and Queries*, CXCV (1950): 223-226. Discusses the question of whether Udall changed his religion for political purposes.

Fowler, Thomas, *The History of Corpus Christi College*. Oxford: Clarendon Press, 1893. Gives valuable background for Udall's early biography.

Hebert, Catherine A. "Udall's *Ralph Roister Doister*," in *Explicator*, 37, No. 2 (Winter 1979): 20. A useful explication of the play.

Herrick, Marvin T. *Italian Comedy in the Renaissance*. Urbana: University of Illinois Press, 1960. An excellent comparison of the devices and structures of Italian and English Renaissance comedy.

Miller, Edwin S. "Roister Doister's Funeralls," in *Studies in Philology*. XLIII (1946): 42-58. A good discussion of topical allusions in Udall's play.

Motter, T. H. *The School Drama in England*. London: Longmans, Green, 1929. Although now somewhat outdated, Motter offers a comprehensive discussion of the kind of atmosphere that spawned *Roister Doister*.

Parrott, Thomas M. and R. H. Ball. *A Short View of Elizabethan Drama*. New York: Charles Scribners' Sons, 1958. Offers a brief discussion of *Ralph Roister Doister* in the context of early English drama.

Plumstead, G. W. "Satirical Parody in *Roister Doister*: A Re-interpretation," in *Studies in Philology*, LX (1963): 141-154. Reviews earlier criticism of Udall's play and discusses the subjects of parody.

Reed, A.W. *Early Tudor Drama*. London: Methuen, 1926. A valuable and engaging study of the drama of Udall's time.

Withington, Robert, "Braggart, Vice and the Devil: A Note on the Development of Comic Characters in the Early English Drama," in *Speculum*, XI (1936): 124-129. Discusses the origins of some of the characters in *Ralph Roister Doister* from Roman and Medieval drama.

Eugene P. Wright
North Texas State University

MIGUEL DE UNAMUNO Y JUGO
1864-1936

Author's Chronology

Born September 29, 1864 in Bilbao, Spain, third of six children of Félix Unamuno, a baker, and Salomé de Jugo, wife and young niece of Félix; completes
secondary school in his native city; *1880-1884* attends University of Madrid where
he receives a doctorate; *1891* marries Concepción Lizarranga, and wins chair of
Greek studies at the University of Salamanca; *1890s* begins to publish essays, a
novel and a play; *1900* is appointed rector of the University of Salamanca, and
continues to publish; *1913* publication of his most important philosophical work,
On the Tragic Sense of Life in Men and Nations; *1914* is dismissed from rectorship
for political reasons; *1924* is exiled to one of the Canary Islands, from where he
flees to France; *1925* settles in Hendaye, France, where he stays until 1930; *1931*
is reappointed to the rectorship of the University of Salamanca by the Republican
government; *1934* retires as professor and is named rector for life; *1936* receives
honorary doctorate from Oxford; denounces Francisco Franco and the anti-
republican Falange; dies, Dec. 31, 1936.

Author's Bibliography

Considered one of the most important representatives of the famous Spanish
'Generation of '98,' Unamuno was a prolific writer of religious and philosophical
essays, historical treatises, novels, poetry, short stories, and plays. In 1895 he
completed his first collection of essays, edited as *On Authentic Tradition* (1905, *En
Torno al casticismo*) and the following year published his first novel, *Peace in War*
(1897, *Paz en la guerra*). In 1898 he wrote his first play, *The Sphinx* (*La esfinge*),
and a second, *The Blindfold*, (*La venda*) the following year. For the next few years,
Unamuno sustained an active writing career in conjunction with his university
duties, completing and publishing his most profound philosophical work, *On the
Tragic Sense of Life in Men and Nations* (1913, *Del sentimiento trágico de la vida
en los hombres y en los pueblos*). In addition to several collections of poetry, three
novels, a number of autobiographical accounts and several essays, Unamuno wrote
several more plays between 1922 and his death in 1936. These are: *Solitude* (1922,
Soledad), *Rachel in Chains* (1922, *Raquel encadenada*), *Dream Shadows* (1926,
Sombras de sueño), *The Other* (1926, *El otro*); *Brother John or the World is a
Stage* (1929, *El hermano Juan o el mundo es teatro*). Unamuno's plays have been
collected and edited in *Teatro Completo*, ed. Manuel García Blanco. Madrid: Ediciones Aguilar, 1959, and Ediciones Escelicer, 1968. Large and important portions
of Unamuno's works, including several plays, have been translated and edited in
the seven-volume Bollingen Series *Selected Works of Miguel de Unamuno*, trans.
Anthony Kerrigan, Allan Lacy and Martin Nozick. Princeton: Princeton University Press, 1967-1984.

Overview of Biographical Sources

Unamuno's complex and varied works have elicited a great deal of interest among English speaking scholars from several academic disciplines. His life, however, has received relatively little attention, perhaps because the details of his biography and career are very well known. Unamuno was an important public figure in Spain, and he lived during a period of active self-examination and self-expression in Iberian letters. While several books contain biographical information, there is only one full-length biography of Unamuno in English, Margaret Thomas Rudd, *The Lone Heretic* (1963). A brief summary of the most important developments in Unamuno's career appears in Martin Nozick, *Miguel de Unamuno* (1971) and in José Ferrater Mora, *Unamuno: A Philosophy of Tragedy* (1962 trans. of *Unamuno: Bosquejo de una filosofía*, 1957).

Evaluation of Selected Biographies

Ferrater Mora, José, *Unamuno. A Philosophy of Tragedy*. trans. Philip Silver. Berkeley: University of California Press, 1962. A succinct version of the writer's life is given in the first twenty-four pages of this personalistic book. In it the author adopts many attitudes based on hindsight, and considers Unamuno an individual who longed "for the eternal and still a victim of the moment." The largest portion of the book is devoted to an examination of Unamuno's philosophical positions; the word tragedy in the title refers to Unamuno's vision of reality as a state of conflict and contradiction rather than to drama or stagecraft.

Nozick, Martin, *Miguel de Unamuno*. New York: Twayne, 1971. A brief and well-informed view of Unamuno's life by a scholar who has devoted many years to the translation and edition of Unamuno's works. The first few pages of this book provide a useful chronology of the highlights of Unamuno's career. The rest of the work discusses in some detail Unamuno's most important works and themes and their relationship to his life and to contemporary events. Nozick considers Unamuno's theater "little more than the perfunctory insertion of his ideas into dramatic outline."

Rudd, Margaret Thomas, *The Lone Heretic*. Austin: University of Texas Press, 1963. A detailed account of the "intimate" side of Unamuno's life, based on research and interviews carried out in Bilbao and Salamanca, the two most prominent cities where Unamuno lived. This biography is a chatty and admiring look at a figure whose ideological inconsistencies and the complexity of his positions are not entirely understood by the biographer. The book attempts to recreate the political mood of Spain, important to the positions adopted by Unamuno, especially during the turbulent decades of the 1920s and 1930s.

Autobiographical Sources

Unamuno wrote about himself often and with deliberation, and he wanted his ideas recorded for future generations. Consequently, there is an impressive amount of autobiographical material in the Unamunian corpus. Some of it is made up by his voluminous correspondence—of which there are no complete published editions and translations—his *Recuerdos de niñez y mocedad* (1908, untranslated; *Memories of Childhood and Youth*); *My Religion and Other Short Essays* (1910), a number of accounts of his travels to Spain and Portugal (1911, 1922). In 1928 he wrote a collection of poems, *Romancero del destierro* (*Ballads of Exile*, untranslated). A collection of personal writings was published posthumously in 1959 in the two-volume *Mi vida y otros recuerdos personales* (*My Life and Other Personal Remembrances*, untranslated). The essays contained in these volumes examine his personal struggles and agonies, his religious doubts and affirmations, his meditations on the art of writing, creativity, fame, immortality, pedagogy, in short, they reflect fully the multifaceted nature of Unamuno's career. He reveals himself as a thinker interested in the judgment of posterity, and as someone who wants his ideas understood and his name and reputation preserved for future generations.

Overview of Critical Sources

Although Unamuno has attracted the attention of critics and scholars for a number of years, most of the studies devoted to his work were completed before the mid-1970s. Some of the problems that most concerned him, such as man's relationship to history and to God, the tension between dreams and reality, and his philosophical speculations regarding the nature of reason, do not appear to enjoy great popularity among scholars today. His novels, especially *Abel Sánchez* (1917) and *The Mist* (1914, *Niebla*) are read and studied in most Spanish literature courses, and literary critics continue to consider him the most important figure of the Generation of '98. His place as dramatist is the least analyzed, perhaps because his dramatic works are not considered good or significant examples of the genre. His plays, overall, have not enjoyed either critical or commercial success; in fact he found it difficult to persuade the theater establishment to present his work, and when his plays were produced, they received poor notices and had to close after only a few performances. The only exception has been the production of *The Other* (*El otro*), a work favorably reviewed and performed a number of times in Spain and Argentina. Unamuno scholars, on the whole, agree that his plays are not good dramatic vehicles. They are used by the writer to present ideas rather than action or spectacle. The characters are not interesting; they do not develop in the course of the action, nor are they able to establish a unique identity. The shortcomings of Unamuno's dramas might account for the fact that his stage work has not generated a single full-length work of criticism in English.

Evaluation of Selected Criticism

Franco, Andrés, *El teatro de Unamuno*. Madrid: Insula, 1971. This is the most complete available study of Unamuno the dramatist. It examines, in detail, ten of the eleven plays of Unamuno, and gives a cogent and sound presentation of his esthetic principles with regard to the theater. Although the author acknowledges Unamuno's shortcomings as a playwright—the indistinguishable characters of all his plays, the visual barrenness of his scenes, the lack of dramatic action and spectacle, the cumbersome dialogues—he nonetheless believes that Unamuno's efforts are worthy of praise because he set out to revitalize Spanish dramaturgy, following a generation of flashy and shallow productions, and to communicate his abstract and profound ideas and ideals through the most popular medium of his time, the stage. The book also includes a useful bibliography.

Zavala, Iris M. *Unamuno y su teatro de conciencia*. Berkeley: University of California Press, 1967. Originally written as a doctoral dissertation, this book studies, in great detail, the content of each of Unamuno's dramatic works without attempting to draw any conclusions about their theatrical or aesthetic merit.

Other Sources

Basdekis, Demetrios, *Unamuno and Spanish Literature*. Berkeley: University of California Press, 1967. One of only a handful of studies in English examining the place of Unamuno in the rich literary tradition of the Iberian Peninsula beginning in the second half of the nineteenth century.

Earle, Peter G. *Unamuno and English Literature*. New York: The Hispanic Institute, 1960. A useful examination of some of the influences on Unamuno's intellectual and esthetic development.

Huertas-Jourda, José, *The Existentialism of Miguel de Unamuno*. Gainesville: University Presses of Florida, 1963. A philosophical study of Unamuno's thought, which places the Spanish writer within the European tradition.

Ilie, Paul, *Unamuno: An Existential View of Self and Society*. Madison: University of Wisconsin Press, 1967. A serious analysis of Unamuno's philosophical ideas, in the light of modern existentialist philosophy, understood, according to the author through the key of psychology.

Lacy, Alan, *Miguel de Unamuno: The Rhetoric of Existence*. The Hague-Paris: ed. Mouton, 1967.

Marías, Julián, *Miguel de Unamuno*. trans. F. M. López-Morillas. Cambridge: Harvard University Press, 1966. Considered the best general approach to the complex ideas of Unamuno. Brief and well-written.

Sedwick, Frank, "Unamuno and Womanhood: His Theater," *Hispania* 43 (1960): 309-313. Interesting early treatment of a current theme.

Turner, David G. *Unamuno's Webs of Fatality*. London: Támesis Books Ltd., 1974. The most recent work on Unamuno to appear in English. The author concentrates exclusively on Unamuno's narrative fiction.

Unamuno Centennial Studies. ed. R. Martínez López. Austin: University of Texas Press, 1966. A collection of scholarly essays, many in English, on various aspects of Unamuno's work.

Valdés, Mario J. *Death in the Literature of Unamuno*. Urbana: University of Illinois Press, 1966.

_____ and Valdés, María Elena de, *An Unamuno Source Book*. Toronto: University of Toronto Press, 1973. A catalogue of Unamuno's library and his techniques for annotating his readings.

Clara Estow
University of Massachusetts
Harbor Campus

RODOLFO USIGLI
1905-1979

Author's Chronology

Born in Mexico City, 1905; *1930s* begin his literary activities as member of the avant-garde literary group, "los contemporáneos;"along with other "contemporáneos" such as Celestino Gorostiza, Xavier Villaurrutia, and Salvador Novo, contributes greatly to the renovation of the Mexican theater during the 1930s and 1940s; translates, among others, George Bernard Shaw, Maxwell Anderson, Elmer Rico, Samuel Behrman, and John Galsworthy; major influences, Eliot (poetry) and Shaw (drama); *1936* receives Rockefeller Fellowship to study drama at Yale University; *1937* begins long and fruitful career as professor of Theater History and Technical Production at the UNAM (National University of Mexico); of his more than 30 dramas, two are universally considered to be his masterpieces: *El gesticulador* 1937, because of its highly critical depiction of post-revolutionary Mexico is not produced until 1947; *Crown of Shadows* 1943, an "anti-historical" interpretation of the motivations underlying Carlota, Maximiliano, and Juárez, also premieres in 1947; *1938* appointed head of the Theater Department of the Fine Arts Section of the Department of Public Education; *1940* establishes the innovative "Teatro de Media Noche" which he hoped would serve as a home for Mexican plays, but was forced to close after six weeks of operation; writes several landmark critical/theoretical essays on theater; *1950-1960s* represents Mexico in various international film/drama festivals; receives several honorary diplomatic posts, in Lebanon and Norway; both as a dramatist and teacher Usigli has served as the spiritual mentor of an important group of younger Mexican dramatists: Emilio Carballido, Jorge Ibargüengoitia, Sergio Magaña, Luisa Josefina Hernández, Hector Mendoza, and others; dies in 1979.

Author's Bibliography

For a more complete bibliography of Usigli's dramatic production see Ruth Lamb's *Bibliografía del teatro mexicano del siglo XX* (Mexico: De Andrea, 1962), pp. 120-21 or Rex Edward Ballinger's student edition of Usigli's *El gesticulador* (New York: Appleton-Century-Crofts, 1963) pp. xi-xiv. The following is a selective bibliography of Usigli's most significant critical writings and plays.

Essays: *Mexico in the Theater* 1932, 1976; *Caminos del teatro en México* 1933; *Itinerario del autor dramático* 1940; *Anatomía del teatro* 1966.

Drama: Usigli's dramatic production can be divided into three stages. Apprenticeship Years (1917-1937) includes: *El apóstol* 1930; *Estado secreto* 1935; *Alcestas* 1936; Mastery Years (1937-1947) includes: *El gesticulador* 1937, 1947 (subsequently translated into English, French, German, Polish, and Russian). In 1953 the Hedgerow Theatre, Moylan, Pennsylvania, produced this play under the title *The Great Gesture;* Studio One of New York City produced a televised version entitled *Another Caesar; Crown of Shadows* 1943, 1947; *El niño y la niebla* 1936, 1951; Mature Years (1947-) includes: *La funcioń de despedida* 1949; *Jano es una muchacha* 1952; *Corona de luz* 1960; *Corona de fuego* 1961.

Overview of Biographical Sources
To date there has been no full-length study in English on Usigli's life. However, for those who read Spanish, *9 dramaturgos hispanoamericanos: Antología del teatro hispanoamericano del siglo XX* (Ottawa: Girol Books, 1979), edited by Frank Dauster, Leon Lyday, and George Woodyard, presents an excellent ten-page historical overview of the contemporary Spanish American theater as well as a three-page bio-bibliographical review of Usigli. Also, Aurora M. Ocampo de Gómez and Ernesto Prado Valázquez' *Diccionario de escritores mexicanos* (Mexico: Universidad Nacional Autónima de México, 1967), pp. 393-395 and Gerardo Luzuriaga and Richard Reeve's *Los clásicos del teatro hispanoamericano* (México: Fondo de Cultura Económica, 1975), pp. 732-733 present a concise synopsis of Usigli's life and literary production.

Evaluation of Selected Biographies
Behind Spanish American Footlights. Austin: University of Texas Press, 1966. This is the most informative source of biographical material of Usigli written in English. Jones not only summarizes Usigli's literary career, but more importantly, places Usigli's life and work in proper perspective vis-a-vis the development of Twentieth-Century Mexican Theater.

Autobiographical Sources
Except for several published personal interviews Usigli has produced very little autobiographical writing that is available in English. His essay, *Mexico in the Theater,* 1932, 1976, although primarily focusing on an historical/critical analysis of Mexican drama, does reveal various aspects of Usigli, the playwright. For those who read Spanish, *Itinerario del autor dramático* 1940 is a beautiful autobiographical description of his development as a dramatist.

Overview of Critical Sources
Usigli is a major literary figure, not only in Mexican, but also Latin American Letters. Along with Xavier Villaurrutia, he is looked upon as the spiritual father of Mexico's Contemporary Theater. His works have been translated and analayzed in many languages. What follows is only a representative selection of the more important critical studies which have been published in English on his drama.

Evaluation of Selected Criticism

Beardsell, Peter R. "Insanity and Poetic Justice in Usigli's *Corona de sombra,*" in *Latin American Theater Review* 10/1 (Fall 1976): 5-14. An intelligent and concise analysis of Usigli's masterpiece.

Gates, Eunice Joiner, "Usigli as Seen in His Prefaces and Epilogues," in *Hispania,* xxxvii, no. 4 (Dec. 1954): 432-439. Gates' study highlights the unique contribution Usigli has made to the Mexican stage, especially regarding his psychological penetration into the Mexican psyche.

Kronik, John W. "Usigli's *El gesticulador* and the Fiction of Truth," in *Latin American Theater Review* 11/1 (Fall 1977): 5-16. Kronik analyzes how Usigli's drama reveals hidden aspects of Mexican reality, and thus serves to lead the public to a deeper awareness of its own identity.

Ragle, Gordon, "Rodolfo Usigli and His Mexican Scene," in *Hispania,* xlvi, no. 2 (May 1972): 307-311. Ragle effectively demonstrates Usigli's gift for penetrating beyond surface reality to unveil the hidden aspects of Mexican society.

Savage, R. Vance, "Rodolfo Usigli's Idea of Mexican Theater," in *Latin American Theater Review,* 4/2 (Spring 1971): 13-20. Savage presents a clear overview of Usigli's analysis of contemporary Mexican drama.

Scott, Wilder P. "Rodolfo Usigli and Contemporary Dramatic Theory," in *Romance Notes,* xi, no. 3 (Spring 1970): 526-530. Scott reviews Usigli's development as a playwright concentrating on the principal theoretical and critical ideas that combined to create his unique literary perspective.

Shaw, Donald L. "Dramatic Techniques in Usigli's *El gesticulador,*" in *Theater Research International* (Glasgow), New Series 1, no. 2 (1976): 125-133. Shaw's analysis of *El gesticulador* focuses on Usigli's technical expertise to create dramatic tension that ultimately leads the public to a deeper self-awareness.

Tilles, Solomon H. "Rodolfo Usigli's Concept of Dramatic Art," in *Latin American Theater Review,* 3/2 (Spring 1970): 31-38. Similar to Scott's article above, Tilles' study focuses on the theortical beliefs underlying Usigli's aesthetics.

Other Sources

Lomeli, Francisco A. "Los mitos de la mexicanidad en la trilogía de Rodolfo Usigli," in *Cuadernos hispanoamericanos,* no. 233 (March 1978): 466-477. Lomeli's study of Usigli's critically acclaimed trilogy *Crown of Shadows, Crown of Light,* and *Crown of Fire* analyzes Usigli's penetration into Mexican history and his attempt to reveal the myths hidden deep within the Mexican psyche.

Richard Keenan
University of Idaho

RAMON MARIA DEL VALLE-INCLAN
1866-1936

Author's Chronology

Ramón Valle Peña born in October (28 or 29), 1866 to Ramón del Valle and Dolores de la Peña y Montenegro in the fishing village of Villanueva de Arosa, province of Pontevedra (Galicia, Spain); *1872-1876* in his childhood, the last Carlist War devastates much of Northern Spain; *1877-1885* studies for the *bachillerato* (high-school equivalency) in Pontevedra; *1885-1890* writing activities begin, a period in which he spent some time in Madrid doing articles and short stories for the Liberal daily *El Globo* and a magazine, *La Ilustración Ibérica*; *1888* begins law studies at the University of Santiago de Compostela (an unfinished enterprise because of his family's economic straits); *1892* visits Mexico; *1895* his first book, *Femeninas*, is published; *1896-1897* settles definitively in Madrid during the winter, after some years of tranquility in Galicia; *1897* publishes *Epitalamio*, followed two years later by *Adega, Cenizas*, and the early serial edition of *La cara de Dios*; *1902* his first significant literary success with *Sonata de otoño*; other parts of this tetralogy appeared over the next three years: *Sonata de estío*, 1903, *Sonata de primavera*, 1904 and *Sonata de invierno*, 1905, comprising the most celebrated works of his characteristic early Modernist period; short story collections also appear in this period; *1907* marries the actress Josefina Blanco and publishes the first of his *Comedias bárbaras, Aguila de blasón* (dramatic works too long for conventional theatrical presentation, hybrids in the vein of the dialogued novel). *1907-1908* visits Navarre, interviewing surviving veterans of the second Carlist War and gathering material for his novelistic cycle on this civil conflict; *1909-1910* enters politics as a candidate for the Spanish Cortes (Parliament) representing a traditionalist party; *1912* two more plays staged in Madrid; during the first World War, serves as a correspondent on the Allied front for the newspaper *El Imparcial*, resulting in a volume of observations, *La media noche* (1917); *1916* publishes *La lámpara maravillosa* and is named Professor of Aesthetics at the School of Fine Arts in Madrid; *1920* undergoes surgery, the beginning of a protracted struggle against the illness of which eventually he would die; *1920s* period of greatest literary and theatrical activity; *1921* second visit to Mexico coincides with the serialization of his most controversial *esperpento, Los cuernos de don Friolera*. *1926-1928* major novels appear; *1927 La hija del capitán* offends the military dictatorship, leading to problems with the authorities, and Valle's arrest and jailing in that year and 1929; *1932* after suffering a severe financial setback due to bankruptcy of his publishers, Valle began to serialize his novel, *Baza de espadas* in *El Sol*, and was definitively separated from his wife; *1933* again undergoes surgery; after the fall of the dictatorship in 1931 was given an official post in Rome by the Republican government; assumes directorship of the Spanish Academy of Fine Arts, but leaves Italy in the autumn of 1934 when his health takes a downturn, returning to Galicia in 1935 to enter a clinic where he dies, January 5, 1936.

Author's Bibliography
The four *Sonatas* appeared in English translation under the joint title, *The Pleasant Memoirs of the Marquis de Bradomín* (1924), and have had a number of editions. There are also translations of *Divinas palabras* (*Divine Words*, 1968) and *Luces de Bohemia* (*Bohemian Lights*, 1976), the latter available in a bilingual edition by A.N. Zahareas and G. Gillespie from the University of Texas Press, which includes an outstanding introduction. *La cabeza del dragón* was translated (1918) as *The Dragon's Head*, and his novel *Tirano Banderas* as *The Tyrant* (1929). Valle's twenty-three theatrical works encompass a wide range of genres, techniques and styles, and given their disparity are most often published in collections with formal affinities (e.g., farces, *esperpentos*). The most widely-used edition of the Complete Works is the *Obras completas* in two volumes (Madrid: Plenitud, 1954); also widely available in Spanish is the *Obras escogidas* (Selected Works, Madrid: Aguilar, 1958 and 1971). Other theatrical pieces include: *El embrujado* (Madrid: J. Izquierdo, 1914); *La pipa de Kif* (Madrid: Clásica española, 1919), a grotesque and lyric dramatization of the circus; *La rosa de papel* (Madrid: *La Novela Semanal*, March 22, 1924); *Tablado de marionetas para educación de príncipes* (Madrid: Rivadeneyra, 1926); *Retablo de la avaricia, la lujuria y la muerte* (Madrid: Rivadeneyra, 1927).

Overview of Biographical Sources
Because Valle tended to falsify biographical information in the process of weaving a literary legend about himself, one must be a good deal more careful than with the average biographical accounts (e.g., many indicate 1870 as his date of birth, and many attributions of quite spurious ancestry and pursuits are repeated in good faith). Melchor Fernández Almagro, *Vida y literatura de Valle-Inclán* (Madrid: Nacional, 1943; rpt. 1966), is a standard early source by a reasonably impartial critic familiar with Valle's literary world. Parts have been superseded by an excellent source in English, Anthony Zahareas (ed.), *Ramón del Valle-Inclán: An Appraisal of his Life and Works* (New York: Las Américas, 1968). More limited biographical considerations are found in Verity Smith, *Ramón del Valle-Inclán* (New York: Twayne Publishers, 1973).

Evaluation of Selected Biographies
In the absence of an authoritative biography, those mentioned above are least plagued by subjectivity and unreliability. However, some additional sources do exist: Francisco Madrid, *La vida altiva de Valle-Inclán* (Buenos Aires: Poseidon, 1943) is the work of an exile shortly after the close of the Spanish Civil War, motivated to a considerable extent by political considerations. Ramón Martínez-López, "A Portrait of Valle-Inclán," in *Valle-Inclán Centennial Studies*, ed. Ricardo Gullón (Austin: University of Texas Press, 1968) provides some personal

recollections and reminiscences. William Fichter in "Génesis de la *Sonata de estíde*" (*Nueva Revista de Filología Hispánica*, VII , 3-4, 526-35) provides a detailed account of the genesis of this short novel which includes some biographical data. The same author's *Publicaciones periodísticas de don Ramón del Valle-Inclán anteriores a 1895* (Mexico: El Colegio de Mexico, 1952) in his long introduction throws some light on Valle's little-known early years. In addition, a number of the centennial studies and special numbers of journals devoted to Valle include personal recollections and biographical anecdotes: see *Cuadernos Hispanoamericanos*, nos. 199-200 (July-Aug. 1966); *La Pluma* (Madrid), IV, 32 (January 1923); *Insula*, nos. 236-37 (July-Aug. 1966); *Papeles de Son Armadans*, XLIII, 127 (October 1966); *Ramón del Valle-Inclán (1866-1966)* (Universidad Nacional de La Plata, 1967), especially the introduction; and *Revista de Occidente*, nos. 44-45 (November-December 1966). Pina, Francisco, *El Valle-Inclán que yo conocí* (Mexico: Universidad Nacional, 1969) includes correspondence and personal anecdotes.

Autobiographical Sources

Valle published an *Autobiografía*, which is at least as fanciful and literary as any of his novels, and tends to exaggerate the sensationalism, picturesqueness and eccentricity which were part of his public image, but bore a negative relationship to his inner self. A limited amount of more reliable autobiographical data can be found in letters and interviews, such as the material published by Dru Dougherty in *Un Valle- Inclán olvidado* (Madrid: Fundamentos, 1983). See especially the interview granted "El Caballero Audaz" (José María Carretero) in *La Esfera* (Madrid, 6 March 1915). Ghiraldo, A., *El archivo de Rubén Darío* (Buenos Aires: Losada, 1943) reprints four letters by Valle, revealing in terms of his early relations with the leader of Hispanic Modernism. Gregorio Martínez Sierra, "Hablando con Valle-Inclán, de él y de su obra," *ABC* (Madrid), 7 diciembre 1928, provides an interview with Valle conducted by an important playwright and director and sheds light on why he turned from the theater to novels in the last years. Francisco Umbral in *Valle-Inclán* (Madrid: Unión Editorial, 1968) includes both biographical and autobiographical material in an unusually well-written introductory overview plagued by a few factual inaccuracies. Carlos del Valle-Inclán, son of the writer, has in his possession a number of unpublished letters and works which he has made available to various investigators.

Overview of Critical Sources

At least two bibliographies of Valle-Inclán criticism are available: José Rubia Barcia, *A Bibliography and Iconography of Valle-Inclán* (Berkeley and Los Angeles: University of California Press, 1960), which although now outdated is indispensable for the time up to 1960; and Robert Lima, *An Annotated Bibliography of Ramón del Valle-Inclán* (University Park, PA: Pennsylvania State University,

1974), with more than 400 pages of text and useful commentaries comprising the flood of material produced with the centennial of Valle's birth and immediately thereafter. There are a few key names in Valle-Inclán criticism, in addtion to those mentioned: Rodolfo Cardona, Sumner Greenfield, and Anthony Zahareas, especially in the area of theater, although most of the important criticism is available only in Spanish.

Evaluation of Selected Criticism

Avalle Arce, J.B. "La esperpentización de Don Juan," *Hispanófila*, 3 (1959); 29-39. Avalle perceptively discusses sources of *Las galas del difunto*. *Modern Spanish Theater*, ed. Michael Benedikt and George Wellwarth (New York: E.P. Dutton, 1969) offers a very readable, brief general introduction (pp. ix-xx) followed by specifics on Valle (pp. 2-3) and Edwin Williams' translation of "Divine Words" (pp. 4-78). Buero Vallejo, Antonio, *Tres maestros ante el público* (Madrid: Alianza, 1973), Spain's leading postwar dramatist, treats Valle, Velázquez and Lorca, pointing out similarities in their ways of involving the public as spectator (pp. 31-54). Díaz-Plaja, Guillermo, *Modernismo Frente a noventa y ocho* (Madrid: Espasa Calpe, 1951) opposes classifying Valle as a member of the "Generation of 1898." In *Las estéticas de Valle-Inclán* (Madrid: Gredos, 1967), the same critic analyzes three periods (which he terms the mythical, the ironical and the degraded) via their expression in a particular character. Flynn, Gerard C., "The Adversary: Bradomín," *Hispanic Review* 29 (1961): 120-133 considers the calculatedly satanic protagonist of the *Sonatas* (which Valle adapted for the stage in 1906 as *El marqués de Bradomín*). Greenfield, Sumner M. "Valle-Inclán," in *Columbia Dictionary of Modern European Literature*, 2 ed. revised (New York: Columbia University Press, 1980) offers an outstanding overview of Valle's works and aesthetics, while in "Stylization and deformation in Valle-Inclán's *La reina castiza*," *Bulletin of Hispanic Studies*, 39 (1962): 78-89, he perspicaciously discusses this farce and its relationship to the *esperpento*. Kuethe, Lourdes Ramos, *Las comedias bárbaras* (Madrid: Editorial Pliegos, 1985), analyzes the trilogy on the Montenegro dynasty as a manifestation of so-called social literature (socio-political criticism). March, María Eugenia, *Forma e idea de los esperpentos de Valle-Inclán* (Madrid: Castalia, 1969) provides a rather general discussion of the *esperpentos*, describing Valle as Expressionist. Pérez Minik, Domingo, *Debates sobre el teatro español contemporáneo* (Santa Cruz de Tenerife: Goya Ediciones, 1953), "Valle-Inclán o la restauración del bululú" (pp. 123-140) studies the author's work in the context of the early historical development of Spanish theater, the Renaissance ambulatory puppet shows of *fantoches* and *títeres*. Francisco Ruiz Ramón, *Historia del teatro español, 2, Siglo XX* (Madrid: Alianza Editorial, 1971), "Valle-Inclán y su teatro en libertad," (98-150) offers an excellent synthesis of Valle's work and significance, by the leading academic expert on Spanish theater as a whole. Seeleman, Rosa, "Folkloric elements in Valle-Inclán," *Hispanic Review*, 3 (1935), 103-118, details the

Galician superstitions so important in Valle's work. Segura Covarsi, Enrique, "Los ciegos en Valle-Inclán," *Clavileño* (Madrid), 3, 17 (1952): 49-52 considers Valle's respect for the blind a reflection of his philosophical ideas, and discusses the use of archetypes. In *"Cara de plata," Revista de literatura,* V, 9-10 (1954), the same critic relates collective characters in the *Comedias bárbaras* to the chorus in Greek tragedy. Smith, Verity, *Ramón del Valle-Inclán* (New York: Twayne, 1973) perceptively discusses Valle's theater within the context of his life and work as a whole. Speratti Piñero, Emma Susana, *De 'Sonata de otoño' al Esperpento* (London: Tamesis, 1968) collects the most important of many previously published articles on Valle. Torrente Ballester, Gonzalo, *Teatro español contemporáneo,* 2 ed. (Madrid: Ediciones Guadarrama, 1968), *"Los cuernos de don Friolera* y dilucidación del esperpento," (188-234) recapitulates the ideas of one of Spain's most perceptive critics and authors on Valle's aesthetics. Sinclair, Alison, *Valle-Inclán's Ruedo Ibérico: A Popular View of Revolution* (London: Tamesis, 1977) studies the *esperpento* narratives of Valle, in which he applies the distorting techniques developed for the theater to the novel. Zahareas, Anthony, ed., *Ramón del Valle-Inclán: An Appraisal of His Life and Works* (New York: Las Americas, 1968), a comprehensive and varied survey of Valle's works by several critics, covering all phases of the author with many excellent articles. Zahareas, Anthony and Rodolfo Cardona, *Visión del esperpento* (Madrid: Castalia, 1970) considers theory and practice of the *esperpento* in great detail. Zamora Vicente, Alonso, *La realidad esperpéntica* (Madrid: Gredos, 1969) provides a very detailed analysis of *Luces de bohemia,* including style and language, the social and political implications, and possible sources.

Janet Pérez
Texas Tech University

MARIO VARGAS LLOSA
1936

Author's Chronology

Born Jorge Mario Pedro Vargas Llosa March 28, 1936, Arequipa, Peru to parents who had already separated; *1937* moves to Cochibamba, Bolivia, to be brought up by his mother and grandparents; *1945* moves to Piura, Peru; *1946* moves to Lima to rejoin parents who have reunited; *1950-1952* resident student at the Leoncio Prado Military Academy; *1952* begins working as a part-time writer for several newspapers, and sees his play *La huida del Inca*, performed at the Teatro Variedades, in Piura; *1955* marries a Bolivian woman Julia Urquidi; *1957* completes his bachelor's degree at the University of San Marcos, Lima; *1958* publishes his first book *Los jefes*, a collection of short stories; *1959* moves to Paris; *1963* publishes his first novel *The Time of the Hero* (tr. 1966); *1965* remarries a Peruvian woman Patricia Llosa; *1966* publishes *The Green House* (tr. 1973) and moves to London where he teaches at the University of London; *1967* publishes novella *The Cubs* (tr. 1979); *1968* writer-in-residence at Washington State University; *1969* publishes third novel *Conversation in the Cathedral* (tr. 1975); *1970* moves to Barcelona and a theatrical adaptation of *The Cubs*, is staged by Alonso Alegria at the Teatro de la Universidad Católica in Lima; *1971* publishes critical study of fellow Colombian novelist, *Gabriel Garcia Márquez: historia de un deicidio*, for which he later receives a doctorate from the University of Madrid; *1973* publishes fourth novel *Pantaleón y las visitadoras*; *1975* publishes a critical study of *Flaubert, La orgía perpetua: Flaubert y "Madame Bovary"*; *1977* teaches at Cambridge University and publishes *Aunt Julia and the Scriptwriter* (tr. 1983); *1978* his admission address into the Language Academy of Peru *José Maria Arguedas, entre sapos y halcones*, is published; *1981* publishes novel *The War of the End of the World* (tr. 1984), first drama *La señorita de Tacna*, and his critical study *Entre Sartre y Camus*; *1983* chairs investigation into allegations that the Peruvian Army killed a group of journalists in Ayacucho, Peru; publishes *Contra viento y marea (1962-1982)*, and his second drama *Kathie y el hipopótamo*; *1984* publishes novel *Historia de Mayta*.

Author's Bibliography (drama)

La huida del Inca, 1952, unpublished; *La señorita de Tacna*, 1981; *Kathie y el hipopótamo*, 1983.

Overview of Biographical Sources

Since Vargas Llosa is still alive few detailed biographical studies have yet been published. Several friends and colleagues have, however, written critical studies which include biographical accounts. Most of these accounts are concerned mainly with the biographical background to Vargas Llosa's works, and specifically the experiences which generated the world-vision of the works themselves.

Evaluation of Selected Biographies

Harss, Luis and Dohnmann, Barbara, 'Mario Vargas Llosa, or the Revolving Door', in *Into the Mainstream. Conversations with Latin-American Writers*. New York: Harper and Row, 1969, pp. 342-376. This essay is an early insightful biographical picture of Vargas Llosa in the sixties. From their interview with Vargas Llosa it is clear that the Peruvian author regards violence as at the root of all human relations and a conditioning and determining factor in human life, and that he sought to express this insight in his work. This essay also gives an insight into how Vargas Llosa saw literature as a means of escape from life and as a means of justifying his life as well.

Oviedo, José Miguel, 'La vida', in *Mario Vargas Llosa: La invención de una realidad*. Barcelona: Barral Editores, 1970, pp. 17-41. This is the most reliable account of Vargas Llosa's life by a critic who knows him well. Unfortunately it is as yet unavailable in English translation. In this essay Oviedo shows how Vargas Llosa came to see literature in his early years as an abnormal, subversive activity, living as he did in a country in which literature is considered as a handicap rather than as a positive achievement.

Standish, Peter, 'The Background to Composition', in *Vargas Llosa: "La ciudad y los perros"*. London: Grant and Cutler, 1982, pp. 9-22. This essay gives a clear, compact account of the major events of Vargas Llosa's life. He emphasizes how Vargas Llosa saw rebellion as the *raison d'être* of the writer, and shows how Vargas Llosa's political views have changed over the years. Standish also provides a lucid account of Vargas Llosa's own theories of the art form.

Urquidi Illanes, Julia, *Lo que Varguitas no dijo*. La Paz, Bolivia: Editorial Khana Cruz, 1983. Untranslated. Revelations by Vargas Llosa's first wife which offer a picture of him that fills out the picture provided by other biographers. She describes their courtship, their subsequent elopement and marriage. She gives a detailed account of their life together in Lima, Madrid, and Paris. She recounts how she gradually became aware that her husband was having an affair with Patricia, a woman he later married after their divorce. She refers significantly to her dismay when Vargas Llosa published *Aunt Julia and the Scriptwriter* since she felt personally implicated. This book is a detailed account of their life together and has the merit of printing for the first time much of the correspondence between Vargas Llosa and his first wife, thereby providing a privileged insight into the early years of the famous Peruvian writer.

Autobiographical Sources

The best autobiographical source is Vargas Llosa's *La historia secreta de una novela* (Barcelona: Tusquets Editor, 1981). In this essay, Vargas Llosa tells of his fascination early on as a young man with a brothel situated on the outskirts of Piura which was called "The Green House," whose name was borrowed for the title of his second novel. He refers to the impact that the Peruvian jungle made upon him when he visited the region of the Upper Marañón in 1958 with the Mexican anthropologist Dr. Juan Comas, and specifically Santa María de Nieva, which became one of the backdrops for his novel. Vargas Llosa further reveals that it was the reading of the chivalry romance *Tirant lo Blanc* in Lima which finally decided him to become a novelist. He also gives a detailed account of the events leading up to the subsequent publication of *The Green House*. This biographical account is a valuable document and gives a picture of Vargas Llosa as a determined, methodical and dedicated writer.

Other autobiographical sources such as they stand are contained in the various interviews which Vargas Llosa has given at various stages throughout his career. Most of these center on the relationship between the author's life and the worlds created in his work. One of the best examples of these interviews is José Miguel Oviedo, 'A Conversation with Mario Vargas Llosa about *La tía Julia y el escribidor*', *Mario Vargas Llosa. A Collection of Essays*, edited by Charles Rossman and Alan Warren Freid (Austin: University of Texas Press, 1978), pp. 152-165. In this interview Vargas Llosa reveals that the main theme of *Aunt Julia and the Scriptwriter* was inspired by a Bolivian writer of soap operas, Raúl Salmón, whom Vargas Llosa knew from 1953 to 1954.

In another significant interview which he gives to Ricardo Cano Gavirio published in *El buitre y el fénix: Conversaciones con Mario Vargas Llosa* (Mexico: Editorial Anagrama, 1972), the Peruvian writer argues against the validity of politics playing a prescriptive role in the creation of the art form. In his interview published by José Miguel Oviedo, 'Mesa redonda: La experiencia de los novelistas', *Revista Iberoamericana*, Vol. 47 (1981): 309-321, Vargas Llosa argues once more on behalf of the individual freedom of the writer. All of these interviews give an inside view of the creative process and are particularly helpful as a means of understanding Vargas Llosa's own work.

Indeed, much of Vargas Llosa's work is firmly rooted in personal experience. *The Time of the Hero*, for example, is based on the author's experience of military life in the Leoncio Prado Military Academy from 1950 to 1952. The book is important as a record of Vargas Llosa's personal perception of the spiritual sterility and moral corruption produced by military life. His book so incensed the authorities of the Military Academy that they attempted to discredit him publicly by publishing details of his poor academic record while at the Academy, and by incinerating one thousand copies of the book in the parade ground outside the Academy shortly after the book was published.

Overview of Critical Sources

Since Vargas Llosa has written more novels than plays, it is inevitable that more critical studies have been devoted to his fiction. There are, however, some essays on Vargas Llosa's drama which are reviewed in the following section. Critics tend overall to explore the extent to which his work is based on lived experience, and also to analyze the various literary techniques used to express his world vision.

Evaluation of Selected Criticism

Frechilla Diaz, Emilio, 'La obra teatral de Vargas Llosa,' in *Archivum, XXXIII (1983): 383-390.* Argues that Vargas Llosa's theater demonstrates the same vision of reality and the same literary obsessions as those explored in his novels. Suggests that the dialogue of the plays lacks the dramatic force of the dialogue in the novels. Temporal disruption is less effective in the theater than in the novels. The main theme of *La señorita de Tacna* is the process of creation of a story; the main theme of *Kathie y el hipopótamo* is the relation between life and fiction. Both plays feature a writer who feels socially outcast because of his profession. This essay is a competent discussion of the salient themes of Vargas Llosa's theater. Only available in Spanish.

Garavito, C. Lucia, '*La señorita de Tacna* o la escritura de una lectura,' in *Latin American Theatre Review*, Vol. 16, No. 1 (Fall 1982): 3-14. Evaluates the role that the reading process plays in the mind of the characters in *La señorita de Tacna*. Only available in Spanish.

Golluscio de Montoya, Eva, 'Los cuentos de *La señorita de Tacna*,' in *Latin American Theatre Review*, 18 (Fall 1984): 35-43. Analyzes the use of literature in *La señorita de Tacna* from a linguistic viewpoint. Applies the theory of speech acts in order to evaluate the overlap of fiction and reality in the play. Only available in Spanish.

Oviedo, José Miguel, '*La señorita de Tacna*,' in *Mario Vargas Llosa: la invención de una realidad*. Madrid: Taurus, 1982, pp. 356-370. Argues that the real theme behind the story line in *La señorita de Tacna* is the betrayal of objective reality by literature. An authoritative discussion of the main themes of the play. Only available in Spanish.

Pérez Blanco, Lucrecio, 'El teatro: Nueva y desventurada obsesión de Vargas Llosa,' in *Cuadernos Americanos*, Vol. 252 (January-February 1984): 202-215. Argues that the main theme of *La señorita de Tacna* is how the writer's liberty is hampered by the uncontrollable 'demon' of inspiration. Suggests that both *La señorita de Tacna* and *Kathie y el hipopótamo* lack dramatic sense. Concludes by assessing Vargas Llosa's view of literature as illusion, referring specifically to the two published plays. Only available in Spanish.

Other Sources

Giacoman, Helmy F. and J.M. Oviedo, ed. *Homenaje a Vargas Llosa. Variaciones interpretativas en torno a su obra*. New York: Las Américas, 1971. Most of the essays collected in this volume deal with specific works by the Peruvian author. Although most of the works studied are the novels of Vargas Llosa, a substantial number of the essays treat seminal themes such as levels of reality in the work of art, the transformation of experience in literature, failure and the relation between art and life. Only available in Spanish.

Oviedo, José Miguel, ed. *Mario Vargas Llosa*. Madrid: Taurus, 1982. A collection of insightful essays which span the range of Vargas Llosa's work. Although only Vargas Llosa's novels are examined, the essays treat general concerns in Vargas Llosa's work such as animalization techniques, freedom, fragmentation and alienation. Only available in Spanish.

Rossman, Charles and Warren Friedman, Alan, ed. *Mario Vargas Llosa. A Collection of Critical Essays*. Austin: University of Texas Press, 1978. A collection of major essays in English on Vargas Llosa's work. Some of the essays examine individual works, and others explore pervasive themes and concerns in Vargas Llosa's work such as myth, Naturalism and the Totalization Impulse. An indispensable guide in English to Vargas Llosa's work.

Solórzano, Carlos, *Teatro latinomericano en el siglo XX*. Mexico: Editorial Pormaca, 1964. An informative guide to twentieth century Latin American theatre by a practicing dramatist. Analyzes how Latin American dramatists, early this century, exposed and explored national problems.

Vargas Llosa, Mario, 'Primitives and Creators,' in *TLS*. No. 3481 (4 November 1968): 1287-1288. Vargas Llosa evaluates the role of primitive instincts in the creative process.

———, *Gabriel García Márquez: historia de un deicidio*. Barcelona: Seix Barral, 1971. Vargas Llosa evolves his theory of the artist as a person who commits deicide by usurping God's role in his ability to create a fictional world. Untranslated.

———, *La orgía perpetua: Flaubert y "Madame Bovary"*. Barcelona: Seix Barral, 1975. In this study Vargas Llosa refers to the enormous impact that *Madame Bovary* had on him when he first read it in 1959. He discusses the sources of Flaubert's masterpiece, and the role of themes such as money and love. He further discusses certain novelistic techniques such as the presentation of time, the omniscient narrator, *style indirect libre* and objectivity, arguing throughout that *Madame Bovary* is the first modern novel. It is clear from this study that Vargas Llosa's understanding of literature was very much influenced by this work. Untranslated.

_____, 'Social Commitment and the Latin American Writer,' in *World Literature Today* (1978): 6-14. A clear statement by the Peruvian writer of his own view of the relation between politics and literature.

_____, 'Seeing with Indian's Eyes,' in *Review*. Nos.25-26 (1980): 52-56. Analyzes the way in which an American Indian view of the world is presented in the fiction of José María Arguedas.

_____, *Entre Sartre y Camus*. Río Piedras P.R.: Ediciones Huracán, 1981. Vargas Llosa evaluates the respective versions of Existentialism of these two French writers. It is clear that Vargas Llosa was influenced by Sartre in particular. Untranslated.

_____, *Contra viento y marea (1962-1982)*. Barcelona: Seix Barral, 1983. Essays on literature and politics, fourteen of which were first published in *Entre Sartre y Camus*. Untranslated.

Selected Dictionaries and Encyclopedias

The Oxford Companion to Spanish Literature, Clarendon Press, 1978. Contains a lucid account of Vargas Llosa's life and works until 1977.

Stephen Hart
Westfield College
University of London

THE WAKEFIELD MASTER
fl. 1420-1450

Author's Chronology

Born sometime during the early 15th century, precise date unknown; believed to be a churchman living in or near Wakefield; *c. 1420-1450* writes *Mactacio Abel* (*The Killing of Abel*), *Processus Noe Cum Filiis* (*Noah*), *Prima Pastorum* (*The First Shepherds' Play*), *Secunda Pastorum* (*The Second Shepherds' Play*), *Magnus Herodes* (*Herod the Great*), *Coliphizacio* (*The Buffeting*) and revises portions of others in the Towneley cycle of mystery plays; date of death unknown.

Author's Bibliography

The Wakefield Pageants in the Towneley Cycle, ed. A. C. Cawley, 1958; *The Wakefield Mystery Plays*, ed. Martial Rose, 1961; *The Towneley Plays*, ed. George England and A. W. Pollard, 1897.

Overview of Biographical Sources

Metrical similarities and other evidence indicate that one man produced six of the thirty-two plays contained in the Towneley cycle, also known as the Wakefield cycle, yet scholars know virtually nothing about the author of the plays, not even his name. Oscar Cargill, perceiving a number of correspondences between the Wakefield Master plays and the *Northern Passion* and the *Turnament of Totenham*, makes a case that Gilbert Pilkington authored the plays in "The Authorship of the *Secunda Pastorum*, *PMLA*, 41 (1926): 810-31; however, Frances A. Foster convincingly disposes of Cargill's theory in "Was Gilbert Pilkington Author of *Secunda Pastorum*?" *PMLA*, 43 (1928): 124-136. If biographers do not know who the Wakefield Master was, they have, at least, some idea of when he wrote. Based on references to fashion and an evaluation of language, Mendal G. Frampton in "The Date of the Flourishing of the 'Wakefield Master,' " *PMLA*, 50 (1935): 630-660, places the Wakefield Master in the North Midlands at the latter end of the period from 1422-1460, in the reign of Henry VI. Still, these few biographical facts provide little assistance in fleshing out the events in the life of this master dramatist of the medieval period.

Most of what is known about the Wakefield Master is gleaned from the plays themselves. Contained in a single manuscript once housed in the Towneley family library in Lancashire, from which the cycle draws its name, the Wakefield plays provide few clues to the identification of the artist. Local references to places in and around Wakefield as well as the dialect have convinced scholars that the author was intimate with the Wakefield area and quite likely a resident. The Wakefield Master's knowledge of Latin and the Bible suggests that he lived as a cleric, though not a friar, and that he did not embrace Lollardry. That one of his characters assumes a southern accent in order to impress his listeners seems to suggest that he had once travelled to the South where he became acquainted with the dialect and turned it to good satirical account.

The pageants reveal something of the character of the man as well. If his plays are any indication, the Wakefield Master must have been a man of great humor and wit. They show a man who understands human nature, someone capable of both tenderness and anger. Certainly not the cloistered mystic, the Wakefield Master appears to be a writer able to bring both his worldly experience and education to bear in the production of his plays. He is devout, but not devoid of humor.

Evaluation of Selected Biographies

Cawley, A. C. *The Wakefield Pagents in the Towneley Cycle*. Manchester: Manchester University Press, 1958. The standard edition of the six Wakefield Master plays, which contains brief sections on the author, date, and dialect.

Rose, Martial, ed. *The Wakefield Mystery Plays*. New York: W. W. Norton, 1961. With no book-length biography published, and none likely, Rose's edition of the Wakefield Master's plays offers the most complete summary of biographical information.

Overview of Critical Sources

Critics of the Towneley cycle have worked to establish its place in the development of English drama, tracing the movement of the pageants from the brief ritual dramatic exchanges which took place during Corpus Christi services to the elaborate outdoor productions staged perhaps over several days. V. A. Kolve in *The Play Called Corpus Christi* (1966) has focused on the creation of the cycle drama and the medieval audience's conception of theater, evaluating the Towneley cycle in the process. Kolve's general study is complemented by a number of more particular investigations concerned with the in-the-round staging techniques used in the Towneley cycle and some morality plays as opposed to the pageant wagons which may have been used in the York cycle. Comparisons between the cycles are undertaken by a number of critics, among them Hardin Craig in *English Religious Drama of the Middle Ages* (1955). Critics have also studied the significant differences between English cycle drama and classical drama. In addition, the concept of unity in the plays has been discussed, especially with reference to the multiple authorship and revisions of the Towneley cycle.

The six plays ascribed to the Wakefield Master have undergone more intensive study than the other plays of the Towneley cycle. Indeed, the Wakefield Master has gained in stature following Millicent Carey's *The Wakefield Group in the Towneley Cycle* (1930), the first book-length study to analyze systematically the Wakefield Master plays. Among the various subsequent efforts are comparisons between the

Wakefield Master and the York Realist, investigations of the Wakefield Master's use of the complicated nine-line stanza, his handling of comic material, his wit, satire, realism, as well as his employment of folk elements. Critics, among them Meyers and Helterman, have discussed typology and symbol in the plays, pointing out the way in which these figures unify the entire cycle. A number of studies have focused on aspects noted in individual plays of the Wakefield Master, particularly *The Second Shepherds' Play*, which critics have acknowledged as his masterpiece.

Evaluation of Selected Criticism

Carey, Millicent, *The Wakefield Group in the Towneley Cycle*. Baltimore: Johns Hopkins Press, 1930. Carey focuses on literary background and popular traditions in this, the first thorough analysis of the Wakefield Master's plays. Four of the plays are investigated in terms of diction, plot, characterization, humor, and realism in an attempt to separate the original from the conventional elements of the pageants. The study concludes that the Wakefield Master employs numerous secular and sacred sources in the production of the plays, resulting in richly complex drama. Carey's work continues to serve as a useful source on the drama of the Wakefield Master.

Craig, Hardin, *English Religious Drama of the Middle Ages*. Oxford: Clarendon Press, 1955. Craig devotes a chapter in his careful study of religious drama to the Wakefield and York cycles, noting their similarities and differences. He traces the history of the unique Towneley manuscript, which apparently served as a formal register of plays from which individual parts were recopied for use by actors at Wakefield. In addition, he considers the various revisions of the cycle. Craig provides a valuable overview of the range of medieval English religious drama.

Gardner, John, *The Construction of the Wakefield Cycle*. Carbondale: Southern Illinois University Press, 1974. Gardner's readable study views the Wakefield cycle as a unified artistic effort evidencing significant interrelationships between plays. He argues that although a number of writers may have been involved in revising the cycle, one man had final responsibility. This controlling intelligence directed revisions intended to heighten dramatic intensity by rewriting dialogue, developing character, and adding both suspense and irony. Gardner concludes that in terms of theme, technique, and language, the entire Towneley cycle shows the influence and intention of the Wakefield Master.

Helterman, Jeffrey, *Symbolic Action in the Plays of the Wakefield Master*. Athens: University of Georgia Press, 1981. The study contends that the Wakefield Master embraced both the temporal and spiritual worlds in his works, allowing symbolic meaning to shift within plays. Reviewing the realistic and symbolic elements of the Wakefield Master, Helterman argues the dramatist's skill in establishing a realistic surface on which the symbolic action takes place. Helterman provides analyses of symbolic action in each of the six Wakefield Master plays.

Kolve, V. A. *The Play Called Corpus Christi*. Stanford: Stanford University Press, 1966. Kolve's important study of the entire range of cycle dramas traditionally staged during the feast of Corpus Christi concerns itself with the principles of construction that motivated the writers and the reactions of the audience who viewed the plays each year. His discussions of the cycle drama as play and game, as well as his discussion of medieval attitudes toward laughter and comedy, are insightful and convincing. Kolve cautions against viewing the plays as purely realistic productions, suggesting instead that the audience easily understood the typological significance of the characters in cycle drama.

Other Sources

Campbell, Josie P. "Farce as Function in the Wakefield Shepherds' Plays," in *Chaucer Review*, 14 (1980): 36-43. Campbell argues that farce serves as a dramatic device through which sacred and secular portions of the cycle are stressed.

Cawley, A. C. and Martin Stevens, *The Towneley Cycle*. Leeds: University of Leeds, 1976. A facsimile edition of the Towneley manuscript now held by the Huntington Library.

Chambers, E. K. *English Literature at the Close of the Middle Ages*. Oxford: Oxford University Press, 1945. This well-respected literary history places the Wakefield plays within the larger context of the late medieval period.

Diller, Hans-Jurgen, "The Craftsmanship of the Wakefield Master," in *Medieval English Drama: Essays Critical and Contextual*. eds. Jerome Taylor and Alan H. Nelson. Chicago: University of Chicago Press, 1972, pp. 245-259. Diller counters the earlier patronizing attitude toward the Wakefield Master, highlighting his genius as a dramatist.

Dunn, E. Catherine, "The Medieval 'Cycle' as History Play: An Approach to the Wakefield Plays," in *Studies in the Renaissance* 7 (1960): 76-89. Using the Wakefield cycle, Dunn postulates a close philosophical relationship between the medieval cycle drama and the later Elizabethan chronicle play. She perceives the unity of the Towneley cycle as existing in the presentation of the universal history of the people of God and the participation of the cycle audience in the design of salvation.

Frampton, Mendal G. "Gilbert Pilkington Once More," in *PMLA*, 47 (1932): 622-35. Recounts the evidence for and against attributing the Wakefield plays to Gilbert Pilkington. Frampton argues that there is no reason to connect Pilkington with the *Turnament of Totenham* and *The Second Shepherds' Play*, since the texts evidence a great geographic separation in the local references employed by the authors.

Mack, Maynard, Jr. "*The Second Shepherds' Play*: A Reconsideration," in *PMLA*, 93 (1978): 78-85. According to Mack, the Wakefield Master skillfully employs dramatic tools to join the sacred and secular material in *The Second Shepherds' Play.*

Meyers, Walter E. *A Figure Given: Typology in the Wakefield Plays.* Pittsburgh: Duquesne University Press, 1970. Meyers examines the use of typology in the Wakefield cycle, finding the plays well structured and sophisticated, not formless and primitive. His study includes chapters on Old Testament and diabolical typology.

Selected Dictionaries and Encyclopedias
Critical Survey of Poetry. Volume 5, Salem Press, 1985. A short biography coupled with a general evaluation and analysis makes this introduction to the Wakefield Master's life and work quite useful.

Kenneth B. Grant
University of Wisconsin Center
Baraboo/Sauk County

JOHN WEBSTER
c.1579-sometime before 1634

Author's Chronology

Born c.1579 in London, England, the son of a prominent coach maker and member of the Merchant Taylors Company; *1587-1597* probably educated at the Merchant Taylors' School near the Webster home; *1597* admitted to the Middle Temple; *1602* collaborates with Middleton, Dekker, Heywood and others on plays for the public theatre, most of them now lost; *1604* writes prefatory verses for two plays; *1605* possibly married to Sara Peniall; collaborates with Dekker on "Westward Ho" and "Northward Ho"; *1606* son baptized at St. Dunstans; *1607* publishes "The Famous History of Sir Thomas Wyatt" and the plays written in previous year with Dekker; *1612* "The White Devil" acted by Red Bull and Company, performance not favorably received, play published by Webster the same year; *1613* publishes a funeral elegy for Henry, Prince of Wales, "A Monumental Column"; "The Duchess of Malfi" acted by the King's Men at Blackfriars Theatre; *1615* admitted to the Merchant Taylors Company; edited the sixth edition of Overbury's "Characters" to which he probably supplied an additional 31 character essays; *c.1617* "The Devil's Law Case" acted; *c.1622* "Appius and Virginia" acted by a company of boys (some date this play as early as 1604); *1623* "The Duchess of Malfi" and "The Devil's Law Case" published; *1624* two collaborations with Ford and others, both plays now lost; "A Cure for a Cuckold," a collaboration with Rowley, acted; "Monuments of Honour" a pageant for the Lord Mayor, written by Webster, performed and published in the same year; died before 1634; *1654* publication of "Appius and Virginia"; *1661* publication of "A Cure for a Cuckold."

Author's Bibliography

The Complete Works of John Webster, 4 vols., ed. by F.L. Lucas, 1927. Ann Arbor, MI: Edwards Brothers, 1966. Useful recent editions of individual plays include: *The White Devil*, ed. by J.R. Brown (Cambridge: Harvard University Press, 1960), *The Duchess of Malfi*, ed. by J.R. Brown (Cambridge: Harvard University Press, 1964), and *The Devil's Law-case*, ed. by Elizabeth Brennan (London: Benn, 1975).

Overview of Biographical Sources

"Of Webster's life we know about nothing less than of Shakespeare's, less than of dramatists as distant as Aeschylus or Sophocles, Euripides or Seneca." (Lucas, *Works*, I, 49.) Since Lucas made these remarks in the introduction to the *Complete Works* in 1927, very little additional information has been discovered about Webster's life. In 1976 Mary Edmond in a series of articles in *TLS* identified him as the son of John Webster, the wealthy coach maker living in West Smithfield. That identification has allowed for certain inferences to be made about his economic background, his education, and his association with the Merchant Taylor's Company. Based upon those discoveries and her intimate knowledge of Elizabethan and Jacobean London, M.C. Bradbrook has written a "biography" which places Webster in the London milieu of the merchant class and political intrigues, and she describes Webster's adult life through references to the theatre world of which he was a part. The most interesting aspect of Webster's career, his collaborations with other writers, will probably never be clearly understood.

Evaluation of Selected Biographies

Bradbrook, Muriel C. *John Webster: Citizen and Dramatist*. London: Weidenfeld and Nicolson, 1980. Using Mary Edmond's discoveries about the Webster family and her identification of John Webster's father as a prosperous coach-maker and Merchant Taylor residing just beyond the old London city wall, Bradbrook weaves together the story of Webster's life by describing four prominent individuals who relate in some way to his life as she imagines it. Two of the figures she describes left their prints on the institutions in which Webster matured—the Merchant Taylors' School and the Middle Temple—while the other two represent the political intrigues taking place in Webster's part of London. In the second half of her study, Bradbrook describes what is known of Webster's career in the theatre and places it in the context of the theatre business of the early Jacobean years. This work provides a lively picture of life in London from 1580-1630 and a plausible picture of Webster's place within it.

Overview of Critical Sources

Webster's work had been performed and anthologized during the 19th century primarily because of the attention paid him first by Charles Lamb in the early years of the century and by Swinbourne at the end of the century. It was not until several years after the publication of Lucas' edition of the *Complete Works* in 1927 that academic interest seriously developed. During the 1950s scholars discussed the Jacobean dramatic writers as a group, showing their undeniable quality which had been obscured by the luminous presence of their contemporary, William Shakespeare. Though united in noting the bizarre theatrical devices and situations used by these writers to depict a bleak world, scholars have been divided in their opinions about the degree of optimism to be found in the Jacobean tragic view. Webster's "The White Devil" and "The Duchess of Malfi" were frequently cited as evidence of the sense of moral decay portrayed in the theatre of the time. Because these two plays assumed an important role in the discussion of Jacobean theatre, they also came to represent the whole of John Webster's career. They were praised for their theatrical style, their powerful poetry, and their honest attention to the human spirit adrift in a sordid world. Many studies have paid attention to the structures of the plays themselves, the psychologically rich characterizations, and Webster's use of sources. Finally, several feminist critics have been drawn to Webster's two tragedies because of their dynamic female central characters.

Evaluation of Selected Criticism

Berry, Ralph, *The Art of John Webster*. Oxford: The Clarendon Press, 1972. Berry places Webster's major plays in the context of continental Baroque aesthetics. He sees "The Duchess of Malfi" as portraying a world in which appearance and reality are separated, a world of meaninglessness and corruption.

Bliss, Lee, *The World's Perspective: John Webster and the Jacobean Drama*. New Brunswick, NJ: Rutgers University Press, 1983. Bliss studies the whole tide of Jacobean drama and theatre life, and sees Webster's work in the context of the intellectual questioning and experimentation with genre occurring between 1604-1625. Webster continued the experimentation with genre begun by Marston, Chapman, Shakespeare and others by shifting the idea of heroism from "the solitary-warrior ideal" to an ideal of spirit which perpetuates love in a confusing and corrupt world. The idealism of the protagonist and his/her visionary power stands against the pragmatic world-view and the pragmatist is found to be deficient, empty and confused.

Boklund, Gunnar, *"The Duchess of Malfi": Sources, Themes, Characters*. Cambridge: Harvard University Press, 1962. Boklund develops his study of the characters in the play from a comprehensive study of the history of the narrative sources which Webster used and the ways in which he relied on them. In a final chapter Boklund studies the play as a dramatic whole in which the sensational effects and the aberrant and violent characters combine to illustrate a world in which virtuous characters have relatively limited power.

Dent, R.W. *John Webster's Borrowing*. Berkeley: University of California Press, 1960. Dent's systematic study concerns Webster's use of sources for details, episodes, and language. The works are examined on a scene-by-scene basis for evidence of debts to other writers, especially his contemporaries writing for the theatre.

Jardine, Lisa, *Still Harping on Daughters*. Sussex: Harvester Press, 1983. In her chapter on "The Duchess of Malfi," Jardine argues that the play is not, as some suppose, the story of the heroism of the strong woman. Using a detailed examination of hereditary rights in the Renaissance, she concludes that the Duchess is shown to be punished for using her power unwisely and disrupting the patriarchal system of inheritance.

Leech, Clifford, *Webster: "The Duchess of Malfi."* Great Neck, NY: Barron's Education Series, 1963. In this brief introductory work, Leech shows the reader how Webster structured the play, how he used sources, how he treated such matters as incest and remarriage, and how he employed various rhetorical devices to produce the tragic effect realized in the play. Because Leech incorporates a good deal of pertinent historical information, this is an excellently balanced introduction to Webster's most famous play.

Moore, Don D. *John Webster and His Critics 1617-1964.* Baton Rouge, LA: Louisiana State University Press, 1966. Moore surveys the critical discussions of Webster's work including reviews of performances, their publication history, and selected 20th century academic commentaries.

Morris, Brian, ed. *John Webster.* Mermaid Critical Commentaries. London: Ernest Benn, 1970. This outstanding collection of critical essays is the result of a University of York Symposium on the plays of Webster. It includes essays on staging the plays, detailed studies of the two tragedies, and essays which interpret Webster's work in the context of the theological questions of his day.

Pearson, Jacqueline, *Tragedy and Tragicomedy in the Plays of John Webster.* Totowa, NJ: Barnes and Noble, 1980. Pearson assesses four of Webster's plays, "The White Devil," "The Duchess of Malfi," "The Devil's Law Case," and "A Cure for a Cuckold," in terms of dramatic form. She discusses the nature of Elizabethan and Jacobean tragicomedy and traces Webster's development from tragedy to tragicomedy. Pearson's work is the only extended treatment of the tragicomedies in the context of both Webster's artistic development and the Jacobean theatre.

Peterson, Joyce E. *Curs'd Example: "The Duchess of Malfi" and Commonweal Tragedy.* Columbia, MO: University of Missouri Press, 1978. Peterson argues against the view that the Duchess is "a transcending individualist trapped in a decadent and evil society" and finds her to be neglecting her public duty to satisfy personal desires. She associates the play with other commonwealth tragedies which illustrate the disastrous consequences which emerge when a public figure neglects his or her responsibility for ruling well. The Duchess is shown to be analogous in many ways to Mary, Queen of Scots, a monarch swayed and controlled by the rule of passion.

Rabkin, Norman, ed. *"The Duchess of Malfi": A Collection of Critical Essays.* Englewood Cliffs, NJ: Prentice-Hall, 1968. Rabkin's introductory essay places Webster among the playwrights who worked during the decline of tragedy, a decline which is evidenced by the increasing helplessness of the heroes. The essays which he collects show no agreement about the moral implications of the play. Some of them argue over the significance and worth of the much disputed fifth act.

Other Sources

Mahaney, William E. *John Webster: A Classified Bibliography.* Institut für Englische Sprache und Literatur. Salzburg, Austria: University of Salzburg, 1973. A comprehensive bibliography of writings by and about Webster including items through 1971. Entries are classified by subject matter including such matters as editions, sources and borrowings, critical commentaries, and performance reviews.

Moore, Don D. ed. *Webster: The Critical Heritage.* London: Routledge and Kegan Paul, 1981. A collection of critical comments on Webster's work from 1612, when he published "The White Devil" and defended it in a preface, through the 19th century revival of interest his work. Moore includes reviews of several 19th century productions of the two major tragedies.

Selected Dictionaries and Encyclopedias

Dictionary of National Biography, London: Macmillan, 1891. The primary source for biographical information until 1976 when some of the conjectures offered here about Webster's early life were proved wrong.

Faye P. Whitaker
Iowa State University

FRANK WEDEKIND
1864-1918

Author's Chronology

Born Benjamin Franklin Wedekind on 24 July 1864 in Hanover, Germany, to Friedrich Wilhelm Wedekind and Emilie Kammerer; *1872* family moves to Switzerland to avoid political persecution; *1886* to Munich to study law, returns to Switzerland as ad man and journalist; after death of father in *1888* inheritance permits travels to Berlin, Munich, Paris, and London and supports Bohemian existence; since *1896* major contributor to the satirical paper "Simplizissimus"; *1899* imprisoned in Germany for political satire; *1901-1902* performances in Munich with popular cabaret troupe "Elf Scharfrichter"; *1902* initial success with *Earth Spirit* after 15 years of artistic anonymity; *1906* marries Tilly Newes, a young actress, birth of daughter Pamela in same year; *1911* daughter Kadidja born; *1914* theatrical celebrations and commemorative book in honor of his 50th birthday; 9 March *1918*, Frank Wedekind dies in Munich of complications following surgery for appendicitis.

Author's Bibliography

Aside from his personality and theatrical innovations, Wedekind's fame rests on the durability of only a few of his plays, primarily *Spring's Awakening* of 1891 (first translated 1923), *Earth Spirit* of 1895 (1923), *The Marquis of Keith* of 1901 (1952), and *Pandora's Box* of 1904 (1923); for this reason there has been no attempt to reissue his collected works in the last half-century. Artur Kutscher and Joachim Friedenthal edited the original *Gesammelte Werke in neun Bänden* from 1920 to 1921, and a revival of interest in Wedekind during the 1960s produced several editions of the major works. Though the more important plays can be found separately or in anthologies, one recommended collection in English is *The Lulu Plays & other Sex Tragedies*, translated by Stephen Spender in 1978, or an earlier version entitled *Five Tragedies of Sex*, (including *Spring's Awakening*) rendered by Frances Fawcett and Stephen Spender with an introduction by Lion Feuchtwanger (n.d.). Volume 58 of The German Library (Continuum Publishing), encompassing both Wedekind and Carl Sternheim, should prove a welcome addition.

Overview of Biographical Sources

Due to his unsavory reputation and the checkered history of his plays, Wedekind has not been the object of enduring popular interest. Long a victim of the censor (and thus anathema for the conservative majority), Wedekind the man and playwright experienced a roller-coaster notoriety: throughout the First World War and again during the Third Reich his works were considered "unpatriotic" and thus seldom performed; at other times his works have merely been tolerated. The task of Wedekind's biographers has thus been one of rehabilitation—to justify the dramatist's personal behavior and to reclaim his "scandalous" plays by demonstrating their seminal contributions to the modern world stage. Although only Artur Kutscher's three-volume *Frank Wedekind: Sein Leben und seine Werke* (1922-1931) and several more-recent monographs in German provide exhaustive treatments of this dramatist, the lengthy studies by Best and Gittleman offer sufficient material in English for the interested reader.

Evaluation of Selected Biographies

Best, Alan, *Frank Wedekind*. Modern German Authors, n.s. IV. London: Oswald Wolff, 1975. Best is arguably the most knowledgeable Wedekind scholar writing in English. His biography gives an excellent impression of the man, but disappoints in its brevity and omission of specifics. In all fairness, however, the book's main purpose is "to illustrate the characteristic themes and techniques of Wedekind's work." This slim volume therefore provides close textual analyses, original interpretations that are sensitive to the ambiguities inherent in Wedekind's works, and insights invaluable for all students of Wedekind. A useful bibliography of secondary sources is appended.

Gittleman, Sol, *Frank Wedekind*. New York: Twayne, 1969. This is the most extensive survey in English of Wedekind's life and works, tracing his origins, influences, reception, and ultimate effect on modern theatre. A thorough chronology offers an overview of the important events of Wedekind's life and work. Each of the dramatic works is discussed at length and interpreted with skill. While Gittleman highlights Wedekind's innovations and strengths, he does not avoid a critical discussion of the dramatist's failings. Too, the major critical literature is incorporated into the text in an unobtrusive fashion. The relationship to Freud and Nietzsche, to Hauptmann and Strindberg, affinities to the circus and to the scandalous are intelligently examined. Gittleman's text is well organized, his style lucid and highly readable.

Autobiographical Sources

Frank Wedekind was not an enthusiastic correspondent, as witnessed by the inclusion of only 479 letters in Fritz Strich's 1924 edition of the *Gesammelte Briefe in zwei Bänden*. The final volume of the collected works contains some essays of personal or philosophical value, though on the whole scholars are endebted to Wedekind's friend and biographer, Artur Kutscher, for many of the details of the dramatist's life.

Overview of Critical Sources

While not as extensive as that in German-language, the critical literature concerning Wedekind's work in English includes examination of specific works and influences, as well as thoughtful evaluation of his place in German drama and on the world stage. As these studies confirm, Wedekind created several mythic characters and established himself as an iconoclast in our century; his appeal and thus his influence is limited, however, by the small number of plays that merit an audience or sustained critical attention.

Evaluation of Selected Criticism

Garten, H. F. "Frank Wedekind," in *Modern German Drama*. London: Oxford University Press, 1959, pp. 87-96. This study measures Wedekind's contributions to German drama, emphasizing the tragedy of adolescence (*Spring's Awakening*); characters and entire plays serve as vehicles for the dramatist's "message," and the dramatic distortions prefigure Expressionist drama. A valuable study of technical innovation and Wedekind's place in the development of 20th-century German drama.

Gittleman, Sol, "Frank Wedekind's Image of America," *German Quarterly*. XX-XIX (1966): 570-580. A fascinating study of Wedekind's distorted perspective on America. Though his parents were naturalized Americans who were so taken with the New World that they named their son Benjamin Franklin Wedekind, the dramatist himself was ambivalent. On the one hand, he saw the country as superior in some aspects, a land of escape from European problems, if remote and thus inaccessible. In his works, however, Wedekind frequently depicted Americans as "defective individuals" and as "destroyers of the ideal."

Jones, Robert A. "Frank Wedekind: Circus Fan," *Monatshefte*, LXI (1969): 139-56. This useful and stimulating essay traces the influence of the circus on Wedekind's tragicomic philosophy of life, as well as on his dramatic techniques and aesthetic principles. This aspect of Wedekind's development, as described by Jones, can be detected in other modern art forms and is especially significant for Expressionist drama as well.

Natan, Alex, "Frank Wedekind," in *German Men of Letters*. II. London: Oswald Wolff, 1963, pp. 103-129. Natan's uneven summary of the major works lauds Wedekind as "the missionary of a new morality," yet dismisses the man as a grotesque clown who flirted with death, as a pessimist who could not construct a positive philosophy of life for the stage.

Shaw, Leroy R. *The Playwright & Historical Change: Dramatic Strategies in Brecht, Hauptmann, Kaiser & Wedekind*. Madison: University of Wisconsin Press, 1970, especially pp. 49-65. Shaw's book primarily concerns change, and therefore he sees Wedekind as an innovator whose "reformulation of traditional concepts opens up a new perspective." Using *Spring's Awakening* as one example, Shaw interprets puberty as a symbol of transition and conscience as man's enemy; the resultant work initiates the "destruction of illusionistic theatre."

Sokel, Walter H. "The Changing Role of Eros in Wedekind's Drama," in *German Quarterly*, XXXIX (1966): 201-207. Despite its brevity, this article offers an excellent survey of the development of Wedekind's attitudes, especially toward Eros and life as seen in his major works. Sokel's insights are masterful in this seminal piece of Wedekind scholarship.

Willeke, Audrone B. "Frank Wedekind and the 'Frauenfrage'," in *Monatshefte*, LXXII (1980): pp. 26-38. This essay posits Wedekind's essential conservatism in regard to women's emancipation, concluding that he felt it necessary to "control" women. As a supposedly liberal dramatist whose female characters have become legendary, Wedekind deserves this sort of investigation. Willeke's detailed and provocative study is a welcome corrective, though not entirely convincing when one considers the vitality and complexity of Wedekind's heroines.

Other Sources

Esslin, Martin, "Modernist Drama: Wedekind to Brecht," in M. Bradbury & James McFarlane, *Modernism 1890-1930*. Pelican Guides to European Literature. Middlesex: Penguin Books, 1976, especially pp. 527-534. The author outlines Wedekind's brand of realism, ties to cabaret, relation to Gerhart Hauptmann and Naturalism, Wedekind's "modernity" and thus his impact on modern theatre. A standard, reliable treatment.

Firda, Richard Arthur, "Wedekind, Nietzsche and the Dionysian Experience," in *Modern Language Notes*. LXXXVII (1972): 720-731. This article traces Wedekind's reception and ultimate rejection of Nietzsche's Dionysian principles; less convincing is the premise that Wedekind's nihilism and view of the absurdity of life prevail.

Heuser, Frederick W. J. "Gerhart Hauptmann and Frank Wedekind," in *Germanic Review*. XX (1945): 54-68. This early study provides a detailed account of the long and tempestuous relationship between these two contemporary greats of the German stage. Both their personal animosities and their aesthetic-philosophical differences are succinctly delineated.

Hibberd, J.L. "Imaginary Numbers and 'Humor' : On Wedekind's *Frühlings Erwachen*," in *Modern Language Review*. LXXIV (1979): 633-647. According to Hibberd, morality (or the purported immorality of Wedekind's plays) is simply a part of a greater, existential issue—one which is not defined, merely indicated in the dramatist's works. Although the question of morality is certainly a central point throughout Wedekind's life and works, its treatment here is vague and offers little enlightenment to serious readers.

Hill, Claude, "Wedekind in Retrospect," in *Modern Drama*, III (1960-1): 82-92. This dated essay portrays Wedekind's personality, work, and his place in German literary history. Hill describes his subject as a lonely "Post-Romanticist with a mania for sex." While correctly postulating Wedekind's dramas as an antidote for mid-20th-century realism (and thus anticipating the Wedekind revival of the 1960s), Hill's individual analyses are less successful.

Todd C. Hanlin
University of Arkansas

OSCAR WILDE
1854-1900

Author's Chronology

Born Oscar Fingall O'Flahertie Wills Wilde in Dublin, Ireland, October 16, 1854; *1871-1874* Trinity College, Dublin; *1878* B.A. Magdalen College, Oxford, where he came under the influence of John Ruskin and Walter Pater; June *1878* wins Newdigate Poetry Prize for *Ravenna*; Christmas Eve, *1881* Wilde sails for America on tour designed to cash in on notoriety resulting from Gilbert and Sullivan's *Patience*; spends one year in US and Canada; January *1883*-May *1884* resides in Paris; May 29, *1884* marries Constance Lloyd; *1887* becomes editor of *Woman's World*; *1891* meets Lord Alfred Douglas; *1892 Lady Windemere's Fan* first theatrical hit; May *1895* sentenced to two years imprisonment for homosexuality, enters Reading Gaol; *1897* after release from prison, leaves England permanently; November 30, *1900* dies in Paris.

Author's Bibliography

Productions: 1883 *Vera*, New York; 1891 *Guido Ferranti: A Tragedy of the XVI Century*, New York; 1892 *Lady Windemere's Fan*, London; 1893 *A Woman of No Importance*; 1895 *The Importance of Being Earnest, An Ideal Husband*; 1896 *Salome*, Paris; 1906 *A Florentine Tragedy*.

Publications: 1881 *Poems*; 1891 *The Picture of Dorian Gray*; 1898 *The Ballad of Reading Gaol*; 1905 *De Profundis* (expurgated); 1908 *First Collected Edition of the Works of Oscar Wilde*; 1913 *The Suppressed Portion of "De Profundis"*; 1948 *The Complete Works of Oscar Wilde*, ed. Vyvyan Holland; 1968 *The Literary Criticism of Oscar Wilde*; 1969 *The Artist as Critic: Critical Writings of Oscar Wilde*.

Overview of Biographical Sources

Oscar Wilde's relatively short but undeniably colorful life has posed a severe problem for his biographers: their subject was so flamboyant and his end so undeniably tragic that Wilde the man is difficult to grasp. Even the best of the biographies, H. Montgomery Hyde's *Oscar Wilde* (New York: Farrar, Straus, and Giroux, 1975), betrays this predilection toward the sensational: fully half the book deals with only the last five years of Wilde's life, with his trials, his imprisonment, and his exile. However, the wealth of biographical treatments tends to make up for the biographers' tendency to dwell on the lurid parts of their subject's life, and the several volumes by Vyvyen Holland, Wilde's son, serve as a useful corrective. These volumes and Hesketh Pearson's *Oscar Wilde: His Life and Wit* (New York: Harper, 1946) make up a complete and reliable corpus of information on the life of a man who was a major literary force and an admittedly controversial figure. Add to these works several others that focus on selected aspects of Wilde's life— his trip to America and his trials in particular—and the body of work dealing with Oscar Wilde ably presents the factual details of Wilde's life, the controversies in which he was involved, and the extraordinary color Wilde lent to his surroundings.

Evaluation of Selected Biographies

Douglas, Lord Alfred, *Oscar Wilde: A Summing Up*. London: Richards, 1950. Alfred Douglas was eighteen years old in 1891, when he and Wilde first met, and it was Douglas' father, the Marquis of Queensberry, who was Wilde's eventual undoing. Douglas's account, rather delayed and certainly circumspect, adds little of factual value, but the person interested in Wilde's downfall cannot avoid this account by one of the principals involved. However, Douglas' book is flawed by the severest of natural tendencies in any autobiography—the autobiographer's wish to maximize his virtues and minimize his faults.

Ericksen, Donald H. *Oscar Wilde*. Boston: Twayne, 1977. For a good, brief summary of a subject's life, Ericksen's book is excellent. The book deals very briefly with the details of Wilde's early life, and then focuses on the period from Wilde's enrollment at Oxford to his death. Ericksen treats Wilde as a major artist, including informative sections on Aestheticism as a reaction against Philistinism and on Wilde's rise to become the figurehead of that movement.

Holland, Vyvyen, *Oscar Wilde and His World*. New York: Charles Scribner's Sons, 1960. Early in life, Vyvyan Wilde changed his last name to Holland to avoid the effects of his father's scandal. This book, however, demonstrates that its author, if he was ever shamed by his father's life, recovered sufficiently to deal forthrightly with that history. Holland argues that his father's work breaks the social barriers of an etiquette-ridden age, coming to the conclusion that, while Wilde was a little ahead of his time, his work broke important ground, especially in the theater, where later dramatists—Shaw in particular—were able to gain acceptance by following in Oscar Wilde's footsteps. This favorably slanted account of Wilde's life is generously supplemented with more than 150 illustrations, including photographs, drawings, and cartoons from every phase of Wilde's life. These pictures help place Wilde in his *milieu*, allowing the reader to get closer to Wilde as a person. The book first appeared as *Oscar Wilde: A Pictorial Biography* (London: Thames & Hudson, 1960).

_____. *Son of Oscar Wilde*. New York: E.P. Dutton, 1954. Though rather gossipy and focused more on the problems Holland had in coming to grips with his father's memory, this book presents a fair portrait of the personal side of Wilde and a very good assessment of the social impact of Wilde's trials and exile.

Hyde, H. Montgomery, *Oscar Wilde*. New York: Farrar, Straus, & Giroux, 1975. Despite its faults, this treatment is the most important biography of Wilde and the one everyone who deals with Wilde's works or his life should read. Hyde presents Wilde's early life, his school years, and his early married years with a completeness and a frankness that previous biographers had either missed or had not considered important. The book is organized into two parts, roughly equal in length, the first of which deals with Wilde's rise to prominence and the second of which focuses on his fall from public grace. The first part is laced with witticisms and anecdotes, sometimes to distraction, and the second part, which treats the trials, weighs the end of Wilde's life, particularly the relationship with Alfred Douglas, too heavily, important as that phase is. Fully half the book is dedicated to the last five years of Wilde's life, and while those years were certainly eventful, they are perhaps less important than the years 1881-1894, when Wilde rose to prominence and wrote most of his finest works.

Pearson, Hesketh, *Oscar Wilde: His Life and Wit*. New York: Harper, 1946. While second to Hyde's biography in importance, this thorough and very readable book, written by a very capable professional biographer, is valuable for its accurate portrait of Wilde from his family background through his exile and death.

Autobiographical Sources

Oscar Wilde's *De Profundis*, in *The Complete Works of Oscar Wilde*. ed. Vyvyen Holland (London: Collins, 1966), written in the form of an impassioned letter to Bosie—Lord Alfred Douglas—seeking a reconciliation, represents Wilde's confessional and his personal and professional credo. *De Profundis* is a critically useful and quite moving self-portrait of a man who put only his talent into his art, but his genius into his life. This *apologia* is supplemented by the excellently edited *The Letters of Oscar Wilde*, edited by Rupert Hart-Davis (New York: Harcourt, Brace & World, 1962). Davis's editing sets out the letters in such a way that they dispel many myths about Wilde as a monster or as a craven money-grubber. Wilde was no sham, and his letters show that fact. Finally, Davis also edited *Selected Letters of Oscar Wilde* (Oxford: Oxford University Press, 1979), a volume that includes most of the important letters from the earlier *Letters*, as well as some which were discovered after the earlier book had already been printed. Altogether, the two volumes of letters and *De Profundis* yield an unusually complete and frank set of autobiographical information.

Overview of Critical Sources

For quite a while, the scandal attendant on Wilde's conviction and exile blocked serious consideration of his work. Later, an influential group of critics, led by Richard Altick and Samuel Chew, tried to dismiss Wilde as an interesting but essentially worthless literary figure. Fortunately, both movements have today been thoroughly countered by excellent critical revaluations of Wilde's fiction, poetry, and drama. What follows is a list of useful and influential assessments of Wilde's achievements. In addition to these works, the interested reader should also seek out two excellent introductions to Wilde's life and works: Donald Ericksen's *Oscar Wilde* (1977), which provides solid introductory chapters on Wilde's poetry, stories, *The Picture of Dorian Gray*, his drama, and *De Profundis*; and Robert Keith Miller's *Oscar Wilde* (1982), which contains not only a sound introduction into Wilde's writings but also a concluding summary of Wilde's critical beliefs—a consideration of his works in light of his own criticism.

Evaluation of Selected Criticism
Beckman, Karl, ed. *Oscar Wilde: The Critical Heritage*. London: Routledge & Kegan Paul, 1970. The standard but extremely useful assembly of selected and exerpted critical assessments from Wilde's contemporaries and from the most influential of critical statements printed since his death.

Bentley, Eric, "The Importance of Being Earnest," in *The Playwright as Thinker*. New York: Reynal & Hitchcock, 1946. Bentley argues that Wilde had a new conception of comedy, using his famous epigrammatic witticisms as comic relief in otherwise bitingly satiric or dark comedies. Wilde's use of masks was an important development toward modern drama.

Bird, Alan, *The Plays of Oscar Wilde*. New York: Barnes & Noble, 1977. Bird argues, convincingly, that Wilde's plays are more worthy of attention than his life. Wilde was a versatile dramatist, a pioneer in the reestablishment of English drama, a force to be reckoned with, and he would have been all these things even if his life had been boring.

Ellman, Richard, ed. *Oscar Wilde: A Collection of Critical Essays*. Englewood Cliffs, NJ: Prentice-Hall, 1969. One of the Twentieth Century Views series, this collection begins with assessments by Yeats and Pater and covers critical responses to Wilde's fiction, poetry, and drama down to the present day. Since no one critic's point of view dominates, this book presents a balanced look at Wilde's position as a writer.

Ericksen, Donald H. *Oscar Wilde*. Boston: Twayne, 1977. This book provides not only a brief biographical summary, but a critical introduction geared toward establishing Wilde as a major artist. The book includes critical introductory chapters organized by genre and a solid overview of Wilde as leader of the Aesthetic movement.

Mickhail, E.H. *Oscar Wilde: An Annotated Bibliography of Criticism*. London: Macmillan, 1978. While this bibliography of works and criticism is less than thorough, as well as imperfectly organized, it represents a good place to start. The book is divided into sections of Wilde's works and contemporary reviews of them, criticism on Wilde—with a cutoff date of 1975—and dissertations written about

Wilde. This book should be supplemented by Fletcher and Stokes' bibliographical essay in *Anglo Irish Literature: A Review of Research* (1976).

Miller, Robert Keith, *Oscar Wilde*. New York: Frederick Ungar, 1982. This Twayne-like introduction includes a biographical summary of Wilde's rise and fall, as well as a critical introduction to his works. What distinguishes this book is its informative summary of Wilde's criticism, including a brief examination of Wilde's works in light of his critical views.

Roditi, Edouard, *Oscar Wilde*. Connecticut: New Directions, 1947. Roditi begins with a look at Wilde's beginnings as a poet, moving to an assessment of Wilde's unique consciousness of the nature of art, and with his attempts to make his poetry incorporate experience. Wilde is a great writer, Roditi argues, because of the ideas expressed in his works.

San Juan, Epifanio, *The Art of Oscar Wilde*. Princeton: Princeton University Press, 1967. San Juan presents a largely convincing and very perceptive argument in favor of Wilde's effect on the novel's and the drama's structures and styles. The book assesses Wilde's value as a serious social critic.

Spininger, Dennis J. "Profiles and Principles: The Sense of the Absurd in *The Importance of Being Earnest*, "in *Papers on Language and Literature* 12 (1976): 49-72. Spininger considers Wilde's use of language as a substitute for reality and his reworking of the melodrama genre so that wit becomes the substance of the play. Wilde "evokes a nihilistic spirit that places (him) closer to Beckett than to Shaw.

Other Sources

Hyde, H. Montgomery, *The Three Trials of Oscar Wilde*. New York: University Books, 1948. Hyde provides an excellent insight into Wilde's legal difficulties, and the book is complete with the transcripts of the court proceedings from Wilde's libel suit against the Marquis of Queensberry and Wilde's two criminal prosecutions—complete from indictment to mistrial to retrial to conviction.

Lewis, Lloyd and H.J. Smith, *Oscar Wilde Discovers America*. New York: Benjamin Blom, 1936; rpt. 1964. An amusing, illustrated account of Wilde in America, this thoroughly documented study is not as anecdotal as most such accounts. The book is laced with actual newspaper and magazine articles and personal recollections of Wilde's passage through America, a passage which was less triumphant than most people think.

Mikhail, E.H. *Oscar Wilde: Interviews and Recollections*. New York: Barnes & Noble, 1979. Mikhail presents a useful assembly of anecdotes and personal memories from people who came into contact with Wilde. The book is thoroughly documented, and the selections are long enough to be of genuine use in assessing public opinion on Wilde throughout his life and after his death.

"Oscar Wilde," in *Dictionary of Literary Biography*, vols. 10, 19, and 34. Ann Arbor: Gale Research, 1984. The entries on Wilde occur in volumes on British dramatists, British poets, and British novelists, respectively. All three entries contain author's bibliographies and selected bibliographies of criticism, as well as reliable, succinct summaries of Wilde's life and his critical reputation. The drama entry, in Volume 10, provides an especially helpful introduction to Wilde's plays, both in performance and as literature.

William Condon
Arkansas Tech University

THORNTON (NIVEN) WILDER
1897-1975

Author's Chronology

Born April 17, 1897, Madison, Wisconsin, to Amos P. and Isabel Niven Wilder; *1905-1909* lives in Shanghai, Hong Kong while father was consul general; *1910-1912* lives in Berkeley, California, starts writing; *1913* graduates Thacher School, Ojai, California; *1915* first three-minute play *The Angel That Troubled the Waters*; *1915-1917* studies classics at Oberlin College; *1917-1918* attends Yale; *1918-1919* joins Coast Artillery; *1919-1920* returns to Yale, on *Yale Literary Magazine*; *1920* A.B. Yale; studies archaeology at the American Academy in Rome; *1921-1928* teaches at Lawrence School; *1926* M.A. Princeton; *1928* wins Pulitzer Price for *The Bridge at San Luis Rey*; tours Europe, studies Continental theatre; *1931* lectures at University of Chicago; *1935* invites Gertrude Stein to lecture at Chicago; *1936* begins career as dramatist; *1938* wins Pulitzer Prize for *Our Town*; *1942-1945* serves with U.S. Air Force, North Africa, Italy; *1943* wins third Pulitzer Prize; *1952* Academy of Arts and Letters gold medal; *1959* MacDowell medal; *1963* Century Association Art medal, Presidential Medal of Freedom; *1968* National Book Award; dies December 7, 1975.

Author's Bibliography (selected)

Fiction: *The Trumpet Shall Sound*, 1919; *Cabala*, 1926; *The Bridge of San Luis Rey*, 1927; *The Woman of Andros*, 1930; *Lucrece*, 1933 (a translation); *Heaven's My Destination*, 1935; *Morts sans Sepulture* (The Victors) (translation), 1945; *The Ides of March* (novel and play), 1940; *Theophilus North*, 1973.

Drama: *The Angel That Troubled the Waters*, 1928; *Our Town*, 1938; *The Merchant of Yonkers*, 1938; *Skin of Our Teeth*, 1941; *A Life in the Sun* (*The Akestiad*), 1955.

Overview of Biographical Sources

Of the three most recent biographies of Thornton Wilder, Richard H. Goldstone's *Thornton Wilder, An Intimate Portrait* (1975) was published while the novelist-playwright was still alive. Wilder, who believed no "literary man of serious intention has a biography written during his lifetime," was unhappy about Goldstone's book, and sent the copy back the author mailed to him, unread. Goldstone had met Wilder in 1942, while they were both in the Service. He had a rare opportunity to see a great deal of Wilder and kept many notes. For this alone this biographer's book deserves respectful consideration. Rex Burbank's *Thornton Wilder* (1978) is not a full biography, but it does contain the most essential information on his life and career, plus critical views. In 156 pages Burbank managaes to capture the spirit of the man and the flavor of his creative output. The work described as the first full-length biography is *The Enthusiast: A Life of Thornton Wilder* by Gilbert A. Harrison (1983). Even though Wilder was not one to keep things helpful to a biographer, Harrison was able to obtain the aid of the writer's sister. Other records and letters were made available to him so that the biography is well documented.

Evaluation of Selected Biographies

Burbank, Rex, *Thornton Wilder*. Boston: Twayne, 1978. Burbank gives a brief but able biographical study of Wilder, considers the criticism his early works received for not springing from American themes, and offers his own assessments. He points out that Wilder believed all a good play needed was a "platform and a passion or two," and that he was successful in "making the ordinary interesting to watch."

Goldstone, Richard H. *Thornton Wilder, An Intimate Portrait*. New York: Saturday Review, 1975. Goldstone met Wilder while in the Air Corps in 1942 and the two had many conversations over the intervening years. He kept notes and his detailed account of Wilder's military service would have pleased Wilder (who was very proud of his military service) had he bothered to read the book. This "intimate portrait" is not free of criticism but the biographer does not present them in a spiteful manner. The book has substantial merit.

Harrison, Gilbert A. *The Enthusiast: A Life of Thornton Wilder*. New Haven: Ticknor and Fields, 1983. The "first full-length" biography of Wilder is both scholarly and highly readable. Harrison received the unstinting help of the Wilder family in gathering material for this biography. He also had free access to the major Wilder documents in Yale's Beinecke Library. Harrison not only covers Wilder's story but considers his works and those who either praised or criticized what he did. It is an excellent biography.

Autobiographical Sources

Wilder did not write an autobiography although he did keep journals (*The Journals of Thornton Wilder, 1939-1961*. Yale University Press, 1985). In a limited sense, something of Wilder's individuality and life experience can be discerned in his *American Characteristics and Other Essays* edited by Donald Callup (Harper and Row, 1979). When his collected letters are eventually published they should provide more information of that nature.

Overview of Critical Sources

While he was alive, and since his death, Wilder attracted the attention of literary critics, and interest in him appears to be increasing. Malcolm Goldstein's *The Art of Thornton Wilder* (1965), is a useful guide to Wilder's novels and plays. Goldstein points out that while Wilder "employs a single theme repeatedly" he was able to bring a new and fresh approach to his stories and plays. *The Plays of Thornton Wilder, A Critical Study* by Donald Haberman (1967) is a thoughtful study of Wilder's artistic skills as a playwright. This is the first thorough study of the plays by Wilder who regarded the theater "as the greatest of all art forms." Haberman's personal encounters with Wilder add extra flavor to this thoughtful study of an artist who helped create new standards in the theater. *Thornton Wilder and His Public* by Amos Niven Wilder (1980) is a tribute to the playwright by his brother. This is largely a work of brotherly admiration in which he questions Goldstein's book in his Foreword. He also generously agrees that "one should be glad that someone has done the spade work represented in the documentation here of many particulars." M.C. Kuner, in his *Thornton Wilder: The Bright and the Dark* (1972), considers both the light and dark qualities in Wilder's writing, and believes the playwright presented the "bright side" more attractively and skillfully. This book captures Wilder as essentially a happy man who rebelled against "well made" plays, who believed that in spite of darkness the sun was still there, and was always a rugged individualist. Rex Burbank's *Thornton Wilder*, while not intended to be either a full biography or critical appraisal, contains much that is essential in appreciating what the playwright achieved.

Evaluation of Selected Criticism

Goldstein, Malcolm, *The Art of Thornton Wilder*. Lincoln: University of Nebraska, 1965. The novels and plays of Wilder are ably considered in this book. Goldstein studies each of the playwright's works and comments on the critics of his time, particularly on the hostile *New Republic* (1930) review by Michael Gold. Gold considered Wilder a snob and above writing on American themes.

Haberman, Donald, *The Plays of Thornton Wilder*. Middletown: Wesleyan University Press, 1967. As an American novelist and playwright who was well read in the classics, Wilder doesn't always appear as a man of humor. Haberman not only reveals that quick humor of his, but examines his plays and novels for their human qualities. This book, an able survey of Wilder's plays, is enlightened by Haberman's incisive comments.

Kuner, M.C. *Thornton Wilder: The Bright and the Dark*. New York: Thomas Crowell, 1972. While Kuner shows that essentially Wilder was a writer who saw the bright and hopeful in life, he was also deeply concerned with the nature of evil. This book does not purport to be the definitive survey of the works of Thornton Wilder, but Kuner had made an impressive start in that direction.

Wilder, Amos Niven, *Thornton Wilder and His Public*. Philadelphia: Fortress Press, 1980. Though he displays a strong sense of loyalty to the memory and achievements of his brother, Amos is civil and fair minded in his reaction to critics who thought Wilder shoulld have done better. The book is of particular interest because it contains observations by a close relative whose comments, while somewhat biased, are still of great value.

Selected Dictionaries and Encyclopedias
Contemporary Literary Criticism, Vol. 6, Gale, 1976, pp. 572-578.

A Library of Literary Criticism, Modern American Literature, Frederick Ungar, 3rd edition, 1965, pp. 527-531.

The Oxford Companion to American Literature. 5th edition. Oxford University Press, 1983, pp. 827.

The Penguin Companion to American Literature, McGraw-Hill, 1971, pp. 268-269.

Robert A. Gates
St. John's University

TENNESSEE WILLIAMS
1911-1983

Author's Chronology

Born Thomas Lanier Williams on March 26, 1911, in Columbus, Mississippi; experiences unhappy childhood plagued by illnesses; *1919* moves with family to St. Louis, Missouri; begins to write as a lifelong means of escape and recognition; *1927* publishes first essay in *Smart Set* magazine; *1928* publishes first story entitled "The Vengeance of Nitocros"; *1929-1930* attends University of Missouri; withdraws due to parental pressure to work as a warehouseman for the International Shoe Company, St. Louis; *1935* suffers first nervous breakdown; spends a year recuperating at the home of grandparents in Memphis, Tennessee; first play is produced by Memphis Garden Players; *1936* enrolls at Washington University, St. Louis; *1937-1938* attends University of Iowa and receives bachelor's degree; *1939* begins to publish under the name Tennessee Williams; wins Group Theatre prize for playwriting; *1940-1944* wanders as an itinerant writer from Florida, to Louisiana, to California, to Mexico, and to New York; *1945* achieves first major success with *The Glass Menagerie*; wins New York Drama Critics Circle Award; *1947* wins the Pulitzer Prize for *A Streetcar Named Desire*; *1952* elected to National Institute of Arts and Letters; *1955* wins second Pulitzer Prize for *Cat on a Hot Tin Roof*; *1963* enters period of severe depression; *1969* converts to Roman Catholicism; continues to travel extensively while maintaining residences in New York City, New Orleans, and Key West, Florida; writes consistently for the remainder of his life for the theatre; dies February 25, 1983 in New York City.

Author's Bibliography (selected)

"The Summer Belvedere" in *Five Young American Poets*, 1944 (poems); *Battle of Angels*, 1945 (play); *The Glass Menagerie*, 1945 (play); *A Streetcar Named Desire*, 1947 (play); *One Arm and Other Stories*, 1948; *Summer and Smoke*, 1948 (play); *The Roman Spring of Mrs. Stone*, 1950 (novel); *Hard Candy: A Book of Stories*, 1954; *Cat on a Hot Tin Roof*, 1955 (play); *In the Winter of Cities*, 1956 (poems); *Suddenly Last Summer*, 1958 (play); *Sweet Bird of Youth*, 1959 (play); *The Night of the Iguana*, 1961 (play); *Moise and the World of Reason*, 1975 (novel); *Memoirs*, 1975 (autobiography); *Androgyne, Mon Amour*, 1977 (poems); *A Lovely Sunday for Creve Coeur*, 1980 (play); *Tennessee Williams: Collected Stories*, 1985 (published posthumously).

Overview of Biographical Sources

Recognized as America's most prolific playwright since Eugene O'Neill and a major figure in contemporary theatre, Tennessee Williams presents an intriguing and complex subject for biographers. Beginning his career as a poet and short story writer, Williams increasingly became more dependent on the theatre as a vehicle to express his unique understanding and compassion of the strength and fragility of the human spirit. Deeply concerned with his critical reputation, Williams consistently struggled to maintain his reputation as a serious artist rather than a public celebrity. In retrospect, the artistic merit of his major plays in conjunction with his flamboyant lifestyle and admitted homosexuality will undoubtedly ensure Williams a distinct position in literary history.

Establishing an accurate picture of Williams' life has long presented a difficult and controversial task for nonacademic readers and scholars. Erroneous biographical information, often introduced by Williams himself, has been repeated to the point of acceptance as fact. This propensity to sacrifice detail for effect is openly acknowledged by Williams as an effort to further elaborate the events of his life. Biographical information is also distorted by commentators attempting to identify autobiographical references in Williams' literary work. This is further complicated by Williams' lifelong habit of rewriting and retitling his material.

Early biographical treatments indicate an increasing demand for information but offer an incomplete perspective of Williams' life, intertwining biographical material with production detail surrounding the plays. A brief but insightful treatment is Gerald Weales' *Tennessee Williams* (Minneapolis: University of Minnesota, 1965), a pamphlet-length study combining biographical data with literary and thematic influences in Williams' work. Capitalizing on friendship with Williams, several authors produced semi-biographical treatments designed for popular rather than scholarly audiences. These include Gilbert Maxwell's *Tennessee Williams and Friends* (Cleveland: World, 1965), Mike Steen's *A Look at Tennessee Williams* (New York: Hawthorn, 1969), and Richard Leavitt's *The World of Tennessee Williams* (New York: G. P. Putnam's Sons, 1978). During his lifetime, Williams refused to authorize a biography and even though several treatments have appeared since his death it is questionable whether or not the "definitive" biography has yet to be written.

Evaluation of Selected Biographies

Rader, Dotson, *Tennessee: Cry of the Heart*. New York: Doubleday, 1985. A close friend of Williams from 1969 until the time of Williams' death, Rader presents a candid and absorbing account of Williams' life, and focuses primarily on the latter period of Williams' literary career. Enhanced by the proximity of their personal relationship, Rader provides an informative and engaging portrait of Williams, abundant in anecdotal commentary which successfully deviates from the more conventional form of biography.

Spoto, Donald, *The Kindness of Strangers: The Life of Tennessee Williams*. Boston: Little, Brown, 1985. An objective, well-documented account of Williams' life and work. Relying heavily on Williams' published and unpublished materials as well as extensive interviews with numerous personal and professional associates of Williams, Spoto offers the most complete Williams biography to date.

Tischler, Nancy M. *Tennessee Williams: Rebellious Puritan*. New York: Citadel, 1961. A well-written and unified critical biography attempting to provide an understanding of the interrelationship between Williams' life and art. Referring to Williams as a "romantic nonconformist," Tischler investigates not only the plays but also the stories, poems, and prose as an autobiographical reflection of the author. Although dated in relation to Williams' body of work, this is considered the most effective early summary of Williams' life and continues as an important resource.

Williams, Dakin and Shepherd Mead. *Tennessee Williams: An Intimate Biography*. New York: Arbor House, 1983. Published shortly after Williams' death, this is a partially successful account of Williams' life coauthored by his brother, Dakin, and Mead, a literary contemporary of Williams. Although respectful of Williams' achievements, this volume suggests a pretentious quality and an apparent need to "set the record straight" concerning the relationship between brothers. Of significance, however, is the intimate knowledge of family background offering insight into Williams' homosexuality, his obsession with illness and death, and his tortured relationship with his sister Rose.

Williams, Edwina Dakin, as told to Lucy Freeman. *Remember Me to Tom*. New York: G. P. Putnam's Sons, 1963. An uneven, self-indulgent attempt at autobiography by Williams' mother, but of interest for biographical information concerning Williams. This provides significant access into Williams' troubled world, while providing clues to the character and themes of his later writing. Also included are some of Williams' early poems, journal entries and letters.

Autobiographical Sources

Published in 1975, Williams' long awaited autobiography entitled *Memoirs* was greeted with disappointment by the majority of critical response. Loosely structured, alternating in time sequence, this is a portrait of the artist as celebrity, providing an illuminating backdrop to the composition and production of his plays, while teasing rather than enlightening his audience concerning his controversial sexuality. Similar to his literary efforts, *Memoirs* unfolds as a confessional, radiating a sensitivity while exposing hidden elements of Williams' artistic and personal development. Although an imperfect, anecdotal account of Williams' life, this represents an immensely readable work and an important piece to the Williams puzzle.

Although Williams' collected letters have yet to be published, an important sampling has been provided by Donald Windham, novelist, early acquaintance, and collaborator with Williams on an early play entitled *You Touched Me*, produced in 1945. *Tennessee Williams' Letters to Donald Windham 1940-1965*, (New York: Holt, Rinehart and Winston, 1977), edited by Windham, is a collection of 159 letters, mostly received during the 1940s and several letters representing the period

1950-1965 when the exchange and friendship ceased. The letters are highly readable, providing information concerning early friendships, liasons, and influences in Williams' career.

Overview of Critical Sources

Due to his renowned stature as a playwright, Williams has been the subject of numerous critical studies attempting to define the parameters of his position in contemporary theatre. Most critical accounts agree on Williams' contributions as a dramatist, primarily his poetic use of language, his exploration of the boundaries of stage production, and his experimentation with sensitive subject material. Negatively, critics argue that Williams was repetitious and lacked serious development as a writer, while glorifying a depraved world of violence, decadence, and sexual perversion. Welcoming his early original talent as daring and innovative, giving objective form to highly subjective experience, Williams fell from grace with many critics who deplored his preoccupation with sensationalism and questioned whether he had sacrificed his talent to popular success.

Although the majority of critical attention is concentrated on Williams' plays, comprehensive studies are increasingly more perceptive at investigating the nondramatic literature for its use of language and thematic elements which would later be formalized in the theatre. Future studies will undoubtedly continue to reevaluate Williams' literary reputation, emphasizing the relationship and importance of Williams' latter plays to his body of work.

Of additional interest, arranged primarily for a scholarly audience, are several bibliographic treatments. These include Delma E. Presley's "Tennessee Williams: Twenty-Five Years of Criticism," *Bulletin of Bibliography* 30 (January-March 1973): 21-29, Drewey Wayne Gunn's *Tennessee Williams: A Bibliography* (Metuchen, NJ: Scarecrow, 1980), and most recently, John S. McCann's *The Critical Reputation of Tennessee Williams: A Reference Guide* (Boston, G. K. Hall, 1983).

Evaluation of Selected Criticism

Falk, Signi Lenea, *Tennessee Williams*. New York: Twayne, 1962. Recognizing Williams' early writing as a primary source for his later work and suggesting its importance as a record of personal experience, Falk devotes a section of this critical study to a discussion of the poems, stories, and short plays. Falk is most successful in discussing Williams' relationship with the rich and varied literature of a Southern Renaissance movement emerging in the middle decades of the twentieth century.

Jackson, Esther Merle, *The Broken World of Tennessee Williams*. Madison: University of Wisconsin, 1965. Concentrating her efforts on Williams' plays, this is generally regarded as an important piece of criticism for its discussion of the existential nature of Williams' work. Jackson reveals Williams' major characters as possessing "anti-heroic" qualities such as the potential for moral and spiritual disintegration, responsibility for their own suffering, sense of guilt, and quest for identity.

Tharpe, Jac, ed. *Tennessee Williams: A Tribute*. Jackson: University Press of Mississippi, 1977. A massive collection of fifty-three essays providing a wide range of criticism and opinion on Williams' work in all genres. Although the quality of essays vary, this is the most significant critical volume to date concerning Williams, and five essays are devoted to the nondramatic prose and poetry. Of exceptional value are Jacob H. Adler's "Tennessee Williams' South: The Culture and the Power," S. Alan Chesler's "Tennessee Williams: Reassessment and Assessment," and Nancy M. Tischler's "A Gallery of Witches." A selected version of the text is also available under the title of *Tennessee Williams: 13 Essays* (Jackson: University Press of Mississippi, 1980).

Other Sources

Bowles, Paul, *Without Stopping: An Autobiography*. New York: G. P. Putnam's Sons, 1972. Distinguished American author and intimate of Williams provides a colorful glimpse into a literary friendship spanning a forty year period.

Buckley, Tom, "Tennessee Williams Survives," in *Atlantic Monthly* 226 (November 1970): 98-108. Interview-commentary highlighting Williams' concern over his public reputation and defending his present position as a productive writer.

Carr, Virginia Spencer, *The Lonely Hunter: A Biography of Carson McCullers*. Garden City, NY: Doubleday, 1975. Considered by Williams as a major writer sharing an affinity with the literary Southern Renaissance, this volume sheds light on the intricate social and professional relationship between McCullers and Williams.

Cohn, Ruby, "Late Tennessee Williams," in *Modern Drama* 27 (September 1984): 336-344. In contrast to the popular critical opinion questioning Williams' effectiveness as a playwright during the last decade of his life, Cohn offers a positive analysis of the period focusing on *The Two-Character Play*, *Vieux Carré*, and *Clothes for a Summer Hotel*.

Vidal, Gore, "Selected Memories of the Glorious Bird and the Golden Age," in *The New York Review of Books* (February 5, 1976): 13-18. Responding to the publication of Williams' *Memoirs*, Vidal presents a vivid portrait of Williams. Noteworthy is the much quoted reference to Williams as a writer "who does not develop; he simply continues."

Selected Dictionaries and Encyclopedias

American Writers: A Collection of Literary Biographies, Charles Scribners' Sons, 1974. Concise overview of Williams' life and works, including an informative section analyzing the nondramatic literature.

Dictionary of Literary Biography, Gale, 1978. General biographical introduction to Williams and discussion of the major plays.

Dictionary of Literary Biography: Documentary Series, Gale, 1984. Volume-length supplement devoted exclusively to Williams expanding the biographical and critical information of the *Dictionary of Literary Biography*. Incorporating materials from all periods of Williams' career as a writer of plays as well as of poetry and fiction, this volume serves as an important addition to the body of literature on the personal and professional life of a major American writer.

Steven Serafin
Long Island University

EGON WOLFF
1926

Author's Chronology

Born in Chile, 1926 of German parents; majors in Chemical Engineering at the Catholic University of Santiago, but is attracted to literature from an early age; at 16 writes a novel entitled *El ocaso; 1957,* encouraged by his wife, enters two plays in a literary competition sponsored by *Teatro Experimental; Mansión de lechuzas* earns honorable mention and is performed in 1958 by the University of Concepción; *Discípulos del miedo* premieres a year later; *1959* writes *Parejas de trapo* which wins the 1960 ITUCH Award for best drama; *1960 Niñamadre* premieres and is regarded as one of the best Chilean plays of the twentieth century both for its psychological penetration and its technical construction; *1961* receives fellowship to study at Yale University where an English translation of *Niñamadre,* under the title *A Touch of Blue,* is performed; *1962* writes *Esas 49 estrellas* and *Los invasores;* the latter play is considered to be his most important work, not because it is arguably his best, but because it marks a new level of literary maturity that continues throughout his literary career; in his three following works, *El signo de Caín* 1971, *Flores de papel* 1971, and *Kindergarten* 1977 Wolff continually reduces the number of characters in his effort to penetrate ever deeper into the psychological depths of twentieth-century Chilean reality; April 16th, 1980 the English translation, *Paper Flowers* 1971, premieres in Vancouver, B.C.; to date Wolff has 13 published or produced plays plus six or seven other unpublished works.

Author's Bibliography

For the most complete bibliographical information concerning Wolff refer to Pedro Shimose's *Diccionario de autores iberoamericanos* (Madrid: Ministerio de Asuntos Exteriores, 1982), p. 446. The following is a selective bibliography of Wolff's most important plays. *Discípulos del miedo* 1957, 1959; *Mansión de Lechuzas* 1957, 1958; *Parejas de trapo* 1960; *A Touch of Blue* 1960, 1961; *Esas 49 estrellas* 1962; *Los invasores* 1962; *El signo de Caín* 1971; *Paper Flowers* 1971; *Kindergarten* 1977; *Espejismos* 1978; *José* 1979.

Overview of Biographical Sources

To date, there is no full-length study in English on Wolff's life; however, Margaret S. Peden's "The Theater of Egon Wolff" focuses on his life and literary development. Willis Knapp Jones in *Behind Spanish American Footlights* also reviews the salient bio-bibliographical facts surrounding Wolff's literary production.

Evaluation of Selected Biographies

Jones, Willis Knapp, *Behind Spanish American Footlights.* Austin: University of Texas Press, 1966, pp. 231-245. Jones dedicates a chapter to "The Contemporary Chilean Theater" and presents a concise overview of Wolff's literary production.

Peden, Margaret S. "The Theater of Egon Wolff," in *Dramatists in Revolt: The New Latin American Theater.* eds. by Leon F. Lyday and George W. Woodyard. Austin: University of Texas Press, 1976, pp. 190-201. This is the most informative study in English on Wolff's literary career.

Wolff is universally regarded as one of Latin America's leading twentieth-century dramatists. Many of his works have been anthologized and scholars throughout the world have critically analyzed his theater. What follows is only a representative sampling of the more important critical studies that have been published in English on his drama.

Evaluation of Selected Criticism

Chrzanowski, Joe, "Theme, Characterization and Structure in *Los invasores,*" in *Latin American Theater Review* 11/2 (Spring 1978): 5-10. This is a thorough critical study of Wolff's landmark drama. Chrzanowski focuses on the psychological depth of the play's characters as well as its circular structure which serves to shock the audience into a deeper awareness of the drama's social relevance.

Lopez, Daniel, "Ambiguity in *Flores de papel,*" in *Latin American Theater Review* 12/1 (Fall 1978): 43-50. Lopez' analysis of *Flores de papel* demonstrates the uncertainty of human relationships and the fragile line that separates the rational from the irrational elements of life.

Lyday, Leon F. "Egon Wolff's *Los invasores:* A Play Within a Dream," in *Latin American Theater Review* 6/1 (Fally 1972): 19-26. Lyday's study focuses on the multidimensional aspects of *Los invasores'* structure. It is specifically Wolff's creative use of dream vs. reality that contributes so much to the play's impact on the audience.

Peden, Margaret S. "*Kindergarten,* A New Play by Egon Wolff," in *Latin American Theater Review* 10/2 (Spring 1977): 5-10. Peden analyzes the psychological aspects of the play's three characters, two brothers and a sister, who live together in a ritualistic world of play and fighting.

_____, "The Theater of Egon Wolff," in *Dramatists in Revolt: The New Latin American Theater.* eds. Leon F. Lyday and George W. Woodyard. Austin: University of Texas Press, 1976, pp. 190-201. To date, this is the most informative essay in English on Wolff's dramatic production. Besides giving a clear overview of Wolff's development into a major Latin American dramatist, Peden focuses in detail on six of his plays: *Mansión de lechuzas, Discípulos del mideo, Niñamadre, Los invasores, El signo de Caín,* and *Flores de papel.*

Other Sources

Castedo-Ellerman, Elena, "Variantes de Egon Wolff: fórmulas dramática y social," in *Hispamérica* V, no. 15 (Dec. 1976): 15-38. This is an excellent study in Spanish of Wolff's dramatic and social perspectives.

Vidal, Hernán, María, de la Luz Hurtado and Carlos Ochsenius, *Teatro chileno de la crisis institucional: 1973-1980 (Antología crítica).* Minneopolis: Minnesota Latin American Series, 1982, pp. 1-99. This critical anthology of contemporary Chilean drama contains two excellent introductory essays on the state of Chilean theater since Pinochet's violent coup d'etat in 1973.

Richard Keenan
University of Idaho

WILLIAM WYCHERLEY
1640?-1716

Author's Chronology

Born near Shrewsbury at Clive, in Shropshire, England in 1640 or 1641, of a family of comfortable means; c. *1655-1659* lives in Paris; c. *1660* studies at Queens College, Oxford, shortly, and thereafter briefly at the Inner Temple receives training in law; *1664* serves with the English fleet abroad; c. *1672-1679* becomes playwright and associates with the Court Wits of King Charles II's court; *1679* or *1680* marries the Countess of Drogheda; *1682* wife dies and Wycherley is jailed for debt; *1686* is pensioned by James II; c. *1687-1715* retires to Clive, writes poetry; *1704* forms friendship with the young Alexander Pope; *1715* deathbed marriage to a girl in her twenties; January 1, 1716 dies.

Author's Bibliography

Wycherly prided himself as a poet, but most of his verse is trifling; he is chiefly remembered for his last two plays. "Hero and Leander", 1669 (burlesque poem, published anonymously); *Love in a Wood*, 1671 (drama); *The Gentleman Dancing Master*, 1672 (drama); *The Country Wife*, 1675 (drama); *The Plain Dealer*, 1676 (drama); "Epistles to the King and Duke", 1683 (verse); he also wrote numbers of minor poems—songs, sonnets, epistles, epigrams, and satires, many published in *Miscellany Poems*, 1704; *The Complete Works of William Wycherley*, 1924, ed. Montague Summers, 4 vols.; *The Complete Plays of William Wycherley*, 1967, ed. Gerald Weales; *The Plays of William Wycherley*, 1979, ed. Arthur Friedman.

Overview of Biographical Sources

Wycherley's life was unfortunate, one long and constant struggle against poverty. Moreover, he lived a largely uneventful life to the age of 75. Very little is known about his early career, or even about the 1670s, the pinnacle when all of his plays were written and produced. An early, sketchy biography was the anonymous (by Charles Gildon?) *Memoirs of the Life of William Wycherley, Esq.* (1718), which included an earlier brief recollection by Lord Lansdowne. In the twentieth century, *The Complete Works of William Wycherley* (New York: Russell and Russell, 1964) includes a reasonable biography by Summers. Only more recently, however, have some details about Wycherley's career been uncovered, such as how much time Wycherley actually spent in Debtor's Prison (W. R. Chadwick, "Wycherley: The Seven Lean Years," *Notes & Queries* 216, 30-34) and what the particulars were concerning his deathbed marriage (Howard P. Vincent, "The Death of William Wycherley," *Harvard Studies and Notes in Philology and Literature* 15 219-42).

Evaluation of Selected Biographies

Connely, Willard, *Brawny Wycherley*. New York: Charles Schribners' Sons, 1930. The first important biography in English in the present century and included in a volume by itself, it provides some new letters and other information. But it is mostly a zesty popular biography, rather than a scholarly one; for it is chiefly concerned to set the scene and environment of the Restoration period, generating some fanciful inventions about Wycherley's life and a good deal of imagined detail and dialogue.

McCarthy, B. Eugene, *William Wycherley; A Biography*. Athens, OH: Ohio University Press, 1979. Clearly this is the best and most authoritative biography yet to appear. The author has engaged in much research in records offices in England, and has produced an abundance of new information. His biography is best commended because it is scholarly, factual, and cautious.

Autobiographical Sources

Wycherley is rarely autobiographical in his creative work; he is fond of maxims and moralizings, but he usually adopts masks or assumes extreme positions through a *persona* or spokesman. And, as is the case with most satirists, he is not to be trusted; his asseverations cannot be taken at face value. Indeed, his seeming aloofness in his writings has fostered ambiguity and dispute: he has been accused of excessive moralism or, more often, of being abandoned and salacious. Most of the poems, furthermore, are poorly written, and revised in his old age.

Overview of Critical Sources

The conventional approach in the late eighteenth century and particularly in the nineteenth was to lump Wycherley with all of the Restoration comic playwrights, perceiving them as frivolous authors of light comedy and entertainment, and condemning them all for immorality and lasciviousnees, and generally ignoring their work. In the present century, there has been an attempt to rehabilitate these comic playwrights—Etherege, Congreve, Wycherley—stressing their skill in surveying manners and social behavior (for example, John L. Palmers, *The Comedy of Manners*, 1913), although it is often conceded that Wycherley's extremism and apparent fury weaken his plays. The most recent criticism has sought to distinguish Wycherley from other playwrights, to stress his uniqueness as a dramatic satirist, and to herald *The Country Wife* and *The Plain Dealer* as masterpieces in their kind.

Evaluation of Selected Criticism

Chadwick, W.R. *The Four Plays of William Wycherley: A Study in the Development of a Dramatist*. The Hague: Mouton, 1975. This study is devoted exclusively to tracing Wycherley's development as a dramatist, pointing out his increasing mastery of plot, character, and action. It includes a useful bibliography. The best sections are those which provide close readings of the two major plays, *A Country Wife* and *The Plain Dealer*.

Holland, Norman N. *The First Modern Comedies: The Significance of Etherege, Wycherley, and Congreve.* Cambridge: Harvard University Press, 1959. Holland employs the new-critical methods of careful analysis, and, like Thomas H. Fujimura (*The Restoration Comedy of Wit.* Princeton: Princeton University Press, 1952) calls for the critical re-evaluation of the playwrights, with attention to their artistry and to the intellectual background of the period.

Zimbardo, Rose A. *Wycherley's Drama. A Link in the Development of English Satire.* New Haven: Yale University Press, 1965. The first full-length book devoted to Wycherley's dramatic work, this study attempts to establish that Wycherley is unique among the other comic playwrights of the period in being essentially a satirist, one participating in the Renaissance, Elizabethan, and Restoration satiric traditions. She pays considerable attention to the *persona* or satiric "spokesman" and to the satiric "structure" of the plays in her discussion.

Other Sources

McCarthy, B. Eugene, *William Wycherley. A Reference Guide.* Boston: G. K. Hall, 1985. An extremely useful annotated bibliography of opinions about and scholarship concerning Wycherley from 1669 to 1982.

Rogers, Katherine M. *William Wycherley.* New York: Twayne, 1972. Providing a brief text treating of the author's life and writings, this is one of the sounder general introductions to the man and his work, together with a short bibliography.

Vernon, P. F. *William Wycherley.* London: Longmans, Green, 1965. One of the terse pamphlets in the "Writers and Their Work" series, this volume offers a brief biography, criticism, and select bibliography.

Selected Dictionaries and Encyclopedias

The Cambridge Guide to English Literature, Cambridge University Press, 1983. Brief life, with critical commentary.

Great Writers of the English Language: Dramatists, St. Martin's Press, 1979. Brief summary of Wycherley's life, a biographical listing of his works, and a critical essay by Gerald Weales.

Magill's Bibliography of Literary Criticism, Salem Press, 1979. Brief bibliographies of criticism of the four plays.

The New Cambridge Bibliography of English Literature, Cambridge University Press, 1969-1977. Brief bibliography of Wycherley's works and of the criticism.

John R. Clark
University of South Florida

ZEAMI MOTOKIYO
Kanze Motokiyo
1363-1443

Author's Chronology

Also known as Zeami, or Seami, born in the province of Yamoto (now Nara Prefecture), Japan, son of Kanze Kiyotsugu (also called Kan'ami, 1333-1384), head of a troup of local performers, precursors of a traditional Japanese theatrical form, Noh; *1374* summoned to the capital, modern-day Kyoto; as a result of performance at Imagumano Shrine, won Shogun, Ashikaga Yoshimitsu's favor and became his protegé at a highly cultivated court; *1378* accompanies Shogun at box seat for annual Gion festival; *1384* at father's death succeeds as head of the Kanze troup; *1394* performs Noh in Nara at Kasuga Shrine, for which occasion Shogun also went to the former capital; *1399* performs Noh at Sambōin, Daigoji Temple, with the now-retired Shogun Yoshimitsu in attendance; *1400-1402* compiles items included in his earliest treatise, Fūshikaden (Teachings on Style and the Flower); *1402* takes monkish name, Zeami, by which he is best-remembered today; *1408* performs before the Emperor Gokomatsu on the occasion of a royal visit to the palace in the northern suburbs of Kyoto; *1422* becomes a Sōtō Zen monk; first son, Motomasa, appointed master of troup; *1429* new Shogun, Ashikaga Yoshinori, bars father and son from his palace; *1430* second son, Motoyoshi, gives up Noh to become a monk; *1432* Motomasa dies, to father's grief; nephew, On'ami, heads troup; *1434* exiled to island of Sado, perhaps for having refused to transmit secret teachings to nephew; returns to Kyoto shortly before death; *1443* son-in-law, Komparu Zenchiku (1405-1468), continues in a line of performers unbroken to the present day.

Author's Bibliography

Besides his work as troup leader, Zeami also left a number of plays, known as *yōkyoku*, "chant pieces," and twenty-three treatises on aesthetic principles, training of actors, and standards of performance. These texts give expression to the received wisdom of Chinese and Japanese poetry, art, religion, and philosophy, as well as the theatrical traditions of medieval Japan.

Because transmission of knowledge and wisdom in medieval Japan was held in secrecy and passed from master to chosen disciple, Zeami's plays and other writings remained unpublished. In the early seventeenth century plays began to appear in wood-block editions. Of the treatises, only a few circulated in surreptitious manuscript copies, with the best texts remaining closely-guarded secrets in the houses of the five main acting families. Only in the twentieth century did the treatises become available. A definitive set of sixteen texts was published by Nose

Asaji, *Zeami jūroku bushū hyōshaku* (Critical Edition of Zeami's Sixteen Treatises) (2 vols., 1940, 1944). A similar set of twenty-three texts, edited by Kawase Kazuma, *Zeami nijū-san bushū* (1945, Zeami's Twenty-three Treatises) appeared, as well. With peace and growing prosperity after 1945 meticulous Japanese scholarship has produced standard editions of Zeami's writings and permitted a fuller view of his life and work than would have been formerly thought possible. The most readily available collection of translated plays, including representative titles ascribed to Zeami, is Donald Keene, ed. *Twenty Plays of the Nō Theatre* (1970). In Japanese standard editions of plays are included in series such as *Nihon koten bungaku taikei* (1955-61), Compendium of Japanese Classical Literature). The *Yōkyoku-shū* (1960, Collected Chant Pieces), edited by Yokomichi Mario and Omote Akira, contains twenty-one plays ascribed to Zeami, including the representative warrior play, *Atsumori* (personal name) and the woman play, *Izutsu* (Well-Curb), translated by Kenneth Yasuda in *Harvard Journal of Asiatic Studies*, 1980, with an impressive critical and scholarly apparatus.

Overview of Biographical Sources

Emphasis in Noh scholarship in Japan and elsewhere has been on the plays and treatises rather than on Zeami's life. There is no full-length biographical study in English. Besides scattered notices in books and articles, beginning with Arthur Waley's *The No Plays of Japan* (1921), the most judicious and detailed treatment of Zeami's life in English is found in Thomas Hare, "Zeami's Style: A Study of the 'mugen' Noh Plays of Zeami Motokiyo" (1981), an unpublished Ph.D. dissertation. In Japanese Nishio Minoru's booklet, *Zeami Motokiyo* (1932), deserves to be consulted. While it is, to some extent, a biography, it also presents Zeami's views of training actors, acting, and performance. Kobayashi Shizuo's brilliant biography, *Zeami* (1943), remains frequently cited. Nogami Toyoichirō's *Zeami Motokiyo* (1943), also emerges from the prewar wave of pioneering modern scholarship on Zeami and the origins of Noh. Nishi Isshō's *Zeami kenkyū* (1967, Research on Z.) and Matsuda Tamotsu, *Zeami to Nō no kenkyū* (1972, Research on Z. and Noh) both utilize the postwar tide of scholarship after the veil of secrecy was removed from primary sources handed down in traditional actors' families. Whether future scholars will place as much value on study of Zeami's life as on aesthetics, criticism, and theatre history, allowing the appearance of a definitive critical biography remains to be seen. This branch of scholarship in Japan is relatively undeveloped.

Evaluation of Selected Biographies (untranslated)

Kitagawa, Tadahiko, *Zeami*. Tokyo: Chūō Kōron Sha, 1972. Kitagawa places Zeami within the history of Noh as a theatrical form, evaluating his contribution to the process by which Noh changed from a popular performing spectacle to an aristocratic theatrical art. Kitagawa begins with Zeami's times and treatment of the facts of Zeami's life as they are known. Then he proceeds to discussion of the plays ascribed to Zeami, to the treatises, mostly composed between 1402 and 1430, and to matters involving Zeami's exile, in 1434, concluding with the continuation of Zeami's theatre troup and transmission of Noh from the middle ages to early modern times. Concise and lucid, Kitagawa, like most recent authors, combines the biographical and critical function.

Kobayashi, Shizuo, *Zeami*. Tokyo: Hinoki Shoten, 1943; revised and expanded, 1958; rpt. 1980. A pioneering book-length (198 pages) overview of Zeami's life and work, Kobayashi's study includes sections on biography, theatre art, treatises, and plays attributed to Zeami, finishing with a chronology. Sound judgment and careful attention to historical detail mark Kobayashi's exposition. Although written in an old-fashioned style of Japanese before the postwar burst of new materials and studies, Kobayashi's work still merits careful attention by scholars interested in Zeami and the origins of Noh. His premature death in military service in the Philippines in 1945 deprived the world of a talented young scholar.

Nishi, Isshō. *Zeami kenkyū* (Research on Z.). Tokyo: Sarubia Shuppan, 1967. A collection of articles originally published 1960-1965, Nishi's book exemplifies the postwar harvest of Japanese historical scholarship that features close philological rigor and attention todocumentary evidence. Nishi's biographical research focuses on Zeami's relations with the Ashikaga political and military rulers who patronized the form of theatre that Kan'ami, Zeami, and their successors developed. Besides biographical essays, Nishi includes a study of the circumstances of composition of Zeami's treatises and an essay on later revisions of a play that survives in a manuscript by Zeami. There is also an annotated bibliography of monographs on Zeami and an extensive list of books and articles.

————, *Zeami-ron* (Essays on Z.). Tokyo: Ōfūsha, 1980. This second collection of articles includes additional essays together with a co-authored study of Noh plays based on material in the early eleventh century court romance, *Genji monogatari* (Tale of Genji). There is also an abbreviated chronology of Zeami. These articles, originally published between 1961 and 1979, extend knowledge of Zeami's associations with his contemporaries and assess Zeami's position as a playwright and aesthetician.

Yashima, Masaharu, *Zeami no Nō to geiron* (Z.: His Noh and his treatises). Tokyo: Mimii Shoten, 1985 (900 pages). An ambitious effort to portray Zeami and evaluate his achievement in aesthetics and theatre criticism, Yashima's book synthesizes prewar and postwar scholarship. Besides dealing with the significance and artistry of the treatises, Yashima examines the plays attributed to Zeami with close attention to the oldest manuscript copies and recent theories about the modular structure of the plays, reconsidering the problem of authorship.

Autobiographical Sources

Other than a few brief and scattered letters, the principal autobiographical source is the treatise, *Sarugaku dangi* (Reflections on Art), translated in Rimer and Yamazaki (1984). Compiled in 1430, the text is based on conversations recorded by Zeami's second son, Motoyoshi. Besides a general section on the art of Noh and passages on actors whose lineage he traces in art, Zeami treats various topics and ramifications of Noh, both spiritual and physical. Personal references, including details about his first son, Motomasa, dot the text. Titles of plays ascribed to Zeami are also mentioned. Problems in deciphering and authenticating letters by Zeami, as well as the paucity of such documents, have so far prevented publication of an edition of the collected letters.

Overview of Critical Sources

Following the discovery and publication of his treatises and the beginning of modern scholarship on Zeami early in the twentieth century, each year has brought new contributions to criticism of Zeami's life and work. For the year 1965, to give an example, the last period covered in Nishi's list in *Zeami kenkyū* (1967), 114 items appear. More recently if anything the tide has swelled. Not only in traditional Japanese theatre but in the fields of intellectual history and aesthetics Zeami's position seems as secure as that of Lady Murasaki, author of the *Tale of Genji*, the most celebrated classic in Japanese literature. Together with his father, Zeami created a composite theatrical art by fusing popular and aristocratic elements. A harmony of dance and mimicry appeals to the eye along with chant and dialogue that entertain the ear. Yet another essential component of Zeami's art involves an intellectual, philosophical, and emotional dimension that touches the heart and soul of spectators. As if this were not enough, the writings on aesthetic principles, training of actors, and standards of performance give expression to the wisdom of Chinese and Japanese poetry, art, religion, and philosophy, as well as the received theatrical traditions. Few people anywhere have equaled Zeami's achievement as playwright, theoretician, and leader of a troup of performers, whose lineage has continued unbroken to the present day. The energy Zeami devoted to scholarship, theatre, and criticism continues to gather force and bear fruit.

Evaluation of Selected Criticism

Nearman, Mark J. "Kakyō: Zeami's Fundamental Principles of Acting," in *Monumenta Nipponica* (Tokyo), 37, 3 (1982): 333-74; 37, 4 (1982): 459-96; 38, 1 (1983): 49-71. Besides a translation of the treatise with the most extensive analysis of how a student actor may become a creative artist, Nearman includes discussion of the treatise's relevance to theatre practice, a commentary longer than the original text, and extensive annotation. Nearman's work reflects familiarity with modern Japanese criticism, with the plays and treatises, and with Chinese and Japanese classical learning that underlies Zeami's writings. It should be read in conjunction with the following title.

Rimer, J. Thomas and Yamnazaki Masakazu, trans. *On the Art of the Nō Drama: The Major Treatises of Zeami*. Princeton: Princeton University Press, 1984. Here translation becomes a form of criticism. Choice of English terminology and syntax to represent the sense of one of the most remarkable bodies of dramaturgy in the world involves exercise of keen critical skill. For the general reader this book offers the best guide to Japanese primary and secondary texts. The treatises included are as follows: 1) *Fūshikaden* (ca. 1402, "Teachings on Style and the Flower"); 2) *Shikadō* (1420, "The True Path to the Flower"); 3) *Sandō* (1423, "The Three Elements in Composing a Play"); 4) *Kakyo* (1424, "A Mirror Held to the Flower" in Rimer and Yamazaki); 5) *Kyūi* (ca. 1424, "Notes on the Nine Levels"); 6) *Yūgaku shūdō fūken* (1424, "Disciplines for the Joy of Art"); 7) *Shūgyoku tokka* (1428, "Finding Gems, Gaining Flower"); 8) *Shūdōsho* (1430, "Learning the Way"); and 9) *Sarugaku dangi* (1430, discussed above under *Autobiographical Sources*). Rimer and Yamazaki's text makes it possible for readers of English to evaluate Zeami's achievement in dramaturgy and aesthetics.

Sekine, Masaru, *Zeami and His Theories of Noh Drama*. Gerrards Cross, Buckinghamshire: Colin Smythe Limited, 1985. Informed discussion and commentary on Zeami's principal treatises is organized into a topical structure that includes the history of Noh, categories of plays, training, acting, playwriting, public competition, audience, and the idea of perfection of skill discussed metaphorically as *hana*, literally "flower," which along with *yūgen*—idealized beauty personified as a woman—stands at the center of Zeami's view of aesthetics. A brief bibliography and an extensive glossary complete the work. The author, who comes from a hereditary Noh family, is familiar with modern Western theatre. The book complements the two above titles.

Other Sources

Keene, Donald, *Nō: The Classical Theatre of Japan*. Tokyo: Kodansha International, 1966. Illustrated and comprehensive introduction to the theatrical form to which Zeami gave impetus.

Komparu, Kunio, *The Noh Theatre: Principles and Perspectives*. trans., Jane Corddry and Stephen Comee. Tokyo: John Weatherhill, 1983. Revised and expanded translation of *Nō e no izanai* (1980, Invitation to Noh), this is an analysis of modern Noh form with passing references to Zeami's theory and practice.

Narukawa, Takeo, *Zeami: Hana no tetsugaku* (Z.: The Philosophy of "Flower"). Tokyo: Tamagawa Daigaku Shuppanbu, 1980. Untranslated. Focus on Zeami's aesthetic concept of true artistic accomplishment.

716

Zeami Motokiyo

O'Neill, P.G. *Early Nō Drama*. London: Lund Humphries, 1958. Detailed account of Japanese theatre until Zeami's time.

Raz, Jacob, *Audience and Actors: A Study of Their Interaction in the Japanese Traditional Theatre*. Leiden: E.J. Brill, 1983. Includes material on Zeami's views on the audience of the Noh theatre.

Toita, Michizō, *Kan'ami to Zeami* (Kan'ami and Z.). Tokyo: Iwanami Shoten, 1969. Interpretive and readable biographical/critical study.

Ueda, Makoto, *Zeami, Bashō, Yeats, and Pound: A Study in Japanese and English Poetics*. The Hague: Mouton, 1965. Chapter One, "Zeami Motokiyo: Imitation, Yūgen, and the Sublime," stands out for imaginative cross-cultural orientation yet to be superseded.

Yamazaki, Masakazu, *Mask and Sword: Two Plays for the Contemporary Japanese Theatre*. New York: Columbia University Press, 1980. trans. J. Thomas Rimer. Includes *Zeami*, Yamazaki's dramatic interpretation of the life and career; originally published in 1974 in book form in Japanese.

Leon Zolbrod
University of British Columbia

INDEX OF AUTHORS AND MAJOR SOURCES REVIEWED

CUMULATIVE INDEX